Blackstone's Statutes on

Employment Law

33rd edition

edited by

Astra Emir

MA, LLM

OXFORD
UNIVERSITY PRESS

OXFORD
UNIVERSITY PRESS

Great Clarendon Street, Oxford, OX2 6DP,
United Kingdom

Oxford University Press is a department of the University of Oxford.
It furthers the University's objective of excellence in research, scholarship,
and education by publishing worldwide. Oxford is a registered trade mark of
Oxford University Press in the UK and in certain other countries

First published by Blackstone Press 1988

Thirtieth edition 2020
Thirty-first edition 2021
Thirty-second edition 2023
Thirty-third edition 2026

Published in the United States of America by Oxford University Press
198 Madison Avenue, New York, NY 10016, United States of America

British Library Cataloguing in Publication Data
Data available

ISBN 978–0–19–792099–2

Printed in the UK by
Bell & Bain Ltd., Glasgow

Contents

Alphabetical contents v
Chronological contents viii
Editor's preface ix
New to this edition x

Part I Statutes of the UK Parliament 1

Health and Safety at Work etc. Act 1974 1
Trade Union and Labour Relations (Consolidation) Act 1992 10
Employment Rights Act 1996 139
Employment Tribunals Act 1996 260
Human Rights Act 1998 269
National Minimum Wage Act 1998 273
Employment Relations Act 1999 284
Employment Act 2002 288
Equality Act 2010 290
Modern Slavery Act 2015 350

Part II Statutory Instruments 351

The Employment Tribunals Extension of Jurisdiction (England and Wales) Order 1994 351
The Employment Protection (Continuity of Employment) Regulations 1996 352
The Working Time Regulations 1998 353
The Management of Health and Safety at Work Regulations 1999 376
The Maternity and Parental Leave etc. Regulations 1999 382
The Part-Time Workers (Prevention of Less Favourable Treatment) Regulations 2000 394
The Fixed-term Employees (Prevention of Less Favourable Treatment) Regulations 2002 400
The Paternity and Adoption Leave Regulations 2002 406
The Information and Consultation of Employees Regulations 2004 418
The Transfer of Undertakings (Protection of Employment) Regulations 2006 427
The Agency Workers Regulations 2010 439
The Employment Relations Act 1999 (Blacklists) Regulations 2010 451
The Equality Act 2010 (Disability) Regulations 2010 456
Shared Parental Leave Regulations 2014 457
The Exclusivity Terms in Zero Hours Contracts (Redress) Regulations 2015 463
The Exclusivity Terms for Zero Hours Workers (Unenforceability and Redress) Regulations 2022 464
The Carer's Leave Regulations 2024 467
The Employment Rights (Increase of Limits) Order 2026 469
The National Minimum Wage (Amendment) Regulations 2026 470

Part III Non-Statutory Materials 471

ACAS Code of Practice 1 Disciplinary and Grievance Procedures (Revised 2015) 471

Equality Act 2010 Statutory Code of Practice on Equal Pay (Issued 2011) 475

Equality Act 2010 Statutory Code of Practice on Employment (Issued 2011) 478

Alphabetical contents

A ACAS Code of Practice 1 (Revised 2015) Disciplinary and Grievance Procedures
paras 1–47 . . . 471–5
Agency Workers Regulations 2010
Contents . . . 439
regs 2–9 . . . 440–6
regs 12–15 . . . 446–8
regs 17–20 . . . 448–50
C Carer's Leave Regulations 2024
regs 2–6 . . . 467–8
E Employment Act 2002
s. 38 . . . 288–9
Sched. 5 . . . 289–90
Employment Protection (Continuity of Employment) Regulations 1996
regs 2–4 . . . 352–3
Employment Relations Act 1999
ss. 10–15 . . . 284–7
s. 34 . . . 287–8
Employment Relations Act 1999 (Blacklists) Regulations 2010
regs 2–11 . . . 451–5
reg. 13 . . . 455–6
Employment Rights Act 1996
Contents . . . 139–42
ss. 1–9 . . . 142–7
ss. 11–27A . . . 147–57
ss. 27BA–BB . . . 157–9
s. 27BE . . . 159–60
ss. 27BG–BK . . . 160–4
ss. 27BN–P . . . 164–6
ss. 27BR–BV . . . 167–9
ss. 27C–D . . . 169–70
ss. 27G–M . . . 170–4
ss. 43A–H . . . 174–7
ss. 43J–L . . . 177–8
s. 44 . . . 178–9
s. 45A . . . 179–80
ss. 47–57 . . . 180–7
ss. 57A–B . . . 188
ss. 61–3 . . . 189–90
ss. 64–8 . . . 190–1
ss. 69–73 . . . 191–5
ss. 75A–B . . . 195–6
s. 80 . . . 196
ss. 80F–I . . . 196–9
ss. 86–95 . . . 199–203
ss. 97–8 . . . 203–5
ss. 99–100 . . . 205–6
s. 101A . . . 206–7
ss. 103–4A . . . 207–8
s. 104C . . . 208
ss. 104F–G . . . 208–9
ss. 104I–K . . . 209–15
ss. 105–8 . . . 215–9
s. 111 . . . 219
ss. 112–24A . . . 219–25
s. 126 . . . 225
ss. 128–32 . . . 225–28
ss. 135–6 . . . 228–9
ss. 138–55 . . . 229–37
ss. 162–5 . . . 237–9
ss. 173–4 . . . 239–40
s. 176 . . . 240–1
ss. 180–2 . . . 241–2
ss. 184–6 . . . 242–3
ss. 191–3 . . . 242–5
ss. 202–5A . . . 245–50
ss. 210–16 . . . 250–3
s. 218 . . . 253
ss. 220–31 . . . 253–8
ss. 234–5 . . . 258–60
Employment Rights (Increase of Limits) Order 2026
Sched. . . . 469
Employment Tribunals Act 1996
s. 4 . . . 260–1
s. 6 . . . 261–2
s. 12A . . . 262–3
s. 15 . . . 263
ss. 18–18A . . . 264–5
ss. 20–2 . . . 265–7
s. 28 . . . 267–8
s. 33 . . . 268
Employment Tribunals Extension of Jurisdiction (England and Wales) Order 1994
Arts 3–5 . . . 351
Arts 7, 8, 10 . . . 352
Equality Act 2010
Contents . . . 290–1
s. 1 . . . 291–3
s. 3 . . . 293
ss. 4–13 . . . 293–5

ss. 15–16 . . . 295–6
ss. 18–21 . . . 296–8
ss. 23–7 . . . 299–301
ss. 39–41 . . . 301–2
ss. 49–55 . . . 302–7
s. 57 . . . 307–8
ss. 60–A . . . 308–11
ss. 64–6 . . . 311–2
ss. 69–74 . . . 312–4
ss. 76–7 . . . 314–5
ss. 79–80 . . . 315–6
s. 83 . . . 316
ss. 108–13 . . . 317–19
s. 120 . . . 319–20
ss. 122–4A . . . 320–1
ss. 127–32 . . . 321–4
ss. 135–6 . . . 324–6
ss. 141–9 . . . 326–31
s. 156 . . . 331
ss. 158–9 . . . 331–2
ss. 193–4 . . . 332–3
ss. 212–13 . . . 333–5
Sched. 1 . . . 335–6
Scheds 7–9 . . . 337–47
Sched. 28 . . . 347–50

Equality Act 2010 (Disability) Regulations 2010
regs 3–7 . . . 456

Equality Act 2010 Statutory Code of Practice on Employment (2011)
Ch. 16, paras 1–2, 4–19, 23–9, 32 . . . 478–82
Ch. 17, paras 8, 11, 12, 16, 17, 20, 25, 32–40, 44, 47, 51 . . . 482–6
Ch 19, paras 3–10 . . . 486–8

Equality Act 2010 Statutory Code of Practice on Equal Pay (2011)
paras 158–71 . . . 475–8

Exclusivity Terms in Zero Hours Contracts (Redress) Regulations 2015
regs 2–4 . . . 463–4

Exclusivity Terms for Zero Hours Workers (Unenforceability and Redress) Regulations 2022
regs 2–9 . . . 464–7

F Fixed-term Employees (Prevention of Less Favourable Treatment) Regulations 2002
regs 1–12 . . . 400–5
reg. 19 . . . 405
Sched. 1 . . . 405–6

H Health and Safety at Work etc. Act 1974
ss. 1–4 . . . 1–3
ss. 6–9 . . . 3–5
ss. 20–22 . . . 6–8
s. 25 . . . 8
s. 33 . . . 8–9
ss. 36–37 . . . 9
s. 47 . . . 10

Human Rights Act 1998
ss. 1–4 . . . 269–70
ss. 7–8 . . . 270–1
ss. 11–13 . . . 271
Sched. 1 . . . 271–3

I Information and Consultation of Employees Regulations 2004
Contents . . . 418
regs 2–3A . . . 418–20
reg. 7 . . . 420–1
regs 11–14 . . . 421–2
reg. 16 . . . 422–3
reg. 18 . . . 423
regs 20–6 . . . 424–7
Sched. 1 . . . 427

M Management of Health and Safety at Work Regulations 1999
Contents . . . 376
reg. 3 . . . 376–7
regs 5–15 . . . 377–81

Maternity and Parental Leave etc. Regulations 1999
reg. 2 . . . 382–3
reg. 4 . . . 383–4
regs 6–11 . . . 384–6
regs 12A–16 . . . 387–8
regs 17–21 . . . 388–91
Sched. 1 . . . 392
Sched. 2 . . . 393–4

Modern Slavery Act 2015
s. 1 . . . 350

N National Minimum Wage Act 1998
Contents . . . 273
s. 1 . . . 274
ss. 17–19A . . . 274–6
ss. 19D–E . . . 276
ss. 23–4 . . . 276–8
s. 28 . . . 278
ss. 31–2 . . . 278–9
ss. 34–7 . . . 279–80
ss. 44–5A . . . 280–2
ss. 48–9 . . . 282–3
ss. 54–5 . . . 283–4

National Minimum Wage (Amendment) Regulations 2026
reg. 2 . . . 470

P Part-time Workers (Prevention of Less Favourable Treatment) Regulations 2000

regs 1–8 . . . 394–9
reg. 9 . . . 399
regs 11–12 . . . 399
Paternity and Adoption Leave Regulations 2002
reg. 2 . . . 406–7
regs 4–6 . . . 408–10
regs 8–10 . . . 410–12
regs 12–15 . . . 412–13
regs 18–20 . . . 413–14
reg. 21A . . . 414
regs 23–4 . . . 414–5
regs 26–30 . . . 415–18
S Shared Parental Leave Regulations 2014
Contents . . . 457
regs 4–9 . . . 457–61
regs 35–6 . . . 461–3
T Trade Union and Labour Relations (Consolidation) Act 1992
Contents . . . 10–14
ss. 1–2 . . . 14
ss. 5–7 . . . 15
ss. 9–12 . . . 15–16
ss. 15–16 . . . 16–18
ss. 20–3 . . . 18–20
ss. 46–7 . . . 20–1
s. 50 . . . 21–2
s. 51 . . . 22
ss. 53–6A . . . 23–5
ss. 62–70ZI . . . 25–34
s..70ZL . . . 34
ss. 71–3 . . . 34–6
ss. 82–7 . . . 36–40
ss. 92–3 . . . 40
ss. 95–6 . . . 40
ss. 108A–C . . . 41–3
ss. 117–22 . . . 43–5
s. 136A . . . 45–6
ss. 137–56 . . . 46–56
ss. 160–8B . . . 56–62
ss. 169–72 . . . 62–4
ss. 173–88 . . . 64–73
ss. 189–92 . . . 73–76
ss. 195–6 . . . 76
s. 198A . . . 76–7
ss. 207, 207A . . . 77–8
ss. 209–12 . . . 78–9
ss. 212B–14 . . . 79
ss. 218–26A . . . 79–85
ss. 227–31A . . . 85–7
ss. 232A–5A . . . 88–92
ss. 236–6B . . . 92–3
ss. 2326D–8A . . . 93–5
ss. 239–48 . . . 95–9
s. 254 . . . 99
ss. 259–60 . . . 99–100
s. 273 . . . 100–1
s. 282 . . . 101
s. 285 . . . 101
ss. 288–9 . . . 102–3
ss. 295–9 . . . 103–6
Sched. A1 . . . 106–37
Sched. A2 . . . 138
Transfer of Undertakings (Protection of Employment) Regulations 2006
regs 2–16 . . . 427–39
reg. 18 . . . 439
W Working Time Regulations 1998
Contents . . . 353–4
regs 2–6A . . . 354–8
regs 8–15 . . . 358–62
regs 15B–16A . . . 363–7
reg. 17 . . . 367
regs 19–24A . . . 368–9
regs 26A–9B . . . 370–2
regs 29E–30 . . . 372–3
reg. 35 . . . 373–4
regs 36–7 . . . 374–5
reg. 42 . . . 375
Sched. 1 . . . 375–6

Chronological contents

1974 Health and Safety at Work etc. Act 1974 ... 1

1992 Trade Union and Labour Relations (Consolidation) Act 1992 ... 10

1994 Employment Tribunals Extension of Jurisdiction (England and Wales) Order 1994 ... 351

1996 Employment Protection (Continuity of Employment) Regulations 1996 ... 352

Employment Rights Act 1996 ... 139

Employment Tribunals Act 1996 ... 260

1998 Human Rights Act 1998 ... 269

National Minimum Wage Act 1998 ... 273

Working Time Regulations 1998 ... 353

1999 Employment Relations Act 1999 ... 284

Management of Health and Safety at Work Regulations 1999 ... 376

Maternity and Parental Leave etc. Regulations 1999 ... 382

2000 Part-Time Workers (Prevention of Less Favourable Treatment) Regulations 2000 ... 394

2002 Employment Act 2002 ... 288

Fixed-term Employees (Prevention of Less Favourable Treatment) Regulations 2002 ... 400

Paternity and Adoption Leave Regulations 2002 ... 406

2004 Information and Consultation of Employees Regulations 2004 ... 418

2006 Transfer of Undertakings (Protection of Employment) Regulations 2006 ... 427

2010 Agency Workers Regulations 2010 ... 439

Employment Relations Act 1999 (Blacklists) Regulations 2010 ... 451

Equality Act 2010 ... 290

Equality Act 2010 (Disability) Regulations 2010 ... 456

2011 Equality Act 2010 Statutory Code of Practice on Equal Pay (Issued 2011) ... 475

Equality Act 2010 Statutory Code of Practice on Employment (Issued 2011) ... 478

2014 Shared Parental Leave Regulations ... 457

2015 ACAS Code of Practice 1 Disciplinary and Grievance Procedures (Revised 2015) ... 471

Exclusivity Terms in Zero Hours Contracts (Redress) Regulations 2015 ... 463

Modern Slavery Act 2015 ... 350

2022 Exclusivity Terms for Zero Hours Workers (Unenforceability and Redress) Regulations 2022 ... 464

2024 Carer's Leave Regulations 2024 ... 467

2026 Employment Rights (Increase of Limits) Order 2026 ... 469

National Minimum Wage (Amendment) Regulations 2026 ... 470

Editor's preface

This collection of statutes is primarily intended for students of employment law and it includes all those statutes and parts of statutes which a student may be referred to in their courses. The collection is necessarily not comprehensive but I hope that I have not omitted anything of relevance. What has been provided covers all the law relevant for students of employment law, discrimination law, and trade union law. The statutes are not, of course, the whole story, but they are an essential prerequisite to appreciating the structure, nature, and purpose of employment law and as the subject is now mainly statutory it is impossible to study it satisfactorily without constant reference to the statutes, for much of the case law depends to a great extent on interpretation.

In the longer statutes, I have included the preliminary index to the sections, and also in those statutes omissions and repeals are indicated in square brackets so readers can tell why a section is not available (and can if curious chase up omissions for themselves).

The text is as amended to April 2026 but some changes may not have been brought into force by the publication date. Many of the changes have been made by the Employment Rights Act 2025. It should be noted that this is an enabling Act. This means that it makes changes to other statutes, or gives a power to make regulations, and so does not appear in the text as a stand-alone statute. Where these changes have already been made, for example to the Employment Rights Act 1996, they appear in the text.

There are further changes still to be made by the Employment Rights Act 2025. Where the text of the relevant statutes has not been changed as at April 2026, these do not yet appear in the book. Important forthcoming changes include the removal of the statutory cap on compensatory award, a six-month rather than two-year qualifying period for unfair dismissal, and the extension of time to bring a tribunal claim from three to six months. The government's expected timetable for the further changes appears online at https://www.gov.uk/government/publications/implementing-the-plan-to-make-work-pay-and-employment-rights-act/plan-to-make-work-pay-and-employment-rights-act-timeline-update#timetable-for-changes-being-introduced-in-2026 (last accessed 14 April 2026).

The task of selection is becoming ever more difficult especially as regulations become even more complex and repetitive. Nevertheless, it is hoped that this book presents within a reasonable compass and at a reasonable price all the major legislation which a student will need to refer to. Finally, I am most grateful to all at Oxford University Press for their help and efficiency.

The statutes are arranged in chronological order (and alphabetically within years) and are set out as amended to April 2026.

Astra Emir

New to this edition

The thirty-third edition of *Blackstone's Statutes on Employment Law* has been fully revised and updated with all relevant new legislation up to April 2026.

This edition includes changes made by the following legislation (in date and then alphabetical order):

- Carer's Leave Act 2023
- Employment (Allocation of Tips) Act 2023
- Employment Relations (Flexible Working) Act 2023
- Employment Rights (Amendment, Revocation and Transitional Provision) Regulations 2023
- Equality Act 2010 (Amendment) Regulations 2023
- Worker Protection (Amendment of Equality Act 2010) Act 2023
- Carer's Leave (Consequential Amendments to Subordinate Legislation) Regulations 2024
- Carer's Leave Regulations 2024
- Maternity Leave, Adoption Leave and Shared Parental Leave (Amendment) Regulations 2024
- Paternity Leave (Amendment) Regulations 2024
- Employment Rights Act 2025
- Employment Rights (Increase of Limits) Order 2026
- National Minimum Wage (Amendment) Regulations 2026
- Employment Rights Act 2025 (Parental and Paternity Leave) (Removal of Qualifying Periods etc.) (Consequential Amendments) Regulations 2026

(Also note the comments on the Employment Rights Act 2025 which are set out in the Preface.)

Blackstone's Statutes
Unsurpassed in authority, reliability, and accuracy

The titles in the Blackstone's Statutes series are a collection of carefully reviewed and selected unannotated legislative material and official documents.

We make every effort to ensure titles in the series meet the needs of their target market. They are reviewed by lecturers to match university courses closely and are expertly edited to be manageable in size, whilst retaining their comprehensive coverage.

The editors only include material from legislation that will be valuable to students and lecturers and it is therefore abridged where necessary.

Conventions used in *Blackstone's Statutes on Employment Law*

Omissions and repeals are indicated in square brackets so readers can tell why a section is not available (and can if curious chase up omissions for themselves). For example:

24–45D [omitted]
88 [repealed]; 89–91 [omitted]

Generally, the author has omitted material which relates only to particular employments (such as dock workers or teachers), together with minor regulatory or empowering provisions.

One feature of current practice is that statutes mainly take effect by amending the two principal Consolidation Acts, so that while a statute may not appear in this book under its own title, nevertheless its provisions are fully incorporated into existing legislation.

The material in this book is reproduced in its most up-to-date form. Supplementary notes and details of amending provisions are generally not included.

All statutes have been enacted but some very recent legislation may not yet be in force.

Part I

Statutes of the UK Parliament

Health and Safety at Work etc. Act 1974

(1974, c. 37)

PART I HEALTH, SAFETY AND WELFARE IN CONNECTION WITH WORK, AND CONTROL OF DANGEROUS SUBSTANCES AND CERTAIN EMISSIONS INTO THE ATMOSPHERE

Preliminary

1 Preliminary.

General duties

2 General duties of employers to their employees.

3 General duties of employers and self-employed to persons other than their employees.

4 General duties of persons concerned with premises to persons other than their employees.

6 General duties of manufacturers etc. as regards articles and substances for use at work.

7 General duties of employees at work.

8 Duty not to interfere with or misuse things provided pursuant to certain provisions.

9 Duty not to charge employees for things done or provided pursuant to certain specific requirements.

Enforcement

20 Powers of inspectors.

21 Improvement notices.

22 Prohibition notices.

25 Power to deal with cause of imminent danger.

Provisions as to offences

33 Offences

36 Offences due to fault of other person.

37 Offences by bodies corporate.

Miscellaneous and supplementary

47 Civil liability.

PART I HEALTH, SAFETY AND WELFARE IN CONNECTION WITH WORK, AND CONTROL OF DANGEROUS SUBSTANCES AND CERTAIN EMISSIONS INTO THE ATMOSPHERE

Preliminary

1 Preliminary

(1) The provisions of this Part shall have effect with a view to—

(a) securing the health, safety and welfare of persons at work;

(b) protecting persons other than persons at work against risks to health or safety arising out of or in connection with the activities of persons at work;

(c) controlling the keeping and use of explosive or highly flammable or otherwise dangerous substances, and generally preventing the unlawful acquisition, possession and use of such substances;

(d) [repealed]

(2) The provisions of this Part relating to the making of health and safety regulations and the preparation and approval of codes of practice shall in particular have effect with a view to enabling the enactments specified in the third column of Schedule 1 and the regulations, orders and other instruments in force under those enactments to be progressively replaced by a system of regulations and approved codes of practice operating in combination with the other provisions of this Part and designed to maintain or improve the standards of health, safety and welfare established by or under those enactments.

(3) For the purposes of this Part risks arising out of or in connection with the activities of persons at work shall be treated as including risks attributable to the manner of conducting an undertaking, the plant or substances used for the purposes of an undertaking and the condition of premises so used or any part of them.

(4) References in this Part to the general purposes of this Part are references to the purposes mentioned in subsection (1) above.

General Duties

2 General duties of employers to their employees

(1) It shall be the duty of every employer to ensure, so far as is reasonably practicable, the health, safety and welfare at work of all his employees.

(2) Without prejudice to the generality of an employer's duty under the preceding subsection, the matters to which that duty extends include in particular—

- (a) the provision and maintenance of plant and systems of work that are, so far as is reasonably practicable, safe and without risks to health;
- (b) arrangements for ensuring, so far as is reasonably practicable, safety and absence of risks to health in connection with the use, handling, storage and transport of articles and substances;
- (c) the provision of such information, instruction, training and supervision as is necessary to ensure, so far as is reasonably practicable, the health and safety at work of his employees;
- (d) so far as is reasonably practicable as regards any place of work under the employer's control, the maintenance of it in a condition that is safe and without risks to health and the provision and maintenance of means of access to and egress from it that are safe and without such risks;
- (e) the provision and maintenance of a working environment for his employees that is, so far as is reasonably practicable, safe, without risks to health, and adequate as regards facilities and arrangements for their welfare at work.

(3) Except in such cases as may be prescribed, it shall be the duty of every employer to prepare and as often as may be appropriate revise a written statement of his general policy with respect to the health and safety at work of his employees and the organisation and arrangements for the time being in force for carrying out that policy, and to bring the statement and any revision of it to the notice of all of his employees.

(4) [omitted]; (5) [repealed]

(6) It shall be the duty of every employer to consult any such representatives with a view to the making and maintenance of arrangements which will enable him and his employees to co-operate effectively in promoting and developing measures to ensure the health and safety at work of the employees, and in checking the effectiveness of such measures.

(7) In such cases as may be prescribed it shall be the duty of every employer, if requested to do so by the safety representatives mentioned in subsection (4) above, to establish, in accordance with regulations made by the Secretary of State, a safety committee having the function of keeping under review the measures taken to ensure the health and safety at work of his employees and such other functions as may be prescribed.

3 General duties of employers and self-employed to persons other than their employees

(1) It shall be the duty of every employer to conduct his undertaking in such a way as to ensure, so far as is reasonably practicable, that persons not in his employment who may be affected thereby are not thereby exposed to risks to their health or safety.

(2) It shall be the duty of every self-employed person who conducts an undertaking of a prescribed description to conduct the undertaking in such a way as to ensure, so far as is reasonably practicable, that he and other persons (not being his employees) who may be affected thereby are not thereby exposed to risks to their health or safety.

(2A) A description of undertaking included in regulations under subsection (2) may be framed by reference to—

(a) the type of activities carried out by the undertaking, where those activities are carried out or any other feature of the undertaking;

(b) whether persons who may be affected by the conduct of the undertaking, other than the self-employed person (or his employees), may thereby be exposed to risks to their health or safety.

(3) In such cases as may be prescribed, it shall be the duty of every employer and every self-employed person, in the prescribed circumstances and in the prescribed manner, to give to persons (not being his employees) who may be affected by the way in which he conducts his undertaking the prescribed information about such aspects of the way in which he conducts his undertaking as might affect their health or safety.

4 General duties of persons concerned with premises to persons other than their employees

(1) This section has effect for imposing on persons duties in relation to those who—

(a) are not their employees; but

(b) use non-domestic premises made available to them as a place of work or as a place where they may use plant or substances provided for their use there,

and applies to premises so made available and other non-domestic premises used in connection with them.

(2) It shall be the duty of each person who has, to any extent, control of premises to which this section applies or of the means of access thereto or egress therefrom or of any plant or substance in such premises to take such measures as it is reasonable for a person in his position to take to ensure, so far as is reasonably practicable, that the premises, all means of access thereto or egress therefrom available for use by persons using the premises, and any plant or substance in the premises or, as the case may be, provided for use there, is or are safe and without risks to health.

(3) Where a person has, by virtue of any contract or tenancy, an obligation of any extent in relation to—

(a) the maintenance or repair of any premises to which this section applies or any means of access thereto or egress therefrom; or

(b) the safety of or the absence of risks to health arising from plant or substances in any such premises;

that person shall be treated, for the purposes of subsection (2) above, as being a person who has control of the matters to which his obligation extends.

(4) Any reference in this section to a person having control of any premises or matter is a reference to a person having control of the premises or matter in connection with the carrying on by him of a trade, business or other undertaking (whether for profit or not).

5 [repealed]

6 General duties of manufacturers etc. as regards articles and substances for use at work

(1) It shall be the duty of any person who designs, manufactures, imports or supplies any article for use at work or any article of fairground equipment—

(a) to ensure, so far as is reasonably practicable, that the article is so designed and constructed that it will be safe and without risks to health at all times when it is being set, used, cleaned or maintained by a person at work;

(b) to carry out or arrange for the carrying out of such testing and examination as may be necessary for the performance of the duty imposed on him by the preceding paragraph;

(c) to take such steps as are necessary to secure that persons supplied by that person with the article are provided with adequate information about the use for which the article is designed or has been tested and about any conditions necessary to ensure that it will be safe and without risks to health at all such times as are mentioned in paragraph (a) above and when it is being dismantled or disposed of; and

(d) to take such steps as are necessary to secure, so far as is reasonably practicable, that persons so supplied are provided with all such revisions of information provided to them by virtue of the preceding paragraph as are necessary by reason of its becoming known that anything gives rise to a serious risk to health or safety.

(1A) [omitted]

(2) It shall be the duty of any person who undertakes the design or manufacture of any article for use at work or of any article of fairground equipment to carry out or arrange for the carrying out of any necessary research with a view to the discovery and, so far as is reasonably practicable, the elimination or minimisation of any risks to health or safety to which the design or article may give rise.

(3) It shall be the duty of any person who erects or installs any article for use at work in any premises where that article is to be used by persons at work or who erects or installs any article of fairground equipment to ensure, so far as is reasonably practicable, that nothing about the way in which the article is erected or installed makes it unsafe or a risk to health at any such time as is mentioned in paragraph (a) of subsection (1) or, as the case may be, in paragraph (a) of subsection (1) or (1A) above.

(4) It shall be the duty of any person who manufactures, imports or supplies any substance—

(a) to ensure, so far as is reasonably practicable, that the substance will be safe and without risks to health at all times when it is being used, handled, processed, stored or transported by a person at work or in premises to which section 4 above applies;

(b) to carry out or arrange for the carrying out of such testing and examination as may be necessary for the performance of the duty imposed on him by the preceding paragraph;

(c) to take such steps as are necessary to secure that persons supplied by that person with the substance are provided with adequate information about any risks to health or safety to which the inherent properties of the substance may give rise, about the results of any relevant tests which have been carried out on or in connection with the substance and about any conditions necessary to ensure that the substance will be safe and without risks to health at all such times as are mentioned in paragraph (a) above and when the substance is being disposed of; and

(d) to take such steps as are necessary to secure, so far as is reasonably practicable, that persons so supplied are provided with all such revisions of information provided to them by virtue of the preceding paragraph as are necessary by reason of its becoming known that anything gives rise to a serious risk to health or safety.

(5) It shall be the duty of any person who undertakes the manufacture of any substance to carry out or arrange for the carrying out of any necessary research with a view to the discovery and, so far as is reasonably practicable, the elimination or minimisation of any risks to health or safety to which the substance may give rise at all such times as are mentioned in paragraph (a) of subsection (4) above.

(6) Nothing in the preceding provisions of this section shall be taken to require a person to repeat any testing, examination or research which has been carried out otherwise than by him or at his instance, in so far as it is reasonable for him to rely on the results thereof for the purposes of those provisions.

(7) Any duty imposed on any person by any of the preceding provisions of this section shall extend only to things done in the course of a trade, business or other undertaking carried on by him (whether for profit or not) and to matters within his control.

(8) Where a person designs, manufactures, imports or supplies an article for use at work or an article of fairground equipment and does so for or to another on the basis of a written undertaking

by that other to take specified steps sufficient to ensure, so far as is reasonably practicable, that the article will be safe and without risks to health at all such times as are mentioned in paragraph (a) of subsection (1) or, as the case may be, in paragraph (a) of subsection (1) or (1A) above, the undertaking shall have the effect of relieving the first-mentioned person from the duty imposed by virtue of that paragraph to such extent as is reasonable having regard to the terms of the undertaking.

(8A) Nothing in subsection (7) or (8) above shall relieve any person who imports any article or substance from any duty in respect of anything which—

(a) in the case of an article designed outside the United Kingdom, was done by and in the course of any trade, profession or other undertaking carried on by, or was within the control of, the person who designed the article; or
(b) in the case of an article or substance manufactured outside the United Kingdom, was done by and in the course of any trade, profession or other undertaking carried on by, or was within the control of, the person who manufactured the article or substance.

(9) Where a person ('the ostensible supplier') supplies any article or substance to another ('the customer') under a hire-purchase agreement, conditional sale agreement or credit-sale agreement, and the ostensible supplier—

(a) carries on the business of financing the acquisition of goods by others by means of such agreements; and
(b) in the course of that business acquired his interest in the article or substance supplied to the customer as a means of financing its acquisition by the customer from a third person ('the effective supplier'),

the effective supplier and not the ostensible supplier shall be treated for the purposes of this section as supplying the article or substance to the customer, and any duty imposed by the preceding provisions of this section on suppliers shall accordingly fall on the effective supplier and not on the ostensible supplier.

(10) For the purposes of this section an absence of safety or a risk to health shall be disregarded in so far as the case in or in relation to which it would arise is shown to be one the occurrence of which could not reasonably be foreseen; and in determining whether any duty imposed by virtue of paragraph (a) of subsection (1), (1A) or (4) above has been performed regard shall be had to any relevant information or advice which has been provided to any person by the person by whom the article has been designed, manufactured, imported or supplied or, as the case may be, by the person by whom the substance has been manufactured, imported or supplied.

7 General duties of employees at work

It shall be the duty of every employee while at work—

(a) to take reasonable care for the health and safety of himself and of other persons who may be affected by his acts or omissions at work; and
(b) as regards any duty or requirement imposed on his employer or any other person by or under any of the relevant statutory provisions, to co-operate with him so far as is necessary to enable that duty or requirement to be performed or complied with.

8 Duty not to interfere with or misuse things provided pursuant to certain provisions

No person shall intentionally or recklessly interfere with or misuse anything provided in the interests of health, safety or welfare in pursuance of any of the relevant statutory provisions.

9 Duty not to charge employees for things done or provided pursuant to certain specific requirements

No employer shall levy or permit to be levied on any employee of his any charge in respect of anything done or provided in pursuance of any specific requirement of the relevant statutory provisions.

10–19 [omitted]

Enforcement

20 Powers of inspectors

(1) Subject to the provisions of section 19 and this section, an inspector may, for the purpose of carrying into effect any of the relevant statutory provisions within the field of responsibility of the enforcing authority which appointed him, exercise the powers set out in subsection (2) below.

(2) The powers of an inspector referred to in the preceding subsection are the following, namely—

- (a) at any reasonable time (or, in a situation which in his opinion is or may be dangerous, at any time) to enter any premises which he has reason to believe it is necessary for him to enter for the purpose mentioned in subsection (1) above;
- (b) to take with him a constable if he has reasonable cause to apprehend any serious obstruction in the execution of his duty;
- (c) without prejudice to the preceding paragraph, on entering any premises by virtue of paragraph (a) above to take with him—
  - (i) any other person duly authorised by his (the inspector's) enforcing authority; and
  - (ii) any equipment or materials required for any purpose for which the power of entry is being exercised;
- (d) to make such examination and investigation as may in any circumstances be necessary for the purpose mentioned in subsection (1) above;
- (e) as regards any premises which he has power to enter, to direct that those premises or any part of them, or anything therein, shall be left undisturbed (whether generally or in particular respects) for so long as is reasonably necessary for the purpose of any examination or investigation under paragraph (d) above;
- (f) to take such measurements and photographs and make such recordings as he considers necessary for the purpose of any examination or investigation under paragraph (d) above;
- (g) to take samples of any articles or substances found in any premises which he has power to enter, and of the atmosphere in or in the vicinity of any such premises;
- (h) in the case of any article or substance found in any premises which he has power to enter, being an article or substance which appears to him to have caused or to be likely to cause danger to health or safety, to cause it to be dismantled or subjected to any process or test (but not so as to damage or destroy it unless this is in the circumstances necessary for the purpose mentioned in subsection (1) above);
- (i) in the case of any such article or substance as is mentioned in the preceding paragraph, to take possession of it and detain it for so long as is necessary for all or any of the following purposes, namely—
  - (i) to examine it and do to it anything which he has power to do under that paragraph;
  - (ii) to ensure that it is not tampered with before his examination of it is completed;
  - (iii) to ensure that it is available for use as evidence in any proceedings for an offence under any of the relevant statutory provisions or any proceedings relating to a notice under section 21 or 22;
- (j) to require any person whom he has reasonable cause to believe to be able to give any information relevant to any examination or investigation under paragraph (d) above to answer (in the absence of persons other than a person nominated by him to be present and any persons whom the inspector may allow to be present) such questions as the inspector thinks fit to ask and to sign a declaration of the truth of his answers;
- (k) to require the production of, inspect, and take copies of or of any entry in—
  - (i) any books or documents which by virtue of any of the relevant statutory provisions are required to be kept; and
  - (ii) any other books or documents which it is necessary for him to see for the purposes of any examination or investigation under paragraph (d) above;

(l) to require any person to afford him such facilities and assistance with respect to any matters or things within that person's control or in relation to which that person has responsibilities as are necessary to enable the inspector to exercise any of the powers conferred on him by this section;

(m) any other power which is necessary for the purpose mentioned in subsection (1) above.

(3) [omitted]

(4) Where an inspector proposes to exercise the power conferred by subsection (2)(h) above in the case of an article or substance found in any premises, he shall, if so requested by a person who at the time is present in and has responsibilities in relation to those premises, cause anything which is to be done by virtue of that power to be done in the presence of that person unless the inspector considers that its being done in that person's presence would be prejudicial to the safety of the State.

(5) Before exercising the power conferred by subsection (2)(h) above in the case of any article or substance, an inspector shall consult such persons as appear to him appropriate for the purpose of ascertaining what dangers, if any, there may be in doing anything which he proposes to do under that power.

(6) Where under the power conferred by subsection (2)(i) above an inspector takes possession of any article or substance found in any premises, he shall leave there, either with a responsible person or, if that is impracticable, fixed in a conspicuous position, a notice giving particulars of that article or substance sufficient to identify it and stating that he has taken possession of it under that power; and before taking possession of any such substance under that power an inspector shall, if it is practicable for him to do so, take a sample thereof and give to a responsible person at the premises a portion of the sample marked in a manner sufficient to identify it.

(7) No answer given by a person in pursuance of a requirement imposed under subsection (2)(j) above shall be admissible in evidence against that person or the spouse or civil partner of that person in any proceedings.

(8) Nothing in this section shall be taken to compel the production by any person of a document of which he would on grounds of legal professional privilege be entitled to withhold production on an order for discovery in an action in the High Court or, as the case may be, on an order for the production of documents in an action in the Court of Session.

(9) [repealed].

(10) [repealed].

21 Improvement notices

If an inspector is of the opinion that a person—

(a) is contravening one or more of the relevant statutory provisions; or

(b) has contravened one or more of those provisions in circumstances that make it likely that the contravention will continue or be repeated,

he may serve on him a notice (in this Part referred to as 'an improvement notice') stating that he is of that opinion, specifying the provision or provisions as to which he is of that opinion, giving particulars of the reasons why he is of that opinion, and requiring that person to remedy the contravention or, as the case may be, the matters occasioning it within such period (ending not earlier than the period within which an appeal against the notice can be brought under section 24) as may be specified in the notice.

22 Prohibition notices

(1) This section applies to any activities which are being or are likely to be carried on by or under the control of any person, being activities to or in relation to which any of the relevant statutory provisions apply or will, if the activities are so carried on, apply.

(2) If as regards any activities to which this section applies an inspector is of the opinion that, as carried on or likely to be carried on by or under the control of the person in question, the activities involve or, as the case may be, will involve a risk of serious personal injury, the inspector may serve on that person a notice (in this Part referred to as 'a prohibition notice').

(3) A prohibition notice shall—

(a) state that the inspector is of the said opinion;

(b) specify the matters which in his opinion give or, as the case may be, will give rise to the said risk;

(c) where in his opinion any of those matters involves or, as the case may be, will involve a contravention of any of the relevant statutory provisions, state that he is of that opinion, specify the provision or provisions as to which he is of that opinion, and give particulars of the reasons why he is of that opinion; and

(d) direct that the activities to which the notice relates shall not be carried on by or under the control of the person on whom the notice is served unless the matters specified in the notice in pursuance of paragraph (b) above and any associated contraventions of provisions so specified in pursuance of paragraph (c) above have been remedied.

(4) A direction contained in a prohibition notice in pursuance of subsection (3)(d) above shall take effect—

(a) at the end of the period specified in the notice; or

(b) if the notice so declares, immediately.

23–24 [omitted]

25 Power to deal with cause of imminent danger

(1) Where, in the case of any article or substance found by him in any premises which he has power to enter, an inspector has reasonable cause to believe that, in the circumstances in which he finds it, the article or substance is a cause of imminent danger of serious personal injury, he may seize it and cause it to be rendered harmless (whether by destruction or otherwise).

(2) Before there is rendered harmless under this section—

(a) any article that forms part of a batch of similar articles; or

(b) any substance,

the inspector shall, if it is practicable for him to do so, take a sample thereof and give to a responsible person at the premises where the article or substance was found by him a portion of the sample marked in a manner sufficient to identify it.

(3) As soon as may be after any article or substance has been seized and rendered harmless under this section, the inspector shall prepare and sign a written report giving particulars of the circumstances in which the article or substance was seized and so dealt with by him, and shall—

(a) give a signed copy of the report to a responsible person at the premises where the article or substance was found by him; and

(b) unless that person is the owner of the article or substance, also serve a signed copy of the report on the owner;

and if, where paragraph (b) above applies, the inspector cannot after reasonable enquiry ascertain the name or address of the owner, the copy may be served on him by giving it to the person to whom a copy was given under the preceding paragraph.

25A–28 [omitted]; 29–32 [repealed]

Provisions as to offences

33 Offences

(1) It is an offence for a person—

(a) to fail to discharge a duty to which he is subject by virtue of sections 2 to 7;

(b) to contravene section 8 or 9;

(c) to contravene any health and safety regulations or any requirement or prohibition imposed under any such regulations (including any requirement or prohibition to which he is subject by virtue of the terms of or any condition or restriction attached to any licence, approval, exemption or other authority issued, given or granted under the regulations);

(d) to contravene any requirement imposed by or under regulations under section 14 or intentionally to obstruct any person in the exercise of his powers under that section;

(e) to contravene any requirement imposed by an inspector under section 20 or 25;
(f) to prevent or attempt to prevent any other person from appearing before an inspector or from answering any question to which an inspector may by virtue of section 20(2) require an answer;
(g) to contravene any requirement or prohibition imposed by an improvement notice or a prohibition notice (including any such notice as modified on appeal);
(h) intentionally to obstruct an inspector in the exercise or performance of his powers or duties or to obstruct a customs officer in the exercise of his powers under section 25A;
(i) to contravene any requirement imposed by a notice under section 27(1);
(j) to use or disclose any information in contravention of section 27(4) or 28;
(k) to make a statement which he knows to be false or recklessly to make a statement which is false where the statement is made—
  (i) in purported compliance with a requirement to furnish any information imposed by or under any of the relevant statutory provisions; or
  (ii) for the purpose of obtaining the issue of a document under any of the relevant statutory provisions to himself or another person;
(l) intentionally to make a false entry in any register, book, notice or other document required by or under any of the relevant statutory provisions to be kept, served or given or, with intent to deceive, to make use of any such entry which he knows to be false;
(m) with intent to deceive, to forge or use a document issued or authorised to be issued under any of the relevant statutory provisions or required for any purpose thereunder or to make or have in his possession a document so closely resembling any such document as to be calculated to deceive;
(n) falsely to pretend to be an inspector;
(o) to fail to comply with an order made by a court under section 42.

(2)–(3) [omitted]; (5)–(6) [repealed]

34–35 [omitted]

36 Offences due to fault of other person

(1) Where the commission by any person of an offence under any of the relevant statutory provisions is due to the act or default of some other person, that other person shall be guilty of the offence, and a person may be charged with and convicted of the offence by virtue of this subsection whether or not proceedings are taken against the first-mentioned person.

(2) Where there would be or have been the commission of an offence under section 33 by the Crown but for the circumstance that that section does not bind the Crown, and that fact is due to the act or default of a person other than the Crown, that person shall be guilty of the offence which, but for that circumstance, the Crown would be committing or would have committed, and may be charged with and convicted of that offence accordingly.

(3) [omitted]

37 Offences by bodies corporate

(1) Where an offence under any of the relevant statutory provisions committed by a body corporate is proved to have been committed with the consent or connivance of, or to have been attributable to any neglect on the part of, any director, manager, secretary or other similar officer of the body corporate or a person who was purporting to act in any such capacity, he as well as the body corporate shall be guilty of that offence and shall be liable to be proceeded against and punished accordingly.

(2) Where the affairs of a body corporate are managed by its members, the preceding subsection shall apply in relation to the acts and defaults of a member in connection with his functions of management as if he were a director of the body corporate.

38–46 [omitted]

Miscellaneous and supplementary

47 Civil liability

(1) Nothing in this Part shall be construed—

(a) as conferring a right of action in any civil proceedings in respect of any failure to comply with any duty imposed by sections 2 to 7 or any contravention of section 8; or

(b) [repealed]

(c) as affecting the operation of section 12 of the Nuclear Installations Act 1965 (right to compensation by virtue of certain provisions of that Act).

(2) Breach of a duty imposed by a statutory instrument containing (whether alone or with other provision) health and safety regulations shall not be actionable except to the extent that regulations under this section so provide.

(2A) Breach of a duty imposed by an existing statutory provision shall not be actionable except to the extent that regulations under this section so provide (including by modifying any of the existing statutory provisions).

(2B) [omitted]

(3) No provision made by virtue of section 15(6)(b) shall afford a defence in any civil proceedings.

(4) Subsections (1)(a) (2) and (2A) above are without prejudice to any right of action which exists apart from the provisions of this Act, and subsection (2B)(a) above is without prejudice to any defence which may be available apart from the provisions of the regulations there mentioned.

(5)–(6) [repealed]; (7) [omitted]

48–85 [omitted]

Trade Union and Labour Relations (Consolidation) Act 1992

(1992, c. 52)

PART I TRADE UNIONS

Chapter I Introductory

Meaning of 'trade union'
1 Meaning of 'trade union'

The list of trade unions
2 The list of trade unions

Certification as independent trade union
5 Meaning of 'independent trade union'
6 Application for certificate of independence
7 Withdrawal or cancellation of certificate

Supplementary
9 Appeal against decision of Certification Officer

Chapter II Status and Property of Trade Unions

General
10 Quasi-corporate status of trade unions
11 Exclusion of common law rules as to restraint of trade

Property of trade union
12 Property to be vested in trustees
15 Prohibition on use of funds to indemnify unlawful conduct
16 Remedy against trustees for unlawful use of union property

Liability of trade unions in proceedings in tort
20 Liability of trade union in certain proceedings in tort
21 Repudiation by union of certain acts
22 Limit on damages awarded against trade unions in actions in tort

Restriction on enforcement against certain property
23 Restriction on enforcement of awards against certain property

Chapter IV Elections for Certain Positions

Duty to hold elections
46 Duty to hold elections for certain positions

Requirements to be satisfied with respect to elections
47 Candidates
50 Entitlement to vote
51 Voting
53 Uncontested elections

Remedy for failure to comply with requirements
54 Remedy for failure to comply with requirements: general
55 Application to Certification Officer
56 Application to court
56A Appeals from Certification Officer

Chapter V Rights of Trade Union Members

Right to a ballot before industrial action
62 Right to a ballot before industrial action

Right not to be denied access to the courts
63 Right not to be denied access to the courts

Right not to be unjustifiably disciplined
64 Right not to be unjustifiably disciplined
65 Meaning of 'unjustifiably disciplined'
66 Complaint of infringement of right
67 Further remedies for infringement of right

Right not to suffer deduction of unauthorised union subscriptions
68 Right not to suffer deduction of unauthorised union subscriptions
68A Complaint of infringement of rights

Right to terminate membership of union
69 Right to terminate membership of union

Supplementary
70 Membership of constituent or affiliated organisation

Chapter 5ZA Right of trade unions to access workplaces

Access agreements: general
70ZA Access agreements

Entering into access agreements
70ZB Access requests and response notices
70ZC Response period and negotiation period
70ZD Entering into access agreement by negotiation
70ZE Determinations by the Central Arbitration Committee
70ZF Determinations by the Central Arbitration Committee: further provision

Variation and revocation of access agreements
70ZG Variation and revocation of access agreements

Enforcement of access agreements
70ZH Enforcement of access agreements: initial complaint
70ZI Enforcement of access agreements: subsequent complaint

General limitations on access agreements etc
70ZL General limitations on access agreements etc

Chapter VI Application of Funds for Political Objects

Restriction on use of funds for certain political objects
71 Restriction on use of funds for political objects
72 Political objects to which restriction applies
72A Application of funds in breach of section 71

Political resolution
73 Passing and effect of political resolution

The political fund
82 Rules as to political fund
83 Assets and liabilities of political fund
84 Contributors to political fund
84A Opt-out Information notices
85 Manner of giving effect to section 84

Duties of employer who deducts union contributions
86 Employer not to deduct contributions where member gives certificate
87 Complaint in respect of employer's failure

Supplementary
92 Manner of making union rules
93 Effect of amalgamation
95 Appeals from Certification Officer
96 Meaning of 'date of the ballot'

Chapter VIIA Breach of Rules

108A Right to apply to Certification Officer
108B Declarations and orders
108C Appeals from Certification Officer

Chapter IX Miscellaneous and General Provisions

Exceptions and adaptations for certain bodies
117 Special register bodies
118 Federated trade unions

Interpretation
119 Expressions relating to trade unions
120 Northern Ireland unions
121 Meaning of 'the court'

PART II EMPLOYERS' ASSOCIATIONS

Introductory
122 Meaning of 'employers' association'

PART III RIGHTS IN RELATION TO UNION MEMBERSHIP AND ACTIVITIES

Statement of trade union rights
136A Right to statement of trade union rights

Access to employment
137 Refusal of employment on grounds related to union membership
138 Refusal of service of employment agency on grounds related to union membership
139 Time limit for proceedings
140 Remedies
141 Complaint against employer and employment agency
142 Awards against third parties
143 Interpretation and other supplementary provisions

Contracts for supply of goods or services
144 Union membership requirement in contract for goods or services void
145 Refusal to deal on union membership grounds prohibited

Inducements
145A Inducements relating to union membership or activities
145B Inducements relating to collective bargaining
145C Time limit for proceedings

145D Consideration of complaint
145E Remedies
145F Interpretation and other supplementary provisions

Detriment

146 Detriment on grounds related to union membership or activities
147 Time limit for proceedings
148 Consideration of complaint
149 Remedies
150 Awards against third parties
151 Interpretation and other supplementary provisions

Dismissal of employee

152 Dismissal of employee on grounds related to union membership or activities
153 Selection for redundancy on grounds related to union membership or activities
154 Disapplication of qualifying period and upper age limit for unfair dismissal
155 Matters to be disregarded in assessing contributory fault
156 Minimum basic award
160 Awards against third parties
161 Application for interim relief
162 Application to be promptly determined
163 Procedure on hearing of application and making of order
164 Order for continuation of contract of employment
165 Application for variation or revocation of order
166 Consequences of failure to comply with order
167 Interpretation and other supplementary provisions

Time off for trade union duties and activities

168 Time off for carrying out trade union duties
168A Time off for union learning representatives
168B Time off for union equality representatives
169 Payment for time off under sections 168 to 168B
170 Time off for trade union activities
171 Time limit for proceedings
172 Remedies
173 Interpretation and other supplementary provisions

Right to membership of trade union

174 Right not to be excluded or expelled from union
175 Time limit for proceedings
176 Remedies
177 Interpretation and other supplementary provisions

PART IV INDUSTRIAL RELATIONS

Chapter I Collective Bargaining

Introductory

178 Collective agreements and collective bargaining

Enforceability of collective agreements

179 Whether agreement intended to be a legally enforceable contract
180 Effect of provisions restricting right to take industrial action

Disclosure of information for purposes of collective bargaining

181 General duty of employers to disclose information
182 Restrictions on general duty
183 Complaint of failure to disclose information
184 Further complaint of failure to comply with declaration
185 Determination of claim and award

Prohibition of union recognition requirements

186 Recognition requirement in contract for goods or services void
187 Refusal to deal on grounds of union exclusion prohibited

Chapter II Procedure for Handling Redundancies

Duty of employer to consult representatives

188 Duty of employer to consult representatives
189 Complaint and protective award
190 Entitlement under protective award
191 Termination of employment during protected period
192 Complaint by employee to employment tribunal

Supplementary provisions

195 Construction of references to dismissal as redundant etc.
196 Construction of references to representatives
198A Employees being transferred to the employer from another undertaking

Chapter III Codes of Practice

Supplementary provisions

207 Effect of failure to comply with Code
207A Effect of failure to comply with Code: adjustment of awards

Chapter IV General

Functions of ACAS

209 General duty to promote improvement of industrial relations
210 Conciliation
211 Conciliation officers
212 Arbitration
212B Dismissal procedures agreements
213 Advice
214 Inquiry

Supplementary provisions

218 Meaning of 'trade dispute' in Part IV

PART V INDUSTRIAL ACTION

Protection of acts in contemplation or furtherance of trade dispute

219 Protection from certain tort liabilities
220 Peaceful picketing

221 Restrictions on grant of injunctions and interdicts

Action excluded from protection

222 Action to enforce trade union membership
223 Action taken because of dismissal for taking unofficial action
224 Secondary action
225 Pressure to impose union recognition requirement

Requirement of ballot before action by trade union

226 Requirement of ballot before action by trade union
226A Notice of ballot and sample voting paper for employers
227 Entitlement to vote in ballot
228 Separate workplace ballots
228A Separate workplaces: single and aggregate ballots
229 Voting paper
230 Conduct of ballot
231 Information as to result of ballot
231A Employers to be informed of ballot result
232A Inducement of member denied entitlement to vote
232B Small accidental failures to be disregarded
233 Calling of industrial action with support of ballot
234 Period after which ballot ceases to be effective

Requirement on trade union to give notice of industrial action

234A Notice to employers of industrial action
235 Construction of references to contract of employment in sections 226 to 234A

Industrial action affecting supply of goods or services to an individual

235A Industrial action affecting supply of goods or services to an individual

No compulsion to work

236 No compulsion to work

Protection against detriment

236A Detriment on grounds of industrial action
236B Time limit for proceedings
236D Remedies

Loss of unfair dismissal protection

237 Dismissal of those taking part in unofficial industrial action
238 Dismissals in connection with other industrial action
238A Participation in official industrial action
239 Supplementary provisions relating to unfair dismissal

Criminal offences

240 Breach of contract involving injury to persons or property
241 Intimidation or annoyance by violence or otherwise
242 Restriction of offence of conspiracy: England and Wales
243 Restriction of offence of conspiracy: Scotland

Supplementary

244 Meaning of 'trade dispute' in Part V
245 Crown employees and contracts
246 Minor definitions

PART VI ADMINISTRATIVE PROVISIONS

ACAS

247 ACAS
248 The Council of ACAS

The Certification Officer

254 The Certification Officer

Central Arbitration Committee

259 The Central Arbitration Committee
260 The members of the Committee

PART VII MISCELLANEOUS AND GENERAL

Crown employment, etc.

273 Crown employment

Excluded classes of employment

282 Fixed term employment
285 Employment outside Great Britain

Contracting out, etc.

288 Restriction on contracting out
289 Employment governed by foreign law

Interpretation

295 Meaning of 'employee' and related expressions
296 Meaning of 'worker' and related expressions
297 Associated employers
297A Meaning of 'voting'
298 Minor definitions: general
299 Index of defined expressions

SCHEDULE A1
COLLECTIVE BARGAINING: RECOGNITION

PART I RECOGNITION

1–3 Introduction
4–7 Request for recognition
10 Parties agree
11 Employer rejects request
12 Negotiations fail
18–19B Appropriate bargaining unit
20–31 Union recognition
32 Method not carried out
35–49 General provisions about admissibility

PART II VOLUNTARY RECOGNITION

52 Agreements for recognition
53–54 Other interpretation
55 Determination of type of agreement
56–57 Termination of agreement for recognition
58–59 Application to CAC to specify method

PART IV DERECOGNITION: GENERAL

96–98 Introduction
104–110 Employer's request to end arrangements
112–114 Workers' application to end arrangements
116A–116L Access agreements
117–121 Ballot on derecognition

PART VIII DETRIMENT

156–160 Detriment
161 Dismissal
162 Selection for redundancy
164 Exclusion of requirement as to qualifying period
165 Meaning of worker's contract

PART IX GENERAL

171 CAC's general duty
171A 'Pay' and other matters subject to collective bargaining

SCHEDULE A2
TRIBUNAL JURISDICTIONS TO WHICH SECTION 207A APPLIES

PART I TRADE UNIONS

Chapter I Introductory

Meaning of 'trade union'

1 Meaning of 'trade union'

In this Act a 'trade union' means an organisation (whether temporary or permanent)—

(a) which consists wholly or mainly of workers of one or more descriptions and whose principal purposes include the regulation of relations between workers of that description or those descriptions and employers or employers' associations; or

(b) which consists wholly or mainly of—

(i) constituent or affiliated organisations which fulfil the conditions in paragraph (a) (or themselves consist wholly or mainly of constituent or affiliated organisations which fulfil those conditions), or

(ii) representatives of such constituent or affiliated organisations,

and whose principal purposes include the regulation of relations between workers and employers or between workers and employers' associations, or the regulation of relations between its constituent or affiliated organisations.

The list of trade unions

2 The list of trade unions

(1) The Certification Officer shall keep a list of trade unions containing the names of—

(a) the organisations whose names were, immediately before the commencement of this Act, duly entered in the list of trade unions kept by him under section 8 of the Trade Union and Labour Relations Act 1974, and

(b) the names of the organisations entitled to have their names entered in the list in accordance with this Part.

(2) The Certification Officer shall keep copies of the list of trade unions, as for the time being in force, available for public inspection at all reasonable hours free of charge.

(3) A copy of the list shall be included in his annual report.

(4) The fact that the name of an organisation is included in the list of trade unions is evidence (in Scotland, sufficient evidence) that the organisation is a trade union.

(5) On the application of an organisation whose name is included in the list, the Certification Officer shall issue it with a certificate to that effect.

(6) A document purporting to be such a certificate is evidence (in Scotland, sufficient evidence) that the name of the organisation is entered in the list.

3–4 [omitted]

Certification as independent trade union

5 Meaning of 'independent trade union'

In this Act an 'independent trade union' means a trade union which—

(a) is not under the domination or control of an employer or group of employers or of one or more employers' associations, and

(b) is not liable to interference by an employer or any such group or association (arising out of the provision of financial or material support or by any other means whatsoever) tending towards such control;

and references to 'independence', in relation to a trade union, shall be construed accordingly.

6 Application for certificate of independence

(1) A trade union whose name is entered on the list of trade unions may apply to the Certification Officer for a certificate that it is independent.

The application shall be made in such form and manner as the Certification Officer may require and shall be accompanied by the prescribed fee.

(2) The Certification Officer shall maintain a record showing details of all applications made to him under this section and shall keep it available for public inspection (free of charge) at all reasonable hours.

(3) If an application is made by a trade union whose name is not entered on the list of trade unions, the Certification Officer shall refuse a certificate of independence and shall enter that refusal on the record.

(4) In any other case, he shall not come to a decision on the application before the end of the period of one month after it has been entered on the record; and before coming to his decision he shall make such enquiries as he thinks fit and shall take into account any relevant information submitted to him by any person.

(5) He shall then decide whether the applicant trade union is independent and shall enter his decision and the date of his decision on the record.

(6) If he decides that the trade union is independent he shall issue a certificate accordingly; and if he decides that it is not, he shall give reasons for his decision.

7 Withdrawal or cancellation of certificate

(1) The Certification Officer may withdraw a trade union's certificate of independence if he is of the opinion that the union is no longer independent.

(2) Where he proposes to do so he shall notify the trade union and enter notice of the proposal in the record.

(3) He shall not come to a decision on the proposal before the end of the period of one month after notice of it was entered on the record; and before coming to his decision he shall make such enquiries as he thinks fit and shall take into account any relevant information submitted to him by any person.

(4) He shall then decide whether the trade union is independent and shall enter his decision and the date of his decision on the record.

(5) He shall confirm or withdraw the certificate accordingly; and if he decides to withdraw it, he shall give reasons for his decision.

(6) Where the name of an organisation is removed from the list of trade unions, the Certification Officer shall cancel any certificate of independence in force in respect of that organisation by entering on the record the fact that the organisation's name has been removed from that list and that the certificate is accordingly cancelled.

8 [omitted]

Supplementary

9 Appeal against decision of Certification Officer

(1) An organisation aggrieved by the refusal of the Certification Officer to enter its name in the list of trade unions, or by a decision of his to remove its name from the list, may appeal to the Employment Appeal Tribunal on any appealable question.

(2) A trade union aggrieved by the refusal of the Certification Officer to issue it with a certificate of independence, or by a decision of his to withdraw its certificate, may appeal to the Employment Appeal Tribunal on any appealable question.

(3) [repealed]

(4) For the purposes of this section, an appealable question is any question of law arising in the proceedings before, or arising from the decision of, the Certification Officer.

Chapter II Status and Property of Trade Unions

General

10 Quasi-corporate status of trade unions

(1) A trade union is not a body corporate but—

(a) it is capable of making contracts;

(b) it is capable of suing and being sued in its own name, whether in proceedings relating to property or founded on contract or tort or any other cause of action; and

(c) proceedings for an offence alleged to have been committed by it or on its behalf may be brought against it in its own name.

(2) A trade union shall not be treated as if it were a body corporate except to the extent authorised by the provisions of this Part.

(3) A trade union shall not be registered—

(a) as a company under the Companies Act 2006; or

(b) under the Friendly Societies Act 1974 or the Co-operative and Community Benefit Societies Act 2014;

and any such registration of a trade union (whenever effected) is void.

11 Exclusion of common law rules as to restraint of trade

(1) The purposes of a trade union are not, by reason only that they are in restraint of trade, unlawful so as—

(a) to make any member of the trade union liable to criminal proceedings for conspiracy or otherwise, or

(b) to make any agreement or trust void or voidable.

(2) No rule of a trade union is unlawful or unenforceable by reason only that it is in restraint of trade.

Property of trade union

12 Property to be vested in trustees

(1) All property belonging to a trade union shall be vested in trustees in trust for it.

(2) A judgment, order or award made in proceedings of any description brought against a trade union is enforceable, by way of execution, diligence, punishment for contempt or otherwise, against any property held in trust for it to the same extent and in the same manner as if it were a body corporate.

(3) Subsection (2) has effect subject to section 23 (restriction on enforcement of awards against certain property).

13–14 [omitted]

15 Prohibition on use of funds to indemnify unlawful conduct

(1) It is unlawful for property of a trade union to be applied in or towards—

(a) the payment for an individual of a penalty which has been or may be imposed on him for an offence or for contempt of court,

(b) the securing of any such payment, or

(c) the provision of anything for indemnifying an individual in respect of such a penalty.

(2) Where any property of a trade union is so applied for the benefit of an individual on whom a penalty has been or may be imposed, then—

(a) in the case of a payment, an amount equal to the payment is recoverable by the union from him, and

(b) in any other case, he is liable to account to the union for the value of the property applied.

(3) If a trade union fails to bring or continue proceedings which it is entitled to bring by virtue of subsection (2), a member of the union who claims that the failure is unreasonable may apply to the court on that ground for an order authorising him to bring or continue the proceedings on the union's behalf and at the union's expense.

(4) In this section 'penalty', in relation to an offence, includes an order to pay compensation and an order for the forfeiture of any property; and references to the imposition of a penalty for an offence shall be construed accordingly.

(5) The Secretary of State may by order designate offences in relation to which the provisions of this section do not apply.

Any such order shall be made by statutory instrument which shall be subject to annulment in pursuance of a resolution of either House of Parliament.

(6) This section does not affect—

(a) any other enactment, any rule of law or any provision of the rules of a trade union which makes it unlawful for the property of a trade union to be applied in a particular way; or

(b) any other remedy available to a trade union, the trustees of its property or any of its members in respect of an unlawful application of the union's property.

(7) In this section 'member', in relation to a trade union consisting wholly or partly of, or of representatives of, constituent or affiliated organisations, includes a member of any of the constituent or affiliated organisations.

16 Remedy against trustees for unlawful use of union property

(1) A member of a trade union who claims that the trustees of the union's property—

(a) have so carried out their functions, or are proposing so to carry out their functions, as to cause or permit an unlawful application of the union's property, or

(b) have complied, or are proposing to comply, with an unlawful direction which has been or may be given, or purportedly given, to them under the rules of the union,

may apply to the court for an order under this section.

(2) In a case relating to property which has already been unlawfully applied, or to an unlawful direction that has already been complied with, an application under this section may be made only by a person who was a member of the union at the time when the property was applied or, as the case may be, the direction complied with.

(3) Where the court is satisfied that the claim is well-founded, it shall make such order as it considers appropriate. The court may in particular—

(a) require the trustees (if necessary, on behalf of the union) to take all such steps as may be specified in the order for protecting or recovering the property of the union;

(b) appoint a receiver of, or in Scotland a judicial factor on, the property of the union;

(c) remove one or more of the trustees.

(4) Where the court makes an order under this section in a case in which—

(a) property of the union has been applied in contravention of an order of any court, or in compliance with a direction given in contravention of such an order, or

(b) the trustees were proposing to apply property in contravention of such an order or to comply with any such direction,

the court shall by its order remove all the trustees except any trustee who satisfies the court that there is a good reason for allowing him to remain a trustee.

(5) Without prejudice to any other power of the court, the court may on an application for an order under this section grant such interlocutory relief (in Scotland, such interim order) as it considers appropriate.

(6) This section does not affect any other remedy available in respect of a breach of trust by the trustees of a trade union's property.

(7) In this section 'member', in relation to a trade union consisting wholly or partly of, or of representatives of, constituent or affiliated organisations, includes a member of any of the constituent or affiliated organisations.

17–19 [omitted]

Liability of trade unions in proceedings in tort

20 Liability of trade union in certain proceedings in tort

(1) Where proceedings in tort are brought against a trade union—

(a) on the ground that an act—

(i) induces another person to break a contract or interferes or induces another person to interfere with its performance, or

(ii) consists in threatening that a contract (whether one to which the union is a party or not) will be broken or its performance interfered with, or that the union will induce another person to break a contract or interfere with its performance, or

(b) in respect of an agreement or combination by two or more persons to do or to procure the doing of an act which, if it were done without any such agreement or combination, would be actionable in tort on such a ground,

then, for the purpose of determining in those proceedings whether the union is liable in respect of the act in question, that act shall be taken to have been done by the union if, but only if, it is to be taken to have been authorised or endorsed by the trade union in accordance with the following provisions.

(2) An act shall be taken to have been authorised or endorsed by a trade union if it was done, or was authorised or endorsed—

(a) by any person empowered by the rules to do, authorise or endorse acts of the kind in question, or

(b) by the principal executive committee or the president or general secretary, or

(c) by any other committee of the union or any other official of the union (whether employed by it or not).

(3) For the purposes of paragraph (c) of subsection (2)—

(a) any group of persons constituted in accordance with the rules of the union is a committee of the union; and

(b) an act shall be taken to have been done, authorised or endorsed by an official if it was done, authorised or endorsed by, or by any member of, any group of persons of which he was at the material time a member, the purposes of which included organising or co-ordinating industrial action.

(4) The provisions of paragraphs (b) and (c) of subsection (2) apply notwithstanding anything in the rules of the union, or in any contract or rule of law, but subject to the provisions of section 21 (repudiation by union of certain acts).

(5) Where for the purposes of any proceedings an act is by virtue of this section taken to have been done by a trade union, nothing in this section shall affect the liability of any other person, in those or any other proceedings, in respect of that act.

(6) In proceedings arising out of an act which is by virtue of this section taken to have been done by a trade union, the power of the court to grant an injunction or interdict includes power to require the union to take such steps as the court considers appropriate for ensuring—

(a) that there is no, or no further, inducement of persons to take part or to continue to take part in industrial action, and

(b) that no person engages in any conduct after the granting of the injunction or interdict by virtue of having been induced before it was granted to take part or to continue to take part in industrial action.

The provisions of subsections (2) to (4) above apply in relation to proceedings for failure to comply with any such injunction or interdict as they apply in relation to the original proceedings.

(7) In this section 'rules', in relation to a trade union, means the written rules of the union and any other written provision forming part of the contract between a member and the other members.

21 Repudiation by union of certain acts

(1) An act shall not be taken to have been authorised or endorsed by a trade union by virtue only of paragraph (c) of section 20(2) if it was repudiated by the executive, president or general secretary as soon as reasonably practicable after coming to the knowledge of any of them.

(2) Where an act is repudiated—

(a) written notice of the repudiation must be given to the committee or official in question, without delay, and

(b) the union must do its best to give individual written notice of the fact and date of repudiation, without delay—

(i) to every member of the union who the union has reason to believe is taking part, or might otherwise take part, in industrial action as a result of the act, and

(ii) to the employer of every such member.

(3) The notice given to members in accordance with paragraph (b)(i) of subsection (2) must contain the following statement—

'Your union has repudiated the call (or calls) for industrial action to which this notice relates and will give no support to unofficial industrial action taken in response to it (or them). If you are dismissed while taking unofficial industrial action, you will have no right to complain of unfair dismissal.'

(4) If subsection (2) or (3) is not complied with, the repudiation shall be treated as ineffective.

(5) An act shall not be treated as repudiated if at any time after the union concerned purported to repudiate it the executive, president or general secretary has behaved in a manner which is inconsistent with the purported repudiation.

(6) The executive, president or general secretary shall be treated as so behaving if, on a request made to any of them within three months of the purported repudiation by a person who—

(a) is a party to a commercial contract whose performance has been or may be interfered with as a result of the act in question, and

(b) has not been given written notice by the union of the repudiation, it is not forthwith confirmed in writing that the act has been repudiated.

(7) In this section 'commercial contract' means any contract other than—

(a) a contract of employment, or

(b) any other contract under which a person agrees personally to do work or perform services for another.

22 Limit on damages awarded against trade unions in actions in tort

(1) This section applies to any proceedings in tort brought against a trade union, except—

(a) proceedings for personal injury as a result of negligence, nuisance or breach of duty;

(b) proceedings for breach of duty in connection with the ownership, occupation, possession, control or use of property;

(c) proceedings brought by virtue of Part I of the Consumer Protection Act 1987 (product liability).

(2) In any proceedings in tort to which this section applies the amount which may be awarded against the union by way of damages shall not exceed the following limit—

Number of members of union	Maximum award of damages
Less than 5,000	£40,000
5,000 or more but less than 25,000	£200,000
25,000 or more but less than 100,000	£500,000
100,000 or more	£1,000,000

(3)–(4) [omitted]

(5) In this section—

'breach of duty' means breach of a duty imposed by any rule of law or by or under any enactment;

'personal injury' includes any disease and any impairment of a person's physical or mental condition; and

'property' means any property, whether real or personal (or in Scotland, heritable or moveable).

Restriction on enforcement against certain property

23 Restriction on enforcement of awards against certain property

(1) Where in any proceedings an amount is awarded by way of damages, costs or expenses—

(a) against a trade union,

(b) against trustees in whom property is vested in trust for a trade union, in their capacity as such (and otherwise than in respect of a breach of trust on their part), or

(c) against members or officials of a trade union on behalf of themselves and all of the members of the union,

no part of that amount is recoverable by enforcement against any protected property.

(2) The following is protected property—

(a) property belonging to the trustees otherwise than in their capacity as such;

(b) property belonging to any member of the union otherwise than jointly or in common with the other members;

(c) property belonging to an official of the union who is neither a member nor a trustee;

(d) property comprised in the union's political fund where that fund—

(i) is subject to rules of the union which prevent property which is or has been comprised in the fund from being used for financing strikes or other industrial action, and

(ii) was so subject at the time when the act in respect of which the proceedings are brought was done;

(e) property comprised in a separate fund maintained in accordance with the rules of the union for the purpose only of providing provident benefits.

(3) For this purpose 'provident benefits' includes—

(a) any payment expressly authorised by the rules of the union which is made—

(i) to a member during sickness or incapacity from personal injury or while out of work, or

(ii) to an aged member by way of superannuation, or

(iii) to a member who has met with an accident or has lost his tools by fire or theft;

(b) a payment in discharge or aid of funeral expenses on the death of a member or the spouse or civil partner of a member or as provision for the children of a deceased member.

24–45D [omitted]

Chapter IV Elections for Certain Positions

Duty to hold elections

46 Duty to hold elections for certain positions

(1) A trade union shall secure—

(a) that every person who holds a position in the union to which this Chapter applies does so by virtue of having been elected to it at an election satisfying the requirements of this Chapter, and

(b) that no person continues to hold such a position for more than five years without being re-elected at such an election.

(2) The positions to which this Chapter applies (subject as mentioned below) are—

(a) member of the executive,

(b) any position by virtue of which a person is a member of the executive,

(c) president, and

(d) general secretary.

(3) In this Chapter 'member of the executive' includes any person who, under the rules or practice of the union, may attend and speak at some or all of the meetings of the executive, otherwise than for the purpose of providing the committee with factual information or with technical or professional advice with respect to matters taken into account by the executive in carrying out its functions.

(4) This Chapter does not apply to the position of president or general secretary if the holder of that position—

(a) is not, in respect of that position, either a voting member of the executive or an employee of the union,

(b) holds that position for a period which under the rules of the union cannot end more than 13 months after he took it up, and

(c) has not held either position at any time in the period of twelve months ending with the day before he took up that position.

(4A) This Chapter also does not apply to the position of president if—

(a) the holder of that position was elected or appointed to it in accordance with the rules of the union,

(b) at the time of his election or appointment as president he held a position mentioned in paragraph (a), (b) or (d) of subsection (2) by virtue of having been elected to it at a qualifying election,

(c) it is no more than five years since—

(i) he was elected, or re-elected, to the position mentioned in paragraph (b) which he held at the time of his election or appointment as president, or

(ii) he was elected to another position of a kind mentioned in that paragraph at a qualifying election held after his election or appointment as president of the union, and

(d) he has, at all times since his election or appointment as president, held a position mentioned in paragraph (a), (b) or (d) of subsection (2) by virtue of having been elected to it at a qualifying election.

(5) In subsection (4) a 'voting member of the executive' means a person entitled in his own right to attend meetings of the executive and to vote on matters on which votes are taken by the executive (whether or not he is entitled to attend all such meetings or to vote on all such matters or in all circumstances).

(5A) In subsection (4A) 'qualifying election' means an election satisfying the requirements of this Chapter.

(5B) The 'requirements of this Chapter' referred to in subsections (1) and (5A) are those set out in sections 47 to 52 below.

(6) The provisions of this Chapter apply notwithstanding anything in the rules or practice of the union; and the terms and conditions on which a person is employed by the union shall be disregarded in so far as they would prevent the union from complying with the provisions of this Chapter.

Requirements to be satisfied with respect to elections

47 Candidates

(1) No member of the trade union shall be unreasonably excluded from standing as a candidate.

(2) No candidate shall be required, directly or indirectly, to be a member of a political party.

(3) A member of a trade union shall not be taken to be unreasonably excluded from standing as a candidate if he is excluded on the ground that he belongs to a class of which all the members are excluded by the rules of the union.

But a rule which provides for such a class to be determined by reference to whom the union chooses to exclude shall be disregarded.

48–49 [omitted]

50 Entitlement to vote

(1) Subject to the provisions of this section, entitlement to vote shall be accorded equally to all members of the trade union.

(2) The rules of the union may exclude entitlement to vote in the case of all members belonging to one of the following classes, or to a class falling within one of the following—

(a) members who are not in employment;

(b) members who are in arrears in respect of any subscription or contribution due to the union;

(c) members who are apprentices, trainees or students or new members of the union.

(3) The rules of the union may restrict entitlement to vote to members who fall within—

(a) a class determined by reference to a trade or occupation,

(b) a class determined by reference to a geographical area, or

(c) a class which is by virtue of the rules of the union treated as a separate section within the union,

or to members who fall within a class determined by reference to any combination of the factors mentioned in paragraphs (a), (b) and (c).

The reference in paragraph (c) to a section of a trade union includes a part of the union which is itself a trade union.

(4) Entitlement may not be restricted in accordance with subsection (3) if the effect is that any member of the union is denied entitlement to vote at all elections held for the purposes of this Chapter otherwise than by virtue of belonging to a class excluded in accordance with subsection (2).

51 Voting

(1) The method of voting must be by the marking of a voting paper by the person voting.

(2) Each voting paper must—

(a) state the name of the independent scrutineer and clearly specify the address to which, and the date by which, it is to be returned,

(b) be given one of a series of consecutive whole numbers every one of which is used in giving a different number in that series to each voting paper printed or otherwise produced for the purposes of the election, and

(c) be marked with its number.

(3) Every person who is entitled to vote at the election must—

(a) be allowed to vote without interference from, or constraint imposed by, the union or any of its members, officials or employees, and

(b) so far as is reasonably practicable, be enabled to do so without incurring any direct cost to himself.

(4) So far as is reasonably practicable, every person who is entitled to vote at the election must—

(a) have sent to him by post, at his home address or another address which he has requested the trade union in writing to treat as his postal address, a voting paper which either lists the candidates at the election or is accompanied by a separate list of those candidates; and

(b) be given a convenient opportunity to vote by post.

(5) The ballot shall be conducted so as to secure that—

(a) so far as is reasonably practicable, those voting do so in secret, and

(b) the votes given at the election are fairly and accurately counted.

For the purposes of paragraph (b) an inaccuracy in counting shall be disregarded if it is accidental and on a scale which could not affect the result of the election.

(6) The ballot shall be so conducted as to secure that the result of the election is determined solely by counting the number of votes cast directly for each candidate.

(7) Nothing in subsection (6) shall be taken to prevent the system of voting used for the election being the single transferable vote, that is, a vote capable of being given so as to indicate the voter's order of preference for the candidates and of being transferred to the next choice—

(a) when it is not required to give a prior choice the necessary quota of votes, or

(b) when, owing to the deficiency in the number of votes given for a prior choice, that choice is eliminated from the list of candidates.

51A–52 [omitted]

53 Uncontested elections

Nothing in this Chapter shall be taken to require a ballot to be held at an uncontested election.

Remedy for failure to comply with requirements

54 Remedy for failure to comply with requirements: general

(1) A person alleging a failure on the part of a trade union to comply with any of the requirements of this Chapter may apply for—

(a) a declaration under section 55 (by the Certification Officer), or

(b) a declaration under section 56 (by the court);

(2) An application for a declaration under section 55 or 56 may be made only—

(a) by a person who is a member of the trade union (provided, where the election has been held, he was also a member at the time when it was held), or

(b) by a person who is or was a candidate at the election;

and the references in those sections to a person having a sufficient interest are to such a person.

(3) Where an election has been held, no application under those sections with respect to that election may be made after the end of the period of one year beginning with the day on which the union announced the result of the election.

55 Application to Certification Officer

(1) Where the Certification Officer is satisfied that a trade union has failed to comply with any of the requirements of this Chapter—

(a) on an application by a person having a sufficient interest (see section 54(2)),

(b) [revoked],

the Officer may make a declaration to that effect.

(2) Before deciding the matter the Certification Officer—

(a) may make such enquiries as the Officer thinks fit,

(b) must give the union and the applicant an opportunity to make written representations, and

(c) may give the union and the applicant an opportunity to make oral representations.

(3) If he makes a declaration he shall specify in it the provisions with which the trade union has failed to comply.

(4) Where he makes a declaration and is satisfied that steps have been taken by the union with a view to remedying the declared failure, or securing that a failure of the same or any similar kind does not occur in future, or that the union has agreed to take such steps, he shall specify those steps in the declaration.

(5) Whether he makes or refuses a declaration, he shall give reasons for his decision in writing; and the reasons may be accompanied by written observations on any matter arising from, or connected with, the proceedings.

(5A) Where the Certification Officer makes a declaration he shall also, unless he considers that to do so would be inappropriate, make an enforcement order, that is, an order imposing on the union one or more of the following requirements—

(a) to secure the holding of an election in accordance with the order;

(b) to take such other steps to remedy the declared failure as may be specified in the order;

(c) to abstain from such acts as may be so specified with a view to securing that a failure of the same or a similar kind does not occur in future.

The Certification Officer shall in an order imposing any such requirement as is mentioned in paragraph (a) or (b) specify the period within which the union is to comply with the requirements of the order.

(5B) Where the Certification Officer makes an order requiring the union to hold a fresh election, he shall (unless he considers that it would be inappropriate to do so in the particular circumstances of the case) require the election to be conducted in accordance with the requirements of this Chapter and such other provisions as may be made by the order.

(5C) Where an enforcement order has been made—

(a) any person who is a member of the union and was a member at the time the order was made, or

(b) any person who is or was a candidate in the election in question,

is entitled to enforce obedience to the order as if he had made an application under this section.

(6) In exercising his functions under this section the Certification Officer shall ensure that, so far as is reasonably practicable, an application made to him is determined within six months of being made.

(7) Where he requests a person to furnish information to him in connection with enquiries made by him under this section, he shall specify the date by which that information is to be furnished and, unless he considers that it would be inappropriate to do so, shall proceed with his determination notwithstanding that the information has not been furnished to him by the specified date.

(8) A declaration made by the Certification Officer under this section may be relied on as if it were a declaration made by the court.

(9) An enforcement order made by the Certification Officer under this section may be enforced (by the Certification Officer, the applicant or a person mentioned in subsection (5C)) in the same way as an order of the court.

(10) The following paragraphs have effect if a person applies under section 56 in relation to an alleged failure—

(a) that person may not apply under this section in relation to that failure;

(b) on an application by a different person under this section in relation to that failure, the Certification Officer shall have due regard to any declaration, order, observations or reasons made or given by the court regarding that failure and brought to the Certification Officer's notice.

56 Application to court

(1) A person having a sufficient interest (see section 54(2)) who claims that a trade union has failed to comply with any of the requirements of this Chapter may apply to the court for a declaration to that effect.

(2) [repealed]

(3) If the court makes the declaration asked for, it shall specify in the declaration the provisions with which the trade union has failed to comply.

(4) Where the court makes a declaration it shall also, unless it considers that to do so would be inappropriate, make an enforcement order, that is, an order imposing on the union one or more of the following requirements—

(a) to secure the holding of an election in accordance with the order;

(b) to take such other steps to remedy the declared failure as may be specified in the order;

(c) to abstain from such acts as may be so specified with a view to securing that a failure of the same or a similar kind does not occur in future.

The court shall in an order imposing any such requirement as is mentioned in paragraph (a) or (b) specify the period within which the union is to comply with the requirements of the order.

(5) where the court makes an order requiring the union to hold a fresh election, the court shall (unless it considers that it would be inappropriate to do so in the particular circumstances of the case) require the election to be conducted in accordance with the requirements of this Chapter and such other provisions as may be made by the order.

(6) Where an enforcement order has been made—

(a) any person who is a member of the union and was a member at the time the order was made, or

(b) any person who is or was a candidate in the election in question,

is entitled to enforce obedience to the order as if he had made the application on which the order was made.

(7) Without prejudice to any other power of the court, the court may on an application under this section grant such interlocutory relief (in Scotland, such interim order) as it considers appropriate.

(8) The following paragraphs have effect if a person applies under section 55 in relation to an alleged failure—

(a) that person may not apply under this section in relation to that failure;

(b) on an application by a different person under this section in relation to that failure, the court shall have due regard to any declaration, order, observations or reasons made or given by the Certification Officer regarding that failure and brought to the court's notice.

56A Appeals from Certification Officer

An appeal lies to the Employment Appeal Tribunal on any question of law arising in proceedings before or arising from any decision of the Certification Officer under section 55.

57–61 [omitted]

Chapter V Rights of Trade Union Members

Right to a ballot before industrial action

62 Right to a ballot before industrial action

(1) A member of a trade union who claims that members of the union, including himself, are likely to be or have been induced by the union to take part or to continue to take part in industrial action which does not have the support of a ballot may apply to the court for an order under this section.

In this section 'the relevant time' means the time when the application is made.

(2) For this purpose the question whether industrial action is regarded as having the support of a ballot shall be determined in accordance with section 226(2).

(3) Where on an application under this section the court is satisfied that the claim is well-founded, it shall make such order as it considers appropriate for requiring the union to take steps for ensuring—

(a) that there is no, or no further, inducement of members of the union to take part or to continue to take part in the industrial action to which the application relates, and

(b) that no member engages in conduct after the making of the order by virtue of having been induced before the making of the order to take part or continue to take part in the action.

(4) Without prejudice to any other power of the court, the court may on an application under this section grant such interlocutory relief (in Scotland, such interim order) as it considers appropriate.

(5) For the purposes of this section an act shall be taken to be done by a trade union if it is authorised or endorsed by the union; and the provisions of section 20(2) to (4) apply for the purpose of determining whether an act is to be taken to be so authorised or endorsed.

Those provisions also apply in relation to proceedings for failure to comply with an order under this section as they apply in relation to the original proceedings.

(6) In this section—

'inducement' includes an inducement which is or would be ineffective, whether because of the member's unwillingness to be influenced by it or for any other reason; and

'industrial action' means a strike or other industrial action by persons employed under contracts of employment.

(7) Where a person holds any office or employment under the Crown on terms which do not constitute a contract of employment between that person and the Crown, those terms shall nevertheless be deemed to constitute such a contract for the purposes of this section.

(8) References in this section to a contract of employment include any contract under which one person personally does work or performs services for another; and related expressions shall be construed accordingly.

(9) Nothing in this section shall be construed as requiring a trade union to hold separate ballots for the purposes of this section and sections 226 to 234 (requirement of ballot before action by trade union).

Right not to be denied access to the courts

63 Right not to be denied access to the courts

(1) This section applies where a matter is under the rules of a trade union required or allowed to be submitted for determination or conciliation in accordance with the rules of the union, but a provision of the rules purporting to provide for that to be a person's only remedy has no effect (or would have no effect if there were one).

(2) Notwithstanding anything in the rules of the union or in the practice of any court, if a member or former member of the union begins proceedings in a court with respect to a matter to which this section applies, then if—

(a) he has previously made a valid application to the union for the matter to be submitted for determination or conciliation in accordance with the union's rules, and

(b) the court proceedings are begun after the end of the period of six months beginning with the day on which the union received the application,

the rules requiring or allowing the matter to be so submitted, and the fact that any relevant steps remain to be taken under the rules, shall be regarded for all purposes as irrelevant to any question whether the court proceedings should be dismissed, stayed or sisted, or adjourned.

(3) An application shall be deemed to be valid for the purposes of subsection (2)(a) unless the union informed the applicant, before the end of the period of 28 days beginning with the date on which the union received the application, of the respects in which the application contravened the requirements of the rules.

(4) If the court is satisfied that any delay in the taking of relevant steps under the rules is attributable to unreasonable conduct of the person who commenced the proceedings, it may treat the period specified in subsection (2)(b) as extended by such further period as it considers appropriate.

(5) In this section—

(a) references to the rules of a trade union include any arbitration or other agreement entered into in pursuance of a requirement imposed by or under the rules; and

(b) references to the relevant steps under the rules, in relation to any matter, include any steps falling to be taken in accordance with the rules for the purposes of or in connection with the determination or conciliation of the matter, or any appeal, review or reconsideration of any determination or award.

(6) This section does not affect any enactment or rule of law by virtue of which a court would apart from this section disregard any such rules of a trade union or any such fact as is mentioned in subsection (2).

Right not to be unjustifiably disciplined

64 Right not to be unjustifiably disciplined

(1) An individual who is or has been a member of a trade union has the right not to be unjustifiably disciplined by the union.

(2) For this purpose an individual is 'disciplined' by a trade union if a determination is made, or purportedly made, under the rules of the union or by an official of the union or a number of persons including an official that—

(a) he should be expelled from the union or a branch or section of the union,

(b) he should pay a sum to the union, to a branch or section of the union or to any other person,

(c) sums tendered by him in respect of an obligation to pay subscriptions or other sums to the union, or to a branch or section of the union, should be treated as unpaid or paid for a different purpose,

(d) he should be deprived to any extent of, or of access to, any benefits, services or facilities which would otherwise be provided or made available to him by virtue of his membership of the union, or a branch or section of the union,

(e) another trade union, or a branch or section of it, should be encouraged or advised not to accept him as a member, or

(f) he should be subjected to some other detriment;

and whether an individual is 'unjustifiably disciplined' shall be determined in accordance with section 65.

(3) Where a determination made in infringement of an individual's right under this section requires the payment of a sum or the performance of an obligation, no person is entitled in any proceedings to rely on that determination for the purpose of recovering the sum or enforcing the obligation.

(4) Subject to that, the remedies for infringement of the right conferred by this section are as provided by sections 66 and 67, and not otherwise.

(5) The right not to be unjustifiably disciplined is in addition to (and not in substitution for) any right which exists apart from this section; and, subject to section 66(4), nothing in this section or sections 65 to 67 affects any remedy for infringement of any such right.

65 Meaning of 'unjustifiably disciplined'

(1) An individual is unjustifiably disciplined by a trade union if the actual or supposed conduct which constitutes the reason, or one of the reasons, for disciplining him is—

(a) conduct to which this section applies, or

(b) something which is believed by the union to amount to such conduct;

but subject to subsection (6) (cases of bad faith in relation to assertion of wrongdoing).

(2) This section applies to conduct which consists in—

(a) failing to participate in or support a strike or other industrial action (whether by members of the union or by others), or indicating opposition to or a lack of support for such action;

(b) failing to contravene, for a purpose connected with such a strike or other industrial action, a requirement imposed on him by or under a contract of employment;

(c) asserting (whether by bringing proceedings or otherwise) that the union, any official or representative of it or a trustee of its property has contravened, or is proposing to contravene, a requirement which is, or is thought to be, imposed by or under the rules of the union or any other agreement or by or under any enactment (whenever passed) or any rule of law;

(d) encouraging or assisting a person—

(i) to perform an obligation imposed on him by a contract of employment, or

(ii) to make or attempt to vindicate any such assertion as is mentioned in paragraph (c);

(e) contravening a requirement imposed by or in consequence of a determination which infringes the individual's or another individual's right not to be unjustifiably disciplined;

(f) failing to agree, or withdrawing agreement, to the making from his wages (in accordance with arrangements between his employer and the union) of deductions representing payments to the union in respect of his membership,
(g) resigning or proposing to resign from the union or from another union, becoming or proposing to become a member of another union, refusing to become a member of another union, or being a member of another union,
(h) working with, or proposing to work with, individuals who are not members of the union or who are or are not members of another union,
(i) working for, or proposing to work for, an employer who employs or who has employed individuals who are not members of the union or who are or are not members of another union, or
(j) requiring the union to do an act which the union is, by any provision of this Act, required to do on the requisition of a member.

(3) This section applies to conduct which involves the Certification Officer being consulted or asked to provide advice or assistance with respect to any matter whatever, or which involves any person being consulted or asked to provide advice or assistance with respect to a matter which forms, or might form, the subject-matter of any such assertion as is mentioned in subsection (2)(c) above.

(4) This section also applies to conduct which consists in proposing to engage in, or doing anything preparatory or incidental to, conduct falling within subsection (2) or (3).

(5) This section does not apply to an act, omission or statement comprised in conduct falling within subsection (2), (3) or (4) above if it is shown that the act, omission or statement is one in respect of which individuals would be disciplined by the union irrespective of whether their acts, omissions or statements were in connection with conduct within subsection (2) or (3) above.

(6) An individual is not unjustifiably disciplined if it is shown—
(a) that the reason for disciplining him, or one of them, is that he made such an assertion as is mentioned in subsection (2)(c), or encouraged or assisted another person to make or attempt to vindicate such an assertion,
(b) that the assertion was false, and
(c) that he made the assertion, or encouraged or assisted another person to make or attempt to vindicate it, in the belief that it was false or otherwise in bad faith,

and that there was no other reason for disciplining him or that the only other reasons were reasons in respect of which he does not fall to be treated as unjustifiably disciplined.

(7) In this section—

'conduct' includes statements, acts and omissions;

'contract of employment', in relation to an individual, includes any agreement between that individual and a person for whom he works or normally works;

'employer' includes such a person and related expressions shall be construed accordingly;

'representative', in relation to a union, means a person acting or purporting to act—
(a) in his capacity as a member of the union, or
(b) on the instructions or advice of a person acting or purporting to act in that capacity or in the capacity of an official of the union.

'require' (on the part of an individual) includes request or apply for, and 'requisition' shall be construed accordingly; and

'wages' shall be construed in accordance with the definitions of 'contract of employment', 'employer' and related expressions.

(8) Where a person holds any office or employment under the Crown on terms which do not constitute a contract of employment between him and the Crown, those terms shall nevertheless be deemed to constitute such a contract for the purposes of this section.

66 Complaint of infringement of right

(1) An individual who claims that he has been unjustifiably disciplined by a trade union may present a complaint against the union to an employment tribunal.

(2) The tribunal shall not entertain such a complaint unless it is presented—

(a) before the end of the period of three months beginning with the date of the making of the determination claimed to infringe the right, or

(b) where the tribunal is satisfied—

(i) that it was not reasonably practicable for the complaint to be presented before the end of that period, or

(ii) that any delay in making the complaint is wholly or partly attributable to a reasonable attempt to appeal against the determination or to have it reconsidered or reviewed,

within such further period as the tribunal considers reasonable.

(2A) [omitted]

(3) Where the tribunal finds the complaint well-founded, it shall make a declaration to that effect.

(4) Where a complaint relating to an expulsion which is presented under this section is declared to be well-founded, no complaint in respect of the expulsion shall be presented or proceeded with under section 174 (right not to be excluded or expelled from trade union).

67 Further remedies for infringement of right

(1) An individual whose complaint under section 66 has been declared to be well-founded may make an application to an employment tribunal for one or both of the following—

(a) an award of compensation to be paid to him by the union;

(b) an order that the union pay him an amount equal to any sum which he has paid in pursuance of any such determination as is mentioned in section 64(2)(b).

(2) [repealed]

(3) An application under this section shall not be entertained if made before the end of the period of four weeks beginning with the date of the declaration or after the end of the period of six months beginning with that date.

(4) [repealed]

(5) The amount of compensation awarded shall, subject to the following provisions, be such as the employment tribunal considers just and equitable in all the circumstances.

(6) In determining the amount of compensation to be awarded, the same rule shall be applied concerning the duty of a person to mitigate his loss as applies to damages recoverable under the common law in England and Wales or Scotland.

(7) Where the employment tribunal finds that the infringement complained of was to any extent caused or contributed to by the action of the applicant, it shall reduce the amount of the compensation by such proportion as it considers just and equitable having regard to that finding.

(8) The amount of compensation awarded calculated in accordance with subsections (5) to (7) shall not exceed the aggregate of—

(a) an amount equal to 30 times the limit for the time being imposed by section 227(1)(a) of the Employment Rights Act 1996 (maximum amount of a week's pay for basic award in unfair dismissal cases), and

(b) an amount equal to the limit for the time being imposed by section 124(1) of that Act (maximum compensatory award in such cases).

(8A) If on the date on which the application was made—

(a) the determination infringing the applicant's right not to be unjustifiably disciplined has not been revoked, or

(b) the union has failed to take all the steps necessary for securing the reversal of anything done for the purpose of giving effect to the determination,

the amount of compensation shall be not less than the amount for the time being specified in section 176(6A).

(9) [repealed]

Right not to suffer deduction of unauthorised union subscriptions

68 Right not to suffer deduction of unauthorised union subscriptions

(1) Where arrangements ('subscription deduction arrangements') exist between the employer of a worker and a trade union relating to the making from workers' wages of deductions representing payments to the union in respect of the workers' membership of the union ('subscription deductions'), the employer shall ensure that no subscription deduction is made from wages payable to the worker on any day unless—

(a) the worker has authorised in writing the making from his wages of subscription deductions; and

(b) the worker has not withdrawn the authorisation.

(2) A worker withdraws an authorisation given for the purposes of subsection (1), in relation to a subscription deduction which falls to be made from wages payable to him on any day, if a written notice withdrawing the authorisation has been received by the employer in time for it to be reasonably practicable for the employer to secure that no such deduction is made.

(3) A worker's authorisation of the making of subscription deductions from his wages shall not give rise to any obligation on the part of the employer to the worker to maintain or continue to maintain subscription deduction arrangements.

(4) In this section and section 68A, 'employer', 'wages' and 'worker' have the same meanings as in the Employment Rights Act 1996.

68A Complaint of infringement of rights

(1) A worker may present a complaint to an employment tribunal that his employer has made a deduction from his wages in contravention of section 68—

(a) within the period of three months beginning with the date of the payment of the wages from which the deduction, or (if the complaint relates to more than one deduction) the last of the deductions, was made, or

(b) where the tribunal is satisfied that it was not reasonably practicable for the complaint to be presented within that period, within such further period as the tribunal considers reasonable.

(1A) [omitted]

(2) Where a tribunal finds that a complaint under this section is well-founded, it shall make a declaration to that effect and shall order the employer to pay to the worker the whole amount of the deduction, less any such part of the amount as has already been paid to the worker by the employer.

(3) Where the making of a deduction from the wages of a worker both contravenes section 68(1) and involves one or more of the contraventions specified in subsection (4) of this section, the aggregate amount which may be ordered by an employment tribunal or court (whether on the same occasion or on different occasions) to be paid in respect of the contraventions shall not exceed the amount, or (where different amounts may be ordered to be paid in respect of different contraventions) the greatest amount, which may be ordered to be paid in respect of any one of them.

(4) The contraventions referred to in subsection (3) are—

(a) a contravention of the requirement not to make a deduction without having given the particulars required by section 8 (itemised pay statements) or 9(1) (standing statements of fixed deductions) of the Employment Rights Act 1996,

(b) a contravention of section 13 of that Act (requirement not to make unauthorised deductions), and

(c) a contravention of section 86(1) or 90(1) of this Act (requirements not to make deductions of political fund contributions in certain circumstances).

Right to terminate membership of union

69 Right to terminate membership of union

In every contract of membership of a trade union, whether made before or after the passing of this Act, a term conferring a right on the member, on giving reasonable notice and complying with any reasonable conditions, to terminate his membership of the union shall be implied.

Supplementary

70 Membership of constituent or affiliated organisation

In this Chapter 'member', in relation to a trade union consisting wholly or partly of, or of representatives of, constituent or affiliated organisations, includes a member of any of the constituent or affiliated organisations.

Chapter 5ZA Right of trade unions to access workplaces

Access agreements: general

70ZA Access agreements

(1) This section applies for the purposes of this Chapter.

(2) An 'access agreement' is an agreement between a qualifying trade union and an employer that—

(a) provides for one or more officials of the union to physically enter a workplace or communicate with workers (or both) for any of the access purposes, and

(b) is entered into under section 70ZD or is treated as having been entered into under section 70ZE.

(3) A 'qualifying trade union' is a trade union that has a certificate of independence.

(4) 'Access' means—

(a) physical entry into a workplace;

(b) communication with workers.

(5) A reference to communication with workers is a reference to communication with workers (including the provision of information to workers) by any means, whether directly or indirectly.

(6) The 'access purposes' are—

(a) to meet, support, represent, recruit or organise workers (whether or not they are members of a trade union);

(b) to facilitate collective bargaining.

(7) But the access purposes do not include organising industrial action.

(8) Sections 70ZB to 70ZF contain provision about entering into access agreements.

(9) Section 70ZG contains provision about the variation or revocation of access agreements.

(10) Sections 70ZH to 70ZK contain provision about the enforcement of access agreements.

(11) Section 70ZL contains general limitations on the provision that may be made under this Chapter, including in access agreements.

Entering into access agreements

70ZB Access requests and response notices

(1) A qualifying trade union may give an employer a request for access by one or more officials of the union for any of the access purposes.

(2) A request under subsection (1)—

(a) may request access on one or more occasions;

(b) may include the terms on which access is requested (including as to what (if any) assistance the employer is requested to provide in relation to the access).

(3) A request under subsection (1) must—

(a) be in the prescribed form;

(b) include the prescribed information;

(c) be given in the prescribed manner.

(4) An employer that has been given a request under subsection (1) may give the union a notice agreeing with the request or disagreeing with the request (in whole or in part).

(5) A notice under subsection (4) must—

(a) be in the prescribed form;

(b) include the prescribed information;

(c) be given in the prescribed manner.

(6) In this Chapter—
'access request' means a request under subsection (1) given in accordance with subsection (3);
'response notice' means a notice under subsection (4) given in accordance with subsection (5).

70ZC Response period and negotiation period

In sections 70ZD and 70ZE—

(a) 'the response period' means a prescribed period beginning with the day on which an access request is given;
(b) 'the negotiation period' means a prescribed period beginning with the day on which a response notice is given.

70ZD Entering into access agreement by negotiation

(1) An access agreement is entered into under this section if—

(a) a qualifying trade union gives an access request to an employer,
(b) the employer gives the union a response notice before the end of the response period,
(c) before the end of the negotiation period, the union and the employer agree in writing terms on which officials of the union are to have access, and
(d) the union and the employer jointly notify the Central Arbitration Committee of those terms in the prescribed form and manner.

(2) See section 70ZE for the case where an access agreement is treated as being entered into by virtue of a determination of the Central Arbitration Committee.

70ZE Determinations by the Central Arbitration Committee

(1) This section applies if a qualifying trade union has given an access request to an employer and either—

(a) the employer has not given a response notice to the union before the end of the response period, or
(b) the employer has given a response notice before the end of the response period and the negotiation period has ended without the union and the employer agreeing in writing terms on which officials of the union are to have access.

(2) The Central Arbitration Committee may, on an application under this section, make a determination that officials of the union are or are not to have access.

(3)–(7) [omitted]

(8) Section 70ZF makes further provision about determinations under this section.

70ZF Determinations by the Central Arbitration Committee: further provision

(1) Subject to regulations under this section, a determination by the Central Arbitration Committee under section 70ZE must be consistent with the access principles.

(2) The access principles are—

(a) officials of a qualifying trade union should be able to physically enter a workplace or communicate with workers (or both) for any of the access purposes in any manner that does not unreasonably interfere with the employer's business;
(b) an employer should take reasonable steps to facilitate access by officials of a qualifying trade union;
(c) physical entry into a workplace should not be refused solely on the basis that communication with workers by means not involving physical entry into a workplace is permitted;
(d) communication with workers by means not involving physical entry into a workplace should not be refused solely on the basis that physical entry into a workplace is permitted;
(e) access should be refused entirely only where it is reasonable in all the circumstances to do so.

(3)–(6) [omitted]

Variation and revocation of access agreements

70ZG Variation and revocation of access agreements

(1) The parties to an access agreement may at any time vary or revoke the agreement.

(2) A variation or revocation of an access agreement must be in writing.

(3) An access agreement that is varied under this section continues to have effect as an access agreement for the purposes of this Chapter.

(4) The effect of an access agreement being revoked is that it ceases to be an access agreement for the purposes of this Chapter.

(5) A variation or revocation of an access agreement takes effect—

(a) only if the parties jointly notify the Central Arbitration Committee of the variation or revocation in the prescribed form and manner;

(b) only in respect of times after the day on which the Central Arbitration Committee is so notified.

Enforcement of access agreements

70ZH Enforcement of access agreements: initial complaint

(1) A party to an access agreement may make a complaint to the Central Arbitration Committee on the ground that—

(a) the other party has breached the agreement;

(b) a person that is not a party to the agreement has taken or is taking steps to prevent access, or has prevented access, from taking place in accordance with the agreement.

(2) A complaint under subsection (1) must be made before the end of the period of three months beginning with the day on which the matter complained of is alleged to have occurred.

(3) On a complaint under subsection (1), the Central Arbitration Committee may—

(a) vary the agreement;

(b) make a declaration that the complaint is or is not well-founded;

(c) if it makes a declaration that the complaint is well-founded, make an order requiring a person to take any steps specified in the order for the purposes of ensuring that access takes place in accordance with the agreement.

(4) An access agreement that is varied under subsection (3)(a) continues to have effect as an access agreement for the purposes of this Chapter.

(5) An order under subsection (3)(c) may, where it appears to the Central Arbitration Committee necessary or appropriate to do so, make provision different from that made in the agreement.

(6) [omitted]

(7) For the purposes of this section, a reference to a person taking steps includes a reference to a person not doing something.

70ZI Enforcement of access agreements: subsequent complaint

(1) This section applies where the Central Arbitration Committee has made a declaration under section 70ZH(3) that a complaint about a person is well-founded.

(2) A party to an access agreement may make a complaint to the Central Arbitration Committee on any of the following grounds—

(a) that the person has, before the end of the relevant period, carried out the conduct complained of under section 70ZH again;

(b) where the complaint under section 70ZH was that the person breached the agreement, that the person has, before the end of the relevant period, breached the agreement again (whether or not in the way complained of under section 70ZH);

(c) that the person has breached an order under section 70ZH(3)(c).

(3) In subsection (2), 'the relevant period' means the period of 12 months beginning with the date of the declaration.

(4) A complaint under subsection (2) must be made before the end of the period of three months beginning with the day on which the alleged conduct occurs.

(5) On a complaint about a person under subsection (2), the Central Arbitration Committee may—

(a) make a declaration that the complaint is or is not well-founded;

(b) if it makes a declaration that the complaint is well-founded, make an order requiring the person to pay an amount to the Central Arbitration Committee.

(6)–(9) [omitted]

(10) For the purposes of this section, a reference to conduct includes a reference to a person not doing something.

70ZJ–70ZK [omitted]

General limitations on access agreements etc

70ZL General limitations on access agreements etc

(1) Nothing in this Chapter requires or authorises any of the following (each, a 'prohibited activity')—

(a) physical entry by any person into a dwelling;

(b) a disclosure of personal data without the consent of the data subject;

(c) a disclosure of information that would contravene the data protection legislation (but, in determining whether a disclosure would do so, the provisions of this Chapter are to be taken into account).

(2) Accordingly—

(a) a term of an access agreement entered into under section 70ZD that requires or authorises a prohibited activity is of no effect for the purposes of this Chapter;

(b) the Central Arbitration Committee may not specify as a term of an access agreement under section 70ZE any term that would require or authorise a prohibited activity;

(c) the Central Arbitration Committee may not exercise any function under sections 70ZH to 70ZK so as to require or authorise a prohibited activity.

(3) In this section—

(a) 'consent' has the same meaning as in the UK GDPR (see Article 4(11) of the UK GDPR);

(b) 'personal data', 'data subject', 'the data protection legislation' and 'the UK GDPR' have the same meaning as in the Data Protection Act 2018 (see section 3 of that Act).

70ZM [omitted]

70ZN–70C [omitted]

Chapter VI Application of Funds for Political Objects

Restriction on use of funds for certain political objects

71 Restriction on use of funds for political objects

(1) The funds of a trade union shall not be applied in the furtherance of the political objects to which this Chapter applies unless—

(a) there is in force in accordance with this Chapter a resolution (a 'political resolution') approving the furtherance of those objects as an object of the union (see sections 73 to 81), and

(b) there are in force rules of the union as to—

(i) the making of payments in furtherance of those objects out of a separate fund, and

(ii) the making of contributions to that fund by members,

which comply with this Chapter (see sections 82, 84 and 85) and have been approved by the Certification Officer.

(2) This applies whether the funds are so applied directly, or in conjunction with another trade union, association or body, or otherwise indirectly.

72 Political objects to which restriction applies

(1) The political objects to which this Chapter applies are the expenditure of money—

(a) on any contribution to the funds of, or on the payment of expenses incurred directly or indirectly by, a political party;

(b) on the provision of any service or property for use by or on behalf of any political party;

(c) in connection with the registration of electors, the candidature of any person, the selection of any candidate or the holding of any ballot by the union in connection with any election to a political office;

(d) on the maintenance of any holder of a political office;

(e) on the holding of any conference or meeting by or on behalf of a political party or of any other meeting the main purpose of which is the transaction of business in connection with a political party;

(f) on the production, publication or distribution of any literature, document, film, sound recording or advertisement the main purpose of which is to persuade people to vote for a political party or candidate or to persuade them not to vote for a political party or candidate.

(2) Where a person attends a conference or meeting as a delegate or otherwise as a participator in the proceedings, any expenditure incurred in connection with his attendance as such shall, for the purposes of subsection (1)(e), be taken to be expenditure incurred on the holding of the conference or meeting.

(3) In determining for the purposes of subsection (1) whether a trade union has incurred expenditure of a kind mentioned in that subsection, no account shall be taken of the ordinary administrative expenses of the union.

(4) In this section—

'candidate' means a candidate for election to a political office and includes a prospective candidate;

'contribution', in relation to the funds of a political party, includes any fee payable for affiliation to, or membership of, the party and any loan made to the party;

'electors' means electors at an election to a political office;

'film' includes any record, however made, of a sequence of visual images, which is capable of being used as a means of showing that sequence as a moving picture;

'local authority' means a local authority within the meaning of section 270 of the Local Government Act 1972 or section 235 of the Local Government (Scotland) Act 1973; and

'political office' means the office of member of Parliament, member of the European Parliament or member of a local authority or any position within a political party.

72A Application of funds in breach of section 71

(1) A person who is a member of a trade union and who claims that it has applied its funds in breach of section 71 may apply to the Certification Officer for a declaration that it has done so.

(1A) Where an application is made under subsection (1), the Certification Officer must ensure that, so far as is reasonably practicable, it is determined within six months of being made.

(2) Where the Certification Officer is satisfied that a trade union has applied its funds in breach of section 71, the Officer may make a declaration to that effect.

(2A) Before deciding the matter the Certification Officer—

(a) may make such enquiries as the Officer thinks fit,

(b) must give the union and the applicant an opportunity to make written representations, and

(c) may give the union and the applicant an opportunity to make oral representations.

(2B) The Certification Officer—

(a) must give reasons for the Officer's decision in writing, and

(b) may make written observations on any matter arising from, or connected with, the proceedings.

(3) If he makes a declaration he shall specify in it—

(a) the provisions of section 71 breached, and

(b) the amount of the funds applied in breach.

(4) If he makes a declaration and is satisfied that the union has taken or agreed to take steps with a view to—

(a) remedying the declared breach, or

(b) securing that a breach of the same or any similar kind does not occur in future,

he shall specify those steps in making the declaration.

(5) If he makes a declaration he may make such order for remedying the breach as he thinks just under the circumstances.

(6) Where the Certification Officer requests a person to furnish information to him in connection with enquiries made by him under this section, he shall specify the date by which that information is to be furnished and, unless he considers that it would be inappropriate to do so, shall proceed with his determination notwithstanding that the information has not been furnished to him by the specified date.

(7) A declaration made by the Certification Officer under this section may be relied on as if it were a declaration made by the court.

(8) Where an order has been made under this section, any person who is a member of the union and was a member at the time it was made is entitled to enforce obedience to the order as if he had made an application under this section.

(9) An order made by the Certification Officer under this section may be enforced (by the Certification Officer, the applicant or a person mentioned in subsection (8)) in the same way as an order of the court.

(10) If a person applies to the Certification Officer under this section in relation to an alleged breach he may not apply to the court in relation to the breach; but nothing in this subsection shall prevent such a person from exercising any right to appeal against or challenge the Certification Officer's decision on the application to him.

(11) If—

(a) a person applies to the court in relation to an alleged breach, and

(b) the breach is one in relation to which he could have made an application to the Certification Officer under this section,

he may not apply to the Certification Officer under this section in relation to the breach.

Political resolution

73 Passing and effect of political resolution

(1) A political resolution must be passed by a majority of those voting on a ballot of the members of the trade union held in accordance with this Chapter.

(2) A political resolution so passed shall take effect as if it were a rule of the union and may be rescinded in the same manner and subject to the same provisions as such a rule.

(3) [repealed]

(4) Where a political resolution ('the old resolution') is in force and a ballot is held on a new political resolution, then—

(a) if the new resolution is passed, the old resolution shall be treated as rescinded, and

(b) if it is not passed, the old resolution shall cease to have effect at the end of the period of two weeks beginning with the date of the ballot.

74–81 [omitted]

The political fund

82 Rules as to political fund

(1) The trade union's rules must provide—

(a) that payments in the furtherance of the political objects to which this Chapter applies shall be made out of a separate fund (the 'political fund' of the union);

(b) that a member of the union who is not a contributor (see section 84) shall not be under any obligation to contribute to the political fund;

(c) that a member shall not by reason of not being a contributor—

(i) be excluded from any benefits of the union, or

(ii) be placed in any respect either directly or indirectly under a disability or at a disadvantage as compared with other members of the union (except in relation to the control or management of the political fund);

(ca) that, if the union has a political fund, any form (including an electronic form) that a person has to complete in order to become a member of the union shall include—

(i) a statement to the effect that the person may opt out of being a contributor to the fund, and

(ii) a statement setting out the effect of paragraph (c); and

(d) that contribution to the political fund shall not be made a condition for admission to the union.

(2) A member of a trade union who claims that he is aggrieved by a breach of any rule made in pursuance of this section may complain to the Certification Officer.

(2A) Where the Certification Officer is satisfied that a breach has been committed, the Officer may make such order for remedying the breach as he thinks just under the circumstances.

(3) Before deciding the matter the Certification Officer—

(a) may make such enquiries as the Officer thinks fit,

(b) must give a representative of the union and the complainant an opportunity to make written representations, and

(c) may give a representative of the union and the complainant an opportunity to make oral representations.

(3A) Where the Certification Officer requests a person to furnish information to him in connection with enquiries made by him under this section, he shall specify the date by which that information is to be furnished and, unless he considers that it would be inappropriate to do so, shall proceed with his determination notwithstanding that the information has not been furnished to him by the specified date.

(4) [repealed]

(4A) Where an order has been made under this section, any person who is a member of the union and was a member at the time it was made is entitled to enforce obedience to the order as if he had made a complaint under this section.

(4B) An order made by the Certification Officer under this section may be enforced (by the Certification Officer, the complainant or a person mentioned in subsection (4A))—

(a) in England and Wales, in the same way as an order of the county court;

(b) in Scotland, in the same way as an order of the sheriff.

83 Assets and liabilities of political fund

(1) There may be added to a union's political fund only—

(a) sums representing contributions made to the fund by members of the union or by any person other than the union itself, and

(b) property which accrues to the fund in the course of administering the assets of the fund.

(2) The rules of the union shall not be taken to require any member to contribute to the political fund at a time when there is no political resolution in force in relation to the union.

(3) No liability of a union's political fund shall be discharged out of any other fund of the union.

This subsection applies notwithstanding any term or condition on which the liability was incurred or that an asset of the other fund has been charged in connection with the liability.

84 Contributors to political fund

(1) For the purposes of this Act, a member of a trade union is a 'contributor' to the political fund of the union unless an opt-out notice given by the member to the union has effect (see subsection (3)).

(2) An 'opt-out notice' is a notice that the member opts out of being a contributor.

(3) An opt-out notice has effect on and after the relevant day unless the member withdraws the notice.

(4) In subsection (3), 'the relevant day' means—

(a) in a case where—

(i) a political resolution is passed on a ballot held at a time when no such resolution is in force, and

(ii) the opt-out notice is given before the end of the period of four weeks beginning with the day on which an opt-out information notice is given to the member under section 84A,

the day on which the opt-out notice is given;

(b) in any other case, the earlier of—

(i) a day specified in, or determined in accordance with, the rules of the union, and

(ii) 1 January in the year following the year in which the opt-out notice is given.

(5) A member of a trade union withdraws an opt-out notice by giving the union notice of the withdrawal (a 'withdrawal notice').

(6) A member of a trade union may give an opt-out notice or a withdrawal notice—

(a) by delivering it (either personally or by an authorised agent or by post) at the head office or a branch office of the union;

(b) by sending it by email to an address that the union has told its members can be used for sending such notices;

(c) by completing an electronic form provided by the union which sets out the notice, and sending it to the union by electronic means in accordance with instructions given by the union;

(d) by such other electronic means as may be prescribed.

(7)–(8) [omitted]

84A Opt-out information notices

(1) A trade union must give an opt-out information notice to each member of the union—

(a) within the period of eight weeks beginning with the day after the day on which a political resolution is passed by the members of the union under section 73, and

(b) within the period of eight weeks beginning with the end of—

(i) the period of ten years beginning with the day on which a political resolution is passed, and

(ii) each successive period of ten years,

unless during that period of ten years the political resolution is rescinded or otherwise ceases to have effect.

(2) An 'opt-out information notice' is a notice stating that—

(a) each member of the union has the right not to be a contributor to the political fund of the union, and

(b) a member may exercise that right by giving an opt-out notice under section 84.

(3) An opt-out information notice must be given in accordance with rules of the union approved for the purpose by the Certification Officer.

(4) In deciding whether to approve those rules, the Certification Officer must have regard in each case to the existing practice and character of the union.

(5) As soon as is reasonably practicable after the end of any period of eight weeks within which an opt-out information notice must be given, a trade union must send to the Certification Officer a copy of—

(a) the opt-out information notice, or

(b) if there is more than one form of opt-out information notice, each form of notice.

(6) A member of a trade union who claims that the union has failed to comply with this section may complain to the Certification Officer.

(7) Where the Certification Officer is satisfied on a complaint under subsection (6) that a trade union has failed to comply with this section, the Officer may make such order for remedying the failure as the Officer thinks just under the circumstances.

(8)–(9) [omitted]

85 Manner of giving effect to section 84

(1) A union that has a political fund must either—

(a) make a separate levy of contributions to that fund from the members who are contributors, or

(b) relieve members who are not contributors from the payment of the appropriate portion of any periodical contribution required from members towards the expenses of the union.

(2) In the latter case, the rules shall provide—

(a) that relief shall be given as far as possible to all members who are not contributors on the occasion of the same periodical payment, and

(b) for enabling each member of the union to know what portion (if any) of any periodical contribution payable by the member is a contribution to the political fund.

Duties of employer who deducts union contributions

86 Employer not to deduct contributions where member gives certificate

(1) If a member of a trade union which has a political fund certifies in writing to his employer that, or to the effect that—

(a) the member is not a contributor to the fund, or

(b) the member has given the union an opt-out notice but it does not yet have effect,

the employer shall ensure that no amount representing a contribution to the political fund is deducted by him from emoluments payable to the member.

(2) The employer's duty under subsection (1) applies from the first day, following the giving of the certificate, on which it is reasonably practicable for him to comply with that subsection, until the certificate is withdrawn.

(3) An employer may not refuse to deduct any union dues from emoluments payable to a person who has given a certificate under this section if he continues to deduct union dues from emoluments payable to other members of the union, unless his refusal is not attributable to the giving of the certificate or otherwise connected with the duty imposed by subsection (1).

87 Complaint in respect of employer's failure

(1) A person who claims his employer has failed to comply with section 86 in deducting or refusing to deduct any amount from emoluments payable to him may present a complaint to an employment tribunal.

(2) A tribunal shall not consider a complaint under subsection (1) unless it is presented—

(a) within the period of three months beginning with the date of the payment of the emoluments or (if the complaint relates to more than one payment) the last of the payments, or

(b) where the tribunal is satisfied that it was not reasonably practicable for the complaint to be presented within that period, within such further period as the tribunal considers reasonable.

(2A) [omitted]

(3) Where on a complaint under subsection (1) arising out of subsection (3) (refusal to deduct union dues) of section 86 the question arises whether the employer's refusal to deduct an amount was attributable to the giving of the certificate or was otherwise connected with the duty imposed by subsection (1) of that section, it is for the employer to satisfy the tribunal that it was not.

(4) Where a tribunal finds that a complaint under subsection (1) is well-founded—

(a) it shall make a declaration to that effect and, where the complaint arises out of subsection (1) of section 86, order the employer to pay to the complainant the amount deducted in contravention of that subsection less any part of that amount already paid to him by the employer, and

(b) it may, if it considers it appropriate to do so in order to prevent a repetition of the failure, make an order requiring the employer to take, within a specified time, the steps specified in the order in relation to emoluments payable by him to the complainant.

(5) A person who claims his employer has failed to comply with an order made under subsection (4)(b) on a complaint presented by him may present a further complaint to an employment tribunal; but only one complaint may be presented under this subsection in relation to any order.

(6) A tribunal shall not consider a complaint under subsection (5) unless it is presented—

(a) after the end of the period of four weeks beginning with the date of the order, but

(b) before the end of the period of six months beginning with that date.

(7) Where on a complaint under subsection (5) a tribunal finds that an employer has, without reasonable excuse, failed to comply with an order made under subsection (4)(b), it shall order the employer to pay to the complainant an amount equal to two weeks' pay.

(8) Chapter II of Part XIV of the Employment Rights Act 1996 (calculation of a week's pay) applies for the purposes of subsection (7) with the substitution for section 225 of the following—

For the purposes of this Chapter in its application to subsection (7) of section 87 of the Trade Union and Labour Relations (Consolidation) Act 1992, the calculation date is the date of the payment, or (if more than one) the last of the payments, to which the complaint related.

88 [repealed]; 89–91 [omitted]

Supplementary

92 Manner of making union rules

If the Certification Officer is satisfied, and certifies, that rules of a trade union made for any of the purposes of this Chapter and requiring approval by him have been approved—

(a) by a majority of the members of the union voting for the purpose, or

(b) by a majority of delegates of the union at a meeting called for the purpose,

the rules shall have effect as rules of the union notwithstanding that the rules of the union as to the alteration of rules or the making of new rules have not been complied with.

93 Effect of amalgamation

(1) Where on an amalgamation of two or more trade unions—

(a) there is in force in relation to each of the amalgamating unions a political resolution and such rules as are required by this Chapter, and

(b) the rules of the amalgamated union in force immediately after the amalgamation include such rules as are required by this Chapter,

the amalgamated union shall be treated for the purposes of this Chapter as having passed a political resolution.

(2) That resolution shall be treated as having been passed on the date of the earliest of the ballots on which the resolutions in force immediately before the amalgamation with respect to the amalgamating unions were passed.

(3) Where one of the amalgamating unions is a Northern Ireland union, the references above to the requirements of this Chapter shall be construed as references to the requirements of the corresponding provisions of the law of Northern Ireland.

94 [omitted]

95 Appeals from Certification Officer

An appeal lies to the Employment Appeal Tribunal on any question of law arising in proceedings before or arising from any decision of the Certification Officer under this Chapter.

96 Meaning of 'date of the ballot'

In this Chapter the 'date of the ballot' means, in the case of a ballot in which votes may be cast on more than one day, the last of those days.

97–108 [omitted]

Chapter VIIA Breach of Rules

108A Right to apply to Certification Officer

(1) A person who claims that there has been a breach or threatened breach of the rules of a trade union relating to any of the matters mentioned in subsection (2) may apply to the Certification Officer for a declaration to that effect, subject to subsections (3) to (7).

(2) The matters are—

(a) the appointment or election of a person to, or the removal of a person from, any office;

(b) disciplinary proceedings by the union (including expulsion);

(c) the balloting of members on any issue other than industrial action;

(d) the constitution or proceedings of any executive committee or of any decision-making meeting;

(e) such other matters as may be specified in an order made by the Secretary of State.

(3) The applicant must be a member of the union, or have been one at the time of the alleged breach or threatened breach.

(4) A person may not apply under subsection (1) in relation to a claim if he is entitled to apply under section 80 in relation to the claim.

(5) No application may be made regarding—

(a) the dismissal of an employee of the union;

(b) disciplinary proceedings against an employee of the union.

(6) An application must be made—

(a) within the period of six months starting with the day on which the breach or threatened breach is alleged to have taken place, or

(b) if within that period any internal complaints procedure of the union is invoked to resolve the claim, within the period of six months starting with the earlier of the days specified in subsection (7).

(7) Those days are—

(a) the day on which the procedure is concluded, and

(b) the last day of the period of one year beginning with the day on which the procedure is invoked.

(8) The reference in subsection (1) to the rules of a union includes references to the rules of any branch or section of the union.

(9) In subsection (2)(c) 'industrial action' means a strike or other industrial action by persons employed under contracts of employment.

(10) For the purposes of subsection (2)(d) a committee is an executive committee if—

(a) it is a committee of the union concerned and has power to make executive decisions on behalf of the union or on behalf of a constituent body,

(b) it is a committee of a major constituent body and has power to make executive decisions on behalf of that body, or

(c) it is a sub-committee of a committee falling within paragraph (a) or (b).

(11) For the purposes of subsection (2)(d) a decision-making meeting is—

(a) a meeting of members of the union concerned (or the representatives of such members) which has power to make a decision on any matter which, under the rules of the union, is final as regards the union or which, under the rules of the union or a constituent body, is final as regards that body, or

(b) a meeting of members of a major constituent body (or the representatives of such members) which has power to make a decision on any matter which, under the rules of the union or the body, is final as regards that body.

(12) For the purposes of subsections (10) and (11), in relation to the trade union concerned—

(a) a constituent body is any body which forms part of the union, including a branch, group, section or region;

(b) a major constituent body is such a body which has more than 1,000 members.

(13) Any order under subsection (2)(e) shall be made by statutory instrument; and no such order shall be made unless a draft of it has been laid before and approved by resolution of each House of Parliament.

(14) If a person applies to the Certification Officer under this section in relation to an alleged breach or threatened breach he may not apply to the court in relation to the breach or threatened breach; but nothing in this subsection shall prevent such a person from exercising any right to appeal against or challenge the Certification Officer's decision on the application to him.

(15) If—

(a) a person applies to the court in relation to an alleged breach or threatened breach, and

(b) the breach or threatened breach is one in relation to which he could have made an application to the Certification Officer under this section,

he may not apply to the Certification Officer under this section in relation to the breach or threatened breach.

108B Declarations and orders

(1) The Certification Officer may refuse to accept an application under section 108A unless he is satisfied that the applicant has taken all reasonable steps to resolve the claim by the use of any internal complaints procedure of the union.

(2) If he accepts an application under section 108A the Certification Officer—

(a) shall make such enquiries as he thinks fit,

(b) shall give the applicant and the union an opportunity to be heard,

(c) shall ensure that, so far as is reasonably practicable, the application is determined within six months of being made,

(d) may make or refuse the declaration asked for, and

(e) shall, whether he makes or refuses the declaration, give reasons for his decision in writing.

(3) Where the Certification Officer makes a declaration he shall also, unless he considers that to do so would be inappropriate, make an enforcement order, that is, an order imposing on the union one or both of the following requirements—

(a) to take such steps to remedy the breach, or withdraw the threat of a breach, as may be specified in the order;

(b) to abstain from such acts as may be so specified with a view to securing that a breach or threat of the same or a similar kind does not occur in future.

(4) The Certification Officer shall in an order imposing any such requirement as is mentioned in subsection (3)(a) specify the period within which the union is to comply with the requirement.

(5) Where the Certification Officer requests a person to furnish information to him in connection with enquiries made by him under this section, he shall specify the date by which that information is to be furnished and, unless he considers that it would be inappropriate to do so, shall proceed with his determination of the application notwithstanding that the information has not been furnished to him by the specified date.

(6) A declaration made by the Certification Officer under this section may be relied on as if it were a declaration made by the court.

(7) Where an enforcement order has been made, any person who is a member of the union and was a member at the time it was made is entitled to enforce obedience to the order as if he had made the application on which the order was made.

(8) An enforcement order made by the Certification Officer under this section may be enforced (by the Certification Officer, the applicant or a person mentioned in subsection (7)) in the same way as an order of the court.

(9) An order under section 108A(2)(e) may provide that, in relation to an application under section 108A with regard to a prescribed matter, the preceding provisions of this section shall apply with such omissions or modifications as may be specified in the order; and a prescribed matter is such matter specified under section 108A(2)(e) as is prescribed under this subsection.

108C Appeals from Certification Officer

An appeal lies to the Employment Appeal Tribunal on any question of law arising in proceedings before or arising from any decision of the Certification Officer under this Chapter.

109–114 [repealed]

Chapter IX Miscellaneous and General Provisions

115–116 [repealed]; 116A [omitted]; 116B [repealed]

Exceptions and adaptations for certain bodies

117 Special register bodies

(1) In this section a 'special register body' means an organisation whose name appeared in the special register maintained under section 84 of the Industrial Relations Act 1971 immediately before 16 September 1974, and which is a company registered under the Companies Act 2006 or is incorporated by charter or letters patent.

(2) The provisions of this Part apply to special register bodies as to other trade unions, subject to the following exceptions and adaptations.

(3) In Chapter II (status and property of trade unions)—

(a) in section 10 (quasi-corporate status of trade unions)—

(i) subsections (1) and (2) (prohibition on trade union being incorporated) do not apply, and

(ii) subsection (3) (prohibition on registration under certain Acts) does not apply so far as it relates to registration as a company under the Companies Act 2006;

(b) section 11 (exclusion of common law rules as to restraint of trade) applies to the purposes or rules of a special register body only so far as they relate to the regulation of relations between employers or employers' associations and workers;

(c) sections 12 to 14 (vesting of property in trustees; transfer of securities) do not apply; and

(d) in section 20 (liability of trade union in certain proceedings in tort) in subsection (7) the reference to the contract between a member and the other members shall be construed as a reference to the contract between a member and the body.

(4) Sections 33 to 35 (appointment and removal of auditors) do not apply to a special register body which is registered as a company under the Companies Act 2006; and sections 36 and 37 (rights and duties of auditors) apply to the auditors appointed by such a body under Chapter 2 of Part 16 of that Act.

(5) Sections 45B and 45C (disqualification) and Chapter IV (elections) apply only to—

(a) the position of voting member of the executive, and

(b) any position by virtue of which a person is a voting member of the executive. In this subsection 'voting member of the executive' has the meaning given by section 46(5).

118 Federated trade unions

(1) In this section a 'federated trade union' means a trade union which consists wholly or mainly of constituent or affiliated organisations, or representatives of such organisations, as described in paragraph (b) of the definition of 'trade union' in section 1.

(2) The provisions of this Part apply to federated trade unions subject to the following exceptions and adaptations.

(3) For the purposes of section 22 (limit on amount of damages) as it applies to a federated trade union, the members of such of its constituent or affiliated organisations as have their head or main office in Great Britain shall be treated as members of the union.

(4) The following provisions of Chapter III (trade union administration) do not apply to a federated trade union which consists wholly or mainly of representatives of constituent or affiliated organisations—

(a) section 27 (duty to supply copy of rules),
(b) section 28 (duty to keep accounting records),
(c) sections 32 to 37 (annual return, statement for members, accounts and audit),
(ca) sections 37A to 37E (investigation of financial affairs), and
(d) sections 38 to 42 (Members' superannuation schemes).

(4A) [omitted]

(5) Sections 29 to 31 (right of member to access to accounting records) do not apply to a federated trade union which has no members other than constituent or affiliated organisations or representatives of such organisations.

(6) Sections 24 to 26 (register of Members' names and addresses) and Chapter IV (elections for certain trade union positions) do not apply to a federated trade union—

(a) if it has no individual members other than representatives of constituent or affiliated organisations, or
(b) if its individual members (other than such representatives) are all merchant seamen and a majority of them are ordinarily resident outside the United Kingdom. For this purpose 'merchant seaman' means a person whose employment, or the greater part of it, is carried out on board sea-going ships.

(7) The provisions of Chapter VI (application of funds for political objects) apply to a trade union which is in whole or part an association or combination of other unions as if the individual members of the component unions were members of that union and not of the component unions.

But nothing in that Chapter prevents a component union from collecting contributions on behalf of the association or combination from such of its members as are contributors to the political fund of the association or combination.

(8) [omitted]

Interpretation

119 Expressions relating to trade unions

In this Act, in relation to a trade union—

'agent' means a banker or solicitor of, or any person employed as an auditor by, the union or any branch or section of the union;

'branch or section', except where the context otherwise requires, includes a branch or section which is itself a trade union;

'executive' means the principal committee of the union exercising executive functions, by whatever name it is called;

'financial affairs' means affairs of the union relating to any fund which is applicable for the purposes of the union (including any fund of a branch or section of the union which is so applicable);

'general secretary' means the official of the union who holds the office of general secretary or, where there is no such office, holds an office which is equivalent, or (except in section 14(4)) the nearest equivalent, to that of general secretary;

'officer' includes—

(a) any member of the governing body of the union, and
(b) any trustee of any fund applicable for the purposes of the union;

'official' means—

(a) an officer of the union or of a branch or section of the union, or
(b) a person elected or appointed in accordance with the rules of the union to be a representative of its members or of some of them,

and includes a person so elected or appointed who is an employee of the same employer as the members or one or more of the members whom he is to represent;

'president' means the official of the union who holds the office of president or, where there is no such office, who holds an office which is equivalent, or (except in section 14(4) or Chapter IV) the nearest equivalent, to that of president; and

'rules', except where the context otherwise requires, includes the rules of any branch or section of the union.

120 Northern Ireland unions

In this Part a 'Northern Ireland union' means a trade union whose principal office is situated in Northern Ireland.

121 Meaning of 'the court'

In this Part 'the court' (except where the reference is expressed to be to the county court or sheriff court) means the High Court or the Court of Session.

PART II EMPLOYERS' ASSOCIATIONS

Introductory

122 Meaning of 'employers' association'

(1) In this Act an 'employers' association' means an organisation (whether temporary or permanent)—

(a) which consists wholly or mainly of employers or individual owners of undertakings of one or more descriptions and whose principal purposes include the regulation of relations between employers of that description or those descriptions and workers or trade unions; or

(b) which consists wholly or mainly of—

(i) constituent or affiliated organisations which fulfil the conditions in paragraph (a) (or themselves consist wholly or mainly of constituent or affiliated organisations which fulfil those conditions), or

(ii) representatives of such constituent or affiliated organisations,

and whose principal purposes include the regulation of relations between employers and workers or between employers and trade unions, or the regulation of relations between its constituent or affiliated organisations.

(2) References in this Act to employers' associations include combinations of employers and employers' associations.

123–136 [omitted]

PART III RIGHTS IN RELATION TO UNION MEMBERSHIP AND ACTIVITIES

Statement of trade union rights

136A Right to statement of trade union rights

(1) A worker's employer must give the worker a written statement that the worker has the right to join a trade union.

(2) The statement must be given—

(a) at the same time as the employer gives the worker a statement under section 1 of the 1996 Act (statement of employment particulars);

(b) at other prescribed times.

(3) The Secretary of State may prescribe—

(a) information that must be included in the statement;

(b) the form which the statement must take;

(c) the manner in which the statement must be given.

(4) The information prescribed may include that the worker has rights conferred by this Part.

(5) For the purposes of this section—

(a) 'worker' and 'employer' have the same meaning as in the 1996 Act (see section 230 of that Act);

(b) in a case where an employer gives a worker a statement under section 1 of the 1996 Act in instalments (see section 2(4) of that Act), that statement is to be treated as given when the first instalment is given;

(c) 'the 1996 Act' means the Employment Rights Act 1996.

(6) [omitted]

(7) See section 38 of the Employment Act 2002 for the effect of failing to give a statement in accordance with this section.

Access to employment

137 Refusal of employment on grounds related to union membership

(1) It is unlawful to refuse a person employment—

(a) because he is, or is not, a member of a trade union, or

(b) because he is unwilling to accept a requirement—

(i) to take steps to become or cease to be, or to remain or not to become, a member of a trade union, or

(ii) to make payments or suffer deductions in the event of his not being a member of a trade union.

(2) A person who is thus unlawfully refused employment has a right of complaint to an employment tribunal.

(3) Where an advertisement is published which indicates, or might reasonably be understood as indicating—

(a) that employment to which the advertisement relates is open only to a person who is, or is not, a member of a trade union, or

(b) that any such requirement as is mentioned in subsection (1)(b) will be imposed in relation to employment to which the advertisement relates,

a person who does not satisfy that condition or, as the case may be, is unwilling to accept that requirement, and who seeks and is refused employment to which the advertisement relates, shall be conclusively presumed to have been refused employment for that reason.

(4) Where there is an arrangement or practice under which employment is offered only to persons put forward or approved by a trade union, and the trade union puts forward or approves only persons who are members of the union, a person who is not a member of the union and who is refused employment in pursuance of the arrangement or practice shall be taken to have been refused employment because he is not a member of the trade union.

(5) A person shall be taken to be refused employment if he seeks employment of any description with a person and that person—

(a) refuses or deliberately omits to entertain and process his application or enquiry, or

(b) causes him to withdraw or cease to pursue his application or enquiry, or

(c) refuses or deliberately omits to offer him employment of that description, or

(d) makes him an offer of such employment the terms of which are such as no reasonable employer who wished to fill the post would offer and which is not accepted, or

(e) makes him an offer of such employment but withdraws it or causes him not to accept it.

(6) Where a person is offered employment on terms which include a requirement that he is, or is not, a member of a trade union, or any such requirement as is mentioned in subsection (1)(b), and he does not accept the offer because he does not satisfy or, as the case may be, is unwilling to accept the requirement, he shall be treated as having been refused employment for that reason.

(7) Where a person may not be considered for appointment or election to an office in a trade union unless he is a member of the union, or of a particular branch or section of the union or of one of a number of particular branches or sections of the union, nothing in this section applies to anything done for the purpose of securing compliance with that condition although as holder of the office he would be employed by the union.

For this purpose an 'office' means any position—

(a) by virtue of which the holder is an official of the union, or

(b) to which Chapter IV of Part I applies (duty to hold elections).

(8) The provisions of this section apply in relation to an employment agency acting, or purporting to act, on behalf of an employer as in relation to an employer.

138 Refusal of service of employment agency on grounds related to union membership

(1) It is unlawful for an employment agency to refuse a person any of its services—

(a) because he is, or is not, a member of a trade union, or

(b) because he is unwilling to accept a requirement to take steps to become or cease to be, or to remain or not to become, a member of a trade union.

(2) A person who is thus unlawfully refused any service of an employment agency has a right of complaint to an employment tribunal.

(2A) Section 12A of the Employment Tribunals Act 1996 (financial penalties) applies in relation to a complaint under this section as it applies in relation to a claim involving an employer and a worker (reading references to an employer as references to the employment agency and references to a worker as references to the complainant).

(3) Where an advertisement is published which indicates, or might reasonably be understood as indicating—

(a) that any service of an employment agency is available only to a person who is, or is not, a member of a trade union, or

(b) that any such requirement as is mentioned in subsection (1)(b) will be imposed in relation to a service to which the advertisement relates,

a person who does not satisfy that condition or, as the case may be, is unwilling to accept that requirement, and who seeks to avail himself of and is refused that service, shall be conclusively presumed to have been refused it for that reason.

(4) A person shall be taken to be refused a service if he seeks to avail himself of it and the agency—

(a) refuses or deliberately omits to make the service available to him, or

(b) causes him not to avail himself of the service or to cease to avail himself of it, or

(c) does not provide the same service, on the same terms, as is provided to others.

(5) Where a person is offered a service on terms which include a requirement that he is, or is not, a member of a trade union, or any such requirement as is mentioned in subsection (1)(b), and he does not accept the offer because he does not satisfy or, as the case may be, is unwilling to accept that requirement, he shall be treated as having been refused the service for that reason.

139 Time limit for proceedings

(1) An employment tribunal shall not consider a complaint under section 137 or 138 unless it is presented to the tribunal—

(a) before the end of the period of three months beginning with the date of the conduct to which the complaint relates, or

(b) where the tribunal is satisfied that it was not reasonably practicable for the complaint to be presented before the end of that period, within such further period as the tribunal considers reasonable.

(2)–(4) [omitted]

140 Remedies

(1) Where the employment tribunal finds that a complaint under section 137 or 138 is well-founded, it shall make a declaration to that effect and may make such of the following as it considers just and equitable—

(a) an order requiring the respondent to pay compensation to the complainant of such amount as the tribunal may determine;

(b) a recommendation that the respondent take within a specified period action appearing to the tribunal to be practicable for the purpose of obviating or reducing the adverse effect on the complainant of any conduct to which the complaint relates.

(2) Compensation shall be assessed on the same basis as damages for breach of statutory duty and may include compensation for injury to feelings.

(3) If the respondent fails without reasonable justification to comply with a recommendation to take action, the tribunal may increase its award of compensation or, if it has not made such an award, make one.

(4) The total amount of compensation shall not exceed the limit for the time being imposed by section 124(1) of the Employment Rights Act 1996 (limit on compensation for unfair dismissal).

141 Complaint against employer and employment agency

(1) Where a person has a right of complaint against a prospective employer and against an employment agency arising out of the same facts, he may present a complaint against either of them or against them jointly.

(2) If a complaint is brought against one only, he or the complainant may request the tribunal to join or sist the other as a party to the proceedings.

The request shall be granted if it is made before the hearing of the complaint begins, but may be refused if it is made after that time; and no such request may be made after the tribunal has made its decision as to whether the complaint is well-founded.

(3) Where a complaint is brought against an employer and an employment agency jointly, or where it is brought against one and the other is joined or sisted as a party to the proceedings, and the tribunal—

(a) finds that the complaint is well-founded as against the employer and the agency, and

(b) makes an award of compensation,

it may order that the compensation shall be paid by the one or the other, or partly by one and partly by the other, as the tribunal may consider just and equitable in the circumstances.

142 Awards against third parties

(1) If in proceedings on a complaint under section 137 or 138 either the complainant or the respondent claims that the respondent was induced to act in the manner complained of by pressure which a trade union or other person exercised on him by calling, organising, procuring or financing a strike or other industrial action, or by threatening to do so, the complainant or the respondent may request the employment tribunal to direct that the person who he claims exercised the pressure be joined or sisted as a party to the proceedings.

(2) The request shall be granted if it is made before the hearing of the complaint begins, but may be refused if it is made after that time; and no such request may be made after the tribunal has made its decision as to whether the complaint is well-founded.

(3) Where a person has been so joined or sisted as a party to the proceedings and the tribunal—

(a) finds that the complaint is well-founded,

(b) makes an award of compensation, and

(c) also finds that the claim in subsection (1) above is well-founded,

it may order that the compensation shall be paid by the person joined instead of by the respondent, or partly by that person and partly by the respondent, as the tribunal may consider just and equitable in the circumstances.

(4) Where by virtue of section 141 (complaint against employer and employment agency) there is more than one respondent, the above provisions apply to either or both of them.

143 Interpretation and other supplementary provisions

(1) In sections 137 to 143—

'advertisement' includes every form of advertisement or notice, whether to the public or not, and references to publishing an advertisement shall be construed accordingly;

'employment' means employment under a contract of employment, and related expressions shall be construed accordingly; and

'employment agency' means a person who, for profit or not, provides services for the purpose of finding employment for workers or supplying employers with workers, but subject to subsection (2) below.

(2) For the purposes of sections 137 to 143 as they apply to employment agencies—

(a) services other than those mentioned in the definition of 'employment agency' above shall be disregarded, and

(b) a trade union shall not be regarded as an employment agency by reason of services provided by it only for, or in relation to, its members.

(3) References in sections 137 to 143 to being or not being a member of a trade union are to being or not being a member of any trade union, of a particular trade union or of one of a number of particular trade unions.

Any such reference includes a reference to being or not being a member of a particular branch or section of a trade union or of one of a number of particular branches or sections of a trade union.

(4) The remedy of a person for conduct which is unlawful by virtue of section 137 or 138 is by way of a complaint to an employment tribunal in accordance with this Part, and not otherwise.

No other legal liability arises by reason that conduct is unlawful by virtue of either of those sections.

Contracts for supply of goods or services

144 Union membership requirement in contract for goods or services void

A term or condition of a contract for the supply of goods or services is void in so far as it purports to require that the whole, or some part, of the work done for the purposes of the contract is done only by persons who are, or are not, members of trade unions or of a particular trade union.

145 Refusal to deal on union membership grounds prohibited

(1) A person shall not refuse to deal with a supplier or prospective supplier of goods or services on union membership grounds.

'Refuse to deal' and 'union membership grounds' shall be construed as follows.

(2) A person refuses to deal with a person if, where he maintains (in whatever form) a list of approved suppliers of goods or services, or of persons from whom tenders for the supply of goods or services may be invited, he fails to include the name of that person in that list.

He does so on union membership grounds if the ground, or one of the grounds, for failing to include his name is that if that person were to enter into a contract with him for the supply of goods or services, work to be done for the purposes of the contract would, or would be likely to, be done by persons who were, or who were not, members of trade unions or of a particular trade union.

(3) A person refuses to deal with a person if, in relation to a proposed contract for the supply of goods or services—

(a) he excludes that person from the group of persons from whom tenders for the supply of the goods or services are invited, or

(b) he fails to permit that person to submit such a tender, or

(c) he otherwise determines not to enter into a contract with that person for the supply of the goods or services.

He does so on union membership grounds if the ground, or one of the grounds, on which he does so is that if the proposed contract were entered into with that person, work to be done for the purposes of the contract would, or would be likely to, be done by persons who were, or who were not, members of trade unions or of a particular trade union.

(4) A person refuses to deal with a person if he terminates a contract with him for the supply of goods or services.

He does so on union membership grounds if the ground, or one of the grounds, on which he does so is that work done, or to be done, for the purposes of the contract has been, or is likely to be, done by persons who are or are not members of trade unions or of a particular trade union.

(5) The obligation to comply with this section is a duty owed to the person with whom there is a refusal to deal and to any other person who may be adversely affected by its contravention; and a breach of the duty is actionable accordingly (subject to the defences and other incidents applying to actions for breach of statutory duty).

Inducements

145A Inducements relating to union membership or activities

(1) A worker has the right not to have an offer made to him by his employer for the sole or main purpose of inducing the worker—

(a) not to be or seek to become a member of an independent trade union,

(b) not to take part, at an appropriate time, in the activities of an independent trade union,

(c) not to make use, at an appropriate time, of trade union services, or

(d) to be or become a member of any trade union or of a particular trade union or of one of a number of particular trade unions.

(2) In subsection (1) 'an appropriate time' means—

(a) a time outside the worker's working hours, or

(b) a time within his working hours at which, in accordance with arrangements agreed with or consent given by his employer, it is permissible for him to take part in the activities of a trade union or (as the case may be) make use of trade union services.

(3) In subsection (2) 'working hours', in relation to a worker, means any time when, in accordance with his contract of employment (or other contract personally to do work or perform services), he is required to be at work.

(4) In subsections (1) and (2)—

(a) 'trade union services' means services made available to the worker by an independent trade union by virtue of his membership of the union, and

(b) references to a worker's 'making use' of trade union services include his consenting to the raising of a matter on his behalf by an independent trade union of which he is a member.

(5) A worker or former worker may present a complaint to an employment tribunal on the ground that his employer has made him an offer in contravention of this section.

145B Inducements relating to collective bargaining

(1) A worker who is a member of an independent trade union which is recognised, or seeking to be recognised, by his employer has the right not to have an offer made to him by his employer if—

(a) acceptance of the offer, together with other workers' acceptance of offers which the employer also makes to them, would have the prohibited result, and

(b) the employer's sole or main purpose in making the offers is to achieve that result.

(2) The prohibited result is that the workers' terms of employment, or any of those terms, will not (or will no longer) be determined by collective agreement negotiated by or on behalf of the union.

(3) It is immaterial for the purposes of subsection (1) whether the offers are made to the workers simultaneously.

(4) Having terms of employment determined by collective agreement shall not be regarded for the purposes of section 145A (or section 146 or 152) as making use of a trade union service.

(5) A worker or former worker may present a complaint to an employment tribunal on the ground that his employer has made him an offer in contravention of this section.

145C Time limit for proceedings

(1) An employment tribunal shall not consider a complaint under section 145A or 145B unless it is presented—

(a) before the end of the period of three months beginning with the date when the offer was made or, where the offer is part of a series of similar offers to the complainant, the date when the last of them was made, or

(b) where the tribunal is satisfied that it was not reasonably practicable for the complaint to be presented before the end of that period, within such further period as it considers reasonable.

(2) [omitted]

145D Consideration of complaint

(1) On a complaint under section 145A it shall be for the employer to show what was his sole or main purpose in making the offer.

(2) On a complaint under section 145B it shall be for the employer to show what was his sole or main purpose in making the offers.

(3) On a complaint under section 145A or 145B, in determining any question whether the employer made the offer (or offers) or the purpose for which he did so, no account shall be taken of any pressure which was exercised on him by calling, organising, procuring or financing a strike or other industrial action, or by threatening to do so; and that question shall be determined as if no such pressure had been exercised.

(4) In determining whether an employer's sole or main purpose in making offers was the purpose mentioned in section 145B(1), the matters taken into account must include any evidence—

- (a) that when the offers were made the employer had recently changed or sought to change, or did not wish to use, arrangements agreed with the union for collective bargaining,
- (b) that when the offers were made the employer did not wish to enter into arrangements proposed by the union for collective bargaining, or
- (c) that the offers were made only to particular workers, and were made with the sole or main purpose of rewarding those particular workers for their high level of performance or of retaining them because of their special value to the employer.

145E Remedies

(1) Subsections (2) and (3) apply where the employment tribunal finds that a complaint under section 145A or 145B is well-founded.

(2) The tribunal—

- (a) shall make a declaration to that effect, and
- (b) shall make an award to be paid by the employer to the complainant in respect of the offer complained of.

(3) The amount of the award shall be £5,993 (subject to any adjustment of the award that may fall to be made under Part 3 of the Employment Act 2002).

(4) Where an offer made in contravention of section 145A or 145B is accepted—

- (a) if the acceptance results in the worker's agreeing to vary his terms of employment, the employer cannot enforce the agreement to vary, or recover any sum paid or other asset transferred by him under the agreement to vary;
- (b) if as a result of the acceptance the worker's terms of employment are varied, nothing in section 145A or 145B makes the variation unenforceable by either party.

(5) Nothing in this section or sections 145A and 145B prejudices any right conferred by section 146 or 149.

(6) In ascertaining any amount of compensation under section 149, no reduction shall be made on the ground—

- (a) that the complainant caused or contributed to his loss, or to the act or failure complained of, by accepting or not accepting an offer made in contravention of section 145A or 145B, or
- (b) that the complainant has received or is entitled to an award under this section.

145F Interpretation and other supplementary provisions

(1) References in sections 145A to 145E to being or becoming a member of a trade union include references—

- (a) to being or becoming a member of a particular branch or section of that union, and
- (b) to being or becoming a member of one of a number of particular branches or sections of that union.

(2) References in those sections—

- (a) to taking part in the activities of a trade union, and
- (b) to services made available by a trade union by virtue of membership of the union, shall be construed in accordance with subsection (1).

(3) In sections 145A to 145E—

'worker' means an individual who works, or normally works, as mentioned in paragraphs (a) to (c) of section 296(1), and

'employer' means—

(a) in relation to a worker, the person for whom he works;

(b) in relation to a former worker, the person for whom he worked.

(4) The remedy of a person for infringement of the right conferred on him by section 145A or 145B is by way of a complaint to an employment tribunal in accordance with this Part, and not otherwise.

Detriment

146 Detriment on grounds related to union membership or activities

(1) A worker has the right not to be subjected to any detriment as an individual by any act, or any deliberate failure to act, by his employer if the act or failure takes place for the sole or main purpose of—

(a) preventing or deterring him from being or seeking to become a member of an independent trade union, or penalising him for doing so,

(b) preventing or deterring him from taking part in the activities of an independent trade union at an appropriate time, or penalising him for doing so,

(ba) preventing or deterring him from making use of trade union services at an appropriate time, or penalising him for doing so, or

(c) compelling him to be or become a member of any trade union or of a particular trade union or of one of a number of particular trade unions.

(2) In subsection (1) 'an appropriate time' means—

(a) a time outside the worker's working hours, or

(b) a time within his working hours at which, in accordance with arrangements agreed with or consent given by his employer, it is permissible for him to take part in the activities of a trade union or (as the case may be) make use of trade union services;

and for this purpose 'working hours', in relation to a worker, means any time when, in accordance with his contract of employment (or other contract personally to do work or perform services), he is required to be at work.

(2A) In this section—

(a) 'trade union services' means services made available to the worker by an independent trade union by virtue of his membership of the union, and

(b) references to a worker's 'making use' of trade union services include his consenting to the raising of a matter on his behalf by an independent trade union of which he is a member.

(2B) If an independent trade union of which a worker is a member raises a matter on his behalf (with or without his consent), penalising the worker for that is to be treated as penalising him as mentioned in subsection (1)(ba).

(2C) A worker also has the right not to be subjected to any detriment as an individual by any act, or any deliberate failure to act, by his employer if the act or failure takes place because of the worker's failure to accept an offer made in contravention of section 145A or 145B.

(2D) For the purposes of subsection (2C), not conferring a benefit that, if the offer had been accepted by the worker, would have been conferred on him under the resulting agreement shall be taken to be subjecting him to a detriment as an individual (and to be a deliberate failure to act).

(3) A worker also has the right not to be subjected to any detriment as an individual by any act, or any deliberate failure to act, by his employer if the act or failure takes place for the sole or main purpose of enforcing a requirement (whether or not imposed by a contract of employment or in writing) that, in the event of his not being a member of any trade union or of a particular trade union or of one of a number of particular trade unions, he must make one or more payments.

(4) For the purposes of subsection (3) any deduction made by an employer from the remuneration payable to a worker in respect of his employment shall, if it is attributable to his not being a member

of any trade union or of a particular trade union or of one of a number of particular trade unions, be treated as a detriment to which he has been subjected as an individual by an act of his employer taking place for the sole or main purpose of enforcing a requirement of a kind mentioned in that subsection.

(5) A worker or former worker may present a complaint to an employment tribunal on the ground that he has been subjected to a detriment by his employer in contravention of this section.

(5A) This section does not apply where—

(a) the worker is an employee; and

(b) the detriment in question amounts to dismissal.

147 Time limit for proceedings

(1) An employment tribunal shall not consider a complaint under section 146 unless it is presented—

(a) before the end of the period of three months beginning with the date of the act or failure to which the complaint relates or, where that act or failure is part of a series of similar acts or failures (or both) the last of them, or

(b) where the tribunal is satisfied that it was not reasonably practicable for the complaint to be presented before the end of that period, within such further period as it considers reasonable.

(2) For the purposes of subsection (1)—

(a) where an act extends over a period, the reference to the date of the act is a reference to the last day of that period;

(b) a failure to act shall be treated as done when it was decided on.

(3) For the purposes of subsection (2), in the absence of evidence establishing the contrary an employer shall be taken to decide on a failure to act—

(a) when he does an act inconsistent with doing the failed act, or

(b) if he has done no such inconsistent act, when the period expires within which he might reasonably have been expected to do the failed act if it was to be done.

(4) [omitted]

148 Consideration of complaint

(1) On a complaint under section 146 it shall be for the employer to show what was the sole or main purpose for which he acted or failed to act.

(2) In determining any question whether the employer acted or failed to act, or the purpose for which he did so, no account shall be taken of any pressure which was exercised on him by calling, organising, procuring or financing a strike or other industrial action, or by threatening to do so; and that question shall be determined as if no such pressure had been exercised.

(3)–(5) [repealed]

149 Remedies

(1) Where the employment tribunal finds that a complaint under section 146 is well-founded, it shall make a declaration to that effect and may make an award of compensation to be paid by the employer to the complainant in respect of the act or failure complained of.

(2) The amount of the compensation awarded shall be such as the tribunal considers just and equitable in all the circumstances having regard to the infringement complained of and to any loss sustained by the complainant which is attributable to the act or failure which infringed his right.

(3) The loss shall be taken to include—

(a) any expenses reasonably incurred by the complainant in consequence of the act or failure complained of, and

(b) loss of any benefit which he might reasonably be expected to have had but for that act or failure.

(4) In ascertaining the loss, the tribunal shall apply the same rule concerning the duty of a person to mitigate his loss as applies to damages recoverable under the common law of England and Wales or Scotland.

(5) In determining the amount of compensation to be awarded no account shall be taken of any pressure which was exercised on the employer by calling, organising, procuring or financing a strike or other industrial action, or by threatening to do so; and that question shall be determined as if no such pressure had been exercised.

(6) Where the tribunal finds that the act or failure complained of was to any extent caused or contributed to by action of the complainant, it shall reduce the amount of the compensation by such proportion as it considers just and equitable having regard to that finding.

150 Awards against third parties

(1) If in proceedings on a complaint under section 146—

(a) the complaint is made on the ground that the complainant has been subjected to detriment by an act or failure by his employer taking place for the sole or main purpose of compelling him to be or become a member of any trade union or of a particular trade union or of one of a number of particular trade unions, and

(b) either the complainant or the employer claims in proceedings before the tribunal that the employer was induced to act or fail to act in the way complained of by pressure which a trade union or other person exercised on him by calling, organising, procuring or financing a strike or other industrial action, or by threatening to do so,

the complainant or the employer may request the tribunal to direct that the person who he claims exercised the pressure be joined or sisted as a party to the proceedings.

(2) The request shall be granted if it is made before the hearing of the complaint begins, but may be refused if it is made after that time; and no such request may be made after the tribunal has made a declaration that the complaint is well-founded.

(3) Where a person has been so joined or sisted as a party to proceedings and the tribunal—

(a) makes an award of compensation, and

(b) finds that the claim mentioned in subsection (1)(b) is well-founded,

it may order that the compensation shall be paid by the person joined instead of by the employer, or partly by that person and partly by the employer, as the tribunal may consider just and equitable in the circumstances.

151 Interpretation and other supplementary provisions

(1) References in sections 146 to 150 to being, becoming or ceasing to remain a member of a trade union include references to being, becoming or ceasing to remain a member of a particular branch or section of that union and to being, becoming or ceasing to remain a member of one of a number of particular branches or sections of that union.

(1A) References in those sections—

(a) to taking part in the activities of a trade union, and

(b) to services made available by a trade union by virtue of membership of the union, shall be construed in accordance with subsection (1).

(1B) In sections 146 to 150—

'worker' means an individual who works, or normally works, as mentioned in paragraphs (a) to (c) of section 296(1), and 'employer' means—

(a) in relation to a worker, the person for whom he works;

(b) in relation to a former worker, the person for whom he worked.

(2) The remedy of a person for infringement of the right conferred on him by section 146 is by way of a complaint to an employment tribunal in accordance with this Part, and not otherwise.

Dismissal of employee

152 Dismissal of employee on grounds related to union membership or activities

(1) For purposes of Part X of the Employment Rights Act 1996 (unfair dismissal) the dismissal of an employee shall be regarded as unfair if the reason for it (or, if more than one, the principal reason) was that the employee—

(a) was, or proposed to become, a member of an independent trade union,
(b) had taken part, or proposed to take part, in the activities of an independent trade union at an appropriate time,
(ba) had made use, or proposed to make use, of trade union services at an appropriate time,
(bb) had failed to accept an offer made in contravention of section 145A or 145B, or
(c) was not a member of any trade union, or of a particular trade union, or of one of a number of particular trade unions, or had refused, or proposed to refuse, to become or remain a member.

(2) In subsection (1) 'an appropriate time' means—
(a) a time outside the employee's working hours, or
(b) a time within his working hours at which, in accordance with arrangements agreed with or consent given by his employer, it is permissible for him to take part in the activities of a trade union or (as the case may be) make use of trade union services;

and for this purpose 'working hours', in relation to an employee, means any time when, in accordance with his contract of employment, he is required to be at work.

(2A) In this section—
(a) 'trade union services' means services made available to the employee by an independent trade union by virtue of his membership of the union, and
(b) references to an employee's 'making use' of trade union services include his consenting to the raising of a matter on his behalf by an independent trade union of which he is a member.

(2B) Where the reason or one of the reasons for the dismissal was that an independent trade union (with or without the employee's consent) raised a matter on behalf of the employee as one of its members, the reason shall be treated as falling within subsection (1)(ba).

(3) Where the reason, or one of the reasons, for the dismissal was—
(a) the employee's refusal, or proposed refusal, to comply with a requirement (whether or not imposed by his contract of employment or in writing) that, in the event of his not being a member of any trade union, or of a particular trade union, or of one of a number of particular trade unions, he must make one or more payments, or
(b) his objection, or proposed objection, (however expressed) to the operation of a provision (whether or not forming part of his contract of employment or in writing) under which, in the event mentioned in paragraph (a), his employer is entitled to deduct one or more sums from the remuneration payable to him in respect of his employment,

the reason shall be treated as falling within subsection (1)(c).

(4) References in this section to being, becoming or ceasing to remain a member of a trade union include references to being, becoming or ceasing to remain a member of a particular branch or section of that union or of one of a number of particular branches or sections of that trade union.

(5) References in this section—
(a) to taking part in the activities of a trade union, and
(b) to services made available by a trade union by virtue of membership of the union,

shall be construed in accordance with subsection (4).

153 Selection for redundancy on grounds related to union membership or activities

Where the reason or principal reason for the dismissal of an employee was that he was redundant, but it is shown—
(a) that the circumstances constituting the redundancy applied equally to one or more other employees in the same undertaking who held positions similar to that held by him and who have not been dismissed by the employer, and
(b) that the reason (or, if more than one, the principal reason) why he was selected for dismissal was one of those specified in section 152(1),

the dismissal shall be regarded as unfair for the purposes of Part X of the Employment Rights Act 1996 (unfair dismissal).

154 Disapplication of qualifying period and upper age limit for unfair dismissal

Sections 108(1) and 109(1) of the Employment Rights Act 1996 (qualifying period and upper age limit for unfair dismissal protection) do not apply to a dismissal which by virtue of section 152 or 153 is regarded as unfair for the purposes of Part 10 of that Act.

155 Matters to be disregarded in assessing contributory fault

(1) Where an employment tribunal makes an award of compensation for unfair dismissal in a case where the dismissal is unfair by virtue of section 152 or 153, the tribunal shall disregard, in considering whether it would be just and equitable to reduce, or further reduce, the amount of any part of the award, any such conduct or action of the complainant as is specified below.

(2) Conduct or action of the complainant shall be disregarded in so far as it constitutes a breach or proposed breach of a requirement—

- (a) to be or become a member of any trade union or of a particular trade union or of one of a number of particular trade unions,
- (b) to cease to be, or refrain from becoming, a member of any trade union or of a particular trade union or of one of a number of particular trade unions,
- (c) not to take part in the activities of any trade union or of a particular trade union or of one of a number of particular trade unions, or
- (d) not to make use of services made available by any trade union or by a particular trade union or by one of a number of particular trade unions.

For the purposes of this subsection a requirement means a requirement imposed on the complainant by or under an arrangement or contract of employment or other agreement.

(2A) Conduct or action of the complainant shall be disregarded in so far as it constitutes acceptance of or failure to accept an offer made in contravention of section 145A or 145B.

(3) Conduct or action of the complainant shall be disregarded in so far as it constitutes a refusal, or proposed refusal, to comply with a requirement of a kind mentioned in section 152(3)(a) (payments in lieu of membership) or an objection, or proposed objection, (however expressed) to the operation of a provision of a kind mentioned in section 152(3)(b) (deductions in lieu of membership).

156 Minimum basic award

(1) Where a dismissal is unfair by virtue of section 152(1) or 153, the amount of the basic award of compensation, before any reduction is made under section 122 of the Employment Rights Act 1996 shall be not less than £9,157.

(2) But where the dismissal is unfair by virtue of section 153, subsection (2) of that section (reduction for contributory fault) applies in relation to so much of the basic award as is payable because of subsection (1) above.

157–159 [repealed]

160 Awards against third parties

(1) If in proceedings before an employment tribunal on a complaint of unfair dismissal either the employer or the complainant claims—

- (a) that the employer was induced to dismiss the complainant by pressure which a trade union or other person exercised on the employer by calling, organising, procuring or financing a strike or other industrial action, or by threatening to do so, and
- (b) that the pressure was exercised because the complainant was not a member of any trade union or of a particular trade union or of one of a number of particular trade unions,

the employer or the complainant may request the tribunal to direct that the person who he claims exercised the pressure be joined or sisted as a party to the proceedings.

(2) The request shall be granted if it is made before the hearing of the complaint begins, but may be refused after that time; and no such request may be made after the tribunal has made an award of compensation for unfair dismissal or an order for reinstatement or re-engagement.

(3) Where a person has been so joined or sisted as a party to the proceedings and the tribunal—

(a) makes an award of compensation for unfair dismissal, and

(b) finds that the claim mentioned in subsection (1) is well-founded,

the tribunal may order that the compensation shall be paid by that person instead of the employer, or partly by that person and partly by the employer, as the tribunal may consider just and equitable.

161 Application for interim relief

(1) An employee who presents a complaint of unfair dismissal alleging that the dismissal is unfair by virtue of section 152 may apply to the tribunal for interim relief.

(2) The tribunal shall not entertain an application for interim relief unless it is presented to the tribunal before the end of the period of seven days immediately following the effective date of termination (whether before, on or after that date).

(3) In a case where the employee relies on section 152(1)(a), (b) or (ba), or on section 152(1)(bb) otherwise than in relation to an offer made in contravention of section 145A(1)(d), the tribunal shall not entertain an application for interim relief unless before the end of that period there is also so presented a certificate in writing signed by an authorised official of the independent trade union of which the employee was or proposed to become a member stating—

(a) that on the date of the dismissal the employee was or proposed to become a member of the union, and

(b) that there appear to be reasonable grounds for supposing that the reason for his dismissal (or, if more than one, the principal reason) was one alleged in the complaint.

(4) An 'authorised official' means an official of the trade union authorised by it to act for the purposes of this section.

(5) A document purporting to be an authorisation of an official by a trade union to act for the purposes of this section and to be signed on behalf of the union shall be taken to be such an authorisation unless the contrary is proved; and a document purporting to be a certificate signed by such an official shall be taken to be signed by him unless the contrary is proved.

(6) For the purposes of subsection (3) the date of dismissal shall be taken to be—

(a) where the employee's contract of employment was terminated by notice (whether given by his employer or by him), the date on which the employer's notice was given, and

(b) in any other case, the effective date of termination.

162 Application to be promptly determined

(1) An employment tribunal shall determine an application for interim relief as soon as practicable after receiving the application and, where appropriate, the requisite certificate.

(2) The tribunal shall give to the employer, not later than seven days before the hearing, a copy of the application and of any certificate, together with notice of the date, time and place of the hearing.

(3) If a request under section 160 (awards against third parties) is made three days or more before the date of the hearing, the tribunal shall also give to the person to whom the request relates, as soon as reasonably practicable, a copy of the application and of any certificate, together with notice of the date, time and place of the hearing.

(4) The tribunal shall not exercise any power it has of postponing the hearing of an application for interim relief except where it is satisfied that special circumstances exist which justify it in doing so.

163 Procedure on hearing of application and making of order

(1) If on hearing an application for interim relief it appears to the tribunal that it is likely that on determining the complaint to which the application relates that it will find that, by virtue of section 152, the complainant has been unfairly dismissed, the following provisions apply.

(2) The tribunal shall announce its findings and explain to both parties (if present) what powers the tribunal may exercise on the application and in what circumstances it will exercise them, and

shall ask the employer (if present) whether he is willing, pending the determination or settlement of the complaint—

(a) to reinstate the employee, that is to say, to treat him in all respects as if he had not been dismissed, or

(b) if not, to re-engage him in another job on terms and conditions not less favourable than those which would have been applicable to him if he had not been dismissed.

(3) For this purpose 'terms and conditions not less favourable than those which would have been applicable to him if he had not been dismissed' means as regards seniority, pension rights and other similar rights that the period prior to the dismissal shall be regarded as continuous with his employment following the dismissal.

(4) If the employer states that he is willing to reinstate the employee, the tribunal shall make an order to that effect.

(5) If the employer states that he is willing to re-engage the employee in another job, and specifies the terms and conditions on which he is willing to do so, the tribunal shall ask the employee whether he is willing to accept the job on those terms and conditions; and—

(a) if the employee is willing to accept the job on those terms and conditions, the tribunal shall make an order to that effect, and

(b) if he is not, then, if the tribunal is of the opinion that the refusal is reasonable, the tribunal shall make an order for the continuation of his contract of employment, and otherwise the tribunal shall make no order.

(6) If on the hearing of an application for interim relief the employer fails to attend before the tribunal, or states that he is unwilling either to reinstate the employee or re-engage him as mentioned in subsection (2), the tribunal shall make an order for the continuation of the employee's contract of employment.

164 Order for continuation of contract of employment

(1) An order under section 163 for the continuation of a contract of employment is an order that the contract of employment continue in force—

(a) for the purposes of pay or any other benefit derived from the employment, seniority, pension rights and other similar matters, and

(b) for the purpose of determining for any purpose the period for which the employee has been continuously employed,

from the date of its termination (whether before or after the making of the order) until the determination or settlement of the complaint.

(2) Where the tribunal makes such an order it shall specify in the order the amount which is to be paid by the employer to the employee by way of pay in respect of each normal pay period, or part of any such period, falling between the date of dismissal and the determination or settlement of the complaint.

(3) Subject as follows, the amount so specified shall be that which the employee could reasonably have been expected to earn during that period, or part, and shall be paid—

(a) in the case of payment for any such period falling wholly or partly after the making of the order, on the normal pay day for that period, and

(b) in the case of a payment for any past period, within such time as may be specified in the order.

(4) If an amount is payable in respect only of part of a normal pay period, the amount shall be calculated by reference to the whole period and reduced proportionately.

(5) Any payment made to an employee by an employer under his contract of employment, or by way of damages for breach of that contract, in respect of a normal pay period or part of any such period shall go towards discharging the employer's liability in respect of that period under subsection (2); and conversely any payment under that subsection in respect of a period shall go towards discharging any liability of the employer under, or in respect of the breach of, the contract of employment in respect of that period.

(6) If an employee, on or after being dismissed by his employer, receives a lump sum which, or part of which, is in lieu of wages but is not referable to any normal pay period, the tribunal shall take the payment into account in determining the amount of pay to be payable in pursuance of any such order.

(7) For the purposes of this section the amount which an employee could reasonably have been expected to earn, his normal pay period and the normal pay day for each such period shall be determined as if he had not been dismissed.

165 Application for variation or revocation of order

(1) At any time between the making of an order under section 163 and the determination or settlement of the complaint, the employer or the employee may apply to an employment tribunal for the revocation or variation of the order on the ground of a relevant change of circumstances since the making of the order.

(2) Sections 161 to 163 apply in relation to such an application as in relation to an original application for interim relief, except that—

- (a) no certificate need be presented to the tribunal under section 161(3), and
- (b) in the case of an application by the employer, section 162(2) (service of copy of application and notice of hearing) has effect with the substitution of a reference to the employee for the reference to the employer.

166 Consequences of failure to comply with order

(1) If on the application of an employee an employment tribunal is satisfied that the employer has not complied with the terms of an order for the reinstatement or re-engagement of the employee under section 163(4) or (5), the tribunal shall—

- (a) make an order for the continuation of the employee's contract of employment, and
- (b) order the employer to pay the employee such compensation as the tribunal considers just and equitable in all the circumstances having regard—
  - (i) to the infringement of the employee's right to be reinstated or re-engaged in pursuance of the order, and
  - (ii) to any loss suffered by the employee in consequence of the non-compliance.

(2) Section 164 applies to an order under subsection (1)(a) as in relation to an order under section 163.

(3) If on the application of an employee an employment tribunal is satisfied that the employer has not complied with the terms of an order for the continuation of a contract of employment, the following provisions apply.

(4) If the non-compliance consists of a failure to pay an amount by way of pay specified in the order, the tribunal shall determine the amount owed by the employer on the date of the determination.

If on that date the tribunal also determines the employee's complaint that he has been unfairly dismissed, it shall specify that amount separately from any other sum awarded to the employee.

(5) In any other case, the tribunal shall order the employer to pay the employee such compensation as the tribunal considers just and equitable in all the circumstances having regard to any loss suffered by the employee in consequence of the non-compliance.

167 Interpretation and other supplementary provisions

(1) Part X of the Employment Rights Act 1996 (unfair dismissal) has effect subject to the provisions of sections 152 to 166 above.

(2) Those sections shall be construed as one with that Part; and in those sections—

'complaint of unfair dismissal' means a complaint under section 111 of the Employment Rights Act 1996;

'award of compensation for unfair dismissal' means an award of compensation for unfair dismissal under section 112(4) or 117(3)(a) of that Act; and

'order for reinstatement or re-engagement' means an order for reinstatement or re-engagement under section 113 of that Act.

(3) Nothing in those sections shall be construed as conferring a right to complain of unfair dismissal from employment of a description to which that Part does not otherwise apply.

Time off for trade union duties and activities

168 Time off for carrying out trade union duties

(1) An employer shall permit an employee of his who is an official of an independent trade union recognised by the employer to take time off during his working hours for the purpose of carrying out any duties of his, as such an official, concerned with—

- (a) negotiations with the employer related to or connected with matters falling within section 178(2) (collective bargaining) in relation to which the trade union is recognised by the employer, or
- (b) the performance on behalf of employees of the employer of functions related to or connected with matters falling within that provision which the employer has agreed may be so performed by the trade union, or
- (c) receipt of information from the employer and consultation by the employer under section 188 (redundancies) or under the Transfer of Undertakings (Protection of Employment) Regulations 2006, or
- (d) negotiations with a view to entering into an agreement under regulation 9 of the Transfer of Undertakings (Protection of Employment) Regulations 2006 that applies to employees of the employer, or
- (e) the performance on behalf of employees of the employer of functions related to or connected with the making of an agreement under that regulation.

(2) He shall also permit such an employee to take time off during his working hours for the purpose of undergoing training in aspects of industrial relations—

- (a) relevant to the carrying out of such duties as are mentioned in subsection (1), and
- (b) approved by the Trades Union Congress or by the independent trade union of which he is an official.

(3) The amount of time off which an employee is to be permitted to take under this section and the purposes for which, the occasions on which and any conditions subject to which time off may be so taken are those that are reasonable in all the circumstances having regard to any relevant provisions of a Code of Practice issued by ACAS.

(3A) An employer that permits an employee to take time off as required by this section must, where requested by the employee, provide the employee with such accommodation and other facilities for carrying out the duties or undergoing the training for which the employee takes time off as is reasonable in all the circumstances, having regard to any relevant provisions of a Code of Practice issued by ACAS.

(4) An employee may present a complaint to an employment tribunal that the employer has failed—

- (a) to permit the employee to take time off, or
- (b) to provide the employee with facilities,

as required by this section.

(5) On a complaint under subsection (4)(a), it is for the employer to show that the amount of time off which the employee proposed to take was not a reasonable amount of time off.

168A Time off for union learning representatives

(1) An employer shall permit an employee of his who is—

- (a) a member of an independent trade union recognised by the employer, and
- (b) a learning representative of the trade union,

to take time off during his working hours for any of the following purposes.

(2) The purposes are—

- (a) carrying on any of the following activities in relation to qualifying members of the trade union—
  - (i) analysing learning or training needs,

(ii) providing information and advice about learning or training matters,
(iii) arranging learning or training, and
(iv) promoting the value of learning or training,

(b) consulting the employer about carrying on any such activities in relation to such members of the trade union,

(c) preparing for any of the things mentioned in paragraphs (a) and (b).

(3)–(6) [omitted]

(7) If an employer is required to permit an employee to take time off under subsection (1), he shall also permit the employee to take time off during his working hours for the following purposes—

(a) undergoing training which is relevant to his functions as a learning representative, and

(b) where the trade union has in the last six months given the employer notice under subsection (4)(b) in relation to the employee, undergoing such training as is mentioned in subsection (4)(a).

(8) The amount of time off which an employee is to be permitted to take under this section and the purposes for which, the occasions on which and any conditions subject to which time off may be so taken are those that are reasonable in all the circumstances having regard to any relevant provision of a Code of Practice issued by ACAS or the Secretary of State.

(8A) An employer that permits an employee to take time off as required by this section must, where requested by the employee, provide the employee with such accommodation and other facilities for the purposes for which the employee takes time off as is reasonable in all the circumstances, having regard to any relevant provisions of a Code of Practice issued by ACAS.

(9) An employee may present a complaint to an employment tribunal that his employer has failed to permit him to take time off as required by this section.

(9) An employee may present a complaint to an employment tribunal that the employer has failed—

(a) to permit the employee to take time off, or

(b) to provide the employee with facilities,

as required by this section.

(10) [omitted]

(11) For the purposes of this section, a person is a learning representative of a trade union if he is appointed or elected as such in accordance with its rules.

168B Time off for union equality representatives

(1) An employer must permit an employee who is—

(a) a member of an independent trade union recognised by the employer, and

(b) an equality representative of the trade union,

to take time off during the employee's working hours for any of the following purposes.

(2) The purposes are—

(a) carrying out activities for the purpose of promoting the value of equality in the workplace;

(b) arranging learning or training on matters relating to equality in the workplace;

(c) providing information, advice or support to qualifying members of the trade union in relation to matters relating to equality in the workplace;

(d) consulting with the employer on matters relating to equality in the workplace;

(e) obtaining and analysing information relating to equality in the workplace;

(f) preparing for any of the things mentioned in paragraphs (a) to (e).

(3)–(6) [omitted]

(7) If an employer is required to permit an employee to take time off under subsection (1), the employer must also permit the employee to take time off during the employee's working hours for the following purposes—

(a) undergoing training which is relevant to the employee's functions as an equality representative, and

(b) where the trade union has in the last six months given the employer notice under subsection (4)(b) in relation to the employee, undergoing such training as is mentioned in subsection (4)(a).

(8) The amount of time off which an employee is to be permitted to take under this section and the purposes for which, the occasions on which and any conditions subject to which time off may be so taken are those that are reasonable in all the circumstances, having regard to any relevant provision of a Code of Practice issued by ACAS or the Secretary of State.

(9) An employer that permits an employee to take time off as required by this section must, where requested by the employee, provide the employee with such accommodation and other facilities in relation to the purposes for which the employee takes time off as is reasonable in all the circumstances, having regard to any relevant provisions of a Code of Practice issued by ACAS.

(10) An employee may present a complaint to an employment tribunal that the employer has failed—

(a) to permit the employee to take time off, or

(b) to provide the employee with facilities,

as required by this section.

(11) [omitted]

(12) For the purposes of this section—

(a) a person is an equality representative of a trade union if the person is appointed or elected as such in accordance with its rules;

(b) 'equality', in relation to a workplace, means—

(i) the elimination of discrimination, harassment and victimisation, each of which is to be read in accordance with the Equality Act 2010, and of any other conduct that is prohibited by or under that Act;

(ii) the advancement of equality of opportunity between persons who share a relevant protected characteristic and persons who do not share it;

(iii) the fostering of good relations between persons who share a relevant protected characteristic and persons who do not share it;

(c) 'relevant protected characteristic' means age, disability, gender reassignment, pregnancy and maternity, race, religion or belief, sex or sexual orientation, each of which is to be read in accordance with the Equality Act 2010;

(d) a reference to qualifying members of the trade union is a reference to members of the trade union—

(i) who are employees of the employer of a description in respect of which the union is recognised by the employer, and

(ii) in relation to whom it is the function of the equality representative to act as such.

169 Payment for time off under sections 168 to 168B

(1) An employer who permits an employee to take time off under section 168, 168A or 168B shall pay him for the time taken off pursuant to the permission.

(2) Where the employee's remuneration for the work he would ordinarily have been doing during that time does not vary with the amount of work done, he shall be paid as if he had worked at that work for the whole of that time.

(3) Where the employee's remuneration for the work he would ordinarily have been doing during that time varies with the amount of work done, he shall be paid an amount calculated by reference to the average hourly earnings for that work.

The average hourly earnings shall be those of the employee concerned or, if no fair estimate can be made of those earnings, the average hourly earnings for work of that description of persons in comparable employment with the same employer or, if there are no such persons, a figure of average hourly earnings which is reasonable in the circumstances.

(4) A right to be paid an amount under this section does not affect any right of an employee in relation to remuneration under his contract of employment, but—

(a) any contractual remuneration paid to an employee in respect of a period of time off to which this section applies shall go towards discharging any liability of the employer under this section in respect of that period, and

(b) any payment under this section in respect of a period shall go towards discharging any liability of the employer to pay contractual remuneration in respect of that period.

(5) An employee may present a complaint to an employment tribunal that his employer has failed to pay him in accordance with this section.

170 Time off for trade union activities

(1) An employer shall permit an employee of his who is a member of an independent trade union recognised by the employer in respect of that description of employee to take time off during his working hours for the purpose of taking part in—

(a) any activities of the union, and

(b) any activities in relation to which the employee is acting as a representative of the union.

(2) The right conferred by subsection (1) does not extend to activities which themselves consist of industrial action, whether or not in contemplation or furtherance of a trade dispute.

(2A) The right conferred by subsection (1) does not extend to time off for the purpose of acting as, or having access to services provided by, a learning representative or an equality representative of a trade union.

(2B) An employer shall permit an employee of his who is a member of an independent trade union recognised by the employer in respect of that description of employee to take time off during his working hours for the purpose of having access to services provided by a person in his capacity as a learning representative or an equality representative of the trade union.

(2C) Subsection (2B) only applies—

(a) in relation to a learning representative, if the learning representative would be entitled to time off under subsection (1) of section 168A for the purpose of carrying on in relation to the employee activities of the kind mentioned in subsection (2) of that section.

(b) in relation to an equality representative, if the equality representative would be entitled to time off under subsection (1) of section 168B for the purpose of carrying on in relation to the employee activities of the kind mentioned in subsection (2) of that section.

(3) The amount of time off which an employee is to be permitted to take under this section and the purposes for which, the occasions on which and any conditions subject to which time off may be so taken are those that are reasonable in all the circumstances having regard to any relevant provisions of a Code of Practice issued by ACAS.

(4) An employee may present a complaint to an employment tribunal that his employer has failed to permit him to take time off as required by this section.

(5) For the purposes of this section—

(a) a person is a learning representative or an equality representative of a trade union if he is appointed or elected as such in accordance with its rules, and

(b) a person who is a learning representative of a trade union acts as such if he carries on the activities mentioned in section 168A(2) in that capacity and

(c) a person who is an equality representative of a trade union acts as such if the person carries on the activities mentioned in section 168B(2) in that capacity.

171 Time limit for proceedings

(1) An employment tribunal shall not consider a complaint under section 168, 168A, 168B, 169 or 170 unless it is presented to the tribunal—

(a) within three months of the date when the failure occurred, or

(b) where the tribunal is satisfied that it was not reasonably practicable for the complaint to be presented within that period, within such further period as the tribunal considers reasonable.

(2) [omitted]

172 Remedies

(1) Where the tribunal finds a complaint under section 168, 168A, 168B or 170 is well-founded, it shall make a declaration to that effect and may make an award of compensation to be paid by the employer to the employee.

(2) The amount of the compensation shall be such as the tribunal considers just and equitable in all the circumstances having regard to the employer's default and to any loss sustained by the employee which is attributable to the matters complained of.

(3) Where on a complaint under section 169 the tribunal finds that the employer has failed to pay the employee in accordance with that section, it shall order him to pay the amount which it finds to be due.

172A–172B [omitted]

173 Interpretation and other supplementary provisions

(1) For the purposes of sections 168, 168A, 168B and 170 the working hours of an employee shall be taken to be any time when in accordance with his contract of employment he is required to be at work.

(2) The remedy of an employee for infringement of the rights conferred on him by section 168, 168A, 168B, 169 or 170 is by way of complaint to an employment tribunal in accordance with this Part, and not otherwise.

(3)–(4) [omitted]

Right to membership of trade union

174 Right not to be excluded or expelled from union

(1) An individual shall not be excluded or expelled from a trade union unless the exclusion or expulsion is permitted by this section.

(2) The exclusion or expulsion of an individual from a trade union is permitted by this section if (and only if)—

(a) he does not satisfy, or no longer satisfies, an enforceable membership requirement contained in the rules of the union,

(b) he does not qualify, or no longer qualifies, for membership of the union by reason of the union operating only in a particular part or particular parts of Great Britain,

(c) in the case of a union whose purpose is the regulation of relations between its members and one particular employer or a number of particular employers who are associated, he is not, or is no longer, employed by that employer or one of those employers, or

(d) the exclusion or expulsion is entirely attributable to conduct of his (other than excluded conduct) and the conduct to which it is wholly or mainly attributable is not protected conduct.

(3) A requirement in relation to membership of a union is 'enforceable' for the purposes of subsection (2)(a) if it restricts membership solely by reference to one or more of the following criteria—

(a) employment in specified trade, industry or profession,

(b) occupational description (including grade, level or category of appointment), and

(c) possession of specified trade, industrial or professional qualifications or work experience.

(4) For the purposes of subsection (2)(d) 'excluded conduct', in relation to an individual, means—

(a) conduct which consists in his being or ceasing to be, or having been or ceased to be, a member of another trade union,

(b) conduct which consists in his being or ceasing to be, or having been or ceased to be, employed by a particular employer or at a particular place, or

(c) conduct to which section 65 (conduct for which an individual may not be disciplined by a union) applies or would apply if the references in that section to the trade union which is relevant for the purposes of that section were references to any trade union.

(4A) For the purposes of subsection (2)(d) 'protected conduct' is conduct which consists in the individual's being or ceasing to be, or having been or ceased to be, a member of a political party.

(4B) Conduct which consists of activities undertaken by an individual as a member of a political party is not conduct falling within subsection (4A).

(4C) Conduct which consists in an individual's being or having been a member of a political party is not conduct falling within subsection (4A) if membership of that political party is contrary to—

(a) a rule of the trade union, or

(b) an objective of the trade union.

(4D) For the purposes of subsection (4C)(b) in the case of conduct consisting in an individual's being a member of a political party, an objective is to be disregarded—

(a) in relation to an exclusion, if it is not reasonably practicable for the objective to be ascertained by a person working in the same trade, industry or profession as the individual;

(b) in relation to an expulsion, if it is not reasonably practicable for the objective to be ascertained by a member of the union.

(4E) For the purposes of subsection (4C)(b) in the case of conduct consisting in an individual's having been a member of a political party, an objective is to be disregarded—

(a) in relation to an exclusion, if at the time of the conduct it was not reasonably practicable for the objective to be ascertained by a person working in the same trade, industry or profession as the individual;

(b) in relation to an expulsion, if at the time of the conduct it was not reasonably practicable for the objective to be ascertained by a member of the union.

(4F) Where the exclusion or expulsion of an individual from a trade union is wholly or mainly attributable to conduct which consists of an individual's being or having been a member of a political party but which by virtue of subsection (4C) is not conduct falling within subsection (4A), the exclusion or expulsion is not permitted by virtue of subsection (2)(d) if any one or more of the conditions in subsection (4G) apply.

(4G) Those conditions are—

(a) the decision to exclude or expel is taken otherwise than in accordance with the union's rules;

(b) the decision to exclude or expel is taken unfairly;

(c) the individual would lose his livelihood or suffer other exceptional hardship by reason of not being, or ceasing to be, a member of the union.

(4H) For the purposes of subsection (4G)(b) a decision to exclude or expel an individual is taken unfairly if (and only if)—

(a) before the decision is taken the individual is not given—

(i) notice of the proposal to exclude or expel him and the reasons for that proposal, and

(ii) a fair opportunity to make representations in respect of that proposal, or

(b) representations made by the individual in respect of that proposal are not considered fairly.

(5) An individual who claims that he has been excluded or expelled from a trade union in contravention of this section may present a complaint to an employment tribunal.

175 Time limit for proceedings

(1) An employment tribunal shall not entertain a complaint under section 174 unless it is presented—

(a) before the end of the period of six months beginning with the date of the exclusion or expulsion, or

(b) where the tribunal is satisfied that it was not reasonably practicable for the complaint to be presented before the end of that period, within such further period as the tribunal considers reasonable.

(2) [omitted]

176 Remedies

(1) Where the employment tribunal finds a complaint under section 174 is well-founded, it shall make a declaration to that effect.

(1A) If a tribunal makes a declaration under subsection (1) and it appears to the tribunal that the exclusion or expulsion was mainly attributable to conduct falling within section 174(4A) it shall make a declaration to that effect.

(1B) If a tribunal makes a declaration under subsection (1A) and it appears to the tribunal that the other conduct to which the exclusion or expulsion was attributable consisted wholly or mainly of conduct of the complainant which was contrary to—

(a) a rule of the union, or
(b) an objective of the union,

it shall make a declaration to that effect.

(1C) For the purposes of subsection (1B), it is immaterial whether the complainant was a member of the union at the time of the conduct contrary to the rule or objective.

(1D) A declaration by virtue of subsection (1B)(b) shall not be made unless the union shows that, at the time of the conduct of the complainant which was contrary to the objective in question, it was reasonably practicable for that objective to be ascertained—

(a) if the complainant was not at that time a member of the union, by a person working in the same trade, industry or profession as the complainant, and
(b) if he was at that time a member of the union, by a member of the union.

(2) An individual whose complaint has been declared to be well-founded may make an application to an employment tribunal for an award of compensation to be paid to him by the union.

(3) The application shall not be entertained if made—

(a) before the end of the period of four weeks beginning with the date of the declaration under subsection (1), or
(b) after the end of the period of six months beginning with that date.

(4) The amount of compensation awarded shall, subject to the following provisions, be such as the employment tribunal considers just and equitable in all the circumstances.

(5) Where the employment tribunal finds that the exclusion or expulsion complained of was to any extent caused or contributed to by the action of the applicant, it shall reduce the amount of the compensation by such proportion as it considers just and equitable having regard to that finding.

(6) The amount of compensation calculated in accordance with subsections (4) and (5) shall not exceed the aggregate of—

(a) an amount equal to thirty times the limit for the time being imposed by section 227(1)(a) of the Employment Rights Act 1996 (maximum amount of a week's pay for basic award in unfair dismissal cases), and
(b) an amount equal to the limit for the time being imposed by section 124(1) of that Act (maximum compensatory award in such cases).

(6A) If on the date on which the application was made the applicant had not been admitted or re-admitted to the union, the award shall less than £13,986.

(6B) Subsection (6A) does not apply in a case where the tribunal which made the declaration under subsection (1) also made declarations under subsections (1A) and (1B).

(7)–(8) [repealed]

177 Interpretation and other supplementary provisions

(1) For the purposes of section 174—

(a) 'trade union' does not include an organisation falling within paragraph (b) of section 1,
(b) 'conduct' includes statements, acts and omissions, and
(c) 'employment' includes any relationship whereby an individual personally does work or performs services for another person (related expressions being construed accordingly).

(2) For the purposes of sections 174 to 176—

(a) if an individual's application for membership of a trade union is neither granted nor rejected before the end of the period within which it might reasonably have been expected to be granted if it was to be granted, he shall be treated as having been excluded from the union on the last day of that period, and

(b) an individual who under the rules of a trade union ceases to be a member of the union on the happening of an event specified in the rules shall be treated as having been expelled from the union.

(3) The remedy of an individual for infringement of the rights conferred by section 174 is by way of a complaint to an employment tribunal in accordance with that section, sections 175 and 176 and this section, and not otherwise.

(4) Where a complaint relating to an expulsion which is presented under section 174 is declared to be well-founded, no complaint in respect of the expulsion shall be presented or proceeded with under section 66 (complaint of infringement of right not to be unjustifiably disciplined).

(5) The rights conferred by section 174 are in addition to, and not in substitution for, any right which exists apart from that section; and, subject to subsection (4), nothing in that section, section 175 or 176 or this section affects any remedy for infringement of any such right.

PART IV INDUSTRIAL RELATIONS

Chapter I Collective Bargaining

Introductory

178 Collective agreements and collective bargaining

(1) In this Act 'collective agreement' means any agreement or arrangement made by or on behalf of one or more trade unions and one or more employers or employers' associations and relating to one or more of the matters specified below; and 'collective bargaining' means negotiations relating to or connected with one or more of those matters.

(2) The matters referred to above are—

(a) terms and conditions of employment, or the physical conditions in which any workers are required to work;

(b) engagement or non-engagement, or termination or suspension of employment or the duties of employment, of one or more workers;

(c) allocation of work or the duties of employment between workers or groups of workers;

(d) matters of discipline;

(e) a worker's membership or non-membership of a trade union;

(f) facilities for officials of trade unions; and

(g) machinery for negotiation or consultation, and other procedures, relating to any of the above matters, including the recognition by employers or employers' associations of the right of a trade union to represent workers in such negotiation or consultation or in the carrying out of such procedures.

(3) In this Act 'recognition', in relation to a trade union, means the recognition of the union by an employer, or two or more associated employers, to any extent, for the purpose of collective bargaining; and 'recognised' and other related expressions shall be construed accordingly.

Enforceability of collective agreements

179 Whether agreement intended to be a legally enforceable contract

(1) A collective agreement shall be conclusively presumed not to have been intended by the parties to be a legally enforceable contract unless the agreement—

(a) is in writing, and

(b) contains a provision which (however expressed) states that the parties intend that the agreement shall be a legally enforceable contract.

(2) A collective agreement which does satisfy those conditions shall be conclusively presumed to have been intended by the parties to be a legally enforceable contract.

(3) If a collective agreement is in writing and contains a provision which (however expressed) states that the parties intend that one or more parts of the agreement specified in that provision, but not the whole of the agreement, shall be a legally enforceable contract, then—

(a) the specified part or parts shall be conclusively presumed to have been intended by the parties to be a legally enforceable contract, and

(b) the remainder of the agreement shall be conclusively presumed not to have been intended by the parties to be such a contract.

(4) A part of a collective agreement which by virtue of subsection (3)(b) is not a legally enforceable contract may be referred to for the purpose of interpreting a part of the agreement which is such a contract.

180 Effect of provisions restricting right to take industrial action

(1) Any terms of a collective agreement which prohibit or restrict the right of workers to engage in a strike or other industrial action, or have the effect of prohibiting or restricting that right, shall not form part of any contract between a worker and the person for whom he works unless the following conditions are met.

(2) The conditions are that the collective agreement—

(a) is in writing,

(b) contains a provision expressly stating that those terms shall or may be incorporated in such a contract,

(c) is reasonably accessible at his place of work to the worker to whom it applies and is available for him to consult during working hours, and

(d) is one where each trade union which is a party to the agreement is an independent trade union;

and that the contract with the worker expressly or impliedly incorporates those terms in the contract.

(3) The above provisions have effect notwithstanding anything in section 179 and notwithstanding any provision to the contrary in any agreement (including a collective agreement or a contract with any worker).

Disclosure of information for purposes of collective bargaining

181 General duty of employers to disclose information

(1) An employer who recognises an independent trade union shall, for the purposes of all stages of collective bargaining about matters, and in relation to descriptions of workers, in respect of which the union is recognised by him, disclose to representatives of the union, on request, the information required by this section.

In this section and sections 182 to 185 'representative', in relation to a trade union, means an official or other person authorised by the union to carry on such collective bargaining.

(2) The information to be disclosed is all information relating to the employer's undertaking (including information relating to use of agency workers in that undertaking) which is in his possession, or that of an associated employer, and is information—

(a) without which the trade union representatives would be to a material extent impeded in carrying on collective bargaining with him, and

(b) which it would be in accordance with good industrial relations practice that he should disclose to them for the purposes of collective bargaining.

(3) A request by trade union representatives for information under this section shall, if the employer so requests, be in writing or be confirmed in writing.

(4) In determining what would be in accordance with good industrial relations practice, regard shall be had to the relevant provisions of any Code of Practice issued by ACAS, but not so as to exclude any other evidence of what that practice is.

(5) Information which an employer is required by virtue of this section to disclose to trade union representatives shall, if they so request, be disclosed or confirmed in writing.

182 Restrictions on general duty

(1) An employer is not required by section 181 to disclose information—

(a) the disclosure of which would be against the interests of national security, or

(b) which he could not disclose without contravening a prohibition imposed by or under an enactment, or

(c) which has been communicated to him in confidence, or which he has otherwise obtained in consequence of the confidence reposed in him by another person, or

(d) which relates specifically to an individual (unless that individual has consented to its being disclosed), or

(e) the disclosure of which would cause substantial injury to his undertaking for reasons other than its effect on collective bargaining, or

(f) obtained by him for the purpose of bringing, prosecuting or defending any legal proceedings.

In formulating the provisions of any Code of Practice relating to the disclosure of information, ACAS shall have regard to the provisions of this subsection.

(2) In the performance of his duty under section 181 an employer is not required—

(a) to produce, or allow inspection of, any document (other than a document prepared for the purpose of conveying or confirming the information) or to make a copy of or extracts from any document, or

(b) to compile or assemble any information where the compilation or assembly would involve an amount of work or expenditure out of reasonable proportion to the value of the information in the conduct of collective bargaining.

183 Complaint of failure to disclose information

(1) A trade union may present a complaint to the Central Arbitration Committee that an employer has failed—

(a) to disclose to representatives of the union information which he was required to disclose to them by section 181, or

(b) to confirm such information in writing in accordance with that section.

The complaint must be in writing and in such form as the Committee may require.

(2) If on receipt of a complaint the Committee is of the opinion that it is reasonably likely to be settled by conciliation, it shall refer the complaint to ACAS and shall notify the trade union and employer accordingly, whereupon ACAS shall seek to promote a settlement of the matter.

If a complaint so referred is not settled or withdrawn and ACAS is of the opinion that further attempts at conciliation are unlikely to result in a settlement, it shall inform the Committee of its opinion.

(3) If the complaint is not referred to ACAS or, if it is so referred, on ACAS informing the Committee of its opinion that further attempts at conciliation are unlikely to result in a settlement, the Committee shall proceed to hear and determine the complaint and shall make a declaration stating whether it finds the complaint well-founded, wholly or in part, and stating the reasons for its findings.

(4) On the hearing of a complaint any person who the Committee considers has a proper interest in the complaint is entitled to be heard by the Committee, but a failure to accord a hearing to a person other than the trade union and employer directly concerned does not affect the validity of any decision of the Committee in those proceedings.

(5) If the Committee finds the complaint wholly or partly well-founded, the declaration shall specify—

(a) the information in respect of which the Committee finds that the complaint is well-founded,

(b) the date (or, if more than one, the earliest date) on which the employer refused or failed to disclose or, as the case may be, to confirm in writing, any of the information in question, and

(c) a period (not being less than one week from the date of the declaration) within which the employer ought to disclose that information, or, as the case may be, to confirm it in writing.

(6) On a hearing of a complaint under this section a certificate signed by or on behalf of a Minister of the Crown and certifying that a particular request for information could not be complied with except by disclosing information the disclosure of which would have been against the interests of national security shall be conclusive evidence of that fact.

A document which purports to be such a certificate shall be taken to be such a certificate unless the contrary is proved.

184 Further complaint of failure to comply with declaration

(1) After the expiration of the period specified in a declaration under section 183(5)(c) the trade union may present a further complaint to the Central Arbitration Committee that the employer has failed to disclose or, as the case may be, to confirm in writing to representatives of the union information specified in the declaration.

The complaint must be in writing and in such form as the Committee may require.

(2) On receipt of a further complaint the Committee shall proceed to hear and determine the complaint and shall make a declaration stating whether they find the complaint well-founded, wholly or in part, and stating the reasons for their finding.

(3) On the hearing of a further complaint any person who the Committee consider has a proper interest in that complaint shall be entitled to be heard by the Committee, but a failure to accord a hearing to a person other than the trade union and employer directly concerned shall not affect the validity of any decision of the Committee in those proceedings.

(4) If the Committee find the further complaint wholly or partly well-founded the declaration shall specify the information in respect of which the Committee find that that complaint is well-founded.

185 Determination of claim and award

(1) On or after presenting a further complaint under section 184 the trade union may present to the Central Arbitration Committee a claim, in writing, in respect of one or more descriptions of employees (but not workers who are not employees) specified in the claim that their contracts should include the terms and conditions specified in the claim.

(2) The right to present a claim expires if the employer discloses or, as the case may be, confirms in writing, to representatives of the trade union the information specified in the declaration under section 183(5) or 184(4); and a claim presented shall be treated as withdrawn if the employer does so before the Committee make an award on the claim.

(3) If the Committee find, or have found, the further complaint wholly or partly well-founded, they may, after hearing the parties, make an award that in respect of any description of employees specified in the claim the employer shall, from a specified date, observe either—

(a) the terms and conditions specified in the claim; or

(b) other terms and conditions which the Committee consider appropriate.

The date specified may be earlier than that on which the award is made but not earlier than the date specified in accordance with section 183(5)(b) in the declaration made by the Committee on the original complaint.

(4) An award shall be made only in respect of a description of employees, and shall comprise only terms and conditions relating to matters in respect of which the trade union making the claim is recognised by the employer.

(5) Terms and conditions which by an award under this section an employer is required to observe in respect of an employee have effect as part of the employee's contract of employment as from the date specified in the award, except in so far as they are superseded or varied—

(a) by a subsequent award under this section,

(b) by a collective agreement between the employer and the union for the time being representing that employee, or

(c) by express or implied agreement between the employee and the employer so far as that agreement effects an improvement in terms and conditions having effect by virtue of the award.

(6) Where—

(a) by virtue of any enactment, other than one contained in this section, providing for minimum remuneration or terms and conditions, a contract of employment is to have effect as modified by an award, order or other instrument under that enactment, and

(b) by virtue of an award under this section any terms and conditions are to have effect as part of that contract,

that contract shall have effect in accordance with that award, order or other instrument or in accordance with the award under this section, whichever is the more favourable, in respect of any terms and conditions of that contract, to the employee.

(7) No award may be made under this section in respect of terms and conditions of employment which are fixed by virtue of any enactment.

Prohibition of union recognition requirements

186 Recognition requirement in contract for goods or services void

A term or condition of a contract for the supply of goods or services is void in so far as it purports to require a party to the contract—

(a) to recognise one or more trade unions (whether or not named in the contract) for the purpose of negotiating on behalf of workers, or any class of worker, employed by him, or

(b) to negotiate or consult with, or with an official of, one or more trade unions (whether or not so named).

187 Refusal to deal on grounds of union exclusion prohibited

(1) A person shall not refuse to deal with a supplier or prospective supplier of goods or services if the ground or one of the grounds for his action is that the person against whom it is taken does not, or is not likely to—

(a) recognise one or more trade unions for the purpose of negotiating on behalf of workers, or any class of worker, employed by him, or

(b) negotiate or consult with, or with an official of, one or more trade unions.

(2) A person refuses to deal with a person if—

(a) where he maintains (in whatever form) a list of approved suppliers of goods or services, or of persons from whom tenders for the supply of goods or services may be invited, he fails to include the name of that person in that list; or

(b) in relation to a proposed contract for the supply of goods or services—

(i) he excludes that person from the group of persons from whom tenders for the supply of the goods or services are invited, or

(ii) he fails to permit that person to submit such a tender, or

(iii) he otherwise determines not to enter into a contract with that person for the supply of the goods or services; or

(c) he terminates a contract with that person for the supply of goods or services.

(3) The obligation to comply with this section is a duty owed to the person with whom there is a refusal to deal and to any other person who may be adversely affected by its contravention; and a breach of the duty is actionable accordingly (subject to the defences and other incidents applying to actions for breach of statutory duty).

Chapter II Procedure for Handling Redundancies

Duty of employer to consult representatives

188 Duty of employer to consult representatives

(A1) Subsection (1) applies where an employer is proposing to dismiss as redundant within a period of 90 days or less—

(a) at least the threshold number of employees (see section 195A), or

(b) 20 or more employees at one establishment.

(1) Where an employer is proposing to dismiss as redundant 20 or more employees at one establishment within a period of 90 days or less, the employer shall consult about the dismissals all the persons who are appropriate representatives of any of the employees who may be affected by the proposed dismissals or may be affected by measures taken in connection with those dismissals.

(1A) The consultation shall begin in good time and in any event—

(a) where the employer is proposing to dismiss 100 or more employees as mentioned in subsection (A1), at least 45 days, and

(b) otherwise, at least 30 days,

before the first of the dismissals takes effect.

(1B) For the purposes of this section the appropriate representatives of any affected employees are—

(a) if the employees are of a description in respect of which an independent trade union is recognised by their employer, representatives of the trade union, or

(b) in any other case, whichever of the following employee representatives the employer chooses—

(i) employee representatives appointed or elected by the affected employees otherwise than for the purposes of this section, who (having regard to the purposes for and the method by which they were appointed or elected) have authority from those employees to receive information and to be consulted about the proposed dismissals on their behalf;

(ii) employee representatives elected by the affected employees, for the purposes of this section, in an election satisfying the requirements of section 188A(1).

(2) The consultation shall include consultation about ways of—

(a) avoiding the dismissals,

(b) reducing the numbers of employees to be dismissed, and

(c) mitigating the consequences of the dismissals,

and shall be undertaken by the employer with a view to reaching agreement with the appropriate representatives.

(2A) This section does not require the employer to—

(a) consult all of the appropriate representatives together, or

(b) undertake the consultation with a view to reaching the same agreement with all of the appropriate representatives.

(3) In determining how many employees an employer is proposing to dismiss as redundant no account shall be taken of employees in respect of whose proposed dismissals consultation has already begun.

(4) For the purposes of the consultation the employer shall disclose in writing to the appropriate representatives—

(a) the reasons for his proposals,

(b) the numbers and descriptions of employees whom it is proposed to dismiss as redundant,

(c) where the employees whom it is proposed to dismiss as redundant are at only one establishment, the total number of employees of any such description employed by the employer at the establishment in question,

(ca) where the employees whom it is proposed to dismiss as redundant are at more than one establishment—

(i) the total number of employees of any such description employed by the employer, and

(ii) details of the establishments at which those employees are employed,

(d) the proposed method of selecting the employees who may be dismissed,

(e) the proposed method of carrying out the dismissals, with due regard to any agreed procedure, including the period over which the dismissals are to take effect,

(f) the proposed method of calculating the amount of any redundancy payments to be made (otherwise than in compliance with an obligation imposed by or by virtue of any enactment) to employees who may be dismissed,
(g) the number of agency workers working temporarily for and under the supervision and direction of the employer,
(h) the parts of the employer's undertaking in which those agency workers are working, and
(i) the type of work those agency workers are carrying out.

(5) That information shall be given to each of the appropriate representatives by being delivered to them or sent by post to an address notified by them to the employer, or (in the case of representatives of a trade union) sent by post to the union at the address of its head or main office.

(5A) The employer shall allow the appropriate representatives access to the affected employees and shall afford to those representatives such accommodation and other facilities as may be appropriate.

(6) [repealed]

(7) If in any case there are special circumstances which render it not reasonably practicable for the employer to comply with a requirement of subsection (1A), (2) or (4), the employer shall take all such steps towards compliance with that requirement as are reasonably practicable in those circumstances. Where the decision leading to the proposed dismissals is that of a person controlling the employer (directly or indirectly), a failure on the part of that person to provide information to the employer shall not constitute special circumstances rendering it not reasonably practicable for the employer to comply with such a requirement.

(7A) Where—
(a) the employer has invited any of the affected employees to elect employee representatives, and
(b) the invitation was issued long enough before the time when the consultation is required by subsection (1A)(a) or (b) to begin to allow them to elect representatives by that time,

the employer shall be treated as complying with the requirements of this section in relation to those employees if he complies with those requirements as soon as is reasonably practicable after the election of the representatives.

(7B) If, after the employer has invited affected employees to elect representatives, the affected employees fail to do so within a reasonable time, he shall give to each affected employee the information set out in subsection (4).

(8) This section does not confer any rights on a trade union, a representative or an employee except as provided by sections 189 to 192 below.

188A [omitted]

189 Complaint and protective award

(1) Where an employer has failed to comply with a requirement of section 188 or section 188A, a complaint may be presented to an employment tribunal on that ground—
(a) in the case of a failure relating to the election of employee representatives, by any of the affected employees or by any of the employees who have been dismissed as redundant;
(b) in the case of any other failure relating to employee representatives, by any of the employee representatives to whom the failure related;
(c) in the case of failure relating to representatives of a trade union, by the trade union; and
(d) in any other case, by any of the affected employees or by any of the employees who have been dismissed as redundant.

(1A) If on a complaint under subsection (1) a question arises as to whether or not any employee representative was an appropriate representative for the purposes of section 188, it shall be for the employer to show that the employee representative had the authority to represent the affected employees.

(1B) On a complaint under subsection (1)(a) it shall be for the employer to show that the requirements in section 188A have been satisfied.

(2) If the tribunal finds the complaint well-founded it shall make a declaration to that effect and may also make a protective award.

(3) A protective award is an award in respect of one or more descriptions of employees—

(a) who has been dismissed as redundant, or whom it is proposed to dismiss as redundant, and

(b) in respect of whose dismissal or proposed dismissal the employer has failed to comply with a requirement of section 188,

ordering the employer to pay remuneration for the protected period.

(4) The protected period—

(a) begins with the date on which the first of the dismissals to which the complaint relates takes effect, or the date of the award, whichever is the earlier, and

(b) is of such length as the tribunal determines to be just and equitable in all the circumstances having regard to the seriousness of the employer's default in complying with any requirement of section 188;

but shall not exceed 180 days.

(5) An employment tribunal shall not consider a complaint under this section unless it is presented to the tribunal—

(a) before the date on which the last of the dismissals to which the complaint relates takes effect, or

(b) during the period of three months beginning with that date, or

(c) where the tribunal is satisfied that it was not reasonably practicable for the complaint to be presented within the period of three months, within such further period as it considers reasonable.

(5A) [omitted]

(6) If on a complaint under this section a question arises—

(a) whether there were special circumstances which rendered it not reasonably practicable for the employer to comply with any requirement of section 188, or

(b) whether he took all such steps towards compliance with that requirement as were reasonably practicable in those circumstances,

it is for the employer to show that there were and that he did.

190 Entitlement under protective award

(1) Where an employment tribunal has made a protective award, every employee of a description to which the award relates is entitled, subject to the following provisions and to section 191, to be paid remuneration by his employer for the protected period.

(2) The rate of remuneration payable is a week's pay for each week of the period; and remuneration in respect of a period less than one week shall be calculated by reducing proportionately the amount of a week's pay.

(3) [repealed]

(4) An employee is not entitled to remuneration under a protective award in respect of a period during which he is employed by the employer unless he would be entitled to be paid by the employer in respect of that period—

(a) by virtue of his contract of employment, or

(b) by virtue of sections 87 to 91 of the Employment Rights Act 1996 (rights of employee in period of notice),

if that period fell within the period of notice required to be given by section 86(1) of that Act.

(5) Chapter II of Part XIV of the Employment Rights Act 1996 applies with respect to the calculation of a week's pay for the purposes of this section.

The calculation date for the purposes of that Chapter is the date on which the protective award was made or, in the case of an employee who was dismissed before the date on which the protective award was made, the date which by virtue of section 226(5) is the calculation date for the purpose of computing the amount of a redundancy payment in relation to that dismissal (whether or not the employee concerned is entitled to any such payment).

(6) If an employee of a description to which a protective award relates dies during the protected period, the award has effect in his case as if the protected period ended on his death.

191 Termination of employment during protected period

(1) Where the employee is employed by the employer during the protected period and—

(a) he is fairly dismissed by his employer otherwise than as redundant, or

(b) he unreasonably terminates the contract of employment,

then, subject to the following provisions, he is not entitled to remuneration under the protective award in respect of any period during which but for that dismissal or termination he would have been employed.

(2) If an employer makes an employee an offer (whether in writing or not and whether before or after the ending of his employment under the previous contract) to renew his contract of employment, or to re-engage him under a new contract, so that the renewal or re-engagement would take effect before or during the protected period, and either—

(a) the provisions of the contract as renewed, or of the new contract, as to the capacity and place in which he would be employed, and as to the other terms and conditions of his employment, would not differ from the corresponding provisions of the previous contract, or

(b) the offer constitutes an offer of suitable employment in relation to the employee,

the following subsections have effect.

(3) If the employee unreasonably refuses the offer, he is not entitled to remuneration under the protective award in respect of a period during which but for that refusal he would have been employed.

(4) If the employee's contract of employment is renewed, or he is re-engaged under a new contract of employment, in pursuance of such an offer as is referred to in subsection (2)(b), there shall be a trial period in relation to the contract as renewed, or the new contract (whether or not there has been a previous trial period under this section).

(5) The trial period begins with the ending of his employment under the previous contract and ends with the expiration of the period of four weeks beginning with the date on which he starts work under the contract as renewed, or the new contract, or such longer period as may be agreed in accordance with subsection (6) for the purpose of retraining the employee for employment under that contract.

(6) Any such agreement—

(a) shall be made between the employer and the employee or his representative before the employee starts work under the contract as renewed or, as the case may be, the new contract,

(b) shall be in writing,

(c) shall specify the date of the end of the trial period, and

(d) shall specify the terms and conditions of employment which will apply in the employee's case after the end of that period.

(7) If during the trial period—

(a) the employee, for whatever reason, terminates the contract, or gives notice to terminate it and the contract is thereafter, in consequence, terminated, or

(b) the employer, for a reason connected with or arising out of the change to the renewed, or new, employment, terminates the contract, or gives notice to terminate it and the contract is thereafter, in consequence, terminated,

the employee remains entitled under the protective award unless, in a case falling within paragraph (a), he acted unreasonably in terminating or giving notice to terminate the contract.

192 Complaint by employee to employment tribunal

(1) An employee may present a complaint to an employment tribunal on the ground that he is an employee of a description to which a protective award relates and that his employer has failed, wholly or in part, to pay him remuneration under the award.

(2) An employment tribunal shall not entertain a complaint under this section unless it is presented to the tribunal—

(a) before the end of the period of three months beginning with the day (or, if the complaint relates to more than one day, the last of the days) in respect of which the complaint is made of failure to pay remuneration, or

(b) where the tribunal is satisfied that it was not reasonably practicable for the complaint to be presented within the period of three months, within such further period as it may consider reasonable.

(2A) [omitted]

(3) Where the tribunal finds a complaint under this section well-founded it shall order the employer to pay the complainant the amount of remuneration which it finds is due to him.

(4) The remedy of an employee for infringement of his right to remuneration under a protective award is by way of complaint under this section, and not otherwise.

193–194 [omitted]

Supplementary provisions

195 Construction of references to dismissal as redundant etc.

(1) In this Chapter references to dismissal as redundant are references to dismissal for a reason not related to the individual concerned or for a number of reasons all of which are not so related.

(2) For the purposes of any proceedings under this Chapter, where an employee is or is proposed to be dismissed it shall be presumed, unless the contrary is proved, that he is or is proposed to be dismissed as redundant.

195A [omitted]

196 Construction of references to representatives

(1) For the purposes of this Chapter persons are employee representatives if—

(a) they have been elected by employees for the specific purpose of being consulted by their employer about dismissals proposed by him, or

(b) having been elected or appointed by employees (whether before or after dismissals have been proposed by their employer) otherwise than for that specific purpose, it is appropriate (having regard to the purposes for which they were elected) for the employer to consult them about dismissals proposed by him,

and (in either case) they are employed by the employer at the time when they are elected or appointed.

(2) References in this Chapter to representatives of a trade union, in relation to an employer, are to officials or other persons authorised by the trade union to carry on collective bargaining with the employer.

(3) References in this Chapter to affected employees are to employees who may be affected by the proposed dismissals or who may be affected by measures taken in connection with such dismissals.

197–198 [omitted]

198A Employees being transferred to the employer from another undertaking

(1) This section applies where the following conditions are met—

(a) there is to be, or is likely to be, a relevant transfer,

(b) the transferee is proposing to dismiss as redundant 20 or more employees at one establishment within a period of 90 days or less, and

(c) the individuals who work for the transferor and who are to be (or are likely to be) transferred to the transferee's employment under the transfer ('transferring individuals') include one or more individuals who may be affected by the proposed dismissals or by measures taken in connection with the proposed dismissals.

(2) Where this section applies, the transferee may elect to consult, or to start to consult, representatives of affected transferring individuals about the proposed dismissals before the transfer takes place ('pre-transfer consultation').

(3) Any such election—

(a) may be made only if the transferor agrees to it, and

(b) must be made by way of written notice to the transferor.

(4) [omitted]

(5) A transferee who elects to carry out pre-transfer consultation may cancel that election at any time by written notice to the transferor.

(6) [omitted]

(7) For the purposes of this section and section 198B—

'affected transferring individual' means a transferring individual who may be affected by the proposed dismissals or who may be affected by measures taken in connection with the proposed dismissals;

'pre-transfer consultation' has the meaning given in subsection (2);

'relevant transfer' means—

(a) a relevant transfer under the Transfer of Undertakings (Protection of Employment) Regulations 2006,

(b) anything else regarded, by virtue of an enactment, as a relevant transfer for the purposes of those Regulations, or

(c) where an enactment provides a power to make provision which is the same as or similar to those Regulations, any other novation of a contract of employment effected in the exercise of that power,

and 'transferor' and 'transferee' are to be construed accordingly;

'transferring individual' has the meaning given in subsection (1)(c).

198B [omitted]

Chapter III Codes of Practice

199–206 [omitted]

Supplementary provisions

207 Effect of failure to comply with Code

(1) A failure on the part of any person to observe any provision of a Code of Practice issued under this Chapter shall not of itself render him liable to any proceedings.

(2) In any proceedings before an employment tribunal or the Central Arbitration Committee any Code of Practice issued under this Chapter by ACAS shall be admissible in evidence, and any provision of the Code which appears to the tribunal or Committee to be relevant to any question arising in the proceedings shall be taken into account in determining that question.

(3) In any proceedings before a court or employment tribunal or the Central Arbitration Committee any Code of Practice issued under this Chapter by the Secretary of State shall be admissible in evidence, and any provision of the Code which appears to the court, tribunal or Committee to be relevant to any question arising in the proceedings shall be taken into account in determining that question.

207A Effect of failure to comply with Code: adjustment of awards

(1) This section applies to proceedings before an employment tribunal relating to a claim by an employee under any of the jurisdictions listed in Schedule A2.

(2) If, in the case of proceedings to which this section applies, it appears to the employment tribunal that—

(a) the claim to which the proceedings relate concerns a matter to which a relevant Code of Practice applies,

(b) the employer has failed to comply with that Code in relation to that matter, and
(c) that failure was unreasonable,

the employment tribunal may, if it considers it just and equitable in all the circumstances to do so, increase any award it makes to the employee by no more than 25%.

(3) If, in the case of proceedings to which this section applies, it appears to the employment tribunal that—

(a) the claim to which the proceedings relate concerns a matter to which a relevant Code of Practice applies,
(b) the employee has failed to comply with that Code in relation to that matter, and
(c) that failure was unreasonable,

the employment tribunal may, if it considers it just and equitable in all the circumstances to do so, reduce any award it makes to the employee by no more than 25%.

(4) In subsections (2) and (3), 'relevant Code of Practice' means a Code of Practice issued under this Chapter which relates exclusively or primarily to procedure for the resolution of disputes.

(5) Where an award falls to be adjusted under this section and under section 38 of the Employment Act 2002, the adjustment under this section shall be made before the adjustment under that section.

(6)–(9) [omitted]

208 [omitted]

Chapter IV General

Functions of ACAS

209 General duty to promote improvement of industrial relations

It is the general duty of ACAS to promote the improvement of industrial relations.

210 Conciliation

(1) Where a trade dispute exists or is apprehended ACAS may, at the request of one or more parties to the dispute or otherwise, offer the parties to the dispute its assistance with a view to bringing about a settlement.

(2) The assistance may be by way of conciliation or by other means, and may include the appointment of a person other than an officer or servant of ACAS to offer assistance to the parties to the dispute with a view to bringing about a settlement.

(3) In exercising its functions under this section ACAS shall have regard to the desirability of encouraging the parties to a dispute to use any appropriate agreed procedures for negotiation or the settlement of disputes.

210A [omitted]

211 Conciliation officers

(1) ACAS shall designate some of its officers to perform the functions of conciliation officers under any enactment (whenever passed) relating to matters which are or could be the subject of proceedings before an employment tribunal.

(2) References in any such enactment to a conciliation officer are to an officer designated under this section.

212 Arbitration

(1) Where a trade dispute exists or is apprehended ACAS may, at the request of one or more of the parties to the dispute and with the consent of all the parties to the dispute, refer all or any of the matters to which the dispute relates for settlement to the arbitration of—

(a) one or more persons appointed by ACAS for that purpose (not being officers or employees of ACAS), or
(b) the Central Arbitration Committee.

(2) In exercising its functions under this section ACAS shall consider the likelihood of the dispute being settled by conciliation.

(3) Where there exist appropriate agreed procedures for negotiation or the settlement of disputes, ACAS shall not refer a matter for settlement to arbitration under this section unless—

(a) those procedures have been used and have failed to result in a settlement, or

(b) there is, in ACAS's opinion a special reason which justifies arbitration under this section as an alternative to those procedures.

(4) Where a matter is referred to arbitration under subsection (1)(a)—

(a) if more than one arbitrator or arbiter is appointed, ACAS shall appoint one of them to act as chairman; and

(b) the award may be published if ACAS so decides and all the parties consent.

(5) Nothing in any of sections 1 to 15 of and schedule 1 to the Arbitration (Scotland) Act 2010 or Part I of the Arbitration Act 1996 (general provisions as to arbitration) applies to an arbitration under this section.

212A [omitted]

212B Dismissal procedures agreements

ACAS may, in accordance with any dismissal procedures agreement (within the meaning of the Employment Rights Act 1996), refer any matter to the arbitration of a person appointed by ACAS for the purpose (not being an officer or employee of ACAS).

213 Advice

(1) ACAS may, on request or otherwise, give employers, employers' associations, workers and trade unions such advice as it thinks appropriate on matters concerned with or affecting or likely to affect industrial relations.

(2) ACAS may also publish general advice on matters concerned with or affecting or likely to affect industrial relations.

214 Inquiry

(1) ACAS may, if it thinks fit, inquire into any question relating to industrial relations generally or to industrial relations in any particular industry or in any particular undertaking or part of an undertaking.

(2) The findings of an inquiry under this section, together with any advice given by ACAS in connection with those findings, may be published by ACAS if—

(a) it appears to ACAS that publication is desirable for the improvement of industrial relations, either generally or in relation to the specific question inquired into, and

(b) after sending a draft of the findings to all parties appearing to be concerned and taking account of their views, it thinks fit.

Supplementary provisions

215–217 [omitted]

218 Meaning of 'trade dispute' in Part IV

(1) In this Part 'trade dispute' means a dispute between employers and workers, or between workers and workers, which is connected with one or more of the following matters—

(a) terms and conditions of employment, or the physical conditions in which any workers are required to work;

(b) engagement or non-engagement, or termination or suspension of employment or the duties of employment, of one or more workers;

(c) allocation of work or the duties of employment as between workers or groups of workers;

(d) matters of discipline;

(e) the membership or non-membership of a trade union on the part of a worker;

(f) facilities for officials of trade unions; and

(g) machinery for negotiation or consultation, and other procedures, relating to any of the foregoing matters, including the recognition by employers or employers' associations of the right of a trade union to represent workers in any such negotiation or consultation or in the carrying out of such procedures.

(2) A dispute between a Minister of the Crown and any workers shall, notwithstanding that he is not the employer of those workers, be treated for the purposes of this Part as a dispute between an employer and those workers if the dispute relates—

(a) to matters which have been referred for consideration by a joint body on which, by virtue of any provision made by or under any enactment, that Minister is represented, or

(b) to matters which cannot be settled without that Minister exercising a power conferred on him by or under an enactment.

(3) There is a trade dispute for the purpose of this Part even though it relates to matters occurring outside Great Britain.

(4) A dispute to which a trade union or employer's association is a party shall be treated for the purposes of this Part as a dispute to which workers or, as the case may be, employers are parties.

(5) In this section—

'employment' includes any relationship whereby one person personally does work or performs services for another; and

'worker', in relation to a dispute to which an employer is a party, includes any worker even if not employed by that employer.

PART V INDUSTRIAL ACTION

Protection of acts in contemplation or furtherance of trade dispute

219 Protection from certain tort liabilities

(1) An act done by a person in contemplation or furtherance of a trade dispute is not actionable in tort on the ground only—

(a) that it induces another person to break a contract or interferes or induces another person to interfere with its performance, or

(b) that it consists in his threatening that a contract (whether one to which he is a party or not) will be broken or its performance interfered with, or that he will induce another person to break a contract or interfere with its performance.

(2) An agreement or combination by two or more persons to do or procure the doing of an act in contemplation or furtherance of a trade dispute is not actionable in tort if the act is one which if done without any such agreement or combination would not be actionable in tort.

(3) Nothing in subsections (1) and (2) prevents an act done in the course of picketing from being actionable in tort unless it is done in the course of attendance declared lawful by section 220 (peaceful picketing).

(4) Subsections (1) and (2) have effect subject to—

(a) sections 222 to 225 (action excluded from protection),

(b) section 226 (requirement of ballot before action by trade union), and

(c) section 234A (requirement of notice to employer of industrial action);

and in those sections 'not protected' means excluded from the protection afforded by this section or, where the expression is used with reference to a particular person, excluded from that protection as respects that person.

220 Peaceful picketing

(1) It is lawful for a person in contemplation or furtherance of a trade dispute to attend—

(a) at or near his own place of work, or

(b) if he is an official of a trade union, at or near the place of work of a member of the union whom he is accompanying and whom he represents, for the purpose only of peacefully obtaining or communicating information, or peacefully persuading any person to work or abstain from working.

(2) If a person works or normally works—

(a) otherwise than at any one place, or

(b) at a place the location of which is such that attendance there for a purpose mentioned in subsection (1) is impracticable,

his place of work for the purposes of that subsection shall be any premises of his employer from which he works or from which his work is administered.

(3) In the case of a worker not in employment where—

(a) his last employment was terminated in connection with a trade dispute, or

(b) the termination of his employment was one of the circumstances giving rise to a trade dispute,

in relation to that dispute his former place of work shall be treated for the purposes of subsection (1) as being his place of work.

(4) A person who is an official of a trade union by virtue only of having been elected or appointed to be a representative of some of the members of the union shall be regarded for the purposes of subsection (1) as representing only those members; but otherwise an official of a union shall be regarded for those purposes as representing all its members.

220A [repealed]

221 Restrictions on grant of injunctions and interdicts

(1) Where—

(a) an application for an injunction or interdict is made to a court in the absence of the party against whom it is sought or any representative of his, and

(b) he claims, or in the opinion of the court would be likely to claim, that he acted in contemplation or furtherance of a trade dispute,

the court shall not grant the injunction or interdict unless satisfied that all steps which in the circumstances were reasonable have been taken with a view to securing that notice of the application and an opportunity of being heard with respect to the application have been given to him.

(2) Where—

(a) an application for an interlocutory injunction is made to a court pending the trial of an action, and

(b) the party against whom it is sought claims that he acted in contemplation or furtherance of a trade dispute,

the court shall, in exercising its discretion whether or not to grant the injunction, have regard to the likelihood of that party's succeeding at the trial of the action in establishing any matter which would afford a defence to the action under section 219 (protection from certain tort liabilities) or section 220 (peaceful picketing).

This subsection does not extend to Scotland.

Action excluded from protection

222 Action to enforce trade union membership

(1) An act is not protected if the reason, or one of the reasons, for which it is done is the fact or belief that a particular employer—

(a) is employing, has employed or might employ a person who is not a member of a trade union, or

(b) is failing, has failed or might fail to discriminate against such a person.

(2) For the purposes of subsection (1)(b) an employer discriminates against a person if, but only if, he ensures that his conduct in relation to—

(a) persons, or persons of any description, employed by him, or who apply to be, or are, considered by him for employment, or

(b) the provision of employment for such persons,

is different, in some or all cases, according to whether or not they are members of a trade union, and is more favourable to those who are.

(3) An act is not protected if it constitutes, or is one of a number of acts which together constitute, an inducement or attempted inducement of a person—

(a) to incorporate in a contract to which that person is a party, or a proposed contract to which he intends to be a party, a term or condition which is or would be void by virtue of section 144 (union membership requirement in contract for goods or services), or

(b) to contravene section 145 (refusal to deal with person on grounds relating to union membership).

(4) References in this section to an employer employing a person are to a person acting in the capacity of the person for whom a worker works or normally works.

(5) References in this section to not being a member of a trade union are to not being a member of any trade union, of a particular trade union or of one of a number of particular trade unions.

Any such reference includes a reference to not being a member of a particular branch or section of a trade union or of one of a number of particular branches or sections of a trade union.

223 Action taken because of dismissal for taking unofficial action

An act is not protected if the reason, or one of the reasons, for doing it is the fact or belief that an employer has dismissed one or more employees in circumstances such that by virtue of section 237 (dismissal in connection with unofficial action) they have no right to complain of unfair dismissal.

224 Secondary action

(1) An act is not protected if one of the facts relied on for the purpose of establishing liability is that there has been secondary action which is not lawful picketing.

(2) There is secondary action in relation to a trade dispute when, and only when, a person—

(a) induces another to break a contract of employment or interferes or induces another to interfere with its performance, or

(b) threatens that a contract of employment under which he or another is employed will be broken or its performance interfered with, or that he will induce another to break a contract of employment or to interfere with its performance,

and the employer under the contract of employment is not the employer party to the dispute.

(3) Lawful picketing means acts done in the course of such attendance as is declared lawful by section 220 (peaceful picketing)—

(a) by a worker employed (or, in the case of a worker not in employment, last employed) by the employer party to the dispute, or

(b) by a trade union official whose attendance is lawful by virtue of subsection (1)(b) of that section.

(4) For the purposes of this section an employer shall not be treated as party to a dispute between another employer and workers of that employer; and where more than one employer is in dispute with his workers, the dispute between each employer and his workers shall be treated as a separate dispute.

In this subsection 'worker' has the same meaning as in section 244 (meaning of 'trade dispute').

(5) An act in contemplation or furtherance of a trade dispute which is primary action in relation to that dispute may not be relied on as secondary action in relation to another trade dispute.

Primary action means such action as is mentioned in paragraph (a) or (b) of subsection (2) where the employer under the contract of employment is the employer party to the dispute.

(6) In this section 'contract of employment' includes any contract under which one person personally does work or performs services for another, and related expressions shall be construed accordingly.

225 Pressure to impose union recognition requirement

(1) An act is not protected if it constitutes, or is one of a number of acts which together constitute, an inducement or attempted inducement of a person—

(a) to incorporate in a contract to which that person is a party, or a proposed contract to which he intends to be a party, a term or condition which is or would be void by virtue of section 186 (recognition requirement in contract for goods or services), or

(b) to contravene section 187 (refusal to deal with person on grounds of union exclusion).

(2) An act is not protected if—

(a) it interferes with the supply (whether or not under a contract) of goods or services, or can reasonably be expected to have that effect, and

(b) one of the facts relied upon for the purpose of establishing liability is that a person has—

(i) induced another to break a contract of employment or interfered or induced another to interfere with its performance, or

(ii) threatened that a contract of employment under which he or another is employed will be broken or its performance interfered with, or that he will induce another to break a contract of employment or to interfere with its performance, and

(c) the reason, or one of the reasons, for doing the act is the fact or belief that the supplier (not being the employer under the contract of employment mentioned in paragraph (b)) does not, or might not—

(i) recognise one or more trade unions for the purpose of negotiating on behalf of workers, or any class of worker, employed by him, or

(ii) negotiate or consult with, or with an official of, one or more trade unions.

Requirement of ballot before action by trade union

226 Requirement of ballot before action by trade union

(1) An act done by a trade union to induce a person to take part, or continue to take part, in industrial action—

(a) is not protected unless the industrial action has the support of a ballot, and

(b) where section 226A falls to be complied with in relation to the person's employer, is not protected as respects the employer unless the trade union has complied with section 226A in relation to him.

In this section 'the relevant time', in relation to an act by a trade union to induce a person to take part, or continue to take part, in industrial action, means the time at which proceedings are commenced in respect of the act.

(2) Industrial action shall be regarded as having the support of a ballot only if—

(a) the union has held a ballot in respect of the action—

(i) in relation to which the requirements of section 226B so far as applicable before and during the holding of the ballot were satisfied,

(ii) in relation to which the requirements of sections 227 to 231 were satisfied,

(iia) in which at least 50% of those who were entitled to vote in the ballot did so, and

(iii) in which the majority voting in the ballot answered 'Yes' to the question applicable in accordance with section 229(2) to industrial action of the kind to which the act of inducement relates;

(b) such of the requirements of the following sections as have fallen to be satisfied at the relevant time have been satisfied, namely—

(i) section 226B so far as applicable after the holding of the ballot, and

(ii) section 231B;

(bb) section 232A does not prevent the industrial action from being regarded as having the support of the ballot; and

(c) the requirements of section 233 (calling of industrial action with support of ballot) are satisfied.

Any reference in this subsection to a requirement of a provision which is disapplied or modified by section 232 has effect subject to that section.

(2A)–(2F) [repealed]

(3) Where separate workplace ballots are held by virtue of section 228(1)—

(a) industrial action shall be regarded as having the support of a ballot if the conditions specified in subsection (2) are satisfied, and

(b) the trade union shall be taken to have complied with the requirements relating to a ballot imposed by section 226A if those requirements are complied with, in relation to the ballot for the place of work of the person induced to take part, or continue to take part, in the industrial action.

(3A) If the requirements of section 231A fall to be satisfied in relation to an employer, as respects that employer industrial action shall not be regarded as having the support of a ballot unless those requirements are satisfied in relation to that employer.

(4) For the purposes of this section an inducement, in relation to a person, includes an inducement which is or would be ineffective, whether because of his unwillingness to be influenced by it or for any other reason.

226A Notice of ballot and sample voting paper for employers

(1) The trade union must take such steps as are reasonably necessary to ensure that—

(a) not later than the seventh day before the opening day of the ballot, the notice specified in subsection (2), and

(b) not later than the third day before the opening day of the ballot, the sample voting paper specified in subsection (2F),

is received by every person who it is reasonable for the union to believe (at the latest time when steps could be taken to comply with paragraph (a)) will be the employer of persons who will be entitled to vote in the ballot.

(2) The notice referred to in paragraph (a) of subsection (1) is a notice in writing—

(a) stating that the union intends to hold the ballot,

(b) specifying the date which the union reasonably believes will be the opening day of the ballot, and

(c) containing—

(i) the lists mentioned in subsection (2A) and the number mentioned in subsection (2B), or

(ii) where some or all of the employees concerned are employees from whose wages the employer makes deductions representing payments to the union, either those lists and that number or the information mentioned in subsection (2C).

(2A) The lists are—

(a) a list of the categories of employee to which the employees concerned belong, and

(b) a list of the workplaces at which the employees concerned work.

(2B) The number is the total number of employees concerned.

(2C) The information referred to in subsection (2)(c)(ii) is such information as will enable the employer readily to deduce—

(a) the total number of employees concerned,

(b) the categories of employee to which the employees concerned belong, and

(c) the workplaces at which the employees concerned work.

(2D) The lists and the number supplied under this section, or the information mentioned in subsection (2C) that is so supplied, must be as accurate as is reasonably practicable in the light of the information in the possession of the union at the time when it complies with subsection (1)(a).

(2E) For the purposes of subsection (2D) information is in the possession of the union if it is held, for union purposes—

(a) in a document, whether in electronic form or any other form, and

(b) in the possession or under the control of an officer or employee of the union.

(2F) The sample voting paper referred to in paragraph (b) of subsection (1) is—

(a) a sample of the form of voting paper which is to be sent to the employees concerned, or

(b) where the employees concerned are not all to be sent the same form of voting paper, a sample of each form of voting paper which is to be sent to any of them.

(2G) Nothing in this section requires a union to supply an employer with the names of the employees concerned.

(2H) In this section references to the 'employees concerned' are references to those employees of the employer in question who the union reasonably believes will be entitled to vote in the ballot.

(2I) For the purposes of this section, the workplace at which an employee works is—

(a) in relation to an employee who works at or from a single set of premises, those premises, and

(b) in relation to any other employee, the premises with which his employment has the closest connection.

(3)–(3B) [repealed]

(4) In this section references to the opening day of the ballot are references to the first day when a voting paper is sent to any person entitled to vote in the ballot.

(5) This section in its application to a ballot in which merchant seamen to whom section 230(2A) applies are entitled to vote, shall have effect with the substitution in subsection (2F), for references to the voting paper which is to be sent to the employees, of references to the voting paper which is to be sent or otherwise provided to them.

226B–226C [omitted]

227 Entitlement to vote in ballot

(1) Entitlement to vote in the ballot must be accorded equally to all the members of the trade union who it is reasonable at the time of the ballot for the union to believe will be induced by the union to take part or, as the case may be, to continue to take part in the industrial action in question, and to no others.

(2) [repealed]

228 Separate workplace ballots

(1) Subject to subsection (2), this section applies if the members entitled to vote in a ballot by virtue of section 227 do not all have the same workplace.

(2) This section does not apply if the union reasonably believes that all those members have the same workplace.

(3) Subject to section 228A, a separate ballot shall be held for each workplace; and entitlement to vote in each ballot shall be accorded equally to, and restricted to, members of the union who—

(a) are entitled to vote by virtue of section 227, and

(b) have that workplace.

(4) In this section and section 228A 'workplace' in relation to a person who is employed means—

(a) if the person works at or from a single set of premises, those premises, and

(b) in any other case, the premises with which the person's employment has the closest connection.

228A Separate workplaces: single and aggregate ballots

(1) Where section 228(3) would require separate ballots to be held for each workplace, a ballot may be held in place of some or all of the separate ballots if one of subsections (2) to (4) is satisfied in relation to it.

(2) This subsection is satisfied in relation to a ballot if the workplace of each member entitled to vote in the ballot is the workplace of at least one member of the union who is affected by the dispute.

(3) This subsection is satisfied in relation to a ballot if entitlement to vote is accorded to, and limited to, all the members of the union who—

(a) according to the union's reasonable belief have an occupation of a particular kind or have any of a number of particular kinds of occupation, and

(b) are employed by a particular employer, or by any of a number of particular employers, with whom the union is in dispute.

(4) This subsection is satisfied in relation to a ballot if entitlement to vote is accorded to, and limited to, all the members of the union who are employed by a particular employer, or by any of a number of particular employers, with whom the union is in dispute.

(5) For the purposes of subsection (2) the following are members of the union affected by a dispute—

(a) if the dispute relates (wholly or partly) to a decision which the union reasonably believes the employer has made or will make concerning a matter specified in subsection (1)(a), (b) or (c) of section 244 (meaning of 'trade dispute'), members whom the decision directly affects,

(b) if the dispute relates (wholly or partly) to a matter specified in subsection (1)(d) of that section, members whom the matter directly affects,

(c) if the dispute relates (wholly or partly) to a matter specified in subsection (2)(e) of that section, persons whose membership or non-membership is in dispute,

(d) if the dispute relates (wholly or partly) to a matter specified in subsection (1)(f) of that section, officials of the union who have used or would use the facilities concerned in the dispute.

229 Voting paper

(1) The method of voting in a ballot must be by the marking of a voting paper by the person voting.

(1A) Each voting paper must—

(a) state the name of the independent scrutineer,

(b) clearly specify the address to which, and the date by which, it is to be returned,

(c) be given one of a series of consecutive whole numbers every one of which is used in giving a different number in that series to each voting paper printed or otherwise produced for the purposes of the ballot, and

(d) be marked with its number.

This subsection, in its application to a ballot in which merchant seamen to whom section 230(2A) applies are entitled to vote, shall have effect with the substitution, for the reference to the address to which the voting paper is to be returned, of a reference to the ship to which the seamen belong.

(2) The voting paper must contain at least one of the following questions—

(a) a question (however framed) which requires the person answering it to say, by answering 'Yes' or 'No', whether he is prepared to take part or, as the case may be, to continue to take part in a strike;

(b) a question (however framed) which requires the person answering it to say, by answering 'Yes' or 'No', whether he is prepared to take part or, as the case may be, to continue to take part in industrial action short of a strike.

(2A) For the purposes of subsection (2) an overtime ban and a call-out ban constitute industrial action short of a strike.

(2B)–(2D) [repealed]

(3) The voting paper must specify who, in the event of a vote in favour of industrial action, is authorised for the purposes of section 233 to call upon members to take part or continue to take part in the industrial action.

The person or description of persons so specified need not be authorised under the rules of the union but must be within section 20(2) (persons for whose acts the union is taken to be responsible).

(4) The following statement must (without being qualified or commented upon by anything else on the voting paper) appear on every voting paper—

'If you take part in a strike or other industrial action, you may be in breach of your contract of employment.

However, if you are dismissed for taking part in strike or other industrial action which is called officially and is otherwise lawful, the dismissal will be unfair.

230 Conduct of ballot

(1) Every person who is entitled to vote in the ballot must—

(a) be allowed to vote without interference from, or constraint imposed by, the union or any of its members, officials or employees, and

(b) so far as is reasonably practicable, be enabled to do so without incurring any direct cost to himself.

(2) Except as regards persons falling within subsection (2A), so far as is reasonably practicable, every person who is entitled to vote in the ballot must—

(a) have a voting paper sent to him by post at his home address or any other address which he has requested the trade union in writing to treat as his postal address, and

(b) be given a convenient opportunity to vote by post.

(2A) Subsection (2B) applies to a merchant seaman if the trade union reasonably believes that—

(a) he will be employed in a ship either at sea or at a place outside Great Britain at some time in the period during which votes may be cast, and

(b) it will be convenient for him to receive a voting paper and to vote while on the ship or while at a place where the ship is rather than in accordance with subsection (2).

(2B) Where this subsection applies to a merchant seaman he shall, if it is reasonably practicable—

(a) have a voting paper made available to him while on the ship or while at a place where the ship is, and

(b) be given an opportunity to vote while on the ship or while at a place where the ship is.

(2C) In subsections (2A) and (2B) 'merchant seaman' means a person whose employment, or the greater part of it, is carried out on board sea-going ships.

(3) [repealed]

(4) A ballot shall be conducted so as to secure that—

(a) so far as is reasonably practicable, those voting do so in secret, and

(b) the votes given in the ballot are fairly and accurately counted.

For the purposes of paragraph (b) an inaccuracy in counting shall be disregarded if it is accidental and on a scale which could not affect the result of the ballot.

231 Information as to result of ballot

As soon as is reasonably practicable after the holding of the ballot, the trade union shall take such steps as are reasonably necessary to ensure that all persons entitled to vote in the ballot are told—

(a) the number of individuals who were entitled to vote in the ballot,

(b) the number of votes cast in the ballot,

(c) the number of individuals answering 'Yes' to the question, or as the case may be, to each question,

(d) the number of individuals answering 'No' to the question, or as the case may be, to each question,

(e) the number of spoiled or otherwise invalid voting papers returned, and

(f) whether or not the number of votes cast in the ballot is at least 50% of the number of individuals who were entitled to vote in the ballot.

(g) [repealed]

231A Employers to be informed of ballot result

(1) As soon as reasonably practicable after the holding of the ballot, the trade union shall take such steps as are reasonably necessary to ensure that every relevant employer is informed of the matters mentioned in section 231.

(2) In subsection (1) 'relevant employer' means a person who it is reasonable for the trade union to believe (at the time when the steps are taken) was at the time of the ballot the employer of any persons entitled to vote.

231B–232 [omitted]

232A Inducement of member denied entitlement to vote

Industrial action shall not be regarded as having the support of a ballot if the following conditions apply in the case of any person—

(a) he was a member of the trade union at the time when the ballot was held,
(b) it was reasonable at that time for the trade union to believe he would be induced to take part or, as the case may be, to continue to take part in the industrial action,
(c) he was not accorded entitlement to vote in the ballot, and
(d) he was induced by the trade union to take part or, as the case may be, to continue to take part in the industrial action.

232B Small accidental failures to be disregarded

(1) If—

(a) in relation to a ballot there is a failure (or there are failures) to comply with a provision mentioned in subsection (2) or with more than one of those provisions, and
(b) the failure is accidental and on a scale which is unlikely to affect the result of the ballot or, as the case may be, the failures are accidental and taken together are on a scale which is unlikely to affect the result of the ballot,

the failure (or failures) shall be disregarded for all purposes (including, in particular, those of section 232A(c)).

(2) The provisions are section 227(1), section 230(2) and section 230(2B).

233 Calling of industrial action with support of ballot

(1) Industrial action shall be regarded as having the support of a ballot only if—

(a) it is called by a person specified or of a description specified in the voting paper for the ballot in accordance with section 229(3), and
(b) there was no call by the trade union to take part or continue to take part in industrial action to which the ballot relates, or any authorisation or endorsement by the union of any such industrial action, before the date of the ballot.

(2)–(3) [repealed]

(4) For the purposes of this section a call shall be taken to have been made by a trade union if it was authorised or endorsed by the union; and the provisions of section 20(2) to (4) apply for the purpose of determining whether a call, or industrial action, is to be taken to have been so authorised or endorsed.

234 Period after which ballot ceases to be effective

(1) Industrial action that is regarded as having the support of a ballot shall cease to be so regarded at the end of the period of 12 months beginning with the date of the ballot.

(1A) Subsection (1) has effect—

(a) without prejudice to the possibility of the industrial action getting the support of a fresh ballot; and
(b) subject to the following provisions.

(2) Where for the whole or part of that period the calling or organising of industrial action is prohibited—

(a) by virtue of a court order which subsequently lapses or is discharged, recalled or set aside, or
(b) by virtue of an undertaking given to a court by any person from which he is subsequently released or by which he ceases to be bound,

the trade union may apply to the court for an order that the period during which the prohibition had effect shall not count towards the period referred to in subsection (1).

(3) The application must be made forthwith upon the prohibition ceasing to have effect—

(a) to the court by virtue of whose decision it ceases to have effect, or
(b) where an order lapses or an undertaking ceases to bind without any such decision, to the court by which the order was made or to which the undertaking was given.

(4) The court shall not make an order if it appears to the court—

(a) that the result of the ballot no longer represents the views of the union members concerned, or

(b) that an event is likely to occur as a result of which those members would vote against industrial action if another ballot were to be held.

(5) No appeal lies from the decision of the court to make or refuse an order under this section.

(6) The period between the making of an application under this section and its determination does not count towards the period referred to in subsection (1).

Requirement on trade union to give notice of industrial action

234A Notice to employers of industrial action

(1) An act done by a trade union to induce a person to take part, or continue to take part, in industrial action is not protected as respects his employer unless the union has taken or takes such steps as are reasonably necessary to ensure that the employer receives within the appropriate period a relevant notice covering the act.

(2) Subsection (1) imposes a requirement in the case of an employer only if it is reasonable for the union to believe, at the latest time when steps could be taken to ensure that he receives such a notice, that he is the employer of persons who will be or have been induced to take part, or continue to take part, in the industrial action.

(3) For the purposes of this section a relevant notice is a notice in writing which—

(a) contains—

(i) the lists mentioned in subsection (3A) and the figures mentioned in subsection (3B), together with an explanation of how those figures were arrived at, or

(ii) where some or all of the affected employees are employees from whose wages the employer makes deductions representing payments to the union, either those lists and figures and that explanation or the information mentioned in subsection (3C), and

(b) states whether industrial action is intended to be continuous or discontinuous and specifies—

(i) where it is to be continuous, the intended date for any of the affected employees to begin to take part in the action,

(ii) where it is to be discontinuous, the intended dates for any of the affected employees to take part in the action.

(3A) The lists referred to in subsection (3)(a) are—

(a) a list of the categories of employee to which the affected employees belong, and

(b) a list of the workplaces at which the affected employees work.

(3B) The figures referred to in subsection (3)(a) are—

(a) the total number of the affected employees,

(b) [repealed], and

(c) the number of the affected employees who work at each workplace in the list mentioned in subsection (3A)(b).

(3C) The information referred to in subsection (3)(a)(ii) is such information as will enable the employer readily to deduce—

(a) the total number of the affected employees,

(b) the categories of employee to which the affected employees, and

(c) the workplaces at which the affected employees work and the number of them who work at each of those workplaces.

(3D) The lists and figures supplied under this section, or the information mentioned in subsection (3C) that is so supplied, must be as accurate as is reasonably practicable in the light of the information in the possession of the union at the time when it complies with subsection (1).

(3E) For the purposes of subsection (3D) information is in the possession of the union if it is held, for union purposes—

(a) in a document, whether in electronic form or any other form, and
(b) in the possession or under the control of an officer or employee of the union.

(3F) Nothing in this section requires a union to supply an employer with the names of the affected employees.

(4) For the purposes of subsection (1) the appropriate period is the period—
(a) beginning with the day when the union satisfies the requirement of section 231A in relation to the ballot in respect of the industrial action, and
(b) ending with the tenth day before the day, or before the first of the days, specified in the relevant notice.

In paragraph (b) 'starting date' means the day, or the first of the days, specified in the relevant notice.

(5) For the purposes of subsection (1) a relevant notice covers an act done by the union if the person induced falls within a notified category of employee and the workplace at which he works is a notified workplace and—
(a) where he is induced to take part or continue to take part in industrial action which the union intends to be continuous, if—
 (i) the notice states that the union intends the industrial action to be continuous, and
 (ii) there is no participation by him in the industrial action before the date specified in the notice in consequence of any inducement by the union not covered by a relevant notice; and
(b) where he is induced to take part or continue to take part in industrial action which the union intends to be discontinuous, if there is no participation by him in the industrial action on a day not so specified in consequence of any inducement by the union not covered by a relevant notice.

(5A) [repealed]

(5B) In subsection (5)—
(a) a 'notified category of employee' means—
 (i) a category of employee that is listed in the notice, or
 (ii) where the notice contains the information mentioned in subsection (3C), a category of employee that the employer (at the time he receives the notice) can readily deduce from the notice is a category of employee to which some or all of the affected employees belong, and
(b) a 'notified workplace' means—
 (i) a workplace that is listed in the notice, or
 (ii) where the notice contains the information mentioned in subsection (3C), a workplace that the employer (at the time he receives the notice) can readily deduce from the notice is the workplace at which some or all of the affected employees work.

(5C) In this section references to the 'affected employees' are references to those employees of the employer who the union reasonably believes will be induced by the union, or have been so induced, to take part or continue to take part in the industrial action.

(5D) For the purposes of this section, the workplace at which an employee works is—
(a) in relation to an employee who works at or from a single set of premises, those premises, and
(b) in relation to any other employee, the premises with which his employment has the closest connection.

(6) For the purposes of this section—
(a) a union intends industrial action to be discontinuous if it intends it to take place only on some days on which there is an opportunity to take the action, and
(b) a union intends industrial action to be continuous if it intends it to be not so restricted.

(7) Subject to subsections (7A) and (7B) where—
(a) continuous industrial action which has been authorised or endorsed by a union ceases to be so authorised or endorsed, and

(b) the industrial action has at a later date again been authorised or endorsed by the union (whether as continuous or discontinuous action),

no relevant notice covering acts done to induce persons to take part in the earlier action shall operate to cover acts done to induce persons to take part in the action authorised or endorsed at the later date and this section shall apply in relation to an act to induce a person to take part, or continue to take part, in the industrial action after that date as if the references in subsection (3)(b)(i) to the industrial action were to the industrial action taking place after that date.

(7A) Subsection (7) shall not apply where industrial action ceases to be authorised or endorsed in order to enable the union to comply with a court order or an undertaking given to a court.

(7B) Subsection (7) shall not apply where—

(a) a union agrees with an employer, before industrial action ceases to be authorised or endorsed, that it will cease to be authorised or endorsed with effect from a date specified in the agreement ('the suspension date') and that it may again be authorised or endorsed with effect from a date not earlier than a date specified in the agreement ('the resumption date'),

(b) the action ceases to be authorised or endorsed with effect from the suspension date, and

(c) the action is again authorised or endorsed with effect from a date which is not earlier than the resumption date or such later date as may be agreed between the union and the employer.

(8) The requirement imposed on a trade union by subsection (1) shall be treated as having been complied with if the steps were taken by other relevant persons or committees whose acts were authorised or endorsed by the union and references to the belief or intention of the union in subsection (2) or as the case may be, subsections (3), (5), (5C) and (6) shall be construed as references to the belief or the intention of the person or committee taking the steps.

(9) The provisions of section 20(2) to (4) apply for the purpose of determining for the purposes of subsection (1) who are relevant persons or committees and whether the trade union is to be taken to have authorised or endorsed the steps the person or committee took and for the purposes of subsections (7) to (7B) whether the trade union is to be taken to have authorised or endorsed the industrial action.

234B–G [repealed]

235 Construction of references to contract of employment in sections 226 to 234A

In sections 226 to 234A references to a contract of employment include any contract under which one person personally does work or performs services for another; and 'employer' and other related expressions shall be construed accordingly.

Industrial action affecting supply of goods or services to an individual

235A Industrial action affecting supply of goods or services to an individual

(1) Where an individual claims that—

(a) any trade union or other person has done, or is likely to do, an unlawful act to induce any person to take part, or to continue to take part, in industrial action, and

(b) an effect, or a likely effect, of the industrial action is or will be to—

(i) prevent or delay the supply of goods or services, or

(ii) reduce the quality of goods or services supplied, to the individual making the claim,

he may apply to the High Court or the Court of Session for an order under this section.

(2) For the purposes of this section an act to induce any person to take part, or to continue to take part, in industrial action is unlawful—

(a) if it is actionable in tort by any one or more persons, or

(b) (where it is or would be the act of a trade union) if it could form the basis of an application by a member under section 62.

(3) In determining whether an individual may make an application under this section it is immaterial whether or not the individual is entitled to be supplied with the goods or services in question.

(4) Where on an application under this section the court is satisfied that the claim is well-founded, it shall make such order as it considers appropriate for requiring the person by whom the act of inducement has been, or is likely to be, done to take steps for ensuring—

(a) that no, or no further, act is done by him to induce any persons to take part or to continue to take part in the industrial action, and

(b) that no person engages in conduct after the making of the order by virtue of having been induced by him before the making of the order to take part or continue to take part in the industrial action.

(5) Without prejudice to any other power of the court, the court may on an application under this section grant such interlocutory relief (in Scotland, such interim order) as it considers appropriate.

(6) For the purposes of this section an act of inducement shall be taken to be done by a trade union if it is authorised or endorsed by the union; and the provisions of section 20(2) to (4) apply for the purposes of determining whether such an act is to be taken to be so authorised or endorsed.

Those provisions also apply in relation to proceedings for failure to comply with an order under this section as they apply in relation to the original proceedings.

235B–235C [repealed]

No compulsion to work

236 No compulsion to work

No court shall, whether by way of—

(a) an order for specific performance or specific implement of a contract of employment, or

(b) an injunction or interdict restraining a breach or threatened breach of such a contract,

compel an employee to do any work or attend at any place for the doing of any work.

Protection against detriment

236A Detriment on grounds of industrial action

(1) A worker has the right not to be subjected as an individual to detriment of a prescribed description by any act, or any deliberate failure to act, by the worker's employer, if the act or failure takes place for the sole or main purpose of preventing or deterring the worker from taking protected industrial action, or penalising the worker for doing so.

(2) For that purpose, a worker takes protected industrial action if the worker commits an act which, or a series of acts each of which, the worker is induced to commit by an act which by virtue of section 219 is not actionable in tort.

(3) But no account may be taken of the repudiation of any act by a trade union as mentioned in section 21 in relation to anything which occurs before the end of the next working day after the day on which the repudiation takes place.

(4) [omitted]

(5) Subsection (1) does not apply where the worker is an employee and the detriment in question amounts to dismissal (but see sections 237 to 239).

(6) A worker or former worker may present a complaint to an employment tribunal on the ground that the worker or former worker has been subjected to a detriment by an employer in contravention of this section.

(7) A worker or former worker has no other remedy for infringement of the right conferred by this section.

(8) In this section and sections 236B to 236D—

'employer' means—

(a) in relation to a worker, the person for whom the worker works;

(b) in relation to a former worker, the person for whom the former worker worked;

'worker' means an individual who works, or normally works, as mentioned in paragraphs (a) to (c) of section 296(1);

'working day' means any day which is not a Saturday or Sunday, Christmas Day, Good Friday or a bank holiday under the Banking and Financial Dealings Act 1971.

236B Time limit for proceedings

(1) An employment tribunal may not consider a complaint under section 236A unless it is presented—

(a) before the end of the period of six months beginning with the date of the act or failure to which the complaint relates or, where that act or failure is part of a series of similar acts or failures (or both), the last of them, or

(b) where the tribunal is satisfied that it was not reasonably practicable for the complaint to be presented before the end of that period, within such further period as it considers reasonable.

(2) For the purposes of subsection (1)—

(a) where an act extends over a period, the reference to the date of the act is a reference to the last day of that period;

(b) a failure to act is to be treated as done when it was decided on.

(3) For the purposes of subsection (2), in the absence of evidence establishing the contrary, an employer is to be taken to decide on a failure to act—

(a) when the employer does an act inconsistent with doing the failed act, or

(b) if the employer has done no such inconsistent act, when the period expires within which the employer might reasonably have been expected to do the failed act if it was to be done.

(4) [omitted]

236C [omitted]

236D Remedies

(1) Where the employment tribunal finds that a complaint under section 236A is well-founded, the tribunal—

(a) must make a declaration to that effect, and

(b) may make an award of compensation to be paid by the employer to the complainant in respect of the act or failure complained of.

(2) The amount of the compensation awarded is to be an amount which the tribunal considers just and equitable in all the circumstances having regard to the infringement complained of and to any loss sustained by the complainant which is attributable to the act or failure.

(3)–(5) [omitted]

Loss of unfair dismissal protection

237 Dismissal of those taking part in unofficial industrial action

(1) An employee has no right to complain of unfair dismissal if at the time of dismissal he was taking part in an unofficial strike or other unofficial industrial action.

(1A) Subsection (1) does not apply to the dismissal of the employee if it is shown that the reason (or, if more than one, the principal reason) for the dismissal or, in a redundancy case, for selecting the employee for dismissal was one of those specified in or under—

(a) section 98B, 99, 100, 101A(d), 103, 103A, 104C, 104D, or 104E of the Employment Rights Act 1996 (dismissal in jury service, family, health and safety, working time, employee representative, protected disclosure, flexible working, pension scheme membership, and study and training cases),

(b) section 104 of that Act in its application in relation to time off under section 57A of that Act (dependants); and a reference to a specified reason for dismissal includes a reference to specified circumstances of dismissal.

(2) A strike or other industrial action is unofficial in relation to an employee unless—

(a) he is a member of a trade union and the action is authorised or endorsed by that union, or

(b) he is not a member of a trade union but there are among those taking part in the industrial action members of a trade union by which the action has been authorised or endorsed.

Provided that, a strike or other industrial action shall not be regarded as unofficial if none of those taking part in it are members of a trade union.

(3) The provisions of section 20(2) apply for the purpose of determining whether industrial action is to be taken to have been authorised or endorsed by a trade union.

(4) The question whether industrial action is to be so taken in any case shall be determined by reference to the facts as at the time of dismissal.

Provided that, where an act is repudiated as mentioned in section 21, industrial action shall not thereby be treated as unofficial before the end of the next working day after the day on which the repudiation takes place.

(5) In this section the 'time of dismissal' means—

(a) where the employee's contract of employment is terminated by notice, when the notice is given,

(b) where the employee's contract of employment is terminated without notice, when the termination takes effect, and

(c) where the employee is employed under a contract for a fixed term which expires without being renewed under the same contract, when that term expires;

and a 'working day' means any day which is not a Saturday or Sunday, Christmas Day, Good Friday or a bank holiday under the Banking and Financial Dealings Act 1971.

(6) For the purposes of this section membership of a trade union for purposes unconnected with the employment in question shall be disregarded; but an employee who was a member of a trade union when he began to take part in industrial action shall continue to be treated as a member for the purpose of determining whether that action is unofficial in relation to him or another notwithstanding that he may in fact have ceased to be a member.

238 Dismissals in connection with other industrial action

(1) This section applies in relation to an employee who has a right to complain of unfair dismissal (the 'complainant') and who claims to have been unfairly dismissed, where at the date of the dismissal—

(a) the employer was conducting or instituting a lock-out, or

(b) the complainant was taking part in a strike or other industrial action.

(2) In such a case an employment tribunal shall not determine whether the dismissal was fair or unfair unless it is shown—

(a) that one or more relevant employees of the same employer have not been dismissed, or

(b) that a relevant employee has before the expiry of the period of three months beginning with the date of his dismissal been offered re-engagement and that the complainant has not been offered re-engagement.

(2A) Subsection (2) does not apply to the dismissal of the employee if it is shown that the reason (or, if more than one, the principal reason) for the dismissal or, in a redundancy case, for selecting the employee for dismissal was one of those specified in or under—

(a) section 98B, 99, 100, 101A(d), 103, 104C, 104D or 104E of the Employment Rights Act 1996 (dismissal in jury service, family, health and safety, working time, employee representative, flexible working, pension scheme membership, and study and training cases),

(b) section 104 of that Act in its application in relation to time off under section 57A of that Act (dependants); and a reference to a specified reason for dismissal includes a reference to specified circumstances of dismissal.

(2B) Subsection (2) does not apply in relation to an employee who is regarded as unfairly dismissed by virtue of section 238A below.

(3) For this purpose 'relevant employees' means—

(a) in relation to a lock-out, employees who were directly interested in the dispute in contemplation or furtherance of which the lock-out occurred, and

(b) in relation to a strike or other industrial action, those employees at the establishment of the employer at or from which the complainant works who at the date of his dismissal were taking part in the action.

Nothing in section 237 (dismissal of those taking part in unofficial industrial action) affects the question who are relevant employees for the purposes of this section.

(4) An offer of re-engagement means an offer (made either by the original employer or by a successor of that employer or an associated employer) to re-engage an employee, either in the job which he held immediately before the date of dismissal or in a different job which would be reasonably suitable in his case.

(5) In this section 'date of dismissal' means—

(a) where the employee's contract of employment was terminated by notice, the date on which the employer's notice was given, and

(b) in any other case, the effective date of termination.

238A Participation in official industrial action

(1) For the purposes of this section an employee takes protected industrial action if he commits an act which, or a series of acts each of which, he is induced to commit by an act which by virtue of section 219 is not actionable in tort.

(2) An employee who is dismissed shall be regarded for the purposes of Part X of the Employment Rights Act 1996 (unfair dismissal) as unfairly dismissed if—

(a) the reason (or, if more than one, the principal reason) for the dismissal is that the employee took protected industrial action.

(b) [repealed]

(3)–(7D) [repealed]

(8) For the purposes of this section no account shall be taken of the repudiation of any act by a trade union as mentioned in section 21 in relation to anything which occurs before the end of the next working day (within the meaning of section 237) after the day on which the repudiation takes place.

(9) [repealed].

238B [repealed]

239 Supplementary provisions relating to unfair dismissal

(1) Sections 237 to 238A (loss of unfair dismissal protection in connection with industrial action) shall be construed as one with Part X of the Employment Rights Act 1996 (unfair dismissal); but sections 108 and 109 of that Act (qualifying period and age limit) shall not apply in relation to section 238A of this Act.

(2) In relation to a complaint to which section 238 or 238A applies, section 111(2) of that Act (time limit for complaint) does not apply, but an employment tribunal shall not consider the complaint unless it is presented to the tribunal—

(a) before the end of the period of six months beginning with the date of the complainant's dismissal (as defined by section 238(5)), or

(b) where the tribunal is satisfied that it was not reasonably practicable for the complaint to be presented before the end of that period, within such further period as the tribunal considers reasonable.

(3) Where it is shown that the condition referred to in section 238(2)(b) is fulfilled (discriminatory re-engagement), the references in—

(a) sections 98 to 106 of the Employment Rights Act 1996, and

(b) sections 152 and 153 of this Act,

to the reason or principal reason for which the complainant was dismissed shall be read as references to the reason or principal reason he has not been offered re-engagement.

(4) In relation to a complaint under section 111 of the 1996 Act (unfair dismissal: complaint to employment tribunal) that a dismissal was unfair by virtue of section 238A of this Act—

(a) no order shall be made under section 113 of the 1996 Act (reinstatement or re-engagement) until after the conclusion of protected industrial action by any employee in relation to the relevant dispute,

(b) regulations under section 7 of the Employment Tribunals Act 1996 may make provision about the adjournment and renewal of applications (including provision requiring adjournment in specified circumstances), and

(c) regulations under section 9 of that Act may require a pre-hearing review to be carried out in specified circumstances.

Criminal offences

240 Breach of contract involving injury to persons or property

(1) A person commits an offence who wilfully and maliciously breaks a contract of service or hiring, knowing or having reasonable cause to believe that the probable consequences of his so doing, either alone or in combination with others, will be—

(a) to endanger human life or cause serious bodily injury, or

(b) to expose valuable property, whether real or personal, to destruction or serious injury.

(2) Subsection (1) applies equally whether the offence is committed from malice conceived against the person endangered or injured or, as the case may be, the owner of the property destroyed or injured, or otherwise.

(3) A person guilty of an offence under this section is liable on summary conviction to a fine not exceeding level 2 on the standard scale.

(4) This section does not apply to seamen.

241 Intimidation or annoyance by violence or otherwise

(1) A person commits an offence who, with a view to compelling another person to abstain from doing or to do any act which that person has a legal right to do or abstain from doing, wrongfully and without legal authority—

(a) uses violence to or intimidates that person or his spouse or civil partner or children, or injures his property,

(b) persistently follows that person about from place to place,

(c) hides any tools, clothes or other property owned or used by that person, or deprives him of or hinders him in the use thereof,

(d) watches or besets the house or other place where that person resides, works, carries on business or happens to be, or the approach to any such house or place, or

(e) follows that person with two or more other persons in a disorderly manner in or through any street or road.

(2) A person guilty of an offence under this section is liable on summary conviction to imprisonment for a term not exceeding six months or a fine not exceeding level 5 on the standard scale, or both.

(3) [repealed]

242 Restriction of offence of conspiracy: England and Wales

(1) Where in pursuance of any such agreement as is mentioned in section 1(1) of the Criminal Law Act 1977 (which provides for the offence of conspiracy) the acts in question in relation to an offence are to be done in contemplation or furtherance of a trade dispute, the offence shall be disregarded for the purposes of that subsection if it is a summary offence which is not punishable with imprisonment.

(2) This section extends to England and Wales only.

243 Restriction of offence of conspiracy: Scotland

(1) An agreement of combination by two or more persons to do or procure to be done an act in contemplation or furtherance of a trade dispute is not indictable as a conspiracy if that act committed by one person would not be punishable as a crime.

(2) A crime for this purpose means an offence punishable on indictment, or an offence punishable on summary conviction, and for the commission of which the offender is liable under the statute making the offence punishable to be imprisoned either absolutely or at the discretion of the court as an alternative for some other punishment.

(3) Where a person is convicted of any such agreement or combination as is mentioned above to do or procure to be done an act which is punishable only on summary conviction, and is sentenced to imprisonment, the imprisonment shall not exceed three months or such longer time as may be prescribed by the statute for the punishment of the act when committed by one person.

(4) Nothing in this section—

- (a) exempts from punishment a person guilty of a conspiracy for which a punishment is awarded by an Act of Parliament, or
- (b) affects the law relating to riot, unlawful assembly, breach of the peace, or any offence against the State or the Sovereign.

(5) This section extends to Scotland only.

Supplementary

244 Meaning of 'trade dispute' in Part V

(1) In this Part a 'trade dispute' means a dispute between workers and their employer which relates wholly or mainly to one or more of the following—

- (a) terms and conditions of employment, or the physical conditions in which any workers are required to work;
- (b) engagement or non-engagement, or termination or suspension of employment or the duties of employment, of one or more workers;
- (c) allocation of work or the duties of employment between workers or groups of workers;
- (d) matters of discipline;
- (e) a worker's membership or non-membership of a trade union;
- (f) facilities for officials of trade unions; and
- (g) machinery for negotiation or consultation, and other procedures, relating to any of the above matters, including the recognition by employers or employers' associations of the right of a trade union to represent workers in such negotiation or consultation or in the carrying out of such procedures.

(2) A dispute between a Minister of the Crown and any workers shall, notwithstanding that he is not the employer of those workers, be treated as a dispute between those workers and their employer if the dispute relates to matters which—

- (a) have been referred for consideration by a joint body on which, by virtue of provision made by or under any enactment, he is represented, or
- (b) cannot be settled without him exercising a power conferred on him by or under an enactment.

(3) There is a trade dispute even though it relates to matters occurring outside the United Kingdom, so long as the person or persons whose actions in the United Kingdom are said to be in contemplation or furtherance of a trade dispute relating to matters occurring outside the United Kingdom are likely to be affected in respect of one or more of the matters specified in subsection (1) by the outcome of the dispute.

(4) An act, threat or demand done or made by one person or organisation against another which, if resisted, would have led to a trade dispute with that other, shall be treated as being done or made in contemplation of a trade dispute with that other, notwithstanding that because that other submits to the act or threat or accedes to the demand no dispute arises.

(5) In this section—

'employment' includes any relationship whereby one person personally does work or performs services for another; and

'worker', in relation to a dispute with an employer, means—

(a) a worker employed by that employer; or
(b) a person who has ceased to be so employed if his employment was terminated in connection with the dispute or if the termination of his employment was one of the circumstances giving rise to the dispute.

245 Crown employees and contracts

Where a person holds any office or employment under the Crown on terms which do not constitute a contract of employment between that person and the Crown, those terms shall nevertheless be deemed to constitute such a contract for the purposes of—

(a) the law relating to liability in tort of a person who commits an act which—
  (i) induces another person to break a contract, interferes with the performance of a contract or induces another person to interfere with its performance, or
  (ii) consists in a threat that a contract will be broken or its performance interfered with, or that any person will be induced to break a contract or interfere with its performance, and
(b) the provisions of this or any other Act which refer (whether in relation to contracts generally or only in relation to contracts of employment) to such an act.

246 Minor definitions

In this Part—

'date of the ballot' means, in the case of a ballot in which votes may be cast on more than one day, the last of those days;

'strike' means (except for the purposes of section 229(2) (see section 229(2A)) any concerted stoppage of work;

'working hours', in relation to a person, means any time when under his contract of employment, or other contract personally to do work or perform services, he is required to be at work.

PART VI ADMINISTRATIVE PROVISIONS

ACAS

247 ACAS

(1) There shall continue to be a body called the Advisory, Conciliation and Arbitration Service (referred to in this Act as 'ACAS').

(2) ACAS is a body corporate of which the corporators are the members of its Council.

(3) Its functions, and those of its officers and servants, shall be performed on behalf of the Crown, but not so as to make it subject to directions of any kind from any Minister of the Crown as to the manner in which it is to exercise its functions under any enactment.

(4) For the purposes of civil proceedings arising out of those functions the Crown Proceedings Act 1947 applies to ACAS as if it were a government department and the Crown Suits (Scotland) Act 1857 applies to it as if it were a public department.

(5)–(6) [omitted]

248 The Council of ACAS

(1) ACAS shall be directed by a Council which, subject to the following provisions, shall consist of a chairman and nine ordinary members appointed by the Secretary of State.

(2) Before appointing those ordinary members of the Council, the Secretary of State shall—

(a) as to three of them, consult such organisations representing employers as he considers appropriate, and

(b) as to three of them, consult such organisations representing workers as he considers appropriate.

(3) The Secretary of State may, if he thinks fit, appoint a further two ordinary members of the Council (who shall be appointed so as to take office at the same time); and before making those appointments he shall—

(a) as to one of them, consult such organisations representing employers as he considers appropriate, and

(b) as to one of them, consult such organisations representing workers as he considers appropriate.

(4) The Secretary of State may appoint up to three deputy chairmen who may be appointed from the ordinary members, or in addition to those members.

(5) The Council shall determine its own procedure, including the quorum necessary for its meetings.

(6) If the Secretary of State has not appointed a deputy chairmen, the Council may choose a member to act as chairman in the absence or incapacity of the chairman.

(7) The validity of proceedings of the Council is not affected by any vacancy among the members of the Council or by any defect in the appointment of any of them.

249–253 [omitted]

The Certification Officer

254 The Certification Officer

(1) There shall continue to be an officer called the Certification Officer.

(2) The Certification Officer shall be appointed by the Secretary of State after consultation with ACAS (but is not subject to directions of any kind from any Minister of the Crown as to the manner in which he is to exercise his functions).

(3) The Certification Officer may appoint one or more assistant certification officers and shall appoint an assistant certification officer for Scotland.

(4) The Certification Officer may delegate to an assistant certification officer such functions as he thinks appropriate, and in particular may delegate to the assistant certification officer for Scotland such functions as he thinks appropriate in relation to organisations whose principal office is in Scotland.

References to the Certification Officer in enactments relating to his functions shall be construed accordingly.

(5) ACAS shall provide for the Certification Officer the requisite staff (from among the officers and servants of ACAS) and the requisite accommodation, equipment and other facilities.

(5A) ACAS shall pay to the Certification Officer such sums as he may require for the performance of any of his functions.

(6) [repealed]

255–258 [omitted]

Central Arbitration Committee

259 The Central Arbitration Committee

(1) There shall continue to be a body called the Central Arbitration Committee.

(2) The functions of the Committee shall be performed on behalf of the Crown, but not so as to make it subject to directions of any kind from any Minister of the Crown as to the manner in which it is to exercise its functions.

(3) ACAS shall provide for the Committee the requisite staff (from among the officers and servants of ACAS) and the requisite accommodation, equipment and other facilities.

260 The members of the Committee

(1) The Central Arbitration Committee shall consist of members appointed by the Secretary of State.

(2) The Secretary of State shall appoint a member as chairman, and may appoint a member as deputy chairman or members as deputy chairmen.

(3) The Secretary of State may appoint as members only persons experienced in industrial relations, and they shall include some persons whose experience is as representatives of employers and some whose experience is as representatives of workers.

(3A) Before making an appointment under subsection (1) or (2) the Secretary of State shall consult ACAS and may consult other persons.

(4) At any time when the chairman of the Committee is absent or otherwise incapable of acting, or there is a vacancy in the office of chairman, and the Committee has a deputy chairman or deputy chairmen—

(a) the deputy chairman, if there is only one, or

(b) if there is more than one, such of the deputy chairmen as they may agree or in default of agreement as the Secretary of State may direct,

may perform any of the functions of chairman of the Committee.

(5) At any time when every person who is chairman or deputy chairman is absent or otherwise incapable of acting, or there is no such person, such member of the Committee as the Secretary of State may direct may perform any of the functions of the chairman of the Committee.

(6) The validity of any proceedings of the Committee shall not be affected by any vacancy among the members of the Committee or by any defect in the appointment of a member of the Committee.

261–265 [omitted]; 266–271 [repealed]; 272 [omitted]

PART VII MISCELLANEOUS AND GENERAL

Crown employment, etc.

273 Crown employment

(1) The provisions of this Act have effect (except as mentioned below) in relation to Crown employment and persons in Crown employment as in relation to other employment and other workers or employees.

(2) The following provisions are excepted from subsection (1)—

section 87(4)(b) (power of tribunal to make order in respect of employer's failure to comply with duties as to union contributions);

sections 184 and 185 (remedy for failure to comply with declaration as to disclosure of information);

Chapter II of Part IV (procedure for handling redundancies).

(3) In this section 'Crown employment' means employment under or for the purposes of a government department or any officer or body exercising on behalf of the Crown functions conferred by an enactment.

(4) For the purposes of the provisions of this Act as they apply in relation to Crown employment or persons in Crown employment—

(a) 'employee' and 'contract of employment' mean a person in Crown employment and the terms of employment of such a person (but subject to subsection (5) below);

(b) 'dismissal' means the termination of Crown employment;

(c) [repealed]

(d) the reference in 182(1)(e) (disclosure of information for collective bargaining: restrictions on general duty) to the employer's undertaking shall be construed as a reference to the national interest; and

(e) any other reference to an undertaking shall be construed, in relation to a Minister of the Crown, as a reference to his functions or (as the context may require) to the department of which he is in charge, and in relation to a government department, officer or body shall be construed as a reference to the functions of the department, officer or body or (as the context may require) to the department, officer or body.

(5) Sections 137 to 143 (rights in relation to trade union membership: access to employment) apply in relation to Crown employment otherwise than under a contract only where the terms of employment correspond to those of a contract of employment.

(6) This section has effect subject to section 274 (armed forces) and section 275 (exemption on grounds of national security).

274–280 [omitted]

Excluded classes of employment

281 [repealed]

282 Fixed term employment

(1) In this section, 'fixed term contract' means a contract of employment that, under its provisions determining how it will terminate in the normal course, will terminate—

(a) on the expiry of a specific term,

(b) on the completion of a particular task, or

(c) on the occurrence or non-occurrence of any other specific event other than the attainment by the employee of any normal and bona fide retiring age in the establishment for an employee holding the position held by him.

(2) The provisions of Chapter II of Part IV (procedure for handling redundancies) do not apply to employment under a fixed term contract unless—

(a) the employer is proposing to dismiss the employee as redundant; and

(b) the dismissal will take effect before the expiry of the specific term, the completion of the particular task or the occurrence or non-occurrence of the specific event (as the case may be).

283 [repealed]; 284 [omitted]

285 Employment outside Great Britain

(1) The following provisions of this Act do not apply to employment where under his contract of employment an employee ordinarily works, or in the case of a prospective employee would ordinarily work, outside Great Britain—

In Part III (rights in relation to trade union membership and activities)—

sections 137 to 143 (access to employment),

sections 145A to 151 (inducements and detriment), and

sections 168 to 173 (time off for trade union duties and activities);

In Part IV, sections 193 to 194 (duty to notify Secretary of State of certain redundancies).

(1A) Sections 145A to 151 do not apply to employment where under his contract personally to do work or perform services a worker who is not an employee ordinarily works outside Great Britain.

(1B) For the purposes of subsection (1) as it relates to sections 193 to 194, employment on board a ship registered in the United Kingdom or a GB-linked ship shall be treated as employment where under his contract a person ordinarily works in Great Britain.

(2) For the other purposes of subsection (1) and the purposes of subsection (1A) employment on board a ship registered in the United Kingdom shall be treated as employment where under his contract a person ordinarily works in Great Britain unless—

(a) the ship is registered at a port outside Great Britain, or

(b) the employment is wholly outside Great Britain, or

(c) the employee or, as the case may be, the worker or the person seeking employment or seeking to avail himself of a service of an employment agency, is not ordinarily resident in Great Britain.

(3)–(7) [omitted]

286–287 [omitted]

Contracting out, etc.

288 Restriction on contracting out

(1) Any provision in an agreement (whether a contract of employment or not) is void in so far as it purports—

- (a) to exclude or limit the operation of any provision of this Act, or
- (b) to preclude a person from bringing—
  - (i) proceedings before an employment tribunal or the Central Arbitration Committee under any provision of this Act.
  - (ii) [repealed]

(2) Subsection (1) does not apply to an agreement to refrain from instituting or continuing proceedings where a conciliation officer has taken action under any of sections 18A to 18C of the Employment Tribunals Act 1996 (conciliation).

(2A) Subsection (1) does not apply to an agreement to refrain from instituting or continuing any proceedings, other than excepted proceedings, specified in subsection (1)(b) of that section before an employment tribunal if the conditions regulating settlement agreements under this Act are satisfied in relation to the agreement.

(2B) The conditions regulating compromise agreements under this Act are that—

- (a) the agreement must be in writing;
- (b) the agreement must relate to the particular proceedings;
- (c) the complainant must have received advice from a relevant independent adviser as to the terms and effect of the proposed agreement and in particular its effect on his ability to pursue his rights before an employment tribunal;
- (d) there must be in force, when the adviser gives the advice, a contract of insurance, or an indemnity provided for members of a profession or professional body covering the risk of a claim by the complainant in respect of loss arising in consequence of the advice;
- (e) the agreement must identify the adviser; and
- (f) the agreement must state that the conditions regulating settlement agreements under this Act are satisfied.

(2C) The proceedings excepted from subsection (2A) are proceedings on a complaint of non-compliance with section 188.

(3) Subsection (1) does not apply—

- (a) to such an agreement as is referred to in section 185(5)(b) or (c) to the extent that it varies or supersedes an award under that section;
- (b) to any provision in a collective agreement excluding rights under Chapter II of Part IV (procedure for handling redundancies), if an order under section 198 is in force in respect of it.

(4) A person is a relevant independent adviser for the purposes of subsection (2B)(c)—

- (a) if he is a qualified lawyer,
- (b) if he is an officer, official, employee or member of an independent trade union who has been certified in writing by the trade union as competent to give advice and as authorised to do so on behalf of the trade union,
- (c) if he works at an advice centre (whether as an employee or a volunteer) and has been certified in writing by the centre as competent to give advice and as authorised to do so on behalf of the centre, or
- (d) if he is a person of a description specified in an order made by the Secretary of State.

(4A) But a person is not a relevant independent adviser for the purposes of subsection (2B)(c) in relation to the complainant—

- (a) if he is, is employed by or is acting in the matter for the other party or a person who is connected with the other party,
- (b) in the case of a person within subsection (4)(b) or (c), if the trade union or advice centre is the other party or a person who is connected with the other party,

(c) in the case of a person within subsection (4)(c), if the complainant makes a payment for the advice received from him, or

(d) in the case of a person of a description specified in an order under subsection (4)(d), if any condition specified in the order in relation to the giving of advice by persons of that description is not satisfied.

(4B) In subsection (4)(a) 'qualified lawyer' means—

(a) as respects England and Wales, a person who, for the purposes of the Legal Services Act 2007, is an authorised person in relation to an activity which constitutes the exercise of a right of audience or the conduct of litigation (within the meaning of that Act), and

(b) as respects Scotland, an advocate (whether in practice as such or employed to give legal advice), or a solicitor who holds a practising certificate.

(4C) An order under subsection (4)(d) shall be made by statutory instrument which shall be subject to annulment in pursuance of a resolution of either House of Parliament.

(5) For the purposes of subsection (4A) any two persons are to be treated as connected—

(a) if one is a company of which the other (directly or indirectly) has control, or

(b) if both are companies of which a third person (directly or indirectly) has control.

(6) An agreement under which the parties agree to submit a dispute to arbitration—

(a) shall be regarded for the purposes of subsections (2) and (2A) as being an agreement to refrain from instituting or continuing proceedings if—

(i) the dispute is covered by a scheme having effect by virtue of an order under section 212A, and

(ii) the agreement is to submit it to arbitration in accordance with the scheme, but

(b) shall be regarded for those purposes as neither being nor including such an agreement in any other case.

289 Employment governed by foreign law

For the purposes of this Act it is immaterial whether the law which (apart from this Act) governs any person's employment is the law of the United Kingdom, or of a part of the United Kingdom, or not.

290–291 [repealed]; 292–294 [omitted]

Interpretation

295 Meaning of 'employee' and related expressions

(1) In this Act—

'contract of employment' means a contract of service or of apprenticeship,

'employee' means an individual who has entered into or works under (or, where the employment has ceased, worked under) a contract of employment, and

'employer', in relation to an employee, means the person by whom the employee is (or, where the employment has ceased, was) employed.

(2) Subsection (1) has effect subject to section 235 and other provisions conferring a wider meaning on 'contract of employment', or related expressions.

296 Meaning of 'worker' and related expressions

(1) In this Act 'worker' means an individual who works, or normally works or seeks to work—

(a) under a contract of employment, or

(b) under any other contract whereby he undertakes to do or perform personally any work or services for another party to the contract who is not a professional client of his, or

(c) in employment under or for the purposes of a government department (otherwise than as a member of the naval, military or air forces of the Crown) in so far as such employment does not fall within paragraph (a) or (b) above.

(2) In this Act 'employer', in relation to a worker, means a person for whom one or more workers work, or have worked or normally work or seek to work.

(3) This section shall have effect subject to sections 68(4), 145F(3), 151(1B) and 236A(8).

297 Associated employers

For the purposes of this Act any two employers shall be treated as associated if—

(a) one is a company of which the other (directly or indirectly) has control, or

(b) both are companies of which a third person (directly or indirectly) has control; and 'associated employer' shall be construed accordingly.

297A Meaning of 'voting'

For the purposes of this Act, the number of persons voting in a ballot includes those who return ballot papers that are spoiled or otherwise invalid.

297B [repealed]

298 Minor definitions: general

In this Act, unless the context otherwise requires—

'act' and 'action' each includes omission, and references to doing an act or taking action shall be construed accordingly;

'agency worker' has the meaning given in regulation 3 of the Agency Workers Regulations 2010;

'certificate of independence' means a certificate issued under—

(a) section 6(6), or

(b) section 101A(4);

'contravention' includes a failure to comply, and cognate expressions shall be construed accordingly;

'dismiss', 'dismissal' and 'effective date of termination', in relation to an employee, shall be construed in accordance with Part X of the Employment Rights Act 1996;

'legal professional privilege', as respects Scotland, means confidentiality of communications;

'tort', as respects Scotland, means delict, and cognate expressions shall be construed accordingly.

299 Index of defined expressions

In this Act the expressions listed below are defined by or otherwise fall to be construed in accordance with the provisions indicated—

ACAS	section 247(1)
act and action	section 298
advertisement (in sections 137 to 143)	section 143(1)
affected employees (in Part IV, Chapter II)	section 196(3)
'affected transferring individual' (in sections 198A and 198B)	section 198A(7)
agency worker	section 298
agent (of trade union)	section 119
appropriately qualified actuary (in sections 38 to 41)	section 42
associated employer	section 297
branch or section (of trade union)	section 119
certificate of independence	section 298
collective agreement and collective bargaining	section 178(1)
contract of employment	
– generally	section 295(1)
– in sections 226 to 234A	section 235
– in relation to Crown employment	section 273(4)(a)
– in relation to House of Lords or House of Commons staff	sections 277(4) and 278(4)(a)

(Cont.)

contravention	section 298
contributor (in relation to the political fund of a trade union)	section 84(1)
the court (in Part I)	section 121
date of the ballot (in Part V)	section 246
dismiss and dismissal	
– generally	section 298
– in relation to Crown employment	section 273(4)(c)
– in relation to House of Commons staff	section 278(4)(b)
the duty of confidentiality, in the context of a scrutineer or independent person	section 24A(3)
effective date of termination	section 298
employee	
– generally	section 295(1)
– in relation to Crown employment	section 273(4)(a)
– in relation to House of Commons staff	section 278(4)(a)
– excludes police service	section 280
employee representatives (in Part IV, Chapter II)	section 196(1)
employer	
– in relation to an employee	section 295(1)
– in relation to a worker	section 296(2)
– in relation to health service practitioners	section 279
employment and employment agency (in sections 137 to 143)	section 143(1)
executive (of trade union)	section 119
financial affairs (of trade union)	section 119
financial year (in Part VI)	section 272
general secretary	section 119
independent trade union (and related expressions)	section 5
legal professional privilege (as respects Scotland)	section 298
list	
– of trade unions	section 2
– of employers' associations	section 123
Northern Ireland union (in Part I)	section 120
not protected (in sections 222 to 226 and 234A)	section 219(4)
officer	
– of trade union	section 119
– of employers' association	section 136
official (of trade union)	section 119

(Cont.)

offshore employment	section 287
political fund	section 82(1)(a)
political resolution	section 82(1)(a)
prescribed	section 293(1)
president	section 119
'pre-transfer consultation' (in sections 198A and 198B)	section 198A(7)
recognised, recognition and related expressions	section 178(3)
'relevant transfer' (in sections 198A and 198B)	section 198A(7)
representatives of trade union (in Part IV, Chapter II)	section 196(2)
rules (of trade union)	section 119
strike (in Part V)	section 246
tort (as respects Scotland)	section 298
trade dispute	
– in Part IV	section 218
– in Part V	section 244
trade union	section 1
'transferee' and 'transferor' (in sections 198A and 198B)	section 198A(7)
'transferring individual' (in sections 198A and 198B)	section 198A(7)
undertaking (of employer)	
– in relation to Crown employment	section 273(4)(e) and (f)
– in relation to House of Commons staff	section 278(4)(c) and (d)
voting	section 297A
worker	
– generally	section 296(1)
– includes health service practitioners	section 279
– excludes police service	section 280
working hours (in Part V)	section 246

300–302 [omitted]

SCHEDULE A1

COLLECTIVE BARGAINING: RECOGNITION

PART I RECOGNITION

Introduction

1. A trade union (or trade unions) seeking recognition to be entitled to conduct collective bargaining on behalf of a group or groups of workers may make a request in accordance with this Part of this

Schedule.

2.—(1) This paragraph applies for the purposes of this Part of this Schedule.

(2) References to the bargaining unit are to the group of workers concerned (or the groups taken together).

(3) References to the proposed bargaining unit are to the bargaining unit proposed in the request for recognition.

(3A) References to an appropriate bargaining unit's being decided by the CAC are to a bargaining unit's being decided by the CAC to be appropriate under paragraph 19(2) or (3) or 19A(2) or (3).

(4) References to the employer are to the employer of the workers constituting the bargaining unit concerned.

(5) References to the parties are to the union (or unions) and the employer.

3.—(1) This paragraph applies for the purposes of this part of this Schedule.

(2) The meaning of collective bargaining given by section 178(1) shall not apply.

(3) References to collective bargaining are to negotiations relating to pay, hours and holidays; but this has effect subject to sub-paragraph (4).

(4) If the parties agree matters as the subject of collective bargaining, references to collective bargaining are to negotiations relating to the agreed matters; and this is the case whether the agreement is made before or after the time when the CAC issues a declaration, or the parties agree, that the union is (or unions are) entitled to conduct collective bargaining on behalf of a bargaining unit.

(5) Sub-paragraph (4) does not apply in construing paragraph 31(3).

(6) Sub-paragraphs (2) to (5) do not apply in construing paragraph 35 or 44.

Request for recognition

4.—(1) The union or unions seeking recognition must make a request for recognition to the employer.

(2) Paragraphs 5 to 9 apply to the request.

5. The request is not valid unless it is received by the employer.

6. The request is not valid unless the union (or each of the unions) has a certificate of independence.

7.—(1) The request is not valid unless the employer, taken with any associated employer or employers, employs—

(a) at least 21 workers on the day the employer receives the request, or

(b) an average of at least 21 workers in the 13 weeks ending with that day.

(2)–(8) [omitted]

8.–9. [omitted]

Parties agree

10.—(1) If before the end of the first period the parties agree a bargaining unit and that the union is (or unions are) to be recognised as entitled to conduct collective bargaining on behalf of the unit, no further steps are to be taken under this Part of this Schedule.

(2) If before the end of the first period the employer informs the union (or unions) that the employer does not accept the request but is willing to negotiate, sub-paragraph (3) applies.

(3) The parties may conduct negotiations with a view to agreeing a bargaining unit and that the union is (or unions are) to be recognised as entitled to conduct collective bargaining on behalf of the unit.

(4) If such an agreement is made before the end of the second period no further steps are to be taken under this Part of this Schedule.

(5) The employer and the union (or unions) may request ACAS to assist in conducting the negotiations.

(6) The first period is the period of 10 working days starting with the day after that on which the employer receives the request for recognition.

(7) The second period is—

(a) the period of 20 working days starting with the day after that on which the first period ends, or

(b) such longer period (so starting) as the parties may from time to time agree.

Employer rejects request

11.—(1) This paragraph applies if—

(a) before the end of the first period the employer fails to respond to the request, or

(b) before the end of the first period the employer informs the union (or unions) that the employer does not accept the request (without indicating a willingness to negotiate).

(2) The union (or unions) may apply to the CAC to decide both these questions—

(a) whether the proposed bargaining unit is appropriate;

(b) whether the union has (or unions have) the support of a majority of the workers constituting the appropriate bargaining unit.

Negotiations fail

12.—(1) Sub-paragraph (2) applies if—

(a) the employer informs the union (or unions) under paragraph 10(2), and

(b) no agreement is made before the end of the second period.

(2) The union (or unions) may apply to the CAC to decide both these questions—

(a) whether the proposed bargaining unit is appropriate;

(b) whether the union has (or unions have) the support of a majority of the workers constituting the appropriate bargaining unit.

(3) Sub-paragraph (4) applies if—

(a) the employer informs the union (or unions) under paragraph 10(2), and

(b) before the end of the second period the parties agree a bargaining unit but not that the union is (or unions are) to be recognised as entitled to conduct collective bargaining on behalf of the unit.

(4) The union (or unions) may apply to the CAC to decide the question whether the union has (or unions have) the support of a majority of the workers constituting the bargaining unit.

(5) But no application may be made under this paragraph if within the period of 10 working days starting with the day after that on which the employer informs the union (or unions) under paragraph 10(2) the employer proposes that ACAS be requested to assist in conducting the negotiations and—

(a) the union rejects (or unions reject) the proposals, or

(b) the union fails (or unions fail) to accept the proposal within the period of 10 working days starting with the day after that on which the employer makes the proposal.

13.–17. [omitted]

Appropriate bargaining unit

18.—(1) If the CAC accepts an application under paragraph 11(2) or 12(2) it must try to help the parties to reach within the appropriate period an agreement as to what the appropriate bargaining unit is.

(2) The appropriate period is (subject to any notice under sub-paragraph (3), (4) or (5))—

(a) the period of 20 working days starting with the day after that on which the CAC gives notice of acceptance of the application, or

(b) such longer period (so starting) as the CAC may specify to the parties by notice containing reasons for the extension.

(3) If, during the appropriate period, the CAC concludes that there is no reasonable prospect of the parties' agreeing an appropriate bargaining unit before the time when (apart from this sub-paragraph) the appropriate period would end, the CAC may, by a notice given to the parties, declare that the appropriate period ends with the date of the notice.

(4) If, during the appropriate period, the parties apply to the CAC for a declaration that the appropriate period is to end with a date (specified in the application) which is earlier than the date with which it would otherwise end, the CAC may, by a notice given to the parties, declare that the appropriate period ends with the specified date.

(5) If the CAC has declared under sub-paragraph (4) that the appropriate period ends with a specified date, it may before that date by a notice given to the parties specify a later date with which the appropriate period ends.

(6) A notice under sub-paragraph (3) must contain reasons for reaching the conclusion mentioned in that sub-paragraph.

(7) A notice under sub-paragraph (5) must contain reasons for the extension of the appropriate period.

18A.—(1) This paragraph applies if the CAC accepts an application under paragraph 11(2) or 12(2).

(2) Within 5 working days starting with the day after that on which the CAC gives the employer notice of acceptance of the application, the employer must supply the following information to the union (or unions) and the CAC—

- (a) a list of the categories of worker in the proposed bargaining unit,
- (b) a list of the workplaces at which the workers in the proposed bargaining unit work, and
- (c) the number of workers the employer reasonably believes to be in each category at each workplace.

(3) The lists and numbers supplied under this paragraph must be as accurate as is reasonably practicable in the light of the information in the possession of the employer at the time when he complies with sub-paragraph (2).

(4) The lists and numbers supplied to the union (or unions) and to the CAC must be the same.

(5) For the purposes of this paragraph, the workplace at which a worker works is—

- (a) if the person works at or from a single set of premises, those premises, and
- (b) in any other case, the premises with which the worker's employment has the closest connection.

19.—(1) This paragraph applies if—

- (a) the CAC accepts an application under paragraph 11(2) or 12(2),
- (b) the parties have not agreed an appropriate bargaining unit at the end of the appropriate period (defined by paragraph 18), and
- (c) at the end of that period either no request under paragraph 19A(1)(b) has been made or such a request has been made but the condition in paragraph 19A(1)(c) has not been met.

(2) Within the decision period, the CAC must decide whether the proposed bargaining unit is appropriate.

(3) If the CAC decides that the proposed bargaining unit is not appropriate, it must also decide within the decision period a bargaining unit which is appropriate.

(4) The decision period is—

- (a) the period of 10 working days starting with the day after that with which the appropriate period ends, or
- (b) such longer period (so starting) as the CAC may specify to the parties by notice containing reasons for the extension.

19A.—(1) This paragraph applies if—

- (a) the CAC accepts an application under paragraph 11(2) or 12(2),
- (b) during the appropriate period (defined by paragraph 18), the CAC is requested by the union (or unions) to make a decision under this paragraph, and
- (c) the CAC is, either at the time the request is made or at a later time during the appropriate period, of the opinion that the employer has failed to comply with the duty imposed by paragraph 18A.

(2) Within the decision period, the CAC must decide whether the proposed bargaining unit is appropriate.

(3) If the CAC decides that the proposed bargaining unit is not appropriate, it must also decide within the decision period a bargaining unit which is appropriate.

(4) The decision period is—

- (a) the period of 10 working days starting with the day after the day on which the request is made, or
- (b) such longer period (so starting) as the CAC may specify to the parties by notice containing reasons for the extension.

19B.—(1) This paragraph applies if the CAC has to decide whether a bargaining unit is appropriate for the purposes of paragraph 19(2) or (3) or 19A(2) or (3).

(2) The CAC must take these matters into account—

(a) the need for the unit to be compatible with effective management;

(b) the matters listed in sub-paragraph (3), so far as they do not conflict with that need.

(3) The matters are—

(a) the views of the employer and of the union (or unions);

(b) existing national and local bargaining arrangements;

(c) the desirability of avoiding small fragmented bargaining units within an undertaking;

(d) the characteristics of workers falling within the bargaining unit under consideration and of any other employees of the employer whom the CAC considers relevant;

(e) the location of workers.

(4) In taking an employer's views into account for the purpose of deciding whether the proposed bargaining unit is appropriate, the CAC must take into account any view the employer has about any other bargaining unit that he considers would be appropriate.

(5) The CAC must give notice of its decision to the parties.

19C.–19P. [omitted]

Union recognition

20.—(1) This paragraph applies if—

(a) the CAC accepts an application under paragraph 11(2) or 12(2),

(b) the parties have agreed an appropriate bargaining unit at the end of the appropriate period (defined by paragraph 18), or the CAC has decided an appropriate bargaining unit, and

(c) that bargaining unit differs from the proposed bargaining unit.

(2) Within the decision period the CAC must decide whether the application is invalid within the terms of paragraphs 43 to 50.

(3) In deciding whether the application is invalid, the CAC must consider any evidence which it has been given by the employer or the union (or unions).

(4) If the CAC decides that the application is invalid—

(a) the CAC must give notice of its decision to the parties,

(b) the CAC must not proceed with the application, and

(c) no further steps are to be taken under this part of this Schedule.

(5) If the CAC decides that the application is not invalid it must—

(a) proceed with the application, and

(b) give notice to the parties that it is so proceeding.

(6) The decision period is—

(a) the period of 10 working days starting with the day after that on which the parties agree an appropriate bargaining unit or the CAC decides an appropriate bargaining unit, or

(b) such longer period (so starting) as the CAC may specify to the parties by notice containing reasons for the extension.

21.—(1) This paragraph applies if—

(a) the CAC accepts an application under paragraph 11(2) or 12(2),

(b) the parties have agreed an appropriate bargaining unit at the end of the appropriate period (defined by paragraph 18), or the CAC has decided an appropriate bargaining unit, and

(c) that bargaining unit is the same as the proposed bargaining unit.

(2) This paragraph also applies if the CAC accepts an application under paragraph 12(4).

(3) The CAC must proceed with the application.

22.—(1) This paragraph applies if—

(a) the CAC proceeds with an application in accordance with paragraph 20 or 21 (and makes no declaration under paragraph 19F(5)), and

(b) the CAC is satisfied that a majority of the workers constituting the bargaining unit are members of the union (or unions).

(2) The CAC must issue a declaration that the union is (or unions are) recognised as entitled to conduct collective bargaining on behalf of the workers constituting the bargaining unit.

(3) But if any of the three qualifying conditions is fulfilled, instead of issuing a declaration under sub-paragraph (2) the CAC must give notice to the parties that it intends to arrange for the holding of a secret ballot in which the workers constituting the bargaining unit are asked whether they want the union (or unions) to conduct collective bargaining on their behalf.

(4) These are the three qualifying conditions—

(a) the CAC is satisfied that a ballot should be held in the interests of good industrial relations;

(b) the CAC has evidence, which it considers to be credible, from a significant number of the union members within the bargaining unit that they do not want the union (or unions) to conduct collective bargaining on their behalf;

(c) membership evidence is produced which leads the CAC to conclude that there are doubts whether a significant number of the union members within the bargaining unit want the union (or unions) to conduct collective bargaining on their behalf.

(5) For the purposes of sub-paragraph (4)(c) membership evidence is—

(a) evidence about the circumstances in which union members became members;

(b) evidence about the length of time for which union members have been members, in a case where the CAC is satisfied that such evidence should be taken into account.

23.—(1) This paragraph applies if—

(a) the CAC proceeds with an application in accordance with paragraph 20 or 21 (and makes no declaration under paragraph 19F(5)), and

(b) the CAC is not satisfied that a majority of the workers constituting the bargaining unit are members of the union (or unions).

(2) The CAC must give notice to the parties that it intends to arrange for the holding of a secret ballot in which the workers constituting the bargaining unit are asked whether they want the union (or unions) to conduct collective bargaining on their behalf.

24. [omitted]

25.—(1) This paragraph applies if the CAC arranges under paragraph 24 for the holding of a ballot.

(2) The ballot must be conducted by a qualified independent person appointed by the CAC.

(3) The ballot must be conducted within—

(a) the period of 20 working days starting with the day after that on which the qualified independent person is appointed, or

(b) such longer period (so starting) as the CAC may decide.

(4) The ballot must be conducted—

(a) at a workplace or workplaces decided by the CAC,

(b) by post, or

(c) by a combination of the methods described in sub-paragraphs (a) and (b), depending on the CAC's preference.

(5) In deciding how the ballot is to be conducted the CAC must take into account—

(a) the likelihood of the ballot being affected by unfairness or malpractice if it were conducted at a workplace or workplaces;

(b) costs and practicality;

(c) such other matters as the CAC considers appropriate.

(6) The CAC may not decide that the ballot is to be conducted as mentioned in sub-paragraph (4)(c) unless there are special factors making such a decision appropriate; and special factors include—

(a) factors arising from the location of workers or the nature of their employment;

(b) factors put to the CAC by the employer or the union (or unions).

(6A) If the CAC decides that the ballot must (in whole or in part) be conducted at a workplace (or workplaces), it may require arrangements to be made for workers—

(a) who (but for the arrangements) would be prevented by the CAC's decision from voting by post, and

(b) who are unable, for reasons relating to those workers as individuals, to cast their votes in the ballot at the workplace (or at any of them),

to be given the opportunity (if they request it far enough in advance of the ballot for this to be practicable) to vote by post; and the CAC's imposing such a requirement is not to be treated for the purposes of sub-paragraph (6) as a decision that the ballot be conducted as mentioned in sub-paragraph (4)(c).

(7)–(9) [omitted]

26.—(1) An employer who is informed by the CAC under paragraph 25 (9) must comply with the following five duties.

(2) The first duty is to co-operate generally, in connection with the ballot, with the union (or unions) and the person appointed to conduct the ballot; and the second and third duties are not to prejudice the generality of this.

(3) The second duty is to give to the union (or unions) such access to the workers constituting the bargaining unit as is reasonable to enable the union (or unions) to inform the workers of the object of the ballot and to seek their support and their opinions on the issues involved.

(4) The third duty is to do the following (so far as it is reasonable to expect the employer to do so)—

(a) to give to the CAC, within the period of 10 working days starting with the day after that on which the employer is informed under paragraph 25(9), the names and home addresses of the workers constituting the bargaining unit;

(b) to give to the CAC, as soon as is reasonably practicable, the name and home address of any worker who joins the unit after the employer has complied with paragraph (a);

(c) to inform the CAC, as soon as is reasonably practicable, of any worker whose name has been given to the CAC under paragraph 19D or paragraph (a) or (b) of this sub-paragraph and who ceases to be within the unit.

(4A) The fourth duty is to refrain from making any offer to any or all of the workers constituting the bargaining unit which—

(a) has or is likely to have the effect of inducing any or all of them not to attend any relevant meeting between the union (or unions) and the workers constituting the bargaining unit, and

(b) is not reasonable in the circumstances.

(4B) The fifth duty is to refrain from taking or threatening to take any action against a worker solely or mainly on the grounds that he—

(a) attended or took part in any relevant meeting between the union (or unions) and the workers constituting the bargaining unit, or

(b) indicated his intention to attend or take part in such a meeting.

(4C) A meeting is a relevant meeting in relation to a worker for the purposes of sub-paragraphs (4A) and (4B) if—

(a) it is organised in accordance with any agreement reached concerning the second duty or as a result of a step ordered to be taken under paragraph 27 to remedy a failure to comply with that duty, and

(b) it is one which the employer is, by such an agreement or order as is mentioned in paragraph (a), required to permit the worker to attend.

(4D) Without prejudice to the generality of the second duty imposed by this paragraph, an employer is to be taken to have failed to comply with that duty if—

(a) he refuses a request for a meeting between the union (or unions) and any or all of the workers constituting the bargaining unit to be held in the absence of the employer or any representative of his (other than one who has been invited to attend the meeting) and it is not reasonable in the circumstances for him to do so,

(b) he or a representative of his attends such a meeting without having been invited to do so,

(c) he seeks to record or otherwise be informed of the proceedings at any such meeting and it is not reasonable in the circumstances for him to do so, or

(d) he refuses to give an undertaking that he will not seek to record or otherwise be informed of the proceedings at any such meeting unless it is reasonable in the circumstances for him to do either of those things.

(4E) The fourth and fifth duties do not confer any rights on a worker; but that does not affect any other right which a worker may have.

(4F)–(4H) [omitted]

(5) As soon as is reasonably practicable after the CAC receives any information under sub-paragraph (4) it must pass it on to the person appointed to conduct the ballot.

(6) If asked to do so by the union (or unions) the person appointed to conduct the ballot must send to any worker—

(a) whose name and home address have been given under sub-paragraph (5), and

(b) who is still within the unit (so far as the person so appointed is aware), any information supplied by the union (or unions) to the person so appointed.

(7) The duty under sub-paragraph (6) does not apply unless the union bears (or unions bear) the cost of sending the information.

(8)–(9) [omitted]

27.—(1) If the CAC is satisfied that the employer has failed to fulfil any of the duties imposed on him by paragraph 26, and the ballot has not been held, the CAC may order the employer—

(a) to take such steps to remedy the failure as the CAC considers reasonable and specifies in the order, and

(b) to do so within such period as the CAC considers reasonable and specifies in the order.

(2) If the CAC is satisfied that the employer has failed to comply with an order under sub-paragraph (1), and the ballot has not been held, the CAC may issue a declaration that the union is (or unions are) recognised as entitled to conduct collective bargaining on behalf of the bargaining unit.

(3) If the CAC issues a declaration under sub-paragraph (2) it shall take steps to cancel the holding of the ballot; and if the ballot is held it shall have no effect.

27A.—(1) Each of the parties informed by the CAC under paragraph 25(9) must refrain from using any unfair practice.

(2) A party uses an unfair practice if, with a view to influencing the result of the ballot, the party—

(a) offers to pay money or give money's worth to a worker entitled to vote in the ballot in return for the worker's agreement to vote in a particular way or to abstain from voting,

(b) makes an outcome-specific offer to a worker entitled to vote in the ballot,

(c) coerces or attempts to coerce a worker entitled to vote in the ballot to disclose—

(i) whether he intends to vote or to abstain from voting in the ballot, or

(ii) how he intends to vote, or how he has voted, in the ballot,

(d) dismisses or threatens to dismiss a worker,

(e) takes or threatens to take disciplinary action against a worker,

(f) subjects or threatens to subject a worker to any other detriment, or
(g) uses or attempts to use undue influence on a worker entitled to vote in the ballot.

(3) For the purposes of sub-paragraph (2)(b) an 'outcome-specific offer' is an offer to pay money or give money's worth which—
(a) is conditional on the issuing by the CAC of a declaration that—
(i) the union is (or unions are) recognised as entitled to conduct collective bargaining on behalf of the bargaining unit, or
(ii) the union is (or unions are) not entitled to be so recognised, and
(b) is not conditional on anything which is done or occurs as a result of the declaration in question.

(4) The duty imposed by this paragraph does not confer any rights on a worker; but that does not affect any other right which a worker may have.

(5) [omitted]

27B.—(1) A party may complain to the CAC that another party has failed to comply with paragraph 27A.

(2) A complaint under sub-paragraph (1) must be made on or before the first working day after—
(a) the date of the ballot, or
(b) if votes may be cast in the ballot on more than one day, the last of those days.

(3) Within the decision period the CAC must decide whether the complaint is well-founded.

(4) A complaint is well-founded if—
(a) the CAC finds that the party complained against used an unfair practice, and
(b) the CAC is satisfied that the use of that practice changed or was likely to change, in the case of a worker entitled to vote in the ballot—
(i) his intention to vote or to abstain from voting,
(ii) his intention to vote in a particular way, or
(iii) how he voted.

(5) The decision period is—
(a) the period of 10 working days starting with the day after that on which the complaint under sub-paragraph (1) was received by the CAC, or
(b) such longer period (so starting) as the CAC may specify to the parties by a notice containing reasons for the extension.

(6) If, at the beginning of the decision period, the ballot has not begun, the CAC may by notice to the parties and the qualified independent person postpone the date on which it is to begin until a date which falls after the end of the decision period.

27C.—(1) This paragraph applies if the CAC decides that a complaint under paragraph 27B is well-founded.

(2) The CAC must, as soon as is reasonably practicable, issue a declaration to that effect.

(3) The CAC may do either or both of the following—
(a) order the party concerned to take any action specified in the order within such period as may be so specified, or
(b) give notice to the employer and to the union (or unions) that it intends to arrange for the holding of a secret ballot in which the workers constituting the bargaining unit are asked whether they want the union (or unions) to conduct collective bargaining on their behalf.

(4) The CAC may give an order or a notice under sub-paragraph (3) either at the same time as it issues the declaration under sub-paragraph (2) or at any other time before it acts under paragraph 29.

(5) The action specified in an order under sub-paragraph (3)(a) shall be such as the CAC considers reasonable in order to mitigate the effect of the failure of the party concerned to comply with the duty imposed by paragraph 27A.

(6) The CAC may give more than one order under sub-paragraph (3)(a).

27D.—(1) This paragraph applies if the CAC issues a declaration under paragraph 27C(2) and the declaration states that the unfair practice used consisted of or included—

(a) the use of violence, or

(b) the dismissal of a union official.

(2) This paragraph also applies if the CAC has made an order under paragraph 27C(3)(a) and—

(a) it is satisfied that the party subject to the order has failed to comply with it, or

(b) it makes another declaration under paragraph 27C(2) in relation to a complaint against that party.

(3) If the party concerned is the employer, the CAC may issue a declaration that the union is (or unions are) recognised as entitled to conduct collective bargaining on behalf of the bargaining unit.

(4) If the party concerned is a union, the CAC may issue a declaration that the union is (or unions are) not entitled to be so recognised.

(5) The powers conferred by this paragraph are in addition to those conferred by paragraph 27C(3).

27E.—(1) This paragraph applies if the CAC issues a declaration that a complaint under paragraph 27B is well-founded and—

(a) gives a notice under paragraph 27C(3)(b), or

(b) issues a declaration under paragraph 27D.

(2) If the ballot in connection with which the complaint was made has not been held, the CAC shall take steps to cancel it.

(3) If that ballot is held, it shall have no effect.

27F.—(1) This paragraph applies if the CAC gives a notice under paragraph 27C(3)(b).

(2) Paragraphs 24 to 29 apply in relation to that notice as they apply in relation to a notice given under paragraph 22(3) or 23(2) but with the modifications specified in sub-paragraphs (3) to (6).

(3) In each of sub-paragraphs (5)(a) and (6)(a) of paragraph 24 for '10 working days' substitute '5 working days'.

(4) An employer's duty under paragraph (a) of paragraph 26(4) is limited to—

(a) giving the CAC the names and home addresses of any workers in the bargaining unit which have not previously been given to it in accordance with that duty;

(b) giving the CAC the names and home addresses of those workers who have joined the bargaining unit since he last gave the CAC information in accordance with that duty;

(c) informing the CAC of any change to the name or home address of a worker whose name and home address have previously been given to the CAC in accordance with that duty; and

(d) informing the CAC of any worker whose name had previously been given to it in accordance with that duty who has ceased to be within the bargaining unit.

(5) Any order given under paragraph 27(1) or 27C(3)(a) for the purposes of the cancelled or ineffectual ballot shall have effect (to the extent that the CAC specifies in a notice to the parties) as if it were made for the purposes of the ballot to which the notice under paragraph 27C(3)(b) relates.

(6) The gross costs of the ballot shall be borne by such of the parties and in such proportions as the CAC may determine and, accordingly, sub-paragraphs (2) and (3) of paragraph 28 shall be omitted and the reference in sub-paragraph (4) of that paragraph to the employer and the union (or each of the unions) shall be construed as a reference to the party or parties which bear the costs in accordance with the CAC's determination.

28. [omitted]

29.—(1) As soon as is reasonably practicable after the CAC is informed of the result of a ballot by the person conducting it, the CAC must act under this paragraph.

(1A) The duty in sub-paragraph (1) does not apply if the CAC gives a notice under paragraph 27C(3)(b).

(2) The CAC must inform the employer and the union (or unions) of the result of the ballot.

(3) If the result is that the union is (or unions are) supported by a majority of the workers voting, the CAC must issue a declaration that the union is (or unions are) recognised as entitled to conduct collective bargaining on behalf of the bargaining unit.

(4) If the result is otherwise the CAC must issue a declaration that the union is (or unions are) not entitled to be so recognised.

(5)–(7) [repealed]

30.—(1) This paragraph applies if the CAC issues a declaration under this Part of this Schedule that the union is (or unions are) recognised as entitled to conduct collective bargaining on behalf of a bargaining unit.

(2) The parties may in the negotiation period conduct negotiations with a view to agreeing a method by which they will conduct collective bargaining.

(3) If no agreement is made in the negotiation period the employer or the union (or unions) may apply to the CAC for assistance.

(4) The negotiation period is—

(a) the period of 30 working days starting with the start day, or

(b) such longer period (so starting) as the parties may from time to time agree.

(5) The start day is the day after that on which the parties are notified of the declaration.

31.—(1) This paragraph applies if an application for assistance is made to the CAC under paragraph 30.

(2) The CAC must try to help the parties to reach in the agreement period an agreement on a method by which they will conduct collective bargaining.

(3) If at the end of the agreement period the parties have not made such an agreement the CAC must specify to the parties the method by which they are to conduct collective bargaining.

(4) Any method specified under sub-paragraph (3) is to have effect as if it were contained in a legally enforceable contract made by the parties.

(5) But if the parties agree in writing—

(a) that sub-paragraph (4) shall not apply, or shall not apply to particular parts of the method specified by the CAC, or

(b) to vary or replace the method specified by the CAC,

the written agreement shall have effect as a legally enforceable contract made by the parties.

(6) Specific performance shall be the only remedy available for breach of anything which is a legally enforceable contract by virtue of this paragraph.

(7) If at any time before a specification is made under sub-paragraph (3) the parties jointly apply to the CAC requesting it to stop taking steps under this paragraph, the CAC must comply with the request.

(8) The agreement period is—

(a) the period of 20 working days starting with the day after that on which the CAC receives the application under paragraph 30, or

(b) such longer period (so starting) as the CAC may decide with the consent of the parties.

Method not carried out

32.—(1) This paragraph applies if—

(a) the CAC issues a declaration under this Part of this Schedule that the union is (or unions are) recognised as entitled to conduct collective bargaining on behalf of a bargaining unit,

(b) the parties agree a method by which they will conduct collective bargaining, and
(c) one or more of the parties fails to carry out the agreement.

(2) the employer or the union (or unions) may apply to the CAC for assistance.

(3) Paragraph 31 applies as if 'paragraph 30' (in each place) read 'paragraph 30 or paragraph 32'.

General provisions about admissibility

33.–34. [omitted]

35.—(1) An application under paragraph 11 or 12 is not admissible if the CAC is satisfied that there is already in force a collective agreement under which a union is (or unions are) recognised as entitled to conduct collective bargaining on behalf of any workers falling within the relevant bargaining unit.

(2) But sub-paragraph (1) does not apply to an application under paragraph 11 or 12 if—

(a) the union (or unions) recognised under the collective agreement and the union (or unions) making the application under paragraph 11 or 12 are the same, and
(b) the matters in respect of which the union is (or unions are) entitled to conduct collective bargaining do not include all of the following: pay, hours and holidays ('the core topics').

(3) A declaration of recognition which is the subject of a declaration under paragraph 83(2) must for the purposes of sub-paragraph (1) be treated as ceasing to have effect to the extent specified in paragraph 83(2) on the making of the declaration under paragraph 83(2).

(4) In applying sub-paragraph (1) an agreement for recognition (the agreement in question) must be ignored if—

(a) the union does not have (or none of the unions has) a certificate of independence,
(b) at some time there was an agreement (the old agreement) between the employer and the union under which the union (whether alone or with other unions) was recognised as entitled to conduct collective bargaining on behalf of a group of workers which was the same or substantially the same as the group covered by the agreement in question, and
(c) the old agreement ceased to have effect in the period of three years ending with the date of the agreement in question.

(5) It is for the CAC to decide whether one group of workers is the same or substantially the same as another, but in deciding the CAC may take account of the views of any person it believes has an interest in the matter.

(5A) In applying sub-paragraph (1) an agreement for recognition (the agreement in question) must be ignored if—

(a) the union recognised under the agreement in question does not have (or none of the unions recognised under the agreement in question has) a certificate of independence,
(b) the union (or unions) making the application under paragraph 11 or 12 made the application before the end of the period of reflection, and
(c) the agreement in question was entered into during the restricted period.

(5B) The period of reflection is the period of 20 working days starting with the first day after the end of—

(a) the first period referred to in paragraph 10(6), in the case of an application under paragraph 11, or
(b) the second period referred to in paragraph 10(7), in the case of an application under paragraph 12.

(5C) The restricted period is the period—

(a) starting with the day on which the employer receives a valid request for recognition under paragraph 4, and
(b) ending with the day on which the CAC makes a decision under paragraph 15.

(6) The relevant bargaining unit is—

(a) the proposed bargaining unit, where the application is under paragraph 11(2) or 12(2);

(b) the agreed bargaining unit, where the application is under paragraph 12(4).

36.—(1) An application under paragraph 11 or 12 is not admissible unless the CAC decides that members of the union (or unions) constitute at least the required percentage (see paragraph 171B) of the workers constituting the relevant bargaining unit.

(2) The relevant bargaining unit is—

(a) the proposed bargaining unit, where the application is under paragraph 11(2) or 12(2);

(b) the agreed bargaining unit, where the application is under paragraph 12(4).

(3) The CAC must give reasons for the decision.

37.—(1) This paragraph applies to an application made by more than one union under paragraph 11 or 12.

(2) The application is not admissible unless—

(a) the unions show that they will co-operate with each other in a manner likely to secure and maintain stable and effective collective bargaining arrangements, and

(b) the unions show that, if the employer wishes, they will enter into arrangements under which collective bargaining is conducted by the unions acting together on behalf of the workers constituting the relevant bargaining unit.

(3) The relevant bargaining unit is—

(a) the proposed bargaining unit, where the application is under paragraph 11(2) or 12(2);

(b) the agreed bargaining unit, where the application is under paragraph 12(4).

38. [omitted]

39.—(1) This paragraph applies if the CAC accepts a relevant application relating to a bargaining unit or proceeds under paragraph 20 with an application relating to a bargaining unit.

(2) Another relevant application is not admissible if—

(a) the application is made within the period of 3 years starting with the day after that on which the CAC gave notice of acceptance of the application mentioned in sub-paragraph (1),

(b) the relevant bargaining unit is the same or substantially the same as the bargaining unit mentioned in sub-paragraph (1), and

(c) the application is made by the union (or unions) which made the application mentioned in sub-paragraph (1).

(3) A relevant application is an application under paragraph 11 or 12.

(4) The relevant bargaining unit is—

(a) the proposed bargaining unit, where the application is under paragraph 11(2) or 12(2);

(b) the agreed bargaining unit, where the application is under paragraph 12(4).

(5) This paragraph does not apply if paragraph 40 or 41 applies.

40.—(1) This paragraph applies if the CAC issues a declaration under paragraph 27D(4) or 29(4) that a union is (or unions are) not entitled to be recognised as entitled to conduct collective bargaining on behalf of a bargaining unit; and this is so whether the ballot concerned is arranged under this Part or Part III of this Schedule.

(2) An application under paragraph 11 or 12 is not admissible if—

(a) the application is made within the period of 3 years starting with the day after that on which the declaration was issued,

(b) the relevant bargaining unit is the same or substantially the same as the bargaining unit mentioned in sub-paragraph (1), and

(c) the application is made by the union (or unions) which made the application leading to the declaration.

(3) The relevant bargaining unit is—

(a) the proposed bargaining unit, where the application is under paragraph 11(2) or 12 (2);

(b) the agreed bargaining unit, where the application is under paragraph 12(4).

41.—(1) This paragraph applies if the CAC issues a declaration under paragraph 119D(4), 119H(5) or 121(3) that bargaining arrangements are to cease to have effect; and that is so whether the ballot concerned is arranged under Part IV or Part V of this Schedule.

(2) An application under paragraph 11 or 12 is not admissible if—

(a) the application is made within the period of 3 years starting with the day after that on which the declaration was issued,

(b) the relevant bargaining unit is the same or substantially the same as the bargaining unit to which the bargaining arrangements mentioned in sub-paragraph (1) relate, and

(c) the application is made by the union which was a party (or unions which were parties) to the proceedings leading to the declaration.

(3) The relevant bargaining unit is—

(a) the proposed bargaining unit, where the application is under paragraph 11(2) or 12 (2);

(b) the agreed bargaining unit, where the application is under paragraph 12(4).

42. [omitted]

43.—(1) Paragraphs 44 to 50 apply if the CAC has to decide under paragraph 20 whether an application is valid.

(2) In those paragraphs—

(a) references to the application in question are to that application, and

(b) references to the relevant bargaining unit are to the bargaining unit agreed by the parties or decided by the CAC.

44.—(1) The application in question is invalid if the CAC is satisfied that there is already in force a collective agreement under which a union is (or unions are) recognised as entitled to conduct collective bargaining on behalf of any workers falling within the relevant bargaining unit.

(2) But sub-paragraph (1) does not apply to the application in question if—

(a) the union (or unions) recognised under the collective agreement and the union (or unions) making the application in question are the same, and

(b) the matters in respect of which the union is (or unions are) entitled to conduct collective bargaining do not include all of the following: pay, hours and holidays ('the core topics').

(3)–(5) [omitted]

(6) In applying sub-paragraph (1) an agreement for recognition (the agreement in question) must be ignored if—

(a) the union recognised under the agreement in question does not have (or none of the unions recognised under the agreement in question has) a certificate of independence,

(b) the union (or unions) making the application under paragraph 11 or 12 made the application before the end of the period of reflection, and

(c) the agreement in question was entered into during the restricted period.

(7) The period of reflection is the period of 20 working days starting with the first day after the end of—

(a) the first period referred to in paragraph 10(6), in the case of an application under paragraph 11, or

(b) the second period referred to in paragraph 10(7), in the case of an application under paragraph 12.

(8) The restricted period is the period—

(a) starting with the day on which the employer receives a valid request for recognition under paragraph 4, and

(b) ending with the day on which the CAC makes a decision under paragraph 20.

45.—(1) The application in question is invalid unless the CAC decides that members of the union (or unions) constitute at least the required percentage (see paragraph 171B) of the workers constituting the relevant bargaining unit.

(2) For the purposes of sub-paragraph (1), any worker who joined the relevant bargaining unit after the application day is to be disregarded.

46. [omitted]

47.—(1) This paragraph applies if the CAC accepts an application under paragraph 11 or 12 relating to a bargaining unit or proceeds under paragraph 20 with an application relating to a bargaining unit.

(2) The application in question is invalid if—

(a) the application is made within the period of 3 years starting with the day after that on which the CAC gave notice of acceptance of the application mentioned in sub-paragraph (1),

(b) the relevant bargaining unit is the same or substantially the same as the bargaining unit mentioned in sub-paragraph (1), and

(c) the application is made by the union (or unions) which made the application mentioned in sub-paragraph (1).

(3) This paragraph does not apply if paragraph 48 or 49 applies.

48.—(1) This paragraph applies if the CAC issues a declaration under paragraph 27D(4) or 29(4) that a union is (or unions are) not entitled to be recognised as entitled to conduct collective bargaining on behalf of a bargaining unit; and this is so whether the ballot concerned is arranged under this Part or Part III of this Schedule.

(2) The application in question is invalid if—

(a) the application is made within the period of 3 years starting with the date of the declaration,

(b) the relevant bargaining unit is the same or substantially the same as the bargaining unit mentioned in sub-paragraph (1), and

(c) the application is made by the union (or unions) which made the application leading to the declaration.

49.—(1) This paragraph applies if the CAC issues a declaration under paragraph 119D(4), 119H(5) or 121(3) that bargaining arrangements are to cease to have effect; and this is so whether the ballot concerned is arranged under Part IV or Part V of this Schedule.

(2) The application in question is invalid if—

(a) the application is made within the period of 3 years starting with the day after that on which the declaration was issued,

(b) the relevant bargaining unit is the same or substantially the same as the bargaining unit to which the bargaining arrangements mentioned in sub-paragraph (1) relate, and

(c) the application is made by the union which was a party (or unions which were parties) to the proceedings leading to the declaration.

50.–51. [omitted]

PART II VOLUNTARY RECOGNITION

Agreements for recognition

52.—(1) This paragraph applies for the purposes of this Part of this Schedule.

(2) An agreement is an agreement for recognition if the following conditions are fulfilled in relation to it—

(a) the agreement is made in the permitted period between a union (or unions) and an employer in consequence of a request made under paragraph 4 and valid within the terms of paragraphs 5 to 9;

(b) under the agreement the union is (or unions are) recognised as entitled to conduct collective bargaining on behalf of a group or groups of workers employed by the employer;

(c) if sub-paragraph (5) applies to the agreement, it is satisfied.

(3) The permitted period is the period which begins with the day on which the employer receives the request and ends when the first of the following occurs—

(a) the union withdraws (or unions withdraw) the request;

(b) the union withdraws (or unions withdraw) any application under paragraph 11 or 12 made in consequence of the request;

(c) the CAC gives notice of a decision under paragraph 14(7) which precludes it from accepting such an application under paragraph 11 or 12;

(d) the CAC gives notice under paragraph 15(4)(a) or 20(4)(a) in relation to such an application under paragraph 11 or 12;

(e) the parties give notice to the CAC under paragraph 17(2) in relation to such an application under paragraph 11 or 12;

(f) the CAC issues a declaration under paragraph 19F(5) or 22(2) in consequence of such an application under paragraph 11 or 12;

(g) the CAC is notified under paragraph 24(2) in relation to such an application under paragraph 11 or 12;

(h) the last day of the notification period ends (the notification period being that defined by paragraph 24(6) and arising from such an application under paragraph 11 or 12).

(i) the CAC is required under paragraph 51(3) to cancel such an application under paragraph 11 or 12.

(4) Sub-paragraph (5) applies to an agreement if—

(a) at the time it is made the CAC has received an application under paragraph 11 or 12 in consequence of the request mentioned in sub-paragraph (2), and

(b) the CAC has not decided whether the application is admissible or it has decided that it is admissible.

(5) This sub-paragraph is satisfied if, in relation to the application under paragraph 11 or 12, the parties give notice to the CAC under paragraph 17 before the final event (as defined in paragraph 17) occurs.

Other interpretation

53.—(1) This paragraph applies for the purposes of this Part of this Schedule.

(2) In relation to an agreement for recognition, references to the bargaining unit are to the group of workers (or the groups taken together) to which the agreement for recognition relates.

(3) In relation to an agreement for recognition, references to the parties are to the union (or unions) and the employer who are parties to the agreement.

54.—(1) This paragraph applies for the purposes of this Part of this Schedule.

(2) The meaning of collective bargaining given by section 178(1) shall not apply.

(3) Except in paragraph 63(2), in relation to an agreement for recognition references to collective bargaining are to negotiations relating to the matters in respect of which the union is (or unions are) recognised as entitled to conduct negotiations under the agreement for recognition.

(4) In paragraph 63(2) the reference to collective bargaining is to negotiations relating to pay, hours and holidays.

Determination of type of agreement

55.—(1) This paragraph applies if one or more of the parties to an agreement applies to the CAC for a decision whether or not the agreement is an agreement for recognition.

(2) The CAC must give notice of receipt of an application under sub-paragraph (1) to any parties to the agreement who are not parties to the application.

(3) The CAC must within the decision period decide whether the agreement is an agreement for recognition.

(4) If the CAC decides that the agreement is an agreement for recognition it must issue a declaration to that effect.

(5) If the CAC decides that the agreement is not an agreement for recognition it must issue a declaration to that effect.

(6) The decision period is—

(a) the period of 10 working days starting with the day after that on which the CAC receives the application under sub-paragraph (1), or

(b) such longer period (so starting) as the CAC may specify to the parties to the agreement by notice containing reasons for the extension.

Termination of agreement for recognition

56.—(1) The employer may not terminate an agreement for recognition before the relevant period ends.

(2) After that period ends the employer may terminate the agreement, with or without the consent of the union (or unions).

(3) The union (or unions) may terminate an agreement for recognition at any time, with or without the consent of the employer.

(4) Sub-paragraphs (1) to (3) have effect subject to the terms of the agreement or any other agreement of the parties.

(5) The relevant period is the period of three years starting with the day after the date of the agreement.

57.—(1) If an agreement for recognition is terminated, as from the termination the agreement and any provisions relating to the collective bargaining method shall cease to have effect.

(2) For this purpose provisions relating to the collective bargaining method are—

(a) any agreement between the parties as to the method by which collective bargaining is to be conducted with regard to the bargaining unit, or

(b) anything effective as, or as if contained in, a legally enforceable contract and relating to the method by which collective bargaining is to be conducted with regard to the bargaining unit.

Application to CAC to specify method

58.—(1) This paragraph applies if the parties make an agreement for recognition.

(2) The parties may in the negotiation period conduct negotiations with a view to agreeing a method by which they will conduct collective bargaining.

(3) If no agreement is made in the negotiation period the employer or the union (or unions) may apply to the CAC for assistance.

(4) The negotiation period is—

(a) the period of 30 working days starting with the start day, or

(b) such longer period (so starting) as the parties may from time to time agree.

(5) The start day is the day after that on which the agreement is made.

59.—(1) This paragraph applies if—

(a) the parties to an agreement for recognition agree a method by which they will conduct collective bargaining, and

(b) one or more of the parties fails to carry out the agreement as to a method.

(2) The employer or the union (or unions) may apply to the CAC for assistance.

60.–95. [omitted]

PART IV DERECOGNITION: GENERAL

Introduction

96.—(1) This part of this Schedule applies if the CAC has issued a declaration that a union is (or unions are) recognised as entitled to conduct collective bargaining on behalf of a bargaining unit.

(2) In such a case references in this Part of this Schedule to the bargaining arrangements are to the declaration and to the provisions relating to the collective bargaining method.

(3) For this purpose the provisions relating to the collective bargaining method are—

(a) the parties' agreement as to the method by which collective bargaining is to be conducted,

(b) anything effective as, or as if contained in, a legally enforceable contract and relating to the method by which collective bargaining is to be conducted, or

(c) any provision of Part III of this Schedule that a method of collective bargaining is to have effect.

97. For the purposes of this Part of this Schedule the relevant date is the date of the expiry of the period of 3 years starting with the date of the CAC's declaration.

98. References in this Part of this Schedule to the parties are to the employer and the union (or unions) concerned.

99.–103. [omitted]

Employer's request to end arrangements

104.—(1) This paragraph and paragraphs 105 to 111 apply if after the relevant date the employer requests the union (or each of the unions) to agree to end the bargaining arrangements.

(2) The request is not valid unless it—

(a) is in writing,

(b) is received by the union (or each of the unions),

(c) identifies the bargaining arrangements, and

(d) states that it is made under this Schedule.

105. [omitted]

106.—(1) This paragraph applies if—

(a) before the end of the first period the union fails (or unions fail) to respond to the request, or

(b) before the end of the first period the union informs the employer that it does not (or unions inform the employer that they do not) accept the request (without indicating a willingness to negotiate).

(2) The employer may apply to the CAC for the holding of a secret ballot to decide whether the bargaining arrangements should be ended.

107.—(1) This paragraph applies if—

(a) the union informs (or unions inform) the employer under paragraph 105(2), and

(b) no agreement is made before the end of the second period.

(2) The employer may apply to the CAC for the holding of a secret ballot to decide whether the bargaining arrangements should be ended.

(3) But no application may be made if within the period of 10 working days starting with the day after that on which the union informs (or unions inform) the employer under paragraph 105(2) the union proposes (or unions propose) that ACAS be requested to assist in conducting the negotiations and—

(a) the employer rejects the proposal, or

(b) the employer fails to accept the proposal within the period of 10 working days starting with the day after that on which the union makes (or unions make) the proposal.

108.–109. [omitted]

110.—(1) An application under paragraph 106 or 107 is not admissible unless the CAC decides that—

(a) at least 10 per cent of the workers constituting the bargaining unit favour an end of the bargaining arrangements, and

(b) a majority of the workers constituting the bargaining unit would be likely to favour an end of the bargaining arrangements.

(2) The CAC must give reasons for the decision.

111. [omitted]

Workers' application to end arrangements

112.—(1) A worker or workers falling within the bargaining unit may after the relevant date apply to the CAC to have the bargaining arrangements ended.

(2) An application is not admissible unless—

(a) it is made in such form as the CAC specifies, and

(b) it is supported by such documents as the CAC specifies.

(3) An application is not admissible unless the worker gives (or workers give) to the employer and to the union (or each of the unions)—

(a) notice of the application, and

(b) a copy of the application and any documents supporting it.

113.—(1) An application under paragraph 112 is not admissible if—

(a) a relevant application was made, or a notice under paragraph 99(2) was given, within the period of 3 years prior to the date of the application under paragraph 112,

(b) the relevant application, or notice under paragraph 99(2), and the application under paragraph 112 relate to the same bargaining unit, and

(c) the CAC accepted the relevant application or (as the case may be) decided under paragraph 100 that the notice complied with paragraph 99(3).

(2) A relevant application is an application made to the CAC—

(a) [repealed],

(b) by the employer under paragraph 106, 107 or 128, or

(c) by a worker (or workers) under paragraph 112.

114.—(1) An application under paragraph 112 is not admissible unless the CAC decides that—

(a) at least 10 per cent of the workers constituting the bargaining unit favour an end of the bargaining arrangements, and

(b) a majority of the workers constituting the bargaining unit would be likely to favour an end of the bargaining arrangements.

(2) The CAC must give reasons for the decision.

115.–116. [omitted]

Access agreements

116A.—(1) This paragraph applies if—

(a) the CAC accepts an application under paragraph 106, 107 or 112, and

(b) the application is in progress.

(2) The union (or unions) may, by giving notice to the CAC and the employer within the access request period, request access to the workers constituting the bargaining unit in connection with the application.

(3) The access request period is the period of 5 working days starting with the day after the day on which the CAC gives the union (or unions) notice under paragraph 111(5) or 115(5) that the application is accepted.

(4) For the purposes of this paragraph and paragraphs 116B to 116E, an application under paragraph 106, 107 or 112 is in progress if none of the following has occurred—

(a) in the case of an application under paragraph 106 or 107, the withdrawal of the application;

(b) in the case of an application under paragraph 112, an agreement or withdrawal as described in paragraph 116(1);

(c) the CAC refusing the application under paragraph 116E(4)(a), 116K(4)(a) or (6) or 119(2);

(d) the CAC notifying the union (or unions) of a declaration issued under paragraph 116E(5) or 116K(5) in relation to the application;

(e) the holding of any ballot arising from the application

16B.—(1) This paragraph applies if—

(a) the CAC accepts an application under paragraph 106, 107 or 112,

(b) the union requests (or unions request) access to the workers constituting the bargaining unit under paragraph 116A(2) in connection with the application, and

(c) the application is in progress.

(2) The CAC must try to help the parties to reach agreement within the negotiation period as to terms on which the union is (or unions are) to have access to the workers.

(3) The negotiation period is, subject to any notice under sub-paragraph (4) or (6)—

(a) the period of 20 working days starting with the day after the day on which the CAC gives the union (or unions) notice under paragraph 111(5) or 115(5) that the application is accepted, or

(b) such longer period (so starting) as the CAC may specify to the parties by notice containing reasons for the extension.

(4) If, during the negotiation period, the CAC concludes that there is no reasonable prospect of the parties' agreeing terms on which the union is (or unions are) to have access to the workers before the time when (apart from this sub-paragraph) the negotiation period would end, the CAC may, by a notice given to the parties, declare that the negotiation period ends with the date of the notice.

(5) A notice under sub-paragraph (4) must contain reasons for reaching the conclusion mentioned in that sub-paragraph.

(6) If, during the negotiation period, the parties apply to the CAC for a declaration that the negotiation period is to end with a date (specified in the application) which is earlier or later than the date with which it would otherwise end, the CAC may, by a notice given to the parties, declare that the negotiation period ends with the specified date.

116C.—(1) This paragraph applies if—

(a) the CAC accepts an application under paragraph 106, 107 or 112,

(b) the union requests (or unions request) access to the workers constituting the bargaining unit under paragraph 116A(2) in connection with the application,

(c) the parties have not within the negotiation period agreed terms on which the union is (or unions are) to have access to the workers, and

(d the application is in progress.

(2) Within the adjudication period, the CAC must—

(a) decide the terms on which the union is (or unions are) to have access to the workers, or

(b) decide that the union is (or unions are) not to have access to the workers.

(3) The adjudication period is—

(a) the period of 10 working days starting with the day after the day with which the negotiation period ends, or

(b) such longer period (so starting) as the CAC may specify to the parties by notice containing reasons for the extension.

(4) Any terms decided by the CAC must be terms that the CAC regards as allowing such access to the workers constituting the bargaining unit as is reasonable to enable the union (or unions) to—

(a) inform the workers of the object of the application or any ballot arising from it, and

(b) seek their support and their opinions on the issues involved.

116D.—(1) This paragraph applies if—

(a) an access agreement is entered into, and

(b) the application under paragraph 106, 107 or 112 is in progress.

(2) 'Access agreement' means—

(a) terms on which the union is (or unions are) to have access to the workers constituting the bargaining unit and which are agreed between the parties under paragraph 116B during the negotiation period, or

(b) terms on which the union is (or unions are) to have access to the workers constituting the bargaining unit and which are decided by the CAC under paragraph 116C,

and such an agreement is to be treated as 'entered into' when the terms are so agreed or decided.

(3) The parties must comply with the access agreement.

(4) The employer must refrain from making any offer to any or all of the workers constituting the bargaining unit which—

(a) has or is likely to have the effect of inducing any or all of them not to attend any relevant meeting between the union (or unions) and the workers constituting the bargaining unit, and

(b) is not reasonable in the circumstances.

(5) The employer must refrain from taking, or threatening to take, any action against a worker solely or mainly on the grounds that the worker—

(a) attended or took part in any relevant meeting between the union (or unions) and the workers constituting the bargaining unit, or

(b) indicated an intention to attend or take part in such a meeting.

(6) A meeting is a relevant meeting in relation to a worker for the purposes of sub-paragraphs (4) and (5) if—

(a) it is organised in accordance with an access agreement or as a result of a step ordered to be taken under paragraph 116E to remedy a failure to comply with the duty in sub-paragraph (3), and

(b) it is one which the employer is, by such an agreement or order as is mentioned in paragraph (a), required to permit the worker to attend.

(7) The duties imposed by sub-paragraphs (4) and (5) do not confer any rights on a worker; but that does not affect any other right which a worker may have.

(8) Any provision of an access agreement that would require personal data relating to any of the relevant workers to be disclosed to a person other than a person appointed under paragraph 117 to conduct a ballot is of no effect for the purposes of this Part of this Schedule.

(9) 'Personal data' has the same meaning as in the Data Protection Act 2018 (see section 3 of that Act).

(10) An access agreement is to be conclusively presumed not to have been intended by the parties to be a legally enforceable contract; and, accordingly, where an access agreement is, or is part of, a collective agreement, section 179(2) and (3)(a) do not apply to the access agreement.

116E.—(1) Sub-paragraph (2) applies if—

(a) the CAC is satisfied that a party has failed to fulfil any of the duties imposed on that party by paragraph 116D, and

(b) the application under paragraph 106, 107 or 112 is in progress.

(2) The CAC may order the party—

(a) to take such steps to remedy the failure as the CAC considers reasonable and specifies in the order, and

(b) to do so within such period as the CAC considers reasonable and specifies in the order.

(3) Sub-paragraphs (4) and (5) apply if—

(a) the CAC is satisfied that a party has failed to comply with an order under sub-paragraph (2), and

(b) the application under paragraph 106, 107 or 112 is in progress.

(4) If the party that has failed to comply is the employer, the CAC may—

(a) refuse the employer's application under paragraph 106 or 107;

(b) order the employer to refrain from any campaigning in relation to an application under paragraph 112.

(5) If the party that has failed to comply is a union, the CAC may issue a declaration that the bargaining arrangements are to cease to have effect; and the bargaining arrangements cease to have effect accordingly.

116F.—(1) This paragraph applies if the CAC has made an order under paragraph 116E(4)(b) in relation to an application under paragraph 112.

(2) [omitted]

116G. [omitted]

116H.—(1) Each of the parties informed by the CAC under paragraph 111(5) or 115(5) that an application under paragraph 106, 107 or 112 is accepted must refrain from using any unfair practice in relation to the application.

(2) A party uses an unfair practice if, with a view to influencing the outcome of the application, the party does any of the following—

- (a) dismisses, or threatens to dismiss, a worker;
- (b) takes, or threatens to take, disciplinary action against a worker;
- (c) subjects, or threatens to subject, a worker to any other detriment;
- (d) offers to pay money, or give money's worth, to a relevant worker in return for the worker's agreement to vote in a particular way, or to abstain from voting, in a relevant ballot;
- (e) makes an outcome-specific offer to a relevant worker;
- (f) coerces, or attempts to coerce, a relevant worker to disclose—
    - (i) whether the worker intends to vote, or to abstain from voting, in any relevant ballot, or
    - (ii) how the worker intends to vote, or has voted, in any relevant ballot;
- (g) uses, or attempts to use, undue influence on a relevant worker.

(3) In sub-paragraph (2)—

- (a) 'relevant ballot' means any ballot that is or may be held in which workers are asked whether the bargaining arrangements should be ended, and
- (b) 'relevant worker' means any worker who is or would be entitled to vote in a relevant ballot.

(4) For the purposes of sub-paragraph (2)(e) an 'outcome-specific offer' is an offer to pay money, or give money's worth, which—

- (a) is conditional on—
    - (i) the issuing by the CAC of a declaration that the bargaining arrangements are to cease to have effect, or
    - (ii) the refusal by the CAC of an application under paragraph 106, 107 or 112, and
- (b) is not conditional on anything which is done or occurs as a result of that declaration, or, as the case may be, of that refusal.

(5) For the purposes of this paragraph and paragraphs 116I to 116K as they apply in relation to an application under paragraph 112, references to a party are to be read as including references to the worker or workers making the application.

(6) The duty imposed by this paragraph does not confer any rights on a worker; but that does not affect any other right which a worker may have.

(7) [omitted]

116I.—(1) A party may complain to the CAC that another party has failed to comply with paragraph 116H.

(2) A complaint under sub-paragraph (1) may not be made after—

- (a) in the case of an application under paragraph 106 or 107, the application is withdrawn;
- (b) in the case of an application under paragraph 112, an agreement or withdrawal as described in paragraph 116(1);
- (c) the CAC refuses the application under paragraph 116E(4)(a), 116K(4)(a) or (6) or 119(2);

(d) the CAC notifies the union (or unions) of a declaration issued under paragraph 116E(5) or 116K(5) in relation to the application;

(e) if the CAC informs the union (or unions) under paragraph 117(11) of a ballot, the fifth working day after—

(i) the date of the ballot, or

(ii) if votes may be cast in the ballot on more than one day, the last of those days.

(3) Within the decision period the CAC must decide whether the complaint is well-founded.

(4) A complaint is well-founded if the CAC finds that the party complained against used an unfair practice.

(5) [omitted]

116j.—(1) This paragraph applies if the CAC decides that a complaint under paragraph 116I is well-founded.

(2) The CAC must, as soon as is reasonably practicable, issue a declaration to that effect.

(3) The CAC may order the party concerned to take any action specified in the order within such period as may be so specified.

(4) Sub-paragraph (5) applies if the CAC has at any time informed the union (or unions) under paragraph 117(11) of a ballot in relation to the application (including a ballot that was cancelled or is ineffective).

(5) The CAC may make arrangements for the holding of a secret ballot in which the workers constituting the bargaining unit are asked whether the bargaining arrangements should be ended.

(6) The CAC may make an order under sub-paragraph (3), or make arrangements under sub-paragraph (5), either at the same time as it issues the declaration under sub-paragraph (2) or at any other time before any of the following occurs—

(a) in the case of an application under paragraph 106 or 107, the withdrawal of the application;

(b) in the case of an application under paragraph 112, an agreement or withdrawal as described in paragraph 116(1);

(c) the CAC refusing the application under paragraph 116E(4)(a), 116K(4)(a) or (6) or 119(2);

(d) the CAC notifying the union (or unions) of a declaration issued under paragraph 116E(5) or 116K(5) in relation to the application;

(e) if the CAC informs the union (or unions) under paragraph 117(11) of a ballot, the CAC acting under paragraph 121 in relation to the ballot.

(7) The action specified in an order under sub-paragraph (3) must be such as the CAC considers reasonable in order to mitigate the effect of the failure of the party concerned to comply with the duty imposed by paragraph 116H.

(8) The CAC may make more than one order under sub-paragraph (3).

116K.—(1) Sub-paragraphs (4) to (7) apply if—

(a) the CAC issues a declaration under paragraph 116J(2) that a complaint that a party has failed to comply with paragraph 116H is well-founded,

(b) the application under paragraph 106, 107 or 112 has not been withdrawn or, in the case of an application under paragraph 112, there has been no agreement as described in paragraph 116(1),

(c) the CAC has not refused the application under paragraph 116E(4)(a), 116K(4)(a) or (6) or 119(2),

(d) the CAC has not notified the union (or unions) of a declaration issued under paragraph 116E(5) or 116K(5) in relation to the application, and

(e) sub-paragraph (2) or (3) applies.

(2) This sub-paragraph applies if the declaration states that the unfair practice used consisted of or included—

(a) the use of violence, or.

(b) the dismissal of a union official.

(3) This sub-paragraph applies if the CAC has made an order under paragraph 116J(3) and—

(a) it is satisfied that the party subject to the order has failed to comply with it, or

(b) it makes another declaration under paragraph 116J(2) in relation to a complaint against that party.

(4) If the party that has failed to comply is the employer, the CAC may—

(a) refuse the employer's application under paragraph 106 or 107;

(b) order the employer to refrain from any campaigning in relation to an application under paragraph 112.

(5) If the party that has failed to comply is a union, the CAC may issue a declaration that the bargaining arrangements are to cease to have effect on a date specified by the CAC in the declaration; and the bargaining arrangements cease to have effect accordingly.

(6) If the party that has failed to comply is the worker making an application under paragraph 112 (or any of the workers making an application under paragraph 112), the CAC may refuse the application.

(7) The powers conferred by this paragraph are in addition to those conferred by paragraph 116J.

116L.—(1) This paragraph applies if the CAC has made an order against the employer under paragraph 116J(3) or 116K(4)(b) in relation to an application under paragraph 112.

(2) The worker making the application (or each of the workers making the application) and the union (or each of the unions) are entitled to enforce obedience to the order.

(3) The order may be enforced—

(a) in England and Wales, in the same way as an order of the county court;

(b) in Scotland, in the same way as an order of the sheriff.

Ballot on derecognition

117.—(1) This paragraph applies if the CAC accepts an application under paragraph 106 or 107.

(2) This paragraph also applies if—

(a) the CAC accepts an application under paragraph 112, and

(b) in the period mentioned in paragraph 116(1) there is no agreement or withdrawal as there described.

(3) The CAC must arrange for the holding of a secret ballot in which the workers constituting the bargaining unit are asked whether the bargaining arrangements should be ended.

(4) The ballot must be conducted by a qualified independent person appointed by the CAC.

(5) The ballot must be conducted within—

(a) the period of 20 working days starting with the day after that on which the qualified independent person is appointed, or

(b) such longer period (so starting) as the CAC may decide.

(6) The ballot must be conducted—

(a) at a workplace or workplaces decided by the CAC,

(b) by post, or

(c) by a combination of the methods described in sub-paragraphs (a) and (b), depending on the CAC's preference.

(7) In deciding how the ballot is to be conducted the CAC must take into account—

(a) the likelihood of the ballot being affected by unfairness or malpractice if it were conducted at a workplace or workplaces;

(b) costs and practicality;

(c) such other matters as the CAC considers appropriate.

(8) The CAC may not decide that the ballot is to be conducted as mentioned in sub-paragraph (6)(c) unless there are special factors making such a decision appropriate; and special factors include—

(a) factors arising from the location of workers or the nature of their employment;

(b) factors put to the CAC by the employer or the union (or unions).

(8A) If the CAC decides that the ballot must (in whole or in part) be conducted at a workplace (or workplaces), it may require arrangements to be made for workers—

(a) who (but for the arrangements) would be prevented by the CAC's decision from voting by post, and

(b) who are unable, for reasons relating to those workers as individuals, to cast their votes in the ballot at the workplace (or at any of them),

to be given the opportunity (if they request it far enough in advance of the ballot for this to be practicable) to vote by post; and the CAC's imposing such a requirement is not to be treated for the purposes of sub-paragraph (8) as a decision that the ballot be conducted as mentioned in sub-paragraph (6)(c).

(9)–(11) [omitted]

118.—(1) An employer who is informed by the CAC under paragraph 117(11) must comply with the following five duties.

(2) The first duty is to co-operate generally, in connection with the ballot, with the union (or unions) and the person appointed to conduct the ballot; and the second and third duties are not to prejudice the generality of this.

(3) The second duty is to give to the union (or unions) such access to the workers constituting the bargaining unit as is reasonable to enable the union (or unions) to inform the workers of the object of the ballot and to seek their support and their opinions on the issues involved.

(4) The third duty is to do the following (so far as it is reasonable to expect the employer to do so)—

(a) to give to the CAC, within the period of 10 working days starting with the day after that on which the employer is informed under paragraph 117(11), the names and home addresses of the workers constituting the bargaining unit;

(b) to give to the CAC, as soon as is reasonably practicable, the name and home address of any worker who joins the unit after the employer has complied with paragraph (a);

(c) to inform the CAC, as soon as is reasonably practicable, of any worker whose name has been given to the CAC under paragraph (a) or (b) but who ceases to be within the unit.

(4A) The fourth duty is to refrain from making any offer to any or all of the workers constituting the bargaining unit which—

(a) has or is likely to have the effect of inducing any or all of them not to attend any relevant meeting between the union (or unions) and the workers constituting the bargaining unit, and

(b) is not reasonable in the circumstances.

(4B) The fifth duty is to refrain from taking or threatening to take any action against a worker solely or mainly on the grounds that he—

(a) attended or took part in any relevant meeting between the union (or unions) and the workers constituting the bargaining unit, or

(b) indicated his intention to attend or take part in such a meeting.

(4C) A meeting is a relevant meeting in relation to a worker for the purposes of sub-paragraph (4A) and (4B) if—

(a) it is organised in accordance with any agreement reached concerning the second duty or as a result of a step ordered to be taken under paragraph 119 to remedy a failure to comply with that duty, and

(b) it is one which the employer is, by such an agreement or order as is mentioned in paragraph (a), required to permit the worker to attend.

(4D) Without prejudice to the generality of the second duty imposed by this paragraph, an employer is to be taken to have failed to comply with that duty if—

(a) he refuses a request for a meeting between the union (or unions) and any or all of the workers constituting the bargaining unit to be held in the absence of the employer or any representative of his (other than one who has been invited to attend the meeting) and it is not reasonable in the circumstances for him to do so,

(b) he or a representative of his attends such a meeting without having been invited to do so,

(c) he seeks to record or otherwise be informed of the proceedings at any such meeting and it is not reasonable in the circumstances for him to do so, or

(d) he refuses to give an undertaking that he will not seek to record or otherwise be informed of the proceedings at any such meeting unless it is reasonable in the circumstances for him to do either of those things.

(4E) The fourth and fifth duties do not confer any rights on a worker; but that does not affect any other right which a worker may have.

(5) As soon as is reasonably practicable after the CAC receives any information under sub-paragraph (4) it must pass it on to the person appointed to conduct the ballot.

(6) If asked to do so by the union (or unions) the person appointed to conduct the ballot must send to any worker—

(a) whose name and home address have been given under sub-paragraph (5), and

(b) who is still within the unit (so far as the person so appointed is aware),

any information supplied by the union (or unions) to the person so appointed.

(7) the duty under sub-paragraph (6) does not apply unless the union bears (or unions bear) the cost of sending the information.

(8)–(9) [omitted]

119.—(1) If the CAC is satisfied that the employer has failed to fulfil any of the duties imposed on him by paragraph 118, and the ballot has not been held, the CAC may order the employer—

(a) to take such steps to remedy the failure as the CAC considers reasonable and specifies in the order, and

(b) to do so within such period as the CAC considers reasonable and specifies in the order.

(2) If—

(a) the ballot has been arranged in consequence of an application under paragraph 106 or 107,

(b) the CAC is satisfied that the employer has failed to comply with an order under sub-paragraph (1), and

(c) the ballot has not been held, the CAC may refuse the application.

(3) [repealed]

(4) If the CAC refuses an application under sub-paragraph (2) it shall take steps to cancel the holding of the ballot; and if the ballot is held it shall have no effect.

119A.—(1) Each of the parties informed by the CAC under paragraph 117(11) must refrain from using any unfair practice.

(2) A party uses an unfair practice if, with a view to influencing the result of the ballot, the party—

(a) offers to pay money or give money's worth to a worker entitled to vote in the ballot in return for the worker's agreement to vote in a particular way or to abstain from voting,

(b) makes an outcome-specific offer to a worker entitled to vote in the ballot,

(c) coerces or attempts to coerce a worker entitled to vote in the ballot to disclose—

(i) whether he intends to vote or to abstain from voting in the ballot, or

(ii) how he intends to vote, or how he has voted, in the ballot,

(d) dismisses or threatens to dismiss a worker,

(e) takes or threatens to take disciplinary action against a worker,

(f) subjects or threatens to subject a worker to any other detriment, or

(g) uses or attempts to use undue influence on a worker entitled to vote in the ballot.

(3) For the purposes of sub-paragraph (2)(b) an 'outcome-specific offer' is an offer to pay money or give money's worth which—

(a) is conditional on—

(i) the issuing by the CAC of a declaration that the bargaining arrangements are to cease to have effect, or

(ii) the refusal by the CAC of an application under paragraph 106, 107 or 112, and

(b) is not conditional on anything which is done or occurs as a result of that declaration or, as the case may be, of that refusal.

(4) The duty imposed by this paragraph does not confer any rights on a worker; but that does not affect any other right which a worker may have.

(5) [omitted]

119B.—(1) A party may complain to the CAC that another party has failed to comply with paragraph 119A.

(2) A complaint under sub-paragraph (1) must be made on or before the first working day after—

(a) the date of the ballot, or

(b) if votes may be cast in the ballot on more than one day, the last of those days.

(3) Within the decision period the CAC must decide whether the complaint is well-founded.

(4) A complaint is well-founded if—

(a) the CAC finds that the party complained against used an unfair practice, and

(b) the CAC is satisfied that the use of that practice changed or was likely to change, in the case of a worker entitled to vote in the ballot—

(i) his intention to vote or to abstain from voting,

(ii) his intention to vote in a particular way, or

(iii) how he voted.

(5) The decision period is—

(a) the period of 10 working days starting with the day after that on which the complaint under sub-paragraph (1) was received by the CAC, or

(b) such longer period (so starting) as the CAC may specify to the parties by a notice containing reasons for the extension.

(6) If, at the beginning of the decision period, the ballot has not begun, the CAC may by notice to the parties and the qualified independent person postpone the date on which it is to begin until a date which falls after the end of the decision period.

119C.—(1) This paragraph applies if the CAC decides that a complaint under paragraph 119B is well-founded.

(2) The CAC must, as soon as is reasonably practicable, issue a declaration to that effect.

(3) The CAC may do either or both of the following—

(a) order the party concerned to take any action specified in the order within such period as may be so specified, or

(b) make arrangements for the holding of a secret ballot in which the workers constituting the bargaining unit are asked whether the bargaining arrangements should be ended.

(4) The CAC may give an order or make arrangements under sub-paragraph (3) either at the same time as it issues the declaration under sub-paragraph (2) or at any other time before it acts under paragraph 121.

(5) The action specified in an order under sub-paragraph (3)(a) shall be such as the CAC considers reasonable in order to mitigate the effect of the failure of the party complained against to comply with the duty imposed by paragraph 119A.

(6) The CAC may give more than one order under sub-paragraph (3)(a).

119D.—(1) This paragraph applies if the CAC issues a declaration under paragraph 119C(2) and the declaration states that the unfair practice used consisted of or included—

(a) the use of violence, or

(b) the dismissal of a union official.

(2) This paragraph also applies if the CAC has made an order under paragraph 119C(3)(a) and—

(a) it is satisfied that the party subject to the order has failed to comply with it, or

(b) it makes another declaration under paragraph 119C(2) in relation to a complaint against that party.

(3) If the party concerned is the employer, the CAC may refuse the employer's application under paragraph 106 or 107.

(4) If the party concerned is a union, the CAC may issue a declaration that the bargaining arrangements are to cease to have effect on a date specified by the CAC in the declaration.

(5) If a declaration is issued under sub-paragraph (4) the bargaining arrangements shall cease to have effect accordingly.

(6) The powers conferred by this paragraph are in addition to those conferred by paragraph 119C(3).

119E.—(1) This paragraph applies if the CAC issues a declaration that a complaint under paragraph 119B is well-founded and—

(a) makes arrangements under paragraph 119C(3)(b),

(b) refuses under paragraph 119D(3) or 119H(6) an application under paragraph 106, 107 or 112, or

(c) issues a declaration under paragraph 119D(4) or 119H(5).

(2) If the ballot in connection with which the complaint was made has not been held, the CAC shall take steps to cancel it.

(3) If that ballot is held, it shall have no effect.

119F.—(1) This paragraph applies if the CAC makes arrangements under paragraph 119C(3)(b).

(2) Paragraphs 117(4) to (11) and 118 to 121 apply in relation to those arrangements as they apply in relation to arrangements made under paragraph 117(3) but with the modifications specified in sub-paragraphs (3) to (5).

(3) An employer's duty under paragraph (a) of paragraph 118(4) is limited to—

(a) giving the CAC the names and home addresses of any workers in the bargaining unit which have not previously been given to it in accordance with that duty;

(b) giving the CAC the names and home addresses of those workers who have joined the bargaining unit since he last gave the CAC information in accordance with that duty;

(c) informing the CAC of any change to the name or home address of a worker whose name and home address have previously been given to the CAC in accordance with that duty; and

(d) informing the CAC of any worker whose name had previously been given to it in accordance with that duty who has ceased to be within the bargaining unit.

(4) Any order given under paragraph 119(1) or 119C(3)(a) for the purposes of the cancelled or ineffectual ballot shall have effect (to the extent that the CAC specifies in a notice to the parties) as if it were made for the purposes of the ballot for which arrangements are made under paragraph 119C(3)(b).

(5) The gross costs of the ballot shall be borne by such of the parties and in such proportions as the CAC may determine and, accordingly, sub-paragraphs (2) and (3) of paragraph 120 shall be omitted and the reference in sub-paragraph (4) of that paragraph to the employer and the union (or each of the unions) shall be construed as a reference to the party or parties which bear the costs in accordance with the CAC's determination.

119G.—(1) Paragraphs 119A to 119C, 119E and 119F apply in relation to an application under paragraph 112 as they apply in relation to an application under paragraph 106 or 107 but with the modifications specified in this paragraph.

(2) References in those paragraphs (and, accordingly, in paragraph 119H(3)) to a party shall be read as including references to the applicant worker or workers; but this is subject to sub-paragraph (3).

(3) The reference in paragraph 119A(1) to a party informed under paragraph 117(11) shall be read as including a reference to the applicant worker or workers.

119H.—(1) This paragraph applies in relation to an application under paragraph 112 in the cases specified in sub-paragraphs (2) and (3).

(2) The first case is where the CAC issues a declaration under paragraph 119C(2) and the declaration states that the unfair practice used consisted of or included—

(a) the use of violence, or

(b) the dismissal of a union official.

(3) The second case is where the CAC has made an order under paragraph 119C(3)(a) and—

(a) it is satisfied that the party subject to the order has failed to comply with it, or

(b) it makes another declaration under paragraph 119C(2) in relation to a complaint against that party.

(4) If the party concerned is the employer, the CAC may order him to refrain from further campaigning in relation to the ballot.

(5) If the party concerned is a union, the CAC may issue a declaration that the bargaining arrangements are to cease to have effect on a date specified by the CAC in the declaration.

(6) If the party concerned is the applicant worker (or any of the applicant workers), the CAC may refuse the application under paragraph 112.

(7) If a declaration is issued under sub-paragraph (5) the bargaining arrangements shall cease to have effect accordingly.

(8) The powers conferred by this paragraph are in addition to those conferred by paragraph 119C(3).

119I.—(1) This paragraph applies if—

(a) a ballot has been arranged in consequence of an application under paragraph 112,

(b) the CAC has given the employer an order under paragraph 119(1), 119C(3) or 119H (4), and

(c) the ballot for the purposes of which the order was made (or any other ballot for the purposes of which it has effect) has not been held.

(2) The applicant worker (or each of the applicant workers) and the union (or each of the unions) is entitled to enforce obedience to the order.

(3) The order may be enforced—

(a) in England and Wales, in the same way as an order of the county court;

(b) in Scotland, in the same way as an order of the sheriff.

120. [omitted]

121.—(1) As soon as is reasonably practicable after the CAC is informed of the result of a ballot by the person conducting it, the CAC must act under this paragraph.

(1A) The duty in sub-paragraph (1) does not apply if the CAC makes arrangements under paragraph 119C(3)(b).

(2) The CAC must inform the employer and the union (or unions) of the result of the ballot.

(3) If the result is that the proposition that the bargaining arrangements should be ended is supported by—

(a) a majority of the workers voting, and

(b) at least 40 per cent of the workers constituting the bargaining unit,

the CAC must issue a declaration that the bargaining arrangements are to cease to have effect on a date specified by the CAC in the declaration.

(4) If the result is otherwise the CAC must refuse the application under paragraph 106, 107 or 112.

(5) If a declaration is issued under sub-paragraph (3) the bargaining arrangements shall cease to have effect accordingly.

(6)–(8) [omitted]

122.–155. [omitted]

PART VIII DETRIMENT

Detriment

156.—(1) A worker has a right not to be subjected to any detriment by any act, or any deliberate failure to act, by his employer if the act or failure takes place on any of the grounds set out in sub-paragraph (2).

(2) The grounds are that—

(a) the worker acted with a view to obtaining or preventing recognition of a union (or unions) by the employer under this Schedule;

(b) the worker indicated that he supported or did not support recognition of a union (or unions) by the employer under this Schedule;

(c) the worker acted with a view to securing or preventing the ending under this Schedule of bargaining arrangements;

(d) the worker indicated that he supported or did not support the ending under this Schedule of bargaining arrangements;

(e) the worker influenced or sought to influence the way in which votes were to be cast by other workers in a ballot arranged under this Schedule;

(f) the worker influenced or sought to influence other workers to vote or to abstain from voting in such a ballot;

(g) the worker voted in such a ballot;

(h) the worker proposed to do, failed to do, or proposed to decline to do, any of the things referred to in paragraphs (a) to (g).

(3) A ground does not fall within sub-paragraph (2) if it constitutes an unreasonable act or omission by the worker.

(4) This paragraph does not apply if the worker is an employee and the detriment amounts to dismissal within the meaning of the Employment Rights Act 1996.

(5) A worker may present a complaint to an employment tribunal on the ground that he has been subjected to a detriment in contravention of this paragraph.

(6) Apart from the remedy by way of complaint as mentioned in sub-paragraph (5), a worker has no remedy for infringement of the right conferred on him by this paragraph.

157.—(1) An employment tribunal shall not consider a complaint under paragraph 156 unless it is presented—

(a) before the end of the period of 3 months starting with the date of the act or failure to which the complaint relates or, if that act or failure is part of a series of similar acts or failures (or both), the last of them, or

(b) where the tribunal is satisfied that it was not reasonably practicable for the complaint to be presented before the end of that period, within such further period as it considers reasonable.

(2) For the purposes of sub-paragraph (1)—

(a) where an act extends over a period, the reference to the date of the act is a reference to the last day of that period;

(b) a failure to act shall be treated as done when it was decided on.

(3) For the purposes of sub-paragraph (2), in the absence of evidence establishing the contrary an employer must be taken to decide on a failure to act—

(a) when he does an act inconsistent with doing the failed act, or

(b) if he has done no such inconsistent act, when the period expires within which he might reasonably have been expected to do the failed act if it was to be done.

(4) [omitted]

158. On a complaint under paragraph 156 it shall be for the employer to show the ground on which he acted or failed to act.

159.—(1) If the employment tribunal finds that a complaint under paragraph 156 is well-founded it shall make a declaration to that effect and may make an award of compensation to be paid by the employer to the complainant in respect of the act or failure complained of.

(2) The amount of the compensation awarded shall be such as the tribunal considers just and equitable in all the circumstances having regard to the infringement complained of and to any loss sustained by the complainant which is attributable to the act or failure which infringed his right.

(3) The loss shall be taken to include—

(a) any expenses reasonably incurred by the complainant in consequence of the act or failure complained of, and

(b) loss of any benefit which he might reasonably be expected to have had but for that act or failure.

(4) In ascertaining the loss, the tribunal shall apply the same rule concerning the duty of a person to mitigate his loss as applies to damages recoverable under the common law of England and Wales or Scotland.

(5) If the tribunal finds that the act or failure complained of was to any extent caused or contributed to by action of the complainant, it shall reduce the amount of the compensation by such proportion as it considers just and equitable having regard to the finding.

160.—(1) If the employment tribunal finds that a complaint under paragraph 156 is well-founded and—

(a) the detriment of which the worker has complained is the termination of his worker's contract, but

(b) that contract was not a contract of employment,

any compensation awarded under paragraph 159 must not exceed the limit specified in sub-paragraph (2).

(2) The limit is the total of—

(a) the sum which would be the basic award for unfair dismissal, calculated in accordance with section 119 of the Employment Rights Act 1996, if the worker had been an employee and the contract terminated had been a contract of employment, and

(b) the sum for the time being specified in section 124(1) of that Act which is the limit for a compensatory award to a person calculated in accordance with section 123 of that Act.

Dismissal

161.—(1) For the purposes of Part X of the Employment Rights Act 1996 (unfair dismissal) the dismissal of an employee shall be regarded as unfair if the dismissal was made—

(a) for a reason set out in sub-paragraph (2), or

(b) for reasons the main one of which is one of those set out in sub-paragraph (2).

(2) The reasons are that—

(a) the employee acted with a view to obtaining or preventing recognition of a union (or unions) by the employer under this Schedule;

(b) the employee indicated that he supported or did not support recognition of a union (or unions) by the employer under this Schedule;

(c) the employee acted with a view to securing or preventing the ending under this Schedule of bargaining arrangements;

(d) the employee indicated that he supported or did not support the ending under this Schedule of bargaining arrangements;

(e) the employee influenced or sought to influence the way in which votes were to be cast by other workers in a ballot arranged under this Schedule;

(f) the employee influenced or sought to influence other workers to vote or to abstain from voting in such a ballot;

(g) the employee voted in such a ballot;

(h) the employee proposed to do, failed to do, or proposed to decline to do, any of the things referred to in paragraphs (a) to (g).

(3) A reason does not fall within sub-paragraph (2) if it constitutes an unreasonable act or omission by the employee.

Selection for redundancy

162. For the purposes of Part X of the Employment Rights Act 1996 (unfair dismissal) the dismissal of an employee shall be regarded as unfair if the reason or principal reason for the dismissal was that he was redundant but it is shown—

(a) that the circumstances constituting the redundancy applied equally to one or more other employees in the same undertaking who held positions similar to that held by him and who have not been dismissed by the employer, and

(b) that the reason (or, if more than one, the principal reason) why he was selected for dismissal was one falling within paragraph 161(2).

Employees with fixed-term contracts

163. [omitted]

Exclusion of requirement as to qualifying period

164. Sections 108 and 109 of the Employment Rights Act 1996 (qualifying period and upper age limit for unfair dismissal protection) do not apply to a dismissal which by virtue of paragraph 161 or 162 is regarded as unfair for the purposes of Part X of that Act.

Meaning of worker's contract

165. References in this Part of this Schedule to a worker's contract are to the contract mentioned in paragraph (a) or (b) of section 296(1) or the arrangements for the employment mentioned in paragraph (c) of section 296(1).

PART IX GENERAL

165A.–170A. [omitted]

CAC's general duty

171. In exercising functions under this Schedule in any particular case the CAC must have regard to the object of encouraging and promoting fair and efficient practices and arrangements in the workplace, so far as having regard to that object is consistent with applying other provisions of this Schedule in the case concerned.

'Pay' and other matters subject to collective bargaining

171A.—(1) In this Schedule 'pay' does not include terms relating to a person's membership of or rights under, or his employer's contributions to—

(a) an occupational pension scheme (as defined by section 1 of the Pension Schemes Act 1993), or

(b) a personal pension scheme (as so defined).

(2)–(7) [omitted]

172. [omitted]

Section 207A

SCHEDULE A2

TRIBUNAL JURISDICTIONS TO WHICH SECTION 207A APPLIES

Section 145A of this Act (inducements relating to union membership or activities).

Section 145B of this Act (inducements relating to collective bargaining).

Section 146 of this Act (detriment in relation to union membership and activities).

Section 189 of this Act (failure to follow consultation requirements).

Paragraph 156 of Schedule A1 to this Act (detriment in relation to union recognition rights).

Section 23 of the Employment Rights Act 1996 (c. 18) (unauthorised deductions and payments).

Section 27K of that Act (complaints about tips etc).

Section 27N of that Act (complaints about information).

Section 48 of that Act (detriment in employment).

Section 111 of that Act (unfair dismissal).

Section 163 of that Act (redundancy payments).

Section 24 of the National Minimum Wage Act 1998 (c. 39) (detriment in relation to national minimum wage).

Sections 120 and 127 of the Equality Act 2010 (discrimination etc. in work cases).

The Employment Tribunal Extension of Jurisdiction (England and Wales) Order 1994 (SI 1994/1623) (breach of employment contract and termination).

The Employment Tribunal Extension of Jurisdiction (Scotland) Order 1994 (SI 1994/1624) (corresponding provision for Scotland).

Regulation 30 of the Working Time Regulations 1998 (SI 1998/1833) (breach of regulations).

Regulation 32 of the Transnational Information and Consultation of Employees Regulations 1999 (SI 1999/3323) (detriment relating to European Works Councils).

Regulation 45 of the European Public Limited-Liability Company Regulations 2004 (SI 2004/2326) (detriment in employment).

Regulation 33 of the Information and Consultation of Employees Regulations 2004 (SI 2004/3426) (detriment in employment).

Paragraph 8 of the Schedule to the Occupational and Personal Pension Schemes (Consultation by Employers and Miscellaneous Amendment) Regulations 2006 (SI 2006/349) (detriment in employment).

Regulation 34 of the European Cooperative Society (Involvement of Employees) Regulations 2006 (SI 2006/2059) (detriment in relation to involvement in a European Cooperative Society).

Regulation 17 of the Cross-border Railway Services (Working Time) Regulations 2008 (SI 2008/1660) (breach of regulations).

Regulation 9 of the Employment Relations Act 1999 (Blacklists) Regulations 2010 (SI 2010/493) (detriment connected with prohibited list).

Sections 120 and 127 of the Equality Act 2010 (discrimination etc in work cases).

SCHEDULES A3 AND A4 [OMITTED]

Employment Rights Act 1996

(1996, c. 18)

PART I EMPLOYMENT PARTICULARS

Right to statements of employment particulars

1 Statement of initial employment particulars
2 Statement of initial particulars: supplementary
3 Note about disciplinary procedures and pensions
4 Statement of changes
5 Exclusion from rights to statements
6 Reasonably accessible document or collective agreement
7 Power to require particulars of further matters
7A Use of alternative documents to give particulars
7B Giving of alternative documents before start of employment

Right to itemised pay statement

8 Itemised pay statement
9 Standing statement of fixed deductions

Enforcement

11 References to employment tribunals
12 Determination of references

PART II PROTECTION OF WAGES

Deductions by employer

13 Right not to suffer unauthorised deductions
14 Excepted deductions

Payments to employer

15 Right not to have to make payments to employer
16 Excepted payments

Cash shortages and stock deficiencies in retail employment

17 Introductory
18 Limits on amount and time of deductions
19 Wages determined by reference to shortages etc.
20 Limits on method and timing of payments
21 Limit on amount of payments
22 Final instalments of wages

Enforcement

23 Complaints to employment tribunals
24 Determination of complaints
25 Determinations: supplementary
26 Complaints and other remedies

Supplementary

27 Meaning of 'wages' etc.

PART 2A ZERO HOURS WORKERS AND SIMILAR

Exclusivity terms and other restrictions

27A Exclusivity terms unenforceable in zero hours contracts

Chapter II Right to guaranteed hours

Guaranteed hours offers

27BA Right for qualifying workers to be offered guaranteed hours
27BB Requirements relating to a guaranteed hours offer
27BE Acceptance or rejection of a guaranteed hours offer

Enforcement

27BG Complaints to employment tribunals: grounds
27BH Complaints to employment tribunals: time limits
27BI Remedies

Shifts: rights to reasonable notice

27BJ Right to reasonable notice of a shift
27BK Right to reasonable notice of cancellation of or change to a shift
27BN Complaints to employment tribunals
27BO Remedies

Right to payment for cancelled, moved and curtailed shifts

27BP Right to payment for a cancelled, moved or curtailed shift
27BR Exceptions to duty to make payment for a cancelled, moved or curtailed shift
27BS Contractual remuneration
27BT Complaints to employment tribunal
27BU Remedies

Agency workers: guaranteed hours and rights relating to shifts

27BV Agency workers

PART 2B TIPS, GRATUITIES AND SERVICE CHARGES

Requirement to deal with tips, gratuities and service charges

27C Qualifying tips, gratuities and service charges
27D How tips etc must be dealt with
27G When tips etc must be dealt with
27H Agency workers

Information

27I Written policy
27J Records

Enforcement

27K Complaints to employment tribunal about tips etc
27L Determination of complaints about tips etc
27M Compensation: dealing with tips etc

PART IVA PROTECTED DISCLOSURES

43A Meaning of 'protected disclosure'
43B Disclosures qualifying for protection
43C Disclosure to employer or other responsible person

43D Disclosure to legal adviser
43E Disclosure to Minister of the Crown
43F Disclosure to prescribed person
43G Disclosure in other cases
43H Disclosure of exceptionally serious failure
43J Contractual duties of confidentiality
43K Extension of meaning of 'worker' etc. for Part IVA
43L Other interpretative provisions.

PART V PROTECTION FROM SUFFERING DETRIMENT IN EMPLOYMENT

Rights not to suffer detriment
44 Health and safety cases
45A Working time cases
47 Employee representatives
47A Employees exercising right to time off work for study or training
47B Protected disclosures
47C Leave for family and domestic reasons
47E Flexible working
47G Employee shareholder status

Enforcement
48 Complaints to employment tribunals
49 Remedies

PART VI TIME OFF WORK

Public duties
50 Right to time off for public duties
51 Complaints to employment tribunals

Looking for work and making arrangements for training
52 Right to time off to look for work or arrange training
53 Right to remuneration for time off under section 52
54 Complaints to employment tribunals

Ante-natal care
55 Right to time off for ante-natal care
56 Right to remuneration for time off under section 55
57 Complaints to employment tribunals

Dependants
57A Time off for dependants
57B Complaint to employment tribunal

Employee representatives
61 Right to time off for employee representatives
62 Right to remuneration for time off under section 61
63 Complaints to employment tribunals

PART VII SUSPENSION FROM WORK

Suspension on medical grounds
64 Right to remuneration on suspension on medical grounds
65 Exclusions from right to remuneration

Suspension on maternity grounds
66 Meaning of suspension on maternity grounds
67 Right to offer of alternative work
68 Right to remuneration

General
69 Calculation of remuneration
69A Calculation of remuneration (agency workers)
70 Complaints to employment tribunals
70A Complaints to employment tribunals: agency workers

PART VIII

Chapter I Maternity Leave
71 Ordinary maternity leave
72 Compulsory maternity leave
73 Additional maternity leave

Chapter 1A Adoption Leave
75A Ordinary adoption leave
75B Additional adoption leave

Chapter II Parental Leave
80 Complaint to employment tribunal

PART 8A FLEXIBLE WORKING
80F Statutory right to request contract variation
80G Employer's duties in relation to application under section 80F
80H Complaints to employment tribunals
80I Remedies

PART 8B CARER'S LEAVE
80J Carer's leave
80K Rights during and after carer's leave
80L Special cases
80M Part 8B: supplemental
80N Complaint to employment tribunal

PART IX TERMINATION OF EMPLOYMENT

Minimum period of notice
86 Rights of employer and employee to minimum notice
87 Rights of employee in period of notice
88 Employments with normal working hours
89 Employments without normal working hours
90 Short-term incapacity benefit, contributory employment and support allowance and industrial injury benefit
91 Supplementary

Written statement of reasons for dismissal
92 Right to written statement of reasons for dismissal
93 Complaints to employment tribunal

PART X UNFAIR DISMISSAL

Chapter I Right not to be Unfairly Dismissed

The right
94 The right

Dismissal
95 Circumstances in which an employee is dismissed
97 Effective date of termination

Fairness
98 General

Other dismissals
99 Leave for family reasons
100 Health and safety cases
101A Working time cases
103 Employee representatives
103A Protected disclosure
104 Assertion of statutory right
104A The national minimum wage
104C Flexible working
104F Blacklists
104G Employee shareholder status
104I Contracts of employment: restricted variations
104J Contracts of employment: variations that are not restricted variations
104K Redundancy: replacement of employees with people who are not employees
105 Redundancy
106 Replacements
107 Pressure on employer to dismiss unfairly

Exclusion of right
108 Qualifying period of employment

Chapter II Remedies for Unfair Dismissal

Introductory
111 Complaints to employment tribunal
112 The remedies: orders and compensation

Orders for reinstatement or re-engagement
113 The orders
114 Order for reinstatement
115 Order for re-engagement
116 Choice of order and its terms
117 Enforcement of order and compensation

Compensation
118 General
119 Basic award
120 Basic award: minimum in certain cases
121 Basic award of two weeks' pay in certain cases
122 Basic award: reductions
123 Compensatory award
124 Limit of compensatory award etc.
124A Adjustments under the Employment Act 2002
126 Acts which are both unfair dismissal and discrimination

Interim relief
128 Interim relief pending determination of complaint
129 Procedure on hearing of application and making of order
130 Order for continuation of contract of employment
131 Application for variation or revocation of order
132 Consequence of failure to comply with order

PART XI REDUNDANCY PAYMENTS ETC.

Chapter I Right to Redundancy Payment

135 The right

Chapter II Right on Dismissal by Reason of Redundancy

Dismissal by reason of redundancy
136 Circumstances in which an employee is dismissed
138 No dismissal in cases of renewal of contract or re-engagement
139 Redundancy

Exclusions
140 Summary dismissal
141 Renewal of contract or re-engagement
142 Employee anticipating expiry of employer's notice
143 Strike during currency of employer's notice
144 Provisions supplementary to section 143

Supplementary
145 The relevant date
146 Provisions supplementing sections 138 and 141

Chapter III Right by Reason of Lay-Off or Short-Time

Lay-off and short-time
147 Meaning of 'lay-off' and 'short-time'
148 Eligibility by reason of lay-off or short-time

Exclusions
149 Counter-notices
150 Resignation
151 Dismissal
152 Likelihood of full employment

Supplementary
153 The relevant date
154 Provisions supplementing sections 148 and 152

Chapter IV General Exclusions from Right

155 Qualifying period of employment

Chapter V Other Provisions about Redundancy Payments

162 Amount of a redundancy payment
163 References to employment tribunals
164 Claims for redundancy payment
165 Written particulars of redundancy payment

Chapter VII Supplementary

Application of Part to particular cases
173 Employees paid by person other than employer

Death of employer or employee
174 Death of employer: dismissal
176 Death of employee

Other supplementary provisions
180 Offences
181 Interpretation

PART XII INSOLVENCY OF EMPLOYERS
182 Employee's rights on insolvency of employer
184 Debts to which Part applies
185 The appropriate date
186 Limit on amount payable under section 182

PART XIII MISCELLANEOUS

Chapter I Particular Types of Employment
Crown employment etc.
191 Crown employment
192 Armed forces
193 National security

Chapter II Other Miscellaneous Matters
Restrictions on disclosure of information
202 National security
Harassment and discrimination: contractual duties of confidentiality
202A Contractual duties of confidentiality relating to harassment and discrimination
Contracting out etc. and remedies
203 Restrictions on contracting out
204 Law governing employment
205 Remedy for infringement of certain rights
Employee shareholder status
205A Employee shareholders

PART XIV INTERPRETATION

Chapter I Continuous Employment
210 Introductory
211 Period of continuous employment
212 Weeks counting in computing period
213 Intervals in employment
214 Special provisions for redundancy payments
215 Employment abroad etc.
216 Industrial disputes
218 Change of employer

Chapter II A Week's Pay
Introductory
220 Introductory
Employments with normal working hours
221 General
222 Remuneration varying according to time of work
223 Supplementary
Employments with no normal working hours
224 Employments with no normal working hours
The calculation date
225 Rights during employment
226 Rights on termination
Maximum amount of week's pay
227 Maximum amount
Miscellaneous
228 New employments and other special cases
229 Supplementary

Chapter III Other Interpretation Provisions
230 Employees, workers etc.
231 Associated employers
234 Normal working hours
235 Other definitions

PART I EMPLOYMENT PARTICULARS

Right to statements of employment particulars

1 Statement of initial employment particulars

(1) Where a worker begins employment with an employer, the employer shall give to the worker a written statement of particulars of employment.

(2) Subject to sections 2(2) to (4)—

(a) the particulars required by subsections (3) and (4) must be included in a single document; and

(b) the statement must be given not later than the beginning of the employment.

(3) The statement shall contain particulars of—

(a) the names of the employer and worker,

(b) the date when the employment began, and

(c) in the case of a statement given to an employee the date on which the employee's period of continuous employment began (taking into account any employment with a previous employer which counts towards that period).

(4) The statement shall also contain particulars, as at a specified date not more than seven days before the statement (or the instalment of a statement given under section 2(4) containing them) is given, of—

(a) the scale or rate of remuneration or the method of calculating remuneration,

(b) the intervals at which remuneration is paid (that is, weekly, monthly or other specified intervals),

(c) any terms and conditions relating to hours of work including any terms and conditions relating to—

(i) normal working hours,

(ii) the days of the week the worker is required to work, and

(iii) whether or not such hours or days may be variable, and if they may be how they vary or how that variation is to be determined.

(d) any terms and conditions relating to any of the following—

(i) entitlement to holidays, including public holidays, and holiday pay (the particulars given being sufficient to enable the worker's entitlement, including any entitlement to accrued holiday pay on the termination of employment, to be precisely calculated),

(ii) incapacity for work due to sickness or injury, including any provision for sick pay,

(iia) any other paid leave, and

(iii) pensions and pension schemes,

(da) any other benefits provided by the employer that do not fall within another paragraph of this subsection,

(e) the length of notice which the worker is obliged to give and entitled to receive to terminate his contract of employment or other worker's contract,

(f) the title of the job which the worker is employed to do or a brief description of the work for which he is employed,

(g) where the employment is not intended to be permanent, the period for which it is expected to continue or, if it is for a fixed term, the date when it is to end,

(ga) any probationary period, including any conditions and its duration,

(h) either the place of work or, where the worker is required or permitted to work at various places, an indication of that and of the address of the employer,

(j) any collective agreements which directly affect the terms and conditions of the employment including, where the employer is not a party, the persons by whom they were made,

(k) where the worker is required to work outside the United Kingdom for a period of more than one month—

(i) the period for which he is to work outside the United Kingdom,

(ii) the currency in which remuneration is to be paid while he is working outside the United Kingdom,

(iii) any additional remuneration payable to him, and any benefits to be provided to or in respect of him, by reason of his being required to work outside the United Kingdom, and

(iv) any terms and conditions relating to his return to the United Kingdom,

(l) any training entitlement provided by the employer,

(m) any part of that training entitlement which the employer requires the worker to complete, and

(n) any other training which the employer requires the worker to complete and which the employer will not bear the cost of.

(5) Subsection (4)(d)(iii) does not apply to a worker of a body or authority if—

(a) the worker's pension rights depend on the terms of a pension scheme established under any provision contained in or having effect under any Act, and

(b) any such provision requires the body or authority to give to a new worker information concerning the worker's pension rights or the determination of questions affecting those rights.

(6) In this section 'probationary period' means a temporary period specified in the contract of employment or other worker's contract between a worker and an employer that—

(a) commences at the beginning of the employment, and

(b) is intended to enable the employer to assess the worker's suitability for the employment.

2 Statement of initial particulars: supplementary

(1) If, in the case of a statement under section 1, there are no particulars to be entered under any of the heads of paragraph (d) or (k) of subsection (4) of that section, or under any of the other paragraphs of subsection (3) or (4) of that section, that fact shall be stated.

(2) A statement under section 1 may refer the worker for particulars of any of the matters specified in subsection (4)(d)(ii) to (iii) and (l) of that section to the provisions of some other document which is reasonably accessible to the worker.

(3) A statement under section 1 may refer the worker for particulars of either of the matters specified in subsection (4)(e) of that section to the law or to the provisions of any collective agreement directly affecting the terms and conditions of the employment which is reasonably accessible to the worker.

(4) A statement, insofar as it relates to the particulars required by section 1(4)(d)(iii), (j) and (l) and the note required by section 3—

(a) may be given in instalments; and

(b) must be given not later than two months after the beginning of the employment, even where the employment ends before that date.

(5) Where before the end of the period of two months after the beginning of a worker's employment the worker is to begin to work outside the United Kingdom for a period of more than one month, any instalment of a statement given under subsection (4) shall be given to him not later than the time when he leaves the United Kingdom in order to begin so to work.

(6) [repealed]

3 Note about disciplinary procedures and pensions

(1) A statement under section 1 shall include a note—

(a) specifying any disciplinary rules applicable to the worker or referring the worker to the provisions of a document specifying such rules which is reasonably accessible to the worker,

(aa) specifying any procedure applicable to the taking of disciplinary decisions relating to the worker, or to a decision to dismiss the worker, or referring the worker to the provisions of a document specifying such a procedure which is reasonably accessible to the worker,

(b) specifying (by description or otherwise)—

(i) a person to whom the worker can apply if dissatisfied with any disciplinary decision relating to him, or any decision to dismiss him, and

(ii) a person to whom the worker can apply for the purpose of seeking redress of any grievance relating to his employment, and the manner in which any such application should be made, and

(c) where there are further steps consequent on any such application, explaining those steps or referring to the provisions of a document explaining them which is reasonably accessible to the worker.

(2) Subsection (1) does not apply to rules, disciplinary decisions, decisions to dismiss, grievances or procedures relating to health or safety at work.

(3)–(5) [repealed]

4 Statement of changes

(1) If, after the material date, there is a change in any of the matters particulars of which are required by sections 1 to 3 to be included or referred to in a statement under section 1, the employer shall give to the worker a written statement containing particulars of the change.

(2) For the purposes of subsection (1)—

(a) in relation to a matter particulars of which are included or referred to in a statement given under section 1, the material date is the date to which the statement relates,

(b) in relation to a matter particulars of which—

(i) are included or referred to in an instalment of a statement given under section 2(4),

(ii) [repealed]

the material date is the date to which the instalment relates, and

(c) in relation to any other matter, the material date is the date by which a statement under section 1 is required to be given.

(3) A statement under subsection (1) shall be given at the earliest opportunity and, in any event, not later than—

(a) one month after the change in question, or

(b) where that change results from the worker being required to work outside the United Kingdom for a period of more than one month, the time when he leaves the United Kingdom in order to begin so to work, if that is earlier.

(4) A statement under subsection (1) may refer the worker to the provisions of some other document which is reasonably accessible to the worker for a change in any of the matters specified in sections 1(4)(d)(ii) to (iii) and 3(1)(a) and (c).

(5) A statement under subsection (1) may refer the worker for a change in either of the matters specified in section 1(4)(e) to the law or to the provisions of any collective agreement directly affecting the terms and conditions of the employment which is reasonably accessible to the worker.

(6) Where, after an employer has given to a worker a statement under section 1, either—

(a) the name of the employer (whether an individual or a body corporate or partnership) is changed without any change in the identity of the employer, or

(b) in the case of a statement given to an employee the identity of the employer is changed in circumstances in which the continuity of the employee's period of employment is not broken,

and subsection (7) applies in relation to the change, the person who is the employer immediately after the change is not required to give to the worker a statement under section 1; but the change shall be treated as a change falling within subsection (1) of this section.

(7) This subsection applies in relation to a change if it does not involve any change in any of the matters (other than the names of the parties) particulars of which are required by sections 1 to 3 to be included or referred to in the statement under section 1.

(8) A statement under subsection (1) which informs an employee of a change such as is referred to in subsection (6)(b) shall specify the date on which the employee's period of continuous employment began.

5 Exclusion from rights to statements

(1) Sections 1 to 4 apply to a worker who at any time comes or ceases to come within the exceptions from those sections provided by section 199, and under section 209, as if his employment with his employer terminated or began at that time.

(2) The fact that section 1 is directed by subsection (1) to apply to a worker as if his employment began on his ceasing to come within the exceptions referred to in that subsection does not affect the obligation under section 1(3)(b) to specify the date on which his employment actually began.

6 Reasonably accessible document or collective agreement

In sections 2 to 4 references to a document or collective agreement which is reasonably accessible to a worker are references to a document or collective agreement which—

(a) the worker has reasonable opportunities of reading in the course of his employment, or

(b) is made reasonably accessible to the worker in some other way.

7 Power to require particulars of further matters

The Secretary of State may by order provide that section 1 shall have effect as if particulars of such further matters as may be specified in the order were included in the particulars required by that section; and, for that purpose, the order may include such provisions amending that section as appear to the Secretary of State to be expedient.

7A Use of alternative documents to give particulars

(1) Subsections (2) and (3) apply where—

(a) an employer gives a worker a document in writing in the form of a contract of employment or other worker's contract or letter of engagement,

(b) the document contains information which, were the document in the form of a statement under section 1, would meet the employer's obligation under that section in relation to the matters mentioned in that section save for the particulars specified in section 2(4), and

(c) the document is given not later than the beginning of the employment.

(2) The employer's duty under section 1 in relation to any matter shall be treated as met if the document given to the worker contains information which, were the document in the form of a statement under that section, would meet the employer's obligation under that section in relation to that matter.

(3) The employer's duty under section 3 shall be treated as met if the document given to the worker contains information which, were the document in the form of a statement under section 1 and the information included in the form of a note, would meet the employer's obligation under section 3.

(4) For the purposes of this section a document to which subsection (1)(a) applies shall be treated, in relation to information in respect of any of the matters mentioned in section 1(4), as specifying the date on which the document is given to the worker as the date as at which the information applies.

(5) Where subsection (2) applies in relation to any matter, the date on which the document by virtue of which that subsection applies is given to the worker shall be the material date in relation to that matter for the purposes of section 4(1).

(6) Where subsection (3) applies, the date on which the document by virtue of which that subsection applies is given to the worker shall be the material date for the purposes of section 4(1) in relation to the matters of which particulars are required to be given under section 3.

(7) The reference in section 4(6) to an employer having given a statement under section 1 shall be treated as including his having given a document by virtue of which his duty to give such a statement is treated as met.

7B Giving of alternative documents before start of employment

A document in the form of a contract of employment or other worker's contract or letter of engagement given by an employer to a worker before the beginning of the worker's employment with the employer shall, when the employment begins, be treated for the purposes of section 7A as having been given at that time.

Right to itemised pay statement

8 Itemised pay statement

(1) A worker has the right to be given by his employer, at or before the time at which any payment of wages or salary is made to him, a written itemised pay statement.

(2) The statement shall contain particulars of—

(a) the gross amount of the wages or salary,

(b) the amounts of any variable, and (subject to section 9) any fixed, deductions from that gross amount and the purposes for which they are made,
(c) the net amount of wages or salary payable,
(d) where different parts of the net amount are paid in different ways, the amount and method of payment of each part-payment, and
(e) where the amount of wages or salary varies by reference to time worked, the total number of hours worked in respect of the variable amount of wages or salary either as—
(i) a single aggregate figure, or
(ii) separate figures for different types of work or different rates of pay.

9 Standing statement of fixed deductions

(1) A pay statement given in accordance with section 8 need not contain separate particulars of a fixed deduction if—
(a) it contains instead an aggregate amount of fixed deductions, including that deduction, and
(b) the employer has given to the worker, at or before the time at which the pay statement is given, a standing statement of fixed deductions which satisfies subsection (2).

(2) A standing statement of fixed deductions satisfies this subsection if—
(a) it is in writing,
(b) it contains, in relation to each deduction comprised in the aggregate amount of deductions, particulars of—
(i) the amount of the deduction,
(ii) the intervals at which the deduction is to be made, and
(iii) the purpose for which it is made, and
(c) it is (in accordance with subsection (5)) effective at the date on which the pay statement is given.

(3) A standing statement of fixed deductions may be amended, whether by—
(a) addition of a new deduction,
(b) a change in the particulars, or
(c) cancellation of an existing deduction,
by notice in writing, containing particulars of the amendment, given by the employer to the worker.

(4) An employer who has given to a worker a standing statement of fixed deductions shall—
(a) within the period of twelve months beginning with the date on which the first standing statement was given, and
(b) at intervals of not more than twelve months afterwards,
re-issue it in a consolidated form incorporating any amendments notified in accordance with subsection (3).

(5) For the purposes of subsection (2)(c) a standing statement of fixed deductions—
(a) becomes effective on the date on which it is given to the worker, and
(b) ceases to be effective at the end of the period of twelve months beginning with that date or, where it is re-issued in accordance with subsection (4), with the end of the period of twelve months beginning with the date of the last re-issue.

10 [omitted]

Enforcement

11 References to employment tribunals

(1) Where an employer does not give a worker a statement as required by section 1, 4 or 8 (either because the employer gives the worker no statement or because the statement the employer gives does not comply with what is required), the worker may require a reference to be made to an employment tribunal to determine what particulars ought to have been included or referred to in a statement so as to comply with the requirements of the section concerned.

(2) Where—

(a) a statement purporting to be a statement under section 1 or 4, or a pay statement or a standing statement of fixed deductions purporting to comply with section 8 or 9, has been given to a worker, and

(b) a question arises as to the particulars which ought to have been included or referred to in the statement so as to comply with the requirements of this Part,

either the employer or the worker may require the question to be referred to and determined by an employment tribunal.

(3) For the purposes of this section—

(a) [repealed]

(b) a question as to the particulars which ought to have been included in a pay statement or standing statement of fixed deductions does not include a question solely as to the accuracy of an amount stated in any such particulars.

(4) An employment tribunal shall not consider a reference under this section in a case where the employment to which the reference relates has ceased unless an application requiring the reference to be made was made—

(a) before the end of the period of three months beginning with the date on which the employment ceased, or

(b) within such further period as the tribunal considers reasonable in a case where it is satisfied that it was not reasonably practicable for the application to be made before the end of that period of three months.

(5) [repealed]

(6) [omitted]

12 Determination of references

(1) Where, on a reference under section 11(1), an employment tribunal determines particulars as being those which ought to have been included or referred to in a statement given under section 1 or 4, the employer shall be deemed to have given to the worker a statement in which those particulars were included, or referred to, as specified in the decision of the tribunal.

(2) On determining a reference under section 11(2) relating to a statement purporting to be a statement under section 1 or 4, an employment tribunal may—

(a) confirm the particulars as included or referred to in the statement given by the employer,

(b) amend those particulars, or

(c) substitute other particulars for them,

as the tribunal may determine to be appropriate; and the statement shall be deemed to have been given by the employer to the worker in accordance with the decision of the tribunal.

(3) Where on a reference under section 11 an employment tribunal finds—

(a) that an employer has failed to give a worker any pay statement in accordance with section 8, or

(b) that a pay statement or standing statement of fixed deductions does not, in relation to a deduction, contain the particulars required to be included in that statement by that section or section 9,

the tribunal shall make a declaration to that effect.

(4) Where on a reference in the case of which subsection (3) applies the tribunal further finds that any unnotified deductions have been made from the pay of the worker during the period of thirteen weeks immediately preceding the date of the application for the reference (whether or not the deductions were made in breach of the contract of employment), the tribunal may order the employer to pay the worker a sum not exceeding the aggregate of the unnotified deductions so made.

(5) For the purposes of subsection (4) a deduction is an unnotified deduction if it is made without the employer giving the worker, in any pay statement or standing statement of fixed deductions, the particulars of the deduction required by section 8 or 9.

PART II PROTECTION OF WAGES

Deductions by employer

13 Right not to suffer unauthorised deductions

(1) An employer shall not make a deduction from wages of a worker employed by him unless—

(a) the deduction is required or authorised to be made by virtue of a statutory provision or a relevant provision of the worker's contract, or

(b) the worker has previously signified in writing his agreement or consent to the making of the deduction.

(2) In this section 'relevant provision', in relation to a worker's contract, means a provision of the contract comprised—

(a) in one or more written terms of the contract of which the employer has given the worker a copy on an occasion prior to the employer making the deduction in question, or

(b) in one or more terms of the contract (whether express or implied and, if express, whether oral or in writing) the existence and effect, or combined effect, of which in relation to the worker the employer has notified to the worker in writing on such an occasion.

(3) Where the total amount of wages paid on any occasion by an employer to a worker employed by him is less than the total amount of the wages properly payable by him to the worker on that occasion (after deductions), the amount of the deficiency shall be treated for the purposes of this Part as a deduction made by the employer from the worker's wages on that occasion.

(4) Subsection (3) does not apply in so far as the deficiency is attributable to an error of any description on the part of the employer affecting the computation by him of the gross amount of the wages properly payable by him to the worker on that occasion.

(5) For the purposes of this section a relevant provision of a worker's contract having effect by virtue of a variation of the contract does not operate to authorise the making of a deduction on account of any conduct of the worker, or any other event occurring, before the variation took effect.

(6) For the purposes of this section an agreement or consent signified by a worker does not operate to authorise the making of a deduction on account of any conduct of the worker, or any other event occurring, before the agreement or consent was signified.

(7) This section does not affect any other statutory provision by virtue of which a sum payable to a worker by his employer but not constituting 'wages' within the meaning of this Part is not to be subject to a deduction at the instance of the employer.

(8) In relation to deductions from amounts of qualifying tips, gratuities and service charges allocated to workers under Part 2B, subsection (1) applies as if—

(a) in paragraph (a), the words 'or a relevant provision of the worker's contract' were omitted, and

(b) paragraph (b) were omitted.

14 Excepted deductions

(1) Section 13 does not apply to a deduction from a worker's wages made by his employer where the purpose of the deduction is the reimbursement of the employer in respect of—

(a) an overpayment of wages, or

(b) an overpayment in respect of expenses incurred by the worker in carrying out his employment,

made (for any reason) by the employer to the worker.

(2) Section 13 does not apply to a deduction from a worker's wages made by his employer in consequence of any disciplinary proceedings if those proceedings were held by virtue of a statutory provision.

(3) Section 13 does not apply to a deduction from a worker's wages made by his employer in pursuance of a requirement imposed on the employer by a statutory provision to deduct and pay over to a public authority amounts determined by that authority as being due to it from the worker if the deduction is made in accordance with the relevant determination of that authority.

(4) Section 13 does not apply to a deduction from a worker's wages made by his employer in pursuance of any arrangements which have been established—

(a) in accordance with a relevant provision of his contract to the inclusion of which in the contract the worker has signified his agreement or consent in writing, or

(b) otherwise with the prior agreement or consent of the worker signified in writing,

and under which the employer is to deduct and pay over to a third person amounts notified to the employer by that person as being due to him from the worker, if the deduction is made in accordance with the relevant notification by that person.

(5) Section 13 does not apply to a deduction from a worker's wages made by his employer where the worker has taken part in a strike or other industrial action and the deduction is made by the employer on account of the worker's having taken part in that strike or other action.

(6) Section 13 does not apply to a deduction from a worker's wages made by his employer with his prior agreement or consent signified in writing where the purpose of the deduction is the satisfaction (whether wholly or in part) of an order of a court or tribunal requiring the payment of an amount by the worker to the employer.

Payments to employer

15 Right not to have to make payments to employer

(1) An employer shall not receive a payment from a worker employed by him unless—

(a) the payment is required or authorised to be made by virtue of a statutory provision or a relevant provision of the worker's contract, or

(b) the worker has previously signified in writing his agreement or consent to the making of the payment.

(2) In this section 'relevant provision', in relation to a worker's contract, means a provision of the contract comprised—

(a) in one or more written terms of the contract of which the employer has given the worker a copy on an occasion prior to the employer receiving the payment in question, or

(b) in one or more terms of the contract (whether express or implied and, if express, whether oral or in writing) the existence and effect, or combined effect, of which in relation to the worker the employer has notified to the worker in writing on such an occasion.

(3) For the purposes of this section a relevant provision of a worker's contract having effect by virtue of a variation of the contract does not operate to authorise the receipt of a payment on account of any conduct of the worker, or any other event occurring, before the variation took effect.

(4) For the purposes of this section an agreement or consent signified by a worker does not operate to authorise the receipt of a payment on account of any conduct of the worker, or any other event occurring, before the agreement or consent was signified.

(5) Any reference in this Part to an employer receiving a payment from a worker employed by him is a reference to his receiving such a payment in his capacity as the worker's employer.

16 Excepted payments

(1) Section 15 does not apply to a payment received from a worker by his employer where the purpose of the payment is the reimbursement of the employer in respect of—

(a) an overpayment of wages, or

(b) an overpayment in respect of expenses incurred by the worker in carrying out his employment,

made (for any reason) by the employer to the worker.

(2) Section 15 does not apply to a payment received from a worker by his employer in consequence of any disciplinary proceedings if those proceedings were held by virtue of a statutory provision.

(3) Section 15 does not apply to a payment received from a worker by his employer where the worker has taken part in a strike or other industrial action and the payment has been required by the employer on account of the worker's having taken part in that strike or other action.

(4) Section 15 does not apply to a payment received from a worker by his employer where the purpose of the payment is the satisfaction (whether wholly or in part) of an order of a court or tribunal requiring the payment of an amount by the worker to the employer.

Cash shortages and stock deficiencies in retail employment

17 Introductory

(1) In the following provisions of this Part—

'cash shortage' means a deficit arising in relation to amounts received in connection with retail transactions, and

'stock deficiency' means a stock deficiency arising in the course of retail transactions.

(2) In the following provisions of this Part 'retail employment', in relation to a worker, means employment involving (whether or not on a regular basis)—

- (a) the carrying out by the worker of retail transactions directly with members of the public or with fellow workers or other individuals in their personal capacities, or
- (b) the collection by the worker of amounts payable in connection with retail transactions carried out by other persons directly with members of the public or with fellow workers or other individuals in their personal capacities.

(3) References in this section to a 'retail transaction' are to the sale or supply of goods or the supply of services (including financial services).

(4) References in the following provisions of this Part to a deduction made from wages of a worker in retail employment, or to a payment received from such a worker by his employer, on account of a cash shortage or stock deficiency include references to a deduction or payment so made or received on account of—

- (a) any dishonesty or other conduct on the part of the worker which resulted in any such shortage or deficiency, or
- (b) any other event in respect of which he (whether or not together with any other workers) has any contractual liability and which so resulted,

in each case whether or not the amount of the deduction or payment is designed to reflect the exact amount of the shortage or deficiency.

(5) References in the following provisions of this Part to the recovery from a worker of an amount in respect of a cash shortage or stock deficiency accordingly include references to the recovery from him of an amount in respect of any such conduct or event as is mentioned in subsection (4)(a) or (b).

(6) In the following provisions of this Part 'pay day', in relation to a worker, means a day on which wages are payable to the worker.

18 Limits on amount and time of deductions

(1) Where (in accordance with section 13) the employer of a worker in retail employment makes, on account of one or more cash shortages or stock deficiencies, a deduction or deductions from wages payable to the worker on a pay day, the amount or aggregate amount of the deduction or deductions shall not exceed one-tenth of the gross amount of the wages payable to the worker on that day.

(2) Where the employer of a worker in retail employment makes a deduction from the worker's wages on account of a cash shortage or stock deficiency, the employer shall not be treated as making the deduction in accordance with section 13 unless (in addition to the requirements of that section being satisfied with respect to the deduction)—

(a) the deduction is made, or

(b) in the case of a deduction which is one of a series of deductions relating to the shortage or deficiency, the first deduction in the series was made,

not later than the end of the relevant period.

(3) In subsection (2) 'the relevant period' means the period of twelve months beginning with the date when the employer established the existence of the shortage or deficiency or (if earlier) the date when he ought reasonably to have done so.

19 Wages determined by reference to shortages etc.

(1) This section applies where—

(a) by virtue of an agreement between a worker in retail employment and his employer, the amount of the worker's wages or any part of them is or may be determined by reference to the incidence of cash shortages or stock deficiencies, and

(b) the gross amount of the wages payable to the worker on any pay day is, on account of any such shortages or deficiencies, less than the gross amount of the wages that would have been payable to him on that day if there had been no such shortages or deficiencies.

(2) The amount representing the difference between the two amounts referred to in subsection (1)(b) shall be treated for the purposes of this Part as a deduction from the wages payable to the worker on that day made by the employer on account of the cash shortages or stock deficiencies in question.

(3) The second of the amounts referred to in subsection (1)(b) shall be treated for the purposes of this Part (except subsection (1)) as the gross amount of the wages payable to him on that day.

(4) Accordingly—

(a) section 13, and

(b) if the requirements of section 13 and subsection (2) of section 18 are satisfied, subsection (1) of section 18,

have effect in relation to the amount referred to in subsection (2) of this section.

20 Limits on method and timing of payments

(1) Where the employer of a worker in retail employment receives from the worker a payment on account of a cash shortage or stock deficiency, the employer shall not be treated as receiving the payment in accordance with section 15 unless (in addition to the requirements of that section being satisfied with respect to the payment) he has previously—

(a) notified the worker in writing of the worker's total liability to him in respect of that shortage or deficiency, and

(b) required the worker to make the payment by means of a demand for payment made in accordance with the following provisions of this section.

(2) A demand for payment made by the employer of a worker in retail employment in respect of a cash shortage or stock deficiency—

(a) shall be made in writing, and

(b) shall be made on one of the worker's pay days.

(3) A demand for payment in respect of a particular cash shortage or stock deficiency, or (in the case of a series of such demands) the first such demand, shall not be made—

(a) earlier than the first pay day of the worker following the date when he is notified of his total liability in respect of the shortage or deficiency in pursuance of subsection (1)(a) or, where he is so notified on a pay day, earlier than that day, or

(b) later than the end of the period of twelve months beginning with the date when the employer established the existence of the shortage or deficiency or (if earlier) the date when he ought reasonably to have done so.

(4) For the purposes of this Part a demand for payment shall be treated as made by the employer on one of a worker's pay days if it is given to the worker or posted to, or left at, his last known address—

(a) on that pay day, or
(b) in the case of a pay day which is not a working day of the employer's business, on the first such working day following that pay day.

(5) Legal proceedings by the employer of a worker in retail employment for the recovery from the worker of an amount in respect of a cash shortage or stock deficiency shall not be instituted by the employer after the end of the period referred to in subsection (3)(b) unless the employer has within that period made a demand for payment in respect of that amount in accordance with this section.

21 Limit on amount of payments

(1) Where the employer of a worker in retail employment makes on any pay day one or more demands for payment in accordance with section 20, the amount or aggregate amount required to be paid by the worker in pursuance of the demand or demands shall not exceed—

(a) one-tenth of the gross amount of the wages payable to the worker on that day, or
(b) where one or more deductions falling within section 18(1) are made by the employer from those wages, such amount as represents the balance of that one-tenth after subtracting the amount or aggregate amount of the deduction or deductions.

(2) Once an amount has been required to be paid by means of a demand for payment made in accordance with section 20 on any pay day, that amount shall not be taken into account under subsection (1) as it applies to any subsequent pay day, even though the employer is obliged to make further requests for it to be paid.

(3) Where in any legal proceedings the court finds that the employer of a worker in retail employment is (in accordance with section 15 as it applies apart from section 20(1)) entitled to recover an amount from the worker in respect of a cash shortage or stock deficiency, the court shall, in ordering the payment by the worker to the employer of that amount, make such provision as appears to the court to be necessary to ensure that it is paid by the worker at a rate not exceeding that at which it could be recovered from him by the employer in accordance with this section.

22 Final instalments of wages

(1) In this section 'final instalment of wages', in relation to a worker, means—

(a) the amount of wages payable to the worker which consists of or includes an amount payable by way of contractual remuneration in respect of the last of the periods for which he is employed under his contract prior to its termination for any reason (but excluding any wages referable to any earlier such period), or
(b) where an amount in lieu of notice is paid to the worker later than the amount referred to in paragraph (a), the amount so paid,

in each case whether the amount in question is paid before or after the termination of the worker's contract.

(2) Section 18(1) does not operate to restrict the amount of any deductions which may (in accordance with section 13(1)) be made by the employer of a worker in retail employment from the worker's final instalment of wages.

(3) Nothing in section 20 or 21 applies to a payment falling within section 20(1) which is made on or after the day on which any such worker's final instalment of wages is paid; but (even if the requirements of section 15 would otherwise be satisfied with respect to it) his employer shall not be treated as receiving any such payment in accordance with that section if the payment was first required to be made after the end of the period referred to in section 20(3)(b).

(4) Section 21 (3) does not apply to an amount which is to be paid by a worker on or after the day on which his final instalment of wages is paid.

Enforcement

23 Complaints to employment tribunals

(1) A worker may present a complaint to an employment tribunal—

(a) that his employer has made a deduction from his wages in contravention of section 13 (including a deduction made in contravention of that section as it applies by virtue of section 18(2)),
(b) that his employer has received from him a payment in contravention of section 15 (including a payment received in contravention of that section as it applies by virtue of section 20(1)),
(c) that his employer has recovered from his wages by means of one or more deductions falling within section 18(1) an amount or aggregate amount exceeding the limit applying to the deduction or deductions under that provision, or
(d) that his employer has received from him in pursuance of one or more demands for payment made (in accordance with section 20) on a particular pay day, a payment or payments of an amount or aggregate amount exceeding the limit applying to the demand or demands under section 21(1).

(2) Subject to subsection (4), an employment tribunal shall not consider a complaint under this section unless it is presented before the end of the period of three months beginning with—
(a) in the case of a complaint relating to a deduction by the employer, the date of payment of the wages from which the deduction was made, or
(b) in the case of a complaint relating to a payment received by the employer, the date when the payment was received.

(3) Where a complaint is brought under this section in respect of—
(a) a series of deductions or payments, or
(b) a number of payments falling within subsection (1)(d) and made in pursuance of demands for payment subject to the same limit under section 21(1) but received by the employer on different dates,

the references in subsection (2) to the deduction or payment are to the last deduction or payment in the series or to the last of the payments so received.

(3A) [omitted]

(4) Where the employment tribunal is satisfied that it was not reasonably practicable for a complaint under this section to be presented before the end of the relevant period of three months, the tribunal may consider the complaint if it is presented within such further period as the tribunal considers reasonable.

(4A) An employment tribunal is not (despite subsections (3) and (4)) to consider so much of a complaint brought under this section as relates to a deduction where the date of payment of the wages from which the deduction was made was before the period of two years ending with the date of presentation of the complaint.

(4B) Subsection (4A) does not apply so far as a complaint relates to a deduction from wages that are of a kind mentioned in section 27(1)(b) to (j).

(5) No complaint shall be presented under this section in respect of any deduction made in contravention of section 86 of the Trade Union and Labour Relations (Consolidation) Act 1992 (deduction of political fund contribution where certificate of exemption or objection has been given).

24 Determination of complaints

(1) Where a tribunal finds a complaint under section 23 well-founded, it shall make a declaration to that effect and shall order the employer—
(a) in the case of a complaint under section 23(1)(a), to pay to the worker the amount of any deduction made in contravention of section 13,
(b) in the case of a complaint under section 23(1)(b), to repay to the worker the amount of any payment received in contravention of section 15,
(c) in the case of a complaint under section 23(1)(c), to pay to the worker any amount recovered from him in excess of the limit mentioned in that provision, and
(d) in the case of a complaint under section 23(1)(d), to repay to the worker any amount received from him in excess of the limit mentioned in that provision.

(2) Where a tribunal makes a declaration under subsection (1), it may order the employer to pay to the worker (in addition to any amount ordered to be paid under that subsection) such amount as the tribunal considers appropriate in all the circumstances to compensate the worker for any financial loss sustained by him which is attributable to the matter complained of.

25 Determinations: supplementary

(1) Where, in the case of any complaint under section 23(1)(a), a tribunal finds that, although neither of the conditions set out in section 13(1)(a) and (b) was satisfied with respect to the whole amount of the deduction, one of those conditions was satisfied with respect to any lesser amount, the amount of the deduction shall for the purposes of section 24(a) be treated as reduced by the amount with respect to which that condition was satisfied.

(2) Where, in the case of any complaint under section 23(1)(b), a tribunal finds that, although neither of the conditions set out in section 15(1)(a) and (b) was satisfied with respect to the whole amount of the payment, one of those conditions was satisfied with respect to any lesser amount, the amount of the payment shall for the purposes of section 24(b) be treated as reduced by the amount with respect to which that condition was satisfied.

(3) An employer shall not under section 24 be ordered by a tribunal to pay or repay to a worker any amount in respect of a deduction or payment, or in respect of any combination of deductions or payments, in so far as it appears to the tribunal that he has already paid or repaid any such amount to the worker.

(4) Where a tribunal has under section 24 ordered an employer to pay or repay to a worker any amount in respect of a particular deduction or payment falling within section 23(1)(a) to (d), the amount which the employer is entitled to recover (by whatever means) in respect of the matter in relation to which the deduction or payment was originally made or received shall be treated as reduced by that amount.

(5) Where a tribunal has under section 24 ordered an employer to pay or repay to a worker any amount in respect of any combination of deductions or payments falling within section 23(1)(c) or (d), the aggregate amount which the employer is entitled to recover (by whatever means) in respect of the cash shortages or stock deficiencies in relation to which the deductions or payments were originally made or required to be made shall be treated as reduced by that amount.

26 Complaints and other remedies

Section 23 does not affect the jurisdiction of an employment tribunal to consider a reference under section 11 in relation to any deduction from the wages of a worker; but the aggregate of any amounts ordered by an employment tribunal to be paid under section 12(4) and under section 24 (whether on the same or different occasions) in respect of a particular deduction shall not exceed the amount of the deduction.

Supplementary

27 Meaning of 'wages' etc.

(1) In this Part 'wages', in relation to a worker, means any sums payable to the worker in connection with his employment, including—

- (a) any fee, bonus, commission, holiday pay or other emolument referable to his employment, whether payable under his contract or otherwise,
- (b) statutory sick pay under Part XI of the Social Security Contributions and Benefits Act 1992,
- (c) statutory maternity pay under Part XII of that Act,
- (ca) statutory paternity pay under Part 12ZA of that Act,
- (cb) statutory adoption pay under Part 12ZB of that Act,
- (cc) statutory shared parental pay under Part 12ZC of that Act,
- (cd) statutory parental bereavement pay under Part 12ZD of that Act,
- (ce) statutory neonatal care pay under Part 12ZE of that Act,
- (ce) any amount of qualifying tips, gratuities and service charges allocated to the worker under Part 2B of this Act,

(d) a guarantee payment (under section 28 of this Act),
(e) any payment for time off under Part VI of this Act or section 169 of the Trade Union and Labour Relations (Consolidation) Act 1992 (payment for time off for carrying out trade union duties etc.),
(f) remuneration on suspension on medical grounds under section 64 of this Act and remuneration on suspension on maternity grounds under section 68 of this Act,
(fa) remuneration on ending the supply of an agency worker on maternity grounds under section 68C of this Act,
(g) any sum payable in pursuance of an order for reinstatement or re-engagement under section 113 of this Act,
(h) any sum payable in pursuance of an order for the continuation of a contract of employment under section 130 of this Act or section 164 of the Trade Union and Labour Relations (Consolidation) Act 1992, and
(j) remuneration under a protective award under section 189 of that Act, but excluding any payments within subsection (2).

(2) Those payments are—
(a) any payment by way of an advance under an agreement for a loan or by way of an advance of wages (but without prejudice to the application of section 13 to any deduction made from the worker's wages in respect of any such advance),
(b) any payment in respect of expenses incurred by the worker in carrying out his employment,
(c) any payment by way of a pension, allowance or gratuity in connection with the worker's retirement or as compensation for loss of office,
(d) any payment referable to the worker's redundancy, and
(e) any payment to the worker otherwise than in his capacity as a worker.

(3) Where any payment in the nature of a non-contractual bonus is (for any reason) made to a worker by his employer, the amount of the payment shall for the purposes of this Part—
(a) be treated as wages of the worker, and
(b) be treated as payable to him as such on the day on which the payment is made.

(4) In this Part 'gross amount', in relation to any wages payable to a worker, means the total amount of those wages before deductions of whatever nature.

(5) For the purposes of this Part any monetary value attaching to any payment or benefit in kind furnished to a worker by his employer shall not be treated as wages of the worker except in the case of any voucher, stamp or similar document which is—
(a) of a fixed value expressed in monetary terms, and
(b) capable of being exchanged (whether on its own or together with other vouchers, stamps or documents, and whether immediately or only after a time) for money, goods or services (or for any combination of two or more of those things).

PART 2A ZERO HOURS WORKERS AND SIMILAR

Chapter 1 Exclusivity terms and other restrictions

27A Exclusivity terms unenforceable in zero hours contracts

(1) In this section 'zero hours contract' means a contract of employment or other worker's contract under which—
(a) the undertaking to do or perform work or services is an undertaking to do so conditionally on the employer making work or services available to the worker, and
(b) there is no certainty that any such work or services will be made available to the worker.

(2) For this purpose, an employer makes work or services available to a worker if the employer requests or requires the worker to do the work or perform the services.

(3) Any provision of a zero hours contract which—

(a) prohibits the worker from doing work or performing services under another contract or under any other arrangement, or

(b) prohibits the worker from doing so without the employer's consent,

is unenforceable against the worker.

(4) Subsection (3) is to be disregarded for the purposes of determining any question whether a contract is a contract of employment or other worker's contract.

27B [omitted]

Chapter 2 Right to guaranteed hours

27BA Right for qualifying workers to be offered guaranteed hours

(1) An employer must make a guaranteed hours offer to a worker in accordance with section 27BB after the end of every period—

(a) that is a reference period in relation to that worker and that employer, and

(b) in relation to which the worker is a qualifying worker of the employer.

(2) Section 27BD makes provision for exceptions to this duty, including in certain cases where the worker ceases to be employed by the employer.

(3) A worker is a qualifying worker of an employer in relation to a reference period if—

(a) during the reference period the worker was employed by the employer under one or more worker's contracts (whether or not continuously) and either—

(i) the worker's contract was, or the worker's contracts were, a zero hours contract or entered into in accordance with a zero hours arrangement, or

(ii) the worker's contract, or the worker's contracts (taken together), required the employer, or were entered into in accordance with an arrangement that required the employer, to make work available to the worker during the reference period for a number of hours ('the minimum number of hours') not exceeding a specified number of hours,

(b) during the reference period the worker worked under the worker's contract or the worker's contracts (taken together) for a number of hours (the 'reference period hours'),

(c) where paragraph (a)(ii) applies, the reference period hours exceeded the minimum number of hours,

(d) the reference period hours satisfy such conditions (or, where paragraph (a)(ii) applies, such further conditions) as to number, regularity or otherwise as are specified, and

(e) when the worker worked the reference period hours, it was not as an excluded worker or an agency worker (but see Part 1 of Schedule A1 for provision about guaranteed hours and agency workers).

(4) In relation to a worker and the worker's employer, each of the following is a 'reference period'—

(a) the initial reference period, and

(b) each subsequent reference period.

(5) 'The initial reference period', in relation to a worker and the worker's employer, means the period—

(a) beginning with—

(i) where the worker is employed by the employer on the day on which subsection (1) comes into force ('the commencement day'), the commencement day, or

(ii) where the worker is not so employed, the first day after the commencement day on which the worker is employed by the employer, and

(b) ending with the specified day.

(6) A 'subsequent reference period', in relation to a worker and the worker's employer, means a period beginning and ending with the specified days.

(7) See paragraph 6(4) of Schedule A1 for provision about when the initial reference period is not a reference period in relation to a worker who is a former agency worker and that worker's employer.

(8) For the purposes of this Chapter—

(a) references to a 'qualifying worker' are to a worker who is a qualifying worker of an employer in relation to a reference period by virtue of subsection (3), and

(b) the reference period in relation to which the worker is a qualifying worker of the employer is referred to as 'the relevant reference period'.

(9) If, during a reference period—

(a) a worker was employed by an employer under one or more worker's contracts of the type described in subsection (3)(a)(i) and one or more worker's contracts of the type described in subsection (3)(a)(ii), and

(b) the hours that the worker worked under the worker's contract, or the worker's contracts, that are of the type described in subsection (3)(a)(ii) did not exceed the minimum number of hours,

the worker's contract, or the worker's contracts, that are of the type described in subsection (3)(a)(ii) are to be disregarded in the application of this Chapter (other than this subsection) in relation to the worker and the reference period (and accordingly that worker's contract, or those worker's contracts, are to be treated as not existing).

(10) Subsection (11) applies where—

(a) a worker's contract or arrangement requires an employer to make work available to a worker for a number of hours, and

(b) some or all of those hours may be made available either on days falling within a reference period or on days falling within another period (all of the days on which the hours may be so made available together forming the 'longer period').

In subsection (11), 'the unassigned hours' are the hours that may be made available at any time during the longer period as described in paragraph (b).

(11) Where this subsection applies—

(a) subsection (3)(a)(ii) is to apply as if the contract or arrangement required the employer to make work available to the worker during the reference period for the apportioned number of the unassigned hours (in addition to any other hours that the employer is required to make available to the worker during the reference period);

(b) 'the apportioned number' of the unassigned hours is—

$$\frac{H \times D1}{D2}$$

where—

H is the number of the unassigned hours,

D1 is the number of days in the reference period that fall within the longer period, and

D2 is the number of days in the longer period.

(12) Where there is more than one longer period in relation to the same reference period, subsection (11) is to be applied separately in relation to each longer period.

(13) Nothing in this Chapter prevents an employer from making one or more other offers to a qualifying worker, to vary the worker's terms and conditions of employment or enter into a new worker's contract, at the same time as making a guaranteed hours offer.

(14)–(15) [omitted]

27BB Requirements relating to a guaranteed hours offer

(1) An offer by an employer to a qualifying worker is a guaranteed hours offer for the purposes of this Chapter if it is an offer—

(a) to vary the worker's terms and conditions of employment (but see subsection (6)), or

(b) to enter into a new worker's contract,

and the terms and conditions as varied or (as the case may be) the new worker's contract will require the employer to provide the qualifying worker with work, and the qualifying worker to do work, for a number of hours that reflects the reference period hours in the relevant reference period.

(2) The Secretary of State may by regulations provide that an offer by an employer to a qualifying worker is a guaranteed hours offer for the purposes of this Chapter only if it also satisfies the condition in subsection (3).

(3) The condition referred to in subsection (2) is that—

(a) the offer sets out—

(i) the days of the week, and the times on those days, when the offered number of hours are to be provided and worked, or

(ii) a working pattern of days, and times of day, by reference to which the offered number of hours are to be provided and worked, and

(b) those days and times reflect, or that pattern reflects, when the qualifying worker worked the reference period hours in the relevant reference period.

(4) Where no regulations are in force under subsection (2) that apply in relation to an offer by an employer to a qualifying worker, the offer is a guaranteed hours offer for the purposes of this Chapter only if it also proposes terms and conditions relating to when the offered number of hours are to be provided and worked (which need not be on particular days of the week, or at particular times on those days, or by reference to a particular working pattern of days or times of day)

(5)–(13) [omitted]

26BC–27BD [omitted]

27BE Acceptance or rejection of a guaranteed hours offer

(1) Where an employer makes a guaranteed hours offer to a qualifying worker and the offer is not treated as having been withdrawn by virtue of section 27BD(2) or regulations under section 27BD(6), the qualifying worker may, by giving notice to the employer before the end of the response period, accept or reject the offer.

(2) Where the guaranteed hours offer takes the form of an offer to vary the qualifying worker's terms and conditions of employment and the qualifying worker gives notice under subsection (1) accepting the offer, the variation (assuming the worker's contract that was in force when the guaranteed hours offer was made is still in force) is to be treated as taking effect on the day after the day on which notice is given (but this is subject to subsection (6)).

(3) If the guaranteed hours offer takes the form of an offer to vary the qualifying worker's terms and conditions of employment but the worker's contract that was in force when the guaranteed hours offer was made ceases to be in force during the response period—

(a) the qualifying worker may (if the offer is not treated as having been withdrawn by virtue of section 27BD(2) or regulations under section 27BD(6)) still give notice under subsection (1) accepting the offer, and

(b) if the qualifying worker does so—

(i) the qualifying worker and the employer are to be treated as entering into a worker's contract on the day after the day on which notice is given (but this is subject to subsection (6)), and

(ii) the terms of the contract are to be treated as being the terms of the worker's contract that was in force when the guaranteed hours offer was made as varied in accordance with the terms of the offer.

(4) Where the guaranteed hours offer takes the form of an offer to enter into a new worker's contract and the qualifying worker gives notice under subsection (1) accepting the offer—

(a) the qualifying worker and the employer are to be treated as entering into a worker's contract in the terms of the offer on the day after the day on which notice is given (but this is subject to subsection (6)), and

(b) that worker's contract is to be treated as replacing any other worker's contract entered into between the qualifying worker and the employer that is in force on that day.

(5) But where, by virtue of subsection (4)(b), a new worker's contract replaces another worker's contract of a qualifying worker who is an employee—

(a) that is not to be treated for the purposes of this Act as breaking the continuity of a period of employment of the qualifying worker;

(b) the worker's contract that is replaced is not to be treated for the purposes of Part 10 as having terminated.

(6) A qualifying worker and an employer may agree, for the purposes of subsection (2), (3) or (4), that the variation of the qualifying worker's terms and conditions of employment is to be treated as taking effect, or (as the case may be) the new worker's contract is to be treated as being entered into, on a later day than the day mentioned in the subsection (and, in subsection (4)(b), the reference to 'that day' is then to be read as a reference to the later agreed day).

(7) If a qualifying worker to whom a guaranteed hours offer has been made does not give notice under subsection (1) before the end of the response period, the qualifying worker is to be treated as having rejected the offer.

(8) [omitted]

(9) In this section, 'the response period' has the same meaning as in section 27BD.

(10) Where—

(a) an employer is permitted by section 27BY(3) to withdraw a guaranteed hours offer (withdrawal of offer following incorporation of terms of collective agreement), and

(b) the employer withdraws the offer by giving notice under that section,

subsection (1) of this section ceases to apply in relation to the offer when the notice is given.

27BF [omitted]

Enforcement

27BG Complaints to employment tribunals: grounds

(1) A worker may present a complaint to an employment tribunal that—

(a) the duty imposed by section 27BA(1) applies to the worker's employer in relation to the worker and a particular reference period, but

(b) by the end of the last day of the offer period, the employer has not made an offer to vary the worker's terms and conditions of employment or to enter into a new worker's contract in compliance (or purported compliance) with that duty (whether because the employer does not consider that the worker is a qualifying worker in relation to the reference period or for any other reason).

(2) A worker may present a complaint to an employment tribunal that—

(a) the duty imposed by section 27BA(1) applies to the worker's employer in relation to the worker and a particular reference period, but

(b) the offer that the employer has made to the worker in relation to that reference period to vary the worker's terms and conditions of employment or to enter into a new worker's contract is not a guaranteed hours offer as described in—

(i) where regulations are in force under subsection (2) of section 27BB that apply in relation to the offer, subsections (1) and (3) of that section (read with any regulations in force under subsection (5)(a) or (b) of that section), or

(ii) where no regulations are in force under subsection (2) of section 27BB that apply in relation to the offer, subsections (1) and (4) of that section (read with any regulations in force under subsection (5)(a) of that section).

(3) A worker may present a complaint to an employment tribunal that—

(a) the duty imposed by section 27BA(1) applies to the worker's employer in relation to the worker and a particular reference period, but

(b) the guaranteed hours offer that the employer has made to the worker in relation to that reference period—

(i) takes the form of an offer to vary the worker's terms and conditions of employment where that is prohibited by section 27BB(6),

(ii) does not comply with section 27BB(7), or

(iii) does not comply with section 27BB(8).

(4) A worker may present a complaint to an employment tribunal that—

(a) the duty imposed by section 27BA(1) applies to the worker's employer in relation to the worker and a particular reference period, but

(b) the guaranteed hours offer that the employer has made to the worker in relation to that reference period is on terms requiring the employer to provide, and the worker to do, less work than would have been the case if the employer had not, during that reference period—

(i) limited (by whatever means, including termination of a worker's contract or an arrangement) the number of hours of work made available to the worker, or

(ii) decided to make work available to the worker in the way that the employer did,

for the sole or main purpose of being able to comply with the duty by making such a reduced offer.

(5) A worker may present a complaint to an employment tribunal that the duty imposed by section 27BA(1) would have applied to the worker's employer in relation to the worker and a particular reference period if the employer had not, during that reference period—

(a) limited (by whatever means, including termination of a worker's contract or an arrangement) the number of hours of work made available to the worker, or

(a) decided to make work available to the worker in the way that the employer did,

for the sole or main purpose of preventing the worker from satisfying, in relation to that reference period, one or more of the conditions in section 27BA(3)(b) to (d).

(6) A complaint under subsection (2), (3) or (4)—

(a) may be presented whether or not the offer in question has been accepted by the worker, but

(b) may not be presented in relation to an offer that is—

(i) treated as having been withdrawn by virtue of section 27BD(2) or regulations under section 27BD(6), or

(ii) withdrawn in accordance with section 27BY(3) (withdrawal of offer following incorporation of terms of collective agreement).

(7) A worker may present a complaint to an employment tribunal that the worker's employer—

(a) has failed to give to the worker a notice under section 27BD(8) or (9);

(b) has given to the worker a notice under section 27BD(8) or (9)(b) in circumstances in which the employer should not have done so;

(c) has given to the worker a notice in purported compliance with section 27BD(9) that does not refer to any provision of the regulations or refers to the wrong provision.

(8) A worker may present a complaint to an employment tribunal that the worker's employer has failed to comply with—

(a) the duty imposed by section 27BF(1);

(b) the duty imposed by section 27BF(2).

(9) In this section 'the last day of the offer period', in relation to a reference period, means the day specified under section 27BB(11)(a) as the last day on which a guaranteed hours offer may be made in relation to that reference period.

27BH Complaints to employment tribunals: time limits

(1) An employment tribunal must not consider a complaint under section 27BG(1) unless it is presented before the end of the period of six months beginning with the day after the last day of the offer period (as defined in section 27BG(9)).

(2) An employment tribunal must not consider a complaint under section 27BG(2) unless it is presented before the end of the period of six months beginning with the day after the day when the offer referred to in that provision is made.

(3) An employment tribunal must not consider a complaint under section 27BG(3) or (4) unless it is presented before the end of the period of six months beginning with the day after the day when the guaranteed hours offer referred to in that provision is made.

(4) An employment tribunal must not consider a complaint under section 27BG(5) unless it is presented before the end of the period of six months beginning with the day after what would have been the last day of the offer period (as defined in section 27BG(9)) if the duty imposed by section 27BA(1) had applied.

(5) An employment tribunal must not consider a complaint under section 27BG(7)(a) relating to a notice unless it is presented before the end of the period of six months beginning with the day after the day on or before which the notice should have been given (see section 27BD(8) and (10)).

(6) An employment tribunal must not consider a complaint under section 27BG(7)(b) or (c) relating to a notice unless it is presented before the end of the period of six months beginning with the day after the day on which the notice is given.

(7) An employment tribunal must not consider a complaint under section 27BG(8)(a)unless it is presented before the end of the period of six months beginning with the day after the last day of the initial information period (see section 27BF(3) and (4)).

(8) An employment tribunal must not consider a complaint under section 27BG(8)(b) unless it is presented before the end of the period of six months beginning with the day on which the worker first becomes aware of the failure to which the complaint relates.

(9) But, if the employment tribunal is satisfied that it was not reasonably practicable for a complaint under section 27BG to be presented before the end of the relevant period of six months, the tribunal may consider the complaint if it is presented within such further period as the tribunal considers reasonable.

(10) Section 207B (extension of time limits to facilitate conciliation before institution of proceedings) applies for the purposes of subsections (1) to (8).

27BI Remedies

(1) Where an employment tribunal finds a complaint under section 27BG well-founded, the tribunal—

(a) must make a declaration to that effect, and

(b) may make an award of compensation to be paid by the employer to the worker.

(2) The amount of compensation under subsection (1)(b) is to be such amount, not exceeding the permitted maximum, as the tribunal considers just and equitable in all the circumstances to compensate the worker for any financial loss sustained by the worker which is attributable to the matter complained of.

(3) In ascertaining the financial loss sustained, the tribunal must apply the same rule concerning the duty of a person to mitigate their loss as applies to damages recoverable under the common law of England and Wales or (as the case may be) Scotland.

(4) For the purposes of subsection (2), 'the permitted maximum' is—

(a) where the complaint is under section 27BG(1), (2), (3), (7) or (8), such number of weeks' pay as the Secretary of State may specify in regulations;

(b) where the complaint is under section 27BG(4) or (5), such amount as the Secretary of State may specify in regulations.

(5) In calculating a week's pay for the purposes of determining the permitted maximum for an award of compensation to a worker who is not an employee, Chapter 2 of Part 14 is to apply as if—

(a) references in that Chapter and in section 234 (normal working hours) to an employee were references to a worker;

(b) references in that Chapter and in section 234 to a contract of employment were references to a worker's contract;

(c) 'week' meant—

(i) in relation to a worker whose remuneration is calculated weekly by a week ending with a day other than a Saturday, a week ending with that other day, and

(ii) in relation to any other worker, a week ending with Saturday.

Chapter 3 Shifts: rights to reasonable notice

27BJ Right to reasonable notice of a shift

(1) An employer must give to a worker reasonable notice of a shift that the employer requests or requires the worker to work if—

(a) the worker is (or is to be) employed by the employer under a zero hours contract, or

(b) the worker is (or is to be) employed by the employer under a worker's contract of a specified description that requires the employer to make some work available to the worker but does not provide on what days and at what times, or in accordance with what pattern of days and times, that work is to be done by the worker,

and the shift is to be worked under the contract referred to in paragraph (a) or (b).

(2) An employer must give to a worker reasonable notice of a shift that the employer requests or requires the worker to work if—

(a) the worker is (or is to be) employed by the employer under a worker's contract of a specified description that requires the employer to make some work available to the worker,

(b) the contract provides on what days and at what times, or in accordance with what pattern of days and times, that work, or some of that work, is to be done by the worker, and

(c) the shift is to be worked under that contract but no part of it corresponds to the time of a shift provided for by the contract as described in paragraph (b).

(3) An employer must give to an individual reasonable notice of a shift that the employer requests the individual to work if—

(a) the individual would, if they worked the shift, be employed by the employer under a worker's contract, and

(b) the worker's contract would be entered into in accordance with a zero hours arrangement that is in place between the employer and the individual.

(4) It is to be presumed, unless the contrary is shown, that notice of a shift is not reasonable notice for the purposes of subsections (1) to (3) if it is given less than a specified amount of time before the shift is due to start.

(5) [omitted]

(6) Where—

(a) the conditions in subsection (2)(a) and (b) are met in relation to a worker and a worker's contract,

(b) the worker is to work (or is working) a shift under that contract all or part of which corresponds to the time of a shift (a 'guaranteed shift') provided for by the contract as described in subsection (2)(b),

(c) the employer requests or requires the worker to start earlier, or end later, than is provided for by the contract (as described in subsection (2)(b)) in relation to the guaranteed shift, and

(d) the earlier start or later end is to result in an additional number of hours being worked above the number of hours to be worked in the guaranteed shift,

the additional hours are to be treated for the purposes of this Chapter as a separate shift (and accordingly as one that meets the condition in subsection (2)(c)).

(7) For the purposes of this Chapter—

'employer', in relation to an individual and a shift, includes a person by whom the individual would be (or would have been) employed if the individual worked the shift;

'worker', in relation to a shift, includes an individual who would be (or would have been) a worker if the individual worked the shift.

(8) In this section, 'notice of a shift' means notice of how many hours are to be worked and when the shift is to start and end.

27BK Right to reasonable notice of cancellation of or change to a shift

(1) Subsection (2) applies in relation to an employer and a worker where—

(a) the employer has given notice of a shift to the worker,

(b) the shift is one that the worker was entitled to reasonable notice of under section 27BJ(1), (2) or (3), and

(c) where the shift is one that the employer has requested (rather than required) the worker to work, the worker has agreed to work it.

(2) The employer must give reasonable notice to the worker of—

(a) the cancellation of the shift by the employer;

(b) any change requested or required by the employer consisting of—

(i) a change to when the shift is to start or end;

(ii) a reduction in the number of hours to be worked during the shift because of a break in the shift;

(but this is subject to section 27BM).

(3) It is to be presumed, unless the contrary is shown, that—

(a) notice of the cancellation of a shift is not reasonable notice for the purposes of subsection (2) if it is given less than a specified amount of time before the shift would have started (if the shift had not been cancelled);

(b) notice of a change to when a shift is to start is not reasonable notice for the purposes of subsection (2) if it is given less than a specified amount of time before the earlier of—

(i) when the shift would have started (if the shift had not been changed), and

(ii) when the shift is due to start (having been changed);

(c) notice of any other change to a shift is not reasonable notice for the purposes of subsection (2) if it is given—

(i) less than a specified amount of time before the shift is due to start;

(ii) on or after the start of the shift.

(4) In this section, 'notice of a shift' has the same meaning as in section 27BJ.

27BL–27 BM [omitted]

27BN Complaints to employment tribunals

(1) A worker may present a complaint to an employment tribunal that the worker's employer has failed to comply with a duty imposed by section 27BJ or 27BK.

(2) Where, in determining whether a complaint under this section is well-founded, the tribunal must determine whether reasonable notice has been given, the tribunal must have regard, in particular, to such of the specified matters as are appropriate in the circumstances.

(3) An employment tribunal must not consider a complaint under this section unless it is presented before the end of the period of six months beginning with—

(a) where the complaint is that the employer failed to comply with a duty imposed by section 27BJ(1), (2) or (3) in relation to a shift, the day on which the shift was due to start;

(b) where the complaint is that the employer failed to comply with the duty imposed by section 27BK(2) in relation to the cancellation of a shift, the day on which the shift would have started (if the shift had not been cancelled);

(c) where the complaint is that the employer failed to comply with the duty imposed by section 27BK(2) in relation to a change to a shift, the day on which the shift as changed was due to start or, where the shift was changed on or after its start, the day on which the shift started.

(4) But, if the employment tribunal is satisfied that it was not reasonably practicable for a complaint to be presented before the end of the relevant period of six months, the tribunal may consider the complaint if it is presented within such further period as the tribunal considers reasonable.

(5) Section 207B (extension of time limits to facilitate conciliation before institution of proceedings) applies for the purposes of subsection (3).

27BO Remedies

(1) Where an employment tribunal finds a complaint under section 27BN well-founded, the tribunal—

(a) must make a declaration to that effect, and

(b) may make an award of compensation to be paid by the employer to the worker.

(2) The amount of compensation under subsection (1)(b) in relation to a complaint is to be such amount, not exceeding the specified amount, as the tribunal considers just and equitable in all the circumstances to compensate the worker for any financial loss sustained by the worker which is attributable to the matter complained of.

(3) In ascertaining the financial loss sustained, the tribunal must apply the same rule concerning the duty of a person to mitigate their loss as applies to damages recoverable under the common law of England and Wales or (as the case may be) Scotland.

Chapter 4 Right to payment for cancelled, moved and curtailed shifts

27BP Right to payment for a cancelled, moved or curtailed shift

(1) An employer must make a payment of a specified amount to a worker each time that the employer cancels, moves or curtails at short notice a qualifying shift—

(a) that the employer has informed the worker they are required to work,

(b) that the employer has requested the worker to work and the worker has agreed to work, or

(c) that the worker has suggested working and the employer has agreed to the worker working,

(but see section 27BR for exceptions to this duty).

(2) A shift is a 'qualifying shift', in relation to a worker and an employer, if it would be (or would have been) worked, or is being worked, by the worker for the employer under—

(a) a zero hours contract,

(b) a worker's contract entered into in accordance with a zero hours arrangement, or

(c) a worker's contract of a specified description that requires the employer to make some work available to the worker but does not provide on what days and at what times, or in accordance with what pattern of days and times, that work is to be done by the worker.

(3) A shift is also a 'qualifying shift', in relation to a worker and an employer, if—

(a) it would be (or would have been) worked, or is being worked, by the worker for the employer under a worker's contract of a specified description that requires the employer to make some work available to the worker,

(b) the contract provides on what days and at what times, or in accordance with what pattern of days and times, that work, or some of that work, is to be done by the worker, and

(c) no part of the shift corresponds to the time of a shift provided for by the contract as described in paragraph (b).

(4) Where—

(a) the conditions in subsection (3)(a) and (b) are met in relation to a shift,

(b) all or part of the shift corresponds to the time of a shift (a 'guaranteed shift') provided for by the contract as described in subsection (3)(b),

(c) the employer requests or requires, or the worker suggests, that the worker starts earlier, or ends later, than is provided for by the contract (as described in subsection (3)(b)) in relation to the guaranteed shift, and

(d) the earlier start or later end is to result in an additional number of hours being worked above the number of hours to be worked in the guaranteed shift,

the additional hours are to be treated for the purposes of this Chapter as a separate shift (and accordingly as a 'qualifying shift').

(5) A payment that an employer is required to make under subsection (1) must be made by no later than the specified day.

(6) For the purposes of this Chapter, 'short notice' means—

(a) in relation to the cancellation of a shift, notice given less than a specified amount of time before the shift would have started (if the shift had not been cancelled);

(b) in relation to the movement of a shift, or the movement and curtailment (at the same time) of a shift, notice given—

(i) less than a specified amount of time before the earlier of when the shift would have started (if the shift had not been moved, or moved and curtailed) and when the shift is due to start (having been moved, or moved and curtailed);

(ii) on or after the start of the shift;

(c) in relation to the curtailment of a shift where there is a change to when the shift is to start (but there is no movement of the shift), notice given less than a specified amount of time before the earlier of—

(i) when the shift would have started (if there had not been the change), and

(ii) when the shift is due to start (the change having been made);

(d) in relation to the curtailment of a shift where there is no change to when the shift is to start, notice given—

(i) less than a specified amount of time before the shift is due to start;

(ii) on or after the start of the shift.

(7) [omitted]

(8) For the purposes of this Chapter—

'employer', in relation to an individual and a shift, includes a person by whom the individual would be (or would have been) employed if the individual worked the shift;

'worker', in relation to a shift, includes an individual who would be (or would have been) a worker if the individual worked the shift.

(9) For the purposes of this Chapter, references to the movement of a shift (however expressed)—

(a) are to any change to the time at which the shift is to start that is a change of more than a specified amount of time;

(b) include—

(i) where a shift is in two or more parts, a change of more than a specified amount of time to the time at which the second (or a subsequent) part is to start, and

(ii) a division of a shift into two or more parts where the time between the parts is more than a specified amount of time,

but only if the change or division (as the case may be) results in the shift ending later.

(10) In this Chapter, references to a request to work a shift made by an employer to a worker include a request (a 'multi-worker request') made by the employer to the worker and one or more others in circumstances where the employer does not need the shift to be worked by all of those to whom the request is made.

(11) For the purposes of this Chapter, where an employer has made a multi-worker request to a worker in relation to a shift, references to the cancellation of the shift (however expressed) include the worker not being needed to work the shift because one or more others have agreed to work it.

27BQ [omitted]

27BR Exceptions to duty to make payment for a cancelled, moved or curtailed shift

(1) The requirement to make a payment under section 27BP(1) does not apply—

(a) in relation to a shift that would be (or would have been) worked, or is being worked, by a worker as an agency worker (but see Part 3 of Schedule A1 for provision about rights of agency workers to payment for cancelled, moved and curtailed shifts);

(b) in relation to the cancellation, movement or curtailment of a shift that an employer has requested a worker to work, unless the worker reasonably believed, whether on agreeing to work the shift or at some later time before the cancellation, movement or curtailment, that they would be needed to work the shift;

(c) in other specified circumstances.

(2)–(5) [omitted]

(6) The duty in subsection (2) is to be taken not to have applied if—

(a) the employer pays to the worker an amount in relation to a number of hours that is at least equal to the amount of the payment that the employer would have been required to make to the worker under section 27BP(1) in relation to the same number of hours but for regulations made under subsection (1)(c), and

(b) the payment is made on or before the day on which the payment under section 27BP(1) would have had to be made if the employer had been required to make it.

(7) Subsection (4) of section 27BS applies for the purposes of subsection (6) of this section as it applies for the purposes of subsections (2) and (3) of that section.

27BS Contractual remuneration

(1) The right of a worker to receive a payment from an employer under section 27BP(1) does not affect any right of the worker in relation to remuneration under a worker's contract entered into between the worker and the employer ('contractual remuneration').

(2) Any contractual remuneration paid to a worker by an employer in relation to a number of hours goes towards discharging any liability of the employer to make a payment to the worker under section 27BP(1) in relation to the same hours.

(3) Any payment made by an employer to a worker under section 27BP(1) in relation to a number of hours goes towards discharging any liability of the employer to pay contractual remuneration to the worker in relation to the same hours.

(4) For the purposes of subsections (2) and (3), the hours to which a payment under section 27BP(1) relates are—

(a) where a shift has been cancelled, the hours that would have been worked if the shift had not been cancelled;

(b) where a shift has been moved, or moved and curtailed (at the same time), and no part of the shift as moved, or as moved and curtailed, corresponds to the time of the shift ('the original shift') before it was moved, or moved and curtailed, the hours that would have been worked during the original shift;

(c) where a shift has been moved, or moved and curtailed (at the same time), and part of the shift as moved, or as moved and curtailed, corresponds to the time of the original shift (but part does not), the hours that would have been worked during the part of the original shift that does not correspond to the shift as moved, or as moved and curtailed;

(d) where a shift has been—

(i) curtailed but not moved, or

(ii) moved and curtailed (at the same time) and the shift as moved and curtailed is to start and end within the time of the original shift,

the hours that would have been worked if the shift had not been curtailed, or moved and curtailed.

27BT Complaints to employment tribunal

(1) A worker may present a complaint to an employment tribunal that the worker's employer—

(a) has failed to make the whole or any part of a payment that the employer is liable to make to the worker under section 27BP(1);

(b) has unreasonably failed to give to the worker a notice under section 27BR(2);

(c) has given to the worker a notice in purported compliance with section 27BR(2) that—

(i) does not refer to any provision of the regulations;

(ii) does not contain an explanation or contains an explanation that is inadequate or untrue.

(2) An employment tribunal must not consider a complaint under subsection (1)(a) relating to a payment unless it is presented before the end of the period of six months beginning with the day after the day on or before which the payment should have been made (see section 27BP(5)).

(3) An employment tribunal must not consider a complaint under subsection (1)(b) relating to a notice unless it is presented before the end of the period of six months beginning with the day after the day on or before which the notice should have been given (see section 27BR(5)(b)).

(4) An employment tribunal must not consider a complaint under subsection (1)(c) relating to a notice unless it is presented before the end of the period of six months beginning with the day after the day on which the notice is given.

(5) But, if the employment tribunal is satisfied that it was not reasonably practicable for a complaint under this section to be presented before the end of the relevant period of six months, the tribunal may consider the complaint if it is presented within such further period as the tribunal considers reasonable.

(6) Section 207B (extension of time limits to facilitate conciliation before institution of proceedings) applies for the purposes of subsections (2) to (4).

27BU Remedies

(1) Where an employment tribunal finds a complaint under section 27BT(1)(a) well-founded, the tribunal must—

(a) make a declaration to that effect, and

(b) order the employer to pay to the worker the amount of the payment under section 27BP(1) which it finds is due to the worker.

(2) Where an employment tribunal finds a complaint under section 27BT(1)(b) or (c) well-founded, the tribunal—

(a) must make a declaration to that effect, and

(b) may order the employer to make a payment to the worker of such amount, not exceeding the specified amount, as the tribunal considers just and equitable in all the circumstances.

(3) But an employment tribunal may not make an order under subsection (2)(b) relating to a notice given in purported compliance with section 27BR(2) if the tribunal makes an order under subsection (1)(b) relating to the same payment to which the notice related.

(4) In determining—

(a) whether to make an order under subsection (2)(b), and

(b) if so, how much to order the employer to pay,

an employment tribunal must have regard, in particular, to the seriousness of the matter complained of.

Chapter 5 Agency workers: guaranteed hours and rights relating to shifts

27BV Agency workers

(1) In this Part, 'agency worker' means an individual—

(a) who has a worker's contract or an arrangement with a work-finding agency by virtue of which the individual is (or is to be) supplied to work for and under the supervision and direction of another person,

(b) who does not do (or is not to do) the work under a worker's contract with the other person, and

(c) who is not (or is not to be) a party to a contract under which the individual undertakes to do the work for another party to the contract whose status is, by virtue of the contract, that of a client or customer of any profession or business undertaking carried on by the individual.

(2) In this Part—

(a) references to an agency worker include, where the context requires, a former agency worker, and

(b) where that is the case, references in relation to the agency worker to a work-finding agency, and references (however expressed) to a person for and under the supervision and direction of whom the agency worker works, are to be read accordingly.

(3) An individual is an 'agency worker' for the purposes of this Part—

(a) whether the individual is (or is to be) supplied to work for and under the supervision and direction of another person—

(i) by the work-finding agency referred to in subsection (1)(a), or

(ii) by a person other than the work-finding agency;

(b) whether the individual is (or is to be) paid, for work done for and under the supervision and direction of another person—

(i) by the work-finding agency referred to in subsection (1)(a), or

(ii) by a person other than the work-finding agency.

(4) In this Part, 'work-finding agency' means a person carrying on the business (whether or not with a view to profit and whether or not in conjunction with any other business) of finding, or seeking to find, work for individuals to do for and under the supervision and direction of other persons (but not in the employment of those other persons).

(5) Part 1 of Schedule A1 contains provision about guaranteed hours and agency workers.

(6) Part 2 of Schedule A1 contains provision about rights of agency workers to reasonable notice in relation to shifts.

(7) Part 3 of Schedule A1 contains provision about rights of agency workers to payment for shifts that are cancelled, moved or curtailed at short notice.

27BW–27BZ3 [omitted]

PART 2B TIPS, GRATUITIES AND SERVICE CHARGES

Requirement to deal with tips, gratuities and service charges

27C Qualifying tips, gratuities and service charges

(1) This Part makes provision for—

(a) how employers must deal with qualifying tips, gratuities and service charges,

(b) [omitted]

(2) In this Part 'qualifying tips, gratuities and service charges' means—

(a) employer-received tips, and

(b) worker-received tips which—

(i) are subject to employer control, or

(ii) are connected with any other worker-received tips which are subject to employer control.

(3) An 'employer-received tip' is an amount paid by a customer of an employer by way of a tip, gratuity or service charge (however described) which—

(a) is received upon its payment or subsequently by the employer or an associated person, or
(b) is received upon its payment by a person under a payment arrangement made between the employer and that person.

(4) A 'worker-received tip' is an amount paid by a customer of an employer by way of a tip, gratuity or service charge (however described) which—

(a) is received upon its payment by a worker of the employer, and
(b) is not subsequently received by the employer or an associated person.

(5) For the purposes of subsection (2)(b)—

(a) a worker-received tip is subject to employer control if the employer or an associated person exercises control or significant influence over the allocation of the tip;
(b) a worker-received tip ('tip A') is connected with another worker-received tip which is subject to employer control ('tip B') if—
(i) both tips are paid at, or are otherwise attributable to, the same place of business, and
(ii) tip A is paid later in the week, or in the week following the week, in which tip B is paid.

(6) In this section the 'amount paid by a customer of an employer by way of a tip, gratuity or service charge' means the actual amount paid by the customer (and accordingly any deductions from the amount paid, whether deducted by the employer or any other person, are to be disregarded when determining the amount paid by the customer).

(7) An amount paid by a customer of an employer is not paid by way of a tip, gratuity or service charge to the extent that the amount represents payment of value added tax.

(8) If an amount is not paid in money, it can be a qualifying tip, gratuity or service charge only if it is paid in the form of a voucher, stamp, token or similar item which is—

(a) of a fixed value expressed in monetary terms, and
(b) capable of being exchanged (whether on its own or together with other vouchers, stamps, tokens or items, and whether immediately or only after a time) for money, goods or services (or for any combination of two or more of those things).

(9) In this section—

'payment arrangement' means an arrangement between an employer and another person under which payments made by customers of the employer are to be received by the other person instead of the employer;

'week' means any period of seven days beginning with a Monday (and ending with a Sunday).

27D How tips etc must be dealt with

(1) An employer must ensure that the total amount of the qualifying tips, gratuities and service charges paid at, or otherwise attributable to, a place of business of the employer is allocated fairly between workers of the employer at that place of business.

(2) Where a worker is allocated an amount of employer-received tips in accordance with subsection (1), that amount is payable to the worker by the employer.

(3) In determining what would be a fair allocation of qualifying tips, gratuities and service charges under this section or section 27E (non-public places of business), regard must be had to the relevant provisions of any code of practice issued under this Part.

(4) [omitted]

27E–27F [omitted]

27G When tips etc must be dealt with

The employer must—

(a) ensure that a qualifying tip, gratuity or service charge is allocated in accordance with section 27D(1), and

(b) make any payment that the employer is required to make to a worker under section 27D(2) as a result of that allocation,

no later than the end of the month following the month in which the tip, gratuity or service charge was paid by the customer.

27H Agency workers

(1) In this Part an 'eligible agency worker' is an individual—

(a) who is supplied by a person (the 'agent') to do work for another person (the 'principal') under a contract or other arrangements made between the agent and the principal, but

(b) who is not, as respects that work, a worker of the principal because of the absence of a worker's contract between the individual and the principal, and

(c) who is not a party to a contract under which the individual undertakes to do the work for another party to the contract whose status is, by virtue of the contract, that of a client or customer of any profession or business undertaking carried on by the individual.

(2) Where an eligible agency worker does work for the principal at a place of business of the principal, this Part applies as if—

(a) the eligible agency worker were a worker of the principal, and

(b) the principal were the employer of the eligible agency worker.

(3) Where an amount is payable to an eligible agency worker under section 27D(2)—

(a) the amount may instead be paid to the agent (within the period specified in section 27G);

(b) the employer must not make any unauthorised deductions from the amount (whether or not the amount is paid to the agent under paragraph (a)).

(4) Where an amount is paid to the agent under subsection (3)—

(a) the amount becomes payable to the eligible agency worker by the agent before the end of the month after the month in which the agent is paid the amount under subsection (3), and

(b) the agent must not make any unauthorised deductions from the amount.

(5) In this section 'unauthorised deduction' means a deduction that is not required or authorised to be made by virtue of a statutory provision.

(6) In this Part a reference to an eligible agency worker includes, where the context requires, a reference to a former eligible agency worker.

Information

27I Written policy

(1) Where qualifying tips, gratuities and service charges are paid at, or are otherwise attributable to, a place of business of an employer on more than an occasional and exceptional basis, the employer must have a written policy on dealing with qualifying tips, gratuities and service charges for the place of business.

(2) A written policy for a place of business must include the following information—

(a) whether the employer requires or encourages customers to pay tips, gratuities and service charges at the place of business;

(b) how the employer ensures that all qualifying tips, gratuities and service charges paid at, or otherwise attributable to, the place of business are dealt with in accordance with this Part, including how the employer allocates qualifying tips, gratuities and service charges between workers at the place of business.

(3) Where an employer is required by this section to have a written policy for a place of business, the employer must make the written policy available to all workers of the employer at the place of business.

(4) Subsection (5) applies in a case where—

(a) an employer is not required by this section to have a written policy for a place of business, but

(b) the employer would be required by this section to have such a written policy if worker-received tips paid at, or otherwise attributable to, the place of business were qualifying tips, gratuities and service charges.

(5) In that case, the employer must make the following information available to all workers of the employer at the place of business—

(a) the fact that the employer is not required by this section to have a written policy for the place of business, and

(b) the reasons why the employer is not required by this section to have such a written policy.

(6) Where—

(a) an employer makes a written policy available to workers at a place of business under this section, and

(b) the employer subsequently amends that policy,

the employer must make the amended version of the policy available to all workers of the employer at the place of business.

27J Records

(1) Where qualifying tips, gratuities and service charges are paid at, or are otherwise attributable to, a place of business of an employer on more than an occasional and exceptional basis, the employer must—

(a) create a record of how every qualifying tip, gratuity and service charge paid at, or otherwise attributable to, the place of business has been dealt with in accordance with this Part, and

(b) maintain that record for a period of three years beginning with the date on which the qualifying tip, gratuity or service charge was paid.

(2) The record required by subsection (1) must include—

(a) the amount of qualifying tips, gratuities and service charges paid at, or otherwise attributable to, the place of business;

(b) the amount of those qualifying tips, gratuities and service charges—

(i) that the employer allocated to workers of the employer at the place of business;

(ii) that the employer arranged to be allocated to workers of the employer at the place of business by an independent tronc operator in accordance with section 27F.

(3) A worker of an employer may make a written request for the employer to provide the following records for a period specified in the request in relation to a place of business of the employer that the worker worked at—

(a) the amount of qualifying tips, gratuities and service charges paid at, or otherwise attributable to, the place of business;

(b) the amount of those qualifying tips, gratuities and service charges—

(i) that the employer allocated to the worker;

(ii) that the employer arranged to be allocated to workers of the employer at the place of business by an independent tronc operator in accordance with section 27F.

(4) Where—

(a) an employer receives a request from a worker under subsection (3) for records in relation to a place of business of the employer, and

(b) the employer is required by this section to maintain those records,

the employer must, within the response period, provide the worker with the requested records in respect of the period specified in the request or a substantially similar period.

(5) Subsection (6) applies in a case where—

(a) an employer receives a request from a worker under subsection (3) for records in relation to a place of business of the employer,

(b) the employer is not required by this section to maintain those records, but

(c) the employer would be required by this section to maintain those records if worker-received tips paid at, or otherwise attributable to, the place of business were qualifying tips, gratuities and service charges.

(6) In that case, the employer must, within the response period, notify the worker—

(a) that the employer is not required by this section to maintain the requested records, and

(b) of the reasons why the employer is not required by this section to maintain those records.

(7) A worker may request records under this section in respect of a period only if—

(a) the period is a period of one month or two or more consecutive months,

(b) the period begins no more than three years before the date of the request,

(c) the period ends before the date of the request, and

(d) the worker worked for the employer at any time during each month that forms part of the request.

(8) A worker may not make more than one request for records under this section in any three month period.

(9) Except as provided by subsection (10), a disclosure of information required by subsection (4) does not breach—

(a) any obligation of confidence owed by the person making the disclosure, or

(b) any other restriction on the disclosure of information (however imposed).

(10) Subsection (4) does not require a disclosure of information that would contravene the data protection legislation (but in determining whether a disclosure would do so, the duty imposed by that subsection is to be taken into account).

(11) In this section—

'the data protection legislation' has the same meaning as in the Data Protection Act 2018 (see section 3(9) of that Act);

'date of the request' means the date that the request is received by the employer;

'response period' means the period of four weeks beginning with the date of the request.

Enforcement

27K Complaints to employment tribunal about tips etc

(1) A worker may present a complaint to an employment tribunal that the worker's employer has failed to comply with—

(a) section 27D (how tips etc must be dealt with), or

(b) section 27G (when tips etc must be dealt with),

in relation to the worker.

(2) An eligible agency worker may also present a complaint to an employment tribunal that an agent has failed to comply with the requirement to make a payment to the eligible agency worker that the agent was required to make under section 27H(4).

(3) An employment tribunal must not consider a complaint under this section unless it is presented before the end of the period of twelve months beginning with the date of the failure to comply.

(4) But, if the employment tribunal is satisfied that it was not reasonably practicable for a complaint to be presented before the end of the relevant period of twelve months, the tribunal may consider the complaint if it is presented within such further period as the tribunal considers reasonable.

(5) If a complaint is presented under this section in respect of a series of failures to comply, the reference in subsection (3) to the date of the failure to comply is to the date of the last failure in the series.

(6) An eligible agency worker may present a complaint under subsection (2) whether or not the eligible agency worker also presents a complaint under subsection (1).

(7) Section 207B (extension of time limits to facilitate conciliation before institution of proceedings) applies for the purposes of subsection (3).

27L Determination of complaints about tips etc

(1) If an employment tribunal finds a complaint under section 27K well founded—

(a) it must make a declaration to that effect, and

(b) it may—

(i) in the case of a complaint under section 27K(1), make an order requiring the employer to deal with qualifying tips, gratuities and service charges that were paid at, or were otherwise attributable to, a place of business of the employer in accordance with this Part;

(ii) in the case of a complaint under section 27K(2), make an order requiring the agent to make a payment to the eligible agency worker of the amount that the agent was required under section 27H to pay to the eligible agency worker.

(2) An order made under subsection (1)(b)(i) may in particular—

(a) require the employer to revise an allocation made by the employer under section 27D;

(b) make a recommendation to the employer regarding that allocation;

(c) require the employer to make a payment to one or more workers of the employer in accordance with this Part (including a worker who is not the complainant).

(3) A recommendation made under subsection (2)(b) is not binding on an employer, but is to be admissible in evidence in proceedings before an employment tribunal; and any provision of the recommendation which appears to the tribunal to be relevant to any question arising in the proceedings is to be taken into account in determining that question.

(4) An order made under subsection (1)(b)(i) following a complaint presented by a worker does not prevent a different worker from presenting a complaint under this Part in relation to the same employer or the same qualifying tips, gratuities and service charges.

27M Compensation: dealing with tips etc

(1) If an employment tribunal makes a declaration under section 27L(1)(a), it may order the employer or agent (as the case may be) to pay to the complainant such amount, not exceeding £5,366, as the tribunal considers appropriate in all the circumstances to compensate the complainant for any financial loss sustained by the complainant which is attributable to the matter complained of.

(2) The tribunal may make an order under this section whether or not an order under section 27L(1)(b) has been made.

27N–43ZB [omitted]

PART IVA PROTECTED DISCLOSURES

43A Meaning of 'protected disclosure'

In this Act a 'protected disclosure' means a qualifying disclosure (as defined by section 43B) which is made by a worker in accordance with any of sections 43C to 43H.

43B Disclosures qualifying for protection

(1) In this Part a 'qualifying disclosure' means any disclosure of information which, in the reasonable belief of the worker making the disclosure, is made in the public interest and tends to show one or more of the following—

(a) that a criminal offence has been committed, is being committed or is likely to be committed,

(b) that a person has failed, is failing or is likely to fail to comply with any legal obligation to which he is subject,

(c) that a miscarriage of justice has occurred, is occurring or is likely to occur,

(d) that the health or safety of any individual has been, is being or is likely to be endangered,
(da) that sexual harassment has occurred, is occurring or is likely to occur,
(e) that the environment has been, is being or is likely to be damaged, or
(f) that information tending to show any matter falling within any one of the preceding paragraphs has been, is being or is likely to be deliberately concealed.

(2) For the purposes of subsection (1), it is immaterial whether the relevant failure occurred, occurs or would occur in the United Kingdom or elsewhere, and whether the law applying to it is that of the United Kingdom or of any other country or territory.

(3) A disclosure of information is not a qualifying disclosure if the person making the disclosure commits an offence by making it.

(4) A disclosure of information in respect of which a claim to legal professional privilege (or, in Scotland, to confidentiality as between client and professional legal adviser) could be maintained in legal proceedings is not a qualifying disclosure if it is made by a person to whom the information had been disclosed in the course of obtaining legal advice.

(5) In this Part 'the relevant failure', in relation to a qualifying disclosure, means the matter falling within paragraphs (a) to (f) of subsection (1).

43C Disclosure to employer or other responsible person

(1) A qualifying disclosure is made in accordance with this section if the worker makes the disclosure—

(a) to his employer, or
(b) where the worker reasonably believes that the relevant failure relates solely or mainly to—
  (i) the conduct of a person other than his employer, or
  (ii) any other matter for which a person other than his employer has legal responsibility,

to that other person.

(2) A worker who, in accordance with a procedure whose use by him is authorised by his employer, makes a qualifying disclosure to a person other than his employer, is to be treated for the purposes of this Part as making the qualifying disclosure to his employer.

43D Disclosure to legal adviser

A qualifying disclosure is made in accordance with this section if it is made in the course of obtaining legal advice.

43E Disclosure to Minister of the Crown

A qualifying disclosure is made in accordance with this section if—

(a) the worker's employer is—
  (i) an individual appointed under any enactment (including any enactment comprised in, or in an instrument made under, an Act of the Scottish Parliament) by a Minister of the Crown or a member of the Scottish Executive, or
  (ii) a body any of whose members are so appointed, and
(b) the disclosure is made to a Minister of the Crown or a member of the Scottish Executive.

43F Disclosure to prescribed person

(1) A qualifying disclosure is made in accordance with this section if the worker—

(a) makes the disclosure to a person prescribed by an order made by the Secretary of State for the purposes of this section, and
(b) reasonably believes—
  (i) that the relevant failure falls within any description of matters in respect of which that person is so prescribed, and
  (ii) that the information disclosed, and any allegation contained in it, are substantially true.

(2) An order prescribing persons for the purposes of this section may specify persons or descriptions of persons and shall specify the descriptions of matters in respect of which each person, or persons of each description, is or are prescribed.

43FA [omitted]

43G Disclosure in other cases

(1) A qualifying disclosure is made in accordance with this section if—

(a) [repealed]

(b) the worker reasonably believes that the information disclosed, and any allegation contained in it, are substantially true,

(c) he does not make the disclosure for purposes of personal gain,

(d) any of the conditions in subsection (2) is met, and

(e) in all the circumstances of the case, it is reasonable for him to make the disclosure.

(2) The conditions referred to in subsection (1)(d) are—

(a) that, at the time he makes the disclosure, the worker reasonably believes that he will be subjected to a detriment by his employer if he makes a disclosure to his employer or in accordance with section 43F,

(b) that, in a case where no person is prescribed for the purposes of section 43F in relation to the relevant failure, the worker reasonably believes that it is likely that evidence relating to the relevant failure will be concealed or destroyed if he makes a disclosure to his employer, or

(c) that the worker has previously made a disclosure of substantially the same information—

(i) to his employer, or

(ii) in accordance with section 43F.

(3) In determining for the purposes of subsection (1)(e) whether it is reasonable for the worker to make the disclosure, regard shall be had, in particular, to—

(a) the identity of the person to whom the disclosure is made,

(b) the seriousness of the relevant failure,

(c) whether the relevant failure is continuing or is likely to occur in the future,

(d) whether the disclosure is made in breach of a duty of confidentiality owed by the employer to any other person,

(e) in a case falling within subsection (2)(c)(i) or (ii), any action which the employer or the person to whom the previous disclosure in accordance with section 43F was made has taken or might reasonably be expected to have taken as a result of the previous disclosure, and

(f) in a case falling within subsection (2)(c)(i), whether in making the disclosure to the employer the worker complied with any procedure whose use by him was authorised by the employer.

(4) For the purposes of this section a subsequent disclosure may be regarded as a disclosure of substantially the same information as that disclosed by a previous disclosure as mentioned in subsection (2)(c) even though the subsequent disclosure extends to information about action taken or not taken by any person as a result of the previous disclosure.

43H Disclosure of exceptionally serious failure

(1) A qualifying disclosure is made in accordance with this section if—

(a) [repealed]

(b) the worker reasonably believes that the information disclosed, and any allegation contained in it, are substantially true,

(c) he does not make the disclosure for purposes of personal gain,

(d) the relevant failure is of an exceptionally serious nature, and

(e) in all the circumstances of the case, it is reasonable for him to make the disclosure.

(2) In determining for the purposes of subsection (1)(e) whether it is reasonable for the worker to make the disclosure, regard shall be had, in particular, to the identity of the person to whom the disclosure is made.

43J Contractual duties of confidentiality

(1) Any provision in an agreement to which this section applies is void in so far as it purports to preclude the worker from making a protected disclosure.

(2) This section applies to any agreement between a worker and his employer (whether a worker's contract or not), including an agreement to refrain from instituting or continuing any proceedings under this Act or any proceedings for breach of contract.

43K Extension of meaning of 'worker' etc. for Part IVA

(1) For the purposes of this Part 'worker' includes an individual who is not a worker as defined by section 230(3) but who—

- (a) works or worked for a person in circumstances in which—
  - (i) he is or was introduced or supplied to do that work by a third person, and
  - (ii) the terms on which he is or was engaged to do the work are or were in practice substantially determined not by him but by the person for whom he works or worked, by the third person or by both of them,
- (b) contracts or contracted with a person, for the purposes of that person's business, for the execution of work to be done in a place not under the control or management of that person and would fall within section 230(3)(b) if for 'personally' in that provision there were substituted '(whether personally or otherwise)',
- (ba) works or worked as a person performing services under a contract entered into by him with NHS England under section 83(2), 84, 92, 100, 107, 115(4), 117 or 134 of, or Schedule 12, to the National Health Service Act 2006 or with a Local Health Board under section 41(2)(b), 42, 50, 57, 64 or 92 of, or Schedule 7, to the National Health Service (Wales) Act 2006,
- (bb) works or worked as a person performing services under a contract entered into by him with a Health Board under section 17J or 17Q of the National Health Service (Scotland) Act 1978,
- (c) works or worked as a person providing services in accordance with arrangements made—
  - (i) by the National Health Service Commissioning Board under section 126 of the National Health Service Act 2006, or Local Health Board under section 71 or 80 of the National Health Service (Wales) Act 2006, or
  - (ii) by a Health Board under section 2C, 17AA, 17C, 25, 26 or 27 of the National Health Service (Scotland) Act 1978,
- (ca) [repealed]
- (cb) is or was provided with work experience provided pursuant to a course of education or training approved by, or under arrangements with, the Nursing and Midwifery Council in accordance with article 15(6)(a) of the Nursing and Midwifery Order 2001 (SI 2002/253), or
- (d) is or was provided with work experience provided pursuant to a training course or programme or with training for employment (or with both) otherwise than—
  - (i) under a contract of employment, or
  - (ii) by an educational establishment on a course run by that establishment;

  and any reference to a worker's contract, to employment or to a worker being 'employed' shall be construed accordingly.

(2) For the purposes of this Part 'employer' includes—

- (a) in relation to a worker falling within paragraph (a) of subsection (1), the person who substantially determines or determined the terms on which he is or was engaged,

(aa) in relation to a worker falling within paragraph (ba) of that subsection, NHS England, or the Local Health Board referred to in that paragraph,
(ab) in relation to a worker falling within paragraph (bb) of that subsection, the Health Board referred to in that paragraph,
(b) in relation to a worker falling within paragraph (c) of that subsection, NHS England or board referred to in that paragraph,
(ba) [repealed]
(c) in relation to a worker falling within paragraph (cb) or (d) of that subsection, the person providing the work experience or training.

(3) In this section 'educational establishment' includes any university, college, school or other educational establishment.

(4)–(5) [omitted]

43KA [omitted]

43L Other interpretative provisions

(1) In this Part—

'qualifying disclosure' has the meaning given by section 43B;

'the relevant failure', in relation to a qualifying disclosure, has the meaning given by section 43B(5),

'sexual harassment' means harassment of the kind described in section 26(2) of the Equality Act 2010 (unwanted conduct of a sexual nature).

(2) In determining for the purposes of this Part whether a person makes a disclosure for purposes of personal gain, there shall be disregarded any reward payable by or under any enactment.

(3) Any reference in this Part to the disclosure of information shall have effect, in relation to any case where the person receiving the information is already aware of it, as a reference to bringing the information to his attention.

PART V PROTECTION FROM SUFFERING DETRIMENT IN EMPLOYMENT

Rights not to suffer detriment

43M [omitted]

44 Health and safety cases

(1) An employee has the right not to be subjected to any detriment by any act, or any deliberate failure to act, by his employer done on the ground that—

(a) having been designated by the employer to carry out activities in connection with preventing or reducing risks to health and safety at work, the employee carried out (or proposed to carry out) any such activities,
(b) being a representative of workers on matters of health and safety at work or member of a safety committee—
(i) in accordance with arrangements established under or by virtue of any enactment, or
(ii) by reason of being acknowledged as such by the employer, the employee performed (or proposed to perform) any functions as such a representative or a member of such a committee,
(ba) the employee took part (or proposed to take part) in consultation with the employer pursuant to the Health and Safety (Consultation with Employees) Regulations 1996 or in an election of representatives of employee safety within the meaning of those Regulations (whether as a candidate or otherwise),

(c) being an employee at a place where—
  (i) there was no such representative or safety committee, or
  (ii) there was such a representative or safety committee but it was not reasonably practicable for the employee to raise the matter by those means,

he brought to his employer's attention, by reasonable means, circumstances connected with his work which he reasonably believed were harmful or potentially harmful to health or safety,

(d) and (e) [repealed]

(1A) A worker has the right not to be subjected to any detriment by any act, or any deliberate failure to act, by his or her employer done on the ground that—

(a) in circumstances of danger which the worker reasonably believed to be serious and imminent and which he or she could not reasonably have been expected to avert, he or she left (or proposed to leave) or (while the danger persisted) refused to return to his or her place of work or any dangerous part of his or her place of work, or
(b) in circumstances of danger which the worker reasonably believed to be serious and imminent, he or she took (or proposed to take) appropriate steps to protect himself or herself or other persons from the danger.

(2) For the purposes of subsection (1A)(b) whether steps which a worker took (or proposed to take) were appropriate is to be judged by reference to all the circumstances including, in particular, his knowledge and the facilities and advice available to him at the time.

(3) A worker is not to be regarded as having been subjected to any detriment on the ground specified in subsection (1A)(b) if the employer shows that it was (or would have been) so negligent for the worker to take the steps which he took (or proposed to take) that a reasonable employer might have treated him as the employer did.

(4) This section does not apply where the worker is an employee and the detriment in question amounts to dismissal (within the meaning of Part X).

45–45ZA [omitted]

45A Working time cases

(1) A worker has the right not to be subjected to any detriment by any act, or any deliberate failure to act, by his employer done on the ground that the worker—

(a) refused (or proposed to refuse) to comply with a requirement which the employer imposed (or proposed to impose) in contravention of the Working Time Regulations 1998,
(b) refused (or proposed to refuse) to forgo a right conferred on him by those Regulations,
(c) failed to sign a workforce agreement for the purposes of those Regulations, or to enter into, or agree to vary or extend, any other agreement with his employer which is provided for in those Regulations,
(d) being—
  (i) a representative of members of the workforce for the purposes of Schedule 1 to those Regulations, or
  (ii) a candidate in an election in which any person elected will, on being elected, be such a representative,

performed (or proposed to perform) any functions or activities as such a representative or candidate,

(e) brought proceedings against the employer to enforce a right conferred on him by those Regulations, or
(f) alleged that the employer had infringed such a right.

(2) It is immaterial for the purposes of subsection (1)(e) or (f)—

(a) whether or not the worker has the right, or

(b) whether or not the right has been infringed, but, for those provisions to apply, the claim to the right and that it has been infringed must be made in good faith.

(3) It is sufficient for subsection (1)(f) to apply that the worker, without specifying the right, made it reasonably clear to the employer what the right claimed to have been infringed was.

(4) This section does not apply where a worker is an employee and the detriment in question amounts to dismissal within the meaning of Part X.

(5) [omitted]

46 [omitted]

47 Employee representatives

(1) An employee has the right not to be subjected to any detriment by any act, or any deliberate failure to act, by his employer done on the ground that, being—

(a) an employee representative for the purposes of Chapter II of Part IV of the Trade Union and Labour Relations (Consolidation) Act 1992 (redundancies) or Regulations 9, 13 and 15 of the Transfer of Undertakings (Protection of Employment) Regulations 2006, or

(b) a candidate in an election in which any person elected will, on being elected, be such an employee representative,

he performed (or proposed to perform) any functions or activities as such an employee representative or candidate.

(1A) An employee has the right not to be subjected to any detriment by any act, or by any deliberate failure to act, by his employer done on the ground of his participation in an election of employee representatives for the purposes of Chapter II of Part IV of the Trade Union and Labour Relations (Consolidation) Act 1992 (redundancies) or Regulations 9, 13 and 15 of the Transfer of Undertakings (Protection of Employment) Regulations 2006.

(2) This section does not apply where the detriment in question amounts to a dismissal (within the meaning of Part X).

47A Employees exercising right to time off work for study or training

(1) An employee has the right not to be subjected to any detriment by any act, or any deliberate failure to act, by his employer or the principal (within the meaning of section 63A(3)) done on the ground that, being a person entitled to—

(a) time off under section 63A(1) or (3), and

(b) remuneration under section 63B(1) in respect of that time taken off, the employee exercised (or proposed to exercise) that right or received (or sought to receive) such remuneration.

(2) This section does not apply where the detriment in question amounts to dismissal (within the meaning of Part X).

47B Protected disclosures

(1) A worker has the right not to be subjected to any detriment by any act, or any deliberate failure to act, by his employer done on the ground that the worker has made a protected disclosure.

(1A) A worker ('W') has the right not to be subjected to any detriment by any act, or any deliberate failure to act, done—

(a) by another worker of W's employer in the course of that other worker's employment, or

(b) by an agent of W's employer with the employer's authority,

on the ground that W has made a protected disclosure.

(1B) Where a worker is subjected to detriment by anything done as mentioned in subsection (1A), that thing is treated as also done by the worker's employer.

(1C) For the purposes of subsection (1B), it is immaterial whether the thing is done with the knowledge or approval of the worker's employer.

(1D) In proceedings against W's employer in respect of anything alleged to have been done as mentioned in subsection (1A)(a), it is a defence for the employer to show that the employer took all reasonable steps to prevent the other worker—

(a) from doing that thing, or
(b) from doing anything of that description.

(1E) A worker or agent of W's employer is not liable by reason of subsection (1A) for doing something that subjects W to detriment if—

(a) the worker or agent does that thing in reliance on a statement by the employer that doing it does not contravene this Act, and
(b) it is reasonable for the worker or agent to rely on the statement.

But this does not prevent the employer from being liable by reason of subsection (1B).

(2) This section does not apply where—

(a) the worker is an employee, and
(b) the detriment in question amounts to dismissal (within the meaning of Part X).

(3) For the purposes of this section, and of sections 48 and 49 so far as relating to this section, 'worker', 'worker's contract', 'employment' and 'employer' have the extended meaning given by section 43K.

47C Leave for family and domestic reasons

(1) An employee has the right not to be subjected to any detriment by any act, or any deliberate failure to act, by his employer done for a prescribed reason.

(2) A prescribed reason is one which is prescribed by regulations made by the Secretary of State and which relates to—

(a) pregnancy, childbirth or maternity,
(aa) time off under section 57ZE,
(ab) time off under section 57ZJ or 57ZL,
(b) ordinary, compulsory or additional maternity leave,
(ba) ordinary or additional adoption leave,
(bb) shared parental leave,
(bc) carer's leave,
(c) parental leave,
(ca) paternity leave,
(cb) parental bereavement leave,
(cc) neonatal care leave, or
(d) time off under section 57A.

(3) A reason prescribed under this section in relation to parental leave may relate to action which an employee takes, agrees to take or refuses to take under or in respect of a collective or workforce agreement.

(4)–(7) [omitted]

47D [omitted]

47E Flexible working

(1) An employee has the right not to be subjected to any detriment by any act, or any deliberate failure to act, by his employer done on the ground that the employee—

(a) made (or proposed to make) an application under section 80F,
(b) [repealed]
(c) brought proceedings against the employer under section 80H, or
(d) alleged the existence of any circumstance which would constitute a ground for bringing such proceedings.

(2) This section does not apply where the detriment in question amounts to dismissal within the meaning of Part 10.

47F [omitted]

47G Employee shareholder status

(1) An employee has the right not to be subjected to a detriment by any act, or any deliberate failure to act, by the employee's employer done on the ground that the employee refused to accept an offer by the employer for the employee to become an employee shareholder (within the meaning of section 205A).

(2) This section does not apply if the detriment in question amounts to dismissal within the meaning of Part 10.

Enforcement

48 Complaints to employment tribunals

(1) An employee may present a complaint to an employment tribunal that he has been subjected to a detriment in contravention of section 43M, 44(1), 45, 46, 47, 47A, 47C(1), 47E, 47F or 47G.

(1XA) A worker may present a complaint to an employment tribunal that the worker has been subjected to a detriment in contravention of section 44(1A).

(1YA) A shop worker may present a complaint to an employment tribunal that he or she has been subjected to a detriment in contravention of section 45ZA.

(1ZA) A worker may present a complaint to an employment tribunal that he has been subjected to a detriment in contravention of section 45A.

(1A) A worker may present a complaint to an employment tribunal that he has been subjected to a detriment in contravention of section 47B.

(1AA) [omitted]

(1B) A person may present a complaint to an employment tribunal that he has been subjected to a detriment in contravention of section 47D.

(2) On a complaint under subsection (1), (1XA), (1ZA), (1A), or (1B) it is for the employer to show the ground on which any act, or deliberate failure to act, was done.

(2A) [omitted]

(3) An employment tribunal shall not consider a complaint under this section unless it is presented—

- (a) before the end of the period of three months beginning with the date of the act or failure to act to which the complaint relates or, where that act or failure is part of a series of similar acts or failures, the last of them, or
- (b) within such further period as the tribunal considers reasonable in a case where it is satisfied that it was not reasonably practicable for the complaint to be presented before the end of that period of three months.

(4) For the purposes of subsection (3)—

- (a) where an act extends over a period, the 'date of the act' means the last day of that period, and
- (b) a deliberate failure to act shall be treated as done when it was decided on;

and, in the absence of evidence establishing the contrary, an employer, a temporary work agency or a hirer shall be taken to decide on a failure to act when he does an act inconsistent with doing the failed act or, if he has done no such inconsistent act, when the period expires within which he might reasonably have been expected to do the failed act if it was to be done.

(4A) [omitted]

(5) In this section and section 49 any reference to the employer includes—

- (a) where a person complains that he has been subjected to a detriment in contravention of section 47A, the principal (within the meaning of section 63A(3)),
- (b) in the case of proceedings against a worker or agent under section 47B(1A), the worker or agent.

(6) In this section and section 49 the following have the same meaning as in the Agency Workers Regulations 2010 (SI 2010/93)—

'agency worker';
'hirer';
'temporary work agency'.

49 Remedies

(1) Where an employment tribunal finds a complaint under section 48(1), (1XA), (1ZA), (1A), or (1B) well-founded, the tribunal—

(a) shall make a declaration to that effect, and
(b) may make an award of compensation to be paid by the employer to the complainant in respect of the act or failure to act to which the complaint relates.

(1A) [omitted]

(2) Subject to subsections (5ZA), (5A) and (6) the amount of the compensation awarded shall be such as the tribunal considers just and equitable in all the circumstances having regard to—

(a) the infringement to which the complaint relates, and
(b) any loss which is attributable to the act, or failure to act, which infringed the complainant's right.

(3) The loss shall be taken to include—

(a) any expenses reasonably incurred by the complainant in consequence of the act, or failure to act, to which the complaint relates, and
(b) loss of any benefit which he might reasonably be expected to have had but for that act or failure to act.

(4) In ascertaining the loss the tribunal shall apply the same rule concerning the duty of a person to mitigate his loss as applies to damages recoverable under the common law of England and Wales or (as the case may be) Scotland.

(5) Where the tribunal finds that the act, or failure to act, to which the complaint relates was to any extent caused or contributed to by action of the complainant, it shall reduce the amount of the compensation by such proportion as it considers just and equitable having regard to that finding.

(5ZA) Where—

(a) the complaint is made under section 48(1XA),
(b) the detriment to which the worker is subjected is the termination of his or her contract, and
(c) that contract is not a contract of employment,

any compensation must not exceed the compensation that would be payable under Chapter II of Part X if the worker had been an employee and had been dismissed for the reason specified in section 100.

(5A) Where—

(a) the complaint is made under section 48(1ZA),
(b) the detriment to which the worker is subjected is the termination of his worker's contract, and
(c) that contract is not a contract of employment,

any compensation must not exceed the compensation that would be payable under Chapter II of Part X if the worker had been an employee and had been dismissed for the reason specified in section 101A.

(6) Where—

(a) the complaint is made under section 48(1A),
(b) the detriment to which the worker is subjected is the termination of his worker's contract, and
(c) that contract is not a contract of employment,

any compensation must not exceed the compensation that would be payable under Chapter II of Part X if the worker had been an employee and had been dismissed for the reason specified in section 103A.

(6A) Where—

(a) the complaint is made under section 48(1A), and

(b) it appears to the tribunal that the protected disclosure was not made in good faith,

the tribunal may, if it considers it just and equitable in all the circumstances to do so, reduce any award it makes to the worker by no more than 25%.

(7) Where—

(a) the complaint is made under section 48(1B) by a person who is not an employee, and

(b) the detriment to which he is subjected is the termination of his contract with the person who is his employer for the purposes of section 25 of the Tax Credits Act 2002,

any compensation must not exceed the compensation that would be payable under Chapter 2 of Part 10 if the complainant had been an employee and had been dismissed for the reason specified in section 104B.

49A–49D [omitted]

PART VI TIME OFF WORK

Public duties

50 Right to time off for public duties

(1) An employer shall permit an employee of his who is—

(a) a justice of the peace, or

(b) an independent prison monitor appointed in accordance with section 7B(2) of the Prisons (Scotland) Act 1989,

to take time off during the employee's working hours for the purpose of performing any of the duties of the office.

(2) An employer shall permit an employee of his who is a member of—

(a) a local authority,

(b) a statutory tribunal,

(c) [repealed]

(ca) [repealed]

(d) an independent monitoring board for a prison,

(e) a relevant health body,

(f) a relevant education body,

(g) the Environment Agency or the Scottish Environment Protection Agency,

(h) Scottish Water,

(i) a panel of lay observers appointed in accordance with section 81(1)(b) of the Criminal Justice Act 1991,

(j) a Visiting Committee appointed in accordance with section 152(1) of the Immigration and Asylum Act 1999, or

(k) a Visiting Committee appointed by the Secretary of State for a short-term holding facility (within the meaning given by section 147 of the Immigration and Asylum Act 1999)

to take time off during the employee's working hours for the purposes specified in subsection (3).

(3) The purposes referred to in subsection (2) are—

(a) attendance at a meeting of the body or any of its committees or subcommittees, and

(b) the doing of any other thing approved by the body, or anything of a class so approved, for the purpose of the discharge of the functions of the body or of any of its committees or sub-committees, and

(c) in the case of a local authority which are operating executive arrangements—

(i) attendance at a meeting of the executive of that local authority or committee of that executive; and

(ii) the doing of any other thing, by an individual member of that executive, for the purposes of the discharge of any function which is to any extent the responsibility of that executive.

(4) The amount of time off which an employee is to be permitted to take under this section, and the occasions on which and any conditions subject to which time off maybe so taken, are those that are reasonable in all the circumstances having regard, in particular, to—

(a) how much time off is required for the performance of the duties of the office or as a member of the body in question, and how much time off is required for the performance of the particular duty,

(b) how much time off the employee has already been permitted under this section or sections 168 and 170 of the Trade Union and Labour Relations (Consolidation) Act 1992 (time off for trade union duties and activities), and

(c) the circumstances of the employer's business and the effect of the employee's absence on the running of that business.

(5)–(10) [omitted]

(11) For the purposes of this section the working hours of an employee shall be taken to be any time when, in accordance with his contract of employment, the employee is required to be at work.

51 Complaints to employment tribunals

(1) An employee may present a complaint to an employment tribunal that his employer has failed to permit him to take time off as required by section 50.

(2) An employment tribunal shall not consider a complaint under this section that an employer has failed to permit an employee to take time off unless it is presented—

(a) before the end of the period of three months beginning with the date on which the failure occurred, or

(b) within such further period as the tribunal considers reasonable in a case where it is satisfied that it was not reasonably practicable for the complaint to be presented before the end of that period of three months.

(2A) [omitted]

(3) Where an employment tribunal finds a complaint under this section well-founded, the tribunal—

(a) shall make a declaration to that effect, and

(b) may make an award of compensation to be paid by the employer to the employee.

(4) The amount of the compensation shall be such as the tribunal considers just and equitable in all the circumstances having regard to—

(a) the employer's default in failing to permit time off to be taken by the employee, and

(b) any loss sustained by the employee which is attributable to the matters to which the complaint relates.

Looking for work and making arrangements for training

52 Right to time off to look for work or arrange training

(1) An employee who is given notice of dismissal by reason of redundancy is entitled to be permitted by his employer to take reasonable time off during the employee's working hours before the end of his notice in order to—

(a) look for new employment, or

(b) make arrangements for training for future employment.

(2) An employee is not entitled to take time off under this section unless, on whichever is the later of—

(a) the date on which the notice is due to expire, and

(b) the date on which it would expire were it the notice required to be given by section 86(1),

he will have been (or would have been) continuously employed for a period of two years or more.

(3) For the purposes of this section the working hours of an employee shall be taken to be any time when, in accordance with his contract of employment, the employee is required to be at work.

53 Right to remuneration for time off under section 52

(1) An employee who is permitted to take time off under section 52 is entitled to be paid remuneration by his employer for the period of absence at the appropriate hourly rate.

(2) The appropriate hourly rate, in relation to an employee, is the amount of one week's pay divided by the number of normal working hours in a week for that employee when employed under the contract of employment in force on the day when the notice of dismissal was given.

(3) But where the number of normal working hours differs from week to week or over a longer period, the amount of one week's pay shall be divided instead by the average number of normal working hours calculated by dividing by twelve the total number of the employee's normal working hours during the period of twelve weeks ending with the last complete week before the day on which the notice was given.

(4) If an employer unreasonably refuses to permit an employee to take time off from work as required by section 52, the employee is entitled to be paid an amount equal to the remuneration to which he would have been entitled under subsection (1) if he had been permitted to take the time off.

(5) The amount of an employer's liability to pay remuneration under subsection (1) shall not exceed, in respect of the notice period of any employee, forty per cent. of a week's pay of that employee.

(6) A right to any amount under subsection (1) or (4) does not affect any right of an employee in relation to remuneration under his contract of employment ('contractual remuneration').

(7) Any contractual remuneration paid to an employee in respect of a period of time off under section 52 goes towards discharging any liability of the employer to pay remuneration under subsection (1) in respect of that period; and, conversely, any payment of remuneration under subsection (1) in respect of a period goes towards discharging any liability of the employer to pay contractual remuneration in respect of that period.

54 Complaints to employment tribunals

(1) An employee may present a complaint to an employment tribunal that his employer—

(a) has unreasonably refused to permit him to take time off as required by section 52, or

(b) has failed to pay the whole or any part of any amount to which the employee is entitled under section 53(1) or (4).

(2) An employment tribunal shall not consider a complaint under this section unless it is presented—

(a) before the end of the period of three months beginning with the date on which it is alleged that the time off should have been permitted, or

(b) within such further period as the tribunal considers reasonable in a case where it is satisfied that it was not reasonably practicable for the complaint to be presented before the end of that period of three months.

(2A) [omitted]

(3) Where an employment tribunal finds a complaint under this section well-founded, the tribunal shall—

(a) make a declaration to that effect, and

(b) order the employer to pay to the employee the amount which it finds due to him.

(4) The amount which may be ordered by a tribunal to be paid by an employer under subsection (3) (or, where the employer is liable to pay remuneration under section 53, the aggregate of that amount and the amount of that liability) shall not exceed, in respect of the notice period of any employee, forty per cent. of a week's pay of that employee.

Ante-natal care

55 Right to time off for ante-natal care

(1) An employee who—

(a) is pregnant, and

(b) has, on the advice of a registered medical practitioner, registered midwife or F1registered nurse, made an appointment to attend at any place for the purpose of receiving ante-natal care,

is entitled to be permitted by her employer to take time off during the employee's working hours in order to enable her to keep the appointment.

(2) An employee is not entitled to take time off under this section to keep an appointment unless, if her employer requests her to do so, she produces for his inspection—

(a) a certificate from a registered medical practitioner, registered midwife or F1registered nurse stating that the employee is pregnant, and

(b) an appointment card or some other document showing that the appointment has been made.

(3) Subsection (2) does not apply where the employee's appointment is the first appointment during her pregnancy for which she seeks permission to take time off in accordance with subsection (1).

(4) For the purposes of this section the working hours of an employee shall be taken to be any time when, in accordance with her contract of employment, the employee is required to be at work.

(5) References in this section to a registered nurse are to such a nurse—

(a) who is also registered in the Specialist Community Public Health Nurses' Part of the register maintained under article 5 of the Nursing and Midwifery Order 2001, and

(b) whose entry in that Part of the register is annotated to show that he holds a qualification in health visiting.

56 Right to remuneration for time off under section 55

(1) An employee who is permitted to take time off under section 55 is entitled to be paid remuneration by her employer for the period of absence at the appropriate hourly rate.

(2) The appropriate hourly rate, in relation to an employee, is the amount of one week's pay divided by the number of normal working hours in a week for that employee when employed under the contract of employment in force on the day when the time off is taken.

(3)–(6) [omitted]

57 Complaints to employment tribunals

(1) An employee may present a complaint to an employment tribunal that her employer—

(a) has unreasonably refused to permit her to take time off as required by section 55, or

(b) has failed to pay the whole or any part of any amount to which the employee is entitled under section 56.

(2) An employment tribunal shall not consider a complaint under this section unless it is presented—

(a) before the end of the period of three months beginning with the date of the appointment concerned, or

(b) within such further period as the tribunal considers reasonable in a case where it is satisfied that it was not reasonably practicable for the complaint to be presented before the end of that period of three months.

(2A) [omitted]

57ZA–57ZS [omitted]

Dependants

57A Time off for dependants

(1) An employee is entitled to be permitted by his employer to take a reasonable amount of time off during the employee's working hours in order to take action which is necessary—

(a) to provide assistance on an occasion when a dependant falls ill, gives birth or is injured or assaulted,

(b) to make arrangements for the provision of care for a dependant who is ill or injured,

(c) in consequence of the death of a dependant,

(d) because of the unexpected disruption or termination of arrangements for the care of a dependant, or

(e) to deal with an incident which involves a child of the employee and which occurs unexpectedly in a period during which an educational establishment which the child attends is responsible for him.

(2) Subsection (1) does not apply unless the employee—

(a) tells his employer the reason for his absence as soon as reasonably practicable, and

(b) except where paragraph (a) cannot be complied with until after the employee has returned to work, tells his employer for how long he expects to be absent.

(3) Subject to subsections (4) and (5), for the purposes of this section 'dependant' means, in relation to an employee—

(a) a spouse or civil partner,

(b) a child,

(c) a parent,

(d) a person who lives in the same household as the employee, otherwise than by reason of being his employee, tenant, lodger or boarder.

(4) For the purposes of subsection (1)(a) or (b) 'dependant' includes, in addition to the persons mentioned in subsection (3), any person who reasonably relies on the employee—

(a) for assistance on an occasion when the person falls ill or is injured or assaulted, or

(b) to make arrangements for the provision of care in the event of illness or injury.

(5) For the purposes of subsection (1)(d) 'dependant' includes, in addition to the persons mentioned in subsection (3), any person who reasonably relies on the employee to make arrangements for the provision of care.

(6) A reference in this section to illness or injury includes a reference to mental illness or injury.

57B Complaint to employment tribunal

(1) An employee may present a complaint to an employment tribunal that his employer has unreasonably refused to permit him to take time off as required by section 57A.

(2) An employment tribunal shall not consider a complaint under this section unless it is presented—

(a) before the end of the period of three months beginning with the date when the refusal occurred, or

(b) within such further period as the tribunal considers reasonable in a case where it is satisfied that it was not reasonably practicable for the complaint to be presented before the end of that period of three months.

(2A) [omitted]

(3) Where an employment tribunal finds a complaint under subsection (1) well-founded, it—

(a) shall make a declaration to that effect, and

(b) may make an award of compensation to be paid by the employer to the employee.

(4) the amount of compensation shall be such as the tribunal considers just and equitable in all the circumstances having regard to—

(a) the employer's default in refusing to permit time off to be taken by the employee, and

(b) any loss sustained by the employee which is attributable to the matters complained of.

58–60 [omitted]

Employee representatives

61 Right to time off for employee representatives

(1) An employee who is—

(a) an employee representative for the purposes of Chapter II of Part IV of the Trade Union and Labour Relations (Consolidation) Act 1992 (redundancies) or Regulations 9, 13 and 15 of the Transfer of Undertakings (Protection of Employment) Regulations 2006, or

(b) a candidate in an election in which any person elected will, on being elected, be such an employee representative,

is entitled to be permitted by his employer to take reasonable time off during the employee's working hours in order to perform his functions as such an employee representative or candidate or in order to undergo training to perform such functions.

(2) For the purposes of this section the working hours of an employee shall be taken to be any time when, in accordance with his contract of employment, the employee is required to be at work.

62 Right to remuneration for time off under section 61

(1) An employee who is permitted to take time off under section 61 is entitled to be paid remuneration by his employer for the time taken off at the appropriate hourly rate.

(2) The appropriate hourly rate, in relation to an employee, is the amount of one week's pay divided by the number of normal working hours in a week for that employee when employed under the contract of employment in force on the day when the time off is taken.

(3) But where the number of normal working hours differs from week to week or over a longer period, the amount of one week's pay shall be divided instead by—

(a) the average number of normal working hours calculated by dividing by twelve the total number of the employee's normal working hours during the period of twelve weeks ending with the last complete week before the day on which the time off is taken, or

(b) where the employee has not been employed for a sufficient period to enable the calculation to be made under paragraph (a), a number which fairly represents the number of normal working hours in a week having regard to such of the considerations specified in subsection (4) as are appropriate in the circumstances.

(4) The considerations referred to in subsection (3)(b) are—

(a) the average number of normal working hours in a week which the employee could expect in accordance with the terms of his contract, and

(b) the average number of normal working hours of other employees engaged in relevant comparable employment with the same employer.

(5) A right to any amount under subsection (1) does not affect any right of an employee in relation to remuneration under his contract of employment ('contractual remuneration').

(6) Any contractual remuneration paid to an employee in respect of a period of time off under section 61 goes towards discharging any liability of the employer to pay remuneration under subsection (1) in respect of that period; and, conversely, any payment of remuneration under subsection (1) in respect of a period goes towards discharging any liability of the employer to pay contractual remuneration in respect of that period.

63 Complaints to employment tribunals

(1) An employee may present a complaint to an employment tribunal that his employer—

(a) has unreasonably refused to permit him to take time off as required by section 61, or

(b) has failed to pay the whole or any part of any amount to which the employee is entitled under section 62.

(2) An employment tribunal shall not consider a complaint under this section unless it is presented—

(a) before the end of the period of three months beginning with the day on which the time off was taken or on which it is alleged the time off should have been permitted, or
(b) within such further period as the tribunal considers reasonable in a case where it is satisfied that it was not reasonably practicable for the complaint to be presented before the end of that period of three months.

(2A) [omitted]

(3) Where an employment tribunal finds a complaint under this section well-founded, the tribunal shall make a declaration to that effect.

(4) If the complaint is that the employer has unreasonably refused to permit the employee to take time off, the tribunal shall also order the employer to pay to the employee an amount equal to the remuneration to which he would have been entitled under section 62 if the employer had not refused.

(5) If the complaint is that the employer has failed to pay the employee the whole or part of any amount to which he is entitled under section 62, the tribunal shall also order the employer to pay to the employee the amount which it finds due to him.

63A–63K [omitted]

PART VII SUSPENSION FROM WORK

Suspension on medical grounds

64 Right to remuneration on suspension on medical grounds

(1) An employee who is suspended from work by his employer on medical grounds is entitled to be paid by his employer remuneration while he is so suspended for a period not exceeding twenty-six weeks.

(2) For the purposes of this Part an employee is suspended from work on medical grounds if he is suspended from work in consequence of—
(a) a requirement imposed by or under a provision of an enactment or of an instrument made under an enactment, or
(b) a recommendation in a provision of a code of practice issued or approved under section 16 of the Health and Safety at Work etc. Act 1974,

and the provision is for the time being specified in subsection (3).

(3) The provisions referred to in subsection (2) are—

Regulation 16 of the Control of Lead at Work Regulations 1980,
Regulation 25 of the Ionising Radiations Regulation 2017 [SI 2017/1075], and
Regulation 11 of the Control of Substances Hazardous to Health Regulations 1988.

(4) The Secretary of State may by order add provisions to or remove provisions from the list of provisions specified in subsection (3).

(5) For the purposes of this Part an employee shall be regarded as suspended from work on medical grounds only if and for so long as he—
(a) continues to be employed by his employer, but
(b) is not provided with work or does not perform the work he normally performed before the suspension.

65 Exclusions from right to remuneration

(1) An employee is not entitled to remuneration under section 64 unless he has been continuously employed for a period of not less than one month ending with the day before that on which the suspension begins.

(2) [repealed]

(3) An employee is not entitled to remuneration under section 64 in respect of any period during which he is incapable of work by reason of disease or bodily or mental disablement.

(4) An employee is not entitled to remuneration under section 64 in respect of any period if—

(a) his employer has offered to provide him with suitable alternative work during the period (whether or not it is work which the employee is under his contract, or was under the contract in force before the suspension, employed to perform) and the employee has unreasonably refused to perform that work, or

(b) he does not comply with reasonable requirements imposed by his employer with a view to ensuring that his services are available.

Suspension on maternity grounds

66 Meaning of suspension on maternity grounds

(1) For the purposes of this Part an employee is suspended from work on maternity grounds if, in consequence of any relevant requirement or relevant recommendation, she is suspended from work by her employer on the ground that she is pregnant, has recently given birth or is breast-feeding a child.

(2) In subsection (1)—

'relevant requirement' means a requirement imposed by or under a specified provision of an enactment or of an instrument made under an enactment, and

'relevant recommendation' means a recommendation in a specified provision of a code of practice issued or approved under section 16 of the Health and Safety at Work etc. Act 1974;

and in this subsection 'specified provision' means a provision for the time being specified in an order made by the Secretary of State under this subsection.

(3) For the purposes of this Part an employee shall be regarded as suspended from work on maternity grounds only if and for so long as she—

(a) continues to be employed by her employer, but

(b) is not provided with work or (disregarding alternative work for the purposes of section 67) does not perform the work she normally performed before the suspension.

67 Right to offer of alternative work

(1) Where an employer has available suitable alternative work for an employee, the employee has a right to be offered to be provided with the alternative work before being suspended from work on maternity grounds.

(2) For alternative work to be suitable for an employee for the purposes of this section—

(a) the work must be of a kind which is both suitable in relation to her and appropriate for her to do in the circumstances, and

(b) the terms and conditions applicable to her for performing the work, if they differ from the corresponding terms and conditions applicable to her for performing the work she normally performs under her contract of employment, must not be substantially less favourable to her than those corresponding terms and conditions.

68 Right to remuneration

(1) An employee who is suspended from work on maternity grounds is entitled to be paid remuneration by her employer while she is so suspended.

(2) An employee is not entitled to remuneration under this section in respect of any period if—

(a) her employer has offered to provide her during the period with work which is suitable alternative work for her for the purposes of section 67, and

(b) the employee has unreasonably refused to perform that work.

68A–68D [omitted]

General

69 Calculation of remuneration

(1) The amount of remuneration payable by an employer to an employee under section 64 or 68 is a week's pay in respect of each week of the period of suspension; and if in any week

remuneration is payable in respect of only part of that week the amount of a week's pay shall be reduced proportionately.

(2) A right to remuneration under section 64 or 68 does not affect any right of an employee in relation to remuneration under the employee's contract of employment ('contractual remuneration').

(3) Any contractual remuneration paid by an employer to an employee in respect of any period goes towards discharging the employer's liability under section 64 or 68 in respect of that period; and, conversely, any payment of remuneration in discharge of an employer's liability under section 64 or 68 in respect of any period goes towards discharging any obligation of the employer to pay contractual remuneration in respect of that period.

69A Calculation of remuneration (agency workers)

(1) The amount of remuneration payable by a temporary work agency to an agency worker under section 68C is a week's pay in respect of each week for which remuneration is payable in accordance with section 68C; and if in any week remuneration is payable in respect of only part of that week the amount of a week's pay shall be reduced proportionately.

(2) A right to remuneration under section 68C does not affect any right of the agency worker in relation to remuneration under the contract with the temporary work agency ('contractual remuneration').

(3) Any contractual remuneration paid by the temporary work agency to an agency worker in respect of any period goes towards discharging the temporary work agency's liability under section 68C in respect of that period; and, conversely, any payment of remuneration in discharge of a temporary work agency's liability under section 68C in respect of any period goes towards discharging any obligation of the temporary work agency to pay contractual remuneration in respect of that period.

(4) For the purposes of subsection (1), a week's pay is the weekly amount that would have been payable to the agency worker for performing the work, according to the terms of the contract with the temporary work agency, but for the fact that the supply of the agency worker to the hirer was ended on maternity grounds.

(5) Expressions used in this section and sections 68A to 68C have the same meaning as in those sections (see section 68D).

70 Complaints to employment tribunals

(1) An employee may present a complaint to an employment tribunal that his or her employer has failed to pay the whole or any part of remuneration to which the employee is entitled under section 64 or 68.

(2) An employment tribunal shall not consider a complaint under subsection (1) relating to remuneration in respect of any day unless it is presented—

- (a) before the end of the period of three months beginning with that day, or
- (b) within such further period as the tribunal considers reasonable in a case where it is satisfied that it was not reasonably practicable for the complaint to be presented within that period of three months.

(3) Where an employment tribunal finds a complaint under subsection (1) well-founded, the tribunal shall order the employer to pay the employee the amount of remuneration which it finds is due to him or her.

(4) An employee may present a complaint to an employment tribunal that in contravention of section 67 her employer has failed to offer to provide her with work.

(5) An employment tribunal shall not consider a complaint under subsection (4) unless it is presented—

- (a) before the end of the period of three months beginning with the first day of the suspension, or

(b) within such further period as the tribunal considers reasonable in a case where it is satisfied that it was not reasonably practicable for the complaint to be presented within that period of three months.

(6) Where an employment tribunal finds a complaint under subsection (4) well-founded, the tribunal may make an award of compensation to be paid by the employer to the employee.

(7) The amount of the compensation shall be such as the tribunal considers just and equitable in all the circumstances having regard to—

(a) the infringement of the employee's right under section 67 by the failure on the part of the employer to which the complaint relates, and

(b) any loss sustained by the employee which is attributable to that failure.

(8) [omitted]

70A Complaints to employment tribunals: agency workers

(1) An agency worker may present a complaint to an employment tribunal that the temporary work agency has failed to pay the whole or any part of remuneration to which the agency worker is entitled under section 68C.

(2) An employment tribunal shall not consider a complaint under subsection (1) relating to remuneration in respect of any day unless it is presented—

(a) before the end of the period of three months beginning with the day on which the supply of the agency worker to a hirer was ended on maternity grounds, or

(b) within such further period as the tribunal considers reasonable in a case where it is satisfied that it was not reasonably practicable for the complaint to be presented within that period of three months.

(3) Where an employment tribunal finds a complaint under subsection (1) well-founded, the tribunal shall order the temporary work agency to pay the agency worker the amount of remuneration which it finds is due to her.

(4) An agency worker may present a complaint to an employment tribunal that in contravention of section 68B the temporary work agency has failed to offer to propose the agency worker to a hirer that has suitable alternative work available.

(5) An employment tribunal shall not consider a complaint under subsection (4) unless it is presented—

(a) before the end of the period of three months beginning with the day on which the supply of the agency worker to a hirer was ended on maternity grounds, or

(b) within such further period as the tribunal considers reasonable in a case where it is satisfied that it was not reasonably practicable for the complaint to be presented within that period of three months.

(6) Where an employment tribunal finds a complaint under subsection (4) well-founded, the tribunal shall order the temporary work agency to pay the agency worker the amount of compensation which it finds is due to her.

(7) The amount of the compensation shall be such as the tribunal considers just and equitable in all the circumstances having regard to—

(a) the infringement of the agency worker's right under section 68B by the failure on the part of the temporary work agency to which the complaint relates, and

(b) any loss sustained by the agency worker which is attributable to that failure.

(7A) [omitted]

(8) Expressions used in this section and sections 68A to 68C have the same meaning as in those sections (see section 68D).

PART VIII

Chapter I Maternity Leave

71 Ordinary maternity leave

(1) An employee may, provided that she satisfies any conditions which may be prescribed, be absent from work at any time during an ordinary maternity leave period.

(2) An ordinary maternity leave period is a period calculated in accordance with regulations made by the Secretary of State.

(3)–(3A) [omitted]

(4) Subject to section 74, an employee who exercises her right under subsection (1)—

(a) is entitled for such purposes and to such extent as may be prescribed to the benefit of the terms and conditions of employment which would have applied if she had not been absent,

(b) is bound for such purposes and to such extent as may be prescribed by any obligations arising under those terms and conditions (except in so far as they are inconsistent with subsection (1)), and

(c) is entitled to return from leave to a job of a prescribed kind.

(5) In subsection (4)(a) 'terms and conditions of employment'—

(a) includes matters connected with an employee's employment whether or not they arise under her contract of employment, but

(b) does not include terms and conditions about remuneration.

(6)–(7) [omitted]

72 Compulsory maternity leave

(1) An employer shall not permit an employee who satisfies prescribed conditions to work during a compulsory maternity leave period.

(2) A compulsory maternity leave period is a period calculated in accordance with regulations made by the Secretary of State.

(3) [omitted]

(4) Subject to subsection (5), any provision of or made under the Health and Safety at Work etc. Act 1974 shall apply in relation to the prohibition under subsection (1) as if it were imposed by regulations under section 15 of that Act.

(5) Section 33(1)(c) of the 1974 Act shall not apply in relation to the prohibition under subsection (1); and an employer who contravenes that subsection shall be—

(a) guilty of an offence, and

(b) liable on summary conviction to a fine not exceeding level 2 on the standard scale.

73 Additional maternity leave

(1) An employee who satisfies prescribed conditions may be absent from work at any time during an additional maternity leave period.

(2) An additional maternity leave period is a period calculated in accordance with regulations made by the Secretary of State.

(3)–(3A) [omitted]

(4) Subject to section 74, an employee who exercises her right under subsection (1)—

(a) is entitled, for such purposes and to such extent as may be prescribed, to the benefit of the terms and conditions of employment which would have applied if she had not been absent,

(b) is bound, for such purposes and to such extent as may be prescribed, by obligations arising under those terms and conditions (except in so far as they are inconsistent with subsection (1)), and

(c) is entitled to return from leave to a job of a prescribed kind.

(5) In subsection (4)(a) 'terms and conditions of employment'—

(a) includes matters connected with an employee's employment whether or not they arise under her contract of employment, but

(b) does not include terms and conditions about remuneration.

(5A) In subsection (4)(c), the reference to return from leave includes, where appropriate, a reference to a continuous period of absence attributable partly to additional maternity leave and partly to ordinary maternity leave.

(6)–(7) [omitted]

74–75 [omitted]

Chapter 1A Adoption Leave

75A Ordinary adoption leave

(1) An employee who satisfies prescribed conditions may be absent from work at any time during an ordinary adoption leave period.

(1A)–(2B) [omitted]

(3) Subject to section 75C, an employee who exercises his right under subsection (1)—

(a) is entitled, for such purposes and to such extent as may be prescribed, to the benefit of the terms and conditions of employment which would have applied if he had not been absent,

(b) is bound, for such purposes and to such extent as may be prescribed, by any obligations arising under those terms and conditions (except in so far as they are inconsistent with subsection (1)), and

(c) is entitled to return from leave to a job of a prescribed kind.

(4) In subsection (3)(a) 'terms and conditions of employment'—

(a) includes matters connected with an employee's employment whether or not they arise under his contract of employment, but

(b) does not include terms and conditions about remuneration.

(5) In subsection (3)(c), the reference to return from leave includes, where appropriate, a reference to a continuous period of absence attributable partly to ordinary adoption leave and partly to maternity leave.

(6)–(8) [omitted]

75B Additional adoption leave

(1) An employee who satisfies prescribed conditions may be absent from work at any time during an additional adoption leave period.

(2) An additional adoption leave period is a period calculated in accordance with regulations made by the Secretary of State.

(3)–(3A) [omitted]

(4) Subject to section 75C, an employee who exercises his right under subsection (1)—

(a) is entitled, for such purposes and to such extent as may be prescribed, to the benefit of the terms and conditions of employment which would have applied if he had not been absent,

(b) is bound, for such purposes and to such extent as may be prescribed, by obligations arising under those terms and conditions (except in so far as they are inconsistent with subsection (1)), and

(c) is entitled to return from leave to a job of a prescribed kind.

(5) In subsection (4)(a) 'terms and conditions of employment'—

(a) includes matters connected with an employee's employment whether or not they arise under his contract of employment, but

(b) does not include terms and conditions about remuneration.

(6) In subsection (4)(c), the reference to return from leave includes, where appropriate, a reference to a continuous period of absence attributable partly to additional adoption leave and partly to—

(a) maternity leave, or

(b) ordinary adoption leave,

or to both.

(7)–(9) [omitted]

75C–75K [omitted]

Chapter II Parental Leave

76–79 [omitted]

80 Complaint to employment tribunal

(1) An employee may present a complaint to an employment tribunal that his employer—

(a) has unreasonably postponed a period of parental leave requested by the employee, or

(b) has prevented or attempted to prevent the employee from taking parental leave.

(2) An employment tribunal shall not consider a complaint under this section unless it is presented—

(a) before the end of the period of three months beginning with the date (or last date) of the matters complained of, or

(b) within such further period as the tribunal considers reasonable in a case where it is satisfied that it was not reasonably practicable for the complaint to be presented before the end of that period of three months.

(2A) [omitted]

(3) Where an employment tribunal finds a complaint under this section well-founded it—

(a) shall make a declaration to that effect, and

(b) may make an award of compensation to be paid by the employer to the employee.

(4) The amount of compensation shall be such as the tribunal considers just and equitable in all the circumstances having regard to—

(a) the employer's behaviour, and

(b) any loss sustained by the employee which is attributable to the matters complained of.

80A [omitted]; 80AA [repealed]; 80B [omitted]; 80BB [repealed]; 80C–80EI [omitted]

PART 8A FLEXIBLE WORKING

80F Statutory right to request contract variation

(1) A qualifying employee may apply to his employer for a change in his terms and conditions of employment if—

(a) the change relates to—

(i) the hours he is required to work,

(ii) the times when he is required to work,

(iii) where, as between his home and a place of business of his employer, he is required to work, or

(iv) such other aspect of his terms and conditions of employment as the Secretary of State may specify by regulations.

(b) [repealed]

(2) An application under this section must—

(a) state that it is such an application,

(b) specify the change applied for and the date on which it is proposed the change should become effective, and
(c) [repealed]
(d) [repealed]

(3) [repealed]

(4) An employee may not—
(a) make more than two applications under this section to the same employer during any period of 12 months;
(b) make an application under this section to an employer if another such application to the same employer is proceeding.

(4A) For the purposes of this section an application is 'proceeding' during any of these periods—
(a) the period—
(i) beginning when the application is made, and
(ii) ending when the application is concluded;
(b) any period—
(i) beginning when an appeal against a decision to refuse the application is brought, and
(ii) ending when the appeal is concluded;
(c) any period—
(i) beginning when, in accordance with section 80G(1C)(b), the decision period for an application or appeal is extended with retrospective effect, and
(ii) ending when the application or appeal is concluded.

(4B) For the purposes of this section an application or appeal is 'concluded' when any of these events occurs—
(a) a decision is made on the application or appeal under section 80G;
(b) the application or appeal is withdrawn;
(c) the application or appeal is disposed of by agreement;
(d) the decision period specified in section 80G for the application or appeal ends without a decision, withdrawal or agreed disposal.

(5) [omitted]; (6) and (7) [repealed]

(8) For the purposes of this section, an employee is—
(a) a qualifying employee if he—
(i) satisfies such conditions as to duration of employment as the Secretary of State may specify by regulations, and
(ii) is not an agency worker (other than an agency worker who is returning to work from a period of parental leave under regulations under section 76);
(b) an agency worker if he is supplied by a person ('the agent') to do work for another ('the principal') under a contract or other arrangement made between the agent and the principal.

(9) Regulations under this section may make different provision for different cases.

(10) [repealed]

80G Employer's duties in relation to application under section 80F

(1) An employer to whom an application under section 80F is made—
(a) shall deal with the application in a reasonable manner,
(aza) shall not refuse the application unless the employee has been consulted about the application,
(aa) shall notify the employee of the decision on the application within the decision period, and shall deal with the application in accordance with regulations made by the Secretary of State, and
(b) may refuse the application only if—

(i) the employer considers that the application should be refused on a ground or grounds listed in subsection (1ZA), and

(ii) it is reasonable for the employer to refuse the application on that ground or those grounds.

(1ZA) The grounds mentioned in subsection (1)(b) are—

(a) the burden of additional costs;

(b) detrimental effect on ability to meet customer demand;

(c) inability to re-organise work among existing staff;

(d) inability to recruit additional staff;

(e) detrimental impact on quality;

(f) detrimental impact on performance;

(g) insufficiency of work during the periods the employee proposes to work;

(h) planned structural changes;

(i) any other grounds specified by the Secretary of State in regulations.

(1ZB) If an employer refuses an application under section 80F, the notification under subsection (1)(aa) must—

(a) state the ground or grounds for refusing the application, and

(b) explain why the employer considers that it is reasonable to refuse the application on that ground or those grounds.

(1A)–(1E) [omitted]; (2)–(4) [repealed]

80H Complaints to employment tribunals

(1) An employee who makes an application under section 80F may present a complaint to an employment tribunal—

(a) that his employer has failed in relation to the application to act in accordance with section 80G(1),

(b) that a decision by his employer to reject the application was based on incorrect facts, or

(c) that the employer's notification under section 80G(1D) was given in circumstances that did not satisfy one of the requirements in section 80G(1D)(a) and (b).

(2) No complaint under subsection (1)(a) or (b) may be made in respect of an application which has been disposed of by agreement or withdrawn.

(3) In the case of an application which has not been disposed of by agreement or withdrawn, no complaint under subsection (1)(a) or (b) may be made until—

(a) the employer notifies the employee of the employer's decision on the application, or

(b) if the decision period applicable to the application (see section 80G(1B)) comes to an end without the employer notifying the employee of the employer's decision on the application, the end of the decision period.

(3A)–(3C) [omitted]; (4) [repealed]

(5) An employment tribunal shall not consider a complaint under this section unless it is presented—

(a) before the end of the period of three months beginning with the relevant date, or

(b) within such further period as the tribunal considers reasonable in a case where it is satisfied that it was not reasonably practicable for the complaint to be presented before the end of that period of three months.

(6) In subsection (5)(a), the reference to the relevant date is a reference to the first date on which the employee may make a complaint under subsection (1)(a), (b) or (c), as the case may be.

(7) [omitted]

80I Remedies

(1) Where an employment tribunal finds a complaint under section 80H well-founded it shall make a declaration to that effect and may—

(a) make an order for reconsideration of the application, and

(b) make an award of compensation to be paid by the employer to the employee.

(2) The amount of compensation shall be such amount, not exceeding the permitted maximum, as the tribunal considers just and equitable in all the circumstances.

(3) For the purposes of subsection (2), the permitted maximum is such number of weeks' pay as the Secretary of State may specify by regulations.

(4) Where an employment tribunal makes an order under subsection (1)(a), section 80G shall apply as if the application had been made on the date of the order.

80J–80N [omitted]

81–85 [repealed]

PART IX TERMINATION OF EMPLOYMENT

Minimum period of notice

86 Rights of employer and employee to minimum notice

(1) The notice required to be given by an employer to terminate the contract of employment of a person who has been continuously employed for one month or more—

(a) is not less than one week's notice if his period of continuous employment is less than two years,

(b) is not less than one week's notice for each year of continuous employment if his period of continuous employment is two years or more but less than twelve years, and

(c) is not less than twelve weeks' notice if his period of continuous employment is twelve years or more.

(2) The notice required to be given by an employee who has been continuously employed for one month or more to terminate his contract of employment is not less than one week.

(3) Any provision for shorter notice in any contract of employment with a person who has been continuously employed for one month or more has effect subject to subsections (1) and (2); but this section does not prevent either party from waiving his right to notice on any occasion or from accepting a payment in lieu of notice.

(4) Any contract of employment of a person who has been continuously employed for three months or more which is a contract for a term certain of one month or less shall have effect as if it were for an indefinite period; and, accordingly, subsections (1) and (2) apply to the contract.

(5) [repealed]

(6) This section does not affect any right of either party to a contract of employment to treat the contract as terminable without notice by reason of the conduct of the other party.

87 Rights of employee in period of notice

(1) If an employer gives notice to terminate the contract of employment of a person who has been continuously employed for one month or more, the provisions of sections 88 to 91 have effect as respects the liability of the employer for the period of notice required by section 86(1).

(2) If an employee who has been continuously employed for one month or more gives notice to terminate his contract of employment, the provisions of sections 88 to 91 have effect as respects the liability of the employer for the period of notice required by section 86(2).

(3) In sections 88 to 91 'period of notice' means—

(a) where notice is given by an employer, the period of notice required by section 86(1), and

(b) where notice is given by an employee, the period of notice required by section 86(2).

(4) This section does not apply in relation to a notice given by the employer or the employee if the notice to be given by the employer to terminate the contract must be at least one week more than the notice required by section 86(1).

88 Employments with normal working hours

(1) If an employee has normal working hours under the contract of employment in force during the period of notice and during any part of those normal working hours—

(a) the employee is ready and willing to work but no work is provided for him by his employer,

(b) the employee is incapable of work because of sickness or injury,

(c) the employee is absent from work wholly or partly because of pregnancy or childbirth or on adoption leave, shared parental leave, carer's leave, parental bereavement leave, neonatal care leave, parental leave or paternity leave, or,

(d) the employee is absent from work in accordance with the terms of his employment relating to holidays,

the employer is liable to pay the employee for the part of normal working hours covered by any of paragraphs (a), (b), (c) and (d) a sum not less than the amount of remuneration for that part of normal working hours calculated at the average hourly rate of remuneration produced by dividing a week's pay by the number of normal working hours.

(2) Any payments made to the employee by his employer in respect of the relevant part of the period of notice (whether by way of sick pay, statutory sick pay, maternity pay, statutory maternity pay, paternity pay, statutory paternity pay, adoption pay, statutory adoption pay, shared parental pay, statutory shared parental pay, parental bereavement pay, statutory parental bereavement pay, neonatal care pay, statutory neonatal care pay, holiday pay or otherwise) go towards meeting the employer's liability under this section.

(3) Where notice was given by the employee, the employer's liability under this section does not arise unless and until the employee leaves the service of the employer in pursuance of the notice.

89 Employments without normal working hours

(1) If an employee does not have normal working hours under the contract of employment in force in the period of notice, the employer is liable to pay the employee for each week of the period of notice a sum not less than a week's pay.

(2) The employer's liability under this section is conditional on the employee being ready and willing to do work of a reasonable nature and amount to earn a week's pay.

(3) Subsection (2) does not apply—

(a) in respect of any period during which the employee is incapable of work because of sickness or injury,

(b) in respect of any period during which the employee is absent from work wholly or partly because of pregnancy or childbirth or on adoption leave, shared parental leave, carer's leave, parental bereavement leave, neonatal care leave, parental leave or paternity leave, or

(c) in respect of any period during which the employee is absent from work in accordance with the terms of his employment relating to holidays.

(4) Any payment made to an employee by his employer in respect of a period within subsection (3) (whether by way of sick pay, statutory sick pay, maternity pay, statutory maternity pay, paternity pay, statutory paternity pay, adoption pay, statutory adoption pay, shared parental pay, statutory shared parental pay, parental bereavement pay, statutory parental bereavement pay, neonatal care pay, statutory neonatal care pay, holiday pay or otherwise) shall be taken into account for the purposes of this section as if it were remuneration paid by the employer in respect of that period.

(5) Where notice was given by the employee, the employer's liability under this section does not arise unless and until the employee leaves the service of the employer in pursuance of the notice.

90 Short-term incapacity benefit, contributory employment and support allowance and industrial injury benefit

(1) This section has effect where the arrangements in force relating to the employment are such that—

- (a) payments by way of sick pay are made by the employer to employees to whom the arrangements apply, in cases where any such employees are incapable of work because of sickness or injury, and
- (b) in calculating any payment so made to any such employee an amount representing, or treated as representing, short-term incapacity benefit, contributory employment and support allowance or industrial injury benefit is taken into account, whether by way of deduction or by way of calculating the payment as a supplement to that amount.

(2) If—

- (a) during any part of the period of notice the employee is incapable of work because of sickness or injury,
- (b) one or more payments by way of sick pay are made to him by the employer in respect of that part of the period of notice, and
- (c) in calculating any such payment such an amount as is referred to in paragraph (b) of subsection (1) is taken into account as mentioned in that paragraph,

for the purposes of section 88 or 89 the amount so taken into account shall be treated as having been paid by the employer to the employee by way of sick pay in respect of that part of that period, and shall go towards meeting the liability of the employer under that section accordingly.

91 Supplementary

(1) An employer is not liable under section 88 or 89 to make any payment in respect of a period during which an employee is absent from work with the leave of the employer granted at the request of the employee, including any period of time off taken in accordance with—

- (a) Part VI of this Act, or
- (b) section 168 or 170 of the Trade Union and Labour Relations (Consolidation) Act 1992 (trade union duties and activities).

(2) No payment is due under section 88 or 89 in consequence of a notice to terminate a contract given by an employee if, after the notice is given and on or before the termination of the contract, the employee takes part in a strike of employees of the employer.

(3) If, during the period of notice, the employer breaks the contract of employment, payments received under section 88 or 89 in respect of the part of the period after the breach go towards mitigating the damages recoverable by the employee for loss of earnings in that part of the period of notice.

(4) If, during the period of notice, the employee breaks the contract and the employer rightfully treats the breach as terminating the contract, no payment is due to the employee under section 88 or 89 in respect of the part of the period falling after the termination of the contract.

(5) If an employer fails to give the notice required by section 86, the rights conferred by sections 87 to 90 and this section shall be taken into account in assessing his liability for breach of the contract.

(6) Sections 86 to 90 and this section apply in relation to a contract all or any of the terms of which are terms which take effect by virtue of any provision contained in or having effect under an Act (whether public or local) as in relation to any other contract; and the reference in this subsection to an Act includes, subject to any express provision to the contrary, an Act passed after this Act.

Written statement of reasons for dismissal

92 Right to written statement of reasons for dismissal

(1) An employee is entitled to be provided by his employer with a written statement giving particulars of the reasons for the employee's dismissal—

(a) if the employee is given by the employer notice of termination of his contract of employment,

(b) if the employee's contract of employment is terminated by the employer without notice, or

(c) if the employee is employed under a limited-term contract and the contract terminates by virtue of the limiting event without being renewed under the same contract.

(2) Subject to subsections (4) and (4A), an employee is entitled to a written statement under this section only if he makes a request for one; and a statement shall be provided within fourteen days of such a request.

(3) Subject to subsections (4) and (4A), an employee is not entitled to a written statement under this section unless on the effective date of termination he has been, or will have been, continuously employed for a period of not less than two years ending with that date.

(4) An employee is entitled to a written statement under this section without having to request it and irrespective of whether she has been continuously employed for any period if she is dismissed—

(a) at any time while she is pregnant, or

(b) after childbirth in circumstances in which her ordinary or additional maternity leave period ends by reason of the dismissal.

(4A) An employee who is dismissed while absent from work during an ordinary or additional adoption leave period is entitled to a written statement under this section without having to request it and irrespective of whether he has been continuously employed for any period if he is dismissed in circumstances in which that period ends by reason of the dismissal.

(5) A written statement under this section is admissible in evidence in any proceedings.

(6) Subject to subsection (7), in this section 'the effective date of termination'—

(a) in relation to an employee whose contract of employment is terminated by notice, means the date on which the notice expires,

(b) in relation to an employee whose contract of employment is terminated without notice, means the date on which the termination takes effect, and

(c) in relation to an employee who is employed under a limited-term contract which terminates by virtue of the limiting event without being renewed under the same contract, means the date on which the termination takes effect.

(7) Where—

(a) the contract of employment is terminated by the employer, and

(b) the notice required by section 86 to be given by an employer would, if duly given on the material date, expire on a date later than the effective date of termination (as defined by subsection (6)),

the later date is the effective date of termination.

(8) In subsection (7)(b) 'the material date' means—

(a) the date when notice of termination was given by the employer, or

(b) where no notice was given, the date when the contract of employment was terminated by the employer.

93 Complaints to employment tribunal

(1) A complaint may be presented to an employment tribunal by an employee on the ground that—

(a) the employer unreasonably failed to provide a written statement under section 92, or

(b) the particulars of reasons given in purported compliance with that section are inadequate or untrue.

(2) Where an employment tribunal finds a complaint under this section well-founded, the tribunal—

(a) may make a declaration as to what it finds the employer's reasons were for dismissing the employee, and

(b) shall make an award that the employer pay to the employee a sum equal to the amount of two weeks' pay.

(3) An employment tribunal shall not consider a complaint under this section relating to the reasons for a dismissal unless it is presented to the tribunal at such a time that the tribunal would, in accordance with section 111, consider a complaint of unfair dismissal in respect of that dismissal presented at the same time.

PART X UNFAIR DISMISSAL

Chapter I Right not to be Unfairly Dismissed

The right

94 The right

(1) An employee has the right not to be unfairly dismissed by his employer.

(2) Subsection (1) has effect subject to the following provisions of this Part (in particular sections 108 to 110) and to the provisions of the Trade Union and Labour Relations (Consolidation) Act 1992 (in particular sections 237 to 239).

Dismissal

95 Circumstances in which an employee is dismissed

(1) For the purposes of this Part an employee is dismissed by his employer if (and, subject to subsection (2), only if)—

(a) the contract under which he is employed is terminated by the employer (whether with or without notice),

(b) he is employed under a limited-term contract and that contract terminates by virtue of the limiting event without being renewed under the same contract, or

(c) the employee terminates the contract under which he is employed (with or without notice) in circumstances in which he is entitled to terminate it without notice by reason of the employer's conduct.

(2) An employee shall be taken to be dismissed by his employer for the purposes of this Part if—

(a) the employer gives notice to the employee to terminate his contract of employment, and

(b) at a time within the period of that notice the employee gives notice to the employer to terminate the contract of employment on a date earlier than the date on which the employer's notice is due to expire;

and the reason for the dismissal is to be taken to be the reason for which the employer's notice is given.

96 [repealed]

97 Effective date of termination

(1) Subject to the following provisions of this section, in this Part 'the effective date of termination'—

(a) in relation to an employee whose contract of employment is terminated by notice, whether given by his employer or by the employee, means the date on which the notice expires,

(b) in relation to an employee whose contract of employment is terminated without notice, means the date on which the termination takes effect, and

(c) in relation to an employee who is employed under a limited-term contract which terminates by virtue of the limiting event without being renewed under the same contract, means the date on which the termination takes effect.

(2) Where—

(a) the contract of employment is terminated by the employer, and

(b) the notice required by section 86 to be given by an employer would, if duly given on the material date, expire on a date later than the effective date of termination (as defined by subsection (1)),

for the purposes of sections 108(1), 119(1) and 227(3) the later date is the effective date of termination.

(3) In subsection (2)(b) 'the material date' means—

(a) the date when notice of termination was given by the employer, or

(b) where no notice was given, the date when the contract of employment was terminated by the employer.

(4) Where—

(a) the contract of employment is terminated by the employee,

(b) the material date does not fall during a period of notice given by the employer to terminate that contract, and

(c) had the contract been terminated not by the employee but by notice given on the material date by the employer, that notice would have been required by section 86 to expire on a date later than the effective date of termination (as defined by subsection (1)),

for the purposes of sections 108(1), 119(1) and 227(3) the later date is the effective date of termination.

(5) In subsection (4) 'the material date' means—

(a) the date when notice of termination was given by the employee, or

(b) where no notice was given, the date when the contract of employment was terminated by the employee.

(6) [repealed]

Fairness

98 General

(1) In determining for the purposes of this Part whether the dismissal of an employee is fair or unfair, it is for the employer to show—

(a) the reason (or, if more than-one, the principal reason) for the dismissal, and

(b) that it is either a reason falling within subsection (2) or some other substantial reason of a kind such as to justify the dismissal of an employee holding the position which the employee held.

(2) A reason falls within this subsection if it—

(a) relates to the capability or qualifications of the employee for performing work of the kind which he was employed by the employer to do,

(b) relates to the conduct of the employee,

(ba) [repealed]

(c) is that the employee was redundant, or

(d) is that the employee could not continue to work in the position which he held without contravention (either on his part or on that of his employer) of a duty or restriction imposed by or under an enactment.

(2A) [repealed]

(3) In subsection (2)(a)—

(a) 'capability', in relation to an employee, means his capability assessed by reference to skill, aptitude, health or any other physical or mental quality, and

(b) 'qualifications', in relation to an employee, means any degree, diploma or other academic, technical or professional qualification relevant to the position which he held.

(3A) [repealed]

(4) Where the employer has fulfilled the requirements of subsection (1), the determination of the question whether the dismissal is fair or unfair (having regard to the reason shown by the employer)—

(a) depends on whether in the circumstances (including the size and administrative resources of the employer's undertaking) the employer acted reasonably or unreasonably in treating it as a sufficient reason for dismissing the employee, and

(b) shall be determined in accordance with equity and the substantial merits of the case.

(5) [repealed]

(6) Subsection (4) is subject to—

(a) sections 98A to 107 of this Act, and

(b) sections 152, 153, 238 and 238A of the Trade Union and Labour Relations (Consolidation) Act 1992 (dismissal on ground of trade union membership or activities or in connection with industrial action).

98ZA–98ZH [repealed]

Other dismissals

98A [repealed]; 98B [omitted]

99 Leave for family reasons

(1) An employee who is dismissed shall be regarded for the purposes of this Part as unfairly dismissed if—

(a) the reason or principal reason for the dismissal is of a prescribed kind, or

(b) the dismissal takes place in prescribed circumstances.

(2) In this section 'prescribed' means prescribed by regulations made by the Secretary of State.

(3) A reason or set of circumstances prescribed under this section must relate to—

(a) pregnancy, childbirth or maternity,

(aa) time off under section 57ZE,

(ab) time off under section 57ZJ or 57ZL,

(b) ordinary, compulsory or additional maternity leave,

(ba) ordinary or additional adoption leave,

(bb) shared parental leave,

(bc) carer's leave,

(c) parental leave,

(ca) paternity leave,

(cb) parental bereavement leave,

(cc) neonatal care leave, or

(d) time off under section 57A;

and it may also relate to redundancy or other factors.

(4) A reason or set of circumstances prescribed under subsection (1) satisfies subsection (3)(c) or (d) if it relates to action which an employee—

(a) takes,

(b) agrees to take, or

(c) refuses to take,

under or in respect of a collective or workforce agreement which deals with parental leave.

(5) [omitted]

100 Health and safety cases

(1) An employee who is dismissed shall be regarded for the purposes of this Part as unfairly dismissed if the reason (or, if more than one, the principal reason) for the dismissal is that—

(a) having been designated by the employer to carry out activities in connection with preventing or reducing risks to health and safety at work, the employee carried out (or proposed to carry out) any such activities,

(b) being a representative of workers on matters of health and safety at work or member of a safety committee—

(i) in accordance with arrangements established under or by virtue of any enactment, or

(ii) by reason of being acknowledged as such by the employer, the employee performed (or proposed to perform) any functions as such a representative or a member of such a committee,

(ba) the employee took part (or proposed to take part) in consultation with the employer pursuant to the Health and Safety (Consultation with Employees) Regulations 1996 or in an election of representatives of employee safety within the meaning of those Regulations (whether as a candidate or otherwise),

(c) being an employee at a place where—

(i) there was no such representative or safety committee, or

(ii) there was such a representative or safety committee but it was not reasonably practicable for the employee to raise the matter by those means,

he brought to his employer's attention, by reasonable means, circumstances connected with his work which he reasonably believed were harmful or potentially harmful to health or safety,

(d) in circumstances of danger which the employee reasonably believed to be serious and imminent and which he could not reasonably have been expected to avert, he left (or proposed to leave) or (while the danger persisted) refused to return to his place of work or any dangerous part of his place of work, or

(e) in circumstances of danger which the employee reasonably believed to be serious and imminent, he took (or proposed to take) appropriate steps to protect himself or other persons from the danger.

(2) For the purposes of subsection (1)(e) whether steps which an employee took (or proposed to take) were appropriate is to be judged by reference to all the circumstances including, in particular, his knowledge and the facilities and advice available to him at the time.

(3) Where the reason (or, if more than one, the principal reason) for the dismissal of an employee is that specified in subsection (1)(e), he shall not be regarded as unfairly dismissed if the employer shows that it was (or would have been) so negligent for the employee to take the steps which he took (or proposed to take) that a reasonable employer might have dismissed him for taking (or proposing to take) them.

101–101ZA [omitted]

101A Working time cases

(1) An employee who is dismissed shall be regarded for the purposes of this Part as unfairly dismissed if the reason (or, if more than one, the principal reason) for the dismissal is that the employee—

(a) refused (or proposed to refuse) to comply with a requirement which the employer imposed (or proposed to impose) in contravention of the Working Time Regulations 1998,

(b) refused (or proposed to refuse) to forgo a right conferred on him by those Regulations,

(c) failed to sign a workforce agreement for the purposes of those Regulations, or to enter into, or agree to vary or extend, any other agreement with his employer which is provided for in those Regulations, or

(d) being—

(i) a representative of members of the workforce for the purposes of Schedule 1 to those Regulations, or

(ii) a candidate in an election in which any person elected will, on being elected, be such a representative,

performed (or proposed to perform) any functions or activities as such a representative or candidate.

(2) [omitted]

101B and 102 [omitted]

103 Employee representatives

(1) An employee who is dismissed shall be regarded for the purposes of this Part as unfairly dismissed if the reason (or, if more than one, the principal reason) for the dismissal is that the employee, being—

(a) an employee representative for the purposes of Chapter II of Part IV of the Trade Union and Labour Relations (Consolidation) Act 1992 (redundancies) or Regulations 9, 13 and 15 of the Transfer of Undertakings (Protection of Employment) Regulations 2006, or

(b) a candidate in an election in which any person elected will, on being elected, be such an employee representative,

performed (or proposed to perform) any functions or activities as such an employee representative or candidate.

(2) An employee who is dismissed shall be regarded for the purposes of this Part as unfairly dismissed if the reason (or, if more than one, the principal reason) for the dismissal is that the employee took part in an election of employee representatives for the purposes of Chapter II of Part IV of the Trade Union and Labour Relations (Consolidation) Act 1992 (redundancies) or Regulations 9, 13 and 15 of the Transfer of Undertakings (Protection of Employment) Regulations 2006.

103A Protected disclosure

An employee who is dismissed shall be regarded for the purposes of this Part as unfairly dismissed if the reason (or, if more than one, the principal reason) for the dismissal is that the employee made a protected disclosure.

104 Assertion of statutory right

(1) An employee who is dismissed shall be regarded for the purposes of this Part as unfairly dismissed if the reason (or, if more than one, the principal reason) for the dismissal is that the employee—

(a) brought proceedings against the employer to enforce a right of his which is a relevant statutory right, or

(b) alleged that the employer had infringed a right of his which is a relevant statutory right.

(2) It is immaterial for the purposes of subsection (1)—

(a) whether or not the employee has the right, or

(b) whether or not the right has been infringed;

but, for that subsection to apply, the claim to the right and that it has been infringed must be made in good faith.

(3) It is sufficient for subsection (1) to apply that the employee, without specifying the right, made it reasonably clear to the employer what the right claimed to have been infringed was.

(4) The following are relevant statutory rights for the purposes of this section—

(a) any right conferred by this Act for which the remedy for its infringement is by way of a complaint or reference to an employment tribunal,

(b) the right conferred by section 86 of this Act,

(c) the rights conferred by sections 68, 86, 145A, 145B, 146, 168, 168A, 169, 170 and 236A of the Trade Union and Labour Relations (Consolidation) Act 1992 (deductions from pay, union activities and time off),

(d) the rights conferred by the Working Time Regulations 1998, the Merchant Shipping (Maritime Labour Convention) (Hours of Work) Regulations 2018 (SI 2018/58), the Merchant Shipping (Working Time: Inland Waterways) Regulations 2003, the Fishing Vessels (Working Time: Sea-fisherman) Regulations 2004 or the Cross-border Railway Services (Working Time) Regulations 2008, and

(e) the rights conferred by the Transfer of Undertakings (Protection of Employment) Regulations 2006.

(5) In this section any reference to an employer includes, where the right in question is conferred by section 63A, the principal (within the meaning of section 63A(3)).

104A The national minimum wage

(1) An employee who is dismissed shall be regarded for the purposes of this Part as unfairly dismissed if the reason (or, if more than one, the principal reason) for the dismissal is that—

(a) any action was taken, or was proposed to be taken, by or on behalf of the employee with a view to enforcing, or otherwise securing the benefit of, a right of the employee's to which this section applies, or

(b) the employer was prosecuted for an offence under section 31 of the National Minimum Wage Act 1998 as a result of action taken by or on behalf of the employee for the purpose of enforcing, or otherwise securing the benefit of, a right of the employee's to which this section applies, or

(c) the employee qualifies, or will or might qualify, for the national minimum wage or for a particular rate of national minimum wage.

(2) It is immaterial for the purposes of paragraph (a) or (b) of subsection (1) above—

(a) whether or not the employee has the right, or

(b) whether or not the right has been infringed, but, for that subsection to apply, the claim to the right and, if applicable, the claim that it has been infringed must be made in good faith.

(3) The following are the rights to which this section applies—

(a) any right conferred by, or by virtue of, any provision of the National Minimum Wage Act 1998 for which the remedy for its infringement is by way of a complaint to an employment tribunal, and

(b) any right conferred by section 17 of the National Minimum Wage Act 1998 (worker receiving less than national minimum wage entitled to additional remuneration).

104B [omitted]

104C Flexible working

An employee who is dismissed shall be regarded for the purposes of this Part as unfairly dismissed if the reason (or, if more than one, the principal reason) for the dismissal is that the employee—

(a) made (or proposed to make) an application under section 80F,

(b) [repealed]

(c) brought proceedings against the employer under section 80H, or

(d) alleged the existence of any circumstance which would constitute a ground for bringing such proceedings.

104D–104E [omitted]

104F Blacklists

(1) An employee who is dismissed shall be regarded for the purposes of this Part as unfairly dismissed if the reason (or, if more than one, the principal reason) for the dismissal relates to a prohibited list, and either—

(a) the employer contravenes regulation 3 of the 2010 Regulations in relation to that prohibited list, or

(b) the employer—

(i) relies on information supplied by a person who contravenes that regulation in relation to that list, and
(ii) knows or ought reasonably to know that the information relied on is supplied in contravention of that regulation.

(2) If there are facts from which the tribunal could conclude, in the absence of any other explanation, that the employer—
(a) contravened regulation 3 of the 2010 Regulations, or
(b) relied on information supplied in contravention of that regulation,
the tribunal must find that such a contravention or reliance on information occurred, unless the employer shows that it did not.

(3) In this section—
'the 2010 Regulations' means the Employment Relations Act 1999 (Blacklists) Regulations 2010, and
'prohibited list' has the meaning given in those Regulations (see regulation 3(2)).

104G Employee shareholder status

An employee who is dismissed is to be regarded for the purposes of this Part as unfairly dismissed if the reason (or, if more than one, the principal reason) for the dismissal is that the employee refused to accept an offer by the employer for the employee to become an employee shareholder (within the meaning of section 205A).

104H [omitted]

104I Contracts of employment: restricted variations

(1) An employee who is dismissed is to be regarded for the purposes of this Part as unfairly dismissed if—
(a) the employee was employed for the purposes of a business carried on by the employer, and
(b) the reason (or, if more than one, the principal reason) for the dismissal is a reason within subsection (2) or (3).

(2) The reason within this subsection is that—
(a) the employer sought to vary the employee's contract of employment to make a restricted variation (see subsection (5)), and
(b) the employee—
(i) did not agree to the restricted variation, or
(ii) where the employer sought to make more than one variation, did not agree to a number of variations that included the restricted variation.

(3) The reason within this subsection is to enable the employer to employ another person, or to re-engage the employee, under a varied contract of employment to carry out the same duties, or substantially the same duties, as the employee carried out before being dismissed.

(4) For the purposes of subsection (3), a contract of employment is a 'varied' contract of employment if—
(a) the terms of the contract are not the same as the terms of the contract of employment under which the employee worked before being dismissed, and
(b) one or more of the differences between the two sets of terms constitutes a restricted variation (see subsection (5));
and, in a case where subsection (3) applies, any reference in this section to the restricted variation is to be read accordingly.

(5) In this section 'restricted variation' means any of the following—
(a) a reduction of, or removal of an entitlement to, any sum payable to an employee in connection with the employment (but see subsection (6));
(b) where the amount of any sum payable to an employee in connection with the employment is determined by reference to a measure of the amount of work done by the

employee (including a measure referable to results achieved by the employee), a variation of that measure;

(c) a variation of any term or condition relating to pensions or pension schemes;

(d) a variation of the number of hours which an employee is required to work;

(e) a variation of the timing or duration of a shift which meets such conditions as may be specified in regulations made by the Secretary of State;

(f) a reduction in the amount of time off which an employee is entitled to take;

(g) a variation of a description specified in regulations made by the Secretary of State;

(h) the inclusion in a contract of employment of a term enabling the employer to make any variation within any of the preceding paragraphs without the employee's agreement.

(6) [omitted]

(7) Subsection (1) does not apply in relation to an employee if on the effective date of termination the employee has not yet started work.

(8) In the case of an employer that is not a local authority, subsection (1) does not apply in relation to an employee if the employer shows that—

(a) the reason for the restricted variation was to eliminate, prevent or significantly reduce, or significantly mitigate the effect of, any financial difficulties which at the time of the dismissal were affecting, or were likely in the immediate future to affect—

(i) the employer's ability to carry on the business as a going concern, or

(ii) where the employer is a public sector employer, the financial sustainability of carrying out the employer's statutory functions, and

(b) in all the circumstances the employer could not reasonably have avoided the need to make the restricted variation.

(9) In the case of an employer that is a local authority, subsection (1) does not apply in relation to an employee if—

(a) at the time of the dismissal, a relevant intervention direction has effect in relation to the authority,

(b) the relevant intervention direction—

(i) specifies that the reason, or one of the reasons, for the giving of the direction is that the authority is undergoing financial difficulties, and

(ii) contains provision relating to the financial management or financial governance of the authority, and

(c) the authority shows that—

(i) the reason for the restricted variation was to eliminate or significantly reduce, or significantly mitigate the effect of, any of the financial difficulties referred to in paragraph (b)(i), and

(ii) in all the circumstances the authority could not reasonably have avoided the need to make the restricted variation.

(10) In determining whether—

(a) in the case of a public sector employer (other than a local authority), subsection (8)(b) is met, or

(b) in the case of a local authority, subsection (9)(c)(ii) is met,

an employment tribunal must apply the same principles as would be applied by a court on an application for judicial review.

(11) Where the employer shows that the conditions in paragraphs (a) and (b) of subsection (8) are met, or (where the employer is a local authority) the conditions in paragraphs (a), (b) and (c) of subsection (9) are met, the matters that must be considered in determining the question whether the dismissal is fair or unfair include the following—

(a) any consultation carried out by the employer with the employee about varying the employee's contract of employment;

(b) if the employee is of a description in respect of which an independent trade union is recognised by the employer, any consultation carried out by the employer with that trade union;

(c) if the employee is not of a description in respect of which an independent trade union is recognised by the employer, any consultation carried out by the employer with any other person representing the interests of the employee that, at the time of the dismissal, had authority to receive information and to be consulted about the dismissal on the employee's behalf;

(d) anything offered to the employee by the employer in return for agreeing to the restricted variation;

(e) any matters specified for the purposes of this subsection in regulations made by the Secretary of State.

(12) In this section—

'English local authority' means—

(a) a county council or district council in England;

(b) a London borough council;

(c) the Greater London Authority;

(d) the Council of the Isles of Scilly;

(e) the Common Council of the City of London in its capacity as a local authority, a police authority or a port health authority;

(f) a combined authority established under section 103 of the Local Democracy, Economic Development and Construction Act 2009;

(g) a combined county authority established under section 9(1) of the Levelling-up and Regeneration Act 2023;

'local authority' means—

(a) an English local authority,

(b) a Welsh local authority, or

(c) a Scottish local authority;

'public sector employer' means a person that—

(a) is wholly or mainly funded from public funds,

(b) is under a statutory duty to carry out any functions of a public nature, and

(c) so far as carrying out those functions, does not operate on a commercial basis;

'recognised', in relation to a trade union, has the same meaning as in the Trade Union and Labour Relations (Consolidation) Act 1992 (see section 178 of that Act);

relevant intervention direction' means—

(a) in the case of an English local authority, a direction under section 15(5) or (6)(a) of the Local Government Act 1999 (powers to deal with failure to comply with duties relating to best value authorities);

(b) in the case of a Welsh local authority, a direction under section 106 or 107 of the Local Government and Elections (Wales) Act 2021 (asc 1) (intervention powers of Welsh Ministers);

(c) in the case of a Scottish local authority, an enforcement direction under section 24 of the Local Government in Scotland Act 2003 (asp 1) relating wholly or partly to a failure of the authority to comply with its duties under section 1 of that Act (local authorities' duty to secure best value);

'Scottish local authority' means a council constituted under section 2 of the Local Government etc. (Scotland) Act 1994;

'statutory duty' means a duty imposed by or under any enactment, including—

(a) a Measure or Act of the National Assembly for Wales or an Act of Senedd Cymru, and

(b) an Act of the Scottish Parliament;

'statutory functions', in relation to a public sector employer, means functions of a public nature which the employer is under a statutory duty to carry out;

'Welsh local authority' means—

(a) a county council or county borough council in Wales;

(b) a corporate joint committee established under Part 5 of the Local Government and Elections (Wales) Act 2021.

(13) [omitted]

104J Contracts of employment: variations that are not restricted variations

(1) This section applies to the dismissal of an employee if—

(a) the employee was employed for the purposes of a business carried on by the employer, and

(b) the reason (or, if more than one, the principal reason) for the dismissal is a reason within subsection (2) or (3).

(2) The reason within this subsection is that—

(a) the employer sought to vary the employee's contract of employment,

(b) the variation was not a restricted variation or, where the employer sought to make more than one variation, none of the variations was a restricted variation, and

(c) the employee did not agree to the variation.

(3) The reason within this subsection is to enable the employer to employ another person, or to re-engage the employee, under a varied contract of employment to carry out the same duties, or substantially the same duties, as the employee carried out before being dismissed.

(4) For the purposes of subsection (3), a contract of employment is a 'varied' contract of employment if—

(a) the terms of the contract are not the same as the terms of the contract of employment under which the employee worked before being dismissed, and

(b) none of the differences between the two sets of terms constitutes a restricted variation;

and, in a case where subsection (3) applies, any reference in this section to the variation is to be read accordingly.

(5) The matters that must be considered in determining the question whether the dismissal is fair or unfair include the following—

(a) the reason for the variation;

(b) any consultation carried out by the employer with the employee about varying the employee's contract of employment;

(c) if the employee is of a description in respect of which an independent trade union is recognised by the employer, any consultation carried out by the employer with that trade union;

(d) if the employee is not of a description in respect of which an independent trade union is recognised by the employer, any consultation carried out by the employer with any other person representing the interests of the employee that, at the time of the dismissal, had authority to receive information and to be consulted about the dismissal on the employee's behalf;

(e) anything offered to the employee by the employer in return for agreeing to the variation;

(f) any matters specified for the purposes of this subsection in regulations made by the Secretary of State.

(6) In this section—

'recognised', in relation to a trade union, has the same meaning as in the Trade Union and Labour Relations (Consolidation) Act 1992 (see section 178 of that Act);

'restricted variation' has the same meaning as in section 104I.

104K Redundancy: replacement of employees with people who are not employees

(1) An employee who is dismissed is to be regarded for the purposes of this Part as unfairly dismissed if—

(a) the employee was employed for the purposes of a business carried on by the employer, and

(b) the reason (or, if more than one, the principal reason) for the dismissal is to enable the employer to replace the employee with an individual who is not an employee of the employer.

(2) For the purposes of this section—

(a) an employer replaces an employee with an individual who is not an employee of the employer if (and only if)—

(i) the individual, or the individual taken together with one or more employees of the employer or other individuals, is to carry out activities, in pursuance of a relevant contract, for the purposes of the employer's business,

(ii) those activities are the same, or substantially the same, activities as the employee, or the employee taken together with one or more other employees of the employer, carried out before being dismissed, and

(iii) the employee's dismissal is not wholly or mainly attributable to the fact that the requirements of the employer's business for those activities to be carried out have ceased or diminished or are expected to cease or diminish;

and any reference in this section to replacing an employee is to be read accordingly;

(b) a reference to replacing an employee with an individual who is not an employee of the employer includes the case where the individual is the one who has been dismissed;

(c) 'relevant contract', in relation to an employer, means a contract, other than a contract of employment, to which the employer is a party (whether or not the individual carrying out activities in pursuance of the contract is a party to it).

(3) Subsection (1) does not apply in relation to an employee if on the effective date of termination the employee has not yet started work.

(4) In the case of an employer that is not a local authority, subsection (1) does not apply in relation to an employee if the employer shows that—

(a) the reason for the replacement was to eliminate, prevent or significantly reduce, or significantly mitigate the effect of, any financial difficulties which at the time of the dismissal were affecting, or were likely in the immediate future to affect—

(i) the employer's ability to carry on the business as a going concern, or

(ii) where the employer is a public sector employer, the financial sustainability of carrying out the employer's statutory functions, and

(b) in all the circumstances the employer could not reasonably have avoided the need to replace the employee.

(5) In the case of an employer that is a local authority, subsection (1) does not apply in relation to an employee if—

(a) at the time of the dismissal, a relevant intervention direction has effect in relation to the authority,

(b) the relevant intervention direction—

(i) specifies that the reason, or one of the reasons, for the giving of the direction is that the authority is undergoing financial difficulties, and

(ii) contains provision relating to the financial management or financial governance of the authority, and

(c) the authority shows that—

(i) the reason for the replacement was to eliminate or significantly reduce, or significantly mitigate the effect of, any of the financial difficulties referred to in paragraph (b)(i), and

(ii) in all the circumstances the authority could not reasonably have avoided the need to replace the employee.

(6) In determining whether—

(a) in the case of a public sector employer (other than a local authority), subsection (4)(b) is met, or

(b) in the case of a local authority, subsection (5)(c)(ii) is met,

an employment tribunal must apply the same principles as would be applied by a court on an application for judicial review.

(7) Where the employer shows that the conditions in paragraphs (a) and (b) of subsection (4) are met, or (where the employer is a local authority) the conditions in paragraphs (a), (b) and (c) of subsection (5) are met, the matters that must be considered in determining the question whether the dismissal is fair or unfair include the following—

(a) any consultation carried out by the employer with the employee about replacing the employee;

(b) if the employee is of a description in respect of which an independent trade union is recognised by the employer, any consultation carried out by the employer with that trade union;

(c) if the employee is not of a description in respect of which an independent trade union is recognised by the employer, any consultation carried out by the employer with any other person representing the interests of the employee that, at the time of the dismissal, had authority to receive information and to be consulted about the dismissal on the employee's behalf;

(d) any matters specified for the purposes of this subsection in regulations made by the Secretary of State.

(8) In this section—

'contract' means a contract whether express or implied and (if it is express) whether oral or in writing;

'English local authority' means—

(a) a county council or district council in England;

(b) a London borough council;

(c) the Greater London Authority;

(d) the Council of the Isles of Scilly;

(e) the Common Council of the City of London in its capacity as a local authority, a police authority or a port health authority;

(f) a combined authority established under section 103 of the Local Democracy, Economic Development and Construction Act 2009;

(g) a combined county authority established under section 9(1) of the Levelling-up and Regeneration Act 2023;

'local authority' means—

(a) an English local authority,

(b) a Welsh local authority, or

(c) a Scottish local authority;

'public sector employer' means a person that—

(a) is wholly or mainly funded from public funds,

(b) is under a statutory duty to carry out any functions of a public nature, and

(c) so far as carrying out those functions, does not operate on a commercial basis;

'recognised', in relation to a trade union, has the same meaning as in the Trade Union and Labour Relations (Consolidation) Act 1992 (see section 178 of that Act);

'relevant intervention direction' means—

(a) in the case of an English local authority, a direction under section 15(5) or (6)(a) of the Local Government Act 1999 (powers to deal with failure to comply with duties relating to best value authorities);

(b) in the case of a Welsh local authority, a direction under section 106 or 107 of the Local Government and Elections (Wales) Act 2021 (asc 1) (intervention powers of Welsh Ministers);

(c) in the case of a Scottish local authority, an enforcement direction under section 24 of the Local Government in Scotland Act 2003 (asp 1) relating wholly or partly to a failure of the authority to comply with its duties under section 1 of that Act (local authorities' duty to secure best value);

'Scottish local authority' means a council constituted under section 2 of the Local Government etc. (Scotland) Act 1994;

'statutory duty' means a duty imposed by or under any enactment, including—

(a) a Measure or Act of the National Assembly for Wales or an Act of Senedd Cymru, and

(b) an Act of the Scottish Parliament;

'statutory functions', in relation to a public sector employer, means functions of a public nature which the employer is under a statutory duty to carry out;

'Welsh local authority' means—

(a) a county council or county borough council in Wales;

(b) a corporate joint committee established under Part 5 of the Local Government and Elections (Wales) Act 2021.

(9) The reference in subsection (5)(a) to a relevant intervention direction includes a relevant intervention direction given before the day on which the Employment Rights Act 2025 was passed.

105 Redundancy

(1) An employee who is dismissed shall be regarded for the purposes of this Part as unfairly dismissed if—

(a) the reason (or, if more than one, the principal reason) for the dismissal is that the employee was redundant,

(b) it is shown that the circumstances constituting the redundancy applied equally to one or more other employees in the same undertaking who held positions similar to that held by the employee and who have not been dismissed by the employer, and

(c) it is shown that any of subsections (2A) to (7N) apply.

(2) [repealed]

(2A) [omitted]

(3) This subsection applies if the reason (or, if more than one, the principal reason) for which the employee was selected for dismissal was one of those specified in subsection (1) of section 100 (read with subsections (2) and (3) of that section).

(4) This subsection applies if either—

(a) the employee was a protected shop worker or an opted-out shop worker, or a protected betting worker or an opted-out betting worker, and the reason (or, if more than one, the principal reason) for which the employee was selected for dismissal was that specified in subsection (1) of section 101 (read with subsection (2) of that section), or

(b) the employee was a shop worker or a betting worker and the reason (or, if more than one, the principal reason) for which the employee was selected for dismissal was that specified in subsection (3) of that section.

(4A) This subsection applies if the reason (or, if more than one, the principal reason) for which the employee was selected for dismissal was one of those specified in section 101A.

(4B) This subsection applies if the reason (or, if more than one, the principal reason) for which the employee was selected for dismissal was that specified in section 101B.

(5) This subsection applies if the reason (or, if more than one, the principal reason) for which the employee was selected for dismissal was that specified in section 102(1).

(6) This subsection applies if the reason (or, if more than one, the principal reason) for which the employee was selected for dismissal was that specified in section 103.

(6A) This subsection applies if the reason (or, if more than one, the principal reason) for which the employee was selected for dismissal was that specified in section 103A.

(7) This subsection applies if the reason (or, if more than one, the principal reason) for which the employee was selected for dismissal was one of those specified in subsection (1) of section 104 (read with subsections (2) and (3) of that section).

(7A) This subsection applies if the reason (or, if more than one, the principal reason) for which the employee was selected for dismissal was one of those specified in subsection (1) of section 104A (read with subsection (2) of that section).

(7B) This subsection applies if the reason (or, if more than one, the principal reason) for which the employee has selected for dismissal was one of those specified in subsection (1) of section 104B (read with subsection (2) of that section).

(7BA) This subsection applies if the reason (or, if more than one, the principal reason) for which the employee was selected for dismissal was one of those specified in section 104C.

(7BB) This subsection applies if the reason (or, if more than one, the principal reason) for which the employee was selected for dismissal was one of those specified in section 104E.

(7BC) [omitted]

(7C) This subsection applies if—

(a) the reason (or, if more than one, the principal reason) for which the employee was selected for dismissal was the reason mentioned in section 238A(2) of the Trade Union and Labour Relations (Consolidation) Act 1992 (participation in official industrial action), and

(b) subsection (3), (4) or (5) of that section applies to the dismissal.

(7D) This subsection applies if the reason (or, if more than one, the principal reason) for which the employee was selected for dismissal was one specified in paragraph (3) or (6) of regulation 28 of the Transnational Information and Consultation of Employees Regulations 1999 (read with paragraphs (4) and (7) of that regulation).

(7E) This subsection applies if the reason (or, if more than one, the principal reason) for which the employee was selected for dismissal was one specified in paragraph (3) of regulation 7 of the Part-time Workers (Prevention of Less Favourable Treatment) Regulations 2000 (unless the case is one to which paragraph (4) of that regulation applies).

(7F) This subsection applies if the reason (or, if more than one, the principal reason) for which the employee was selected for dismissal was one specified in paragraph (3) of regulation 6 of the Fixed-term Employees (Prevention of Less Favourable Treatment) Regulations 2002 (unless the case is one to which paragraph (4) of that regulation applies).

(7G) [omitted]

(7H) This subsection applies if the reason (or, if more than one, the principal reason) for which the employee was selected for dismissal was one specified in paragraph (3) or (6) of regulation 30 of the Information and Consultation of Employees Regulations 2004 (read with paragraphs (4) and (7) of that regulation).

(7I) This subsection applies if the reason (or, if more than one, the principal reason) for which the employee was selected for dismissal was one specified in paragraph 5(3) or (5) of the Schedule to the Occupational and Personal Pension Schemes (Consultation by Employers and Miscellaneous Amendment) Regulations 2006 (read with paragraph 5(6) of that Schedule).

(7IA) [repealed]

(7J) This subsection applies if the reason (or, if more than one, the principal reason) for which the employee was selected for dismissal was one specified in paragraph (3) or (6) of regulation 31 of the European Cooperative Society (Involvement of Employees) Regulations 2006 (read with paragraphs (4) and (7) of that regulation).

(7JA) This subsection applies if the reason (or, if more than one, the principal reason) for which the employee was selected for dismissal was one of those specified in subsection (1) of section 104D (read with subsection (2) of that section).

(7K) [repealed]

(7L) This subsection applies if the reason (or, if more than one, the principal reason) for which the employee was selected for dismissal was one specified in paragraph (3) or (6) of regulation 29 of the European Public Limited-Liability Company (Employee Involvement) (Great Britain) Regulations 2009 (SI 2009/2401) (read with paragraphs (4) and (7) of that regulation).

(7M) This subsection applies if—

(a) the reason (or, if more than one, the principal reason) for which the employee was selected for dismissal was the one specified in the opening words of section 104F(1), and

(b) the condition in paragraph (a) or (b) of that subsection was met.

(7N) This subsection applies if the reason (or, if more than one, the principal reason) for which the employee was selected for dismissal was one specified in—

(a) paragraph (3) of regulation 17 of the Agency Workers Regulations 2010 (unless the case is one to which paragraph (4) of that regulation applies); or

(b) paragraph (3) of regulation 5 of the Agency Workers (Amendment) Regulations 2019 (unless the case is one to which paragraph (4) of that regulation applies).

(8) For the purposes of section 36(2)(b) or 41(1)(b), the appropriate date in relation to this section is the effective date of termination.

(9) In this Part 'redundancy case' means a case where paragraphs (a) and (b) of subsection (1) of this section are satisfied.

106 Replacements

(1) Where this section applies to an employee he shall be regarded for the purposes of section 98(1)(b) as having been dismissed for a substantial reason of a kind such as to justify the dismissal of an employee holding the position which the employee held.

(2) This section applies to an employee where—

(a) on engaging him the employer informs him in writing that his employment will be terminated on the resumption of work by another employee who is, or will be, absent wholly or partly because of pregnancy or childbirth, or on adoption leave or shared parental leave, and

(b) the employer dismisses him in order to make it possible to give work to the other employee.

(3) This section also applies to an employee where—

(a) on engaging him the employer informs him in writing that his employment will be terminated on the end of a suspension of another employee from work on medical grounds or maternity grounds (within the meaning of Part VII), and

(b) the employer dismisses him in order to make it possible to allow the resumption of work by the other employee.

(4) Subsection (1) does not affect the operation of section 98(4) in a case to which this section applies.

107 Pressure on employer to dismiss unfairly

(1) This section applies where there falls to be determined for the purposes of this Part a question—

(a) as to the reason, or principal reason, for which an employee was dismissed,

(b) whether the reason or principal reason for which an employee was dismissed was a reason fulfilling the requirement of section 98(1)(b), or

(c) whether an employer acted reasonably in treating the reason or principal reason for which an employee was dismissed as a sufficient reason for dismissing him.

(2) In determining the question no account shall be taken of any pressure which by calling, organising, procuring or financing a strike or other industrial action, or threatening to do so, was exercised on the employer to dismiss the employee; and the question shall be determined as if no such pressure had been exercised.

Exclusion of right

108 Qualifying period of employment

(1) Section 94 does not apply to the dismissal of an employee unless he has been continuously employed for a period of not less than two years ending with the effective date of termination.

(2) If an employee is dismissed by reason of any such requirement or recommendation as is referred to in section 64(2), subsection (1) has effect in relation to that dismissal as if for the words 'two years' there were substituted the words 'one month'.

(3) Subsection (1) does not apply if—

(a) [repealed]

(aa) [omitted]

(b) subsection (1) of section 99 (read with any regulation made under that section) applies,

(c) subsection (1) of section 100 (read with subsections (2) and (3) of that section) applies,

(d) subsection (1) of section 101 (read with subsection (2) of that section) or subsection (3) of that section applies,

(da) subsection (2) of section 101ZA applies (read with subsection (3) of that section) or subsection (4) of that section applies,

(dd) section 101A applies,

(de) section 101B applies,

(e) section 102 applies,

(f) section 103 applies,

(ff) section 103A applies,

(g) subsection (1) of section 104 (read with subsections (2) and (3) of that section) applies,

(gg) subsection (1) of section 104A (read with subsection (2) of that section) applies,

(gh) subsection (1) of section 104B (read with subsection (2) of that section) applies,

(gi) section 104C applies,

(gj) subsection (1) of section 104D (read with subsection (2) of that section) applies,

(gk) section 104E applies,

(gl) subsection (1) of section 104F (read with subsection (2) of that section) applies.

(gm) section 104G applies,

(gn) section 104H applies,

(h) section 105 applies,

(hh) paragraph (3) or (6) of regulation 28 of the Transnational Information and Consultation of Employees Regulations 1999 (read with paragraphs (4) and (7) of that regulation) applies,

(i) paragraph (1) of regulation 7 of the Part-time Workers (Prevention of Less Favourable Treatment) Regulations 2000 applies,

(j) paragraph (1) of regulation 6 of the Fixed-term Employees (Prevention of Less Favourable Treatment) Regulations 2002 applies,

(k) paragraph (3) or (6) of regulation 42 of the European Public Limited-Liability Company Regulations 2004,

(l) paragraph (3) or (6) of regulation 30 of the Information and Consultation of Employees Regulations 2004 (read with paragraphs (4) and (7) of that regulation) applies,

(m) paragraph 5(3) or (5) of the Schedule to the Occupational and Personal Pension Schemes (Consultation by Employers and Miscellaneous Amendment) Regulations 2006 (read with paragraph 5(6) of that Schedule) applies,

(n) [repealed]

(o) paragraph (3) or (6) of regulation 31 of the European Cooperative Society (Involvement of Employees) Regulations 2006 (read with paragraphs (4) and (7) of that regulation) applies,

(p) [repealed]

(q) paragraph (1)(a) or (b) of regulation 29 of the European Public Limited-Liability Company (Employee Involvement) (Great Britain) Regulations 2009 (SI 2009/2401) applies, or

(r) paragraph (1) of regulation 17 of the Agency Workers Regulations 2010 applies.

(4) Subsection (1) does not apply if the reason (or, if more than one, the principal reason) for the dismissal is, or relates to, the employee's political opinions or affiliation.

(5) Subsection (1) does not apply if the reason (or, if more than one, the principal reason) for the dismissal is, or is connected with, the employee's membership of a reserve force (as defined in section 374 of the Armed Forces Act 2006).

109 [repealed]; 110 [omitted]

Chapter II Remedies for Unfair Dismissal

Introductory

111 Complaints to employment tribunal

(1) A complaint may be presented to an employment tribunal against an employer by any person that he was unfairly dismissed by the employer.

(2) Subject to the following provisions of this section, an employment tribunal shall not consider a complaint under this section unless it is presented to the tribunal—

(a) before the end of the period of three months beginning with the effective date of termination, or

(b) within such further period as the tribunal considers reasonable in a case where it is satisfied that it was not reasonably practicable for the complaint to be presented before the end of that period of three months.

(2A) [omitted]

(3) Where a dismissal is with notice, an employment tribunal shall consider a complaint under this section if it is presented after the notice is given but before the effective date of termination.

(4) In relation to a complaint which is presented as mentioned in subsection (3), the provisions of this Act, so far as they relate to unfair dismissal, have effect as if—

(a) references to a complaint by a person that he was unfairly dismissed by his employer included references to a complaint by a person that his employer has given him notice in such circumstances that he will be unfairly dismissed when the notice expires,

(b) references to reinstatement included references to the withdrawal of the notice by the employer,

(c) references to the effective date of termination included references to the date which would be the effective date of termination on the expiry of the notice, and

(d) references to an employee ceasing to be employed included references to an employee having been given notice of dismissal.

(5) Where the dismissal is alleged to be unfair by virtue of section 104F (blacklists),

(a) subsection (2)(b) does not apply, and

(b) an employment tribunal may consider a complaint that is otherwise out of time if, in all the circumstances of the case, it considers that it is just and equitable to do so.

111A [omitted]

112 The remedies: orders and compensation

(1) This section applies where, on a complaint under section 111, an employment tribunal finds that the grounds of the complaint are well-founded.

(2) The tribunal shall—

(a) explain to the complainant what orders may be made under section 113 and in what circumstances they may be made, and

(b) ask him whether he wishes the tribunal to make such an order.

(3) If the complainant expresses such a wish, the tribunal may make an order under section 113.

(4) If no order is made under section 113, the tribunal shall make an award of compensation for unfair dismissal (calculated in accordance with sections 118 to 126) to be paid by the employer to the employee.

(5)–(6) [repealed]

Orders for reinstatement or re-engagement

113 The orders

An order under this section may be—

(a) an order for reinstatement (in accordance with section 114), or

(b) an order for re-engagement (in accordance with section 115), as the tribunal may decide.

114 Order for reinstatement

(1) An order for reinstatement is an order that the employer shall treat the complainant in all respects as if he had not been dismissed.

(2) On making an order for reinstatement the tribunal shall specify—

(a) any amount payable by the employer in respect of any benefit which the complainant might reasonably be expected to have had but for the dismissal (including arrears of pay) for the period between the date of termination of employment and the date of reinstatement,

(b) any rights and privileges (including seniority and pension rights) which must be restored to the employee, and

(c) the date by which the order must be complied with.

(3) If the complainant would have benefited from an improvement in his terms and conditions of employment had he not been dismissed, an order for reinstatement shall require him to be treated as if he had benefited from that improvement from the date on which he would have done so but for being dismissed.

(4) In calculating for the purposes of subsection (2)(a) any amount payable by the employer, the tribunal shall take into account, so as to reduce the employer's liability, any sums received by the complainant in respect of the period between the date of termination of employment and the date of reinstatement by way of—

(a) wages in lieu of notice or ex gratia payments paid by the employer, or

(b) remuneration paid in respect of employment with another employer, and such other benefits as the tribunal thinks appropriate in the circumstances.

(5) [repealed]

115 Order for re-engagement

(1) An order for re-engagement is an order, on such terms as the tribunal may decide, that the complainant be engaged by the employer, or by a successor of the employer or by an associated employer, in employment comparable to that from which he was dismissed or other suitable employment.

(2) On making an order for re-engagement the tribunal shall specify the terms on which re-engagement is to take place, including—

(a) the identity of the employer,

(b) the nature of the employment,

(c) the remuneration for the employment,

(d) any amount payable by the employer in respect of any benefit which the complainant might reasonably be expected to have had but for the dismissal (including arrears of pay) for the period between the date of termination of employment and the date of re-engagement,

(e) any rights and privileges (including seniority and pension rights) which must be restored to the employee, and

(f) the date by which the order must be complied with.

(3) In calculating for the purposes of subsection (2)(d) any amount payable by the employer, the tribunal shall take into account, so as to reduce the employer's liability, any sums received by the complainant in respect of the period between the date of termination of employment and the date of re-engagement by way of—

(a) wages in lieu of notice or ex gratia payments paid by the employer, or

(b) remuneration paid in respect of employment with another employer, and such other benefits as the tribunal thinks appropriate in the circumstances.

(4) [repealed]

116 Choice of order and its terms

(1) In exercising its discretion under section 113 the tribunal shall first consider whether to make an order for reinstatement and in so doing shall take into account—

(a) whether the complainant wishes to be reinstated,

(b) whether it is practicable for the employer to comply with an order for reinstatement, and

(c) where the complainant caused or contributed to some extent to the dismissal, whether it would be just to order his reinstatement.

(2) If the tribunal decides not to make an order for reinstatement it shall then consider whether to make an order for re-engagement and, if so, on what terms.

(3) In so doing the tribunal shall take into account—

(a) any wish expressed by the complainant as to the nature of the order to be made,

(b) whether it is practicable for the employer (or a successor or an associated employer) to comply with an order for re-engagement, and

(c) where the complainant caused or contributed to some extent to the dismissal, whether it would be just to order his re-engagement and (if so) on what terms.

(4) Except in a case where the tribunal takes into account contributory fault under subsection (3)(c) it shall, if it orders re-engagement, do so on terms which are, so far as is reasonably practicable, as favourable as an order for reinstatement.

(5) Where in any case an employer has engaged a permanent replacement for a dismissed employee, the tribunal shall not take that fact into account in determining, for the purposes of subsection (1)(b) or (3)(b), whether it is practicable to comply with an order for reinstatement or re-engagement.

(6) Subsection (5) does not apply where the employer shows—

(a) that it was not practicable for him to arrange for the dismissed employee's work to be done without engaging a permanent replacement, or

(b) that—

(i) he engaged the replacement after the lapse of a reasonable period, without having heard from the dismissed employee that he wished to be reinstated or re-engaged, and

(ii) when the employer engaged the replacement it was no longer reasonable for him to arrange for the dismissed employee's work to be done except by a permanent replacement.

117 Enforcement of order and compensation

(1) An employment tribunal shall make an award of compensation, to be paid by the employer to the employee, if—

(a) an order under section 113 is made and the complainant is reinstated or re-engaged, but

(b) the terms of the order are not fully complied with.

(2) Subject to section 124, the amount of the compensation shall be such as the tribunal thinks fit having regard to the loss sustained by the complainant in consequence of the failure to comply fully with the terms of the order.

(2A) There shall be deducted from any award under subsection (1) the amount of any award made under section 112(5) at the time of the order under section 113.

(3) Subject to subsections (1) and (2), if an order under section 113 is made but the complainant is not reinstated or re-engaged in accordance with the order, the tribunal shall make—

(a) an award of compensation for unfair dismissal (calculated in accordance with sections 118 to 126), and

(b) except where this paragraph does not apply, an additional award of compensation of an amount not less than twenty-six nor more than fifty-two weeks' pay,

to be paid by the employer to the employee.

(4) Subsection (3)(b) does not apply where—

(a) the employer satisfies the tribunal that it was not practicable to comply with the order,

(b) [repealed]

(5)–(6) [repealed]

(7) Where in any case an employer has engaged a permanent replacement for a dismissed employee, the tribunal shall not take that fact into account in determining for the purposes of subsection (4)(a) whether it was practicable to comply with the order for reinstatement or re-engagement unless the employer shows that it was not practicable for him to arrange for the dismissed employee's work to be done without engaging a permanent replacement.

(8) Where in any case an employment tribunal finds that the complainant has unreasonably prevented an order under section 113 from being complied with, in making an award of compensation for unfair dismissal it shall take that conduct into account as a failure on the part of the complainant to mitigate his loss.

Compensation

118 General

(1) Where a tribunal makes an award of compensation for unfair dismissal under section 112(4) or 117(3)(a) the award shall consist of—

(a) a basic award (calculated in accordance with sections 119 to 122 and 126), and

(b) a compensatory award (calculated in accordance with sections 123, 124, 124A and 126).

(2)–(4) [repealed]

119 Basic award

(1) Subject to the provisions of this section, sections 120 to 122 and section 126, the amount of the basic award shall be calculated by—

(a) determining the period, ending with the effective date of termination, during which the employee has been continuously employed,

(b) reckoning backwards from the end of that period the number of years of employment falling within that period, and

(c) allowing the appropriate amount for each of those years of employment.

(2) In subsection (1)(c) 'the appropriate amount' means—

(a) one and a half weeks' pay for a year of employment in which the employee was not below the age of forty-one,

(b) one week's pay for a year of employment (not within paragraph (a)) in which he was not below the age of twenty-two, and

(c) half a week's pay for a year of employment not within paragraph (a) or (b).

(3) Where twenty years of employment have been reckoned under subsection (1), no account shall be taken under that subsection of any year of employment earlier than those twenty years.

(4)–(6) [repealed]

120 Basic award: minimum in certain cases

(1) The amount of the basic award (before any reduction under section 122) shall not be less than £9,157 where the reason (or, if more than one, the principal reason)—

(a) in a redundancy case, for selecting the employee for dismissal, or

(b) otherwise, for the dismissal,

is one of those specified in section 100(1)(a) and (b), 101A(d), 102(1) or 103.

(1A)–(1B) [repealed]

(1C) Where an employee is regarded as unfairly dismissed by virtue of section 104F (blacklists) (whether or not the dismissal is unfair or regarded as unfair for any other reason), the amount of the basic award of compensation (before any reduction is made under section 122) shall not be less than £5,000.

(2) [repealed]

121 Basic award of two weeks' pay in certain cases

The amount of the basic award shall be two weeks' pay where the tribunal finds that the reason (or, where there is more than one, the principal reason) for the dismissal of the employee is that he was redundant and the employee—

(a) by virtue of section 138 is not regarded as dismissed for the purposes of Part XI, or

(b) by virtue of section 141 is not, or (if he were otherwise entitled) would not be, entitled to a redundancy payment.

122 Basic award: reductions

(1) Where the tribunal finds that the complainant has unreasonably refused an offer by the employer which (if accepted) would have the effect of reinstating the complainant in his employment in all respects as if he had not been dismissed, the tribunal shall reduce or further reduce the amount of the basic award to such extent as it considers just and equitable having regard to that finding.

(2) Where the tribunal considers that any conduct of the complainant before the dismissal (or, where the dismissal was with notice, before the notice was given) was such that it would be just and equitable to reduce or further reduce the amount of the basic award to any extent, the tribunal shall reduce or further reduce that amount accordingly.

(3) Subsection (2) does not apply in a redundancy case unless the reason for selecting the employee for dismissal was one of those specified in section 100(1)(a) and (b), 101A(d), 102(1) or 103; and in such a case subsection (2) applies only to so much of the basic award as is payable because of section 120.

(3A) Where the complainant has been awarded any amount in respect of the dismissal under a designated dismissal procedures agreement, the tribunal shall reduce or further reduce the amount of the basic award to such extent as it considers just and equitable having regard to that award.

(4) The amount of the basic award shall be reduced or further reduced by the amount of—

(a) any redundancy payment awarded by the tribunal under Part XI in respect of the same dismissal, or

(b) any payment made by the employer to the employee on the ground that the dismissal was by reason of redundancy (whether in pursuance of Part XI or otherwise).

(5) Where a dismissal is regarded as unfair by virtue of section 104F (blacklists), the amount of the basic award shall be reduced or further reduced by the amount of any basic award in respect of the same dismissal under section 156 of the Trade Union and Labour Relations Consolidation) Act 1992 (minimum basic award in case of dismissal on grounds related to trade union membership or activities).

123 Compensatory award

(1) Subject to the provisions of this section and sections 124, 124A and 126, the amount of the compensatory award shall be such amount as the tribunal considers just and equitable in all the circumstances having regard to the loss sustained by the complainant in consequence of the dismissal in so far as that loss is attributable to action taken by the employer.

(2) The loss referred to in subsection (1) shall be taken to include—

(a) any expenses reasonably incurred by the complainant in consequence of the dismissal, and

(b) subject to subsection (3), loss of any benefit which he might reasonably be expected to have had but for the dismissal.

(3) The loss referred to in subsection (1) shall be taken to include in respect of any loss of—

(a) any entitlement or potential entitlement to a payment on account of dismissal by reason of redundancy (whether in pursuance of Part XI or otherwise), or

(b) any expectation of such a payment, only the loss referable to the amount (if any) by which the amount of that payment would have exceeded the amount of a basic award (apart from any reduction under section 122) in respect of the same dismissal.

(4) In ascertaining the loss referred to in subsection (1) the tribunal shall apply the same rule concerning the duty of a person to mitigate his loss as applies to damages recoverable under the common law of England and Wales or (as the case may be) Scotland.

(5) In determining, for the purposes of subsection (1), how far any loss sustained by the complainant was attributable to action taken by the employer, no account shall be taken of any pressure which by—

(a) calling, organising, procuring or financing a strike or other industrial action, or

(b) threatening to do so,

was exercised on the employer to dismiss the employee; and that question shall be determined as if no such pressure had been exercised.

(6) Where the tribunal finds that the dismissal was to any extent caused or contributed to by any action of the complainant, it shall reduce the amount of the compensatory award by such proportion as it considers just and equitable having regard to that finding.

(6A) Where—

(a) the reason (or principal reason) for the dismissal is that the complainant made a protected disclosure, and

(b) it appears to the tribunal that the disclosure was not made in good faith,

the tribunal may, if it considers it just and equitable in all the circumstances to do so, reduce any award it makes to the complainant by no more than 25%.

(7) If the amount of any payment made by the employer to the employee on the ground that the dismissal was by reason of redundancy (whether in pursuance of Part XI or otherwise) exceeds the amount of the basic award which would be payable but for section 122(4), that excess goes to reduce the amount of the compensatory award.

(8) Where the amount of the compensatory award falls to be calculated for the purposes of an award under section 117(3)(a), there shall be deducted from the compensatory award any award made under section 112(5) at the time of the order under section 113.

124 Limit of compensatory award etc.

(1) The amount of—

(a) any compensation awarded to a person under section 117(1) and (2), or

(b) a compensatory award to a person calculated in accordance with section 123, shall not exceed the amount specified in subsection (1ZA).

(1ZA) The amount specified in this subsection is the lower of—

(a) £123,543 and

(b) 52 multiplied by a week's pay of the person concerned.

(1A) Subsection (1) shall not apply to compensation awarded, or a compensatory award made, to a person in a case where he is regarded as unfairly dismissed by virtue of section 100, 103A, 104H, 105(3) or 105(6A).

(2) [repealed]

(3) In the case of compensation awarded to a person under section 117(1) and (2), the limit imposed by this section may be exceeded to the extent necessary to enable the award fully to reflect the amount specified as payable under section 114(2)(a) or section 115(2)(d).

(4) Where—

(a) a compensatory award is an award under paragraph (a) of subsection (3) of section 117, and

(b) an additional award falls to be made under paragraph (b) of that subsection, the limit imposed by this section on the compensatory award may be exceeded to the extent necessary to enable the aggregate of the compensatory and additional awards fully to reflect the amount specified as payable under section 114(2)(a) or section 115 (2)(d).

(5) The limit imposed by this section applies to the amount which the employment tribunal would, apart from this section, award in respect of the subject matter of the complaint after taking into account—

(a) any payment made by the respondent to the complainant in respect of that matter, and

(b) any reduction in the amount of the award required by any enactment or rule of law.

124A Adjustments under the Employment Act 2002

Where an award of compensation for unfair dismissal falls to be—

(a) reduced or increased under section 207A of the Trade Union and Labour Relations (Consolidation) Act 1992 (effect of failure to comply with Code: adjustment of awards), or

(b) increased under section 38 of that Act (failure to give statement of employment particulars),

the adjustment shall be in the amount awarded under section 118(1)(b) and shall be applied immediately before any reduction under section 123(6) or (7).

125 [repealed]

126 Acts which are both unfair dismissal and discrimination

(1) This section applies where compensation falls to be awarded in respect of any act both under—

(a) the provisions of this Act relating to unfair dismissal, and

(b) the Equality Act 2010.

(2) An employment tribunal shall not award compensation under either of those Acts in respect of any loss or other matter which is or has been taken into account under the other, by the tribunal (or another employment tribunal) in awarding compensation on the same or another complaint in respect of that act.

127 and 127A–127B [repealed]

Interim relief

128 Interim relief pending determination of complaint

(1) An employee who presents a complaint to an employment tribunal that he has been unfairly dismissed and—

(a) that the reason (or if more than one the principal reason) for the dismissal is one of those specified in—

(i) section 100(1)(a) and (b), 101A(1)(d), 102(1), 103 or 103A, or

(ii) paragraph 161(2) of Schedule A1 to the Trade Union and Labour Relations (Consolidation) Act 1992, or

(b) that the reason (or, if more than one, the principal reason) for which the employee was selected for dismissal was the one specified in the opening words of section 104F(1) and the condition in paragraph (a) or (b) of that subsection was met, may apply to the tribunal for interim relief.

(2) The tribunal shall not entertain an application for interim relief unless it is presented to the tribunal before the end of the period of seven days immediately following the effective date of termination (whether before, on or after that date).

(3) The tribunal shall determine the application for interim relief as soon as practicable after receiving the application.

(4) The tribunal shall give to the employer not later than seven days before the date of the hearing a copy of the application together with notice of the date, time and place of the hearing.

(5) The tribunal shall not exercise any power it has of postponing the hearing of an application for interim relief except where it is satisfied that special circumstances exist which justify it in doing so.

129 Procedure on hearing of application and making of order

(1) This section applies where, on hearing an employee's application for interim relief, it appears to the tribunal that it is likely that on determining the complaint to which the application relates the tribunal will find—

- (a) that the reason (or if more than one the principal reason) for the dismissal is one of those specified in—
  - (i) section 100(1)(a) and (b), 101A(1)(d), 102(1), 103 or 103A, or
  - (ii) paragraph 161(2) of Schedule A1 to the Trade Union and Labour Relations (Consolidation) Act 1992, or
- (b) that the reason (or, if more than one, the principal reason) for which the employee was selected for dismissal was the one specified in the opening words of section 104F(1) and the condition in paragraph (a) or (b) of that subsection was met.

(2) The tribunal shall announce its findings and explain to both parties (if present)—

- (a) what powers the tribunal may exercise on the application, and
- (b) in what circumstances it will exercise them.

(3) The tribunal shall ask the employer (if present) whether he is willing, pending the determination or settlement of the complaint—

- (a) to reinstate the employee (that is, to treat him in all respects as if he had not been dismissed), or
- (b) if not, to re-engage him in another job on terms and conditions not less favourable than those which would have been applicable to him if he had not been dismissed.

(4) For the purposes of subsection (3)(b) 'terms and conditions not less favourable than those which would have been applicable to him if he had not been dismissed' means, as regards seniority, pension rights and other similar rights, that the period prior to the dismissal should be regarded as continuous with his employment following the dismissal.

(5) If the employer states that he is willing to reinstate the employee, the tribunal shall make an order to that effect.

(6) If the employer—

- (a) states that he is willing to re-engage the employee in another job, and
- (b) specifies the terms and conditions on which he is willing to do so,

the tribunal shall ask the employee whether he is willing to accept the job on those terms and conditions.

(7) If the employee is willing to accept the job on those terms and conditions, the tribunal shall make an order to that effect.

(8) If the employee is not willing to accept the job on those terms and conditions—

- (a) where the tribunal is of the opinion that the refusal is reasonable, the tribunal shall make an order for the continuation of his contract of employment, and
- (b) otherwise, the tribunal shall make no order.

(9) If on the hearing of an application for interim relief the employer—

- (a) fails to attend before the tribunal, or

(b) states that he is unwilling either to reinstate or re-engage the employee as mentioned in subsection (3),

the tribunal shall make an order for the continuation of the employee's contract of employment.

130 Order for continuation of contract of employment

(1) An order under section 129 for the continuation of a contract of employment is an order that the contract of employment continue in force—

(a) for the purposes of pay or any other benefit derived from the employment, seniority, pension rights and other similar matters, and

(b) for the purposes of determining for any purpose the period for which the employee has been continuously employed,

from the date of its termination (whether before or after the making of the order) until the determination or settlement of the complaint.

(2) Where the tribunal makes such an order it shall specify in the order the amount which is to be paid by the employer to the employee by way of pay in respect of each normal pay period, or part of any such period, falling between the date of dismissal and the determination or settlement of the complaint.

(3) Subject to the following provisions, the amount so specified shall be that which the employee could reasonably have been expected to earn during that period, or part, and shall be paid—

(a) in the case of a payment for any such period falling wholly or partly after the making of the order, on the normal pay day for that period, and

(b) in the case of a payment for any past period, within such time as may be specified in the order.

(4) If an amount is payable in respect only of part of a normal pay period, the amount shall be calculated by reference to the whole period and reduced proportionately.

(5) Any payment made to an employee by an employer under his contract of employment, or by way of damages for breach of that contract, in respect of a normal pay period, or part of any such period, goes towards discharging the employer's liability in respect of that period under subsection (2); and, conversely, any payment under that subsection in respect of a period goes towards discharging any liability of the employer under, or in respect of breach of, the contract of employment in respect of that period.

(6) If an employee, on or after being dismissed by his employer, receives a lump sum which, or part of which, is in lieu of wages but is not referable to any normal pay period, the tribunal shall take the payment into account in determining the amount of pay to be payable in pursuance of any such order.

(7) For the purposes of this section, the amount which an employee could reasonably have been expected to earn, his normal pay period and the normal pay day for each such period shall be determined as if he had not been dismissed.

131 Application for variation or revocation of order

(1) At any time between—

(a) the making of an order under section 129, and

(b) the determination or settlement of the complaint,

the employer or the employee may apply to an employment tribunal for the revocation or variation of the order on the ground of a relevant change of circumstances since the making of the order.

(2) Sections 128 and 129 apply in relation to such an application as in relation to an original application for interim relief except that, in the case of an application by the employer, section 128(4) has effect with the substitution of a reference to the employee for the reference to the employer.

132 Consequence of failure to comply with order

(1) If, on the application of an employee, an employment tribunal is satisfied that the employer has not complied with the terms of an order for the reinstatement or re-engagement of the employee under section 129(5) or (7), the tribunal shall—

(a) make an order for the continuation of the employee's contract of employment, and

(b) order the employer to pay compensation to the employee.

(2) Compensation under subsection (1)(b) shall be of such amount as the tribunal considers just and equitable in all the circumstances having regard—

(a) to the infringement of the employee's right to be reinstated or re-engaged in pursuance of the order, and

(b) to any loss suffered by the employee in consequence of the non-compliance.

(3) Section 130 applies to an order under subsection (1)(a) as in relation to an order under section 129.

(4) If on the application of an employee an employment tribunal is satisfied that the employer has not complied with the terms of an order for the continuation of a contract of employment subsection (5) or (6) applies.

(5) Where the non-compliance consists of a failure to pay an amount by way of pay specified in the order—

(a) the tribunal shall determine the amount owed by the employer on the date of the determination, and

(b) if on that date the tribunal also determines the employee's complaint that he has been unfairly dismissed, it shall specify that amount separately from any other sum awarded to the employee.

(6) In any other case, the tribunal shall order the employer to pay the employee such compensation as the tribunal considers just and equitable in all the circumstances having regard to any loss suffered by the employee in consequence of the non-compliance.

133–134A [omitted]

PART XI REDUNDANCY PAYMENTS ETC.

Chapter I Right to Redundancy Payment

135 The right

(1) An employer shall pay a redundancy payment to any employee of his if the employee—

(a) is dismissed by the employer by reason of redundancy, or

(b) is eligible for a redundancy payment by reason of being laid off or kept on short-time.

(2) Subsection (1) has effect subject to the following provisions of this Part (including, in particular, sections 140 to 144, 149 to 152, 155 to 161 and 164).

Chapter II Right on Dismissal by Reason of Redundancy

Dismissal by reason of redundancy

136 Circumstances in which an employee is dismissed

(1) Subject to the provisions of this section and sections 137 and 138, for the purposes of this Part an employee is dismissed by his employer if (and only if)—

(a) the contract under which he is employed by the employer is terminated by the employer (whether with or without notice),

(b) he is employed under a limited-term contract which terminates by virtue of the limiting event without being renewed under the same contract, or

(c) the employee terminates the contract under which he is employed (with or without notice) in circumstances in which he is entitled to terminate it without notice by reason of the employer's conduct.

(2) Subsection (1)(c) does not apply if the employee terminates the contract without notice in circumstances in which he is entitled to do so by reason of a lock-out by the employer.

(3) An employee shall be taken to be dismissed by his employer for the purposes of this Part if—

(a) the employer gives notice to the employee to terminate his contract of employment, and

(b) at a time within the obligatory period of notice the employee gives notice in writing to the employer to terminate the contract of employment on a date earlier than the date on which the employer's notice is due to expire.

(4) In this Part the 'obligatory period of notice', in relation to notice given by an employer to terminate an employee's contract of employment, means—

(a) the actual period of the notice in a case where the period beginning at the time when the notice is given and ending at the time when it expires is equal to the minimum period which (by virtue of any enactment or otherwise) is required to be given by the employer to terminate the contract of employment, and

(b) the period which—

(i) is equal to the minimum period referred to in paragraph (a), and

(ii) ends at the time when the notice expires, in any other case.

(5) Where in accordance with any enactment or rule of law—

(a) an act on the part of an employer, or

(b) an event affecting an employer (including, in the case of an individual, his death),

operates to terminate a contract under which an employee is employed by him, the act or event shall be taken for the purposes of this Part to be a termination of the contract by the employer.

137 [repealed]

138 No dismissal in cases of renewal of contract or re-engagement

(1) Where—

(a) an employee's contract of employment is renewed, or he is re-engaged under a new contract of employment in pursuance of an offer (whether in writing or not) made before the end of his employment under the previous contract, and

(b) the renewal or re-engagement takes effect either immediately on, or after an interval of not more than four weeks after, the end of that employment, the employee shall not be regarded for the purposes of this Part as dismissed by his employer by reason of the ending of his employment under the previous contract.

(2) Subsection (1) does not apply if—

(a) the provisions of the contract as renewed, or of the new contract, as to—

(i) the capacity and place in which the employee is employed, and

(ii) the other terms and conditions of his employment, differ (wholly or in part) from the corresponding provisions of the previous contract, and

(b) during the period specified in subsection (3)—

(i) the employee (for whatever reason) terminates the renewed or new contract, or gives notice to terminate it and it is in consequence terminated, or

(ii) the employer, for a reason connected with or arising out of any difference between the renewed or new contract and the previous contract, terminates the renewed or new contract, or gives notice to terminate it and it is in consequence terminated.

(3) The period referred to in subsection (2)(b) is the period—

(a) beginning at the end of the employee's employment under the previous contract, and

(b) ending with—

(i) the period of four weeks beginning with the date on which the employee starts work under the renewed or new contract, or

(ii) such longer period as may be agreed in accordance with subsection (6) for the purpose of retraining the employee for employment under that contract;

and is in this Part referred to as the 'trial period'.

(4) Where subsection (2) applies, for the purposes of this Part—

(a) the employee shall be regarded as dismissed on the date on which his employment under the previous contract (or, if there has been more than one trial period, the original contract) ended, and

(b) the reason for the dismissal shall be taken to be the reason for which the employee was then dismissed, or would have been dismissed had the offer (or original offer) of renewed or new employment not been made, or the reason which resulted in that offer being made.

(5) Subsection (2) does not apply if the employee's contract of employment is again renewed, or he is again re-engaged under a new contract of employment, in circumstances such that subsection (1) again applies.

(6) For the purposes of subsection (3)(b)(ii) a period of retraining is agreed in accordance with this subsection only if the agreement—

(a) is made between the employer and the employee or his representative before the employee starts work under the contract as renewed, or the new contract,

(b) is in writing,

(c) specifies the date on which the period of retraining ends, and

(d) specifies the terms and conditions of employment which will apply in the employee's case after the end of that period.

139 Redundancy

(1) For the purposes of this Act an employee who is dismissed shall be taken to be dismissed by reason of redundancy if the dismissal is wholly or mainly attributable to—

(a) the fact that his employer has ceased or intends to cease—

(i) to carry on the business for the purposes of which the employee was employed by him, or

(ii) to carry on that business in the place where the employee was so employed, or

(b) the fact that the requirements of that business—

(i) for employees to carry out work of a particular kind, or

(ii) for employees to carry out work of a particular kind in the place where the employee was employed by the employer,

have ceased or diminished or are expected to cease or diminish.

(2) For the purposes of subsection (1) the business of the employer together with the business or businesses of his associated employers shall be treated as one (unless either of the conditions specified in paragraphs (a) and (b) of that subsection would be satisfied without so treating them).

(3) For the purposes of subsection (1) the activities carried on by a local authority with respect to the schools maintained by it, and the activities carried on by the governing bodies of those schools, shall be treated as one business (unless either of the conditions specified in paragraphs (a) and (b) of that subsection would be satisfied without so treating them).

(4) Where—

(a) the contract under which a person is employed is treated by section 136(5) as terminated by his employer by reason of an act or event, and

(b) the employee's contract is not renewed and he is not re-engaged under a new contract of employment, he shall be taken for the purposes of this Act to be dismissed by reason of redundancy if the circumstances in which his contract is not renewed, and he is not re-engaged, are wholly or mainly attributable to either of the facts stated in paragraphs (a) and (b) of subsection (1).

(5) In its application to a case within subsection (4), paragraph (a)(i) of subsection (1) has effect as if the reference in that subsection to the employer included a reference to any person to whom, in consequence of the act or event, power to dispose of the business has passed.

(6) In subsection (1) 'cease' and 'diminish' mean cease and diminish either permanently or temporarily and for whatever reason.

(7) In subsection (3) 'local authority' has the meaning given by section 579(1) of the Education Act 1996.

Exclusions

140 Summary dismissal

(1) Subject to subsections (2) and (3), an employee is not entitled to a redundancy payment by reason of dismissal where his employer, being entitled to terminate his contract of employment without notice by reason of the employee's conduct, terminates it either—

- (a) without notice,
- (b) by giving shorter notice than that which, in the absence of conduct entitling the employer to terminate the contract without notice, the employer would be required to give to terminate the contract, or
- (c) by giving notice which includes, or is accompanied by, a statement in writing that the employer would, by reason of the employee's conduct, be entitled to terminate the contract without notice.

(2) Where an employee who—

- (a) has been given notice by his employer to terminate his contract of employment, or
- (b) has given notice to his employer under section 148(1) indicating his intention to claim a redundancy payment in respect of lay-off or short-time,

takes part in a strike at any relevant time in circumstances which entitle the employer to treat the contract of employment as terminable without notice, subsection (1) does not apply if the employer terminates the contract by reason of his taking part in the strike.

(3) Where the contract of employment of an employee who—

- (a) has been given notice by his employer to terminate his contract of employment, or
- (b) has given notice to his employer under section 148(1) indicating his intention to claim a redundancy payment in respect of lay-off or short-time,

is terminated as mentioned in subsection (1) at any relevant time otherwise than by reason of his taking part in a strike, an employment tribunal may determine that the employer is liable to make an appropriate payment to the employee if on a reference to the tribunal it appears to the tribunal, in the circumstances of the case, to be just and equitable that the employee should receive it.

(4) In subsection (3) 'appropriate payment' means—

- (a) the whole of the redundancy payment to which the employee would have been entitled apart from subsection (1), or
- (b) such part of that redundancy payment as the tribunal thinks fit.

(5) In this section 'relevant time'—

- (a) in the case of an employee who has been given notice by his employer to terminate his contract of employment, means any time within the obligatory period of notice, and
- (b) in the case of an employee who has given notice to his employer under section 148(1), means any time after the service of the notice.

141 Renewal of contract or re-engagement

(1) This section applies where an offer (whether in writing or not) is made to an employee before the end of his employment—

- (a) to renew his contract of employment, or

(b) to re-engage him under a new contract of employment,

with renewal or re-engagement to take effect either immediately on, or after an interval of not more than four weeks after, the end of his employment.

(2) Where subsection (3) is satisfied, the employee is not entitled to a redundancy payment if he unreasonably refuses the offer.

(3) This subsection is satisfied where—

(a) the provisions of the contract as renewed, or of the new contract, as to—

(i) the capacity and place in which the employee would be employed, and

(ii) the other terms and conditions of his employment, would not differ from the corresponding provisions of the previous contract, or

(b) those provisions of the contract as renewed, or of the new contract, would differ from the corresponding provisions of the previous contract but the offer constitutes an offer of suitable employment in relation to the employee.

(4) The employee is not entitled to a redundancy payment if—

(a) his contract of employment is renewed, or he is re-engaged under a new contract of employment, in pursuance of the offer,

(b) the provisions of the contract as renewed or new contract as to the capacity or place in which he is employed or the other terms and conditions of his employment differ (wholly or in part) from the corresponding provisions of the previous contract,

(c) the employment is suitable in relation to him, and

(d) during the trial period he unreasonably terminates the contract, or unreasonably gives notice to terminate it and it is in consequence terminated.

142 Employee anticipating expiry of employer's notice

(1) Subject to subsection (3), an employee is not entitled to a redundancy payment where—

(a) he is taken to be dismissed by virtue of section 136(3) by reason of giving to his employer notice terminating his contract of employment on a date earlier than the date on which notice by the employer terminating the contract is due to expire,

(b) before the employee's notice is due to expire, the employer gives him a notice such as is specified in subsection (2), and

(c) the employee does not comply with the requirements of that notice.

(2) The employer's notice referred to in subsection (1)(b) is a notice in writing—

(a) requiring the employee to withdraw his notice terminating the contract of employment and to continue in employment until the date on which the employer's notice terminating the contract expires, and

(b) stating that, unless he does so, the employer will contest any liability to pay to him a redundancy payment in respect of the termination of his contract of employment.

(3) An employment tribunal may determine that the employer is liable to make an appropriate payment to the employee if on a reference to the tribunal it appears to the tribunal, having regard to—

(a) the reasons for which the employee seeks to leave the employment, and

(b) the reasons for which the employer requires him to continue in it,

to be just and equitable that the employee should receive the payment.

(4) In subsection (3) 'appropriate payment' means—

(a) the whole of the redundancy payment to which the employee would have been entitled apart from subsection (1), or

(b) such part of that redundancy payment as the tribunal thinks fit.

143 Strike during currency of employer's notice

(1) This section applies where—

(a) an employer has given notice to an employee to terminate his contract of employment ('notice of termination'),

(b) after the notice is given the employee begins to take part in a strike of employees of the employer, and

(c) the employer serves on the employee a notice of extension.

(2) A notice of extension is a notice in writing which—

(a) requests the employee to agree to extend the contract of employment beyond the time of expiry by a period comprising as many available days as the number of working days lost by striking ('the proposed period of extension'),

(b) indicates the reasons for which the employer makes that request, and

(c) states that the employer will contest any liability to pay the employee a redundancy payment in respect of the dismissal effected by the notice of termination unless either—

(i) the employee complies with the request, or

(ii) the employer is satisfied that, in consequence of sickness or injury or otherwise, the employee is unable to comply with it or that (even though he is able to comply with it) it is reasonable in the circumstances for him not to do so.

(3) Subject to subsections (4) and (5), if the employee does not comply with the request contained in the notice of extension, he is not entitled to a redundancy payment by reason of the dismissal effected by the notice of termination.

(4) Subsection (3) does not apply if the employer agrees to pay a redundancy payment to the employee in respect of the dismissal effected by the notice of termination even though he has not complied with the request contained in the notice of extension.

(5) An employment tribunal may determine that the employer is liable to make an appropriate payment to the employee if on a reference to the tribunal it appears to the tribunal that—

(a) the employee has not complied with the request contained in the notice of extension and the employer has not agreed to pay a redundancy payment in respect of the dismissal effected by the notice of termination, but

(b) either the employee was unable to comply with the request or it was reasonable in the circumstances for him not to comply with it.

(6) In subsection (5) 'appropriate payment' means—

(a) the whole of the redundancy payment to which the employee would have been entitled apart from subsection (3), or

(b) such part of that redundancy payment as the tribunal thinks fit.

(7) If the employee—

(a) complies with the request contained in the notice of extension, or

(b) does not comply with it but attends at his proper or usual place of work and is ready and willing to work on one or more (but not all) of the available days within the proposed period of extension,

the notice of termination has effect, and shall be deemed at all material times to have had effect, as if the period specified in it had been appropriately extended; and sections 87 to 91 accordingly apply as if the period of notice required by section 86 were extended to a corresponding extent.

(8) In subsection (7) 'appropriately extended' means—

(a) in a case within paragraph (a) of that subsection, extended beyond the time of expiry by an additional period equal to the proposed period of extension, and

(b) in a case within paragraph (b) of that subsection, extended beyond the time of expiry up to the end of the day (or last of the days) on which he attends at his proper or usual place of work and is ready and willing to work.

144 Provisions supplementary to section 143

(1) For the purposes of section 143 an employee complies with the request contained in a notice of extension if, but only if, on each available day within the proposed period of extension, he—

(a) attends at his proper or usual place of work, and

(b) is ready and willing to work,

whether or not he has signified his agreement to the request in any other way.

(2) The reference in section 143(2) to the number of working days lost by striking is a reference to the number of working days in the period—

(a) beginning with the date of service of the notice of termination, and

(b) ending with the time of expiry,

which are days on which the employee in question takes part in a strike of employees of his employer.

(3) In section 143 and this section—

'available day', in relation to an employee, means a working day beginning at or after the time of expiry which is a day on which he is not taking part in a strike of employees of the employer,

'available day within the proposed period of extension' means an available day which begins before the end of the proposed period of extension,

'time of expiry', in relation to a notice of termination, means the time at which the notice would expire apart from section 143, and

'working day', in relation to an employee, means a day on which, in accordance with his contract of employment, he is normally required to work.

(4) Neither the service of a notice of extension nor any extension by virtue of section 143(7) of the period specified in a notice of termination affects—

(a) any right either of the employer or of the employee to terminate the contract of employment (whether before, at or after the time of expiry) by a further notice or without notice, or

(b) the operation of this Part in relation to any such termination of the contract of employment.

Supplementary

145 The relevant date

(1) For the purposes of the provisions of this Act relating to redundancy payments 'the relevant date' in relation to the dismissal of an employee has the meaning given by this section.

(2) Subject to the following provisions of this section, 'the relevant date'—

(a) in relation to an employee whose contract of employment is terminated by notice, whether given by his employer or by the employee, means the date on which the notice expires,

(b) in relation to an employee whose contract of employment is terminated without notice, means the date on which the termination takes effect, and

(c) in relation to an employee who is employed under a limited-term contract which terminates by virtue of the limiting event without being renewed under the same contract, means the date on which the termination takes effect.

(3) Where the employee is taken to be dismissed by virtue of section 136(3) the 'relevant date' means the date on which the employee's notice to terminate his contract of employment expires.

(4) Where the employee is regarded by virtue of section 138(4) as having been dismissed on the date on which his employment under an earlier contract ended, 'the relevant date' means—

(a) for the purposes of section 164(1), the date which is the relevant date as defined by subsection (2) in relation to the renewed or new contract or, where there has been more than one trial period, the last such contract, and

(b) for the purposes of any other provision, the date which is the relevant date as defined by subsection (2) in relation to the previous contract or, where there has been more than one such trial period, the original contract.

(5) Where—

(a) the contract of employment is terminated by the employer, and

(b) the notice required by section 86 to be given by an employer would, if duly given on the material date, expire on a date later than the relevant date (as defined by the previous provisions of this section), for the purposes of sections 155, 162(1) and 227(3) the later date is the relevant date.

(6) In subsection (5)(b) 'the material date' means—

(a) the date when notice of termination was given by the employer, or

(b) where no notice was given, the date when the contract of employment was terminated by the employer.

(7) [repealed]

146 Provisions supplementing sections 138 and 141

(1) In sections 138 and 141—

(a) references to re-engagement are to re-engagement by the employer or an associated employer, and

(b) references to an offer are to an offer made by the employer or an associated employer.

(2) For the purposes of the application of section 138(1) or 141(1) to a contract under which the employment ends on a Friday, Saturday or Sunday—

(a) the renewal or re-engagement shall be treated as taking effect immediately on the ending of the employment under the previous contract if it takes effect on or before the next Monday after that Friday, Saturday or Sunday, and

(b) the interval of four weeks to which those provisions refer shall be calculated as if the employment had ended on that next Monday.

(3) [repealed]

Chapter III Right by Reason of Lay-Off or Short-Time

Lay-off and short-time

147 Meaning of 'lay-off' and 'short-time'

(1) For the purposes of this Part an employee shall be taken to be laid off for a week if—

(a) he is employed under a contract on terms and conditions such that his remuneration under the contract depends on his being provided by the employer with work of the kind which he is employed to do, but

(b) he is not entitled to any remuneration under the contract in respect of the week because the employer does not provide such work for him.

(2) For the purposes of this Part an employee shall be taken to be kept on short-time for a week if by reason of a diminution in the work provided for the employee by his employer (being work of a kind which under his contract the employee is employed to do) the employee's remuneration for the week is less than half a week's pay.

148 Eligibility by reason of lay-off or short-time

(1) Subject to the following provisions of this Part, for the purposes of this Part an employee is eligible for a redundancy payment by reason of being laid off or kept on short-time if—

(a) he gives notice in writing to his employer indicating (in whatever terms) his intention to claim a redundancy payment in respect of lay-off or short-time (referred to in this Part as 'notice of intention to claim'), and

(b) before the service of the notice he has been laid off or kept on short-time in circumstances in which subsection (2) applies.

(2) This subsection applies if the employee has been laid off or kept on short-time—

(a) for four or more consecutive weeks of which the last before the service of the notice ended on, or not more than four weeks before, the date of service of the notice, or

(b) for a series of six or more weeks (of which not more than three were consecutive) within a period of thirteen weeks, where the last week of the series before the service of the notice ended on, or not more than four weeks before, the date of service of the notice.

Exclusions

149 Counter-notices

Where an employee gives to his employer notice of intention to claim but—

(a) the employer gives to the employee, within seven days after the service of that notice, notice in writing (referred to in this Part as a 'counter-notice') that he will contest any liability to pay to the employee a redundancy payment in pursuance of the employee's notice, and

(b) the employer does not withdraw the counter-notice by a subsequent notice in writing,

the employee is not entitled to a redundancy payment in pursuance of his notice of intention to claim except in accordance with a decision of an employment tribunal.

150 Resignation

(1) An employee is not entitled to a redundancy payment by reason of being laid off or kept on short-time unless he terminates his contract of employment by giving such period of notice as is required for the purposes of this section before the end of the relevant period.

(2) The period of notice required for the purposes of this section—

(a) where the employee is required by his contract of employment to give more than one week's notice to terminate the contract, is the minimum period which he is required to give, and

(b) otherwise, is one week.

(3) In subsection (1) 'the relevant period'—

(a) if the employer does not give a counter-notice within seven days after the service of the notice of intention to claim, is three weeks after the end of those seven days,

(b) if the employer gives a counter-notice within that period of seven days but withdraws it by a subsequent notice in writing, is three weeks after the service of the notice of withdrawal, and

(c) if—

(i) the employer gives a counter-notice within that period of seven days, and does not so withdraw it, and

(ii) a question as to the right of the employee to a redundancy payment in pursuance of the notice of intention to claim is referred to an employment tribunal,

is three weeks after the tribunal has notified to the employee its decision on that reference.

(4) For the purposes of subsection (3)(c) no account shall be taken of—

(a) any appeal against the decision of the tribunal, or

(b) any proceedings or decision in consequence of any such appeal.

151 Dismissal

(1) An employee is not entitled to a redundancy payment by reason of being laid off or kept on short-time if he is dismissed by his employer.

(2) Subsection (1) does not prejudice any right of the employee to a redundancy payment in respect of the dismissal.

152 Likelihood of full employment

(1) An employee is not entitled to a redundancy payment in pursuance of a notice of intention to claim if—

(a) on the date of service of the notice it was reasonably to be expected that the employee (if he continued to be employed by the same employer) would, not later than four weeks after that date, enter on a period of employment of not less than thirteen weeks during which he would not be laid off or kept on short-time for any week, and

(b) the employer gives a counter-notice to the employee within seven days after the service of the notice of intention to claim.

(2) Subsection (1) does not apply where the employee—

(a) continues or has continued, during the next four weeks after the date of service of the notice of intention to claim, to be employed by the same employer, and

(b) is or has been laid off or kept on short-time for each of those weeks.

Supplementary

153 The relevant date

For the purposes of the provisions of this Act relating to redundancy payments 'the relevant date' in relation to a notice of intention to claim or a right to a redundancy payment in pursuance of such a notice—

(a) in a case falling within paragraph (a) of subsection (2) of section 148, means the date on which the last of the four or more consecutive weeks before the service of the notice came to an end, and

(b) in a case falling within paragraph (b) of that subsection, means the date on which the last of the series of six or more weeks before the service of the notice came to an end.

154 Provisions supplementing sections 148 and 152

For the purposes of sections 148(2) and 152(2)—

(a) it is immaterial whether a series of weeks consists wholly of weeks for which the employee is laid off or wholly of weeks for which he is kept on short-time or partly of the one and partly of the other, and

(b) no account shall be taken of any week for which an employee is laid off or kept on short-time where the lay-off or short-time is wholly or mainly attributable to a strike or a lock-out (whether or not in the trade or industry in which the employee is employed and whether in Great Britain or elsewhere).

Chapter IV General Exclusions from Right

155 Qualifying period of employment

An employee does not have any right to a redundancy payment unless he has been continuously employed for a period of not less than two years ending with the relevant date.

156 [repealed]; 157 [omitted]; 158 [repealed]; 159–161 [omitted]

Chapter V Other Provisions about Redundancy Payments

162 Amount of a redundancy payment

(1) The amount of a redundancy payment shall be calculated by—

(a) determining the period, ending with the relevant date, during which the employee has been continuously employed,

(b) reckoning backwards from the end of that period the number of years of employment falling within that period, and

(c) allowing the appropriate amount for each of those years of employment.

(2) In subsection (1)(c) 'the appropriate amount' means—

(a) one and a half weeks' pay for a year of employment in which the employee was not below the age of forty-one,

(b) one week's pay for a year of employment (not within paragraph (a)) in which he was not below the age of twenty-two, and

(c) half a week's pay for each year of employment not within paragraph (a) or (b).

(3) Where twenty years of employment have been reckoned under subsection (1), no account shall be taken under that subsection of any year of employment earlier than those twenty years.

(4)–(5) [repealed]

(6) Subsections (1) to (3) apply for the purposes of any provision of this Part by virtue of which an employment tribunal may determine that an employer is liable to pay to an employee—

(a) the whole of the redundancy payment to which the employee would have had a right apart from some other provision, or

(b) such part of the redundancy payment to which the employee would have had a right apart from some other provision as the tribunal thinks fit,

as if any reference to the amount of a redundancy payment were to the amount of the redundancy payment to which the employee would have been entitled apart from that other provision.

(7)–(8) [repealed]

163 References to employment tribunals

(1) Any question arising under this Part as to—

(a) the right of an employee to a redundancy payment, or

(b) the amount of a redundancy payment,

shall be referred to and determined by an employment tribunal.

(2) For the purposes of any such reference, an employee who has been dismissed by his employer shall, unless the contrary is proved, be presumed to have been so dismissed by reason of redundancy.

(3) Any question whether an employee will become entitled to a redundancy payment if he is not dismissed by his employer and he terminates his contract of employment as mentioned in section 150(1) shall for the purposes of this Part be taken to be a question as to the right of the employee to a redundancy payment.

(4) Where an order under section 157 is in force in respect of an agreement, this section has effect in relation to any question arising under the agreement as to the right of an employee to a payment on the termination of his employment, or as to the amount of such a payment, as if the payment were a redundancy payment and the question arose under this Part.

(5) Where a tribunal determines under subsection (1) that an employee has a right to a redundancy payment it may order the employer to pay to the worker such amount as the tribunal considers appropriate in all the circumstances to compensate the worker for any financial loss sustained by him which is attributable to the non-payment of the redundancy payment.

(6) Where in accordance with Employment Tribunal Procedure Rules an employment tribunal determines in the same proceedings a complaint presented under section 111 (unfair dismissal) and a question referred under this section, subsection (2) has no effect for the purposes of the proceedings in so far as they relate to the complaint under section 111.

164 Claims for redundancy payment

(1) An employee does not have any right to a redundancy payment unless, before the end of the period of six months beginning with the relevant date—

(a) the payment has been agreed and paid,

(b) the employee has made a claim for the payment by notice in writing given to the employer,

(c) a question as to the employee's right to, or the amount of, the payment has been referred to an employment tribunal, or

(d) a complaint relating to his dismissal has been presented by the employee under section 111.

(2) An employee is not deprived of his right to a redundancy payment by subsection (1) if, during the period of six months immediately following the period mentioned in that subsection, the employee—

(a) makes a claim for the payment by notice in writing given to the employer,

(b) refers to an employment tribunal a question as to his right to, or the amount of, the payment, or

(c) presents a complaint relating to his dismissal under section 111, and it appears to the tribunal to be just and equitable that the employee should receive a redundancy payment.

(3) In determining under subsection (2) whether it is just and equitable that an employee should receive a redundancy payment an employment tribunal shall have regard to—

(a) the reason shown by the employee for his failure to take any such step as is referred to in subsection (2) within the period mentioned in subsection (1), and

(b) all the other relevant circumstances.

(4)–(5) [omitted]

165 Written particulars of redundancy payment

(1) On making any redundancy payment, otherwise than in pursuance of a decision of a tribunal which specifies the amount of the payment to be made, the employer shall give to the employee a written statement indicating how the amount of the payment has been calculated.

(2) An employer who without reasonable excuse fails to comply with subsection (1) is guilty of an offence and liable on summary conviction to a fine not exceeding level 1 on the standard scale.

(3) If an employer fails to comply with the requirements of subsection (1), the employee may by notice in writing to the employer require him to give to the employee a written statement complying with those requirements within such period (not being less than one week beginning with the day on which the notice is given) as may be specified in the notice.

(4) An employer who without reasonable excuse fails to comply with a notice under subsection (3) is guilty of an offence and liable on summary conviction to a fine not exceeding level 3 on the standard scale.

166–170 [omitted]

Chapter VII Supplementary

Application of Part to particular cases

171–172 [omitted]

173 Employees paid by person other than employer

(1) For the purposes of the operation of the provisions of this Part (and Chapter I of Part XIV) in relation to any employee whose remuneration is, by virtue of any statutory provision, payable to him by a person other than his employer, each of the references to the employer specified in subsection (2) shall be construed as a reference to the person by whom the remuneration is payable.

(2) The references referred to in subsection (1) are the first reference in section 135(1), the third reference in section 140(3), the first reference in section 142(3) and the first reference in section 143(2)(c) and the references in sections 142(2)(b), 143(4) and (5), 149(a) and (b), 150(3), 152(1)(b), 158(4), 162(6), 164 to 169, 170(1) and 214(5).

Death of employer or employee

174 Death of employer: dismissal

(1) Where the contract of employment of an employee is taken for the purposes of this Part to be terminated by his employer by reason of the employer's death, this Part has effect in accordance with the following provisions of this section.

(2) Section 138 applies as if—

(a) in subsection (1)(a), for the words 'in pursuance' onwards there were substituted 'by a personal representative of the deceased employer',

(b) in subsection (1)(b), for the words 'either immediately' onwards there were substituted 'not later than eight weeks after the death of the deceased employer', and

(c) in subsections (2)(b) and (6)(a), for the word 'employer' there were substituted 'personal representative of the deceased employer'.

(3) Section 141(1) applies as if—

(a) for the words 'before the end of his employment' there were substituted 'by a personal representative of the deceased employer', and

(b) for the words 'either immediately' onwards there were substituted 'not later than eight weeks after the death of the deceased employer'.

(4) For the purposes of section 141—

(a) provisions of the contract as renewed, or of the new contract, do not differ from the corresponding provisions of the contract in force immediately before the death of the deceased employer by reason only that the personal representative would be substituted for the deceased employer as the employer, and

(b) no account shall be taken of that substitution in determining whether refusal of the offer was unreasonable or whether the employee acted reasonably in terminating or giving notice to terminate the new or renewed employment.

(5) Section 146 has effect as if—

(a) subsection (1) were omitted, and

(b) in subsection (2), paragraph (a) were omitted and, in paragraph (b), for the word 'four' there were substituted 'eight'.

(6) For the purposes of the application of this Part (in accordance with section 161(2)) in relation to an employee who was employed as a domestic servant in a private household, references in this section and sections 175 and 218(4) and (5) to a personal representative include a person to whom the management of the household has passed, otherwise than in pursuance of a sale or other disposition for valuable consideration, in consequence of the death of the employer.

175 [omitted]

176 Death of employee

(1) Where an employee whose employer has given him notice to terminate his contract of employment dies before the notice expires, this Part applies as if the contract had been duly terminated by the employer by notice expiring on the date of the employee's death.

(2) Where—

(a) an employee's contract of employment has been terminated by the employer,

(b) (by virtue of subsection (5) of section 145) a date later than the relevant date as defined by the previous provisions of that section is the relevant date for the purposes of certain provisions of this Act, and

(c) the employee dies before that date,

that subsection applies as if the notice to which it refers would have expired on the employee's death.

(3) Where—

(a) an employer has given notice to an employee to terminate his contract of employment and has offered to renew his contract of employment or to re-engage him under a new contract, and

(b) the employee dies without having accepted or refused the offer and without the offer having been withdrawn,

section 141(2) applies as if for the words 'he unreasonably refuses' there were substituted 'it would have been unreasonable on his part to refuse'.

(4) Where an employee's contract of employment has been renewed or he has been re-engaged under a new contract—

(a) if he dies during the trial period without having terminated, or given notice to terminate, the contract, section 141(4) applies as if for paragraph (d) there were substituted—

'(d) it would have been unreasonable for the employee during the trial period to terminate or give notice to terminate the contract.', and

(b) if during that trial period he gives notice to terminate the contract but dies before the notice expires, sections 138(2) and 141(4) apply as if the notice had expired (and the contract had been terminated by its expiry) on the date of the employee's death.

(5) Where in the circumstances specified in paragraphs (a) and (b) of subsection (3) of section 136 the employee dies before the notice given by him under paragraph (b) of that subsection expires—

(a) if he dies before his employer has given him a notice such as is specified in subsection (2) of section 142, subsections (3) and (4) of that section apply as if the employer had given him such a notice and he had not complied with it, and

(b) if he dies after his employer has given him such a notice, that section applies as if the employee had not died but did not comply with the notice.

(6) Where an employee has given notice of intention to claim—

(a) if he dies before he has given notice to terminate his contract of employment and before the relevant period (as defined in subsection (3) of section 150) has expired, that section does not apply, and

(b) if he dies within the period of seven days after the service of the notice of intention to claim, and before the employer has given a counter-notice, Chapter III applies as if the employer had given a counter-notice within that period of seven days.

(7) Where a claim for a redundancy payment is made by a personal representative of a deceased employee—

(a) if the employee died before the end of the period of six months beginning with the relevant date, subsection (1) of section 164, and

(b) if the employee died after the end of the period of six months beginning with the relevant date but before the end of the following period of six months, subsection (2) of that section,

applies as if for the words 'six months' there were substituted 'one year'.

177 [omitted]

Other supplementary provisions

178–179 [omitted]

180 Offences

(1) Where an offence under this Part committed by a body corporate is proved—

(a) to have been committed with the consent or connivance of, or

(b) to be attributable to any neglect on the part of,

any director, manager, secretary or other similar officer of the body corporate, or any person who was purporting to act in any such capacity, he (as well as the body corporate) is guilty of the offence and liable to be proceeded against and punished accordingly.

(2) In this section 'director', in relation to a body corporate established by or under any enactment for the purpose of carrying on under national ownership any industry or part of an industry or undertaking, being a body corporate whose affairs are managed by its members, means a member of that body corporate.

181 Interpretation

(1) In this Part—

'counter-notice' shall be construed in accordance with section 149(a),

'dismissal' and 'dismissed' shall be construed in accordance with sections 136 to 138

'employer's payment' has the meaning given by section 166,

'notice of intention to claim' shall be construed in accordance with section 148(1),

'obligatory period of notice' has the meaning given by section 136(4), and

'trial period' shall be construed in accordance with section 138(3).

(2) In this Part—

(a) references to an employee being laid off or being eligible for a redundancy payment by reason of being laid off, and
(b) references to an employee being kept on short-time or being eligible for a redundancy payment by reason of being kept on short-time,

shall be construed in accordance with sections 147 and 148.

PART XII INSOLVENCY OF EMPLOYERS

182 Employee's rights on insolvency of employer

If, on an application made to him in writing by an employee, the Secretary of State is satisfied that—

(a) the employee's employer has become insolvent,
(b) the employee's employment has been terminated, and
(c) on the appropriate date the employee was entitled to be paid the whole or part of any debt to which this Part applies,

the Secretary of State shall, subject to section 186, pay the employee out of the National Insurance Fund the amount to which, in the opinion of the Secretary of State, the employee is entitled in respect of the debt.

183 [omitted]

184 Debts to which Part applies

(1) This Part applies to the following debts—

(a) any arrears of pay in respect of one or more (but not more than eight) weeks,
(b) any amount which the employer is liable to pay the employee for the period of notice required by section 86(1) or (2) or for any failure of the employer to give the period of notice required by section 86(1),
(c) any holiday pay—
    (i) in respect of a period or periods of holiday not exceeding six weeks in all, and
    (ii) to which the employee became entitled during the twelve months ending with the appropriate date,
(d) any basic award of compensation for unfair dismissal or so much of an award under a designated dismissal procedures agreement as does not exceed any basic award of compensation for unfair dismissal to which the employee would be entitled but for the agreement, and
(e) any reasonable sum by way of reimbursement of the whole or part of any fee or premium paid by an apprentice or articled clerk.

(2) For the purposes of subsection (1)(a) the following amounts shall be treated as arrears of pay—

(a) a guarantee payment,
(b) any payment for time off under Part VI of this Act or section 169 of the Trade Union and Labour Relations (Consolidation) Act 1992 (payment for time off for carrying out trade union duties etc.),
(c) remuneration on suspension on medical grounds under section 64 of this Act and remuneration on suspension on maternity grounds under section 68 of this Act, and
(d) remuneration under a protective award under section 189 of the Trade Union and Labour Relations (Consolidation) Act 1992.

(3) In subsection (1)(c) 'holiday pay', in relation to an employee, means—

(a) pay in respect of a holiday actually taken by the employee, or
(b) any accrued holiday pay which, under the employee's contract of employment, would in the ordinary course have become payable to him in respect of the period of a holiday if his employment with the employer had continued until he became entitled to a holiday.

(4) A sum shall be taken to be reasonable for the purposes of subsection (1)(e) in a case where a trustee in bankruptcy, or (in Scotland) a trustee or interim trustee in the sequestration of an estate under the Bankruptcy (Scotland) Act 2016, or liquidator has been or is required to be appointed—

(a) as respects England and Wales, if it is admitted to be reasonable by the trustee in bankruptcy or liquidator under section 348 of the Insolvency Act 1986 (effect of bankruptcy on apprenticeships etc.), whether as originally enacted or as applied to the winding up of a company by rules under section 411 of that Act, and

(b) as respects Scotland, if it is accepted by the trustee or interim trustee or liquidator for the purposes of the sequestration or winding up.

185 The appropriate date

In this Part 'the appropriate date'—

(a) in relation to arrears of pay (not being remuneration under a protective award made under section 189 of the Trade Union and Labour Relations (Consolidation) Act 1992 and to holiday pay, means the date on which the employer became insolvent,

(b) in relation to a basic award of compensation for unfair dismissal and to remuneration under a protective award so made, means whichever is the latest of—

(i) the date on which the employer became insolvent,

(ii) the date of the termination of the employee's employment, and

(iii) the date on which the award was made, and

(c) in relation to any other debt to which this Part applies, means whichever is the latter of—

(i) the date on which the employer became insolvent, and

(ii) the date of the termination of the employee's employment.

186 Limit on amount payable under section 182

(1) The total amount payable to an employee in respect of any debt to which this Part applies, where the amount of the debt is referable to a period of time, shall not exceed—

(a) £751 in respect of any one week, or

(b) in respect of a shorter period, an amount bearing the same proportion to £751 as that shorter period bears to a week.

(2) [repealed]

187–190 [omitted]

PART XIII MISCELLANEOUS

Chapter I Particular Types of Employment

Crown employment etc.

191 Crown employment

(1) Subject to sections 192 and 193, the provisions of this Act to which this section applies have effect in relation to Crown employment and persons in Crown employment as they have effect in relation to other employment and other employees or workers.

(2) This section applies to—

(a) Parts I to III,

(aa) Part IVA,

(b) Part V, apart from section 45,

(c) Parts 6 to 8A

(d) in Part IX, sections 92 and 93,

(e) Part X, apart from section 101, and

(f) this Part and Parts XIV and XV.

(3) In this Act 'Crown employment' means employment under or for the purposes of a government department or any officer or body exercising on behalf of the Crown functions conferred by a statutory provision.

(4) For the purposes of the application of provisions of this Act in relation to Crown employment in accordance with subsection (1)—

(a) references to an employee or a worker shall be construed as references to a person in Crown employment,

(b) references to a contract of employment, or a worker's contract, shall be construed as references to the terms of employment of a person in Crown employment,

(c) references to dismissal, or to the termination of a worker's contract, shall be construed as references to the termination of Crown employment,

(d) references to redundancy shall be construed as references to the existence of such circumstances as are treated, in accordance with any arrangements falling within section 177(3) for the time being in force, as equivalent to redundancy in relation to Crown employment,

(da) the reference in section 98B(2)(a) to the employer's undertaking shall be construed as a reference to the national interest, and

(e) any other reference to an undertaking shall be construed—

(i) in relation to a Minister of the Crown, as references to his functions or (as the context may require) to the department of which he is in charge, and

(ii) in relation to a government department, officer or body, as references to the functions of the department, officer or body or (as the context may require) to the department, officer or body.

(5) Where the terms of employment of a person in Crown employment restrict his right to take part in—

(a) certain political activities, or

(b) activities which may conflict with his official functions,

nothing in section 50 requires him to be allowed time off work for public duties connected with any such activities.

(6) Sections 159 and 160 are without prejudice to any exemption or immunity of the Crown.

192 Armed forces

(1) Section 191—

(a) applies to service as a member of the naval, military or air forces of the Crown but subject to the following provisions of this section, and

(b) applies to employment by an association established for the purposes of Part XI of the Reserve Forces Act 1996.

(2) The provisions of this Act which have effect by virtue of section 191 in relation to service as a member of the naval, military or air forces of the Crown are—

(a) Part I,

(aa) in Part V, sections 43M, 45A, 47C and 47D, and sections 48 and 49 so far as relating to those sections,

(ab) [repealed]

(b) in Part VI, sections 55 to 57B,

(c) Parts VII and VIII,

(d) in Part IX, sections 92 and 93,

(e) Part X, apart from sections 98B(2) and (3), 100 to 103, 104C, 108(5) and 134, and

(f) this Part and Parts XIV and XV.

(3)–(8) [omitted]

193 National security

Part IVA and section 47B of this Act do not apply in relation to employment for the purposes of—

(a) the Security Service,

(b) the Secret Intelligence Service, or

(c) the Government Communications Headquarters.

194–195 [omitted]; 196–198 [repealed]; 199–201 [omitted]

Chapter II Other Miscellaneous Matters

Restrictions on disclosure of information

202 National security

(1) Where in the opinion of any Minister of the Crown the disclosure of any information would be contrary to the interests of national security—

(a) nothing in any of the provisions to which this section applies requires any person to disclose the information, and

(b) no person shall disclose the information in any proceedings in any court or tribunal relating to any of those provisions.

(2) This section applies to—

(a) Part I, so far as it relates to employment particulars,

(b) in Part V, sections 43M, 44, 45A, 47 and 47C, and sections 48 and 49 so far as relating to those sections,

(c) in Part VI, sections 55 to 57B and 61 to 63,

(d) in Part VII, sections 66 to 68, and sections 69 and 70 so far as relating to those sections,

(e) Part VIII,

(eza) Part 8A,

(ea) Part 8B,

(f) in Part IX, sections 92 and 93 where they apply by virtue of section 92(4),

(g) Part X so far as relating to a dismissal which is treated as unfair—

(i) by section 98B, 99, 100, 101A(d) or 103, or by section 104 in its application in relation to time off under section 57A,

(ii) by subsection (1) of section 105 by reason of the application of subsection (2A), (3) or (6) of that section or by reason of the application of subsection (4A) in so far as it applies where the reason (or, if more than one, the principal reason) for which an employee was selected for dismissal was that specified in section 101A(d), and

(h) this Part and Parts XIV and XV (so far as relating to any of the provisions in paragraphs (a) to (g)).

Harassment and discrimination: contractual duties of confidentiality

202A Contractual duties of confidentiality relating to harassment and discrimination

(1) Any provision in an agreement between an employer and a worker of the employer (whether a worker's contract or not) is void in so far as it purports to preclude the worker from making—

(a) an allegation of, or a disclosure of information relating to, relevant harassment or discrimination, or

(b) an allegation, or a disclosure of information, relating to the response of an employer of the worker to—
(i) relevant harassment or discrimination, or
(ii) the making of an allegation or disclosure within paragraph (a).

(2) Harassment or discrimination is 'relevant' for the purposes of subsection (1) if—
(a) the harassment or discrimination consists of, or is alleged to consist of, conduct engaged in by—
(i) an employer of the worker, or
(ii) another worker of such an employer, or
(b) the person who is, or is alleged to be, the victim of the harassment or discrimination is—
(i) the worker, or
(ii) another worker of an employer of the worker.

(3) Subsection (1) does not apply to provision in an agreement (an 'excepted agreement') that satisfies such conditions as the Secretary of State may specify by regulations.

(4)–(5) [omitted]

(6) In subsection (5), 'relevant contract' means any contract, other than a contract of employment, whether express or implied and (if express) whether oral or in writing, by which an individual undertakes to do or perform (whether personally or otherwise) any work or services for another party to the contract whose status is by virtue of the contract that of a client or customer of any profession or business undertaking carried on by the individual.

(7) [omitted]

(8) For the purposes of this section, the holding, otherwise than under a contract of employment, of the office of constable or an appointment as a police cadet is to be treated as employment by the relevant officer under a contract of employment.

'The relevant officer' has the meaning given by section 43KA(2).

(9) Nothing in this section affects the operation of any other enactment or rule of law by virtue of which provision in an agreement may be void.

(10) In this section—

'discrimination' means discrimination within any of sections 13, 15 to 19A and 21(2) of the Equality Act 2010;

'harassment' means harassment of the kind described in subsection (1), (2) or (3) of section 26 of that Act;

'specified' means specified in the regulations.

Contracting out etc. and remedies

203 Restrictions on contracting out

(1) Any provision in an agreement (whether a contract of employment or not) is void in so far as it purports—
(a) to exclude or limit the operation of any provision of this Act or Schedule 7 to the Coronavirus Act 2020, or
(b) to preclude a person from bringing any proceedings under this Act before an employment tribunal.

(2) Subsection (1)—
(a) does not apply to any provision in a collective agreement excluding rights under section 28 if an order under section 35 is for the time being in force in respect of it,
(b) does not apply to any provision in a dismissal procedures agreement excluding the right under section 94 if that provision is not to have effect unless an order under section 110 is for the time being in force in respect of it,
(c) does not apply to any provision in an agreement if an order under section 157 is for the time being in force in respect of it,

(d) [repealed]
(e) does not apply to any agreement to refrain from instituting or continuing proceedings where a conciliation officer has taken action under any of sections 18A to 18C of the Employment Tribunals Act 1996, and
(f) does not apply to any agreement to refrain from instituting or continuing any proceedings within the following provisions of section 18(1) of the Employment Tribunals Act 1996 (cases where conciliation available)—
  (i) paragraph (b) (proceedings under this Act),
  (ii) paragraph (l) (proceedings arising out of the Part-time Workers (Prevention of Less Favourable Treatment) Regulations 2000),
  (iii) paragraph (m) (proceedings arising out of the Fixed-term Employees (Prevention of Less Favourable Treatment) Regulations 2002),
  (iv) [repealed]

if the conditions regulating settlement agreements under this Act are satisfied in relation to the agreement.

(3) For the purposes of subsection (2)(f) the conditions regulating settlement agreements under this Act are that—
(a) the agreement must be in writing,
(b) the agreement must relate to the particular proceedings,
(c) the employee or worker must have received advice from a relevant independent adviser as to the terms and effect of the proposed agreement and, in particular, its effect on his ability to pursue his rights before an employment tribunal,
(d) there must be in force, when the adviser gives the advice, a contract of insurance, or an indemnity provided for members of a profession or professional body covering the risk of a claim by the employee or worker in respect of loss arising in consequence of the advice,
(e) the agreement must identify the adviser, and
(f) the agreement must state that the conditions regulating compromise agreements under this Act are satisfied.

(3A) A person is a relevant independent adviser for the purposes of subsection (3)(c)—
(a) if he is a qualified lawyer,
(b) if he is an officer, official, employee or member of an independent trade union who has been certified in writing by the trade union as competent to give advice and as authorised to do so on behalf of the trade union,
(c) if he works at an advice centre (whether as an employee or a volunteer) and has been certified in writing by the centre as competent to give advice and as authorised to do so on behalf of the centre, or
(d) if he is a person of a description specified in an order made by the Secretary of State.

(3B) But a person is not a relevant independent adviser for the purposes of subsection (3)(c) in relation to the employee or worker—
(a) if he is, is employed by or is acting in the matter for the employer or an associated employer,
(b) in the case of a person within subsection (3A)(b) or (c), if the trade union or advice centre is the employer or an associated employer,
(c) in the case of a person within subsection (3A)(c), if the employee or worker makes a payment for the advice received from him, or
(d) in the case of a person of a description specified in an order under subsection (3A)(d), if any condition specified in the order in relation to the giving of advice by persons of that description is not satisfied.

(4) In subsection (3A)(a) 'qualified lawyer' means—

(a) as respects England and Wales, a person who, for the purposes of the Legal Services Act 2007, is an authorised person in relation to an activity which constitutes the exercise of a right of audience or the conduct of litigation (within the meaning of that Act), and
(b) as respects Scotland, an advocate (whether in practice as such or employed to give legal advice), or a solicitor who holds a practising certificate.

(5) An agreement under which the parties agree to submit a dispute to arbitration—
(a) shall be regarded for the purposes of subsection (2)(e) and (f) as being an agreement to refrain from instituting or continuing proceedings if—
(i) the dispute is covered by a scheme having effect by virtue of an order under section 212A of the Trade Union and Labour Relations (Consolidation) Act 1992, and
(ii) the agreement is to submit it to arbitration in accordance with the scheme, but
(b) shall be regarded as neither being nor including such an agreement in any other case.

204 Law governing employment

(1) For the purposes of this Act it is immaterial whether the law which (apart from this Act) governs any person's employment is the law of the United Kingdom, or of a part of the United Kingdom, or not.

(2) [repealed]

205 Remedy for infringement of certain rights

(1) The remedy of an employee for infringement of any of the rights conferred by section 8, Part III, Parts V to VIII, section 92, Part X and Part XII is, where provision is made for a complaint or the reference of a question to an employment tribunal, by way of such a complaint or reference and not otherwise.

(1YA) In relation to the right conferred by section 44(1A), the reference in subsection (1) to an employee has effect as a reference to a worker.

(1ZA) In relation to the right conferred by section 45A, the reference in subsection (1) to an employee has effect as a reference to a worker.

(1A) In relation to the right conferred by section 47B, the reference in subsection (1) to an employee has effect as a reference to a worker.

(2) The remedy of a worker in respect of any contravention of section 13, 15, 18(1) or 21(1) is by way of a complaint under section 23 and not otherwise.

Employee shareholder status

205A Employee shareholders

(1) An individual who is or becomes an employee of a company is an 'employee shareholder' if—
(a) the company and the individual agree that the individual is to be an employee shareholder,
(b) in consideration of that agreement, the company issues or allots to the individual fully paid up shares in the company, or procures the issue or allotment to the individual of fully paid up shares in its parent undertaking, which have a value, on the day of issue or allotment, of no less than £2,000,
(c) the company gives the individual a written statement of the particulars of the status of employee shareholder and of the rights which attach to the shares referred to in paragraph (b) ('the employee shares') (see subsection (5)), and
(d) the individual gives no consideration other than by entering into the agreement.

(2) An employee who is an employee shareholder does not have—
(a) the right to make an application under section 63D (request to undertake study or training),
(b) the right to make an application under section 80F (request for flexible working),
(c) the right under section 94 not to be unfairly dismissed, or
(d) the right under section 135 to a redundancy payment.

(3) The following provisions are to be read in the case of an employee who is an employee shareholder as if for '8 weeks' notice', in each place it appears, there were substituted '16 weeks' notice'—

(a) regulation 11 of the Maternity and Parental Leave etc. Regulations 1999 (SI 1999/3312) (requirement for employee to notify employer of intention to return to work during maternity leave period), and

(b) regulation 25 of the Paternity and Adoption Leave Regulations 2002 (SI 2002/2788) (corresponding provision for adoption leave).

(4) Regulation 30 of the Additional Paternity Leave Regulations 2010 (SI 2010/1055) (requirement for employee to notify employer of intention to return to work during additional paternity leave period) is to be read in the case of an employee who is an employee shareholder as if for 'six weeks' notice', in each place it appears, there were substituted '16 weeks' notice'.

(5) The statement referred to in subsection (1)(c) must—

(a) state that, as an employee shareholder, the individual would not have the rights specified in subsection (2),

(b) specify the notice periods that would apply in the individual's case as a result of subsections (3) and (4),

(c) state whether any voting rights attach to the employee shares,

(d) state whether the employee shares carry any rights to dividends,

(e) state whether the employee shares would, if the company were wound up, confer any rights to participate in the distribution of any surplus assets,

(f) if the company has more than one class of shares and any of the rights referred to in paragraphs (c) to (e) attach to the employee shares, explain how those rights differ from the equivalent rights that attach to the shares in the largest class (or next largest class if the class which includes the employee shares is the largest),

(g) state whether the employee shares are redeemable and, if they are, at whose option,

(h) state whether there are any restrictions on the transferability of the employee shares and, if there are, what those restrictions are,

(i) state whether any of the requirements of sections 561 and 562 of the Companies Act 2006 are excluded in the case of the employee shares (existing shareholders' right of pre-emption), and

(j) state whether the employee shares are subject to drag-along rights or tag-along rights and, if they are, explain the effect of the shares being so subject.

(6) Agreement between a company and an individual that the individual is to become an employee shareholder is of no effect unless, before the agreement is made—

(a) the individual, having been given the statement referred to in subsection (1)(c), receives advice from a relevant independent adviser as to the terms and effect of the proposed agreement, and

(b) seven days have passed since the day on which the individual receives the advice.

(7) Any reasonable costs incurred by the individual in obtaining the advice (whether or not the individual becomes an employee shareholder) which would, but for this subsection, have to be met by the individual are instead to be met by the company.

(8) The reference in subsection (2)(b) to making an application under section 80F does not include a reference to making an application within the period of 14 days beginning with the day on which the employee shareholder returns to work from a period of parental leave under regulations under section 76.

(9) The reference in subsection (2)(c) to unfair dismissal does not include a reference to a dismissal—

(a) which is required to be regarded as unfair for the purposes of Part 10 by a provision (whenever made) contained in or made under this or any other Act, or

(b) which amounts to a contravention of the Equality Act 2010.

(10) The reference in subsection (2)(c) to the right not to be unfairly dismissed does not include a reference to that right in a case where section 108(2) (health and safety cases) applies.

(11)–(12) [omitted]

(13) In this section—

'company' means—

(a) a company or overseas company (within the meaning, in each case, of the Companies Act 2006) which has a share capital, or

(b) a United Kingdom Societas (or UK Societas) within the meaning of Council Regulation 2157/2001/EC of 8 October 2001 on the Statute for a European company;

'drag-along rights', in relation to shares in a company, means the right of the holders of a majority of the shares, where they are selling their shares, to require the holders of the minority to sell theirs;

'parent undertaking' has the same meaning as in the Companies Act 2006;

'relevant independent adviser' has the meaning that it has for the purposes of section 203(3)(c);

'tag-along rights', in relation to shares in a company, means the right of the holders of a minority of the shares to sell their shares, where the holders of the majority are selling theirs, on the same terms as those on which the holders of the majority are doing so.

(14) The reference in this section to the value of shares in a company is a reference to their market value within the meaning of the Taxation of Chargeable Gains Act 1992 (see sections 272 and 273 of that Act).

206–207B [omitted]; 208 [repealed]; 209 [omitted]

PART XIV INTERPRETATION

Chapter I Continuous Employment

210 Introductory

(1) References in any provision of this Act to a period of continuous employment are (unless provision is expressly made to the contrary) to a period computed in accordance with this Chapter.

(2) In any provision of this Act which refers to a period of continuous employment expressed in months or years—

(a) a month means a calendar month, and

(b) a year means a year of twelve calendar months.

(3) In computing an employee's period of continuous employment for the purposes of any provision of this Act, any question—

(a) whether the employee's employment is of a kind counting towards a period of continuous employment, or

(b) whether periods (consecutive or otherwise) are to be treated as forming a single period of continuous employment,

shall be determined week by week; but where it is necessary to compute the length of an employee's period of employment it shall be computed in months and years of twelve months in accordance with section 211.

(4) Subject to sections 215 to 217, a week which does not count in computing the length of a period of continuous employment breaks continuity of employment.

(5) A person's employment during any period shall, unless the contrary is shown, be presumed to have been continuous.

211 Period of continuous employment

(1) An employee's period of continuous employment for the purposes of any provision of this Act—

(a) (subject to subsection (3)) begins with the day on which the employee starts work, and

(b) ends with the day by reference to which the length of the employee's period of continuous employment is to be ascertained for the purposes of the provision.

(2) [repealed]

(3) If an employee's period of continuous employment includes one or more periods which (by virtue of section 215, 216 or 217) while not counting in computing the length of the period do not break continuity of employment, the beginning of the period shall be treated as postponed by the number of days falling within that intervening period, or the aggregate number of days falling within those periods, calculated in accordance with the section in question.

212 Weeks counting in computing period

(1) Any week during the whole or part of which an employee's relations with his employer are governed by a contract of employment counts in computing the employee's period of employment.

(2) [repealed]

(3) Subject to subsection (4), any week (not within subsection (1)) during the whole or part of which an employee is—

(a) incapable of work in consequence of sickness or injury,

(b) absent from work on account of a temporary cessation of work, or

(c) absent from work in circumstances such that, by arrangement or custom, he is regarded as continuing in the employment of his employer for any purpose,

(d) [repealed]

(4) Not more than twenty-six weeks count under subsection (3)(a) between any periods falling under subsection (1).

213 Intervals in employment

(1) Where in the case of an employee a date later than the date which would be the effective date of termination by virtue of subsection (1) of section 97 is treated for certain purposes as the effective date of termination by virtue of subsection (2) or (4) of that section, the period of the interval between the two dates counts as a period of employment in ascertaining for the purposes of section 108(1) or 119(1) the period for which the employee has been continuously employed.

(2) Where an employee is by virtue of section 138(1) regarded for the purposes of Part XI as not having been dismissed by reason of a renewal or re-engagement taking effect after an interval, the period of the interval counts as a period of employment in ascertaining for the purposes of section 155 or 162(1) the period for which the employee has been continuously employed (except so far as it is to be disregarded under section 214 or 215).

(3) Where in the case of an employee a date later than the date which would be the relevant date by virtue of subsections (2) to (4) of section 145 is treated for certain purposes as the relevant date by virtue of subsection (5) of that section, the period of the interval between the two dates counts as a period of employment in ascertaining for the purposes of section 155 or 162(1) the period for which the employee has been continuously employed (except so far as it is to be disregarded under section 214 or 215).

214 Special provisions for redundancy payments

(1) This section applies where a period of continuous employment has to be determined in relation to an employee for the purposes of the application of section 155 or 162(1).

(2) The continuity of a period of employment is broken where—

(a) a redundancy payment has previously been paid to the employee (whether in respect of dismissal or in respect of lay-off or short-time), and

(b) the contract of employment under which the employee was employed was renewed (whether by the same or another employer) or the employee was re-engaged under a new contract of employment (whether by the same or another employer).

(3) The continuity of a period of employment is also broken where—

(a) a payment has been made to the employee (whether in respect of the termination of his employment or lay-off or short-time) in accordance with a scheme under section 1 of the Superannuation Act 1972 or arrangements falling within section 177(3), and

(b) he commenced new, or renewed, employment.

(4) The date on which the person's continuity of employment is broken by virtue of this section—

(a) if the employment was under a contract of employment, is the date which was the relevant date in relation to the payment mentioned in subsection (2)(a) or (3)(a), and

(b) if the employment was otherwise than under a contract of employment, is the date which would have been the relevant date in relation to the payment mentioned in subsection (2)(a) or (3)(a) had the employment been under a contract of employment.

(5) For the purposes of this section a redundancy payment shall be treated as having been paid if—

(a) the whole of the payment has been paid to the employee by the employer,

(b) a tribunal has determined liability and found that the employer must pay part (but not all) of the redundancy payment and the employer has paid that part, or

(c) the Secretary of State has paid a sum to the employee in respect of the redundancy payment under section 167.

215 Employment abroad etc.

(1) This Chapter applies to a period of employment—

(a) (subject to the following provisions of this section) even where during the period the employee was engaged in work wholly or mainly outside Great Britain, and

(b) even where the employee was excluded by or under this Act from any right conferred by this Act.

(2) For the purposes of sections 155 and 162(1) a week of employment does not count in computing a period of employment if the employee—

(a) was employed outside Great Britain during the whole or part of the week, and

(b) was not during that week an employed earner for the purposes of the Social Security Contributions and Benefits Act 1992 in respect of whom a secondary Class 1 contribution was payable under that Act (whether or not the contribution was in fact paid).

(3) Where by virtue of subsection (2) a week of employment does not count in computing a period of employment, the continuity of the period is not broken by reason only that the week does not count in computing the period; and the number of days which, for the purposes of section 211(3), fall within the intervening period is seven for each week within this subsection.

(4) Any question arising under subsection (2) whether—

(a) a person was an employed earner for the purposes of the Social Security Contributions and Benefits Act 1992, or

(b) if so, whether a secondary Class 1 contribution was payable in respect of him under that Act,

shall be determined by an officer of the Commissioners of the Inland Revenue.

(5) Part II of the Social Security Contributions (Transfer of Functions, etc.) Act 1999 (decisions and appeals) shall apply in relation to the determination of any issue by the Inland Revenue under subsection (4) as if it were a decision falling within section 8(1) of that Act.

(6) Subsection (2) does not apply in relation to a person who is—

(a) employed as a master or seaman in a British ship, and

(b) ordinarily resident in Great Britain.

216 Industrial disputes

(1) A week does not count under section 212 if during the week, or any part of the week, the employee takes part in a strike.

(2) The continuity of an employee's period of employment is not broken by a week which does not count under this Chapter (whether or not by virtue only of subsection (1)) if during the week, or any part of the week, the employee takes part in a strike; and the number of days which, for the

purposes of section 211(3), fall within the intervening period is the number of days between the last working day before the strike and the day on which work was resumed.

(3) The continuity of an employee's period of employment is not broken by a week if during the week, or any part of the week, the employee is absent from work because of a lock-out by the employer; and the number of days which, for the purposes of section 211(3), fall within the intervening period is the number of days between the last working day before the lock-out and the day on which work was resumed.

217 [omitted]

218 Change of employer

(1) Subject to the provisions of this section, this Chapter relates only to employment by the one employer.

(2) If a trade or business, or an undertaking (whether or not established by or under an Act), is transferred from one person to another—

- (a) the period of employment of an employee in the trade or business or undertaking at the time of the transfer counts as a period of employment with the transferee, and
- (b) the transfer does not break the continuity of the period of employment.

(3) If by or under an Act (whether public or local and whether passed before or after this Act) a contract of employment between any body corporate and an employee is modified and some other body corporate is substituted as the employer—

- (a) the employee's period of employment at the time when the modification takes effect counts as a period of employment with the second body corporate, and
- (b) the change of employer does not break the continuity of the period of employment.

(4) If on the death of an employer the employee is taken into the employment of the personal representatives or trustees of the deceased—

- (a) the employee's period of employment at the time of the death counts as a period of employment with the employer's personal representatives or trustees, and
- (b) the death does not break the continuity of the period of employment.

(5) If there is a change in the partners, personal representatives or trustees who employ any person—

- (a) the employee's period of employment at the time of the change counts as a period of employment with the partners, personal representatives or trustees after the change, and
- (b) the change does not break the continuity of the period of employment.

(6) If an employee of an employer is taken into the employment of another employer who, at the time when the employee enters the second employer's employment, is an associated employer of the first employer—

- (a) the employee's period of employment at that time counts as a period of employment with the second employer, and
- (b) the change of employer does not break the continuity of the period of employment.

(7)–(11) [omitted]

219 [omitted]

Chapter II A Week's Pay

Introductory

220 Introductory

The amount of a week's pay of an employee shall be calculated for the purposes of this Act in accordance with this Chapter.

Employments with normal working hours

221 General

(1) This section and sections 222 and 223 apply where there are normal working hours for the employee when employed under the contract of employment in force on the calculation date.

(2) Subject to section 222, if the employee's remuneration for employment in normal working hours (whether by the hour or week or other period) does not vary with the amount of work done in the period, the amount of a week's pay is the amount which is payable by the employer under the contract of employment in force on the calculation date if the employee works throughout his normal working hours in a week.

(3) Subject to section 222, if the employee's remuneration for employment in normal working hours (whether by the hour or week or other period) does vary with the amount of work done in the period, the amount of a week's pay is the amount of remuneration for the number of normal working hours in a week calculated at the average hourly rate of remuneration payable by the employer to the employee in respect of the period of twelve weeks ending—

(a) where the calculation date is the last day of a week, with that week, and

(b) otherwise, with the last complete week before the calculation date.

(4) In this section references to remuneration varying with the amount of work done includes remuneration which may include any commission or similar payment which varies in amount.

(5) This section is subject to sections 227 and 228.

222 Remuneration varying according to time of work

(1) This section applies if the employee is required under the contract of employment in force on the calculation date to work during normal working hours on days of the week, or at times of the day, which differ from week to week or over a longer period so that the remuneration payable for, or apportionable to, any week varies according to the incidence of those days or times.

(2) The amount of a week's pay is the amount of remuneration for the average number of weekly normal working hours at the average hourly rate of remuneration.

(3) For the purposes of subsection (2)—

(a) the average number of weekly hours is calculated by dividing by twelve the total number of the employee's normal working hours during the relevant period of twelve weeks, and

(b) the average hourly rate of remuneration is the average hourly rate of remuneration payable by the employer to the employee in respect of the relevant period of twelve weeks.

(4) In subsection (3) 'the relevant period of twelve weeks' means the period of twelve weeks ending—

(a) where the calculation date is the last day of a week, with that week, and

(b) otherwise, with the last complete week before the calculation date.

(5) This section is subject to sections 227 and 228.

223 Supplementary

(1) For the purposes of sections 221 and 222, in arriving at the average hourly rate of remuneration, only—

(a) the hours when the employee was working, and

(b) the remuneration payable for, or apportionable to, those hours, shall be brought in.

(2) If for any of the twelve weeks mentioned in sections 221 and 222 no remuneration within subsection (1)(b) was payable by the employer to the employee, account shall be taken of remuneration in earlier weeks so as to bring up to twelve the number of weeks of which account is taken.

(3) Where—

(a) in arriving at the average hourly rate of remuneration, account has to be taken of remuneration payable for, or apportionable to, work done in hours other than normal working hours, and

(b) the amount of that remuneration was greater than it would have been if the work had been done in normal working hours (or, in a case within section 234(3), in normal working hours falling within the number of hours without overtime),

account shall be taken of that remuneration as if the work had been done in such hours and the amount of that remuneration had been reduced accordingly.

Employments with no normal working hours

224 Employments with no normal working hours

(1) This section applies where there are no normal working hours for the employee when employed under the contract of employment in force on the calculation date.

(2) The amount of a week's pay is the amount of the employee's average weekly remuneration in the period of twelve weeks ending—

(a) where the calculation date is the last day of a week, with that week, and

(b) otherwise, with the last complete week before the calculation date.

(3) In arriving at the average weekly remuneration no account shall be taken of a week in which no remuneration was payable by the employer to the employee and remuneration in earlier weeks shall be brought in so as to bring up to twelve the number of weeks of which account is taken.

(4) This section is subject to sections 227 and 228.

The calculation date

225 Rights during employment

(A1) Where the calculation is for the purposes of section 27BI, the calculation date is—

(a) where the complaint is under section 27BG(1), (2), (3) or (7), the latest day of the reference period to which the complaint relates on which the worker was employed by the employer under a worker's contract;

(b) where the complaint is under section 27BG(8)—

(i) the date on which the complaint was presented to the employment tribunal, or

(ii) if the worker was not employed by the employer under a worker's contract on that date, the latest day before that date on which the worker was so employed.

(B1) Where the calculation is for the purposes of section 27BI as applied by section 27BY(6)(a) in relation to a complaint under section 27BY(5), the calculation date is the latest day of the reference period to which the complaint relates on which the worker was employed by the employer under a worker's contract.

(1) Where the calculation is for the purposes of section 30, the calculation date is—

(a) where the employee's contract has been varied, or a new contract entered into, in connection with a period of short-time working, the last day on which the original contract was in force, and

(b) otherwise, the day in respect of which the guarantee payment is payable.

(2) Where the calculation is for the purposes of section 53 or 54, the calculation date is the day on which the employer's notice was given.

(3) Where the calculation is for the purposes of section 56, the calculation date is the day of the appointment.

(3A) Where the calculation is for the purposes of section 57ZF, the calculation date is the day of the appointment.

(3B) Where the calculation is for the purposes of section 57ZK or 57ZM, the calculation date is the day of the appointment.

(4) Where the calculation is for the purposes of section 62, the calculation date is the day on which the time off was taken or on which it is alleged the time off should have been permitted.

(4A) Where the calculation is for the purposes of section 63B, the calculation date is the day on which the time off was taken or on which it is alleged the time off should have been permitted.

(4B) Where the calculation is for the purposes of section 63J, the calculation date is the day on which the section 63D application was made.

(5) Where the calculation is for the purposes of section 69—

(a) in the case of an employee suspended on medical grounds, the calculation date is the day before that on which the suspension begins, and

(b) in the case of an employee suspended on maternity grounds, the calculation date is—

(i) where the day before that on which the suspension begins falls during a period of ordinary or additional maternity leave, the day before the beginning of that period,

(ii) otherwise, the day before that on which the suspension begins.

(6) Where the calculation is for the purposes of section 80I, the calculation date is the day on which the application under section 80F was made.

226 Rights on termination

(1) Where the calculation is for the purposes of section 88 or 89, the calculation date is the day immediately preceding the first day of the period of notice required by section 86(1) or (2).

(2) Where the calculation is for the purposes of section 93, 117 or 125, the calculation date is—

(a) if the dismissal was with notice, the date on which the employer's notice was given, and

(b) otherwise, the effective date of termination.

(3) Where the calculation is for the purposes of section 112, 119, 120, 121 or 124, the calculation date is—

(a) [repealed]

(b) if by virtue of subsection (2) or (4) of section 97 a date later than the effective date of termination as defined in subsection (1) of that section is to be treated for certain purposes as the effective date of termination, the effective date of termination as so defined, and

(c) otherwise, the date specified in subsection (6).

(4) Where the calculation is for the purposes of section 147(2), the calculation date is the day immediately preceding the first of the four, or six, weeks referred to in section 148(2).

(5) Where the calculation is for the purposes of section 162, the calculation date is—

(a) [repealed]

(b) if by virtue of subsection (5) of section 145 a date is to be treated for certain purposes as the relevant date which is later than the relevant date as defined by the previous provisions of that section, the relevant date as so defined, and

(c) otherwise, the date specified in subsection (6).

(6) The date referred to in subsections (3)(c) and (5)(c) is the date on which notice would have been given had—

(a) the contract been terminable by notice and been terminated by the employer giving such notice as is required by section 86 to terminate the contract, and

(b) the notice expired on the effective date of termination, or the relevant date, (whether or not those conditions were in fact fulfilled).

Maximum amount of week's pay

227 Maximum amount

(1) For the purpose of calculating—

(zza) an award of compensation under section 63J(1)(b),

(za) an award of compensation under section 80I(1)(b),

(a) a basic award of compensation for unfair dismissal,
(b) an additional award of compensation for unfair dismissal,
(ba) an award under section 112(5), or
(c) a redundancy payment, the amount of a week's pay shall not exceed £751.

(2)–(4) [repealed]

Miscellaneous

228 New employments and other special cases

(1) In any case in which the employee has not been employed for a sufficient period to enable a calculation to be made under the preceding provisions of this Chapter, the amount of a week's pay is the amount which fairly represents a week's pay.

(2) In determining that amount the employment tribunal—

(a) shall apply as nearly as may be such of the preceding provisions of this Chapter as it considers appropriate, and
(b) may have regard to such of the considerations specified in subsection (3) as it thinks fit.

(3) The considerations referred to in subsection (2)(b) are—

(a) any remuneration received by the employee in respect of the employment in question,
(b) the amount offered to the employee as remuneration in respect of the employment in question,
(c) the remuneration received by other persons engaged in relevant comparable employment with the same employer, and
(d) the remuneration received by other persons engaged in relevant comparable employment with other employers.

(4) The Secretary of State may by regulations provide that in cases prescribed by the regulations the amount of a week's pay shall be calculated in such manner as may be so prescribed.

229 Supplementary

(1) In arriving at—

(a) an average hourly rate of remuneration, or
(b) average weekly remuneration,

under this Chapter, account shall be taken of work for a former employer within the period for which the average is to be taken if, by virtue of Chapter I of this Part, a period of employment with the former employer counts as part of the employee's continuous period of employment.

(2) Where under this Chapter account is to be taken of remuneration or other payments for a period which does not coincide with the periods for which the remuneration or other payments are calculated, the remuneration or other payments shall be apportioned in such manner as may be just.

Chapter III Other Interpretation Provisions

230 Employees, workers etc.

(1) In this Act 'employee' means an individual who has entered into or works under (or, where the employment has ceased, worked under) a contract of employment.

(2) In this Act 'contract of employment' means a contract of service or apprenticeship, whether express or implied, and (if it is express) whether oral or in writing.

(3) In this Act 'worker' (except in the phrases 'shop worker' and 'betting worker') means an individual who has entered into or works under (or, where the employment has ceased, worked under)—

(a) a contract of employment, or
(b) any other contract, whether express or implied and (if it is express) whether oral or in writing, whereby the individual undertakes to do or perform personally any work or services for another party to the contract whose status is not by virtue of the contract that of a client or customer of any profession or business undertaking carried on by the individual;

and any reference to a worker's contract shall be construed accordingly.

(4) In this Act 'employer', in relation to an employee or a worker, means the person by whom the employee or worker is (or, where the employment has ceased, was) employed.

(5) In this Act 'employment'—

(a) in relation to an employee, means (except for the purposes of section 171) employment under a contract of employment, and

(b) in relation to a worker, means employment under his contract; and 'employed' shall be construed accordingly.

(6) This section has effect subject to sections 43K, 47B(3), 49B(10) and 49C(12); and for the purposes of Part XIII so far as relating to Part IVA or section 47B, 'worker', 'worker's contract' and, in relation to a worker, 'employer', 'employment' and 'employed' have the extended meaning given by section 43K.

(7) This section has effect subject to section 75K(3) and (5).

231 Associated employers

For the purposes of this Act any two employers shall be treated as associated if—

(a) one is a company of which the other (directly or indirectly) has control, or

(b) both are companies of which a third person (directly or indirectly) has control; and 'associated employer' shall be construed accordingly.

232–233 [omitted]

234 Normal working hours

(1) Where an employee is entitled to overtime pay when employed for more than a fixed number of hours in a week or other period, there are for the purposes of this Act normal working hours in his case.

(2) Subject to subsection (3), the normal working hours in such a case are the fixed number of hours.

(3) Where in such a case—

(a) the contract of employment fixes the number, or minimum number, of hours of employment in a week or other period (whether or not it also provides for the reduction of that number or minimum in certain circumstances), and

(b) that number or minimum number of hours exceeds the number of hours without overtime,

the normal working hours are that number or minimum number of hours (and not the number of hours without overtime).

235 Other definitions

(1) In this Act, except in so far as the context otherwise requires—

'act' and 'action' each includes omission and references to doing an act or taking action shall be construed accordingly,

'basic award of compensation for unfair dismissal' shall be construed in accordance with section 118,

'bereavement leave' means leave under section 80EA;

'business' includes a trade or profession and includes any activity carried on by a body of persons (whether corporate or unincorporated),

'carer's leave' means leave under section 80J,

'childbirth' means the birth of a living child or the birth of a child whether living or dead after twenty-four weeks of pregnancy,

'collective agreement' has the meaning given by section 178(1) and (2) of the Trade Union and Labour Relations (Consolidation) Act 1992,

'conciliation officer' means an officer designated by the Advisory, Conciliation and Arbitration Service under section 211 of that Act,

'dismissal procedures agreement' means an agreement in writing with respect to procedures relating to dismissal made by or on behalf of one or more independent trade unions and one or more employers or employers' associations, 'employers' association' has the same meaning as in the Trade Union and Labour Relations (Consolidation) Act 1992,

'expected week of childbirth' means the week, beginning with midnight between Saturday and Sunday, in which it is expected that childbirth will occur,

'guarantee payment' has the meaning given by section 28,

'independent trade union' means a trade union which—

(a) is not under the domination or control of an employer or a group of employers or of one or more employers' associations, and

(b) is not liable to interference by an employer or any such group or association (arising out of the provision of financial or material support or by any other means whatever) tending towards such control,

'job', in relation to an employee, means the nature of the work which he is employed to do in accordance with his contract and the capacity and place in which he is so employed,

'local authority', in relation to the placement of children under section 22C of the Children Act 1989, has the same meaning as in that Act (see section 105(1) of that Act);

'local authority foster parent' has the same meaning as in the Children Act 1989 (see section 105(1) of that Act);

'paternity leave' means leave under section 80A or 80B,

'position', in relation to an employee, means the following matters taken as a whole—

(a) his status as an employee,

(b) the nature of his work, and

(c) his terms and conditions of employment,

'protected disclosure' has the meaning given by section 43A,

'redundancy payment' has the meaning given by Part XI,

'relevant date' has the meaning given by sections 145 and 153,

'renewal' includes extension, and any reference to renewing a contract or a fixed term shall be construed accordingly,

'section 63D application' has the meaning given by section 63D(2);

'shared parental leave' means leave under section 75E or 75G,

'statutory provision' means a provision, whether of a general or a special nature, contained in, or in any document made or issued under, any Act, whether of a general or special nature,

'successor', in relation to the employer of an employee, means (subject to subsection (2)) a person who in consequence of a change occurring (whether by virtue of a sale or other disposition or by operation of law) in the ownership of the undertaking, or of the part of the undertaking, for the purposes of which the employee was employed, has become the owner of the undertaking or part,

'trade union' has the meaning given by section 1 of the Trade Union and Labour Relations (Consolidation) Act 1992,

'week'—

(a) in Chapter I of this Part means a week ending with Saturday, and

(b) otherwise, except in sections 75F, 75H, 80A, 80B, 80EA, 80EF, 80J and 86, means, in relation to an employee whose remuneration is calculated weekly by a week ending with a day other than Saturday, a week ending with that other day and, in relation to any other employee, a week ending with Saturday.

(2) The definition of 'successor' in subsection (1) has effect (subject to the necessary modifications) in relation to a case where—

(a) the person by whom an undertaking or part of an undertaking is owned immediately before a change is one of the persons by whom (whether as partners, trustees or otherwise) it is owned immediately after the change, or

(b) the persons by whom an undertaking or part of an undertaking is owned immediately before a change (whether as partners, trustees or otherwise) include the persons by whom, or include one or more of the persons by whom, it is owned immediately after the change, as it has effect where the previous owner and the new owner are wholly different persons.

(2A) For the purposes of this Act a contract of employment or other worker's contract is a 'limited-term contract' if—

(a) the employment under the contract is not intended to be permanent, and
(b) provision is accordingly made in the contract for it to terminate by virtue of a limiting event.

(2B) In this Act, 'limiting event', in relation to a contract of employment or other worker's contract means—

(a) in the case of a contract for a fixed-term, the expiry of the term,
(b) in the case of a contract made in contemplation of the performance of a specific task, the performance of the task, and
(c) in the case of a contract which provides for its termination on the occurrence of an event (or the failure of an event to occur), the occurrence of the event (or the failure of the event to occur).

(3) References in this Act to redundancy, dismissal by reason of redundancy and similar expressions shall be construed in accordance with section 139.

(4) In sections 136(2), 154 and 216(3) and paragraph 14 of Schedule 2 'lock-out' means—

(a) the closing of a place of employment,
(b) the suspension of work, or
(c) the refusal by an employer to continue to employ any number of persons employed by him in consequence of a dispute,

done with a view to compelling persons employed by the employer, or to aid another employer in compelling persons employed by him, to accept terms or conditions of or affecting employment.

(5) In sections 91(2), 140(2) and (3), 143(1), 144(2) and (3), 154 and 216(1) and (2) and paragraph 14 of Schedule 2 'strike' means—

(a) the cessation of work by a body of employed persons acting in combination, or
(b) a concerted refusal, or a refusal under a common understanding, of any number of employed persons to continue to work for an employer in consequence of a dispute,

done as a means of compelling their employer or any employed person or body of employed persons, or to aid other employees in compelling their employer or any employed person or body of employed persons, to accept or not to accept terms or conditions of or affecting employment.

236–245 [omitted]

Employment Tribunals Act 1996

(1996, c. 17)

PART I EMPLOYMENT TRIBUNALS

1–3A [omitted]

Membership etc.

4 Composition of tribunals

(1) An employment tribunal is, for the purpose of deciding any given matter, to be composed of a member or members chosen by the Senior President of Tribunals.

(2) The member, or each member, chosen must belong to a panel of members of employment tribunals appointed in accordance with regulations under section 1(1).

(3) The Senior President of Tribunals (or any person to whom the function under subsection (1) is delegated)—

(a) must act in accordance with regulations under subsection (4);

(b) may choose themselves (if eligible in accordance with regulations under section 1(1)).

(4) The Lord Chancellor must by regulations make provision, in relation to every matter that may fall to be decided by an employment tribunal, for determining the number of members who are to compose the tribunal.

(5) Where regulations under subsection (4) provide for a tribunal to be composed of a single member, the regulations must provide for that member to be an Employment Judge.

(6) Where regulations under subsection (4) provide for a tribunal to be composed of more than one member, the regulations—

(a) must provide for at least one of those members to be an Employment Judge,

(b) must make provision for determining how many (if any) of the other members are to be Employment Judges and how many (if any) are to be members who are not Employment Judges, and

(c) if the tribunal is to include one or more members who are not Employment Judges, may make provision for determining what qualifications (if any) that member or any of those members must have.

(7) A duty under subsection (4) or (6) to provide for the determination of anything may be discharged by providing for the thing to be determined by the Senior President of Tribunals or the President of Employment Tribunals in accordance with any provision made under that subsection.

(8) The power under subsection (6)(c) may be exercised by giving the Senior President of Tribunals or the President of Employment Tribunals power to determine what qualifications are required in accordance with any provision made by the regulations.

(9) Where a tribunal is to be composed of more than one member, the tribunal may proceed in the absence of one or more of the members chosen to compose it if—

(a) the parties to the case agree, and

(b) at least one of the members who is present is an Employment Judge.

(10) Where a person (other than an Employment Judge) is chosen as one of the members composing a tribunal but does not have a qualification required by virtue of subsection (6)(c), the tribunal may still proceed with that person as a member if the parties to the case agree.

(11) Before making regulations under this section, the Lord Chancellor must consult the Senior President of Tribunals.

(12) In this section—

'President of Employment Tribunals'—

(a) in relation to employment tribunals in England and Wales, means the President of Employment Tribunals (England and Wales), and

(b) in relation to employment tribunals in Scotland, means the President of Employment Tribunals (Scotland);

'qualification' includes experience.

5–5D [omitted]

Procedure

6 Conduct of hearings

(1) A person may appear before an employment tribunal in person or be represented by—

(a) counsel or a solicitor,

(b) a representative of a trade union or an employers' association, or

(c) any other person whom he desires to represent him.

(2) Nothing in any of sections 1 to 15 of and schedule 1 to the Arbitration (Scotland) Act 2010 or Part I of the Arbitration Act 1996 applies to any proceedings before an employment tribunal.

7–12 [omitted]

Financial penalties

12A Financial penalties

(1) Where an employment tribunal determining a claim involving an employer and a worker—

(a) concludes that the employer has breached any of the worker's rights to which the claim relates, and

(b) is of the opinion that the breach has one or more aggravating features,

the tribunal may order the employer to pay a penalty to the Secretary of State (whether or not it also makes a financial award against the employer on the claim).

(2) The tribunal shall have regard to an employer's ability to pay—

(a) in deciding whether to order the employer to pay a penalty under this section;

(b) (subject to subsections (3) to (7)) in deciding the amount of a penalty.

(3) The amount of a penalty under this section shall be—

(a) at least £100;

(b) no more than £20,000.

This subsection does not apply where subsection (5) or (7) applies.

(4) Subsection (5) applies where an employment tribunal—

(a) makes a financial award against an employer on a claim, and

(b) also orders the employer to pay a penalty under this section in respect of the claim.

(5) In such a case, the amount of the penalty under this section shall be 50% of the amount of the award, except that—

(a) if the amount of the financial award is less than £200, the amount of the penalty shall be £100;

(b) if the amount of the financial award is more than £40,000, the amount of the penalty shall be £20,000.

(6) Subsection (7) applies, instead of subsection (5), where an employment tribunal—

(a) considers together two or more claims involving different workers but the same employer, and

(b) orders the employer to pay a penalty under this section in respect of any of those claims.

(7) In such a case—

(a) the amount of the penalties in total shall be at least £100;

(b) the amount of a penalty in respect of a particular claim shall be—

(i) no more than £20,000, and

(ii) where the tribunal makes a financial award against the employer on the claim, no more than 50% of the amount of the award.

But where the tribunal makes a financial award on any of the claims and the amount awarded is less than £200 in total, the amount of the penalties in total shall be £100 (and paragraphs (a) and (b) shall not apply).

(8) Two or more claims in respect of the same act and the same worker shall be treated as a single claim for the purposes of this section.

(9) Subsection (5) or (7) does not require or permit an order under subsection (1) (or a failure to make such an order) to be reconsidered or reviewed where the tribunal subsequently awards compensation under—

(a) section 140(3) of the Trade Union and Labour Relations (Consolidation) Act 1992 (failure to comply with tribunal's recommendation),

(b) section 117 of the Employment Rights Act 1996 (failure to reinstate etc.),

(c) section 124(7) of the Equality Act 2010 (failure to comply with tribunal's recommendation), or
(d) any other provision empowering the tribunal to award compensation, or further compensation, for a failure to comply (or to comply fully) with an order or recommendation of the tribunal.

(10) An employer's liability to pay a penalty under this section is discharged if 50% of the amount of the penalty is paid no later than 21 days after the day on which notice of the decision to impose the penalty is sent to the employer.

(11) In this section—

'claim'—

(a) means anything that is referred to in the relevant legislation as a claim, a complaint or a reference, other than a reference made by virtue of section 122(2) or 128(2) of the Equality Act 2010 (reference by court of question about a non-discrimination or equality rule etc.), and
(b) also includes an application, under regulations made under section 45 of the Employment Act 2002, for a declaration that a person is a permanent employee;

'employer' has the same meaning as in Part 4A of the Employment Rights Act 1996, and also—

(a) in relation to an individual seeking to be employed by a person as a worker, includes that person;
(b) in relation to a right conferred by section 47A or 63A of the Employment Rights Act 1996 (right to time off for young person for study or training), includes the principal within the meaning of section 63A(3) of that Act;
(c) in relation to a right conferred by the Agency Workers Regulations 2010 (SI 2010/93), includes the hirer within the meaning of those Regulations and (where the worker is not actually employed by the temporary work agency) the temporary work agency within that meaning;

'financial award' means an award of a sum of money, but does not including anything payable by virtue of section 13;

'worker' has the same meaning as in Part 4A of the Employment Rights Act 1996, and also includes an individual seeking to be employed by a person as a worker.

(12)–(13) [omitted]

Costs etc., interest and enforcement

13–14 [omitted]

15 Enforcement

(1) Any sum payable in pursuance of a decision of an employment tribunal in England and Wales which has been registered in accordance with Procedure Rules shall be recoverable under section 85 of the County Courts Act 1984 or otherwise as if it were payable under an order of the county court.

(2) Any order for the payment of any sum made by an employment tribunal in Scotland (or any copy of such an order certified by the Secretary of the Tribunals) may be enforced as if it were an extract registered decree arbitral bearing a warrant for execution issued by the sheriff court of any sheriffdom in Scotland.

(3) In this section a reference to a decision or order of an employment tribunal—

(a) does not include a decision or order which, on being reconsidered or reviewed, has been revoked by the tribunal, and
(b) in relation to a decision or order which on being reconsidered or reviewed, has been varied by the tribunal shall be construed as a reference to the decision or order as so varied.

16–17 [omitted]

Conciliation

18 Conciliation: relevant proceedings etc.

(1) In this section and sections 18A to 18C 'relevant proceedings' means employment tribunal proceedings—

(a) under section 66, 68A, 70C, 87, 137, 138, 145A, 145B, 146, 168, 168A, 168B, 169, 170, 174, 189, 192 or 236A of, or paragraph 156 of Schedule A1 to, the Trade Union and Labour Relations (Consolidation) Act 1992,

(b) under section 11, 23, 27K, 27N, 34, 63I, 70, 70A, 80(1), 80H, 93, 111, 163 or 177 of the Employment Rights Act 1996, or under Part 5 or 6 of that Act,

(c) under section 11, 19D(1)(a) or 24 of the National Minimum Wage Act 1998,

(d) under section 56 of the Pensions Act 2008,

(e) under section 120 or 127 of the Equality Act 2010,

(f) under regulation 11 of the Safety Representatives and Safety Committees Regulations 1977,

(g) under article 6 of the Employment Tribunals Extension of Jurisdiction (England and Wales) Order 1994,

(h) under article 6 of the Employment Tribunals Extension of Jurisdiction (Scotland) Order 1994,

(i) under paragraph 2 of Schedule 2 to the Health and Safety (Consultation with Employees) Regulations 1996,

(j) under regulation 30 of the Working Time Regulations 1998,

(k) under regulation 27 or 32 of the Transnational Information and Consultation of Employees Regulation 1999,

(l) under regulation 8 of the Part-time Workers (Prevention of Less Favourable Treatment) Regulations 2000,

(m) under regulation 7 or 9 of the Fixed-term Employees (Prevention of Less Favourable Treatment) Regulations 2002,

(n) under regulation 26 of the Merchant Shipping (Maritime Labour Convention) (Hours of Work) Regulations 2018 (SI 2018/58),

(o) under regulation 15 of the Flexible Working (Procedural Requirements) Regulations 2002,

(p) under regulation 18 of the Merchant Shipping (Working Time: Inland Waterways) Regulations 2003,

(q) under regulation 18 of the Civil Aviation (Working Time) Regulations 2004,

(r) under regulation 19 of the Fishing Vessels (Working Time: Sea-fishermen) Regulations 2004,

(s) under regulation 29 or 33 of the Information and Consultation of Employees Regulations 2004,

(t) under paragraphs 4 or 8 of the Schedule to the Occupational and Personal Pension Schemes (Consultation by Employers and Miscellaneous Amendment) Regulations 2006,

(u) under regulation 30 or 34 of the European Cooperative Society (Involvement of Employees) Regulations 2006,

(v) [repealed]

(w) under regulation 17 of the Cross-border Railway Services (Working Time) Regulations 2008,

(x) under regulation 9 of Ecclesiastical Offices (Terms of Service) Regulations 2009,

(y) under regulation 28 or 32 of the European Public Limited-Liability Company (Employee Involvement) (Great Britain) Regulations 2009,

(z) under regulation 18 of the Agency Workers Regulations 2010,

(z1) under regulation 17 of the Employee Study and Training (Procedural Requirements) Regulations 2010,
(z2) under regulation 5, 6 or 9 of the Employment Relations Act 1999 (Blacklists) Regulations 2010.
(z3) under regulation 3 of the Exclusivity Terms in Zero Hours Contracts (Redress) Regulations 2015,
(z4) under regulation 6 of the Posted Workers (Enforcement of Employment Rights) Regulations 2016,
(z5) under regulation 4 of the Employment Rights Act 1996 (NHS Recruitment—Protected Disclosure) Regulations 2018,
(z6) under paragraph (3) of regulation 4 or paragraph (6) of regulation 5 of the Agency Workers (Amendment) Regulations 2019, or
(z7) under regulation 8 of the Exclusivity Terms for Zero Hours Workers (Unenforceability and Redress) Regulations 2022.

(1A) [omitted]; (2)–(5) [repealed]

(6) In proceeding under any of sections 18A to 18C a conciliation officer shall, where appropriate, have regard to the desirability of encouraging the use of other procedures available for the settlement of grievances.

(7) Anything communicated to a conciliation officer in connection with the performance of his functions under any of sections 18A to 18C shall not be admissible in evidence in any proceedings before an employment tribunal, except with the consent of the person who communicated it to that officer.

(8)–(10) [omitted]

18A Requirement to contact ACAS before instituting proceedings

(1) Before a person ('the prospective claimant') presents an application to institute relevant proceedings relating to any matter, the prospective claimant must provide to ACAS prescribed information, in the prescribed manner, about that matter.

This is subject to subsection (7).

(2) On receiving the prescribed information in the prescribed manner, ACAS shall send a copy of it to a conciliation officer.

(3) The conciliation officer shall, during the prescribed period, endeavour to promote a settlement between the persons who would be parties to the proceedings.

(4) If—

(a) during the prescribed period the conciliation officer concludes that a settlement is not possible, or
(b) the prescribed period expires without a settlement having been reached,

the conciliation officer shall issue a certificate to that effect, in the prescribed manner, to the prospective claimant.

(5)–(7) [omitted]

(8) A person who is subject to the requirement in subsection (1) may not present an application to institute relevant proceedings without a certificate under subsection (4).

(9)–(12) [omitted]

18B–19A [omitted]

PART II THE EMPLOYMENT APPEAL TRIBUNAL

Introductory

20 The Appeal Tribunal

(1) The Employment Appeal Tribunal ('the Appeal Tribunal') shall continue in existence.

(2) The Appeal Tribunal shall have a central office in London but may sit at any time and in any place in Great Britain.

(3) The Appeal Tribunal shall be a superior court of record and shall have an official seal which shall be judicially noticed.

(4) Subsection (2) is subject to regulation 34 of the Transnational Information and Consultation of Employees Regulations 1999, regulation 46(1) of the European Public Limited-Liability Company Regulations 2004, regulation 36(1) of the Information and Consultation of Employees Regulations 2004, and regulation 37(1) of the European Cooperative Society (Involvement of Employees) Regulations 2006, regulation 58(1) of the Companies (Cross-Border Mergers) Regulations 2007 and regulation 33(1) of the European Public Limited-Liability Company (Employee Involvement) (Great Britain) Regulations 2009 (SI 2009/2401).

Jurisdiction

21 Jurisdiction of Appeal Tribunal

(1) An appeal lies to the Appeal Tribunal on any question of law arising from any decision of, or arising in any proceedings before, an employment tribunal under or by virtue of—

- (a)–(c) [repealed]
- (d) the Trade Union and Labour Relations (Consolidation) Act 1992,
- (e) [repealed]
- (f) the Employment Rights Act 1996,
- (fg) [repealed]
- (g) this Act,
- (ga) the National Minimum Wage Act 1998,
- (gb) the Employment Relations Act 1999,
- (gc) the Equality Act 2006,
- (gd) the Pensions Act 2008,
- (ge) the Equality Act 2010,
- (h) the Working Time Regulations,
- (i) the Transnational Information and Consultation of Employees Regulations 1999,
- (j) the Part-time Workers (Prevention of Less Favourable Treatment) Regulations 2000,
- (k) the Fixed-term Employees (Prevention of Less Favourable Treatment) Regulations 2002,
- (l)–(m) [repealed]
- (n) the Merchant Shipping (Working Time: Inland Waterways) Regulations 2003,
- (o) the European Public Limited-Liability Company Regulations 2004,
- (p) the Fishing Vessels (Working Time: Sea Fishermen) Regulations 2004,
- (q) the Information and Consultation of Employees Regulations 2004,
- (r) the Schedule to the Occupational and Personal Pension Schemes (Consultation by Employers and Miscellaneous Amendment) Regulations 2006,
- (s) [repealed]
- (t) the European Cooperative Society (Involvement of Employees) Regulations 2006,
- (u) [repealed]
- (v) the Cross-border Railway Services (Working Time) Regulations 2008,
- (w) the European Public Limited-Liability Company (Employee Involvement) (Great Britain) Regulations 2009 (SI 2009/2401),
- (x) the Employment Relations Act 1999 (Blacklists) Regulations 2010,
- (y) the Agency Workers Regulations 2010, or
- (z) the Merchant Shipping (Maritime Labour Convention) (Hours of Work) Regulations 2018 (SI 2018/58).

(2) No appeal shall lie except to the Appeal Tribunal from any decision of an employment tribunal under or by virtue of the Acts listed or the Regulations referred to in subsection (1).

(3) Subsection (1) does not affect any provision contained in, or made under, any Act which provides for an appeal to lie to the Appeal Tribunal (whether from an employment tribunal, the Certification Officer or any other person or body) otherwise than on a question to which that subsection applies.

(4) The Appeal Tribunal also has any jurisdiction in respect of matters other than appeals which is conferred on it by or under—

(a) the Trade Union and Labour Relations (Consolidation) Act 1992,
(b) this Act, or
(c) any other Act.

Membership etc.

22 Membership of Appeal Tribunal

(1) The Appeal Tribunal shall consist of—

(a) such number of judges as may be nominated from time to time by the Lord Chief Justice, after consulting the Lord Chancellor, from the judges of the High Court and the Court of Appeal and the judges within subsection (2A),
(b) at least one judge of the Court of Session nominated from time to time by the Lord President of the Court of Session, and
(c) such number of other members as may be appointed from time to time by Her Majesty on the joint recommendation of the Lord Chancellor and the Secretary of State ('appointed Members').

(2) The appointed members shall be persons who appear to the Lord Chancellor and the Secretary of State to have special knowledge or experience of industrial relations either—

(a) as representatives of employers, or
(b) as representatives of workers (within the meaning of the Trade Union and Labour Relations (Consolidation) Act 1992).

(2A) [omitted]

(3) The Lord Chief Justice shall appoint one of the judges nominated under subsection (1) to be the President of the Appeal Tribunal.

(3A)–(6) [omitted]

23–25 [omitted]; 26 [repealed]; 27 [omitted]

28 Composition of Appeal Tribunal

(1) The Appeal Tribunal is, for the purpose of deciding any given matter, to be composed of a member or members chosen by the Senior President of Tribunals.

(2) The Senior President of Tribunals (or any person to whom the function under subsection (1) is delegated)—

(a) must act in accordance with regulations under subsection (3);
(b) may choose themselves (if otherwise eligible to sit).

(3) The Lord Chancellor must by regulations make provision, in relation to every matter that may fall to be decided by the Appeal Tribunal, for determining the number of members who are to compose the Tribunal.

(4) Where regulations under subsection (3) provide for the Appeal Tribunal to be composed of a single member, the regulations must provide for that member to be a judge.

(5) Where regulations under subsection (3) provide for the Appeal Tribunal to be composed of more than one member, the regulations—

(a) must provide for at least one of those members to be a judge,
(b) must make provision for determining how many (if any) of the other members are to be judges and how many (if any) are to be appointed members, and
(c) if the Tribunal is to be composed of persons who include one or more appointed members, may make provision for determining what qualifications (if any) that member or any of those members must have.

(6) A duty under subsection (3) or (5) to provide for the determination of anything may be discharged by providing for the thing to be determined by the Senior President of Tribunals or the President of the Appeal Tribunal in accordance with any provision made under that subsection.

(7) The power under subsection (5)(c) may be exercised by giving the Senior President of Tribunals or the President of the Appeal Tribunal power to determine what qualifications are required in accordance with any provision made by the regulations.

(8) Where the Appeal Tribunal is to be composed of more than one member, the Tribunal may proceed in the absence of one or more of the members chosen to compose it if—

(a) the parties to the case agree, and

(b) at least one of the members who is present is a judge.

(9) Where a person (other than a judge) is chosen as one of the members composing the Appeal Tribunal but does not have a qualification required by virtue of subsection (5)(c), the Tribunal may still proceed with that person as a member if the parties to the case agree.

(10) Before making regulations under this section, the Lord Chancellor must consult the Senior President of Tribunals.

(11) In this section, 'qualification' includes experience.

Procedure

29–32 [omitted]

33 Restriction of vexatious proceedings

(1) If, on an application made by the Attorney General or the Lord Advocate under this section, the Appeal Tribunal is satisfied that a person has habitually and persistently and without any reasonable ground—

(a) instituted vexatious proceedings, whether before the Certification Officer, in an employment tribunal or before the Appeal Tribunal, and whether against the same person or against different persons, or

(b) made vexatious applications in any proceedings, whether before the Certification Officer, in an employment tribunal or before the Appeal Tribunal,

the Appeal Tribunal may, after hearing the person or giving him an opportunity of being heard, make a restriction of proceedings order.

(2) A 'restriction of proceedings order' is an order that—

(a) no proceedings shall without the leave of the Appeal Tribunal be instituted before the Certification Officer, in any employment tribunal or before the Appeal Tribunal by the person against whom the order is made,

(b) any proceedings instituted by him before the Certification Officer, in any employment tribunal or before the Appeal Tribunal before the making of the order shall not be continued by him without the leave of the Appeal Tribunal, and

(c) no application (other than one for leave under this section) is to be made by him in any proceedings before the Certification Officer, in any employment tribunal or before the Appeal Tribunal without the leave of the Appeal Tribunal.

(3) A restriction of proceedings order may provide that it is to cease to have effect at the end of a specified period, but otherwise it remains in force indefinitely.

(4) Leave for the institution or continuance of, or for the making of an application in, any proceedings before the Certification Officer, in an employment tribunal or before the Appeal Tribunal by a person who is the subject of a restriction of proceedings order shall not be given unless the Appeal Tribunal is satisfied—

(a) that the proceedings or application are not an abuse of process, and

(b) that there are reasonable grounds for the proceedings or application.

(5) A copy of a restriction of proceedings order shall be published in the London Gazette and the Edinburgh Gazette.

34–48 [omitted]

Human Rights Act 1998

(1998, c. 42)

Introduction

1 The Convention Rights

(1) In this Act 'the Convention rights' means the rights and fundamental freedoms set out in—

(a) Articles 2 to 12 and 14 of the Convention,

(b) Articles 1 to 3 of the First Protocol, and

(c) Article 1 of the Thirteenth Protocol,

as read with Articles 16 to 18 of the Convention.

(2)–(6) [omitted]

2 Interpretation of Convention rights

(1) A court or tribunal determining a question which has arisen in connection with a Convention right must take into account any—

(a) judgment, decision, declaration or advisory opinion of the European Court of Human Rights,

(b) opinion of the Commission given in a report adopted under Article 31 of the Convention,

(c) decision of the Commission in connection with Article 26 or 27(2) of the Convention, or

(d) decision of the Committee of Ministers taken under Article 46 of the Convention,

whenever made or given, so far as, in the opinion of the court or tribunal, it is relevant to the proceedings in which that question has arisen.

(2)–(3) [omitted]

Legislation

3 Interpretation of legislation

(1) So far as it is possible to do so, primary legislation and subordinate legislation must be read and given effect in a way which is compatible with the Convention rights.

(2) This section—

(a) applies to primary legislation and subordinate legislation whenever enacted;

(b) does not affect the validity, continuing operation or enforcement of any incompatible primary legislation; and

(c) does not affect the validity, continuing operation or enforcement of any incompatible subordinate legislation if (disregarding any possibility of revocation) primary legislation prevents removal of the incompatibility.

4 Declaration of incompatibility

(1) Subsection (2) applies in any proceedings in which a court determines whether a provision of primary legislation is compatible with a Convention right.

(2) If the court is satisfied that the provision is incompatible with a Convention right, it may make a declaration of that incompatibility.

(3) Subsection (4) applies in any proceedings in which a court determines whether a provision of subordinate legislation, made in the exercise of a power conferred by primary legislation, is compatible with a Convention right.

(4) If the court is satisfied—

(a) that the provision is incompatible with a Convention right, and

(b) that (disregarding any possibility of revocation) the primary legislation concerned prevents removal of the incompatibility,

it may make a declaration of that incompatibility.

(5) In this section 'court' means—

(a) the Supreme Court;

(b) the Judicial Committee of the Privy Council;
(c) the Court Martial Appeal Court;
(d) in Scotland, the High Court of Justiciary sitting otherwise than as a trial court or the Court of Session;
(e) in England and Wales or Northern Ireland, the High Court or the Court of Appeal;
(f) the Court of Protection, in any matter being dealt with by the President of the Family Division, the Chancellor of the High Court or a puisne judge of the High Court.

(6) A declaration under this section ('a declaration of incompatibility')—
(a) does not affect the validity, continuing operation or enforcement of the provision in respect of which it is given; and
(b) is not binding on the parties to the proceedings in which it is made.

5–6 [omitted]

Public authorities

7 Proceedings

(1) A person who claims that a public authority has acted (or proposes to act) in a way which is made unlawful by section 6(1) may—
(a) bring proceedings against the authority under this Act in the appropriate court or tribunal, or
(b) rely on the Convention right or rights concerned in any legal proceedings,
but only if he is (or would be) a victim of the unlawful act.

(2)–(4) [omitted]

(5) Proceedings under subsection (1)(a) must be brought before the end of—
(a) the period of one year beginning with the date on which the act complained of took place; or
(b) such longer period as the court or tribunal considers equitable having regard to all the circumstances,
but that is subject to any rule imposing a stricter time limit in relation to the procedure in question.

(6) [omitted]

(7) For the purposes of this section, a person is a victim of an unlawful act only if he would be a victim for the purposes of Article 34 of the Convention if proceedings were brought in the European Court of Human Rights in respect of that act.

(8) Nothing in this Act creates a criminal offence.

(9)–(13) [omitted]

7A [omitted]

8 Judicial remedies

(1) In relation to any act (or proposed act) of a public authority which the court finds is (or would be) unlawful, it may grant such relief or remedy, or make such order, within its powers as it considers just and appropriate.

(2) But damages may be awarded only by a court which has power to award damages, or to order the payment of compensation, in civil proceedings.

(3) No award of damages is to be made unless, taking account of all the circumstances of the case, including—
(a) any other relief or remedy granted, or order made, in relation to the act in question (by that or any other court), and
(b) the consequences of any decision (of that or any other court) in respect of that act,
the court is satisfied that the award is necessary to afford just satisfaction to the person in whose favour it is made.

(4) In determining—
(a) whether to award damages, or
(b) the amount of an award,

the court must take into account the principles applied by the European Court of Human Rights in relation to the award of compensation under Article 41 of the Convention.

(5)–(6) [omitted]

9–10 [omitted]

Other rights and proceedings

11 Safeguard for existing human rights

A person's reliance on a Convention right does not restrict—

(a) any other right or freedom conferred on him by or under any law having effect in any part of the United Kingdom; or

(b) his right to make any claim or bring any proceedings which he could make or bring apart from sections 7 to 9.

12 Freedom of expression

(1) This section applies if a court is considering whether to grant any relief which, if granted, might affect the exercise of the Convention right to freedom of expression.

(2) If the person against whom the application for relief is made ('the respondent') is neither present nor represented, no such relief is to be granted unless the court is satisfied—

(a) that the applicant has taken all practicable steps to notify the respondent; or

(b) that there are compelling reasons why the respondent should not be notified.

(3) No such relief is to be granted so as to restrain publication before trial unless the court is satisfied that the applicant is likely to establish that publication should not be allowed.

(4) The court must have particular regard to the importance of the Convention right to freedom of expression and, where the proceedings relate to material which the respondent claims, or which appears to the court, to be journalistic, literary or artistic material (or to conduct connected with such material), to—

(a) the extent to which—

(i) the material has, or is about to, become available to the public; or

(ii) it is, or would be, in the public interest for the material to be published;

(b) any relevant privacy code.

(5) In this section—

'court' includes a tribunal; and

'relief' includes any remedy or order (other than in criminal proceedings).

13 Freedom of thought, conscience and religion

(1) If a court's determination of any question arising under this Act might affect the exercise by a religious organisation (itself or its members collectively) of the Convention right to freedom of thought, conscience and religion, it must have particular regard to the importance of that right.

(2) In this section 'court' includes a tribunal.

Section 1(3)

SCHEDULE 1

THE ARTICLES

PART I THE CONVENTION RIGHTS AND FREEDOMS

Article 4 Prohibition of slavery and forced labour

1. No one shall be held in slavery or servitude.
2. No one shall be required to perform forced or compulsory labour.
3. For the purpose of this Article the term 'forced or compulsory labour' shall not include:

(a) any work required to be done in the ordinary course of detention imposed according to the provisions of Article 5 of this Convention or during conditional release from such detention;
(b) any service of a military character or, in case of conscientious objectors in countries where they are recognised, service exacted instead of compulsory military service;
(c) any service exacted in case of an emergency or calamity threatening the life or well-being of the community;
(d) any work or service which forms part of normal civic obligations.

Article 6 Right to a fair trial

1. In the determination of his civil rights and obligations or of any criminal charge against him, everyone is entitled to a fair and public hearing within a reasonable time by an independent and impartial tribunal established by law. Judgment shall be pronounced publicly but the press and public may be excluded from all or part of the trial in the interest of morals, public order or national security in a democratic society, where the interests of juveniles or the protection of the private life of the parties so require, or to the extent strictly necessary in the opinion of the court in special circumstances where publicity would prejudice the interests of justice.

2. Everyone charged with a criminal offence shall be presumed innocent until proved guilty according to law.

3. Everyone charged with a criminal offence has the following minimum rights:
(a) to be informed promptly, in a language which he understands and in detail, of the nature and cause of the accusation against him;
(b) to have adequate time and facilities for the preparation of his defence;
(c) to defend himself in person or through legal assistance of his own choosing or, if he has not sufficient means to pay for legal assistance, to be given it free when the interests of justice so require;
(d) to examine or have examined witnesses against him and to obtain the attendance and examination of witnesses on his behalf under the same conditions as witnesses against him;
(e) to have the free assistance of an interpreter if he cannot understand or speak the language used in court.

Article 8 Right to respect for private and family life

1. Everyone has the right to respect for his private and family life, his home and his correspondence.

2. There shall be no interference by a public authority with the exercise of this right except such as is in accordance with the law and is necessary in a democratic society in the interests of national security, public safety or the economic well-being of the country, for the prevention of disorder or crime, for the protection of health or morals, or for the protection of the rights and freedoms of others.

Article 9 Freedom of thought, conscience and religion

1. Everyone has the right to freedom of thought, conscience and religion; this right includes freedom to change his religion or belief and freedom, either alone or in community with others and in public or private, to manifest his religion or belief, in worship, teaching, practice and observance.

2. Freedom to manifest one's religion or beliefs shall be subject only to such limitations as are prescribed by law and are necessary in a democratic society in the interests of public safety, for the protection of public order, health or morals, or for the protection of the rights and freedoms of others.

Article 10 Freedom of expression

1. Everyone has the right to freedom of expression. This right shall include freedom to hold opinions and to receive and impart information and ideas without interference by public authority and regardless of frontiers. This Article shall not prevent States from requiring the licensing of broadcasting, television or cinema enterprises.

2. The exercise of these freedoms, since it carries with it duties and responsibilities, may be subject to such formalities, conditions, restrictions or penalties as are prescribed by law and are necessary in a democratic society, in the interests of national security, territorial integrity or public safety, for the prevention of disorder or crime, for the protection of health or morals, for the protection of the reputation or rights of others, for preventing the disclosure of information received in confidence, or for maintaining the authority and impartiality of the judiciary.

Article 11 Freedom of assembly and association

1. Everyone has the right to freedom of peaceful assembly and to freedom of association with others, including the right to form and to join trade unions for the protection of his interests.

2. No restrictions shall be placed on the exercise of these rights other than such as are prescribed by law and are necessary in a democratic society in the interests of national security or public safety, for the prevention of disorder or crime, for the protection of health or morals or for the protection of the rights and freedoms of others. This Article shall not prevent the imposition of lawful restrictions on the exercise of these rights by members of the armed forces, of the police or of the administration of the State.

Article 14 Prohibition of discrimination

The enjoyment of the rights and freedoms set forth in this Convention shall be secured without discrimination on any ground such as sex, race, colour, language, religion, political or other opinion, national or social origin, association with a national minority, property, birth or other status.

Article 16 Restrictions on political activity of aliens

Nothing in Articles 10, 11 and 14 shall be regarded as preventing the High Contracting Parties from imposing restrictions on the political activity of aliens.

National Minimum Wage Act 1998

(1998, c. 39)

Entitlement to the national minimum wage
1 Workers to be paid at least the national minimum wage

Enforcement
17 Non-compliance: worker entitled to additional remuneration
18 Enforcement in the case of special classes of worker
19 Notices of underpayment: arrears
19A Notices of underpayment: financial penalty
19D Non-compliance with notice of underpayment: recovery of arrears
19E Non-compliance with notice of underpayment: recovery of penalty

Rights not to suffer unfair dismissal or other detriment
23 The right not to suffer detriment
24 Enforcement of the right

Civil procedure, evidence and appeals
28 Reversal of burden of proof

Offences
31 Offences
32 Offences by bodies corporate etc.

Special classes of person
34 Agency workers who are not otherwise 'workers'
35 Home workers who are not otherwise 'workers'
36 Crown employment
37 Armed forces

Exclusions
44 Voluntary workers
44A Religious and other communities: resident workers
45 Prisoners
45A Persons discharging fines by unpaid work

Miscellaneous
48 Application of Act to superior employers
49 Restrictions on contracting out

Supplementary
54 Meaning of 'workers', 'employee' etc.
55 Interpretation

Entitlement to the national minimum wage

1 Workers to be paid at least the national minimum wage

(1) A person who qualifies for the national minimum wage shall be remunerated by his employer in respect of his work in any pay reference period at a rate which is not less than the national minimum wage.

(2) A person qualifies for the national minimum wage if he is an individual who—

(a) is a worker;

(b) is working, or ordinarily works, in the United Kingdom under his contract;

(c) has ceased to be of compulsory school age.

(3) The national minimum wage shall be such single hourly rate as the Secretary of State may from time to time prescribe.

(4) For the purposes of this Act a 'pay reference period' is such period as the Secretary of State may prescribe for the purpose.

(5) Subsections (1) to (4) above are subject to the following provisions of this Act.

Regulations relating to the national minimum wage

2–16A [omitted]

Enforcement

17 Non-compliance: worker entitled to additional remuneration

(1) If a worker who qualifies for the national minimum wage is remunerated for any pay reference period by his employer at a rate which is less than the national minimum wage, the worker shall at any time ('the time of determination') be taken to be entitled under his contract to be paid, as additional remuneration in respect of that period whichever is the higher of—

(a) the amount described in subsection (2) below, and

(b) the amount described in subsection (4) below.

(2) The amount referred to in subsection (1)(a) above is the difference between—

(a) the relevant remuneration received by the worker for the pay reference period;

(b) the relevant remuneration which the worker would have received for that period had he been remunerated by the employer at a rate equal to the national minimum wage.

(3) In subsection (2) above, 'relevant remuneration' means remuneration which falls to be brought into account for the purposes of regulations under section 2 above.

(4) The amount referred to in subsection (1)(b) above is the amount determined by the formula—

$$\frac{A}{R1} \times R2$$

where—

A is the amount described in subsection (2) above,

R1 is the rate of national minimum wage which was payable in respect of the worker during the pay reference period, and

R2 is the rate of national minimum wage which would have been payable in respect of the worker during that period had the rate payable in respect of him during that period been determined by reference to regulations under section 1 and 3 above in force at the time of determination.

(5) Subsection (1) above ceases to apply to a worker in relation to any pay reference period when he is at any time paid the additional remuneration for that period to which he is at that time entitled under that subsection.

(6) Where any additional remuneration is paid to the worker under this section in relation to the pay reference period but subsection (1) above has not ceased to apply in relation to him, the

amounts described in subsections (2) and (4) above shall be regarded as reduced by the amount of that remuneration.

18 Enforcement in the case of special classes of worker

(1) If the persons who are the worker and the employer for the purposes of section 17 above would not (apart from this section) fall to be regarded as the worker and the employer for the purposes of—

(a) Part II of the Employment Rights Act 1996 (protection of wages); or

(b) in relation to Northern Ireland, Part IV of the Employment Rights (Northern Ireland) Order 1996;

they shall be so regarded for the purposes of the application of that Part in relation to the entitlement conferred by that section.

(2) In the application by virtue of subsection (1) above of—

(a) Part II of the Employment Rights Act 1996, or

(b) Part IV of the Employment Rights (Northern Ireland) Order 1996,

in a case where there is or was, for the purposes of that Part, no worker's contract between the persons who are the worker and the employer for the purposes of section 17 above, it shall be assumed that there is or, as the case may be, was such a contract.

(3) For the purpose of enabling the amount described as additional remuneration in subsection (1) of section 17 above to be recovered in civil proceedings on a claim in contract in a case where in fact there is or was no worker's contract between the persons who are the worker and the employer for the purposes of that section, it shall be assumed for the purpose of any civil proceedings, so far as relating to that amount, that there is or, as the case may be, was such a contract.

19 Notices of underpayment: arrears

(1) Subsection (2) below applies where an officer acting for the purposes of this Act is of the opinion that, on any day ('the relevant day'), a sum was due under section 17 above for any one or more pay reference periods ending before the relevant day to a worker who at any time qualified for the national minimum wage.

(2) Where this subsection applies, the officer may, subject to this section, serve a notice requiring the employer to pay to the worker, within the 28-day period, the sum due to the worker under section 17 above for any one or more of the pay reference periods referred to in subsection (1) above.

(3) In this Act, 'notice of underpayment' means a notice under this section.

(4) A notice of underpayment must specify, for each worker to whom it relates—

(a) the relevant day in relation to that worker;

(b) the pay reference period or periods in respect of which the employer is required to pay a sum to the worker as specified in subsection (2) above;

(c) the amount described in section 17(2) above in relation to the worker in respect of each such period;

(d) the amount described in section 17(4) above in relation to the worker in respect of each of such period;

(e) the sum due under section 17 above to the worker for each such period.

(5) Where a notice of underpayment relates to more than one worker, the notice may identify the workers by name or by description.

(6) The reference in subsection (1) above to a pay reference period includes (subject to subsection (7) below) a pay reference period ending before the coming into force of this section.

(7) A notice of underpayment may not relate to a pay reference period ending more than six years before the date of service of the notice.

(8) In this section and sections 19A to 19C below 'the 28-day period' means the period of 28 days beginning with the date of service of the notice of underpayment.

19A Notices of underpayment: financial penalty

(1) A notice of underpayment must, subject to this section, require the employer to pay a financial penalty specified in the notice to the Secretary of State within the 28-day period.

(2) The Secretary of State may by directions specify circumstances in which a notice of underpayment is not to impose a requirement to pay a financial penalty.

(3) Directions under subsection (2) may be amended or revoked by further such directions.

(4) The amount of any financial penalty is, subject as follows, to be the total of the amounts for all workers to whom the notice relates calculated in accordance with subsections (5) to (5B).

(5) The amount for each worker to whom the notice relates is the relevant percentage of the amount specified under section 19(4)(c) in respect of each pay reference period specified under section 19(4)(b).

(5A) In subsection (5), 'the relevant percentage', in relation to any pay reference period, means 200%.

(5B) If the amount as calculated under subsection (5) for any worker would be more than £20,000, the amount for the worker taken into account in calculating the financial penalty is to be £20,000.

(6) If a financial penalty as calculated under subsection (4) above would be less than £100, the financial penalty specified in the notice shall be that amount.

(7) [repealed]; (8)–(11) [omitted]

19B–19C [omitted]

19D Non-compliance with notice of underpayment: recovery of arrears

(1) If a requirement to pay a sum to a worker contained in a notice of underpayment is not complied with in whole or in part, an officer acting for the purposes of this Act may, on behalf of any worker to whom the requirement relates—

(a) present a complaint under section 23(1)(a) of the Employment Rights Act 1996 (deductions from worker's wages in contravention of section 13 of that Act) to an employment tribunal in respect of any sums due to the worker by virtue of section 17 above; or

(b) in relation to Northern Ireland, present a complaint under Article 55(1)(a) of the Employment Rights (Northern Ireland) Order 1996 (deductions from worker's wages in contravention of Article 45 of that Order) to an industrial tribunal in respect of any sums due to the worker by virtue of section 17 above; or

(c) commence other civil proceedings for the recovery, on a claim in contract, of any sums due to the worker by virtue of section 17 above.

(2) The powers conferred by subsection (1) above for the recovery of sums due from an employer to a worker shall not be in derogation of any right which the worker may have to recover such sums by civil proceedings.

19E Non-compliance with notice of underpayment: recovery of penalty

A financial penalty payable under a notice of underpayment—

(a) in England and Wales, is recoverable, if the county court so orders, under section 85 of the County Courts Act 1984 or otherwise as if it were payable under an order of that court;

(b) in Scotland, may be enforced in the same manner as an extract registered decree arbitral bearing a warrant for execution issued by the sheriff court of any sheriffdom in Scotland;

(c) in Northern Ireland, is recoverable, if the county court so orders, as if it were payable under an order of that court.

19F–19H [omitted]; 20–22F [repealed]

Rights not to suffer unfair dismissal or other detriment

23 The right not to suffer detriment

(1) A worker has the right not to be subjected to any detriment by any act, or any deliberate failure to act, by his employer, done on the ground that—

(a) any action was taken, or was proposed to be taken, by or on behalf of the worker with a view to enforcing, or otherwise securing the benefit of, a right of the worker's to which this section applies; or

(b) the employer was prosecuted for an offence under section 31 below as a result of action taken by or on behalf of the worker for the purpose of enforcing, or otherwise securing the benefit of, a right of the worker's to which this section applies; or

(c) the worker qualifies, or will or might qualify, for the national minimum wage or for a particular rate of national minimum wage.

(2) It is immaterial for the purposes of paragraph (a) or (b) of subsection (1) above—

(a) whether or not the worker has the right; or

(b) whether or not the right has been infringed;

but, for that subsection to apply, the claim to the right and, if applicable, the claim that it has been infringed must be made in good faith.

(3) The following are the rights to which this section applies—

(a) any right conferred by, or by virtue of, any provision of this Act for which the remedy for its infringement is by way of a complaint to an employment tribunal; and

(b) any right conferred by section 17 above.

(4) This section does not apply where the detriment in question amounts to dismissal within the meaning of—

(a) Part X of the Employment Rights Act 1996 (unfair dismissal); or

(b) Part XI, of the Employment Rights (Northern Ireland) Order 1996 (corresponding provision for Northern Ireland);

except wherein relation to Northern Ireland the person in question is dismissed in circumstances in which by virtue of Article 240 of that Order (fixed term contracts), Part XI does not apply to the dismissal.

24 Enforcement of the right

(1) A worker may present a complaint to an employment tribunal that he has been subjected to a detriment in contravention of section 23 above.

(2) Subject to the following provisions of this section, the provisions of—

(a) sections 48(2) to (4A) and 49 of the Employment Rights Act 1996 (complaints to employment tribunals and remedies), or

(b) in relation to Northern Ireland, Articles 71(2) to (4) and 72 of the Employment Rights (Northern Ireland) Order 1996 (complaints to industrial tribunals and remedies),

shall apply in relation to a complaint under this section as they apply in relation to a complaint under section 48 of that Act or Article 71 of that Order (as the case may be), but taking references in those provisions to the employer as references to the employer within the meaning of section 23(1) above.

(3) Where—

(a) the detriment to which the worker is subjected is the termination of his worker's contract, but

(b) that contract is not a contract of employment,

any compensation awarded under section 49 of the Employment Rights Act 1996 or Article 72 of the Employment Rights (Northern Ireland) Order 1996 by virtue of subsection (2) above must not exceed the limit specified in subsection (4) below.

(4) The limit mentioned in subsection (3) above is the total of—

(a) the sum which would be the basic award for unfair dismissal, calculated in accordance with section 119 of the Employment Rights Act 1996 or Article 153 of the Employment Rights (Northern Ireland) Order 1996 (as the case may be), if the worker had been an employee and the contract terminated had been a contract of employment; and

(b) the sum for the time being specified in section 124(1) of that Act or Article 158(1) of that Order (as the case may be) which is the limit for a compensatory award to a person calculated in accordance with section 123 of that Act or Article 157 of that Order (as the case may be).

(5) Where the worker has been working under arrangements which do not fall to be regarded as a worker's contract for the purposes of—

(a) the Employment Rights Act 1996, or

(b) in relation to Northern Ireland, the Employment Rights (Northern Ireland) Order 1996,

he shall be treated for the purposes of subsections (3) and (4) above as if any arrangements under which he has been working constituted a worker's contract falling within section 230(3)(b) of that Act or Article 3(3)(b) of that Order (as the case may be).

25–27 [omitted]

Civil procedure, evidence and appeals

28 Reversal of burden of proof

(1) Where in any civil proceedings any question arises as to whether an individual qualifies or qualified at any time for the national minimum wage, it shall be presumed that the individual qualifies or, as the case may be, qualified at that time for the national minimum wage unless the contrary is established.

(2) Where—

(a) a complaint is made—

(i) to an employment tribunal under section 23(1)(a) of the Employment Rights Act 1996 (unauthorised deductions from wages), or

(ii) to an industrial tribunal under Article 55(1)(a) of the Employment Rights (Northern Ireland) Order 1996, and

(b) the complaint relates in whole or in part to the deduction of the amount described as additional remuneration in section 17(1) above,

it shall be presumed for the purposes of the complaint, so far as relating to the deduction of that amount, that the worker in question was remunerated at a rate less than the national minimum wage unless the contrary is established.

(3) Where in any civil proceedings a person seeks to recover on a claim in contract the amount described as additional remuneration in section 17(1) above, it shall be presumed for the purposes of the proceedings, so far as relating to that amount, that the worker in question was remunerated at a rate less than the national minimum wage unless the contrary is established.

29–30 [omitted]

Offences

31 Offences

(1) If the employer of a worker who qualifies for the national minimum wage refuses or wilfully neglects to remunerate the worker for any pay reference period at a rate which is at least equal to the national minimum wage, that employer is guilty of an offence.

(2) If a person who is required to keep or preserve any record in accordance with regulations under section 9 above fails to do so, that person is guilty of an offence.

(3) If a person makes, or knowingly causes or allows to be made, in a record required to be kept in accordance with regulations under section 9 above any entry which he knows to be false in a material particular, that person is guilty of an offence.

(4) If a person, for purposes connected with the provisions of this Act, produces or furnishes, or knowingly causes or allows to be produced or furnished, any record or information which he knows to be false in a material particular, that person is guilty of an offence.

(5) If a person—

(a) intentionally delays or obstructs an officer acting for the purposes of this Act in the exercise of any power conferred by this Act, or

(b) refuses or neglects to answer any question, furnish any information or produce any document when required to do so under section 14(1) above,

that person is guilty of an offence.

(6) Where the commission by any person of an offence under subsection (1) or (2) above is due to the act or default of some other person, that other person is also guilty of the offence.

(7) A person may be charged with and convicted of an offence by virtue of subsection (6) above whether or not proceedings are taken against any other person.

(8) In any proceedings for an offence under subsection (1) or (2) above it shall be a defence for the person charged to prove that he exercised all due diligence and took all reasonable precautions to secure that the provisions of this Act, and of any relevant regulations made under it, were complied with by himself and by any person under his control.

(9) A person guilty of an offence under this section shall be liable

(a) on conviction on indictment, to a fine, or

(b) on summary conviction, to a fine not exceeding the statutory maximum.

32 Offences by bodies corporate etc.

(1) This section applies to any offence under this Act.

(2) If an offence committed by a body corporate is proved—

(a) to have been committed with the consent or connivance of an officer of the body, or

(b) to be attributable to any neglect on the part of such an officer,

the officer as well as the body corporate is guilty of the offence and liable to be proceeded against and punished accordingly.

(3) In subsection (2) above 'officer', in relation to a body corporate, means a director, manager, secretary or other similar officer of the body, or a person purporting to act in any such capacity.

(4) If the affairs of a body corporate are managed by its members, subsection (2) above applies in relation to the acts and defaults of a member in connection with his functions of management as if he were a director of the body corporate.

(5) If an offence committed by a partnership in Scotland is proved—

(a) to have been committed with the consent or connivance of a partner, or

(b) to be attributable to any neglect on the part of a partner,

the partner as well as the partnership is guilty of the offence and liable to be proceeded against and punished accordingly.

(6) In subsection (5) above, 'partner' includes a person purporting to act as a partner.

33 [omitted]

Special classes of person

34 Agency workers who are not otherwise 'workers'

(1) This section applies in any case where an individual ('the agency worker')—

(a) is supplied by a person ('the agent') to do work for another ('the principal') under a contract or other arrangements made between the agent and the principal; but

(b) is not, as respects that work, a worker, because of the absence of a worker's contract between the individual and the agent or the principal; and

(c) is not a party to a contract under which he undertakes to do the work for another party to the contract whose status is, by virtue of the contract, that of a client or customer of any profession or business undertaking carried on by the individual.

(2) In a case where this section applies, the other provisions of this Act shall have effect as if there were a worker's contract for the doing of the work by the agency worker made between the agency worker and—

(a) whichever of the agent and the principal is responsible for paying the agency worker in respect of the work; or

(b) if neither the agent nor the principal is so responsible, whichever of them pays the agency worker in respect of the work.

35 Home workers who are not otherwise 'workers'

(1) In determining for the purposes of this Act whether a home worker is or is not a worker, section 54(3)(b) below shall have effect as if for the word 'personally' there were substituted '(whether personally or otherwise)'.

(2) In this section 'home worker' means an individual who contracts with a person, for the purposes of that person's business, for the execution of work to be done in a place not under the control or management of that person.

36 Crown employment

(1) Subject to section 37 below, the provisions of this Act have effect in relation to Crown employment and persons in Crown employment as they have effect in relation to other employment and other workers.

(2) In this Act, subject to section 37 below, 'Crown employment' means employment under or for the purposes of a government department or any officer or body exercising on behalf of the Crown functions conferred by statutory provision.

(3) For the purposes of the application of the other provisions of this Act in relation to Crown employment in accordance with subsection (1) above—

(a) references to an employee or a worker shall be construed as references to a person in Crown employment;

(b) references to a contract of employment or a worker's contract shall be construed as references to the terms of employment of a person in Crown employment; and

(c) references to dismissal, or to the termination of a worker's contract, shall be construed as references to the termination of Crown employment.

37 Armed forces

(1) A person serving as a member of the naval, military or air forces of the Crown does not qualify for the national minimum wage in respect of that service.

(2) Section 36 above applies to employment by an association established for the purposes of Part XI of the Reserve Forces Act 1996, notwithstanding anything in subsection (1) above.

37A–43 [omitted]

Exclusions

44 Voluntary workers

(1) A worker employed by a charity, a voluntary organisation, an associated fund-raising body or a statutory body does not qualify for the national minimum wage in respect of that employment if he receives, and under the terms of his employment (apart from this Act) is entitled to,—

(a) no monetary payments of any description, or no monetary payments except in respect of expenses—

(i) actually incurred in the performance of his duties; or

(ii) reasonably estimated as likely to be or to have been so incurred; and

(iii) no benefits in kind of any description, or no benefits in kind other than the provision of some or all of his subsistence or of such accommodation as is reasonable in the circumstances of the employment.

(1A) For the purposes of subsection (1)(a) above, expenses which—

(a) are incurred in order to enable the worker to perform his duties,

(b) are reasonably so incurred, and

(c) are not accommodation expenses,

are to be regarded as actually incurred in the performance of his duties.

(2) A person who would satisfy the conditions in subsection (1) above but for receiving monetary payments made solely for the purpose of providing him with means of subsistence shall be taken to satisfy those conditions if—

(a) he is employed to do the work in question as a result of arrangements made between a charity acting in pursuance of its charitable purposes and the body for which the work is done; and

(b) the work is done for a charity, a voluntary organisation, an associated fund-raising body or a statutory body.

(3) For the purposes of subsection (1)(b) above—

(a) any training (other than that which a person necessarily acquires in the course of doing his work) shall be taken to be a benefit in kind; but

(b) there shall be left out of account any training provided for the sole or main purpose of improving the worker's ability to perform the work which he has agreed to do.

(4) In this section—

'associated fund-raising body' means a body of persons the profits of which are applied wholly for the purposes of a charity or voluntary organisation;

'charity' means a body of persons, or the trustees of a trust, established for charitable purposes only;

'receive', in relation to a monetary payment or a benefit in kind, means receive in respect of, or otherwise in connection with, the employment in question (whether or not under the terms of the employment);

'statutory body' means a body established by or under an enactment (including an enactment comprised in Northern Ireland legislation);

'subsistence' means such subsistence as is reasonable in the circumstances of the employment in question, and does not include accommodation;

'voluntary organisation' means a body of persons, or the trustees of a trust, which is established only for charitable purposes (whether or not those purposes are charitable within the meaning of any rule of law), benevolent purposes or philanthropic purposes, but which is not a charity.

44A Religious and other communities: resident workers

(1) A residential member of a community to which this section applies does not qualify for the national minimum wage in respect of employment by the community.

(2) Subject to subsection (3), this section applies to a community if—

(a) it is a charity or is established by a charity,

(b) a purpose of the community is to practise or advance a belief of a religious or similar nature, and

(c) all or some of its members live together for that purpose.

(3) This section does not apply to a community which—

(a) is an independent school or an alternative provision Academy that is not an independent school, or

(b) provides a course of further or higher education.

(4) The residential members of a community are those who live together as mentioned in subsection (2)(c).

(5)–(6) [omitted]

45 Prisoners

(1) A prisoner does not qualify for the national minimum wage in respect of any work which he does in pursuance of prison rules.

(2) In this section—

'prisoner' means a person detained in, or on temporary release from, a prison;

'prison' includes any other institution to which prison rules apply;

'prison rules' means—

(a) in relation to England and Wales, rules made under section 47 or 47A of the Prison Act 1952;

(b) in relation to Scotland, rules made under section 39 of the Prisons (Scotland) Act 1989; and

(c) in relation to Northern Ireland, rules made under section 13 of the Prison Act (Northern Ireland) 1953.

45A Persons discharging fines by unpaid work

A person does not qualify for the national minimum wage in respect of any work that he does in pursuance of a work order under Schedule 6 to the Courts Act 2003 (discharge of fines by unpaid work).

45B–47 [omitted]

Miscellaneous

48 Application of Act to superior employers

Where—

(a) the immediate employer of a worker is himself in the employment of some other person, and

(b) the worker is employed on the premises of that other person,

that other person shall be deemed for the purposes of this Act to be the employer of the worker jointly with the immediate employer.

49 Restrictions on contracting out

(1) Any provision in any agreement (whether a worker's contract or not) is void in so far as it purports—

(a) to exclude or limit the operation of any provision of this Act; or

(b) to preclude a person from bringing proceedings under this Act before an employment tribunal.

(2) Subsection (1) above does not apply to any agreement to refrain from instituting or continuing proceedings where a conciliation officer has taken action under—

(a) any of sections 18A to 18C of the Employment Tribunals Act 1996 (conciliation), or

(b) in relation to Northern Ireland, any of Articles 20A to 20C of the Industrial Tribunals (Northern Ireland) Order 1996.

(3) Subsection (1) above does not apply to any agreement to refrain from instituting or continuing before an employment tribunal any proceedings within—

(a) section 18(1)(c) of the Employment Tribunals Act 1996 (proceedings under or by virtue of this Act where conciliation is available), or

(b) in relation to Northern Ireland, Article 20(1)(cc) of the Industrial Tribunals (Northern Ireland) Order 1996,

if the conditions regulating settlement agreements under this Act are satisfied in relation to the agreement.

(4) For the purposes of subsection (3) above the conditions regulating settlement agreements under this Act are that—

(a) the agreement must be in writing,

(b) the agreement must relate to the particular proceedings,

(c) the employee or worker must have received advice from a relevant independent adviser as to the terms and effect of the proposed agreement and, in particular, its effect on his ability to pursue his rights before an employment tribunal,

(d) there must be in force, when the adviser gives the advice, a contract of insurance, or an indemnity provided for members of a profession or a professional body, covering the risk of a claim by the employee or worker in respect of loss arising in consequence of the advice,

(e) the agreement must identify the adviser, and

(f) the agreement must state that the conditions regulating settlement agreements under this Act are satisfied.

(5) A person is a relevant independent adviser for the purposes of subsection (4)(c) above—

(a) if he is a qualified lawyer,

(b) if he is an officer, official, employee or member of an independent trade union who has been certified in writing by the trade union as competent to give advice and as authorised to do so on behalf of the trade union,

(c) if he works at an advice centre (whether as an employee or a volunteer) and has been certified in writing by the centre as competent to give advice and as authorised to do so on behalf of the centre, or

(d) if he is a person of a description specified in an order made by the Secretary of State.

(6) But a person is not a relevant independent adviser for the purposes of subsection (4)(c) above in relation to the employee or worker—

(a) if he is employed by, or is acting in the matter for, the employer or an associated employer,

(b) in the case of a person within subsection (5)(b) or (c) above, if the trade union or advice centre is the employer or an associated employer,

(c) in the case of a person within subsection (5)(c) above, if the employee or worker makes a payment for the advice received from him, or

(d) in the case of a person of a description specified in an order under subsection (5)(d) above, if any condition specified in the order in relation to the giving of advice by persons of that description is not satisfied.

(7) [omitted]

(8) For the purposes of this section any two employers shall be treated as associated if—

(a) one is a company of which the other (directly or indirectly) has control; or

(b) both are companies of which a third person (directly or indirectly) has control; and 'associated employer' shall be construed accordingly.

(8A)–(11) [omitted]

50–53 [omitted]

Supplementary

54 Meaning of 'worker', 'employee' etc.

(1) In this Act 'employee' means an individual who has entered into or works under (or, where the employment has ceased, worked under) a contract of employment.

(2) In this Act 'contract of employment' means a contract of service or apprenticeship, whether express or implied, and (if it is express) whether oral or in writing.

(3) In this Act 'worker' (except in the phrases 'agency worker' and 'home worker') means an individual who has entered into or works under (or, where the employment has ceased, worked under)—

(a) a contract of employment; or

(b) any other contract, whether express or implied and (if it is express) whether oral or in writing, whereby the individual undertakes to do or perform personally any work or services for another party to the contract whose status is not by virtue of the contract that of a client or customer of any profession or business undertaking carried on by the individual;

and any reference to a worker's contract shall be construed accordingly.

(4) In this Act 'employer', in relation to an employee or a worker, means the person by whom the employee or worker is (or, where the employment has ceased, was) employed.

(5) In this Act 'employment'—

(a) in relation to an employee, means employment under a contract of employment; and

(b) in relation to a worker, means employment under his contract; and 'employed' shall be construed accordingly.

55 Interpretation

(1) In this Act, unless the context otherwise requires,—

'civil proceedings' means proceedings before an employment tribunal or civil proceedings before any other court;

'enforcement notice' shall be construed in accordance with section 19 above;

'government department' includes a Northern Ireland department, except in section 52(a) above;

'industrial tribunal' means a tribunal established under Article 3 of the Industrial Tribunals (Northern Ireland) Order 1996;

'notice' means notice in writing;

'pay reference period' shall be construed in accordance with section 1(4) above;

'penalty notice' shall be construed in accordance with section 21 above;

'person who qualifies for the national minimum wage' shall be construed in accordance with section 1(2) above; and related expressions shall be construed accordingly;

'prescribe' means prescribe by regulations;

'regulations' means regulations made by the Secretary of State, except in the case of regulations under section 47(2) or (4) above made by the Secretary of State and the Minister of Agriculture, Fisheries and Food acting jointly or by the Department of Agriculture for Northern Ireland.

(2) Any reference in this Act to a person being remunerated for a pay reference period is a reference to the person being remunerated by his employer in respect of his work in that pay reference period.

(3) Any reference in this Act to doing work includes a reference to performing services; and 'work' and other related expressions shall be construed accordingly.

(4) For the purposes of this Act, a person ceases to be of compulsory school age in Scotland when he ceases to be of school age in accordance with sections 31 and 33 of the Education (Scotland) Act 1980.

(5) Any reference in this Act to a person ceasing to be of compulsory school age shall, in relation to Northern Ireland, be construed in accordance with Article 46 of the Education and Libraries (Northern Ireland) Order 1986.

(6) Any reference in this Act to an employment tribunal shall, in relation to Northern Ireland, be construed as a reference to an industrial tribunal.

56 [omitted]

Employment Relations Act 1999

(1999, c. 26)

1–9 [omitted]

Disciplinary and grievance hearings

10 Right to be accompanied

(1) This section applies where a worker—

(a) is required or invited by his employer to attend a disciplinary or grievance hearing, and

(b) reasonably requests to be accompanied at the hearing.

(2) [repealed]

(2A) Where this section applies, the employer must permit the worker to be accompanied at the hearing by one companion who—

(a) is chosen by the worker; and

(b) is within subsection (3).

(2B) The employer must permit the worker's companion to—

(a) address the hearing in order to do any or all of the following—

(i) put the worker's case;

(ii) sum up that case;

(iii) respond on the worker's behalf to any view expressed at the hearing;

(b) confer with the worker during the hearing.

(2C) Subsection (2B) does not require the employer to permit the worker's companion to—

(a) answer questions on behalf of the worker;

(b) address the hearing if the worker indicates at it that he does not wish his companion to do so; or

(c) use the powers conferred by that subsection in a way that prevents the employer from explaining his case or prevents any other person at the hearing from making his contribution to it.

(3) A person is within this subsection if he is—

(a) employed by a trade union of which he is an official within the meaning of section 1 and 119 of the Trade Union and Labour Relations (Consolidation) Act 1992,

(b) an official of a trade union (within that meaning) whom the union has reasonably certified in writing as having experience of, or as having received training in, acting as a worker's companion at disciplinary or grievance hearings, or

(c) another of the employer's workers.

(4) If—

(a) a worker has a right under this section to be accompanied at a hearing,

(b) his chosen companion will not be available at the time proposed for the hearing by the employer, and

(c) the worker proposes an alternative time which satisfies subsection (5), the employer must postpone the hearing to the time proposed by the worker.

(5) An alternative time must—

(a) be reasonable, and

(b) fall before the end of the period of five working days beginning with the first working day after the day proposed by the employer.

(6) An employer shall permit a worker to take time off during working hours for the purpose of accompanying another of the employer's workers in accordance with a request under subsection (1)(b).

(7) Sections 168(3) and (4) and (5), 169 and 171 to 173 of the Trade Union and Labour Relations (Consolidation) Act 1992 (time off for carrying out trade union duties) shall apply in relation to subsection (6) above as they apply in relation to section 168(1) of that Act.

11 Complaint to employment tribunal

(1) A worker may present a complaint to an employment tribunal that his employer has failed, or threatened to fail, to comply with section 10 (2A), (2B) or (4).

(2) A tribunal shall not consider a complaint under this section in relation to a failure or threat unless the complaint is presented—

(a) before the end of the period of three months beginning with the date of the failure or threat, or

(b) within such further period as the tribunal considers reasonable in a case where it is satisfied that it was not reasonably practicable for the complaint to be presented before the end of that period of three months.

(2A)–(2B) [omitted]

(3) Where a tribunal finds that a complaint under this section is well-founded it shall order the employer to pay compensation to the worker of an amount not exceeding two weeks' pay.

(4) Chapter II of Part XIV of the Employment Rights Act 1996 (calculation of a week's pay) shall apply for the purposes of subsection (3); and in applying that Chapter the calculation date shall be taken to be—

(a) in the case of a claim which is made in the course of a claim for unfair dismissal, the date on which the employer's notice of dismissal was given or, if there was no notice, the effective date of termination, and

(b) in any other case, the date on which the relevant hearing took place (or was to have taken place).

(5) The limit in section 227(1) of the Employment Rights Act 1996 (maximum amount of week's pay) shall apply for the purposes of subsection (3) above.

(6) [repealed]

12 Detriment and dismissal

(1) A worker has the right not to be subjected to any detriment by any act, or any deliberate failure to act, by his employer done on the ground that he—

(a) exercised or sought to exercise the right under section 10(2A), (2B) or (4), or

(b) accompanied or sought to accompany another worker (whether of the same employer or not) pursuant to a request under that section.

(2) Section 48 of the Employment Rights Act 1996 shall apply in relation to contraventions of subsection (1) above as it applies in relation to contraventions of certain sections of that Act.

(3) A worker who is dismissed shall be regarded for the purposes of Part X of the Employment Rights Act 1996 as unfairly dismissed if the reason (or, if more than one, the principal reason) for the dismissal is that he—

(a) exercised or sought to exercise the right under section 10(2A), (2B) or (4), or

(b) accompanied or sought to accompany another worker (whether of the same employer or not) pursuant to a request under that section.

(4) Sections 108 and 109 of that Act (qualifying period of employment and upper age limit) shall not apply in relation to subsection (3) above.

(5) Sections 128 to 132 of that Act (interim relief) shall apply in relation to dismissal for the reason specified in subsection (3)(a) or (b) above as they apply in relation to dismissal for a reason specified in section 128(1)(b) of that Act.

(6) In the application of Chapter II of Part X of that Act in relation to subsection (3) above, a reference to an employee shall be taken as a reference to a worker.

(7) References in this section to a worker having accompanied or sought to accompany another worker include references to his having exercised or sought to exercise any of the powers conferred by section 10(2A) or (2B).

13 Interpretation

(1) In sections 10 to 12 and this section 'worker' means an individual who is—

(a) a worker within the meaning of section 230(3) of the Employment Rights Act 1996,

(b) an agency worker,

(c) a home worker,

(d) a person in Crown employment within the meaning of section 191 of that Act, other than a member of the naval, military, air or reserve forces of the Crown, or

(e) employed as a relevant member of the House of Lords staff or the House of Commons staff within the meaning of section 194(6) or 195(5) of that Act.

(2) In subsection (1) 'agency worker' means an individual who—

(a) is supplied by a person ('the agent') to do work for another ('the principal') by arrangement between the agent and the principal,

(b) is not a party to a worker's contract, within the meaning of section 230(3) of that Act, relating to that work, and

(c) is not a party to a contract relating to that work under which he undertakes to do the work for another party to the contract whose status is, by virtue of the contract, that of a client or customer of any professional or business undertaking carried on by the individual;

and, for the purposes of sections 10 to 12, both the agent and the principal are employers of an agency worker.

(3) In subsection (1) 'home worker' means an individual who—

(a) contracts with a person, for the purposes of the person's business, for the execution of work to be done in a place not under the person's control or management, and

(b) is not a party to a contract relating to that work under which the work is to be executed for another party to the contract whose status is, by virtue of the contract, that of a client or customer of any professional or business undertaking carried on by the individual;

and, for the purposes of sections 10 to 12, the person mentioned in paragraph (a) is the home worker's employer.

(4) For the purposes of section 10 a disciplinary hearing is a hearing which could result in—

(a) the administration of a formal warning to a worker by his employer,

(b) the taking of some other action in respect of a worker by his employer, or

(c) the confirmation of a warning issued or some other action taken.

(5) For the purposes of section 10 a grievance hearing is a hearing which concerns the performance of a duty by an employer in relation to a worker.

(6) For the purposes of section 10(5)(b) in its application to a part of Great Britain a working day is a day other than—

(a) a Saturday or a Sunday,

(b) Christmas Day or Good Friday, or

(c) a day which is a bank holiday under the Banking and Financial Dealings Act 1971 in that part of Great Britain.

14 Contracting out and conciliation

Sections 10 to 13 of this Act shall be treated as provisions of Part V of the Employment Rights Act 1996 for the purposes of—

(a) section 203(1), (2)(e) and (f), (3) and (4) of that Act (restrictions on contracting out), and

(b) section 18(1)(b) of the Employment Tribunals Act 1996 (conciliation).

15 National security employees

Sections 10 to 13 of this Act shall not apply in relation to a person employed for the purposes of—

(a) the Security Service,

(b) the Secret Intelligence Service, or

(c) the Government Communications Headquarters.

16 [omitted]; 17 [repealed]; 18–29 [omitted]

Miscellaneous

30–33 [omitted]

34 Indexation of amounts, etc.

(1) This section applies to the sums specified in the following provisions—

(za) section 27M(1) of the Employment Rights Act 1996 (complaints about tips etc: compensation);

(zb) section 27O(2) of that Act (complaints about information: compensation);

(a) section 31(1) of that Act (guarantee payments: limits);

(b) section 120(1) of that Act (unfair dismissal: minimum amount of basic award);

(c) section 124(1) of that Act (unfair dismissal: limit of compensatory award);

(d) section 186(1)(a) and (b) of that Act (employee's rights on insolvency of employer: maximum amount payable);

(e) section 227(1) of that Act (maximum amount of a week's pay for purposes of certain calculations);

(ea) section 145E(3) of the Trade Union and Labour Relations (Consolidation) Act 1992 (unlawful inducements: amount of award);

(f) section 156(1) of that Act (unfair dismissal: minimum basic award);

(g) section 176(6A) of that Act (right to membership of trade union: remedies).

(2) If the retail prices index for September of a year is higher or lower than the index for the previous September, the Secretary of State shall make an order in relation to each sum mentioned in subsection (1)—

(a) increasing each sum, if the new index is higher, or

(b) decreasing each sum, if the new index is lower,

by the same percentage as the amount of the increase or decrease of the index with effect from the following 6th April.

(3) In making the calculation required by subsection (2) the Secretary of State shall round the result to the nearest whole pound, taking 50p as nearest to the next whole pound above.

(4) [omitted]

(4A) A reference in this section to a sum specified in section 124(1) of the Employment Rights Act 1996 does not include anything specified by virtue of section 15(2)(b)(ii) of the Enterprise and Regulatory Reform Act 2013 (specified number multiplied by a week's pay of the individual concerned).

(4B) As regards a sum specified in section 124(1) of the Employment Rights Act 1996, the duty under subsection (2) to make an order with effect from 6 April in a particular year does not arise where an order varying such a sum with effect from a day within 12 months before that date has been made under section 15(1) of the Enterprise and Regulatory Reform Act 2013.

(5) In this section 'retail prices index' means—

(a) the general index of retail prices (for all items) published by the Statistics Board, or

(b) where that index is not published for a month, any substituted index or figures published by the Board.

(6) [omitted]

35–47 [omitted]

Employment Act 2002

(2002, c. 22)

38 Failure to give statement of employment particulars, etc.

(1) This section applies to proceedings before an employment tribunal relating to a claim by a worker under any of the jurisdictions listed in Schedule 5.

(2) If in the case of proceedings to which this section applies—

(a) the employment tribunal finds in favour of the worker, but makes no award to him in respect of the claim to which the proceedings relate, and

(b) when the proceedings were begun the employer was in breach of his duty to the worker under section 1(1) or 4(1) of the Employment Rights Act 1996 (c. 18) (duty to give a written statement of initial employment particulars or of particulars of change (in the case of a claim by an employee) or under section 41B or 41C of that Act (duty to give a written statement in relation to rights not to work on Sunday)),

the tribunal must, subject to subsection (5), make an award of the minimum amount to be paid by the employer to the worker and may, if it considers it just and equitable in all the circumstances, award the higher amount instead.

(3) If in the case of proceedings to which this section applies—

(a) the employment tribunal makes an award to the worker in respect of the claim to which the proceedings relate, and

(b) when the proceedings were begun the employer was in breach of his duty to the worker under section 1(1) or 4(1) of the Employment Rights Act 1996, or (in the case of a claim by a worker) under section 41B or 41C of that Act,

the tribunal must, subject to subsection (5), increase the award by the minimum amount and may, if it considers it just and equitable in all the circumstances, increase the award by the higher amount instead.

(4) In subsections (2) and (3)—

(a) references to the minimum amount are to an amount equal to two weeks' pay, and

(b) references to the higher amount are to an amount equal to four weeks' pay.

(5) The duty under subsection (2) or (3) does not apply if there are exceptional circumstances which would make an award or increase under that subsection unjust or inequitable.

(6) The amount of a week's pay of a worker shall—

(a) be calculated for the purposes of this section in accordance with Chapter 2 of Part 14 of the Employment Rights Act 1996, and

(b) not exceed the amount for the time being specified in section 227 of that Act (maximum amount of week's pay).

(6A) The provisions referred to in subsection (6) shall apply for the purposes of that subsection—

(a) as if a reference to an employee were a reference to a worker; and

(b) as if a reference to an employee's contract of employment were a reference to a worker's contract of employment or other worker's contract.

(7) For the purposes of Chapter 2 of Part 14 of the Employment Rights Act 1996 as applied by subsection (8), the calculation date shall be taken to be—

(a) if the worker was employed by the employer on the date the proceedings were begun, that date, and

(b) if he was not, in the case of an employee, the effective date of termination as defined by section 97 of that Act or in the case of all other workers the date on which the termination takes effect.

(8) [omitted]

Section 38

SCHEDULE 5

TRIBUNAL JURISDICTIONS TO WHICH SECTION 38 APPLIES

Section 145A of the Trade Union and Labour Relations (Consolidation) Act 1992 (inducements relating to union membership or activities)

Section 145B of that Act (inducements relating to collective bargaining)

Section 146 of that Act (detriment in relation to union membership and activities)

Paragraph 156 of Schedule A1 to that Act (detriment in relation to union recognition rights)

Section 23 of the Employment Rights Act 1996 (c. 18) (unauthorised deductions and payments)

Section 48 of that Act (detriment in employment)

Section 111 of that Act (unfair dismissal)

Section 163 of that Act (redundancy payments)

Section 24 of the National Minimum Wage Act 1998 (c. 39) (detriment in relation to national minimum wage)

Sections 120 and 127 of the Equality Act 2010 (discrimination etc. in work cases)

The Employment Tribunal Extension of Jurisdiction (England and Wales) Order 1994 (SI 1994/1623) (breach of employment contract and termination)

The Employment Tribunal Extension of Jurisdiction (Scotland) Order 1994 (SI 1994/1624) (corresponding provision for Scotland)

Regulation 30 of the Working Time Regulations 1998 (SI 1998/1833) (breach of regulations)

Regulation 32 of the Transnational Information and Consultation of Employees Regulations 1999 (SI 1999/3323) (detriment relating to European Works Councils)

Regulation 45 of the European Public Limited-Liability Company Regulations 2004 (SI 2004/2326) (detriment in employment)

Regulation 33 of the Information and Consultation of Employees Regulations 2004 (SI 2004/3426) (detriment in employment)

Paragraph 8 of the Schedule to the Occupational and Personal Pension Schemes (Consultation by Employers and Miscellaneous Amendment) Regulations 2006 (SI 2006/349) (detriment in employment)

Regulation 34 of the European Cooperative Society (Involvement of Employees) Regulations 2006 (detriment in relation to involvement in a European Cooperative Society)

Regulation 17 of the Cross-border Railways Services (Working Time) Regulations 2008 (breach of regulations)

Sections 120 and 127 of the Equality Act 2010 (discrimination etc in work cases)

Equality Act 2010

(2010, c. 15)

PART 1 SOCIO-ECONOMIC INEQUALITIES

1 Public sector duty regarding socio-economic inequalities
3 Enforcement

PART 2 EQUALITY: KEY CONCEPTS

Chapter 1 Protected Characteristics

4 The protected characteristics
5 Age
6 Disability
7 Gender reassignment
8 Marriage and civil partnership
9 Race
10 Religion or belief
11 Sex
12 Sexual orientation

Chapter 2 Prohibited Conduct

Discrimination
13 Direct discrimination
15 Discrimination arising from disability
16 Gender reassignment discrimination: cases of absence from work
18 Pregnancy and maternity discrimination: work cases
19 Indirect discrimination
19A Indirect discrimination: same disadvantage

Adjustments for disabled persons
20 Duty to make adjustments
21 Failure to comply with duty

Discrimination: supplementary
23 Comparison by reference to circumstances
24 Irrelevance of alleged discriminator's characteristics
25 References to particular strands of discrimination

Other prohibited conduct
26 Harassment
27 Victimisation

PART 5 WORK

Chapter 1 Employment, etc.

Employees
39 Employees and applicants
40 Employees and applicants: harassment
40A Employer duty to prevent sexual harassment of employees
41 Contract workers

Office-holders
49 Personal offices: appointments, etc.
50 Public offices: appointments, etc.
51 Public offices: recommendations for appointments, etc.
52 Interpretation and exceptions

Qualifications
53 Qualifications bodies
54 Interpretation

Employment services
55 Employment service-providers

Trade organisations
57 Trade organisations

Recruitment etc
60 Enquiries about disability and health
60A Discriminatory statements

Chapter 3 Equality of Terms

Sex equality
64 Relevant types of work
65 Equal work
66 Sex equality clause
69 Defence of material factor
70 Exclusion of sex discrimination provisions
71 Sex discrimination in relation to contractual pay

Pregnancy and maternity equality
72 Relevant types of work
73 Maternity equality clause
74 Maternity equality clause: pay
76 Exclusion of pregnancy and maternity discrimination provisions

Disclosure of information
77 Discussions about pay

Supplementary
79 Comparators
80 Interpretation and exceptions

Chapter 4 Supplementary

83 Interpretation and exceptions

PART 8 PROHIBITED CONDUCT: ANCILLARY

108 Relationships that have ended
109 Liability of employers and principals
110 Liability of employees and agents
111 Instructing, causing or inducing contraventions
112 Aiding contraventions

PART 9 ENFORCEMENT

Chapter 1 Introductory

113 Proceedings

Chapter 3 Employment Tribunals

120 Jurisdiction
122 References by court to tribunal, etc.
123 Time limits
124 Remedies: general
124A Remedies: compensation uplift in sexual harassment cases

Chapter 4 Equality of Terms

127 Jurisdiction
128 References by court to tribunal, etc.
129 Time limits
130 Section 129: supplementary
131 Assessment of whether work is of equal value
132 Remedies in non-pensions cases
135 Supplementary

Chapter 5 Miscellaneous

136 Burden of proof
141 Interpretation, etc.

PART 10 CONTRACTS, ETC.

Contracts and other agreements
142 Unenforceable terms
143 Removal or modification of unenforceable terms
144 Contracting out
Collective agreements and rules of undertakings
145 Void and unenforceable terms
146 Declaration in respect of void term, etc.
Supplementary
147 Meaning of 'qualifying settlement agreement'
148 Interpretation

PART 11 ADVANCEMENT OF EQUALITY

Chapter 1 Public Sector Equality Duty

149 Public sector equality duty
156 Enforcement

Chapter 2 Positive Action

158 Positive action: general
159 Positive action: recruitment and promotion

PART 14 GENERAL EXCEPTIONS

193 Charities
194 Charities: supplementary

PART 16 GENERAL AND MISCELLANEOUS

212 General interpretation
213 References to maternity leave, etc.

SCHEDULE 1 DISABILITY: SUPPLEMENTARY PROVISION

Part 1—Determination of disability

SCHEDULE 7 EQUALITY OF TERMS: EXCEPTIONS

Part 1—Terms of work

SCHEDULE 8 WORK: REASONABLE ADJUSTMENTS

Part 1—Introductory
Part 2—Interested disabled person
Part 3—Limitations on the duty

SCHEDULE 9 WORK: EXCEPTIONS

Part 1—Occupational requirements
Part 2—Exceptions relating to age
Part 3—Other exceptions

SCHEDULE 28 INDEX OF DEFINED EXPRESSIONS

PART 1 SOCIO-ECONOMIC INEQUALITIES

1 Public sector duty regarding socio-economic inequalities*

(1) An authority to which this section applies must, when making decisions of a strategic nature about how to exercise its functions, have due regard to the desirability of exercising them in a way that is designed to reduce the inequalities of outcome which result from socio-economic disadvantage.

(2) In deciding how to fulfil a duty to which it is subject under subsection (1), an authority must take into account any guidance issued in accordance with subsection (2A)

(2A) The guidance to be taken into account under subsection (2) is—

(a) in the case of a duty imposed on an authority in relation to devolved Scottish functions, guidance issued by the Scottish Ministers;

* **Editor's Note**: sections 1–3 are in force in Scotland and Wales but not in England. There are two subsections 1(3)—one for England and one for Scotland. Subsection 1(3A) applies to Wales.

(aa) in the case of a duty imposed on an authority in relation to devolved Welsh functions, guidance issued by the Welsh Ministers;
(b) in any other case, guidance issued by a Minister of the Crown.

(3) The authorities to which this section applies are—
(a) a Minister of the Crown;
(b) a government department other than the Security Service, the Secret Intelligence Service or the Government Communications Headquarters;
(ba) a corporate joint committee established by regulations made under Part 5 of the Local Government and Elections (Wales) Act 2021;
(c) a county council or district council in England;
(d) the Greater London Authority;
(e) a London borough council;
(f) the Common Council of the City of London in its capacity as a local authority;
(g) the Council of the Isles of Scilly;
(h)–(j) [repealed]
(k) a police and crime commissioner established for an area in England.

(3) The authorities to which this section applies are—
(a) the Scottish Ministers;
(b) Food Standards Scotland;
(c) Keeper of the Registers of Scotland;
(d) National Records of Scotland;
(e) Revenue Scotland;
(f) Scottish Courts and Tribunals Service;
(g) a council constituted under section 2 of the Local Government etc. (Scotland) Act 1994;
(h) an integration joint board established under section 9(2) of the Public Bodies (Joint Working) (Scotland) Act 2014;
(i) a Health Board constituted under section 2(1)(a) of the National Health Service (Scotland) Act 1978;
(j) a Special Health Board constituted under section 2(1)(b) of that Act;
(k) Scottish Police Authority;
(l) Highlands and Islands Enterprise;
(m) Scottish Enterprise;
(n) Scottish National Investment Bank p.l.c.;
(o) South of Scotland Enterprise.

(3A) This section also applies to the following authorities—
(a) the Welsh Ministers;
(b) a county council or county borough council in Wales;
(c) a Local Health Board established under section 11 of the National Health Service (Wales) Act 2006;
(d) an NHS Trust established under section 18 of the National Health Service (Wales) Act 2006;
(e) a Special Health Authority established under section 22 of the National Health Service (Wales) Act 2006 other than a cross-border Special Health Authority (within the meaning of section 8A(5) of the National Health Service (Wales) Act 2006);
(f) a fire and rescue authority constituted by a scheme under section 2 of the Fire and Rescue Services Act 2004, or a scheme to which section 4 of that Act applies, for an area in Wales;
(g) a National Park authority established by an order under section 63 of the Environment Act 1995 for an area in Wales;
(h) the Welsh Revenue Authority or Awdurdod Cyllid Cymru.

(4) and (5) [repealed]

(6) The reference to inequalities in subsection (1) does not include any inequalities experienced by a person as a result of being a person subject to immigration control within the meaning given by section 115(9) of the Immigration and Asylum Act 1999.

2 [omitted]

3 Enforcement

A failure in respect of a performance of a duty under section 1 does not confer a cause of action at private law.

PART 2 EQUALITY: KEY CONCEPTS

Chapter 1 Protected Characteristics

4 The protected characteristics

The following characteristics are protected characteristics—

age;
disability;
gender reassignment;
marriage and civil partnership;
pregnancy and maternity;
race;
religion or belief;
sex;
sexual orientation.

5 Age

(1) In relation to the protected characteristic of age—

(a) a reference to a person who has a particular protected characteristic is a reference to a person of a particular age group;

(b) a reference to persons who share a protected characteristic is a reference to persons of the same age group.

(2) A reference to an age group is a reference to a group of persons defined by reference to age, whether by reference to a particular age or to a range of ages.

6 Disability

(1) A person (P) has a disability if—

(a) P has a physical or mental impairment, and

(b) the impairment has a substantial and long-term adverse effect on P's ability to carry out normal day-to-day activities.

(2) A reference to a disabled person is a reference to a person who has a disability.

(3) In relation to the protected characteristic of disability—

(a) a reference to a person who has a particular protected characteristic is a reference to a person who has a particular disability;

(b) a reference to persons who share a protected characteristic is a reference to persons who have the same disability.

(4) This Act (except Part 12 and section 190) applies in relation to a person who has had a disability as it applies in relation to a person who has the disability; accordingly (except in that Part and that section)—

(a) a reference (however expressed) to a person who has a disability includes a reference to a person who has had the disability, and

(b) a reference (however expressed) to a person who does not have a disability includes a reference to a person who has not had the disability.

(5)–(6) [omitted]

7 Gender reassignment

(1) A person has the protected characteristic of gender reassignment if the person is proposing to undergo, is undergoing or has undergone a process (or part of a process) for the purpose of reassigning the person's sex by changing physiological or other attributes of sex.

(2) A reference to a transsexual person is a reference to a person who has the protected characteristic of gender reassignment.

(3) In relation to the protected characteristic of gender reassignment—

(a) a reference to a person who has a particular protected characteristic is a reference to a transsexual person;

(b) a reference to persons who share a protected characteristic is a reference to transsexual persons.

8 Marriage and civil partnership

(1) A person has the protected characteristic of marriage and civil partnership if the person is married or is a civil partner.

(2) In relation to the protected characteristic of marriage and civil partnership—

(a) a reference to a person who has a particular protected characteristic is a reference to a person who is married or is a civil partner;

(b) a reference to persons who share a protected characteristic is a reference to persons who are married or are civil partners.

9 Race

(1) Race includes—

(a) colour;

(b) nationality;

(c) ethnic or national origins.

(2) In relation to the protected characteristic of race—

(a) a reference to a person who has a particular protected characteristic is a reference to a person of a particular racial group;

(b) a reference to persons who share a protected characteristic is a reference to persons of the same racial group.

(3) A racial group is a group of persons defined by reference to race; and a reference to a person's racial group is a reference to a racial group into which the person falls.

(4) The fact that a racial group comprises two or more distinct racial groups does not prevent it from constituting a particular racial group.

(5) A Minister of the Crown—

(a) must by order amend this section so as to provide for caste to be an aspect of race;

(b) may by order amend this Act so as to provide for an exception to a provision of this Act to apply, or not to apply, to caste or to apply, or not to apply, to caste in specified circumstances.

(6) The power under section 207(4)(b), in its application to subsection (5), includes power to amend this Act.

10 Religion or belief

(1) Religion means any religion and a reference to religion includes a reference to a lack of religion.

(2) Belief means any religious or philosophical belief and a reference to belief includes a reference to a lack of belief.

(3) In relation to the protected characteristic of religion or belief—

(a) a reference to a person who has a particular protected characteristic is a reference to a person of a particular religion or belief;

(b) a reference to persons who share a protected characteristic is a reference to persons who are of the same religion or belief.

11 Sex

In relation to the protected characteristic of sex—

(a) a reference to a person who has a particular protected characteristic is a reference to a man or to a woman;

(b) a reference to persons who share a protected characteristic is a reference to persons of the same sex.

12 Sexual orientation

(1) Sexual orientation means a person's sexual orientation towards—

(a) persons of the same sex,

(b) persons of the opposite sex, or

(c) persons of either sex.

(2) In relation to the protected characteristic of sexual orientation—

(a) a reference to a person who has a particular protected characteristic is a reference to a person who is of a particular sexual orientation;

(b) a reference to persons who share a protected characteristic is a reference to persons who are of the same sexual orientation.

Chapter 2 Prohibited Conduct

Discrimination

13 Direct discrimination

(1) A person (A) discriminates against another (B) if, because of a protected characteristic, A treats B less favourably than A treats or would treat others.

(2) If the protected characteristic is age, A does not discriminate against B if A can show A's treatment of B to be a proportionate means of achieving a legitimate aim.

(3) If the protected characteristic is disability, and B is not a disabled person, A does not discriminate against B only because A treats or would treat disabled persons more favourably than A treats B.

(4) If the protected characteristic is marriage and civil partnership, this section applies to a contravention of Part 5 (work) only if the treatment is because it is B who is married or a civil partner.

(5) If the protected characteristic is race, less favourable treatment includes segregating B from others.

(6) If the protected characteristic is sex—

(a) less favourable treatment of a woman includes less favourable treatment of her because she is breast-feeding;

(b) in a case where B is a man, no account is to be taken of special treatment afforded to a woman in connection with pregnancy, childbirth or maternity.

(7) [repealed]

(8) This section is subject to sections 17(6) and 18(7).

14 [omitted]

15 Discrimination arising from disability

(1) A person (A) discriminates against a disabled person (B) if—

(a) A treats B unfavourably because of something arising in consequence of B's disability, and

(b) A cannot show that the treatment is a proportionate means of achieving a legitimate aim.

(2) Subsection (1) does not apply if A shows that A did not know, and could not reasonably have been expected to know, that B had the disability.

16 Gender reassignment discrimination: cases of absence from work

(1) This section has effect for the purposes of the application of Part 5 (work) to the protected characteristic of gender reassignment.

(2) A person (A) discriminates against a transsexual person (B) if, in relation to an absence of B's that is because of gender reassignment, A treats B less favourably than A would treat B if—

(a) B's absence was because of sickness or injury, or

(b) B's absence was for some other reason and it is not reasonable for B to be treated less favourably.

(3) A person's absence is because of gender reassignment if it is because the person is proposing to undergo, is undergoing or has undergone the process (or part of the process) mentioned in section 7(1).

17 [omitted]

18 Pregnancy and maternity discrimination: work cases

(1) This section has effect for the purposes of the application of Part 5 (work) to the protected characteristic of pregnancy and maternity.

(2) A person (A) discriminates against a woman if, in or after the protected period in relation to a pregnancy of hers, A treats her unfavourably—

(a) because of the pregnancy, or

(b) because of illness suffered by her in that protected period as a result of the pregnancy.

(3) A person (A) discriminates against a woman if A treats her unfavourably because she is on compulsory maternity leave or on equivalent compulsory maternity leave.

(4) A person (A) discriminates against a woman if A treats her unfavourably because she is exercising or seeking to exercise, or has exercised or sought to exercise, the right to ordinary or additional maternity leave or a right to equivalent maternity leave.

(5) [repealed]

(6) The protected period, in relation to a woman's pregnancy, begins when the pregnancy begins, and ends—

(a) if she has the right to ordinary and additional maternity leave, at the end of the additional maternity leave period or (if earlier) when she returns to work after the pregnancy;

(aa) if she does not have that right, but has a right to equivalent maternity leave, at the end of that leave period, or (if earlier) when she returns to work after the pregnancy;

(b) if she does not have a right as described in paragraph (a) or (aa) at the end of the period of 2 weeks beginning with the end of the pregnancy.

(6A) For the purposes of this section—

'equivalent compulsory maternity leave' means a period of leave—

(a) which is of a substantially similar nature (regardless of its length) to compulsory maternity leave, and

(b) which is provided for under a statutory or contractual scheme;

'equivalent maternity leave' means a period of leave—

(a) which is of a substantially similar nature (regardless of its length) to ordinary or additional maternity leave or both, and

(b) which is provided for under a statutory or contractual scheme

(7) Section 13, so far as relating to sex discrimination, does not apply to treatment of a woman in so far as—

(a) it is in or after the protected period in relation to her and is for a reason mentioned in paragraph (a) or (b) of subsection (2), or

(b) it is for a reason mentioned in subsection (3) or (4).

19 Indirect discrimination

(1) A person (A) discriminates against another (B) if A applies to B a provision, criterion or practice which is discriminatory in relation to a relevant protected characteristic of B's.

(2) For the purposes of subsection (1), a provision, criterion or practice is discriminatory in relation to a relevant protected characteristic of B's if—

(a) A applies, or would apply, it to persons with whom B does not share the characteristic,

(b) it puts, or would put, persons with whom B shares the characteristic at a particular disadvantage when compared with persons with whom B does not share it,

(c) it puts, or would put, B at that disadvantage, and

(d) A cannot show it to be a proportionate means of achieving a legitimate aim.

(3) The relevant protected characteristics are—

age;
disability;
gender reassignment;
marriage and civil partnership;
race;
religion or belief;
sex;
sexual orientation.

19A Indirect discrimination: same disadvantage

(1) A person (A) discriminates against another (B) if—

(a) A applies to B a provision, criterion or practice,

(b) A also applies, or would apply, the provision, criterion or practice to—

(i) persons who share a relevant protected characteristic, and

(ii) persons who do not share that relevant protected characteristic,

(c) B does not share that relevant protected characteristic,

(d) the provision, criterion or practice puts, or would put, persons with the relevant protected characteristic at a particular disadvantage when compared with persons who do not share the relevant protected characteristic,

(e) the provision, criterion or practice puts, or would put, B at substantively the same disadvantage as persons who do share the relevant protected characteristic, and

(f) A cannot show that the provision, criterion or practice is a proportionate means of achieving a legitimate aim.

(2) The relevant protected characteristics for the purposes of this section are—

age;
disability;
gender reassignment;
marriage and civil partnership;
race;
religion or belief;
sex;
sexual orientation.

Adjustments for disabled persons

20 Duty to make adjustments

(1) Where this Act imposes a duty to make reasonable adjustments on a person, this section, sections 21 and 22 and the applicable Schedule apply; and for those purposes, a person on whom the duty is imposed is referred to as A.

(2) The duty comprises the following three requirements.

(3) The first requirement is a requirement, where a provision, criterion or practice of A's puts a disabled person at a substantial disadvantage in relation to a relevant matter in comparison with persons who are not disabled, to take such steps as it is reasonable to have to take to avoid the disadvantage.

(4) The second requirement is a requirement, where a physical feature puts a disabled person at a substantial disadvantage in relation to a relevant matter in comparison with persons who are not disabled, to take such steps as it is reasonable to have to take to avoid the disadvantage.

(5) The third requirement is a requirement, where a disabled person would, but for the provision of an auxiliary aid, be put at a substantial disadvantage in relation to a relevant matter in

comparison with persons who are not disabled, to take such steps as it is reasonable to have to take to provide the auxiliary aid.

(6) Where the first or third requirement relates to the provision of information, the steps which it is reasonable for A to have to take include steps for ensuring that in the circumstances concerned the information is provided in an accessible format.

(7) A person (A) who is subject to a duty to make reasonable adjustments is not (subject to express provision to the contrary) entitled to require a disabled person, in relation to whom A is required to comply with the duty, to pay to any extent A's costs of complying with the duty.

(8) A reference in section 21 or 22 or an applicable Schedule to the first, second or third requirement is to be construed in accordance with this section.

(9) In relation to the second requirement, a reference in this section or an applicable Schedule to avoiding a substantial disadvantage includes a reference to—

(a) removing the physical feature in question,
(b) altering it, or
(c) providing a reasonable means of avoiding it.

(10) A reference in this section, section 21 or 22 or an applicable Schedule (apart from paragraphs 2 to 4 of Schedule 4) to a physical feature is a reference to—

(a) a feature arising from the design or construction of a building,
(b) a feature of an approach to, exit from or access to a building,
(c) a fixture or fitting, or furniture, furnishings, materials, equipment or other chattels, in or on premises, or
(d) any other physical element or quality.

(11) A reference in this section, section 21 or 22 or an applicable Schedule to an auxiliary aid includes a reference to an auxiliary service.

(12) A reference in this section or an applicable Schedule to chattels is to be read, in relation to Scotland, as a reference to moveable property.

(13) The applicable Schedule is, in relation to the Part of this Act specified in the first column of the Table, the Schedule specified in the second column.

Part of this Act	*Applicable Schedule*
Part 3 (services and public functions)	Schedule 2
Part 4 (premises)	Schedule 4
Part 5 (work)	Schedule 8
Part 6 (education)	Schedule 13
Part 7 (associations)	Schedule 15
Each of the Parts mentioned above	Schedule 21

21 Failure to comply with duty

(1) A failure to comply with the first, second or third requirement is a failure to comply with a duty to make reasonable adjustments.

(2) A discriminates against a disabled person if A fails to comply with that duty in relation to that person.

(3) A provision of an applicable Schedule which imposes a duty to comply with the first, second or third requirement applies only for the purpose of establishing whether A has contravened this Act by virtue of subsection (2); a failure to comply is, accordingly, not actionable by virtue of another provision of this Act or otherwise.

22 [omitted]

Discrimination: supplementary

23 Comparison by reference to circumstances

(1) On a comparison of cases for the purposes of section 13, 14, 19 or 19A there must be no material difference between the circumstances relating to each case.

(2) The circumstances relating to a case include a person's abilities if—

(a) on a comparison for the purposes of section 13, the protected characteristic is disability;

(b) on a comparison for the purposes of section 14, one of the protected characteristics in the combination is disability.

(3) If the protected characteristic is sexual orientation, the fact that one person (whether or not the person referred to as B) is a civil partner while another is married is not a material difference between the circumstances relating to each case.

(4) If the protected characteristic is sexual orientation, the fact that one person (whether or not the person referred to as B) is married to, or the civil partner of, a person of the same sex while another is married to, or the civil partner of, a person of the opposite sex is not a material difference between the circumstances relating to each case.

24 Irrelevance of alleged discriminator's characteristics

(1) For the purpose of establishing a contravention of this Act by virtue of section 13(1), it does not matter whether A has the protected characteristic.

(2) For the purpose of establishing a contravention of this Act by virtue of section 14(1), it does not matter—

(a) whether A has one of the protected characteristics in the combination;

(b) whether A has both.

25 References to particular strands of discrimination

(1) Age discrimination is—

(a) discrimination within section 13 because of age;

(b) discrimination within section 19 or 19A where the relevant protected characteristic is age.

(2) Disability discrimination is—

(a) discrimination within section 13 because of disability;

(b) discrimination within section 15;

(c) discrimination within section 19 or 19A where the relevant protected characteristic is disability;

(d) discrimination within section 21.

(3) Gender reassignment discrimination is—

(a) discrimination within section 13 because of gender reassignment;

(b) discrimination within section 16;

(c) discrimination within section 19 or 19A where the relevant protected characteristic is gender reassignment.

(4) Marriage and civil partnership discrimination is—

(a) discrimination within section 13 because of marriage and civil partnership;

(b) discrimination within section 19 or 19A where the relevant protected characteristic is marriage and civil partnership.

(5) Pregnancy and maternity discrimination is discrimination within section 17 or 18.

(6) Race discrimination is—

(a) discrimination within section 13 because of race;

(b) discrimination within section 19 or 19A where the relevant protected characteristic is race.

(7) Religious or belief-related discrimination is—

(a) discrimination within section 13 because of religion or belief;

(b) discrimination within section 19 or 19A where the relevant protected characteristic is religion or belief.

(8) Sex discrimination is—

(a) discrimination within section 13 because of sex;

(b) discrimination within section 19 or 19A where the relevant protected characteristic is sex.

(9) Sexual orientation discrimination is—

(a) discrimination within section 13 because of sexual orientation;

(b) discrimination within section 19 or 19A where the relevant protected characteristic is sexual orientation.

Other prohibited conduct

26 Harassment

(1) A person (A) harasses another (B) if—

(a) A engages in unwanted conduct related to a relevant protected characteristic, and

(b) the conduct has the purpose or effect of—

(i) violating B's dignity, or

(ii) creating an intimidating, hostile, degrading, humiliating or offensive environment for B.

(2) A also harasses B if—

(a) A engages in unwanted conduct of a sexual nature, and

(b) the conduct has the purpose or effect referred to in subsection (1)(b).

(3) A also harasses B if—

(a) A or another person engages in unwanted conduct of a sexual nature or that is related to gender reassignment or sex,

(b) the conduct has the purpose or effect referred to in subsection (1)(b), and

(c) because of B's rejection of or submission to the conduct, A treats B less favourably than A would treat B if B had not rejected or submitted to the conduct.

(4) In deciding whether conduct has the effect referred to in subsection (1)(b), each of the following must be taken into account—

(a) the perception of B;

(b) the other circumstances of the case;

(c) whether it is reasonable for the conduct to have that effect.

(5) The relevant protected characteristics are—

age;
disability;
gender reassignment;
race;
religion or belief;
sex;
sexual orientation.

27 Victimisation

(1) A person (A) victimises another person (B) if A subjects B to a detriment because—

(a) B does a protected act, or

(b) A believes that B has done, or may do, a protected act.

(2) Each of the following is a protected act—

(a) bringing proceedings under this Act;

(b) giving evidence or information in connection with proceedings under this Act;

(c) doing any other thing for the purposes of or in connection with this Act;

(d) making an allegation (whether or not express) that A or another person has contravened this Act.

(3) Giving false evidence or information, or making a false allegation, is not a protected act if the evidence or information is given, or the allegation is made, in bad faith.

(4) This section applies only where the person subjected to a detriment is an individual.

(5) The reference to contravening this Act includes a reference to committing a breach of an equality clause or rule.

28–38 [omitted]

PART 5 WORK

Chapter 1 Employment, etc.

Employees

39 Employees and applicants

(1) An employer (A) must not discriminate against a person (B)—
(a) in the arrangements A makes for deciding to whom to offer employment;
(b) as to the terms on which A offers B employment;
(c) by not offering B employment.

(2) An employer (A) must not discriminate against an employee of A's (B)—
(a) as to B's terms of employment;
(b) in the way A affords B access, or by not affording B access, to opportunities for promotion, transfer or training or for receiving any other benefit, facility or service;
(c) by dismissing B;
(d) by subjecting B to any other detriment.

(3) An employer (A) must not victimise a person (B)—
(a) in the arrangements A makes for deciding to whom to offer employment;
(b) as to the terms on which A offers B employment;
(c) by not offering B employment.

(4) An employer (A) must not victimise an employee of A's (B)—
(a) as to B's terms of employment;
(b) in the way A affords B access, or by not affording B access, to opportunities for promotion, transfer or training or for any other benefit, facility or service;
(c) by dismissing B;
(d) by subjecting B to any other detriment.

(5) A duty to make reasonable adjustments applies to an employer.

(6) Subsection (1)(b), so far as relating to sex or pregnancy and maternity, does not apply to a term that relates to pay—
(a) unless, were B to accept the offer, an equality clause or rule would have effect in relation to the term, or
(b) if paragraph (a) does not apply, except in so far as making an offer on terms including that term amounts to a contravention of subsection (1)(b) by virtue of section 13, 14 or 18.

(7) In subsections (2)(c) and (4)(c), the reference to dismissing B includes a reference to the termination of B's employment—
(a) by the expiry of a period (including a period expiring by reference to an event or circumstance);
(b) by an act of B's (including giving notice) in circumstances such that B is entitled, because of A's conduct, to terminate the employment without notice.

(8) Subsection (7)(a) does not apply if, immediately after the termination, the employment is renewed on the same terms.

40 Employees and applicants: harassment

(1) An employer (A) must not, in relation to employment by A, harass a person (B)—
(a) who is an employee of A's;
(b) who has applied to A for employment.

(2)–(4) [repealed]

40A Employer duty to prevent sexual harassment of employees

(1) An employer (A) must take reasonable steps to prevent sexual harassment of employees of A in the course of their employment.

(2) 'Sexual harassment' in subsection (1) means harassment of the kind described in section 26(2) (unwanted conduct of a sexual nature).

(3) A contravention of subsection (1) (or a contravention of section 111 or 112 that relates to a contravention of subsection (1)) is enforceable as an unlawful act under Part 1 of the Equality Act 2006 (and, by virtue of section 120(8) and (9), is enforceable only by the Commission under that Part or by an employment tribunal in accordance with section 124A (compensation uplift in employee sexual harassment cases)).

41 Contract workers

(1) A principal must not discriminate against a contract worker—

(a) as to the terms on which the principal allows the worker to do the work;

(b) by not allowing the worker to do, or to continue to do, the work;

(c) in the way the principal affords the worker access, or by not affording the worker access, to opportunities for receiving a benefit, facility or service;

(d) by subjecting the worker to any other detriment.

(2) A principal must not, in relation to contract work, harass a contract worker.

(3) A principal must not victimise a contract worker—

(a) as to the terms on which the principal allows the worker to do the work;

(b) by not allowing the worker to do, or to continue to do, the work;

(c) in the way the principal affords the worker access, or by not affording the worker access, to opportunities for receiving a benefit, facility or service;

(d) by subjecting the worker to any other detriment.

(4) A duty to make reasonable adjustments applies to a principal (as well as to the employer of a contract worker).

(5) A 'principal' is a person who makes work available for an individual who is—

(a) employed by another person, and

(b) supplied by that other person in furtherance of a contract to which the principal is a party (whether or not that other person is a party to it).

(6) 'Contract work' is work such as is mentioned in subsection (5).

(7) A 'contract worker' is an individual supplied to a principal in furtherance of a contract such as is mentioned in subsection (5)(b).

42–48 [omitted]

Office-holders

49 Personal offices: appointments, etc.

(1) This section applies in relation to personal offices.

(2) A personal office is an office or post—

(a) to which a person is appointed to discharge a function personally under the direction of another person, and

(b) in respect of which an appointed person is entitled to remuneration.

(3) A person (A) who has the power to make an appointment to a personal office must not discriminate against a person (B)—

(a) in the arrangements A makes for deciding to whom to offer the appointment;

(b) as to the terms on which A offers B the appointment;

(c) by not offering B the appointment.

(4) A person who has the power to make an appointment to a personal office must not, in relation to the office, harass a person seeking, or being considered for, the appointment.

(5) A person (A) who has the power to make an appointment to a personal office must not victimise a person (B)—

(a) in the arrangements A makes for deciding to whom to offer the appointment;

(b) as to the terms on which A offers B the appointment;
(c) by not offering B the appointment.

(6) A person (A) who is a relevant person in relation to a personal office must not discriminate against a person (B) appointed to the office—

(a) as to the terms of B's appointment;
(b) in the way A affords B access, or by not affording B access, to opportunities for promotion, transfer or training or for receiving any other benefit, facility or service;
(c) by terminating B's appointment;
(d) by subjecting B to any other detriment.

(7) A relevant person in relation to a personal office must not, in relation to that office, harass a person appointed to it.

(8) A person (A) who is a relevant person in relation to a personal office must not victimise a person (B) appointed to the office—

(a) as to the terms of B's appointment;
(b) in the way A affords B access, or by not affording B access, to opportunities for promotion, transfer or training or for receiving any other benefit, facility or service;
(c) by terminating B's appointment;
(d) by subjecting B to any other detriment.

(9) A duty to make reasonable adjustments applies to—

(a) a person who has the power to make an appointment to a personal office;
(b) a relevant person in relation to a personal office.

(10) For the purposes of subsection (2)(a), a person is to be regarded as discharging functions personally under the direction of another person if that other person is entitled to direct the person as to when and where to discharge the functions.

(11) For the purposes of subsection (2)(b), a person is not to be regarded as entitled to remuneration merely because the person is entitled to payments—

(a) in respect of expenses incurred by the person in discharging the functions of the office or post, or
(b) by way of compensation for the loss of income or benefits the person would or might have received had the person not been discharging the functions of the office or post.

(12) Subsection (3)(b), so far as relating to sex or pregnancy and maternity, does not apply to a term that relates to pay—

(a) unless, were B to accept the offer, an equality clause or rule would have effect in relation to the term, or
(b) if paragraph (a) does not apply, except in so far as making an offer on terms including that term amounts to a contravention of subsection (3)(b) by virtue of section 13, 14 or 18.

50 Public offices: appointments, etc.

(1) This section and section 51 apply in relation to public offices.

(2) A public office is—

(a) an office or post, appointment to which is made by a member of the executive;
(b) an office or post, appointment to which is made on the recommendation of, or subject to the approval of, a member of the executive;
(c) an office or post, appointment to which is made on the recommendation of, or subject to the approval of, the House of Commons, the House of Lords, the National Assembly for Wales or the Scottish Parliament;
(d) an office or post, appointment to which is made by the Lord Chief Justice or the Senior President of Tribunals.

(3) A person (A) who has the power to make an appointment to a public office within subsection (2)(a), (b) or (d) must not discriminate against a person (B)—

(a) in the arrangements A makes for deciding to whom to offer the appointment;

(b) as to the terms on which A offers B the appointment;
(c) by not offering B the appointment.

(4) A person who has the power to make an appointment to a public office within subsection (2)(a), (b) or (d) must not, in relation to the office, harass a person seeking, or being considered for, the appointment.

(5) A person (A) who has the power to make an appointment to a public office within subsection (2)(a), (b) or (d) must not victimise a person (B)—

(a) in the arrangements A makes for deciding to whom to offer the appointment;
(b) as to the terms on which A offers B the appointment;
(c) by not offering B the appointment.

(6) A person (A) who is a relevant person in relation to a public office within subsection (2)(a), (b) or (d) must not discriminate against a person (B) appointed to the office—

(a) as to B's terms of appointment;
(b) in the way A affords B access, or by not affording B access, to opportunities for promotion, transfer or training or for receiving any other benefit, facility or service;
(c) by terminating the appointment;
(d) by subjecting B to any other detriment.

(7) A person (A) who is a relevant person in relation to a public office within subsection (2)(c) must not discriminate against a person (B) appointed to the office—

(a) as to B's terms of appointment;
(b) in the way A affords B access, or by not affording B access, to opportunities for promotion, transfer or training or for receiving any other benefit, facility or service;
(c) by subjecting B to any other detriment (other than by terminating the appointment).

(8) A relevant person in relation to a public office must not, in relation to that office, harass a person appointed to it.

(9) A person (A) who is a relevant person in relation to a public office within subsection (2)(a), (b) or (d) must not victimise a person (B) appointed to the office—

(a) as to B's terms of appointment;
(b) in the way A affords B access, or by not affording B access, to opportunities for promotion, transfer or training or for receiving any other benefit, facility or service;
(c) by terminating the appointment;
(d) by subjecting B to any other detriment.

(10) A person (A) who is a relevant person in relation to a public office within subsection (2)(c) must not victimise a person (B) appointed to the office—

(a) as to B's terms of appointment;
(b) in the way A affords B access, or by not affording B access, to opportunities for promotion, transfer or training or for receiving any other benefit, facility or service;
(c) by subjecting B to any other detriment (other than by terminating the appointment).

(11) A duty to make reasonable adjustments applies to—

(a) a relevant person in relation to a public office;
(b) a person who has the power to make an appointment to a public office within subsection (2)(a), (b) or (d).

(12) Subsection (3)(b), so far as relating to sex or pregnancy and maternity, does not apply to a term that relates to pay—

(a) unless, were B to accept the offer, an equality clause or rule would have effect in relation to the term, or
(b) if paragraph (a) does not apply, except in so far as making an offer on terms including that term amounts to a contravention of subsection (3)(b) by virtue of section 13, 14 or 18.

51 Public offices: recommendations for appointments, etc.

(1) A person (A) who has the power to make a recommendation for or give approval to an appointment to a public office within section 50(2)(a), (b) or (d), must not discriminate against a person (B)—

(a) in the arrangements A makes for deciding who to recommend for appointment or to whose appointment to give approval;
(b) by not recommending B for appointment to the office;
(c) by making a negative recommendation of B for appointment to the office;
(d) by not giving approval to the appointment of B to the office.

(2) A person who has the power to make a recommendation for or give approval to an appointment to a public office within section 50(2)(a), (b) or (d) must not, in relation to the office, harass a person seeking or being considered for the recommendation or approval.

(3) A person (A) who has the power to make a recommendation for or give approval to an appointment to a public office within section 50(2)(a), (b) or (d), must not victimise a person (B)—

(a) in the arrangements A makes for deciding who to recommend for appointment or to whose appointment to give approval;
(b) by not recommending B for appointment to the office;
(c) by making a negative recommendation of B for appointment to the office;
(d) by not giving approval to the appointment of B to the office.

(4) A duty to make reasonable adjustments applies to a person who has the power to make a recommendation for or give approval to an appointment to a public office within section 50(2)(a), (b) or (d).

(5) A reference in this section to a person who has the power to make a recommendation for or give approval to an appointment to a public office within section 50(2)(a) or (d) is a reference only to a relevant body which has that power; and for that purpose 'relevant body' means a body established—

(a) by or in pursuance of an enactment, or
(b) by a member of the executive.

52 Interpretation and exceptions

(1) This section applies for the purposes of sections 49 to 51.

(2) 'Personal office' has the meaning given in section 49.

(3) 'Public office' has the meaning given in section 50.

(4) An office or post which is both a personal office and a public office is to be treated as being a public office only.

(5) Appointment to an office or post does not include election to it.

(6) 'Relevant person', in relation to an office, means the person who, in relation to a matter specified in the first column of the table, is specified in the second column (but a reference to a relevant person does not in any case include the House of Commons, the House of Lords, the National Assembly for Wales or the Scottish Parliament).

Matter	*Relevant person*
A term of appointment	The person who has the power to set the term.
Access to an opportunity	The person who has the power to afford access to the opportunity (or, if there is no such person, the person who has the power to make the appointment).
Terminating an appointment	The person who has the power to terminate the appointment.
Subjecting an appointee to any other detriment	The person who has the power in relation to the matter to which the conduct in question relates (or, if there is no such person, the person who has the power to make the appointment).
Harassing an appointee	The person who has the power in relation to the matter to which the conduct in question relates.

(7) A reference to terminating a person's appointment includes a reference to termination of the appointment—

(a) by the expiry of a period (including a period expiring by reference to an event or circumstance);

(b) by an act of the person (including giving notice) in circumstances such that the person is entitled, because of the relevant person's conduct, to terminate the appointment without notice.

(8) Subsection (7)(a) does not apply if, immediately after the termination, the appointment is renewed on the same terms.

(9) [omitted]

Qualifications

53 Qualifications bodies

(1) A qualifications body (A) must not discriminate against a person (B)—

(a) in the arrangements A makes for deciding upon whom to confer a relevant qualification;

(b) as to the terms on which it is prepared to confer a relevant qualification on B;

(c) by not conferring a relevant qualification on B.

(2) A qualifications body (A) must not discriminate against a person (B) upon whom A has conferred a relevant qualification—

(a) by withdrawing the qualification from B;

(b) by varying the terms on which B holds the qualification;

(c) by subjecting B to any other detriment.

(3) A qualifications body must not, in relation to conferment by it of a relevant qualification, harass—

(a) a person who holds the qualification, or

(b) a person who applies for it.

(4) A qualifications body (A) must not victimise a person (B)—

(a) in the arrangements A makes for deciding upon whom to confer a relevant qualification;

(b) as to the terms on which it is prepared to confer a relevant qualification on B;

(c) by not conferring a relevant qualification on B.

(5) A qualifications body (A) must not victimise a person (B) upon whom A has conferred a relevant qualification—

(a) by withdrawing the qualification from B;

(b) by varying the terms on which B holds the qualification;

(c) by subjecting B to any other detriment.

(6) A duty to make reasonable adjustments applies to a qualifications body.

(7) The application by a qualifications body of a competence standard to a disabled person is not disability discrimination unless it is discrimination by virtue of section 19.

54 Interpretation

(1) This section applies for the purposes of section 53.

(2) A qualifications body is an authority or body which can confer a relevant qualification.

(3) A relevant qualification is an authorisation, qualification, recognition, registration, enrolment, approval or certification which is needed for, or facilitates engagement in, a particular trade or profession.

(4) An authority or body is not a qualifications body in so far as—

(a) it can confer a qualification to which section 96 applies,

(b) it is the responsible body of a school to which section 85 applies,

(c) it is the governing body of an institution to which section 91 applies,

(d) it exercises functions under the Education Acts, or

(e) it exercises functions under the Education (Scotland) Act 1980.

(5) A reference to conferring a relevant qualification includes a reference to renewing or extending the conferment of a relevant qualification.

(6) A competence standard is an academic, medical or other standard applied for the purpose of determining whether or not a person has a particular level of competence or ability.

Employment services

55 Employment service-providers

(1) A person (an 'employment service-provider') concerned with the provision of an employment service must not discriminate against a person—

(a) in the arrangements the service-provider makes for selecting persons to whom to provide, or to whom to offer to provide, the service;

(b) as to the terms on which the service-provider offers to provide the service to the person;

(c) by not offering to provide the service to the person.

(2) An employment service-provider (A) must not, in relation to the provision of an employment service, discriminate against a person (B)—

(a) as to the terms on which A provides the service to B;

(b) by not providing the service to B;

(c) by terminating the provision of the service to B;

(d) by subjecting B to any other detriment.

(3) An employment service-provider must not, in relation to the provision of an employment service, harass—

(a) a person who asks the service-provider to provide the service;

(b) a person for whom the service-provider provides the service.

(4) An employment service-provider (A) must not victimise a person (B)—

(a) in the arrangements A makes for selecting persons to whom to provide, or to whom to offer to provide, the service;

(b) as to the terms on which A offers to provide the service to B;

(c) by not offering to provide the service to B.

(5) An employment service-provider (A) must not, in relation to the provision of an employment service, victimise a person (B)—

(a) as to the terms on which A provides the service to B;

(b) by not providing the service to B;

(c) by terminating the provision of the service to B;

(d) by subjecting B to any other detriment.

(6) A duty to make reasonable adjustments applies to an employment service-provider, except in relation to the provision of a vocational service.

(7) The duty imposed by section 29(7)(a) applies to a person concerned with the provision of a vocational service; but a failure to comply with that duty in relation to the provision of a vocational service is a contravention of this Part for the purposes of Part 9 (enforcement).

56 [omitted]

Trade organisations

57 Trade organisations

(1) A trade organisation (A) must not discriminate against a person (B)—

(a) in the arrangements A makes for deciding to whom to offer membership of the organisation;

(b) as to the terms on which it is prepared to admit B as a member;

(c) by not accepting B's application for membership.

(2) A trade organisation (A) must not discriminate against a member (B)—

(a) in the way it affords B access, or by not affording B access, to opportunities for receiving a benefit, facility or service;

(b) by depriving B of membership;

(c) by varying the terms on which B is a member;

(d) by subjecting B to any other detriment.

(3) A trade organisation must not, in relation to membership of it, harass—

(a) a member, or
(b) an applicant for membership.

(4) A trade organisation (A) must not victimise a person (B)—
(a) in the arrangements A makes for deciding to whom to offer membership of the organisation;
(b) as to the terms on which it is prepared to admit B as a member;
(c) by not accepting B's application for membership.

(5) A trade organisation (A) must not victimise a member (B)—
(a) in the way it affords B access, or by not affording B access, to opportunities for receiving a benefit, facility or service;
(b) by depriving B of membership;
(c) by varying the terms on which B is a member;
(d) by subjecting B to any other detriment.

(6) A duty to make reasonable adjustments applies to a trade organisation.

(7) A trade organisation is—
(a) an organisation of workers,
(b) an organisation of employers, or
(c) any other organisation whose members carry on a particular trade or profession for the purposes of which the organisation exists.

58–59 [omitted]

Recruitment etc

60 Enquiries about disability and health

(1) A person (A) to whom an application for work is made must not ask about the health of the applicant (B)—
(a) before offering work to B, or
(b) where A is not in a position to offer work to B, before including B in a pool of applicants from whom A intends (when in a position to do so) to select a person to whom to offer work.

(2) A contravention of subsection (1) (or a contravention of section 111 or 112 that relates to a contravention of subsection (1)) is enforceable as an unlawful act under Part 1 of the Equality Act 2006 (and, by virtue of section 120(8), is enforceable only by the Commission under that Part).

(3) A does not contravene a relevant disability provision merely by asking about B's health; but A's conduct in reliance on information given in response may be a contravention of a relevant disability provision.

(4) Subsection (5) applies if B brings proceedings before an employment tribunal on a complaint that A's conduct in reliance on information given in response to a question about B's health is a contravention of a relevant disability provision.

(5) In the application of section 136 to the proceedings, the particulars of the complaint are to be treated for the purposes of subsection (2) of that section as facts from which the tribunal could decide that A contravened the provision.

(6) This section does not apply to a question that A asks in so far as asking the question is necessary for the purpose of—
(a) establishing whether B will be able to comply with a requirement to undergo an assessment or establishing whether a duty to make reasonable adjustments is or will be imposed on A in relation to B in connection with a requirement to undergo an assessment,
(b) establishing whether B will be able to carry out a function that is intrinsic to the work concerned,
(c) monitoring diversity in the range of persons applying to A for work,

(d) taking action to which section 158 would apply if references in that section to persons who share (or do not share) a protected characteristic were references to disabled persons (or persons who are not disabled) and the reference to the characteristic were a reference to disability, or

(e) if A applies in relation to the work a requirement to have a particular disability, establishing whether B has that disability.

(7) In subsection (6)(b), where A reasonably believes that a duty to make reasonable adjustments would be imposed on A in relation to B in connection with the work, the reference to a function that is intrinsic to the work is to be read as a reference to a function that would be intrinsic to the work once A complied with the duty.

(8) Subsection (6)(e) applies only if A shows that, having regard to the nature or context of the work—

(a) the requirement is an occupational requirement, and

(b) the application of the requirement is a proportionate means of achieving a legitimate aim.

(9) 'Work' means employment, contract work, a position as a partner, a position as a member of an LLP, a pupillage or tenancy, being taken as a devil, membership of a stable, an appointment to a personal or public office, or the provision of an employment service; and the references in subsection (1) to offering a person work are, in relation to contract work, to be read as references to allowing a person to do the work.

(10) A reference to offering work is a reference to making a conditional or unconditional offer of work (and, in relation to contract work, is a reference to allowing a person to do the work subject to fulfilment of one or more conditions).

(11) The following, so far as relating to discrimination within section 13 because of disability, are relevant disability provisions—

(a) section 39(1)(a) or (c);

(b) section 41(1)(b);

(c) section 44(1)(a) or (c);

(d) section 45(1)(a) or (c);

(e) section 47(1)(a) or (c);

(f) section 48(1)(a) or (c);

(g) section 49(3)(a) or (c);

(h) section 50(3)(a) or (c);

(i) section 51(1);

(j) section 55(1)(a) or (c);

(k) section 60A(1).

(12) An assessment is an interview or other process designed to give an indication of a person's suitability for the work concerned.

(13) For the purposes of this section, whether or not a person has a disability is to be regarded as an aspect of that person's health.

(14) This section does not apply to anything done for the purpose of vetting applicants for work for reasons of national security.

60A Discriminatory statements

(1) A person (A) must not make a discriminatory statement in connection with a relevant decision that A makes or might make.

(2) References in this section to a 'relevant decision' are to be determined as follows—

Where A is—	*A relevant decision is—*
An employer	Deciding to whom to offer employment
A principal (as defined by section 41(5))	Deciding whether to allow a contract worker (as defined by section 41(7)) to do, or to continue to do, work
A firm or proposed firm (as defined by section 46(2) and (3))	Deciding to whom to offer a position as a partner (read in accordance with section 44(8))
An LLP or proposed LLP (as defined by section 46(4) and (5))	Deciding to whom to offer a position as a member
A barrister or a barrister's clerk (read in accordance with section 47(8))	Deciding to whom to offer a pupillage or tenancy
An advocate (as defined by section 48(9)) or an advocate's clerk (read in accordance with section 48(8))	Deciding who to take as a devil or to whom to offer membership of a stable
A person with power to make an appointment to a personal office (as defined by section 49(2))	Deciding to whom to offer the appointment
A person with power to make an appointment to a public office within section 50(2)(a), (b) or (d)	Deciding to whom to offer the appointment
A person with power to make a recommendation for or give approval to an appointment to a public office within section 50(2)(a), (b) or (d) (read in accordance with section 51(5))	Deciding who to recommend for appointment or to whose appointment to give approval
A qualifications body (as defined by section 54)	Deciding to whom to confer a relevant qualification (as defined by section 54)
A person concerned with the provision of an employment service (read in accordance with section 56)	Deciding on the selection of persons to whom to provide, or to whom to offer to provide, the employment service
A trade organisation (as defined by section 57(7))	Deciding to whom to offer membership of the organisation.

(3) For the purposes of subsection (1) a statement is discriminatory if—
(a) it is directed to the public or a section of the public, and
(b) were it made in connection with a relevant decision, the making of it would amount to treatment of a person that is direct discrimination.

(4) A statement made by a person (B) who—
(a) is not an employee of A acting in the course of B's employment, and
(b) is not an agent of A acting with A's authority,

is to be treated for the purposes of this section as if made by A if there are reasonable grounds for the public, or a section of the public, to believe that B is capable of exercising decisive influence on the making by A of a relevant decision.

(5) Regard is to be had (among other things) to the factors mentioned in subsection (6) when determining—
(a) whether a statement is made in connection with a relevant decision for the purposes of subsection (1);
(b) whether there are reasonable grounds for the belief mentioned in subsection (4).

(6) The factors are—
(a) the status of the person making the statement at the time it is made;
(b) the nature and content of the statement;
(c) the context in which the statement is made;
(d) in the case of a statement that A is treated as having made by virtue of subsection (4), the steps (if any) taken by A to disassociate A from the statement made by B.

(7) It does not matter for the purposes of this section whether or not—
(a) an individual has or may have been affected by the discriminatory statement in question;

(b) A has made, or plans to make, arrangements which would involve the making of a relevant decision.

(8) A contravention of subsection (1) (or a contravention of section 111 or 112 that relates to a contravention of subsection (1)) is enforceable as an unlawful act under Part 1 of the Equality Act 2006 (and, by virtue of section 120(8), is enforceable only by the Commission under that Part).

(9) In subsection (3) the reference to direct discrimination is to a contravention of this Act by virtue of section 13 or 18.

(10) Nothing in this section limits or otherwise affects—

(a) other prohibitions imposed by this Chapter;

(b) the application of section 109 (liability of employers and principals for acts of employees and agents).

61–63 [omitted]

Chapter 3 Equality of Terms

Sex equality

64 Relevant types of work

(1) Sections 66 to 70 apply where—

(a) a person (A) is employed on work that is equal to the work that a comparator of the opposite sex (B) does;

(b) a person (A) holding a personal or public office does work that is equal to the work that a comparator of the opposite sex (B) does.

(2) The references in subsection (1) to the work that B does are not restricted to work done contemporaneously with the work done by A.

(3) [omitted]

65 Equal work

(1) For the purposes of this Chapter, A's work is equal to that of B if it is—

(a) like B's work,

(b) rated as equivalent to B's work, or

(c) of equal value to B's work.

(2) A's work is like B's work if—

(a) A's work and B's work are the same or broadly similar, and

(b) such differences as there are between their work are not of practical importance in relation to the terms of their work.

(3) So on a comparison of one person's work with another's for the purposes of subsection (2), it is necessary to have regard to—

(a) the frequency with which differences between their work occur in practice, and

(b) the nature and extent of the differences.

(4) A's work is rated as equivalent to B's work if a job evaluation study—

(a) gives an equal value to A's job and B's job in terms of the demands made on a worker, or

(b) would give an equal value to A's job and B's job in those terms were the evaluation not made on a sex-specific system.

(5) A system is sex-specific if, for the purposes of one or more of the demands made on a worker, it sets values for men different from those it sets for women.

(6) A's work is of equal value to B's work if it is—

(a) neither like B's work nor rated as equivalent to B's work, but

(b) nevertheless equal to B's work in terms of the demands made on A by reference to factors such as effort, skill and decision-making.

66 Sex equality clause

(1) If the terms of A's work do not (by whatever means) include a sex equality clause, they are to be treated as including one.

(2) Where this section applies by virtue of section 64(1), a sex equality clause is a provision that has the following effect—

(a) if a term of A's is less favourable to A than a corresponding term of B's is to B, A's term is modified so as not to be less favourable;

(b) if A does not have a term which corresponds to a term of B's that benefits B, A's terms are modified so as to include such a term.

(3) Subsection (2)(a) applies to a term of A's relating to membership of or rights under an occupational pension scheme only in so far as a sex equality rule would have effect in relation to the term.

(4) In the case of work within section 65(1)(b), a reference in subsection (2) above to a term includes a reference to such terms (if any) as have not been determined by the rating of the work (as well as those that have).

(5)–(6) [omitted]

67–68 [omitted]

69 Defence of material factor

(1) The sex equality clause in A's terms has no effect in relation to a difference between A's terms and B's terms if the responsible person shows that the difference is because of a material factor reliance on which—

(a) does not involve treating A less favourably because of A's sex than the responsible person treats B, and

(b) if the factor is within subsection (2), is a proportionate means of achieving a legitimate aim.

(2) A factor is within this subsection if A shows that, as a result of the factor, A and persons of the same sex doing work equal to A's are put at a particular disadvantage when compared with persons of the opposite sex doing work equal to A's.

(3) For the purposes of subsection (1), the long-term objective of reducing inequality between men's and women's terms of work is always to be regarded as a legitimate aim.

(4) [omitted]

(5) 'Relevant matter' has the meaning given in section 67.

(6) For the purposes of this section, a factor is not material unless it is a material difference between A's case and B's.

70 Exclusion of sex discrimination provisions

(1) The relevant sex discrimination provision has no effect in relation to a term of A's that—

(a) is modified by, or included by virtue of, a sex equality clause or rule, or

(b) would be so modified or included but for section 69 or Part 2 of Schedule 7.

(2) Neither of the following is sex discrimination for the purposes of the relevant sex discrimination provision—

(a) the inclusion in A's terms of a term that is less favourable as referred to in section 66(2)(a);

(b) the failure to include in A's terms a corresponding term as referred to in section 66(2)(b).

(3) The relevant sex discrimination provision is, in relation to work of a description given in the first column of the table, the provision referred to in the second column so far as relating to sex.

Description of work	*Provision*
Employment	Section 39(2)
Appointment to a personal office	Section 49(6)
Appointment to a public office	Section 50(6)

71 Sex discrimination in relation to contractual pay

(1) This section applies in relation to a term of a person's work—

(a) that relates to pay, but

(b) in relation to which a sex equality clause or rule has no effect.

(2) The relevant sex discrimination provision (as defined by section 70) has no effect in relation to the term except in so far as treatment of the person amounts to a contravention of the provision by virtue of section 13 or 14.

Pregnancy and maternity equality

72 Relevant types of work

Sections 73 to 76 apply where a woman—

(a) is employed, or

(b) holds a personal or public office.

73 Maternity equality clause

(1) If the terms of the woman's work do not (by whatever means) include a maternity equality clause, they are to be treated as including one.

(2) A maternity equality clause is a provision that, in relation to the terms of the woman's work, has the effect referred to in section 74(1), (6) and (8).

(3) In the case of a term relating to membership of or rights under an occupational pension scheme, a maternity equality clause has only such effect as a maternity equality rule would have.

74 Maternity equality clause: pay

(1) A term of the woman's work that provides for maternity-related pay to be calculated by reference to her pay at a particular time is, if each of the following three conditions is satisfied, modified as mentioned in subsection (5).

(2) The first condition is that, after the time referred to in subsection (1) but before the end of the protected period—

(a) her pay increases, or

(b) it would have increased had she not been on maternity leave.

(3) The second condition is that the maternity-related pay is not—

(a) what her pay would have been had she not been on maternity leave, or

(b) the difference between the amount of statutory maternity pay to which she is entitled and what her pay would have been had she not been on maternity leave.

(4) The third condition is that the terms of her work do not provide for the maternity-related pay to be subject to—

(a) an increase as mentioned in subsection (2)(a), or

(b) an increase that would have occurred as mentioned in subsection (2)(b).

(5) The modification referred to in subsection (1) is a modification to provide for the maternity-related pay to be subject to—

(a) any increase as mentioned in subsection (2)(a), or

(b) any increase that would have occurred as mentioned in subsection (2)(b).

(6) A term of her work that—

(a) provides for pay within subsection (7), but

(b) does not provide for her to be given the pay in circumstances in which she would have been given it had she not been on maternity leave,

is modified so as to provide for her to be given it in circumstances in which it would normally be given.

(7) Pay is within this subsection if it is—

(a) pay (including pay by way of bonus) in respect of times before the woman is on maternity leave,

(b) pay by way of bonus in respect of times when she is on compulsory maternity leave, or

(c) pay by way of bonus in respect of times after the end of the protected period.

(8) A term of the woman's work that—

(a) provides for pay after the end of the protected period, but

(b) does not provide for it to be subject to an increase to which it would have been subject had she not been on maternity leave,

is modified so as to provide for it to be subject to the increase.

(9) Maternity-related pay is pay (other than statutory maternity pay) to which a woman is entitled—

(a) as a result of being pregnant, or

(b) in respect of times when she is on maternity leave.

(10) A reference to the protected period is to be construed in accordance with section 18.

75 [omitted]

76 Exclusion of pregnancy and maternity discrimination provisions

(1) The relevant pregnancy and maternity discrimination provision has no effect in relation to a term of the woman's work that is modified by a maternity equality clause or rule.

(1A) The relevant pregnancy and maternity discrimination provision has no effect in relation to a term of the woman's work—

(a) that relates to pay, but

(b) in relation to which a maternity equality clause or rule has no effect.

(2) The inclusion in the woman's terms of a term that requires modification by virtue of section 73(2) or (3) is not pregnancy and maternity discrimination for the purposes of the relevant pregnancy and maternity discrimination provision.

(3) The relevant pregnancy and maternity discrimination provision is, in relation to a description of work given in the first column of the table, the provision referred to in the second column so far as relating to pregnancy and maternity.

Description of work	*Provision*
Employment	Section 39(2)
Appointment to a personal office	Section 49(6)
Appointment to a public office	Section 50(6)

Disclosure of information

77 Discussions about pay

(1) A term of a person's work that purports to prevent or restrict the person (P) from disclosing or seeking to disclose information about the terms of P's work is unenforceable against P in so far as P makes or seeks to make a relevant pay disclosure.

(2) A term of a person's work that purports to prevent or restrict the person (P) from seeking disclosure of information from a colleague about the terms of the colleague's work is unenforceable against P in so far as P seeks a relevant pay disclosure from the colleague; and 'colleague' includes a former colleague in relation to the work in question.

(3) A disclosure is a relevant pay disclosure if made for the purpose of enabling the person who makes it, or the person to whom it is made, to find out whether or to what extent there is, in relation to the work in question, a connection between pay and having (or not having) a particular protected characteristic.

(4) The following are to be treated as protected acts for the purposes of the relevant victimisation provision—

(a) seeking a disclosure that would be a relevant pay disclosure;

(b) making or seeking to make a relevant pay disclosure;

(c) receiving information disclosed in a relevant pay disclosure.

(5) The relevant victimisation provision is, in relation to a description of work specified in the first column of the table, section 27 so far as it applies for the purposes of a provision mentioned in the second column.

Description of work	*Provision by virtue of which section 27 has effect*
Employment	Section 39(3) or (4)
Appointment to a personal office	Section 49(5) or (8)
Appointment to a public office	Section 50(5) or (9)

78 [omitted]

Supplementary

79 Comparators

(1) This section applies for the purposes of this Chapter.

(2) If A is employed, B is a comparator if subsection (3), (4), (4A) or (4B) applies.

(3) This subsection applies if—

(a) B is employed by A's employer or by an associate of A's employer, and

(b) A and B work at the same establishment.

(4) This subsection applies if—

(a) B is employed by A's employer or an associate of A's employer,

(b) B works at an establishment other than the one at which A works, and

(c) common terms apply at the establishments (either generally or as between A and B).

(4A) This subsection applies if a single body—

(a) is responsible for setting or continuing the terms on which A and B are employed, and

(b) is in a position to ensure equal treatment between A and B in respect of such terms.

(4B) This subsection applies if the terms on which A and B are employed are governed by the same collective agreement.

(5) If A holds a personal or public office, B is a comparator if—

(a) B holds a personal or public office, and

(b) the person responsible for paying A is also responsible for paying B.

(6) If A is a relevant member of the House of Commons staff, B is a comparator if—

(a) B is employed by the person who is A's employer under subsection (6) of section 195 of the Employment Rights Act 1996, or

(b) if subsection (7) of that section applies in A's case, B is employed by the person who is A's employer under that subsection.

(7) If A is a relevant member of the House of Lords staff, B is a comparator if B is also a relevant member of the House of Lords staff.

(8) Section 42 does not apply to this Chapter; accordingly, for the purposes of this Chapter only, holding the office of constable is to be treated as holding a personal office.

(9) For the purposes of this section, employers are associated if—

(a) one is a company of which the other (directly or indirectly) has control, or

(b) both are companies of which a third person (directly or indirectly) has control.

(10) In subsection (4B) 'collective agreement' has the same meaning as in the Trade Union and Labour Relations (Consolidation) Act 1992 (see section 178 of that Act).

80 Interpretation and exceptions

(1) This section applies for the purposes of this Chapter.

(2) The terms of a person's work are—

(a) if the person is employed, the terms of the person's employment that are in the person's contract of employment, contract of apprenticeship or contract to do work personally;

(b) if the person holds a personal or public office, the terms of the person's appointment to the office.

(3) If work is not done at an establishment, it is to be treated as done at the establishment with which it has the closest connection.

(4) A person (P) is the responsible person in relation to another person if—

(a) P is the other's employer;

(b) P is responsible for paying remuneration in respect of a personal or public office that the other holds.

(5) A job evaluation study is a study undertaken with a view to evaluating, in terms of the demands made on a person by reference to factors such as effort, skill and decision-making, the jobs to be done—

(a) by some or all of the workers in an undertaking or group of undertakings, or

(b) in the case of the armed forces, by some or all of the members of the armed forces.

(6) In the case of Crown employment, the reference in subsection (5)(a) to an undertaking is to be construed in accordance with section 191(4) of the Employment Rights Act 1996.

(7) [repealed]; (8) [omitted]

Chapter 4 Supplementary

81–82 [omitted]

83 Interpretation and exceptions

(1) This section applies for the purposes of this Part.

(2) 'Employment' means—

(a) employment under a contract of employment, a contract of apprenticeship or a contract personally to do work;

(b) Crown employment;

(c) employment as a relevant member of the House of Commons staff;

(d) employment as a relevant member of the House of Lords staff.

(3) This Part applies to service in the armed forces as it applies to employment by a private person; and for that purpose—

(a) references to terms of employment, or to a contract of employment, are to be read as including references to terms of service;

(b) references to associated employers are to be ignored.

(4) A reference to an employer or an employee, or to employing or being employed, is (subject to section 212(11)) to be read with subsections (2) and (3); and a reference to an employer also includes a reference to a person who has no employees but is seeking to employ one or more other persons.

(5)–(11) [omitted]

84–107 [omitted]

PART 8 PROHIBITED CONDUCT: ANCILLARY

108 Relationships that have ended

(1) A person (A) must not discriminate against another (B) if—

(a) the discrimination arises out of and is closely connected to a relationship which used to exist between them, and

(b) conduct of a description constituting the discrimination would, if it occurred during the relationship, contravene this Act.

(2) A person (A) must not harass another (B) if—

(a) the harassment arises out of and is closely connected to a relationship which used to exist between them, and

(b) conduct of a description constituting the harassment would, if it occurred during the relationship, contravene this Act.

(3) It does not matter whether the relationship ends before or after the commencement of this section.

(4) A duty to make reasonable adjustments applies to A if B is placed at a substantial disadvantage as mentioned in section 20.

(5) For the purposes of subsection (4), sections 20, 21 and 22 and the applicable Schedules are to be construed as if the relationship had not ended.

(6) For the purposes of Part 9 (enforcement), a contravention of this section relates to the Part of this Act that would have been contravened if the relationship had not ended.

(7) But conduct is not a contravention of this section in so far as it also amounts to victimisation of B by A.

109 Liability of employers and principals

(1) Anything done by a person (A) in the course of A's employment must be treated as also done by the employer.

(2) Anything done by an agent for a principal, with the authority of the principal, must be treated as also done by the principal.

(3) It does not matter whether that thing is done with the employer's or principal's knowledge or approval.

(4) In proceedings against A's employer (B) in respect of anything alleged to have been done by A in the course of A's employment it is a defence for B to show that B took all reasonable steps to prevent A—

(a) from doing that thing, or

(b) from doing anything of that description.

(5) This section does not apply to offences under this Act (other than offences under Part 12 (disabled persons: transport)).

110 Liability of employees and agents

(1) A person (A) contravenes this section if—

(a) A is an employee or agent,

(b) A does something which, by virtue of section 109(1) or (2), is treated as having been done by A's employer or principal (as the case may be), and

(c) the doing of that thing by A amounts to a contravention of this Act by the employer or principal (as the case may be).

(2) It does not matter whether, in any proceedings, the employer is found not to have contravened this Act by virtue of section 109(4).

(3) A does not contravene this section if—

(a) A relies on a statement by the employer or principal that doing that thing is not a contravention of this Act, and
(b) it is reasonable for A to do so.

(4) A person (B) commits an offence if B knowingly or recklessly makes a statement mentioned in subsection (3)(a) which is false or misleading in a material respect.

(5) A person guilty of an offence under subsection (4) is liable on summary conviction to a fine not exceeding level 5 on the standard scale.

(5A) A does not contravene this section if A—
(a) does not conduct a relevant marriage,
(b) is not present at, does not carry out, or does not otherwise participate in, a relevant marriage, or
(c) does not consent to a relevant marriage being conducted, for the reason that the marriage is the marriage of a same sex couple.

(5B) Subsection (5A) applies to A only if A is within the meaning of 'person' for the purposes of section 2 of the Marriage (Same Sex Couples) Act 2013; and other expressions used in subsection (5A) and section 2 of that Act have the same meanings in that subsection as in that section.

(5BA)–(5H) [omitted]

(6) Part 9 (enforcement) applies to a contravention of this section by A as if it were the contravention mentioned in subsection (1)(c).

(7) The reference in subsection (1)(c) to a contravention of this Act does not include a reference to disability discrimination in contravention of Chapter 1 of Part 6 (schools).

111 Instructing, causing or inducing contraventions

(1) A person (A) must not instruct another (B) to do in relation to a third person (C) anything which contravenes Part 3, 4, 5, 6 or 7 or section 108(1) or (2) or 112(1) (a basic contravention).

(2) A person (A) must not cause another (B) to do in relation to a third person (C) anything which is a basic contravention.

(3) A person (A) must not induce another (B) to do in relation to a third person (C) anything which is a basic contravention.

(4) For the purposes of subsection (3), inducement may be direct or indirect.

(5) Proceedings for a contravention of this section may be brought—
(a) by B, if B is subjected to a detriment as a result of A's conduct;
(b) by C, if C is subjected to a detriment as a result of A's conduct;
(c) by the Commission.

(6) For the purposes of subsection (5), it does not matter whether—
(a) the basic contravention occurs;
(b) any other proceedings are, or may be, brought in relation to A's conduct.

(7) This section does not apply unless the relationship between A and B is such that A is in a position to commit a basic contravention in relation to B.

(8) A reference in this section to causing or inducing a person to do something includes a reference to attempting to cause or induce the person to do it.

(9) For the purposes of Part 9 (enforcement), a contravention of this section is to be treated as relating—
(a) in a case within subsection (5)(a), to the Part of this Act which, because of the relationship between A and B, A is in a position to contravene in relation to B;
(b) in a case within subsection (5)(b), to the Part of this Act which, because of the relationship between B and C, B is in a position to contravene in relation to C.

112 Aiding contraventions

(1) A person (A) must not knowingly help another (B) to do anything which contravenes Part 3, 4, 5, 6 or 7 or section 108(1) or (2) or 111 (a basic contravention).

(2) It is not a contravention of subsection (1) if—

(a) A relies on a statement by B that the act for which the help is given does not contravene this Act, and

(b) it is reasonable for A to do so.

(3) B commits an offence if B knowingly or recklessly makes a statement mentioned in subsection (2)(a) which is false or misleading in a material respect.

(4) A person guilty of an offence under subsection (3) is liable on summary conviction to a fine not exceeding level 5 on the standard scale.

(5) For the purposes of Part 9 (enforcement), a contravention of this section is to be treated as relating to the provision of this Act to which the basic contravention relates.

(6) [omitted]

PART 9 ENFORCEMENT

Chapter 1 Introductory

113 Proceedings

(1) Proceedings relating to a contravention of this Act must be brought in accordance with this Part.

(2) Subsection (1) does not apply to proceedings under Part 1 of the Equality Act 2006.

(3) Subsection (1) does not prevent—

(a) a claim for judicial review;

(b) proceedings under the Immigration Acts;

(c) proceedings under the Special Immigration Appeals Commission Act 1997;

(d) in Scotland, an application to the supervisory jurisdiction of the Court of Session.

(4) This section is subject to any express provision of this Act conferring jurisdiction on a court or tribunal.

(5) The reference to a contravention of this Act includes a reference to a breach of an equality clause or rule.

(6) Chapters 2 and 3 do not apply to proceedings relating to an equality clause or rule except in so far as Chapter 4 provides for that.

(7) This section does not apply to—

(a) proceedings for an offence under this Act;

(b) proceedings relating to a penalty under Part 12 (disabled persons: transport).

114–119 [omitted]

Chapter 3 Employment Tribunals

120 Jurisdiction

(1) An employment tribunal has, subject to section 121, jurisdiction to determine a complaint relating to—

(a) a contravention of Part 5 (work);

(b) a contravention of section 108, 111 or 112 that relates to Part 5.

(2) An employment tribunal has jurisdiction to determine an application by a responsible person (as defined by section 61) for a declaration as to the rights of that person and a worker in relation to a dispute about the effect of a non-discrimination rule.

(3) An employment tribunal also has jurisdiction to determine an application by the trustees or managers of an occupational pension scheme for a declaration as to their rights and those of a member in relation to a dispute about the effect of a non-discrimination rule.

(4) An employment tribunal also has jurisdiction to determine a question that—

(a) relates to a non-discrimination rule, and

(b) is referred to the tribunal by virtue of section 122.

(5) In proceedings before an employment tribunal on a complaint relating to a breach of a non-discrimination rule, the employer—

(a) is to be treated as a party, and

(b) is accordingly entitled to appear and be heard.

(6) Nothing in this section affects such jurisdiction as the High Court, the county court, the Court of Session or the sheriff has in relation to a non-discrimination rule.

(7) Subsection (1)(a) does not apply to a contravention of section 53 in so far as the act complained of may, by virtue of an enactment, be subject to an appeal or proceedings in the nature of an appeal.

(8) In subsection (1), the references to Part 5 do not include references to section 40A(1) or 60(1) or 60A(1).

(9) Subsection (8) does not prevent an employment tribunal from considering a contravention of section 40A(1) in accordance with section 124A (compensation uplift in employee sexual harassment cases).

121 [omitted]

122 References by court to tribunal, etc.

(1) If it appears to a court in which proceedings are pending that a claim or counter-claim relating to a non-discrimination rule could more conveniently be determined by an employment tribunal, the court may strike out the claim or counter-claim.

(2) If in proceedings before a court a question arises about a non-discrimination rule, the court may (whether or not on an application by a party to the proceedings)—

(a) refer the question, or direct that it be referred by a party to the proceedings, to an employment tribunal for determination, and

(b) stay or sist the proceedings in the meantime.

123 Time limits

(1) Subject to section 140B proceedings on a complaint within section 120 may not be brought after the end of—

(a) the period of 3 months starting with the date of the act to which the complaint relates, or

(b) such other period as the employment tribunal thinks just and equitable.

(2) Proceedings may not be brought in reliance on section 121(1) after the end of—

(a) the period of 6 months starting with the date of the act to which the proceedings relate, or

(b) such other period as the employment tribunal thinks just and equitable.

(3) For the purposes of this section—

(a) conduct extending over a period is to be treated as done at the end of the period;

(b) failure to do something is to be treated as occurring when the person in question decided on it.

(4) In the absence of evidence to the contrary, a person (P) is to be taken to decide on failure to do something—

(a) when P does an act inconsistent with doing it, or

(b) if P does no inconsistent act, on the expiry of the period in which P might reasonably have been expected to do it.

124 Remedies: general

(1) This section applies if an employment tribunal finds that there has been a contravention of a provision referred to in section 120(1).

(2) The tribunal may—

(a) make a declaration as to the rights of the complainant and the respondent in relation to the matters to which the proceedings relate;

(b) order the respondent to pay compensation to the complainant;
(c) make an appropriate recommendation.

(3) An appropriate recommendation is a recommendation that within a specified period the respondent takes specified steps for the purpose of obviating or reducing the adverse effect on the complainant of any matter to which the proceedings relate.

(4) Subsection (5) applies if the tribunal—
(a) finds that a contravention is established by virtue of section 19 or 19A, but
(b) is satisfied that the provision, criterion or practice was not applied with the intention of discriminating against the complainant.

(5) It must not make an order under subsection (2)(b) unless it first considers whether to act under subsection (2)(a) or (c).

(6) The amount of compensation which may be awarded under subsection (2)(b) corresponds to the amount which could be awarded by the county court or the sheriff under section 119.

(7) If a respondent fails, without reasonable excuse, to comply with an appropriate recommendation, the tribunal may—
(a) if an order was made under subsection (2)(b), increase the amount of compensation to be paid;
(b) if no such order was made, make one.

124A Remedies: compensation uplift in sexual harassment cases

(1) This section applies where—
(a) an employment tribunal has found that there has been a contravention of section 40 (harassment of employees) which involved, to any extent, harassment of the kind described in section 26(2) (sexual harassment), and
(b) the tribunal has ordered the respondent to pay compensation to the complainant under section 124(2)(b).

(2) The tribunal must consider whether and to what extent the respondent has also contravened section 40A(1) (duty to take reasonable steps to prevent harassment of employees).

(3) If the tribunal is satisfied that the respondent has contravened section 40A(1), it may order the respondent to pay an amount to the complainant (a 'compensation uplift') in addition to the compensation amount determined in accordance with section 124(6).

(4) The amount of the compensation uplift—
(a) must reflect the extent to which, in the tribunal's opinion, the respondent has contravened section 40A(1), but
(b) may be no more than 25% of the amount awarded under section 124(2)(b).

125 [repealed]; 126 [omitted]

Chapter 4 Equality of Terms

127 Jurisdiction

(1) An employment tribunal has, subject to subsection (6), jurisdiction to determine a complaint relating to a breach of an equality clause or rule.

(2) The jurisdiction conferred by subsection (1) includes jurisdiction to determine a complaint arising out of a breach of an equality clause or rule; and a reference in this Chapter to a complaint relating to such a breach is to be read accordingly.

(3) An employment tribunal also has jurisdiction to determine an application by a responsible person for a declaration as to the rights of that person and a worker in relation to a dispute about the effect of an equality clause or rule.

(4) An employment tribunal also has jurisdiction to determine an application by the trustees or managers of an occupational pension scheme for a declaration as to their rights and those of a member in relation to a dispute about the effect of an equality rule.

(5) An employment tribunal also has jurisdiction to determine a question that—

(a) relates to an equality clause or rule, and

(b) is referred to the tribunal by virtue of section 128(2).

(6) This section does not apply to a complaint relating to an act done when the complainant was serving as a member of the armed forces unless—

(a) the complainant has made a service complaint about the matter, and

(b) the complaint has not been withdrawn.

(7) Subsections (2) to (6) of section 121 apply for the purposes of subsection (6) of this section as they apply for the purposes of subsection (1) of that section.

(8) In proceedings before an employment tribunal on a complaint relating to a breach of an equality rule, the employer—

(a) is to be treated as a party, and

(b) is accordingly entitled to appear and be heard.

(9) Nothing in this section affects such jurisdiction as the High Court, the county court, the Court of Session or the sheriff has in relation to an equality clause or rule.

128 References by court to tribunal, etc.

(1) If it appears to a court in which proceedings are pending that a claim or counter-claim relating to an equality clause or rule could more conveniently be determined by an employment tribunal, the court may strike out the claim or counter-claim.

(2) If in proceedings before a court a question arises about an equality clause or rule, the court may (whether or not on an application by a party to the proceedings)—

(a) refer the question, or direct that it be referred by a party to the proceedings, to an employment tribunal for determination, and

(b) stay or sist the proceedings in the meantime.

129 Time limits

(1) This section applies to—

(a) a complaint relating to a breach of an equality clause or rule;

(b) an application for a declaration referred to in section 127(3) or (4).

(2) Proceedings on the complaint or application may not be brought in an employment tribunal after the end of the qualifying period.

(3) If the complaint or application relates to terms of work other than terms of service in the armed forces, the qualifying period is, in a case mentioned in the first column of the table, the period mentioned in the second column, subject to section 140B.

Case	*Qualifying period*
A standard case	The period of 6 months beginning with the last day of the employment or appointment.
A stable work case (but not if it is also a concealment or incapacity case (or both))	The period of 6 months beginning with the day on which the stable working relationship ended.
A concealment case (but not if it is also an incapacity case)	The period of 6 months beginning with the day on which the worker discovered (or could with reasonable diligence have discovered) the qualifying fact.
An incapacity case (but not if it is also a concealment case)	The period of 6 months beginning with the day on which the worker ceased to have the incapacity.
A case which is a concealment case and an incapacity case.	The period of 6 months beginning with the later of the days on which the period would begin if the case were merely a concealment or incapacity case.

(4) [omitted]

130 Section 129: supplementary

(1) This section applies for the purposes of section 129.

(2) A standard case is a case which is not—

(a) a stable work case,

(b) a concealment case,

(c) an incapacity case, or

(d) a concealment case and an incapacity case.

(3) A stable work case is a case where the proceedings relate to a period during which there was a stable working relationship between the worker and the responsible person (including any time after the terms of work had expired).

(4) A concealment case in proceedings relating to an equality clause is a case where—

(a) the responsible person deliberately concealed a qualifying fact from the worker, and

(b) the worker did not discover (or could not with reasonable diligence have discovered) the qualifying fact until after the relevant day.

(5) [omitted]

(6) A qualifying fact for the purposes of subsection (4) or (5) is a fact—

(a) which is relevant to the complaint, and

(b) without knowledge of which the worker or member could not reasonably have been expected to bring the proceedings.

(7) An incapacity case in proceedings relating to an equality clause with respect to terms of work other than terms of service in the armed forces is a case where the worker had an incapacity during the period of 6 months beginning with the later of—

(a) the relevant day, or

(b) the day on which the worker discovered (or could with reasonable diligence have discovered) the qualifying fact deliberately concealed from the worker by the responsible person.

(8) An incapacity case in proceedings relating to an equality clause with respect to terms of service in the armed forces is a case where the worker had an incapacity during the period of 9 months beginning with the later of—

(a) the last day of the period of service during which the complaint arose, or

(b) the day on which the worker discovered (or could with reasonable diligence have discovered) the qualifying fact deliberately concealed from the worker by the responsible person.

(9) [omitted]

(10) The relevant day for the purposes of this section is—

(a) the last day of the employment or appointment, or

(b) the day on which the stable working relationship between the worker and the responsible person ended.

131 Assessment of whether work is of equal value

(1) This section applies to proceedings before an employment tribunal on—

(a) a complaint relating to a breach of an equality clause or rule, or

(b) a question referred to the tribunal by virtue of section 128(2).

(2) Where a question arises in the proceedings as to whether one person's work is of equal value to another's, the tribunal may, before determining the question, require a member of the panel of independent experts to prepare a report on the question.

(3) The tribunal may withdraw a requirement that it makes under subsection (2); and, if it does so, it may—

(a) request the panel member to provide it with specified documentation;

(b) make such other requests to that member as are connected with the withdrawal of the requirement.

(4) If the tribunal requires the preparation of a report under subsection (2) (and does not withdraw the requirement), it must not determine the question unless it has received the report.

(5) Subsection (6) applies where—

(a) a question arises in the proceedings as to whether the work of one person (A) is of equal value to the work of another (B), and

(b) A's work and B's work have been given different values by a job evaluation study.

(6) The tribunal must determine that A's work is not of equal value to B's work unless it has reasonable grounds for suspecting that the evaluation contained in the study—

(a) was based on a system that discriminates because of sex, or

(b) is otherwise unreliable.

(7) For the purposes of subsection (6)(a), a system discriminates because of sex if a difference (or coincidence) between values that the system sets on different demands is not justifiable regardless of the sex of the person on whom the demands are made.

(8) A reference to a member of the panel of independent experts is a reference to a person—

(a) who is for the time being designated as such by the Advisory, Conciliation and Arbitration Service (ACAS) for the purposes of this section, and

(b) who is neither a member of the Council of ACAS nor one of its officers or members of staff.

(9) 'Job evaluation study' has the meaning given in section 80(5).

132 Remedies in non-pensions cases

(1) This section applies to proceedings before a court or employment tribunal on a complaint relating to a breach of an equality clause, other than a breach with respect to membership of or rights under an occupational pension scheme.

(2) If the court or tribunal finds that there has been a breach of the equality clause, it may—

(a) make a declaration as to the rights of the parties in relation to the matters to which the proceedings relate;

(b) order an award by way of arrears of pay or damages in relation to the complainant.

(3) The court or tribunal may not order a payment under subsection (2)(b) in respect of a time before the arrears day.

(4) In relation to proceedings in England and Wales, the arrears day is, in a case mentioned in the first column of the table, the day mentioned in the second column.

Case	*Arrears day*
A standard case	The day falling 6 years before the day on which the proceedings were instituted.
A concealment case or an incapacity case (or a case which is both).	The day on which the breach first occurred.

(5) In relation to proceedings in Scotland, the arrears day is the first day of—

(a) the period of 5 years ending with the day on which the proceedings were commenced, or

(b) if the case involves a relevant incapacity, or a relevant fraud or error, the period determined in accordance with section 135(6) and (7).

133–134 [omitted]

135 Supplementary

(1) This section applies for the purposes of sections 132 to 134.

(2) A standard case is a case which is not—

(a) a concealment case,

(b) an incapacity case, or

(c) a concealment case and an incapacity case.

(3) A concealment case in relation to an equality clause is a case where—

(a) the responsible person deliberately concealed a qualifying fact (as defined by section 130) from the worker, and

(b) the worker commenced the proceedings before the end of the period of 6 years beginning with the day on which the worker discovered (or could with reasonable diligence have discovered) the qualifying fact.

(4) [omitted]

(5) An incapacity case is a case where the worker or member—

(a) had an incapacity when the breach first occurred, and

(b) commenced the proceedings before the end of the period of 6 years beginning with the day on which the worker or member ceased to have the incapacity.

(6) A case involves a relevant incapacity or a relevant fraud or error if the period of 5 years referred to in section 132(5)(a) or 134(6)(a) is, as a result of subsection (7) below, reckoned as a period of more than 5 years; and—

(a) if, as a result of subsection (7), that period is reckoned as a period of more than 5 years but no more than 20 years, the period for the purposes of section 132(5)(b) or (as the case may be) section 134(6)(b) is that extended period;

(b) if, as a result of subsection (7), that period is reckoned as a period of more than 20 years, the period for the purposes of section 132(5)(b) or (as the case may be) section 134(6)(b) is a period of 20 years.

(7) For the purposes of the reckoning referred to in subsection (6), no account is to be taken of time when the worker or member—

(a) had an incapacity, or

(b) was induced by a relevant fraud or error to refrain from commencing proceedings (not being a time after the worker or member could with reasonable diligence have discovered the fraud or error).

(8) For the purposes of subsection (7)—

(a) a fraud is relevant in relation to an equality clause if it is a fraud on the part of the responsible person;

(b) an error is relevant in relation to an equality clause if it is induced by the words or conduct of the responsible person;

(c) a fraud is relevant in relation to an equality rule if it is a fraud on the part of the employer or the trustees or managers of the scheme;

(d) an error is relevant in relation to an equality rule if it is induced by the words or conduct of the employer or the trustees or managers of the scheme.

(9) A reference in subsection (8) to the responsible person, the employer or the trustees or managers includes a reference to a person acting on behalf of the person or persons concerned.

(10) In relation to terms of service, a reference in section 132(5) or subsection (3) or (5)(b) of this section to commencing proceedings is to be read as a reference to making a service complaint.

(11) [omitted]

(12) In relation to proceedings before a court—

(a) a reference to a complaint is to be read as a reference to a claim, and

(b) a reference to a complainant is to be read as a reference to a claimant.

Chapter 5 Miscellaneous

136 Burden of proof

(1) This section applies to any proceedings relating to a contravention of this Act.

(2) If there are facts from which the court could decide, in the absence of any other explanation, that a person (A) contravened the provision concerned, the court must hold that the contravention occurred.

(3) But subsection (2) does not apply if A shows that A did not contravene the provision.

(4) The reference to a contravention of this Act includes a reference to a breach of an equality clause or rule.

(5) This section does not apply to proceedings for an offence under this Act.

(6) A reference to the court includes a reference to—

(a) an employment tribunal;
(b) the Asylum and Immigration Tribunal;
(c) the Special Immigration Appeals Commission;
(d) the First-tier Tribunal;
(e) the Education Tribunal for Wales;
(f) the First-tier Tribunal for Scotland Health and Education Chamber.

137 [omitted]; 138 [repealed]; 139–140B [omitted]

141 Interpretation, etc.

(1) This section applies for the purposes of this Part.

(2) A reference to the responsible person, in relation to an equality clause or rule, is to be construed in accordance with Chapter 3 of Part 5.

(3) A reference to a worker is a reference to the person to the terms of whose work the proceedings in question relate; and, for the purposes of proceedings relating to an equality rule or a non-discrimination rule, a reference to a worker includes a reference to a member of the occupational pension scheme in question.

(4) A reference to the terms of a person's work is to be construed in accordance with Chapter 3 of Part 5.

(5) A reference to a member of an occupational pension scheme includes a reference to a prospective member.

(6) In relation to proceedings in England and Wales, a person has an incapacity if the person—

(a) has not attained the age of 18, or
(b) lacks capacity (within the meaning of the Mental Capacity Act 2005).

(7) In relation to proceedings in Scotland, a person has an incapacity if the person—

(a) has not attained the age of 16, or
(b) is incapable (within the meaning of the Adults with Incapacity (Scotland) Act 2000 (asp 4)).

(8) 'Service complaint' means a complaint under section 340A(1) or (2) of the Armed Forces Act 2006.

(9) 'Criminal matter' means—

(a) an investigation into the commission of an alleged offence;
(b) a decision whether to commence criminal proceedings;
(c) criminal proceedings.

PART 10 CONTRACTS, ETC.

Contracts and other agreements

142 Unenforceable terms

(1) A term of a contract is unenforceable against a person in so far as it constitutes, promotes or provides for treatment of that or another person that is of a description prohibited by this Act.

(2) A relevant non-contractual term is unenforceable against a person in so far as it constitutes, promotes or provides for treatment of that or another person that is of a description prohibited by this Act, in so far as this Act relates to disability.

(3) A relevant non-contractual term is a term which—

(a) is a term of an agreement that is not a contract, and

(b) relates to the provision of an employment service within section 56(2)(a) to (e) or to the provision under a group insurance arrangement of facilities by way of insurance.

(4) A reference in subsection (1) or (2) to treatment of a description prohibited by this Act does not include—

(a) a reference to the inclusion of a term in a contract referred to in section 70(2)(a) or 76(2), or

(b) a reference to the failure to include a term in a contract as referred to in section 70(2)(b).

(5) Subsection (4) does not affect the application of section 148(2) to this section.

143 Removal or modification of unenforceable terms

(1) The county court or the sheriff may, on an application by a person who has an interest in a contract or other agreement which includes a term that is unenforceable as a result of section 142, make an order for the term to be removed or modified.

(2) An order under this section must not be made unless every person who would be affected by it—

(a) has been given notice of the application (except where notice is dispensed with in accordance with rules of court), and

(b) has been afforded an opportunity to make representations to the county court or sheriff.

(3) An order under this section may include provision in respect of a period before the making of the order.

144 Contracting out

(1) A term of a contract is unenforceable by a person in whose favour it would operate in so far as it purports to exclude or limit a provision of or made under this Act.

(2) A relevant non-contractual term (as defined by section 142) is unenforceable by a person in whose favour it would operate in so far as it purports to exclude or limit a provision of or made under this Act, in so far as the provision relates to disability.

(3) This section does not apply to a contract which settles a claim within section 114.

(4) This section does not apply to a contract which settles a complaint within section 120 if the contract—

(a) is made with the assistance of a conciliation officer, or

(b) is a qualifying settlement agreement.

(5) A contract within subsection (4) includes a contract which settles a complaint relating to a breach of an equality clause or rule or of a non-discrimination rule.

(6) A contract within subsection (4) includes an agreement by the parties to a dispute to submit the dispute to arbitration if—

(a) the dispute is covered by a scheme having effect by virtue of an order under section 212A of the Trade Union and Labour Relations (Consolidation) Act 1992, and

(b) the agreement is to submit the dispute to arbitration in accordance with the scheme.

Collective agreements and rules of undertakings

145 Void and unenforceable terms

(1) A term of a collective agreement is void in so far as it constitutes, promotes or provides for treatment of a description prohibited by this Act.

(2) A rule of an undertaking is unenforceable against a person in so far as it constitutes, promotes or provides for treatment of the person that is of a description prohibited by this Act.

146 Declaration in respect of void term, etc.

(1) A qualifying person (P) may make a complaint to an employment tribunal that a term is void, or that a rule is unenforceable, as a result of section 145.

(2) But subsection (1) applies only if—

(a) the term or rule may in the future have effect in relation to P, and
(b) where the complaint alleges that the term or rule provides for treatment of a description prohibited by this Act, P may in the future be subjected to treatment that would (if P were subjected to it in present circumstances) be of that description.

(3) If the tribunal finds that the complaint is well-founded, it must make an order declaring that the term is void or the rule is unenforceable.

(4) An order under this section may include provision in respect of a period before the making of the order.

(5) In the case of a complaint about a term of a collective agreement, where the term is one made by or on behalf of a person of a description specified in the first column of the table, a qualifying person is a person of a description specified in the second column.

Description of person who made collective agreement	*Qualifying person*
Employer	A person who is, or is seeking to be, an employee of that employer
Organisation of employers	A person who is, or is seeking to be, an employee of an employer who is a member of that organisation
Association of organisations of employers	A person who is, or is seeking to be, an employee of an employer who is a member of an organisation in that association

(6) In the case of a complaint about a rule of an undertaking, where the rule is one made by or on behalf of a person of a description specified in the first column of the table, a qualifying person is a person of a description specified in the second column.

Description of person who made rule of undertaking	*Qualifying person*
Employer	A person who is, or is seeking to be, an employee of that employer
Trade organisation or qualifications body	A person who is, or is seeking to be, a member of the organisation or body
	A person upon whom the body has conferred a relevant qualification
	A person seeking conferment by the body of a relevant qualification

Supplementary

147 Meaning of 'qualifying settlement agreement'

(1) This section applies for the purposes of this Part.

(2) A qualifying settlement agreement is a contract in relation to which each of the conditions in subsection (3) is met.

(3) Those conditions are that—
(a) the contract is in writing,
(b) the contract relates to the particular complaint,

(c) the complainant has, before entering into the contract, received advice from an independent adviser about its terms and effect (including, in particular, its effect on the complainant's ability to pursue the complaint before an employment tribunal),
(d) on the date of the giving of the advice, there is in force a contract of insurance, or an indemnity provided for members of a profession or professional body, covering the risk of a claim by the complainant in respect of loss arising from the advice,
(e) the contract identifies the adviser, and
(f) the contract states that the conditions in paragraphs (c) and (d) are met.

(4) Each of the following is an independent adviser—
(a) a qualified lawyer;
(b) an officer, official, employee or member of an independent trade union certified in writing by the trade union as competent to give advice and as authorised to do so on its behalf;
(c) a worker at an advice centre (whether as an employee or a volunteer) certified in writing by the centre as competent to give advice and as authorised to do so on its behalf;
(d) a person of such description as may be specified by order.

(5) Despite subsection (4), none of the following is an independent adviser to the complainant in relation to a qualifying settlement agreement—
(a) a person (other than the complainant) who is a party to the contract or the complaint;
(b) a person who is connected to a person within paragraph (a);
(c) a person who is employed by a person within paragraph (a) or (b);
(d) a person who is acting for a person within paragraph (a) or (b) in relation to the contract or the complaint;
(e) a person within subsection (4)(b) or (c), if the trade union or advice centre is a person within paragraph (a) or (b);
(f) a person within subsection (4)(c) to whom the complainant makes a payment for the advice.

(6) A 'qualified lawyer', for the purposes of subsection (4)(a), is—
(a) in relation to England and Wales, a person who, for the purposes of the Legal Services Act 2007, is an authorised person in relation to an activity which constitutes the exercise of a right of audience or the conduct of litigation;
(b) in relation to Scotland, an advocate (whether in practice as such or employed to give legal advice) or a solicitor who holds a practising certificate.

(7) 'Independent trade union' has the meaning given in section 5 of the Trade Union and Labour Relations (Consolidation) Act 1992.

(8) Two persons are connected for the purposes of subsection (5) if—
(a) one is a company of which the other (directly or indirectly) has control, or
(b) both are companies of which a third person (directly or indirectly) has control.

(9) Two persons are also connected for the purposes of subsection (5) in so far as a connection between them gives rise to a conflict of interest in relation to the contract or the complaint.

148 Interpretation

(1) This section applies for the purposes of this Part.

(2) A reference to treatment of a description prohibited by this Act does not include treatment in so far as it is treatment that would contravene—
(a) Part 1 (public sector duty regarding socio-economic inequalities), or
(b) Chapter 1 of Part 11 (public sector equality duty).

(3) 'Group insurance arrangement' means an arrangement between an employer and another person for the provision by that other person of facilities by way of insurance to the employer's employees (or a class of those employees).

(4) 'Collective agreement' has the meaning given in section 178 of the Trade Union and Labour Relations (Consolidation) Act 1992.

(5) A rule of an undertaking is a rule within subsection (6) or (7).

(6) A rule within this subsection is a rule made by a trade organisation or a qualifications body for application to—

(a) its members or prospective members,
(b) persons on whom it has conferred a relevant qualification, or
(c) persons seeking conferment by it of a relevant qualification.

(7) A rule within this subsection is a rule made by an employer for application to—

(a) employees,
(b) persons who apply for employment, or
(c) persons the employer considers for employment.

(8) 'Trade organisation', 'qualifications body' and 'relevant qualification' each have the meaning given in Part 5 (work).

PART 11 ADVANCEMENT OF EQUALITY

Chapter 1 Public Sector Equality Duty

149 Public sector equality duty

(1) A public authority must, in the exercise of its functions, have due regard to the need to—

(a) eliminate discrimination, harassment, victimisation and any other conduct that is prohibited by or under this Act;
(b) advance equality of opportunity between persons who share a relevant protected characteristic and persons who do not share it;
(c) foster good relations between persons who share a relevant protected characteristic and persons who do not share it.

(2) A person who is not a public authority but who exercises public functions must, in the exercise of those functions, have due regard to the matters mentioned in subsection (1).

(3) Having due regard to the need to advance equality of opportunity between persons who share a relevant protected characteristic and persons who do not share it involves having due regard, in particular, to the need to—

(a) remove or minimise disadvantages suffered by persons who share a relevant protected characteristic that are connected to that characteristic;
(b) take steps to meet the needs of persons who share a relevant protected characteristic that are different from the needs of persons who do not share it;
(c) encourage persons who share a relevant protected characteristic to participate in public life or in any other activity in which participation by such persons is disproportionately low.

(4) The steps involved in meeting the needs of disabled persons that are different from the needs of persons who are not disabled include, in particular, steps to take account of disabled persons' disabilities.

(5) Having due regard to the need to foster good relations between persons who share a relevant protected characteristic and persons who do not share it involves having due regard, in particular, to the need to—

(a) tackle prejudice, and
(b) promote understanding.

(6) Compliance with the duties in this section may involve treating some persons more favourably than others; but that is not to be taken as permitting conduct that would otherwise be prohibited by or under this Act.

(7) The relevant protected characteristics are—

age;

disability;
gender reassignment;
pregnancy and maternity;
race;
religion or belief;
sex;
sexual orientation.

(8) A reference to conduct that is prohibited by or under this Act includes a reference to—
(a) a breach of an equality clause or rule;
(b) a breach of a non-discrimination rule.

(9) Schedule 18 (exceptions) has effect.

150–155 [omitted]

156 Enforcement

A failure in respect of a performance of a duty imposed by or under this Chapter does not confer a cause of action at private law.

157 [omitted]

Chapter 2 Positive Action

158 Positive action: general

(1) This section applies if a person (P) reasonably thinks that—
(a) persons who share a protected characteristic suffer a disadvantage connected to the characteristic,
(b) persons who share a protected characteristic have needs that are different from the needs of persons who do not share it, or
(c) participation in an activity by persons who share a protected characteristic is disproportionately low.

(2) This Act does not prohibit P from taking any action which is a proportionate means of achieving the aim of—
(a) enabling or encouraging persons who share the protected characteristic to overcome or minimise that disadvantage,
(b) meeting those needs, or
(c) enabling or encouraging persons who share the protected characteristic to participate in that activity.

(3) Regulations may specify action, or descriptions of action, to which subsection (2) does not apply.

(4) This section does not apply to—
(a) action within section 159(3), or
(b) anything that is permitted by virtue of section 104.

(5) If section 104(7) is repealed by virtue of section 105, this section will not apply to anything that would have been so permitted but for the repeal.

(6) This section does not enable P to do anything that is prohibited by or under an enactment other than this Act.

159 Positive action: recruitment and promotion

(1) This section applies if a person (P) reasonably thinks that—
(a) persons who share a protected characteristic suffer a disadvantage connected to the characteristic, or
(b) participation in an activity by persons who share a protected characteristic is disproportionately low.

(2) Part 5 (work) does not prohibit P from taking action within subsection (3) with the aim of enabling or encouraging persons who share the protected characteristic to—

(a) overcome or minimise that disadvantage, or

(b) participate in that activity.

(3) That action is treating a person (A) more favourably in connection with recruitment or promotion than another person (B) because A has the protected characteristic but B does not.

(4) But subsection (2) applies only if—

(a) A is as qualified as B to be recruited or promoted,

(b) P does not have a policy of treating persons who share the protected characteristic more favourably in connection with recruitment or promotion than persons who do not share it, and

(c) taking the action in question is a proportionate means of achieving the aim referred to in subsection (2).

(5) 'Recruitment' means a process for deciding whether to—

(a) offer employment to a person,

(b) make contract work available to a contract worker,

(c) offer a person a position as a partner in a firm or proposed firm,

(d) offer a person a position as a member of an LLP or proposed LLP,

(e) offer a person a pupillage or tenancy in barristers' chambers,

(f) take a person as an advocate's devil or offer a person membership of an advocate's stable,

(g) offer a person an appointment to a personal office,

(h) offer a person an appointment to a public office, recommend a person for such an appointment or approve a person's appointment to a public office, or

(i) offer a person a service for finding employment.

(6) This section does not enable P to do anything that is prohibited by or under an enactment other than this Act.

160–185 [omitted]; 186 [repealed]; 187–192 [omitted]

PART 14 GENERAL EXCEPTIONS

193 Charities

(1) A person does not contravene this Act only by restricting the provision of benefits to persons who share a protected characteristic if—

(a) the person acts in pursuance of a charitable instrument, and

(b) the provision of the benefits is within subsection (2).

(2) The provision of benefits is within this subsection if it is—

(a) a proportionate means of achieving a legitimate aim, or

(b) for the purpose of preventing or compensating for a disadvantage linked to the protected characteristic.

(3) It is not a contravention of this Act for—

(a) a person who provides supported employment to treat persons who have the same disability or a disability of a prescribed description more favourably than those who do not have that disability or a disability of such a description in providing such employment;

(b) a Minister of the Crown to agree to arrangements for the provision of supported employment which will, or may, have that effect.

(4) If a charitable instrument enables the provision of benefits to persons of a class defined by reference to colour, it has effect for all purposes as if it enabled the provision of such benefits—

(a) to persons of the class which results if the reference to colour is ignored, or

(b) if the original class is defined by reference only to colour, to persons generally.

(5) It is not a contravention of this Act for a charity to require members, or persons wishing to become members, to make a statement which asserts or implies membership or acceptance of a religion or belief; and for this purpose restricting the access by members to a benefit, facility or service to those who make such a statement is to be treated as imposing such a requirement.

(6) Subsection (5) applies only if—

(a) the charity, or an organisation of which it is part, first imposed such a requirement before 18 May 2005, and

(b) the charity or organisation has not ceased since that date to impose such a requirement.

(7) It is not a contravention of section 29 for a person, in relation to an activity which is carried on for the purpose of promoting or supporting a charity, to restrict participation in the activity to persons of one sex.

(8) A charity regulator does not contravene this Act only by exercising a function in relation to a charity in a manner which the regulator thinks is expedient in the interests of the charity, having regard to the charitable instrument.

(9) Subsection (1) does not apply to a contravention of—

(a) section 39;

(b) section 40;

(c) section 41;

(d) section 55, so far as relating to the provision of vocational training.

(10) Subsection (9) does not apply in relation to disability.

194 Charities: supplementary

(1) This section applies for the purposes of section 193.

(2) That section does not apply to race, so far as relating to colour.

(3) 'Charity'—

(a) in relation to England and Wales, has the meaning given by section 1(1) of the Charities Act 2011;

(b) in relation to Scotland, means a body entered in the Scottish Charity Register.

(4) 'Charitable instrument' means an instrument establishing or governing a charity (including an instrument made or having effect before the commencement of this section).

(5) The charity regulators are—

(a) the Charity Commission for England and Wales;

(b) the Scottish Charity Regulator.

(6) Section 107(5) applies to references in subsection (5) of section 193 to members, or persons wishing to become members, of a charity.

(7) 'Supported employment' means facilities provided, or in respect of which payments are made, under section 15 of the Disabled Persons (Employment) Act 1944.

195–211 [omitted]

PART 16 GENERAL AND MISCELLANEOUS

212 General interpretation

(1) In this Act—

'armed forces' means any of the naval, military or air forces of the Crown;

'the Commission' means the Commission for Equality and Human Rights;

'detriment' does not, subject to subsection (5), include conduct which amounts to harassment;

'the Education Acts' has the meaning given in section 578 of the Education Act 1996;

'employment' and related expressions are (subject to subsection (11)) to be read with section 83;

'enactment' means an enactment contained in—

(a) an Act of Parliament,

(b) an Act of the Scottish Parliament,

(c) an Act or Measure of the National Assembly for Wales, or
(d) subordinate legislation;

'equality clause' means a sex equality clause or maternity equality clause;

'equality rule' means a sex equality rule or maternity equality rule;

'man' means a male of any age;

'maternity equality clause' has the meaning given in section 73;

'maternity equality rule' has the meaning given in section 75;

'non-discrimination rule' has the meaning given in section 61;

'occupational pension scheme' has the meaning given in section 1 of the Pension Schemes Act 1993;

'parent' has the same meaning as in—

(a) the Education Act 1996 (in relation to England and Wales);
(b) the Education (Scotland) Act 1980 (in relation to Scotland);

'prescribed' means prescribed by regulations;

'profession' includes a vocation or occupation;

'sex equality clause' has the meaning given in section 66;

'sex equality rule' has the meaning given in section 67;

'subordinate legislation' means—

(a) subordinate legislation within the meaning of the Interpretation Act 1978, or
(b) an instrument made under an Act of the Scottish Parliament or an Act or Measure of the National Assembly for Wales;

'substantial' means more than minor or trivial;

'trade' includes any business;

'woman' means a female of any age.

(2) A reference (however expressed) to an act includes a reference to an omission.

(3) A reference (however expressed) to an omission includes (unless there is express provision to the contrary) a reference to—

(a) a deliberate omission to do something;
(b) a refusal to do it;
(c) a failure to do it.

(4) A reference (however expressed) to providing or affording access to a benefit, facility or service includes a reference to facilitating access to the benefit, facility or service.

(5) Where this Act disapplies a prohibition on harassment in relation to a specified protected characteristic, the disapplication does not prevent conduct relating to that characteristic from amounting to a detriment for the purposes of discrimination within section 13 because of that characteristic.

(6) A reference to occupation, in relation to premises, is a reference to lawful occupation.

(7) The following are members of the executive—

(a) a Minister of the Crown;
(b) a government department;
(c) the Welsh Ministers, the First Minister for Wales or the Counsel General to the Welsh Assembly Government;
(d) any part of the Scottish Administration.

(8) A reference to a breach of an equality clause or rule is a reference to a breach of a term modified by, or included by virtue of, an equality clause or rule.

(9) A reference to a contravention of this Act does not include a reference to a breach of an equality clause or rule, unless there is express provision to the contrary.

(10)–(12) [omitted]

(13) Nothing in section 28, 32, 84, 90, 95 or 100 is to be regarded as an express exception.

213 References to maternity leave, etc.

(1) This section applies for the purposes of this Act.

(2) A reference to a woman on maternity leave is a reference to a woman on—

(a) compulsory maternity leave,

(b) ordinary maternity leave, or

(c) additional maternity leave.

(3) A reference to a woman on compulsory maternity leave is a reference to a woman absent from work because she satisfies the conditions prescribed for the purposes of section 72(1) of the Employment Rights Act 1996.

(4) A reference to a woman on ordinary maternity leave is a reference to a woman absent from work because she is exercising the right to ordinary maternity leave.

(5) A reference to the right to ordinary maternity leave is a reference to the right conferred by section 71(1) of the Employment Rights Act 1996.

(6) A reference to a woman on additional maternity leave is a reference to a woman absent from work because she is exercising the right to additional maternity leave.

(7) A reference to the right to additional maternity leave is a reference to the right conferred by section 73(1) of the Employment Rights Act 1996.

(8) 'Additional maternity leave period' has the meaning given in section 73(2) of that Act.

214–218 [omitted]

SCHEDULE 1

DISABILITY: SUPPLEMENTARY PROVISION

PART 1 DETERMINATION OF DISABILITY

1. [omitted]

Long-term effects

2.—(1) The effect of an impairment is long-term if—

(a) it has lasted for at least 12 months,

(b) it is likely to last for at least 12 months, or

(c) it is likely to last for the rest of the life of the person affected.

(2) If an impairment ceases to have a substantial adverse effect on a person's ability to carry out normal day-to-day activities, it is to be treated as continuing to have that effect if that effect is likely to recur.

(3) For the purposes of sub-paragraph (2), the likelihood of an effect recurring is to be disregarded in such circumstances as may be prescribed.

(4) Regulations may prescribe circumstances in which, despite sub-paragraph (1), an effect is to be treated as being, or as not being, long-term.

Severe disfigurement

3.—(1) An impairment which consists of a severe disfigurement is to be treated as having a substantial adverse effect on the ability of the person concerned to carry out normal day-to-day activities.

(2)–(3) [omitted]

4. [omitted]

Effect of medical treatment

5.—(1) An impairment is to be treated as having a substantial adverse effect on the ability of the person concerned to carry out normal day-to-day activities if—

(a) measures are being taken to treat or correct it, and
(b) but for that, it would be likely to have that effect.

(2) 'Measures' includes, in particular, medical treatment and the use of a prosthesis or other aid.

(3) Sub-paragraph (1) does not apply—
(a) in relation to the impairment of a person's sight, to the extent that the impairment is, in the person's case, correctable by spectacles or contact lenses or in such other ways as may be prescribed;
(b) in relation to such other impairments as may be prescribed, in such circumstances as are prescribed.

Normal day-to-day activities

5A.—(1) This paragraph has effect for the purposes of the application to the protected characteristic of disability of—
(a) Part 5 (work);
(b) Part 8 (prohibited conduct: ancillary), so far as relating to Part 5;
(c) Part 10 (contracts), so far as relating to Part 5;
(d) Schedule 21 (reasonable adjustments: supplementary), so far as applying for the purposes of Schedule 8.

(2) References in the relevant provisions to a person's ability to carry out normal day-to-day activities are to be taken as including references to the person's ability to participate fully and effectively in working life on an equal basis with other workers.

(3) The 'relevant provisions' are—
(a) section 6 (disability);
(b) other provisions of this Schedule;
(c) regulations under this Schedule (whenever made).

Certain medical conditions

6.—(1) Cancer, HIV infection and multiple sclerosis are each a disability.

(2) HIV infection is infection by a virus capable of causing the Acquired Immune Deficiency Syndrome.

7. [omitted]

Progressive conditions

8.—(1) This paragraph applies to a person (P) if—
(a) P has a progressive condition,
(b) as a result of that condition P has an impairment which has (or had) an effect on P's ability to carry out normal day-to-day activities, but
(c) the effect is not (or was not) a substantial adverse effect.

(2) P is to be taken to have an impairment which has a substantial adverse effect if the condition is likely to result in P having such an impairment.

(3) Regulations may make provision for a condition of a prescribed description to be treated as being, or as not being, progressive.

Past disabilities

9.—(1) A question as to whether a person had a disability at a particular time ('the relevant time') is to be determined, for the purposes of section 6, as if the provisions of, or made under, this Act were in force when the act complained of was done had been in force at the relevant time.

(2) The relevant time may be a time before the coming into force of the provision of this Act to which the question relates.

PART 2 [OMITTED]

SCHEDULE 7

EQUALITY OF TERMS: EXCEPTIONS

PART 1 TERMS OF WORK

Compliance with laws regulating employment of women, etc.

1. Neither a sex equality clause nor a maternity equality clause has effect in relation to terms of work affected by compliance with laws regulating—

(a) the employment of women;

(b) the appointment of women to personal or public offices.

Pregnancy, etc.

2. A sex equality clause does not have effect in relation to terms of work affording special treatment to women in connection with pregnancy or childbirth.

PART 2 [OMITTED]

SCHEDULE 8

WORK: REASONABLE ADJUSTMENTS

PART 1 INTRODUCTORY

Preliminary

1. This Schedule applies where a duty to make reasonable adjustments is imposed on A by this Part of this Act.

The duty

2.—(1) A must comply with the first, second and third requirements.

(2) For the purposes of this paragraph—

(a) the reference in section 20(3) to a provision, criterion or practice is a reference to a provision, criterion or practice applied by or on behalf of A;

(b) the reference in section 20(4) to a physical feature is a reference to a physical feature of premises occupied by A;

(c) the reference in section 20(3), (4) or (5) to a disabled person is to an interested disabled person.

(3) In relation to the first and third requirements, a relevant matter is any matter specified in the first column of the applicable table in Part 2 of this Schedule.

(4) In relation to the second requirement, a relevant matter is—

(a) a matter specified in the second entry of the first column of the applicable table in Part 2 of this Schedule, or

(b) where there is only one entry in a column, a matter specified there.

(5) If two or more persons are subject to a duty to make reasonable adjustments in relation to the same interested disabled person, each of them must comply with the duty so far as it is reasonable for each of them to do so.

3.—(1) This paragraph applies if a duty to make reasonable adjustments is imposed on A by section 55 (except where the employment service which A provides is the provision of vocational training within the meaning given by section 56(6)(b)).

(2) The reference in section 20(3), (4) and (5) to a disabled person is a reference to an interested disabled person.

(3) In relation to each requirement, the relevant matter is the employment service which A provides.

(4) Sub-paragraph (5) of paragraph 2 applies for the purposes of this paragraph as it applies for the purposes of that paragraph.

PART 2 INTERESTED DISABLED PERSON

Preliminary

4. An interested disabled person is a disabled person who, in relation to a relevant matter, is of a description specified in the second column of the applicable table in this Part of this Schedule.

Employers (see section 39)

5.—(1) This paragraph applies where A is an employer.

Relevant matter	*Description of disabled person*
Deciding to whom to offer employment.	A person who is, or has notified A that the person may be, an applicant for the employment.
Employment by A.	An applicant for employment by A. An employee of A's.

(2) Where A is the employer of a disabled contract worker (B), A must comply with the first, second and third requirements on each occasion when B is supplied to a principal to do contract work.

(3) In relation to the first requirement (as it applies for the purposes of sub-paragraph (2))—

(a) the reference in section 20(3) to a provision, criterion or practice is a reference to a provision, criterion or practice applied by or on behalf of all or most of the principals to whom B is or might be supplied,

(b) the reference to being put at a substantial disadvantage is a reference to being likely to be put at a substantial disadvantage that is the same or similar in the case of each of the principals referred to in paragraph (a), and

(c) the requirement imposed on A is a requirement to take such steps as it would be reasonable for A to have to take if the provision, criterion or practice were applied by or on behalf of A.

(4) In relation to the second requirement (as it applies for the purposes of sub-paragraph (2))—

(a) the reference in section 20(4) to a physical feature is a reference to a physical feature of premises occupied by each of the principals referred to in sub-paragraph (3)(a),

(b) the reference to being put at a substantial disadvantage is a reference to being likely to be put at a substantial disadvantage that is the same or similar in the case of each of those principals, and

(c) the requirement imposed on A is a requirement to take such steps as it would be reasonable for A to have to take if the premises were occupied by A.

(5) In relation to the third requirement (as it applies for the purposes of sub-paragraph (2))—

(a) the reference in section 20(5) to being put at a substantial disadvantage is a reference to being likely to be put at a substantial disadvantage that is the same or similar in the case of each of the principals referred to in sub-paragraph (3)(a), and

(b) the requirement imposed on A is a requirement to take such steps as it would be reasonable for A to have to take if A were the person to whom B was supplied.

Principals in contract work (see section 41)

6.—(1) This paragraph applies where A is a principal.

Relevant matter	*Description of disabled person*
Contract work that A may make available.	A person who is, or has notified A that the person may be, an applicant to do the work.
Contract work that A makes available.	A person who is supplied to do the work.

(2) A is not required to do anything that a disabled person's employer is required to do by virtue of paragraph 5.

7.–10. [omitted]

Persons making appointments to offices etc. (see sections 49 to 51)

11. This paragraph applies where A is a person who has the power to make an appointment to a personal or public office.

Relevant matter	*Description of disabled person*
Deciding to whom to offer the appointment.	A person who is, or has notified A that the person may be, seeking the appointment. A person who is being considered for the appointment.
Appointment to the office.	A person who is seeking, or being considered for, appointment to the office.

12. This paragraph applies where A is a relevant person in relation to a personal or public office.

Relevant matter	*Description of disabled person*
Appointment to the office.	A person appointed to the office.

13. This paragraph applies where A is a person who has the power to make a recommendation for, or give approval to, an appointment to a public office.

Relevant matter	*Description of disabled person*
Deciding who to recommend or approve for appointment to the office.	A person who is, or has notified A that the person may be, seeking recommendation or approval for appointment to the office. A person who is being considered for recommendation or approval for appointment to the office.
Appointment to the office.	A person who is seeking, or being considered for, appointment to the office in question.

14. In relation to the second requirement in a case within paragraph 11, 12 or 13, the reference in paragraph 2(2)(b) to premises occupied by A is to be read as a reference to premises—

(a) under the control of A, and

(b) at or from which the functions of the office concerned are performed.

Qualifications bodies (see section 53)

15.—(1) This paragraph applies where A is a qualifications body.

Relevant matter	*Description of disabled person*
Deciding upon whom to confer a relevant qualification.	A person who is, or has notified A that the person may be, an applicant for the conferment of the qualification.
Conferment by the body of a relevant qualification.	An applicant for the conferment of the qualification. A person who holds the qualification.

(2) [omitted]

Employment service-providers (see section 55)

16. This paragraph applies where—

(a) A is an employment service-provider, and

(b) the employment service which A provides is vocational training within the meaning given by section 56(6)(b).

Relevant matter	*Description of disabled person*
Deciding to whom to offer to provide the service.	A person who is, or has notified A that the person may be, an applicant for the provision of the service.
Provision by A of the service.	A person who applies to A for the provision of the service. A person to whom A provides the service.

Trade organisations (see section 57)

17. This paragraph applies where A is a trade organisation.

Relevant matter	*Description of disabled person*
Deciding to whom to offer membership of the organisation.	A person who is, or has notified A that the person may be, an applicant for membership.
Membership of the organisation.	An applicant for membership. A member.

18.–19. [omitted]

PART 3 LIMITATIONS ON THE DUTY

Lack of knowledge of disability, etc.

20.—(1) A is not subject to a duty to make reasonable adjustments if A does not know, and could not reasonably be expected to know—

(a) in the case of an applicant or potential applicant, that an interested disabled person is or may be an applicant for the work in question;

(b) in any case referred to in Part 2 of this Schedule, that an interested disabled person has a disability and is likely to be placed at the disadvantage referred to in the first, second or third requirement.

(2) An applicant is, in relation to the description of A specified in the first column of the table, a person of a description specified in the second column (and the reference to a potential applicant is to be construed accordingly).

An employer	*An applicant for employment*
A firm or proposed firm	A candidate for a position as a partner
An LLP or proposed LLP	A candidate for a position as a member
A barrister or barrister's clerk	An applicant for a pupillage or tenancy
An advocate or advocate's clerk	An applicant for being taken as an advocate's devil or for becoming a member of a stable
A relevant person in relation to a personal or public office	A person who is seeking appointment to, or recommendation or approval for appointment to, the office
A qualifications body	An applicant for the conferment of a relevant qualification
An employment service-provider	An applicant for the provision of an employment service
A trade organisation	An applicant for membership

(3) If the duty to make reasonable adjustments is imposed on A by section 55, this paragraph applies only in so far as the employment service which A provides is vocational training within the meaning given by section 56(6)(b).

SCHEDULE 9

WORK: EXCEPTIONS

PART 1 OCCUPATIONAL REQUIREMENTS

General

1.—(1) A person (A) does not contravene a provision mentioned in sub-paragraph (2) by applying in relation to work a requirement to have a particular protected characteristic, if A shows that, having regard to the nature or context of the work—

(a) it is an occupational requirement,
(b) the application of the requirement is a proportionate means of achieving a legitimate aim, and
(c) the person to whom A applies the requirement does not meet it (or A has reasonable grounds for not being satisfied that the person meets it).

(2) The provisions are—

(a) section 39(1)(a) or (c) or (2)(b) or (c);
(b) section 41(1)(b);
(c) section 44(1)(a) or (c) or (2)(b) or (c);
(d) section 45(1)(a) or (c) or (2)(b) or (c);
(e) section 49(3)(a) or (c) or (6)(b) or (c);
(f) section 50(3)(a) or (c) or (6)(b) or (c);
(g) section 51(1);
(h) section 60A(1).

(3) The references in sub-paragraph (1) to a requirement to have a protected characteristic are to be read—

(a) in the case of gender reassignment, as references to a requirement not to be a transsexual person (and section 7(3) is accordingly to be ignored);

(b) in the case of marriage and civil partnership, as references to a requirement not to be married or a civil partner (and section 8(2) is accordingly to be ignored).

(4) In the case of a requirement to be of a particular sex, sub-paragraph (1) has effect as if in paragraph (c), the words from '(or' to the end were omitted.

Religious requirements relating to sex, marriage etc., sexual orientation

2.—(1) A person (A) does not contravene a provision mentioned in sub-paragraph (2) by applying in relation to employment a requirement to which subparagraph (4) applies if A shows that—

(a) the employment is for the purposes of an organised religion,

(b) the application of the requirement engages the compliance or non-conflict principle, and

(c) the person to whom A applies the requirement does not meet it (or A has reasonable grounds for not being satisfied that the person meets it).

(2) The provisions are—

(a) section 39(1)(a) or (c) or (2)(b) or (c);

(b) section 49(3)(a) or (c) or (6)(b) or (c);

(c) section 50(3)(a) or (c) or (6)(b) or (c);

(d) section 51(1);

(e) section 60A(1).

(3) A person does not contravene section 53(1) or (2)(a) or (b) by applying in relation to a relevant qualification (within the meaning of that section) a requirement to which sub-paragraph (4) applies if the person shows that—

(a) the qualification is for the purposes of employment mentioned in sub-paragraph (1)(a), and

(b) the application of the requirement engages the compliance or non-conflict principle.

(4) This sub-paragraph applies to—

(a) a requirement to be of a particular sex;

(b) a requirement not to be a transsexual person;

(c) a requirement not to be married or a civil partner;

(ca) a requirement not to be married to, or the civil partner of, a person of the same sex;

(cb) a requirement not to be the civil partner of a person of the opposite sex;

(d) a requirement not to be married to, or the civil partner of, a person who has a living former spouse or civil partner;

(e) a requirement relating to circumstances in which a marriage or civil partnership came to an end;

(f) a requirement related to sexual orientation.

(5) The application of a requirement engages the compliance principle if the requirement is applied so as to comply with the doctrines of the religion.

(6) The application of a requirement engages the non-conflict principle if, because of the nature or context of the employment, the requirement is applied so as to avoid conflicting with the strongly held religious convictions of a significant number of the religion's followers.

(7) A reference to employment includes a reference to an appointment to a personal or public office.

(8) In the case of a requirement within sub-paragraph (4)(a), sub-paragraph (1) has effect as if in paragraph (c) the words from '(or' to the end were omitted.

Other requirements relating to religion or belief

3. A person (A) with an ethos based on religion or belief does not contravene a provision mentioned in paragraph 1(2) by applying in relation to work a requirement to be of a particular religion or belief if A shows that, having regard to that ethos and to the nature or context of the work—

(a) it is an occupational requirement,

(b) the application of the requirement is a proportionate means of achieving a legitimate aim, and

(c) the person to whom A applies the requirement does not meet it (or A has reasonable grounds for not being satisfied that the person meets it).

4. [omitted]

Employment services

5.—(1) A person (A) does not contravene section 55(1) or (2)or section 60A(1) if A shows that A's treatment of another person relates only to work the offer of which could be refused to that other person in reliance on paragraph 1, 2, 3 or 4.

(2) A person (A) does not contravene section 55(1) or (2) or section 60A(1) if A shows that A's treatment of another person relates only to training for work of a description mentioned in sub-paragraph (1).

(3) A person (A) does not contravene section 55(1) or (2) or section 60A(1) if A shows that—

(a) A acted in reliance on a statement made to A by a person with the power to offer the work in question to the effect that, by virtue of subparagraph (1) or (2), A's action would be lawful, and

(b) it was reasonable for A to rely on the statement.

(4) A person commits an offence by knowingly or recklessly making a statement such as is mentioned in sub-paragraph (3)(a) which in a material respect is false or misleading.

(5) A person guilty of an offence under sub-paragraph (4) is liable on summary conviction to a fine not exceeding level 5 on the standard scale.

Interpretation

6.—(1) This paragraph applies for the purposes of this Part of this Schedule.

(2) A reference to contravening a provision of this Act is a reference to contravening that provision by virtue of section 13.

(3) A reference to work is a reference to employment, contract work, a position as a partner or as a member of an LLP, or an appointment to a personal or public office.

(4) A reference to a person includes a reference to an organisation.

(5) A reference to section 39(2)(b), 44(2)(b), 45(2)(b), 49(6)(b) or 50(6)(b) is to be read as a reference to that provision with the omission of the words 'or for receiving any other benefit, facility or service'.

(6) A reference to section 39(2)(c), 44(2)(c), 45(2)(c), 49(6)(c), 50(6)(c), 53(2)(a) or 55(2)(c) (dismissal, etc.) does not include a reference to that provision so far as relating to sex.

(7) The reference to paragraph (b) of section 41(1), so far as relating to sex, is to be read as if that paragraph read—

'(b) by not allowing the worker to do the work.'

PART 2 EXCEPTIONS RELATING TO AGE

Preliminary

7. For the purposes of this Part of this Schedule, a reference to an age contravention is a reference to a contravention of this Part of this Act, so far as relating to age.

Retirement

8.–9. [repealed]

Benefits based on length of service

10.—(1) It is not an age contravention for a person (A) to put a person (B) at a disadvantage when compared with another (C), in relation to the provision of a benefit, facility or service in so far as the disadvantage is because B has a shorter period of service than C.

(2) If B's period of service exceeds 5 years, A may rely on sub-paragraph (1) only if A reasonably believes that doing so fulfils a business need.

(3) A person's period of service is whichever of the following A chooses—

(a) the period for which the person has been working for A at or above a level (assessed by reference to the demands made on the person) that A reasonably regards as appropriate for the purposes of this paragraph, or

(b) the period for which the person has been working for A at any level.

(4) The period for which a person has been working for A must be based on the number of weeks during the whole or part of which the person has worked for A.

(5) But for that purpose A may, so far as is reasonable, discount—

(a) periods of absence;

(b) periods that A reasonably regards as related to periods of absence.

(6) For the purposes of sub-paragraph (3)(b), a person is to be treated as having worked for A during any period in which the person worked for a person other than A if—

(a) that period counts as a period of employment with A as a result of section 218 of the Employment Rights Act 1996, or

(b) if sub-paragraph (a) does not apply, that period is treated as a period of employment by an enactment pursuant to which the person's employment was transferred to A.

(7) For the purposes of this paragraph, the reference to a benefit, facility or service does not include a reference to a benefit, facility or service which may be provided only by virtue of a person's ceasing to work.

The national minimum wage: young workers

11.—(1) It is not an age contravention for a person to pay a young worker (A) at a lower rate than that at which the person pays an older worker (B) if—

(a) the hourly rate for the national minimum wage for a person of A's age is lower than that for a person of B's age, and

(b) the rate at which A is paid is below the single hourly rate.

(2) A young worker is a person who qualifies for the national minimum wage at a lower rate than the single hourly rate; and an older worker is a person who qualifies for the national minimum wage at a higher rate than that at which the young worker qualifies for it.

(3) The single hourly rate is the rate prescribed under section 1(3) of the National Minimum Wage Act 1998.

The national minimum wage: apprentices

12.—(1) It is not an age contravention for a person to pay an apprentice who does not qualify for the national minimum wage at a lower rate than the person pays an apprentice who does.

(2) An apprentice is a person who—

(a) is employed under a contract of apprenticeship, or

(b) as a result of provision made by virtue of section 3(2)(a) of the National Minimum Wage Act 1998 (persons not qualifying), is treated as employed under a contract of apprenticeship.

Redundancy

13.—(1) It is not an age contravention for a person to give a qualifying employee an enhanced redundancy payment of an amount less than that of an enhanced redundancy payment which the person gives to another qualifying employee, if each amount is calculated on the same basis.

(2) It is not an age contravention to give enhanced redundancy payments only to those who are qualifying employees by virtue of sub-paragraph (3)(a) or (b).

(3) A person is a qualifying employee if the person—

(a) is entitled to a redundancy payment as a result of section 135 of the Employment Rights Act 1996,

(b) agrees to the termination of the employment in circumstances where the person would, if dismissed, have been so entitled,

(c) would have been so entitled but for section 155 of that Act (requirement for two years' continuous employment), or

(d) agrees to the termination of the employment in circumstances where the person would, if dismissed, have been so entitled but for that section.

(4) An enhanced redundancy payment is a payment the amount of which is, subject to sub-paragraphs (5) and (6), calculated in accordance with section 162(1) to (3) of the Employment Rights Act 1996.

(5) A person making a calculation for the purposes of sub-paragraph (4)—

(a) may treat a week's pay as not being subject to a maximum amount;

(b) may treat a week's pay as being subject to a maximum amount above that for the time being specified in section 227(1) of the Employment Rights Act 1996;

(c) may multiply the appropriate amount for each year of employment by a figure of more than one.

(6) Having made a calculation for the purposes of sub-paragraph (4) (whether or not in reliance on sub-paragraph (5)), a person may multiply the amount calculated by a figure of more than one.

(7) In sub-paragraph (5), 'the appropriate amount' has the meaning given in section 162 of the Employment Rights Act 1996, and 'a week's pay' is to be read with Chapter 2 of Part 14 of that Act.

(8) For the purposes of sub-paragraphs (4) to (6), the reference to 'the relevant date' in subsection (1)(a) of section 162 of that Act is, in the case of a person who is a qualifying employee by virtue of sub-paragraph (3)(b) or (d), to be read as reference to the date of the termination of the employment.

14. [omitted]

Child care

15.—(1) A person does not contravene a relevant provision, so far as relating to age, only by providing, or making arrangements for or facilitating the provision of, care for children of a particular age group.

(2) The relevant provisions are—

(a) section 39(2)(b);

(b) section 41(1)(c);

(c) section 44(2)(b);

(d) section 45(2)(b);

(e) section 47(2)(b);

(f) section 48(2)(b);

(g) section 49(6)(b);

(h) section 50(6)(b);

(i) section 57(2)(a);

(j) section 58(3)(a).

(3) Facilitating the provision of care for a child includes—

(a) paying for some or all of the cost of the provision;

(b) helping a parent of the child to find a suitable person to provide care for the child;

(c) enabling a parent of the child to spend more time providing care for the child or otherwise assisting the parent with respect to the care that the parent provides for the child.

(4) A child is a person who has not attained the age of 17.

(5) A reference to care includes a reference to supervision.

16. [omitted]

PART 3 OTHER EXCEPTIONS

Non-contractual payments to women on maternity leave

17.—(1) A person does not contravene section 39(1)(b) or (2), so far as relating to pregnancy and maternity, by depriving a woman who is on maternity leave of any benefit from the terms of her employment relating to pay.

(2) The reference in sub-paragraph (1) to benefit from the terms of a woman's employment relating to pay does not include a reference to—

(a) maternity-related pay (including maternity-related pay that is increase-related),

(b) pay (including increase-related pay) in respect of times when she is not on maternity leave, or

(c) pay by way of bonus in respect of times when she is on compulsory maternity leave.

(3) For the purposes of sub-paragraph (2), pay is increase-related in so far as it is to be calculated by reference to increases in pay that the woman would have received had she not been on maternity leave.

(4) A reference to terms of her employment is a reference to terms of her employment that are not in her contract of employment, her contract of apprenticeship or her contract to do work personally.

(5) 'Pay' means benefits—

(a) that consist of the payment of money to an employee by way of wages or salary, and

(b) that are not benefits whose provision is regulated by the contract referred to in sub-paragraph (4).

(6) 'Maternity-related pay' means pay to which a woman is entitled—

(a) as a result of being pregnant, or

(b) in respect of times when she is on maternity leave.

Benefits dependent on marital status, etc.

18.—(1) A person does not contravene this Part of this Act, so far as relating to sexual orientation, by doing anything which prevents or restricts a person who is not within sub-paragraph (1A) from having access to a benefit, facility or service—

(a) the right to which accrued before 5 December 2005 (the day on which section 1 of the Civil Partnership Act 2004 came into force), or

(b) which is payable in respect of periods of service before that date.

(1A) A person is within this sub-paragraph if the person is—

(a) a man who is married to a woman, or

(b) a woman who is married to a man, or

(c) married to a person of the same sex in a relevant gender change case.

(1B) The reference in sub-paragraph (1A)(c) to a relevant gender change case is a reference to a case where—

(a) the married couple were of the opposite sex at the time of their marriage, and

(b) a full gender recognition certificate has been issued to one of the couple under the Gender Recognition Act 2004.

(1C) [omitted]

(2) A person does not contravene this Part of this Act, so far as relating to sexual orientation, by providing married persons and civil partners (to the exclusion of all other persons) with access to a benefit, facility or service.

Provision of services etc. to the public

19.—(1) A does not contravene a provision mentioned in sub-paragraph (2) in relation to the provision of a benefit, facility or service to B if A is concerned with the provision (for payment or not) of a benefit, facility or service of the same description to the public.

(2) The provisions are—

(a) section 39(2) and (4);

(b) section 41(1) and (3);

(c) sections 44(2) and (6) and 45(2) and (6);

(d) sections 49(6) and (8) and 50(6), (7), (9) and (10).

(3) Sub-paragraph (1) does not apply if—

(a) the provision by A to the public differs in a material respect from the provision by A to comparable persons,
(b) the provision to B is regulated by B's terms, or
(c) the benefit, facility or service relates to training.

(4) 'Comparable persons' means—
(a) in relation to section 39(2) or (4), the other employees;
(b) in relation to section 41(1) or (3), the other contract workers supplied to the principal;
(c) in relation to section 44(2) or (6), the other partners of the firm;
(d) in relation to section 45(2) or (6), the other members of the LLP;
(e) in relation to section 49(6) or (8) or 50(6), (7), (9) or (10), persons holding offices or posts not materially different from that held by B.

(5) 'B's terms' means—
(a) the terms of B's employment,
(b) the terms on which the principal allows B to do the contract work,
(c) the terms on which B has the position as a partner or member, or
(d) the terms of B's appointment to the office.

(6) A reference to the public includes a reference to a section of the public which includes B.

20. [omitted]

SCHEDULE 28

INDEX OF DEFINED EXPRESSIONS

Expression	*Provision*
Accrual of rights, in relation to an occupational pension scheme	Section 212(12)
Additional maternity leave	Section 213(6) and (7)
Additional maternity leave period	Section 213(8)
Age discrimination	Section 25(1)
Age group	Section 5(2)
Armed forces	Section 212(1)
Association	Section 107(2)
Auxiliary aid	Section 20(11)
Belief	Section 10(2)
Breach of an equality clause or rule	Section 212(8)
The Commission	Section 212(1)
Commonhold	Section 38(7)
Compulsory maternity leave	Section 213(3)
Contract work	Section 41(6)
Contract worker	Section 41(7)
Contravention of this Act	Section 212(9)
Crown employment	Section 83(9)
	(Cont.)

Expression	*Provision*
Detriment	Section 212(1) and (5)
Disability	Section 6(1)
Disability discrimination	Section 25(2)
Disabled person	Section 6(2) and (4)
Discrimination	Sections 13 to 19A, 21 and 108
Disposal, in relation to premises	Section 38(3) to (5)
Education Acts	Section 212(1)
Employer, in relation to an occupational pension scheme	Section 212(11)
Employment	Section 212(1)
Enactment	Section 212(1)
Equality clause	Section 212(1)
Equality rule	Section 212(1)
Firm	Section 46(2)
Gender reassignment	Section 7(1)
Gender reassignment discrimination	Section 25(3)
Harassment	Section 26(1)
Independent educational institution	Section 89(7)
LLP	Section 46(4)
Man	Section 212(1)
Marriage and civil partnership	Section 8
Marriage and civil partnership discrimination	Section 25(4)
Maternity equality clause	Section 212(1)
Maternity equality rule	Section 212(1)
Maternity leave	Section 213(2)
Member, in relation to an occupational pension scheme	Section 212(10)
Member of the executive	Section 212(7)
Non-discrimination rule	Section 212(1)
Occupation, in relation to premises	Section 212(6)
Occupational pension scheme	Section 212(1)
Offshore work	Section 82(3)
Ordinary maternity leave	Section 213(4) and (5)
Parent	Section 212(1)
Pension credit member	Section 212(11)
Pensionable service	Section 212(11)

Expression	*Provision*
Pensioner member	Section 212(11)
Personal office	Section 49(2)
Physical feature	Section 20(10)
Pregnancy and maternity discrimination	Section 25(5)
Premises	Section 38(2)
Prescribed	Section 212(1)
Profession	Section 212(1)
Proposed firm	Section 46(3)
Proposed LLP	Section 46(5)
Proprietor, in relation to a school	Section 89(4)
Protected characteristics	Section 4
Protected period, in relation to pregnancy	Section 18(6)
Provision of a service	Sections 31 and 212(4)
Public function	Sections 31(4) and 150(5)
Public office	Sections 50(2) and 52(4)
Pupil	Section 89(3)
Race discrimination	Section 25(6)
Reasonable adjustments, duty to make	Section 20
Relevant member of the House of Commons staff	Section 83(5)
Relevant member of the House of Lords staff	Section 83(6)
Relevant person, in relation to a personal or public office	Section 52(6)
Religion	Section 10(1)
Religious or belief-related discrimination	Section 25(7)
Requirement, the first, second or third	Section 20
Responsible body, in relation to a further or higher education institution	Section 91(12)
Responsible body, in relation to a school	Section 85(9)
School	Section 89(5) and (6)
Service-provider	Section 29(1)
Sex	Section 11
Sex discrimination	Section 25(8)
Sex equality clause	Section 212(1)
Sex equality rule	Section 212(1)
Sexual orientation	Section 12(1)
Sexual orientation discrimination	Section 25(9)
	(Cont.)

Expression	*Provision*
Student	Section 94(3)
Subordinate legislation	Section 212(1)
Substantial	Section 212(1)
Taxi, for the purposes of Part 3 (services and public functions)	Schedule 2, paragraph 4
Taxi, for the purposes of Chapter 1 of Part 12 (disabled persons: transport)	Section 173(1)
Tenancy	Section 38(6)
Trade	Section 212(1)
Transsexual person	Section 7(2)
Trustees or managers, in relation to an occupational pension scheme	Section 212(11)
University	Section 94(4)
Victimisation	Section 27(1)
Vocational training	Section 56(6)
Woman	Section 212(1)

Modern Slavery Act 2015

(2015, c. 30)

1 Slavery, servitude and forced or compulsory labour

(1) A person commits an offence if—

(a) the person holds another person in slavery or servitude and the circumstances are such that the person knows or ought to know that the other person is held in slavery or servitude, or

(b) the person requires another person to perform forced or compulsory labour and the circumstances are such that the person knows or ought to know that the other person is being required to perform forced or compulsory labour.

(2) In subsection (1) the references to holding a person in slavery or servitude or requiring a person to perform forced or compulsory labour are to be construed in accordance with Article 4 of the Human Rights Convention.

(3) In determining whether a person is being held in slavery or servitude or required to perform forced or compulsory labour regard may be had to all the circumstances.

(4) For example, regard may be had—

(a) to any of the person's personal circumstances (such as the person being a child, the person's family relationships, and any mental or physical illness) which may make the person more vulnerable than other persons;

(b) to any work or services provided by the person, including work or services provided in circumstances which constitute exploitation within section 3(3) to (6).

(5) The consent of a person (whether an adult or a child) to any of the acts alleged to constitute holding the person in slavery or servitude, or requiring the person to perform forced or compulsory labour, does not preclude a determination that the person is being held in slavery or servitude, or required to perform forced or compulsory labour.

PART II

Statutory Instruments

The Employment Tribunals Extension of Jurisdiction (England and Wales) Order 1994

(SI 1994 No. 1623)

1.–2. [omitted]

Extension of jurisdiction

3. Proceedings may be brought before an employment tribunal in respect of a claim of an employee for the recovery of damages or any other sum (other than a claim for damages, or for a sum due, in respect of personal injuries) if—

(a) the claim is one to which section 131(2) of the 1978 Act applies and which a court in England and Wales would under the law for the time being in force have jurisdiction to hear and determine;

(b) the claim is not one to which article 5 applies; and

(c) the claim arises or is outstanding on the termination of the employee's employment.

4. Proceedings may be brought before an employment tribunal in respect of a claim of an employer for the recovery of damages or any other sum (other than a claim for damages, or for a sum due, in respect of personal injuries) if—

(a) the claim is one to which section 131(2) of the 1978 Act applies and which a court in England and Wales would under the law for the time being in force have jurisdiction to hear and determine;

(b) the claim is not one to which article 5 applies;

(c) the claim arises or is outstanding on the termination of the employment of the employee against whom it is made; and

(d) proceedings in respect of a claim of that employee have been brought before an employment tribunal by virtue of this Order.

5. This article applies to a claim for breach of a contractual term of any of the following descriptions—

(a) a term requiring the employer to provide living accommodation for the employee;

(b) a term imposing an obligation on the employer or the employee in connection with the provision of living accommodation;

(c) a term relating to intellectual property;

(d) a term imposing an obligation of confidence;

(e) a term which is a covenant in restraint of trade.

In this article, 'intellectual property' includes copyright, rights in performances, moral rights, design right, registered designs, patents and trade marks.

6. [omitted]

Time within which proceedings may be brought

7. Subject to article 8B, an employment tribunal shall not entertain a complaint in respect of an employee's contract claim unless it is presented—

(a) within the period of three months beginning with the effective date of termination of the contract giving rise to the claim, or

(b) where there is no effective date of termination, within the period of three months beginning with the last day upon which the employee worked in the employment which has terminated, or

(ba) where the period within which a complaint must be presented in accordance with paragraph (a) or (b) is extended by regulation 15 of the Employment Act 2002 (Dispute Resolution) Regulations 2004, the period within which the complaint must be presented shall be the extended period rather than the period in paragraph (a) or (b), or

(c) where the tribunal is satisfied that it was not reasonably practicable for the complaint to be presented within whichever of those periods is applicable, within such further period as the tribunal considers reasonable.

8. Subject to article 8B, an employment tribunal shall not entertain a complaint in respect of an employer's contract claim unless—

(a) it is presented at a time when there is before the tribunal a complaint in respect of a contract claim of a particular employee which has not been settled or withdrawn;

(b) it arises out of a contract with that employee; and

(c) it is presented—

  (i) within the period of six weeks beginning with the day, or if more than one the last of the days, on which the employer (or other person who is the respondent party to the employee's contract claim) received from the tribunal a copy of an originating application in respect of a contract claim of that employee; or

  (ii) where the tribunal is satisfied that it was not reasonably practicable for the complaint to be presented within that period, within such further period as the tribunal considers reasonable.

8A.–9. [omitted]

Limit on payment to be ordered

10. An employment tribunal shall not in proceedings in respect of a contract claim, or in respect of a number of contract claims relating to the same contract, order the payment of an amount exceeding £25,000.

The Employment Protection (Continuity of Employment) Regulations 1996

(SI 1996 No. 3147)

Application

2. These Regulations apply to any action taken in relation to the dismissal of an employee which consists of—

(a) his making a claim in accordance with a dismissal procedures agreement designated by an order under section 110 of the Employment Rights Act 1996,

(b) the presentation by him of a relevant complaint of dismissal,

(c) any action taken by a conciliation officer under any of sections 18A to 18C of the Employment Tribunals Act 1996,

(d) the making of a relevant settlement agreement,

(e) the making of an agreement to submit a dispute to arbitration in accordance with a scheme having effect by virtue of an order under section 212A of the Trade Union and Labour Relations (Consolidation) Act 1992,

(f) a decision taken arising out of the use of a statutory dispute resolution procedure contained in Schedule 2 to the Employment Act 2002 in a case where, in accordance with the Employment Act 2002 (Dispute Resolution) Regulations 2004, such a procedure applies, or

(g) a decision taken arising out of the use of the statutory duty to consider procedure contained in Schedule 6 to the Employment Equality (Age) Regulations 2006.

Continuity of employment where employee re-engaged

3.—(1) The provisions of this regulation shall have effect to preserve the continuity of a person's period of employment for the purposes of—

(a) Chapter I of Part XIV of the Employment Rights Act 1996 (continuous employment), and

(b) that Chapter as applied by subsection (2) of section 282 of the Trade Union and Labour Relations (Consolidation) Act 1992 for the purposes of that section.

(2) If in consequence of any action to which these Regulations apply a dismissed employee is reinstated or re-employed by his employer or by a successor or associated employer of the employer—

(a) the continuity of that employee's period of employment shall be preserved,

(b) the period beginning with the date on which the dismissal takes effect and ending with the date of reinstatement or re-engagement shall count in the computation of the employee's period of continuous employment.

Exclusion of operation of section 214 of the Employment Rights Act 1996 where redundancy or equivalent payment repaid

4.—(1) Section 214 of the Employment Rights Act 1996 (continuity broken where employee re-employed after the making of a redundancy payment or equivalent payment) shall not apply where—

(a) in consequence of any action to which these Regulations apply a dismissed employee is reinstated or re-employed by his employer or by a successor or associated employer of the employer,

(b) the terms upon which he is so reinstated or re-engaged include provision for him to repay the amount of a redundancy payment or an equivalent payment paid in respect of the relevant dismissal, and

(c) that provision is complied with.

(2) For the purposes of this regulation the cases in which a redundancy payment shall be treated as having been paid are the cases mentioned in section 214(5) of the Employment Rights Act 1996.

The Working Time Regulations 1998

(SI 1998 No. 1833)

Arrangement of Regulations

PART I GENERAL

2 Interpretation

PART II RIGHTS AND OBLIGATIONS CONCERNING WORKING TIME

3 General
4 Maximum weekly working time
5 Agreement to exclude the maximum
5A Maximum working time for young workers
6 Length of night work
6A Night work by young workers
8 Pattern of work
9 Records
10 Daily rest
11 Weekly rest period
12 Rest breaks
13 Entitlement to annual leave

13A Entitlement to additional annual leave
14 Compensation related to entitlement to leave
15 Dates on which leave is taken
15B Irregular hours workers and part-year workers: entitlement to annual leave
15C Irregular hours workers and part-year workers: annual leave accrued while on sick or statutory leave
15D Irregular hours workers and part-year workers: right to carry forward annual leave
15E Irregular hours workers and part-year workers: compensation related to entitlement to leave
15F Meaning of irregular hours workers and part-year workers
16 Payment in respect of periods of leave
16A Rolled-up holiday pay for irregular hours workers and part-year workers
17 Entitlements under other provisions

PART III EXCEPTIONS
19 Domestic service
20 Unmeasured working time
21 Other special cases
22 Shift workers
23 Collective and workforce agreements
24 Compensatory rest
24A Mobile workers
26A Entitlement to additional annual leave under a relevant agreement
27 Young workers: *force majeure*
27A Other exceptions relating to young workers

PART IV MISCELLANEOUS
28 Enforcement
29 Offences
29A Offences due to fault of other person
29B Offences by bodies corporate
29E Power of court to order cause of offence to be remedied
30 Remedies
35 Restrictions on contracting out

PART V SPECIAL CLASSES OF PERSON
36 Agency workers not otherwise 'workers'
37 Crown employment
42 Non-employed trainees

SCHEDULE 1 WORKFORCE AGREEMENTS

PART I GENERAL

1 [omitted]

2 Interpretation

(1) In these Regulations—

'the 1996 Act' means the Employment Rights Act 1996;

'adult worker' means a worker who has attained the age of 18;

'the armed forces' means any of the naval, military and air forces of the Crown;

'calendar year' means the period of twelve months beginning with 1 January in any year;

'the civil protection services' includes the police, fire brigades and ambulance services, the security and intelligence services, customs and immigration officers, the prison service, the coastguard, and lifeboat crew and other voluntary rescue services;

'collective agreement' means a collective agreement within the meaning of section 178 of the Trade Union and Labour Relations (Consolidation) Act 1992, the trade union parties to which are independent trade unions within the meaning of section 5 of that Act;

'day' means a period of 24 hours beginning at midnight;

'employer', in relation to a worker, means the person by whom the worker is (or, where the employment has ceased, was) employed;

'employment', in relation to a worker, means employment under his contract, and 'employed' shall be construed accordingly;

'fishing vessel' has the same meaning as in section 313 of the Merchant Shipping Act 1995;

'irregular hours worker' has the meaning given by regulation 15F(1);

'mobile worker' means any worker employed as a member of travelling or flying personnel by an undertaking which operates transport services for passengers or goods by road or air;

'night time', in relation to a worker, means a period—

(a) the duration of which is not less than seven hours, and

(b) which includes the period between midnight and 5 a.m.,

which is determined for the purposes of these Regulations by a relevant agreement, or, in default of such a determination, the period between 11 p.m. and 6 a.m.;

'night work' means work during night time;

'night worker' means a worker—

(a) who, as a normal course, works at least three hours of his daily working time during night time, or

(b) who is likely, during night time, to work at least such proportion of his annual working time as may be specified for the purposes of these Regulations in a collective agreement or a workforce agreement,

and, for the purpose of paragraph (a) of this definition, a person works hours as a normal course (without prejudice to the generality of that expression) if he works such hours on the majority of days on which he works;

'offshore work' means work performed mainly on or from offshore installations (including drilling rigs), directly or indirectly in connection with the exploration, extraction or exploitation of mineral resources, including hydrocarbons, and diving in connection with such activities, whether performed from an offshore installation or a vessel, including any such work performed in the territorial waters of the United Kingdom adjacent to Great Britain or in any area (except one or part of one in which the law of Northern Ireland applies) designated under section 1(7) of the Continental Shelf Act 1964;

'relevant agreement', in relation to a worker, means a workforce agreement which applies to him, any provision of a collective agreement which forms part of a contract between him and his employer, or any other agreement in writing which is legally enforceable as between the worker and his employer;

'relevant training' means work experience provided pursuant to a training course or programme, training for employment, or both, other than work experience or training—

(a) the immediate provider of which is an educational institution or a person whose main business is the provision of training, and

(b) which is provided on a course run by that institution or person;

'rest period', in relation to a worker, means a period which is not working time, other than a rest break or leave to which the worker is entitled under these Regulations;

'the restricted period', in relation to a worker, means the period between 10 p.m. and 6 a.m. or, where the worker's contract provides for him to work after 10 p.m., the period between 11 p.m. and 7 a.m.;

'ship' has the same meaning as in section 313 of the Merchant Shipping Act 1995;

'sick leave' means absence from work due to sickness or injury;

'statutory leave' means leave provided for in Part 8 and Part 8B of the 1996 Act;

'worker' means an individual who has entered into or works under (or, where the employment has ceased, worked under)—

(a) a contract of employment, or

(b) any other contract, whether express or implied and (if it is express) whether oral or in writing, whereby the individual undertakes to do or perform personally any work or services for another party to the contract whose status is not by virtue of the contract that of a client or customer of any profession or business undertaking carried on by the individual,

and any reference to a worker's contract shall be construed accordingly;

'worker employed in agriculture' means, in relation to Wales, an agricultural worker within the meaning of section 18 of the Agricultural Sector (Wales) Act 2014 and otherwise has the same meaning as in the Agricultural Wages Act 1948 or the Agricultural Wages (Scotland) Act 1949, and a reference to a worker partly employed in agriculture is to a worker employed in agriculture whose employer also employs him for non-agricultural purposes;

'workforce agreement' means an agreement between an employer and worker employed by him or their representatives in respect of which the conditions set out in Schedule 1 to these Regulations are satisfied;

'working time', in relation to a worker, means—

(a) any period during which he is working, at his employer's disposal and carrying out his activity or duties,

(b) any period during which he is receiving relevant training, and

(c) any additional period which is to be treated as working time for the purpose of these Regulations under a relevant agreement,

and 'work' shall be construed accordingly;

'Working Time Directive' means Council Directive 93/104/EC of 23 November 1993 concerning certain aspects of the organisation of working time;

'young worker' means a worker who has attained the age of 15 but not the age of 18 and who, as respects England and Wales, is over compulsory school age (construed in accordance with section 8 of the Education Act 1996) and, as respects Scotland, is over school age (construed in accordance with section 31 of the Education (Scotland) Act 1980); and

'Young Workers Directive' means Council Directive 94/33/EC of 22 June 1994 on the protection of young people at work.

(2) In the absence of a definition in these Regulations, words and expressions used in particular provisions which are also used in corresponding provisions of the Working Time Directive or the Young Workers Directive have the same meaning as they have in those corresponding provisions.

(3) [omitted]

PART II RIGHTS AND OBLIGATIONS CONCERNING WORKING TIME

3 General

(1) The provisions of this Part have effect subject to the exceptions provided for in Part III of these Regulations.

(2) Where, in this Part, separate provision is made as respects the same matter in relation to workers generally and to young workers, the provision relating to workers generally applies only to adult workers and those young workers to whom, by virtue of any exception in Part 3, the provision relating to young workers does not apply.

4 Maximum weekly working time

(1) Unless his employer has first obtained the worker's agreement in writing to perform such work, a worker's working time, including overtime, in any reference period which is applicable in his case shall not exceed an average of 48 hours for each seven days.

(2) An employer shall take all reasonable steps, in keeping with the need to protect the health and safety of workers, to ensure that the limit specified in paragraph (1) is complied with in the case of each worker employed by him in relation to whom it applies and shall keep up-to-date records of all workers who carry out work to which it does not apply by reason of the fact that the employer has obtained the worker's agreement as mentioned in paragraph (1).

(3) Subject to paragraphs (4) and (5) and any agreement under regulation 23(b), the reference periods which apply in the case of a worker are—

(a) where a relevant agreement provides for the application of this regulation in relation to successive periods of 17 weeks, each such period, or

(b) in any other case, any period of 17 weeks in the course of his employment.

(4) Where a worker has worked for his employer for less than 17 weeks, the reference period applicable in his case is the period that has elapsed since he started work for his employer.

(5) Paragraphs (3) and (4) shall apply to a worker who is excluded from the scope of certain provisions of these Regulations by regulation 21 as if for each reference to 17 weeks there were substituted a reference to 26 weeks.

(6) For the purposes of this regulation, a worker's average working time for each seven days during a reference period shall be determined according to the formula—

$$\frac{A + b}{C}$$

where—

A is the aggregate number of hours comprised in the worker's working time during the course of the reference period;

B is the aggregate number of hours comprised in his working time during the course of the period beginning immediately after the end of the reference period and ending when the number of days in that subsequent period on which he has worked equals the number of excluded days during the reference period; and

C is the number of weeks in the reference period.

(7) In paragraph (6), 'excluded days' means days comprised in—

(a) any period of annual leave taken by the worker in exercise of his entitlement under regulation 13, 13A or 15B;

(b) any period of sick leave taken by the worker;

(c) any period of maternity, paternity, adoption or parental leave taken by the worker; and

(d) any period in respect of which the limit specified in paragraph (1) did not apply in relation to the worker by reason of the fact that the employer has obtained the worker's agreement as mentioned in paragraph (1).

5 Agreement to exclude the maximum

(1) [revoked]

(2) An agreement for the purposes of regulation 4—

(a) may either relate to a specified period or apply indefinitely; and

(b) subject to any provision in the agreement for a different period of notice, shall be terminable by the worker by giving not less than seven days' notice to his employer in writing.

(3) Where an agreement for the purposes of regulation 4 makes provision for the termination of the agreement after a period of notice, the notice period provided for shall not exceed three months.

(4) [revoked]

5A Maximum working time for young workers

(1) A young worker's working time shall not exceed—

(a) eight hours a day, or

(b) 40 hours a week.

(2) If, on any day, or, as the case may be, during any week, a young worker is employed by more than one employer, his working time shall be determined for the purpose of paragraph (1) by aggregating the number of hours worked by him for each employer.

(3) For the purposes of paragraphs (1) and (2), a week starts at midnight between Sunday and Monday.

(4) An employer shall take all reasonable steps, in keeping with the need to protect the health and safety of workers, to ensure that the limits specified in paragraph (1) are complied with in the case of each worker employed by him in relation to whom they apply.

6 Length of night work

(1) A night worker's normal hours of work in any reference period which is applicable in his case shall not exceed an average of eight hours for each 24 hours.

(2) An employer shall take all reasonable steps, in keeping with the need to protect the health and safety of workers, to ensure that the limit specified in paragraph (1) is complied with in the case of each night worker employed by him.

(3) The reference periods which apply in the case of a night worker are—

(a) where a relevant agreement provides for the application of this regulation in relation to successive periods of 17 weeks, each such period, or

(b) in any other case, any period of 17 weeks in the course of his employment.

(4) Where a worker has worked for his employer for less than 17 weeks, the reference period applicable in his case is the period that has elapsed since he started work for his employer.

(5) For the purposes of this regulation, a night worker's average normal hours of work for each 24 hours during a reference period shall be determined according to the formula—

$$\frac{A}{B - C}$$

where—

A is the number of hours during the reference period which are normal working hours for that worker;

B is the number of days during the reference period; and

C is the total number of hours during the reference period comprised in rest periods spent by the worker in pursuance of his entitlement under regulation 11, divided by 24.

(6) [revoked]

(7) An employer shall ensure that no night worker employed by him whose work involves special hazards or heavy physical or mental strain works for more than eight hours in any 24-hour period during which the night worker performs night work.

(8) For the purposes of paragraph (7), the work of a night worker shall be regarded as involving special hazards or heavy physical or mental strain if—

(a) it is identified as such in—

(i) a collective agreement, or

(ii) a workforce agreement, which takes account of the specific effects and hazards of night work, or

(b) it is recognised in a risk assessment made by the employer under regulation 3 of the Management of Health and Safety at Work Regulations 1999 as involving a significant risk to the health or safety of workers employed by him.

6A Night work by young workers

An employer shall ensure that no young worker employed by him works during the restricted period.

7 [omitted]

8 Pattern of work

Where the pattern according to which an employer organises work is such as to put the health and safety of a worker employed by him at risk, in particular because the work is monotonous or the work-rate is predetermined, the employer shall ensure that the worker is given adequate rest breaks.

9 Records

(1) An employer shall—

(a) keep records which are adequate to show whether the employer has complied with the limits specified in regulations 4(1), 5A(1) and 6(1) and (7) and the requirements in regulations 6A and 7(1) and (2);

(b) retain such records for two years from the date on which they were made.

(2) The records referred to in paragraph (1)(a) may be created, maintained and kept in such manner and format as the employer reasonably thinks fit.

(3) An employer need not record each worker's daily working hours in order to comply with paragraph (1) if the employer is able to demonstrate compliance without doing so.

10 Daily rest

(1) A worker is entitled to a rest period of not less than eleven consecutive hours in each 24-hour period during which he works for his employer.

(2) Subject to paragraph (3), a young worker is entitled to a rest period of not less than twelve consecutive hours in each 24-hour period during which he works for his employer.

(3) The minimum rest period provided for in paragraph (2) may be interrupted in the case of activities involving periods of work that are split up over the day or of short duration.

11 Weekly rest period

(1) Subject to paragraph (2), a worker is entitled to an uninterrupted rest period of not less than 24 hours in each seven-day period during which he works for his employer.

(2) If his employer so determines, a worker shall be entitled to either—

(a) two uninterrupted rest periods each of not less than 24 hours in each 14-day period during which he works for his employer; or

(b) one uninterrupted rest period of not less than 48 hours in each such 14-day period,

in place of the entitlement provided for in paragraph (1).

(3) Subject to paragraph (8), a young worker is entitled to a rest period of not less than 48 hours in each seven-day period during which he works for his employer.

(4) For the purpose of paragraphs (1) to (3), a seven-day period or (as the case may be) 14-day period shall be taken to begin—

(a) at such times on such days as may be provided for for the purposes of this regulation in a relevant agreement; or

(b) where there are no provisions of a relevant agreement which apply, at the start of each week or (as the case may be) every other week.

(5) In a case where, in accordance with paragraph (4), 14-day periods are to be taken to begin at the start of every other week, the first such period applicable in the case of a particular worker shall be taken to begin—

(a) if the worker's employment began on or before the date on which these Regulations come into force, on 5th October 1998; or

(b) if the worker's employment begins after the date on which these Regulations come into force, at the start of the week in which that employment begins.

(6) For the purposes of paragraphs (4) and (5), a week starts at midnight between Sunday and Monday.

(7) The minimum rest period to which a worker is entitled under paragraph (1) or (2) shall not include any part of a rest period to which the worker is entitled under regulation 10(1), except where this is justified by objective or technical reasons or reasons concerning the organisation of work.

(8) The minimum rest period to which a young worker is entitled under paragraph (3)—

(a) may be interrupted in the case of activities involving periods of work that are split up over the day or are of short duration; and

(b) may be reduced where this is justified by technical or organisation reasons, but not to less than 36 consecutive hours.

12 Rest breaks

(1) Where a worker's daily working time is more than six hours, he is entitled to a rest break.

(2) The details of the rest break to which a worker is entitled under paragraph (1), including its duration and the terms on which it is granted, shall be in accordance with any provisions for the purposes of this regulation which are contained in a collective agreement or a workforce agreement.

(3) Subject to the provisions of any applicable collective agreement or workforce agreement, the rest break provided for in paragraph (1) is an uninterrupted period of not less than 20 minutes, and the worker is entitled to spend it away from his workstation if he has one.

(4) Where a young worker's daily working time is more than four and a half hours, he is entitled to a rest break of at least 30 minutes, which shall be consecutive if possible, and he is entitled to spend it away from his workstation if he has one.

(5) If, on any day, a young worker is employed by more than one employer, his daily working time shall be determined for the purpose of paragraph (4) by aggregating the number of hours worked by him for each employer.

13 Entitlement to annual leave

(A1) This regulation applies to—

(a) a worker in respect of any leave years beginning before 1st April 2024, and

(b) a worker to whom regulation 15B does not apply in respect of any leave years beginning on or after 1st April 2024.

(1) Subject to paragraph (5), a worker is entitled to four weeks' annual leave in each leave year.

(2) [revoked]

(3) A worker's leave year, for the purposes of this regulation, begins—

(a) on such date during the calendar year as may be provided for in a relevant agreement; or

(b) where there are no provisions of a relevant agreement which apply—

(i) if the worker's employment began on or before 1st October 1998, on that date and each subsequent anniversary of that date; or

(ii) if the worker's employment begins after 1st October 1998, on the date on which that employment begins and each subsequent anniversary of that date.

(4) Paragraph (3) does not apply to a worker to whom Schedule 2 applies (workers employed in agriculture in Wales or Scotland) except where, in the case of a worker partly employed in agriculture in Wales or Scotland, a relevant agreement so provides.

(5) Where the date on which a worker's employment begins is later than the date on which (by virtue of a relevant agreement) his first leave year begins, the leave to which he is entitled in that leave year is a proportion of the period applicable under paragraph (1) equal to the proportion of that leave year remaining on the date on which his employment begins.

(6)–(8) [revoked]

(9) Leave to which a worker is entitled under this regulation may be taken in instalments, but—

(a) subject to the exception in paragraphs (14), (15) and (17), it may only be taken in the leave year in respect of which it is due, and

(b) it may not be replaced by a payment in lieu except where the worker's employment is terminated.

(10)–(13) [repealed]

(14) Where, as a result of taking a period of statutory leave in any leave year, a worker is unable to take some or all of the annual leave to which the worker is entitled in that leave year under this regulation, the worker is entitled to carry forward such untaken leave into the following leave year.

(15) Where, as a result of taking a period of sick leave in any leave year, a worker is unable to take some or all of the annual leave to which the worker is entitled in that leave year under this regulation, the worker is entitled to carry forward such untaken leave into the following leave year provided it is taken by the end of the period of 18 months from the end of the leave year in which the entitlement originally arose.

(16) Paragraph (17) applies where, in any leave year, an employer fails to—

(a) recognise a worker's right to annual leave under this regulation or to payment for that leave in accordance with regulation 16;

(b) give the worker a reasonable opportunity to take the leave to which the worker is entitled under this regulation or encourage them to do so; or

(c) inform the worker that any leave not taken by the end of the leave year, which cannot be carried forward, will be lost.

(17) Where this paragraph applies and subject to paragraph (18), the worker is entitled to carry forward any leave to which the worker is entitled under this regulation which is untaken in that leave year or has been taken but not paid in accordance with regulation 16.

(18) Annual leave that has been carried forward pursuant to paragraph (17) cannot be carried forward beyond the end of the first full leave year in which paragraph (17) does not apply.

13A Entitlement to additional annual leave

(A1) This regulation applies to—

(a) a worker in respect of any leave years beginning before 1st April 2024, and

(b) a worker to whom regulation 15B does not apply in respect of any leave years beginning on or after 1st April 2024.

(1) Subject to regulation 26A and paragraphs (3) and (5), a worker is entitled in each leave year to a period of additional leave determined in accordance with paragraph (2).

(2) The period of additional leave to which a worker is entitled under paragraph (1) is—

(a)–(d) [omitted];

(e) in any leave year beginning on or after 1st April 2009, 1.6 weeks.

(3) The aggregate entitlement provided for in paragraph (2) and regulation 13(1) is subject to a maximum of 28 days.

(4) A worker's leave year begins for the purposes of this regulation on the same date as the worker's leave year begins for the purposes of regulation 13.

(5) Where the date on which a worker's employment begins is later than the date on which his first leave year begins, the additional leave to which he is entitled in that leave year is a proportion of the period applicable under paragraph (2) equal to the proportion of that leave year remaining on the date on which his employment begins.

(6) Leave to which a worker is entitled under this regulation may be taken in instalments, but it may not be replaced by a payment in lieu except where—

(a) the worker's employment is terminated;

(b)–(c) [omitted]

(7) A relevant agreement may provide for any leave to which a worker is entitled under this regulation to be carried forward into the leave year immediately following the leave year in respect of which it is due.

(7A) Where, as a result of taking a period of statutory leave in any leave year, a worker is unable to take some or all of the annual leave to which the worker is entitled in that leave year under this regulation, the worker is entitled to carry forward such untaken leave into the following leave year.

(8) This regulation does not apply to workers to whom the Agricultural Wages (Scotland) Act 1949 applies (as that Act had effect on 1 July 1999).

14 Compensation related to entitlement to leave

(1) Paragraphs (1) to (4) of this regulation apply where—

(a) a worker's employment is terminated during the course of his leave year, and

(b) on the date on which the termination takes effect ('the termination date'), the proportion he has taken of the leave to which he is entitled in the leave year under regulations 13(1) and regulation 13A(1) differs from the proportion of the leave year which has expired.

(2) Where the proportion of leave taken by the worker is less than the proportion of the leave year which has expired, his employer shall make him a payment in lieu of leave in accordance with paragraph (3).

(3) The payment due under paragraph (2) shall be—

(a) such sum as may be provided for for the purposes of this regulation in a relevant agreement, or

(b) where there are no provisions of a relevant agreement which apply, a sum equal to the amount that would be due to the worker under regulation 16 in respect of a period of leave determined according to the formula—

$$(A \times B) - C$$

where—

A is the period of leave to which the worker is entitled under regulation 13 and regulation 13A;

B is the proportion of the worker's leave year which expired before the termination date; and

C is the period of leave taken by the worker between the start of the leave year and the termination date.

(4) A relevant agreement may provide that, where the proportion of leave taken by the worker exceeds the proportion of the leave year which has expired, he shall compensate his employer, whether by a payment, by undertaking additional work or otherwise.

(5) [repealed]

(6) Where a worker's employment is terminated and on the termination date the worker remains entitled to leave in respect of any previous leave year which carried forward under paragraph (14), (15) or (17) of regulation 13 or paragraph (7) or (7A) of regulation 13A, the employer shall make the worker a payment in lieu of leave equal to the sum due under regulation 16 for the period of untaken leave.

15 Dates on which leave is taken

(1) A worker may take leave to which he is entitled under regulations 13, 13A and 15B on such days as he may elect by giving notice to his employer in accordance with paragraph (3), subject to any requirement imposed on him by his employer under paragraph (2).

(2) A worker's employer may require the worker—

(a) to take leave to which the worker is entitled under regulation 13, 13A or 15B; or

(b) not to take such leave,

on particular days, by giving notice to the worker in accordance with paragraph (3).

(3) A notice under paragraph (1) or (2)—

(a) may relate to all or part of the leave to which a worker is entitled in a leave year;

(b) shall specify the days on which leave is or (as the case may be) is not to be taken and, where the leave on a particular day is to be in respect of only part of the day, its duration; and

(c) shall be given to the employer or, as the case may be, the worker before the relevant date.

(4) The relevant date, for the purposes of paragraph (3), is the date—

(a) in the case of a notice under paragraph (1) or (2)(a), twice as many days in advance of the earliest day specified in the notice as the number of days or part-days to which the notice relates, and

(b) in the case of a notice under paragraph (2)(b), as many days in advance of the earliest day so specified as the number of days or part-days to which the notice relates.

(5) Any right or obligation under paragraphs (1) to (4) may be varied or excluded by a relevant agreement.

(6) This regulation does not apply to a worker to whom Schedule 2 applies (workers employed in agriculture in Wales or Scotland) except where, in the case of a worker partly employed in agriculture in Wales or Scotland, a relevant agreement so provides.

15A [omitted]

15B Irregular hours workers and part-year workers: entitlement to annual leave

(1) This regulation applies to an irregular hours worker, or a part-year worker, to whom the Agricultural Wages (Scotland) Act 1949 (as that Act had effect on 1st July 1999) does not apply, in respect of any leave years beginning on or after 1st April 2024.

(2) The amount of annual leave to which an irregular hours worker, or a part-year worker, is entitled at any time during a leave year is the amount of annual leave that they have accrued in that year, plus the amount of annual leave (if any) that they have carried forward into that leave year, less the amount of annual leave (if any) that they have taken during that leave year.

(3) In each leave year, an irregular hours worker, or a part-year worker, accrues annual leave—

(a) during any period of sick leave or statutory leave, in accordance with regulation 15C, and

(b) otherwise, on the last day of each pay period at the rate of 12.07% of the number of hours that they have worked during that pay period.

(4) But a worker cannot, in any leave year, accrue more than 28 days of annual leave under this regulation.

(5) Where the amount of annual leave that has accrued in a particular case includes a fraction of an hour, the fraction is to be treated as zero if it is less than 30 minutes and one hour if it is 30 minutes or more than 30 minutes.

(6) Annual leave to which a worker is entitled under this regulation may be taken in instalments, but it may not be replaced by a payment in lieu except where the worker's employment is terminated.

(7) For the purposes of this regulation, a worker's leave year begins—

(a) on such date during the calendar year as may be provided for in a relevant agreement, or

(b) where there are no provisions of a relevant agreement which apply, on the date on which the worker's employment begins and each subsequent anniversary of that date.

(8) Paragraph (7) does not apply to a worker to whom Schedule 2 (workers employed in agriculture) applies except where, in the case of a worker partly employed in agriculture, a relevant agreement so provides.

15C Irregular hours workers and part-year workers: annual leave accrued while on sick or statutory leave

(1) This regulation applies for the purposes of determining the amount of annual leave which a worker to whom regulation 15B applies, accrues in a pay period during a period of sick leave or statutory leave.

(2) The amount of annual leave is calculated as follows—

Step 1—Calculate the average number of hours per week that the worker worked during the relevant period before the worker started the sick leave or statutory leave.

Step 2—Calculate 12.07% of the number of hours arrived at under Step 1 to find the number of hours of annual leave that the worker accrues during each week of the sick leave or statutory leave.

Step 3—Multiply that number of hours by the number of weeks in a pay period for which the worker is taking sick leave or statutory leave to find the number of hours of annual leave that the worker accrues during each such pay period.

(3) In Step 1, the 'relevant period' means—

(a) the period of 52 weeks ending with the day before the day on which the worker started the sick leave or statutory leave, or

(b) if the worker has been in employment for a period of less than 52 complete weeks before starting that leave, that lesser period.

(4) For the purposes of the calculation under Step 1—

(a) no account is to be taken of any weeks during the relevant period in which a worker was, for any amount of time, on sick leave or statutory leave, but

(b) all other weeks during the relevant period are to be taken into account, including weeks during which the worker did not work any hours.

(5) If, in a case falling within paragraph (3)(a), any weeks are discounted under paragraph (4)(a), earlier weeks shall be taken into account so as to bring the number of weeks to 52 (or as close to 52 as possible).

(6) For the purposes of paragraph (5) no account is to be taken of hours worked in weeks preceding the period of 104 weeks ending—

(a) where the calculation date is the last day of a week, with that week, and

(b) otherwise, with the last complete week before the calculation date.

15D Irregular hours workers and part-year workers: right to carry forward annual leave

(1) Leave to which a worker is entitled under regulation 15B may be taken in instalments but, subject to the exceptions in paragraphs (2), (3), (4) and (6), it may only be taken in the leave year that it accrues.

(2) A relevant agreement may provide for part of the annual leave to which a worker is entitled under regulation 15B to be carried forward into the leave year immediately following the leave year in which it accrued.

(3) Where, as a result of taking a period of statutory leave in any leave year, a worker is unable to take some or all of the annual leave to which the worker is entitled in that leave year under regulation 15B, the worker is entitled to carry forward such untaken leave into the following leave year.

(4) Where, as a result of taking a period of sick leave in any leave year, a worker is unable to take some or all of the annual leave to which the worker is entitled in that leave year under regulation 15B, the worker is entitled to carry forward such untaken leave into the following leave year provided it is taken by the end of the period of 18 months from the end of the leave year in which the entitlement originally arose.

(5) Paragraph (6) applies where, in any leave year, an employer fails to—

(a) recognise a worker's right to annual leave under regulation 15B or to payment for that leave in accordance with regulation 16;

(b) give the worker a reasonable opportunity to take the leave to which the worker is entitled under regulation 15B or encourage them to do so; or

(c) inform the worker that any leave not taken by the end of the leave year, which cannot be carried forward, will be lost.

(6) Where this paragraph applies and subject to paragraph (7), the worker is entitled to carry forward any annual leave to which the worker is entitled under regulation 15B which is untaken in that leave year or has been taken but not paid in accordance with regulation 16.

(7) Annual leave that has been carried forward pursuant to paragraph (6) cannot be carried forward beyond the end of the first full leave year in which paragraph (6) does not apply.

15E Irregular hours workers and part-year workers: compensation related to entitlement to leave

(1) This regulation applies to a worker to whom regulation 15B applies, in respect of any leave years beginning on or after 1st April 2024.

(2) Where—

(a) the worker's employment is terminated during the course of their leave year, and

(b) at the date on which the termination takes effect, the worker has not taken all the annual leave to which they are entitled under regulation 15B(2),

the worker's employer must make the worker a payment in lieu of that untaken leave.

(3) The payment due under paragraph (2) is—

(a) such sum as may be provided for in a relevant agreement for the purposes of this regulation, or

(b) where there are no provisions of a relevant agreement which apply, a sum equal to the amount that would be due under regulation 16 in respect of the untaken leave.

(4) A relevant agreement may provide that, where—

(a) the worker's employment is terminated during the course of their leave year, and

(b) the worker has taken more leave than that to which they are entitled under regulation 15B,

the worker must compensate their employer, whether by a payment, by undertaking additional work or otherwise.

(5) Paragraph (2) does not apply if the worker has in respect of the untaken leave mentioned in that paragraph been paid in the way described in regulation 16A.

15F Meaning of irregular hours workers and part-year workers

(1) For the purposes of these Regulations—

(a) a worker is an irregular hours worker, in relation to a leave year, if the number of paid hours that they will work in each pay period during the term of their contract in that year is, under the terms of their contract, wholly or mostly variable;

(b) a worker is a part-year worker, in relation to a leave year, if, under the terms of their contract, they are required to work only part of that year and there are periods within that year (during the term of the contract) of at least a week which they are not required to work and for which they are not paid.

(2) [omitted]

(3) In determining whether a worker is a part-year worker in relation to a leave year, any period of sick leave or statutory leave taken by the worker in that leave year is to be ignored.

16 Payment in respect of periods of leave

(1) A worker is entitled to be paid in respect of any period of annual leave to which he is entitled under regulations 13, 13A and 15B, at the rate of a week's pay in respect of each week of leave.

(1A) The hourly rate of pay in respect of any period of annual leave to which a worker is entitled under regulation 15B is determined according to the formula—

$$A \div B$$

where—

A is the week's pay mentioned in paragraph (1); and

B is the average number of hours worked by the worker in each week used to calculate A.

(2) Sections 221 to 224 of the 1996 Act shall apply for the purpose of determining the amount of a week's pay for the purposes of this regulation, subject to the modifications set out in paragraph (3), the supplementary provisions in paragraphs (3ZA) to (3ZG) and the exception in paragraph (3A).

(3) The provisions referred to in paragraph (2) shall apply—

(a) as if references to the employee were references to the worker;

(b) as if references to the employee's contract of employment were references to the worker's contract;

(c) as if the calculation date were the first day of the period of leave in question;

(d) as if the references to sections 227 and 228 did not apply.

(da) as if, in the case of entitlement under regulations 13 and 15B, sections 223(3) and 234 did not apply;

(e) subject to the exception in sub-paragraph (f)(ii), as if in sections 221(3), 222(3) and (4), 223(2) and 224(2) and (3) references to twelve were references to—

(i) in the case of a worker who on the calculation date has been employed by their employer for less than 52 complete weeks, the number of complete weeks for which the worker has been employed, or

(ii) in any other case, 52; and

(f) in any case where section 223(2) or 224(3) applies as if—

(i) account were not to be taken of remuneration in weeks preceding the period of 104 weeks ending—

(aa) where the calculation date is the last day of a week, with that week, and

(bb) otherwise, with the last complete week before the calculation date; and

(ii) the period of weeks required for the purposes of sections 221(3), 222(3) and (4) and 224(2) was the number of weeks of which account is taken.

(3ZA) In the case of entitlement under regulations 13 and 15B the following types of payments are to be included when determining the amount of a week's pay for the purposes of this regulation—

(a) payments, including commission payments, which are intrinsically linked to the performance of tasks which a worker is obliged to carry out under the terms of their contract;

(b) payments for professional or personal status relating to length of service, seniority or professional qualifications;

(c) other payments, such as overtime payments, which have been regularly paid to a worker in the 52 weeks preceding the calculation date.

(3ZB) To the extent that the types of payment mentioned in paragraph (3ZA) would not otherwise be accounted for in a calculation of a week's pay under sections 221 to 224 of the 1996 Act (as those sections apply for the purposes of this regulation), those types of payment are to be included by calculating the average weekly amount of those payments payable in the relevant period and adding it to the amount of a week's pay arrived at under those sections.

(3ZC) In the case of a worker who on the calculation date has been employed by their employer for less than 52 complete weeks, the 'relevant period' is the number of complete weeks for which the worker has been employed.

(3ZD) In the case of a worker who on the calculation date has been employed by their employer for 52 or more complete weeks, the 'relevant period' is the period of 52 weeks ending—

(a) where the calculation date is the last day of a week, with that week, and

(b) otherwise, with the last complete week before the calculation date.

(3ZE) In calculating the average weekly amount of payments for the purposes of paragraph (3ZB), no account is to be taken of any weeks during the relevant period in which—

(a) no remuneration was payable to the worker; or

(b) a worker was, for any amount of time, on sick leave or statutory leave.

(3ZF) If, in a case falling within paragraph (3ZD), any weeks are discounted under paragraph (3ZE), earlier weeks shall be taken into account so as to bring the number of weeks to 52 (or as close to 52 as possible).

(3ZG) For the purposes of paragraph (3ZF) no account is to be taken of remuneration in weeks preceding the period of 104 weeks ending—

(a) where the calculation date is the last day of a week, with that week, and

(b) otherwise, with the last complete week before the calculation date.

(3A) In any case where applying sections 221 to 224 of the 1996 Act subject to the modifications set out in paragraph (3) gives no weeks of which account is taken, the amount of a week's pay is not to be determined by applying those sections, but is the amount which fairly represents a week's pay having regard to the considerations specified in section 228(3) as if references in that section to the employee were references to the worker.

(3B) For the purposes of paragraphs (3), (3ZA) to (3ZG) and (3A) 'week' means, in relation to a worker whose remuneration is calculated weekly by a week ending with a day other than Saturday, a week ending with that other day and, in relation to any other worker, a week ending with Saturday.

(4) A right to payment under paragraph (1) does not affect any right of a worker to remuneration under his contract ('contractual remuneration') (and paragraph (1) does not confer a right under that contract).

(5) Any contractual remuneration paid to a worker in respect of a period of leave goes towards discharging any liability of the employer to make payments under this regulation in respect of that period; and, conversely, any payment of remuneration under this regulation in respect of a period goes towards discharging any liability of the employer to pay contractual remuneration in respect of that period.

16A Rolled-up holiday pay for irregular hours workers and part-year workers

(1) This regulation applies in relation to pay due to a worker under regulation 16(1) in respect of leave to which the worker is entitled under regulation 15B.

(2) Such holiday pay may be paid by way of a 12.07% uplift to the worker's remuneration for work done.

(3) Holiday pay paid in accordance with paragraph (2) must be paid at the same time as the worker's remuneration for work done.

(4) A worker—

(a) who is on sick leave or statutory leave, and

(b) who was, before going on sick leave or statutory leave, paid holiday pay in the way described in paragraph (2),

must be paid holiday pay in accordance with paragraph (5) in respect of the annual leave that they accrue during the period of sick leave or statutory leave.

(5) Such holiday pay is to be paid by way of a payment each pay period during the period of sick leave or statutory leave which is equal to the average amount of holiday pay that the worker was paid for each pay period during the relevant period.

(6) In paragraph (5) the 'relevant period' means—

(a) the period of 52 weeks ending with the day before the day on which the worker started the sick leave or statutory leave, or

(b) if the worker has been receiving holiday pay in the way described in paragraph (2) for a period of less than 52 complete weeks before starting the sick leave or statutory leave, that lesser period.

(7) Where an employer pays a worker holiday pay in the way described in paragraph (2) or (5) any itemised pay statement provided by the employer to the worker must indicate the amount of holiday pay that has been paid for the period to which the statement relates.

(8) An employer who, in respect of annual leave to which a worker is entitled under regulation 15B, pays holiday pay to the worker in accordance with paragraph (2) or (5) is discharged from their liability to make payments to the worker in the manner described in regulation 16 in respect of that annual leave.

(9) In paragraph (2) the reference to remuneration is a reference to all types of payments that are to be included when determining the amount of a week's pay for the purposes of regulation 16.

(10) In paragraph (7), the reference to an itemised pay statement is to a statement given to a worker under section 8 of the 1996 Act.

16B [omitted]

17 Entitlements under other provisions

Where during any period a worker is entitled to a rest period, rest break or annual leave both under a provision of these Regulations and under a separate provision (including a provision of his contract), he may not exercise the two rights separately, but may, in taking a rest period, break or leave during that period, take advantage of whichever right is, in any particular respect, the more favourable.

PART III EXCEPTIONS

18 [omitted]

19 Domestic service

Regulations 4(1) and (2), 5A(1) and (4), 6(1), (2) and (7), 6A, 7(1), (2) and (6) and 8 do not apply in relation to a worker employed as a domestic servant in a private household.

20 Unmeasured working time

(1) Regulations 4(1) and (2), 6(1), (2) and (7), 10(1), 11(1) and (2) and 12(1) do not apply in relation to a worker where, on account of the specific characteristics of the activity in which he is engaged, the duration of his working time is not measured or predetermined or can be determined by the worker himself, as may be the case for—

- (a) managing executives or other persons with autonomous decision-taking powers;
- (b) family workers; or
- (c) workers officiating at religious ceremonies in churches and religious communities.

(2) [revoked]

21 Other special cases

Subject to regulation 24, regulations 6(1), (2) and (7), 10(1), 11(1) and (2) and 12(1) do not apply in relation to a worker—

- (a) where the worker's activities are such that his place of work and place of residence are distant from one another, including cases where the worker is employed in offshore work, or his different places of work are distant from one another;
- (b) where the worker is engaged in security and surveillance activities requiring a permanent presence in order to protect property and persons, as may be the case for security guards and caretakers or security firms;
- (c) where the worker's activities involve the need for continuity of service or production, as may be the case in relation to—
  - (i) services relating to the reception, treatment or care provided by hospitals or similar establishments (including the activities of doctors in training), residential institutions and prisons;
  - (ii) work at docks or airports;
  - (iii) press, radio, television, cinematographic production, postal and telecommunications services and civil protection services;
  - (iv) gas, water and electricity production, transmission and distribution, household refuse collection and incineration;
  - (v) industries in which work cannot be interrupted on technical grounds;
  - (vi) research and development activities;
  - (vii) agriculture;
  - (viii) the carriage of passengers on regular urban transport services;
- (d) where there is a foreseeable surge of activity, as may be the case in relation to—
  - (i) agriculture;
  - (ii) tourism; and
  - (iii) postal services;
- (e) where the worker's activities are affected by—
  - (i) an occurrence due to unusual and unforeseeable circumstances, beyond the control of the worker's employer;
  - (ii) exceptional events, the consequences of which could not have been avoided despite the exercise of all due care by the employer; or
  - (iii) an accident or the imminent risk of an accident;
- (f) where the worker works in railway transport and—
  - (i) his activities are intermittent;

(ii) he spends his working time on board trains; or

(iii) his activities are linked to transport timetables and to ensuring the continuity and regularity of traffic.

22 Shift workers

(1) Subject to regulation 24—

(a) regulation 10(1) does not apply in relation to a shift worker when he changes shift and cannot take a daily rest period between the end of one shift and the start of the next one;

(b) paragraphs (1) and (2) of regulation 11 do not apply in relation to a shift worker when he changes shift and cannot take a weekly rest period between the end of one shift and the start of the next one; and

(c) neither regulation 10(1) nor paragraphs (1) and (2) of regulation 11 apply to workers engaged in activities involving periods of work split up over the day, as may be the case for cleaning staff.

(2) For the purposes of this regulation—

'shift worker' means any worker whose work schedule is part of shift work; and

'shift work' means any method of organising work in shifts whereby workers succeed each other at the same workstations according to a certain pattern, including a rotating pattern, and which may be continuous or discontinuous, entailing the need for workers to work at different times over a given period of days or weeks.

23 Collective and workforce agreements

A collective agreement or a workforce agreement may—

(a) modify or exclude the application of regulations 6(1) to (3) and (7), 10(1), 11(1) and (2) and 12(1), and

(b) for objective or technical reasons or reasons concerning the organisation of work, modify the application of regulation 4(3) and (4) by the substitution, for each reference to 17 weeks, of a different period, being a period not exceeding 52 weeks,

in relation to particular workers or groups of workers.

24 Compensatory rest

Where the application of any provision of these Regulations is excluded by regulation 21 or 22, or is modified or excluded by means of a collective agreement or a workforce agreement under regulation 23(a), and a worker is accordingly required by his employer to work during a period which would otherwise be a rest period or rest break—

(a) his employer shall wherever possible allow him to take an equivalent period of compensatory rest, and

(b) in exceptional cases in which it is not possible, for objective reasons, to grant such a period of rest, his employer shall afford him such protection as may be appropriate in order to safeguard the worker's health and safety.

24A Mobile workers

(1) Regulations 6(1), (2) and (7), 10(1), 11(1) and (2) and 12(1) do not apply to a mobile worker in relation to whom the application of those regulations is not excluded by any provision of regulation 18.

(2) A mobile worker, to whom paragraph (1) applies, is entitled to adequate rest, except where the worker's activities are affected by any of the matters referred to in regulation 21(e).

(3) For the purposes of this regulation, 'adequate rest' means that a worker has regular rest periods, the duration of which are expressed in units of time and which are sufficiently long and continuous to ensure that, as a result of fatigue or other irregular working patterns, he does not cause injury to himself, to fellow workers or to others and that he does not damage his health, either in the short term or in the longer term.

25–25B [omitted]; 26 [revoked]

26A Entitlement to additional annual leave under a relevant agreement

(1) Regulation 13A does not apply in relation to a worker whose employer, as at 1st October 2007 and by virtue of a relevant agreement, provides each worker employed by him with an annual leave entitlement of 1.6 weeks or 8 days (whichever is the lesser) in addition to each worker's entitlement under regulation 13, provided that such additional annual leave—

- (a) may not be replaced by a payment in lieu except in relation to a worker whose employment is terminated;
- (b) may not be carried forward into a leave year other than that which immediately follows the leave year in respect of which the leave is due; and
- (c) is leave for which the worker is entitled to be paid at not less than the rate of a week's pay in respect of each week of leave, calculated in accordance with sections 221 to 224 of the 1996 Act, modified such that—
  - (i) references to the employee are references to the worker;
  - (ii) references to the employee's contract of employment are references to the worker's contract;
  - (iii) the calculation date is the first day of the period of leave in question; and
  - (iv) the references to sections 227 and 228 do not apply.

(2) Notwithstanding paragraph (1), any additional annual leave in excess of 1.6 weeks or 8 days (whichever is the lesser) to which a worker is entitled, shall not be subject to the conditions of that paragraph.

(3) This regulation shall cease to apply to a worker from the day when an employer ceases to provide additional annual leave in accordance with the conditions in paragraph (1).

(4) This regulation does not apply to workers to whom the Agricultural Wages (Scotland) Act 1949 applies (as that Act had effect on 1 July 1999).

27 Young workers: *force majeure*

(1) Regulations 5A, 6A, 10(2) and 12(4) do not apply in relation to a young worker where his employer requires him to undertake work which no adult worker is available to perform and which—

- (a) is occasioned by either—
  - (i) an occurrence due to unusual and unforeseeable circumstances, beyond the employer's control, or
  - (ii) exceptional events, the consequences of which could not have been avoided despite the exercise of all due care by the employer;
- (b) is of a temporary nature; and
- (c) must be performed immediately.

(2) Where the application of regulation 5A, 6A, 10(2) or 12(4) is excluded by paragraph (1), and a young worker is accordingly required to work during a period which would otherwise be a rest period or rest break, his employer shall allow him to take an equivalent period of compensatory rest within the following three weeks.

27A Other exceptions relating to young workers

(1) Regulation 5A does not apply in relation to a young worker where—

- (a) the young worker's employer requires him to undertake work which is necessary either to maintain continuity of service or production or to respond to a surge in demand for a service or product;
- (b) no adult worker is available to perform the work; and
- (c) performing the work would not adversely affect the young worker's education or training.

(2) Regulation 6A does not apply in relation to a young worker employed—

- (a) in a hospital or similar establishment, or

(b) in connection with cultural, artistic, sporting or advertising activities,

in the circumstances referred to in paragraph (1).

(3) Regulation 6A does not apply, except in so far as it prohibits work between midnight and 4 a.m., in relation to a young worker employed in—

(a) agriculture;
(b) retail trading;
(c) postal or newspaper deliveries;
(d) a catering business;
(e) a hotel, public house, restaurant, bar or similar establishment; or
(f) a bakery;

in the circumstances referred to in paragraph (1).

(4) Where the application of regulation 6A is excluded by paragraph (2) or (3), and a young worker is accordingly required to work during a period which would otherwise be a rest period or rest break—

(a) he shall be supervised by an adult worker where such supervision is necessary for the young worker's protection; and
(b) he shall be allowed an equivalent period of compensatory rest.

PART IV MISCELLANEOUS

28 Enforcement

(1) In this regulation, regulations 29–29E and Schedule 3—

...

'the relevant requirements' means the following provisions—

(a) regulations 4(2), 5A(4), 6(2) and (7), 6A, 7(1), (2) and (6), 8, 9 and 27A(4)(a);
(b) regulation 24, in so far as it applies where regulation 6(1), (2) or (7) is modified or excluded; and
(c) regulation 24A(2), in so far as it applies where regulations 6(1), (2) or (7) is excluded;

...

29 Offences

(1) An employer who fails to comply with any of the relevant requirements or with regulation 16B(1) shall be guilty of an offence.

(2) The provisions of paragraph (3) shall apply where an inspector is exercising or has exercised any power conferred by Schedule 3.

(3) It is an offence for a person—

(a) to contravene any requirement imposed by the inspector under paragraph 2 of Schedule 3;
(b) to prevent or attempt to prevent any other person from appearing before the inspector or from answering any question to which the inspector may by virtue of paragraph 2(2)(e) of Schedule 3 require an answer;
(c) to contravene any requirement or prohibition imposed by an improvement notice or a prohibition notice (including any such notice as is modified on appeal);
(d) intentionally to obstruct the inspector in the exercise or performance of his powers or duties;
(e) to use or disclose any information in contravention of paragraph 8 of Schedule 3;
(f) to make a statement which he knows to be false or recklessly to make a statement which is false, where the statement is made in purported compliance with a requirement to furnish any information imposed by or under these Regulations.

(4) An employer guilty of an offence under paragraph (1) shall be liable—

(a) on summary conviction, to a fine not exceeding the statutory maximum;
(b) on conviction on indictment, to a fine.

(5) A person guilty of an offence under paragraph (3) shall be liable to the penalty prescribed in relation to that provision by paragraphs (6), (7) or (8) as the case may be.

(6) A person guilty of an offence under sub-paragraph (3)(a), (b) or (d) shall be liable on summary conviction to a fine not exceeding level 5 on the standard scale.

(7) A person guilty of an offence under sub-paragraph (3)(c) shall be liable—

(a) on summary conviction, to imprisonment for a term not exceeding three months, or a fine not exceeding the statutory maximum;

(b) on conviction on indictment, to imprisonment for a term not exceeding two years, or a fine, or both.

(8) A person guilty of an offence under any of the sub-paragraphs of paragraph (3) not falling within paragraphs (6) or (7) above, shall be liable—

(a) on summary conviction, to a fine not exceeding the statutory maximum;

(b) on conviction on indictment—

(i) if the offence is under sub-paragraph (3)(e), to imprisonment for a term not exceeding two years or a fine or both;

(ii) if the offence is not one to which the preceding sub-paragraph applies, to a fine.

(9) The provisions set out in regulations 29A–29E below shall apply in relation to the offences provided for in paragraphs (1) and (3).

29A Offences due to fault of other person

Where the commission by any person of an offence is due to the act or default of some other person, that other person shall be guilty of the offence, and a person may be charged with and convicted of the offence by virtue of this paragraph whether or not proceedings are taken against the first-mentioned person.

29B Offences by bodies corporate

(1) Where an offence committed by a body corporate is proved to have been committed with the consent or connivance of, or to have been attributable to any neglect on the part of, any director, manager, secretary or other similar officer of the body corporate or a person who was purporting to act in any such capacity, he as well as the body corporate shall be guilty of that offence and shall be liable to be proceeded against and punished accordingly.

(2) Where the affairs of a body corporate are managed by its members, the preceding paragraph shall apply in relation to the acts and defaults of a member in connection with his functions of management as if he were a director of the body corporate.

29C–29D [omitted]

29E Power of court to order cause of offence to be remedied

(1) Where a person is convicted of an offence in respect of any matters which appear to the court to be matters which it is in his power to remedy, the court may, in addition to or instead of imposing any punishment, order him, within such time as may be fixed by the order, to take such steps as may be specified in the order for remedying the said matters.

(2) The time fixed by an order under paragraph (1) may be extended or further extended by order of the court on an application made before the end of that time as originally fixed or as extended under this paragraph, as the case may be.

(3) Where a person is ordered under paragraph (1) to remedy any matters, that person shall not be liable under these Regulations in respect of those matters in so far as they continue during the time fixed by the order or any further time allowed under paragraph (2).

30 Remedies

(1) A worker may present a complaint to an employment tribunal that his employer—

(a) has refused to permit him to exercise any right he has under—

(i) regulation 10(1) or (2), 11(1), (2) or (3), 12(1) or (4), 13, 13A, 15B or 15D;
(ii) regulation 24, in so far as it applies where regulation 10(1), 11(1) or (2) or 12(1) is modified or excluded;
(iii) regulation 24A, in so far as it applies where regulation 10(1), 11(1) or (2) or 12(1) is excluded; or
(iv) regulation 25(3), 27A(4)(b) or 27(2); or

(b) has failed to pay him the whole or any part of any amount due to him under regulation 14(2), 15E, 16(1) or 16A.

(2) Subject to regulation 30B, an employment tribunal shall not consider a complaint under this regulation unless it is presented—

(a) before the end of the period of three months (or, in a case to which regulation 38(2) applies, six months) beginning with the date on which it is alleged that the exercise of the right should have been permitted (or in the case of a rest period or leave extending over more than one day, the date on which it should have been permitted to begin) or, as the case may be, the payment should have been made;
(b) within such further period as the tribunal considers reasonable in a case where it is satisfied that it was not reasonably practicable for the complaint to be presented before the end of that period of three or, as the case may be, six months.

(2A) Where the period within which a complaint must be presented in accordance with paragraph (2) is extended by regulation 15 of the Employment Act 2002 (Dispute Resolution) Regulations 2004, the period within which the complaint must be presented shall be the extended period rather than the period in paragraph (2).

(3) Where an employment tribunal finds a complaint under paragraph (1)(a) well-founded, the tribunal—

(a) shall make a declaration to that effect, and
(b) may make an award of compensation to be paid by the employer to the worker.

(4) The amount of the compensation shall be such as the tribunal considers just and equitable in all the circumstances having regard to—

(a) the employer's default in refusing to permit the worker to exercise his right, and
(b) any loss sustained by the worker which is attributable to the matters complained of.

(5) Where on a complaint under paragraph (1)(b) an employment tribunal finds that an employer has failed to pay a worker in accordance with regulation 14(2) or (5), 15E, 16(1) or 16A, it shall order the employer to pay to the worker the amount which it finds to be due to him.

30A–34 [omitted]

35 Restrictions on contracting out

(1) Any provision in an agreement (whether a contract of employment or not) is void in so far as it purports—

(a) to exclude or limit the operation of any provision of these Regulations, save in so far as these Regulations provide for an agreement to have that effect, or
(b) to preclude a person from bringing proceedings under these Regulations before an employment tribunal.

(2) Paragraph (1) does not apply to—

(a) any agreement to refrain from instituting or continuing proceedings where a conciliation officer has taken action under any of sections 18A to 18C of the Employment Tribunals Act 1996 (conciliation); or
(b) any agreement to refrain from instituting or continuing proceedings within section 18(1)(j) of the Employment Tribunals Act 1996 (proceedings under these Regulations where conciliation is available), if the conditions regulating settlement agreements under these Regulations are satisfied in relation to the agreement.

(3) For the purposes of paragraph (2)(b) the conditions regulating settlement agreements under these Regulations are that—

(a) the agreement must be in writing,

(b) the agreement must relate to the particular complaint,

(c) the worker must have received advice from a relevant independent adviser as to the terms and effect of the proposed agreement and, in particular, its effect on his ability to pursue his rights before an employment tribunal,

(d) there must be in force, when the adviser gives the advice, a contract of insurance, or an indemnity provided for members of a profession or professional body, covering the risk of a claim by the worker in respect of loss arising in consequence of the advice,

(e) the agreement must identify the adviser, and

(f) the agreement must state that the conditions regulating settlement agreements under these Regulations are satisfied.

(4)–(7) [omitted]

35A [omitted]

PART V SPECIAL CLASSES OF PERSON

36 Agency workers not otherwise 'workers'

(1) This regulation applies in any case where an individual ('the agency worker')—

(a) is supplied by a person ('the agent') to do work for another ('the principal') under a contract or other arrangements made between the agent and the principal; but

(b) is not, as respects that work, a worker, because of the absence of a worker's contract between the individual and the agent or the principal; and

(c) is not a party to a contract under which he undertakes to do the work for another party to the contract whose status is, by virtue of the contract, that of a client or customer of any profession or business undertaking carried on by the individual.

(2) In a case where this regulation applies, the other provisions of these Regulations shall have effect as if there were a worker's contract for the doing of the work by the agency worker made between the agency worker and—

(a) whichever of the agent and the principal is responsible for paying the agency worker in respect of the work; or

(b) if neither the agent nor the principal is so responsible, whichever of them pays the agency worker in respect of the work,

and as if that person were the agency worker's employer.

37 Crown employment

(1) Subject to paragraph (4) and regulation 38, these Regulations have effect in relation to Crown employment and persons in Crown employment as they have effect in relation to other employment and other workers.

(2) In paragraph (1) 'Crown employment' means employment under or for the purposes of a government department or any officer or body exercising on behalf of the Crown functions conferred by a statutory provision.

(3) For the purposes of the application of the provisions of these Regulations in relation to Crown employment in accordance with paragraph (1)—

(a) references to a worker shall be construed as references to a person in Crown employment; and

(b) references to a worker's contract shall be construed as references to the terms of employment of a person in Crown employment.

(4) No act or omission by the Crown which is an offence under regulation 29 shall make the Crown criminally liable, but the High Court or, in Scotland, the Court of Session may, on the application of a person appearing to the Court to have an interest, declare any such act or omission unlawful.

38–41 [omitted]

42 Non-employed trainees

For the purposes of these Regulations, a person receiving relevant training, otherwise than under a contract of employment, shall be regarded as a worker, and the person whose undertaking is providing the training shall be regarded as his employer.

43 [omitted]

SCHEDULE 1

WORKFORCE AGREEMENTS

1. An agreement is a workforce agreement for the purposes of these Regulations if the following conditions are satisfied—

(a) the agreement is in writing;

(b) it has effect for a specified period not exceeding five years;

(c) it applies either—

(i) to all of the relevant members of the workforce, or

(ii) to all of the relevant members of the workforce who belong to a particular group;

(d) the agreement is signed—

(i) in the case of an agreement of the kind referred to in sub-paragraph (c)(i), by the representatives of the workforce, and in the case of an agreement of the kind referred to in sub-paragraph (c)(ii) by the representatives of the group to which the agreement applies (excluding, in either case, any representative not a relevant member of the workforce on the date on which the agreement was first made available for signature), or

(ii) if the employer employed 20 or fewer workers on the date referred to in sub-paragraph (d)(i), either by the appropriate representatives in accordance with that sub-paragraph or by the majority of the workers employed by him;

(e) before the agreement was made available for signature, the employer provided all the workers to whom it was intended to apply on the date on which it came into effect with copies of the text of the agreement and such guidance as those workers might reasonably require in order to understand it fully.

2. For the purposes of this Schedule—

'a particular group' is a group of the relevant members of a workforce who undertake a particular function, work at a particular workplace or belong to a particular department or unit within their employer's business;

'relevant members of the workforce' are all of the workers employed by a particular employer, excluding any worker whose terms and conditions of employment are provided for, wholly or in part, in a collective agreement;

'representatives of the workforce' are workers duly elected to represent the relevant members of the workforce, 'representatives of the group' are workers duly elected to represent the members of a particular group, and representatives are 'duly elected' if the election at which they were elected satisfied the requirements of paragraph 3 of this Schedule.

3. The requirements concerning elections referred to in paragraph 2 are that—
   (a) the number of representatives to be elected is determined by the employer;
   (b) the candidates for election as representatives of the workforce are relevant members of the workforce, and the candidates for election as representatives of a group are members of the group;
   (c) no worker who is eligible to be a candidate is unreasonably excluded from standing for election;
   (d) all the relevant members of the workforce are entitled to vote for representatives of the workforce, and all the members of a particular group are entitled to vote for representatives of the group;
   (e) the workers entitled to vote may vote for as many candidates as there are representatives to be elected;
   (f) the election is conducted so as to secure that—
      (i) so far as is reasonably practicable, those voting do so in secret, and
      (ii) the votes given at the election are fairly and accurately counted.

The Management of Health and Safety at Work Regulations 1999

(SI 1999 No. 3242)

3 Risk assessment
4 Principles of prevention to be applied
5 Health and safety arrangements
6 Health surveillance
7 Health and safety assistance
8 Procedures for serious and imminent danger and for danger areas
9 Contacts with external services
10 Information for employees
11 Co-operation and co-ordination
12 Persons working in host employers' or self-employed persons' undertakings
13 Capabilities and training
14 Employees' duties
15 Temporary workers

1–2 [omitted]

Risk assessment

3.—(1) Every employer shall make a suitable and sufficient assessment of—
   (a) the risks to the health and safety of his employees to which they are exposed whilst they are at work; and
   (b) the risks to the health and safety of persons not in his employment arising out of or in connection with the conduct by him of his undertaking,

for the purpose of identifying the measures he needs to take to comply with the requirements and prohibitions imposed upon him by or under the relevant statutory provisions.

(2) Every relevant self-employed person shall make a suitable and sufficient assessment of—
   (a) the risks to his own health and safety to which he is exposed whilst he is at work; and
   (b) the risks to the health and safety of persons not in his employment arising out of or in connection with the conduct by him of his undertaking,

for the purpose of identifying the measures he needs to take to comply with the requirements and prohibitions imposed upon him by or under the relevant statutory provisions.

(3) Any assessment such as is referred to in paragraph (1) or (2) shall be reviewed by the employer or relevant self-employed person who made it if—
   (a) there is reason to suspect that it is no longer valid; or

(b) there has been a significant change in the matters to which it relates;

and where as a result of any such review changes to an assessment are required, the employer or relevant self-employed person concerned shall make them.

(3A) In this regulation 'relevant self-employed person' means a self-employed person who conducts an undertaking of a prescribed description for the purposes of section 3(2) of the Health and Safety at Work etc. Act 1974.

(4) An employer shall not employ a young person unless he has, in relation to risks to the health and safety of young persons, made or reviewed an assessment in accordance with paragraphs (1) and (5).

(5) In making or reviewing the assessment, an employer who employs or is to employ a young person shall take particular account of—

(a) the inexperience, lack of awareness of risks and immaturity of young persons;
(b) the fitting-out and layout of the workplace and the workstation;
(c) the nature, degree and duration of exposure to physical, biological and chemical agents;
(d) the form, range, and use of work equipment and the way in which it is handled;
(e) the organisation of processes and activities;
(f) the extent of the health and safety training provided or to be provided to young persons; and
(g) risks from agents, processes and work listed in the Annex to Council Directive 94/33/EC on the protection of young people at work, as amended by Directive 2014/27/EU.

(6) Where the employer employs five or more employees, he shall record—

(a) the significant findings of the assessment; and
(b) any group of his employees identified by it as being especially at risk.

4 [omitted]

Health and safety arrangements

5.—(1) Every employer shall make and give effect to such arrangements as are appropriate, having regard to the nature of his activities and the size of his undertaking, for the effective planning, organisation, control, monitoring and review of the preventive and protective measures.

(2) Where the employer employs five or more employees, he shall record the arrangements referred to in paragraph (1).

Health surveillance

6. Every employer shall ensure that his employees are provided with such health surveillance as is appropriate having regard to the risks to their health and safety which are identified by the assessment.

Health and safety assistance

7.—(1) Every employer shall, subject to paragraphs (6) and (7), appoint one or more competent persons to assist him in undertaking the measures he needs to take to comply with the requirements and prohibitions imposed upon him by or under the relevant statutory provisions.

(2) Where an employer appoints persons in accordance with paragraph (1), he shall make arrangements for ensuring adequate co-operation between them.

(3) The employer shall ensure that the number of persons appointed under paragraph (1), the time available for them to fulfil their functions and the means at their disposal are adequate having regard to the size of his undertaking, the risks to which his employees are exposed and the distribution of those risks throughout the undertaking.

(4) The employer shall ensure that—

(a) any person appointed by him in accordance with paragraph (1) who is not in his employment—

(i) is informed of the factors known by him to affect, or suspected by him of affecting, the health and safety of any other person who may be affected by the conduct of his undertaking, and

(ii) has access to the information referred to in regulation 10; and

(b) any person appointed by him in accordance with paragraph (1) is given such information about any person working in his undertaking who is—

(i) employed by him under a fixed-term contract of employment, or

(ii) employed in an employment business,

as is necessary to enable that person properly to carry out the function specified in that paragraph.

(5) A person shall be regarded as competent for the purposes of paragraphs (1) and (8) where he has sufficient training and experience or knowledge and other qualities to enable him properly to assist in undertaking the measures referred to in paragraph (1).

(6) Paragraph (1) shall not apply to a self-employed employer who is not in partnership with any other person where he has sufficient training and experience or knowledge and other qualities properly to undertake the measures referred to in that paragraph himself.

(7) Paragraph (1) shall not apply to individuals who are employers and who are together carrying on business in partnership where at least one of the individuals concerned has sufficient training and experience or knowledge and other qualities—

(a) properly to undertake the measures he needs to take to comply with the requirements and prohibitions imposed upon him by or under the relevant statutory provisions; and

(b) properly to assist his fellow partners in undertaking the measures they need to take to comply with the requirements and prohibitions imposed upon them by or under the relevant statutory provisions.

(8) Where there is a competent person in the employer's employment, that person shall be appointed for the purposes of paragraph (1) in preference to a competent person not in his employment.

Procedures for serious and imminent danger and for danger areas

8.—(1) Every employer shall—

(a) establish and where necessary give effect to appropriate procedures to be followed in the event of serious and imminent danger to persons at work in his undertaking;

(b) nominate a sufficient number of competent persons to implement those procedures in so far as they relate to the evacuation from premises of persons at work in his undertaking; and

(c) ensure that none of his employees has access to any area occupied by him to which it is necessary to restrict access on grounds of health and safety unless the employee concerned has received adequate health and safety instruction.

(2) Without prejudice to the generality of paragraph (1)(a), the procedures referred to in that sub-paragraph shall—

(a) so far as is practicable, require any persons at work who are exposed to serious and imminent danger to be informed of the nature of the hazard and of the steps taken or to be taken to protect them from it;

(b) enable the persons concerned (if necessary by taking appropriate steps in the absence of guidance or instruction and in the light of their knowledge and the technical means at their disposal) to stop work and immediately proceed to a place of safety in the event of their being exposed to serious, imminent and unavoidable danger; and

(c) save in exceptional cases for reasons duly substantiated (which cases and reasons shall be specified in those procedures), require the persons concerned to be prevented from resuming work in any situation where there is still a serious and imminent danger.

(3) A person shall be regarded as competent for the purposes of paragraph (1)(b) where he has sufficient training and experience or knowledge and other qualities to enable him properly to implement the evacuation procedures referred to in that sub-paragraph.

Contacts with external services

9. Every employer shall ensure that any necessary contacts with external services are arranged, particularly as regards first-aid, emergency medical care and rescue work.

Information for employees

10.—(1) Every employer shall provide his employees with comprehensible and relevant information on—

(a) the risks to their health and safety identified by the assessment;
(b) the preventive and protective measures;
(c) the procedures referred to in regulation 8(1)(a);
(d) the identity of those persons nominated by him in accordance with regulation 8(1)(b); and
(e) the risks notified to him in accordance with regulation 11(1)(c).

(2) Every employer shall, before employing a child, provide a parent of the child with comprehensible and relevant information on—

(a) the risks to his health and safety identified by the assessment;
(b) the preventive and protective measures; and
(c) the risks notified to him in accordance with regulation 11(1)(c).

(3) The reference in paragraph (2) to a parent of the child includes—

(a) in England and Wales, a person who has parental responsibility, within the meaning of section 3 of the Children Act 1989, for him; and
(b) in Scotland, a person who has parental rights, within the meaning of section 8 of the Law Reform (Parent and Child) (Scotland) Act 1986 for him.

Co-operation and co-ordination

11.—(1) Where two or more employers share a workplace (whether on a temporary or a permanent basis) each such employer shall—

(a) co-operate with the other employers concerned so far as is necessary to enable them to comply with the requirements and prohibitions imposed upon them by or under the relevant statutory provisions;
(b) (taking into account the nature of his activities) take all reasonable steps to co-ordinate the measures he takes to comply with the requirements and prohibitions imposed upon him by or under the relevant statutory provisions with the measures the other employers concerned are taking to comply with the requirements and prohibitions imposed upon them by that legislation; and
(c) take all reasonable steps to inform the other employers concerned of the risks to their employees' health and safety arising out of or in connection with the conduct by him of his undertaking.

(2) Paragraph (1) shall apply to employers sharing a workplace with self-employed persons and to self-employed persons sharing a workplace with other self-employed persons as it applies to employers sharing a workplace with other employers; and the references in that paragraph to employers and the reference in the said paragraph to their employees shall be construed accordingly.

Persons working in host employers' or self-employed persons' undertakings

12.—(1) Every employer and every self-employed person shall ensure that the employer of any employees from an outside undertaking who are working in his undertaking is provided with comprehensible information on—

(a) the risks to those employees' health and safety arising out of or in connection with the conduct by that first-mentioned employer or by that self-employed person of his undertaking; and
(b) the measures taken by that first-mentioned employer or by that self-employed person in compliance with the requirements and prohibitions imposed upon him by or under the

relevant statutory provisions in so far as the said requirements and prohibitions relate to those employees.

(2) Paragraph (1) shall apply to a self-employed person who is working in the undertaking of an employer or a self-employed person as it applies to employees from an outside undertaking who are working therein; and the reference in that paragraph to the employer of any employees from an outside undertaking who are working in the undertaking of an employer or a self-employed person and the references in the said paragraph to employees from an outside undertaking who are working in the undertaking of an employer or a self-employed person shall be construed accordingly.

(3) Every employer shall ensure that any person working in his undertaking who is not his employee and every self-employed person (not being an employer) shall ensure that any person working in his undertaking is provided with appropriate instructions and comprehensible information regarding any risks to that person's health and safety which arise out of the conduct by that employer or self-employed person of his undertaking.

(4) Every employer shall—

(a) ensure that the employer of any employees from an outside undertaking who are working in his undertaking is provided with sufficient information to enable that second-mentioned employer to identify any person nominated by that first-mentioned employer in accordance with regulation 8(1)(b) to implement evacuation procedures as far as those employees are concerned; and

(b) take all reasonable steps to ensure that any employees from an outside undertaking who are working in his undertaking receive sufficient information to enable them to identify any person nominated by him in accordance with regulation 8(1)(b) to implement evacuation procedures as far as they are concerned.

(5) Paragraph (4) shall apply to a self-employed person who is working in an employer's undertaking as it applies to employees from an outside undertaking who are working therein; and the reference in that paragraph to the employer of any employees from an outside undertaking who are working in an employer's undertaking and the references in the said paragraph to employees from an outside undertaking who are working in an employer's undertaking shall be construed accordingly.

Capabilities and training

13.—(1) Every employer shall, in entrusting tasks to his employees, take into account their capabilities as regards health and safety.

(2) Every employer shall ensure that his employees are provided with adequate health and safety training—

(a) on their being recruited into the employer's undertaking; and

(b) on their being exposed to new or increased risks because of—

(i) their being transferred or given a change of responsibilities within the employer's undertaking,

(ii) the introduction of new work equipment into or a change respecting work equipment already in use within the employer's undertaking,

(iii) the introduction of new technology into the employer's undertaking, or

(iv) the introduction of a new system of work into or a change respecting a system of work already in use within the employer's undertaking.

(3) The training referred to in paragraph (2) shall—

(a) be repeated periodically where appropriate;

(b) be adapted to take account of any new or changed risks to the health and safety of the employees concerned; and

(c) take place during working hours.

Employees' duties

14.—(1) Every employee shall use any machinery, equipment, dangerous substance, transport equipment, means of production or safety device provided to him by his employer in accordance both with any training in the use of the equipment concerned which has been received by him and the instructions respecting that use which have been provided to him by the said employer in compliance with the requirements and prohibitions imposed upon that employer by or under the relevant statutory provisions.

(2) Every employee shall inform his employer or any other employee of that employer with specific responsibility for the health and safety of his fellow employees—

(a) of any work situation which a person with the first-mentioned employee's training and instruction would reasonably consider represented a serious and immediate danger to health and safety; and

(b) of any matter which a person with the first-mentioned employee's training and instruction would reasonably consider represented a shortcoming in the employer's protection arrangements for health and safety,

in so far as that situation or matter either affects the health and safety of that first mentioned employee or arises out of or in connection with his own activities at work, and has not previously been reported to his employer or to any other employee of that employer in accordance with this paragraph.

Temporary workers

15.—(1) Every employer shall provide any person whom he has employed under a fixed-term contract of employment with comprehensible information on—

(a) any special occupational qualifications or skills required to be held by that employee if he is to carry out his work safely; and

(b) any health surveillance required to be provided to that employee by or under any of the relevant statutory provisions,

and shall provide the said information before the employee concerned commences his duties.

(2) Every employer and every self-employed person shall provide any person employed in an employment business who is to carry out work in his undertaking with comprehensible information on—

(a) any special occupational qualifications or skills required to be held by that employee if he is to carry out his work safely; and

(b) health surveillance required to be provided to that employee by or under any of the relevant statutory provisions.

(3) Every employer and every self-employed person shall ensure that every person carrying on an employment business whose employees are to carry out work in his undertaking is provided with comprehensible information on—

(a) any special occupational qualifications or skills required to be held by those employees if they are to carry out their work safely; and

(b) the specific features of the jobs to be filled by those employees (in so far as those features are likely to affect their health and safety);

and the person carrying on the employment business concerned shall ensure that the information so provided is given to the said employees.

16–30 [omitted]

The Maternity and Parental Leave etc. Regulations 1999

(SI 1999 No. 3312)

PART I GENERAL

1 [omitted]

2 Interpretation

(1) In these Regulations—

'the 1996 Act' means the Employment Rights Act 1996;

'additional adoption leave' means leave under section 75B of the 1996 Act;

'additional maternity leave' means leave under section 73 of the 1996 Act;

'armed forces independence payment' means armed forces independence payment under the Armed Forces and Reserve Forces (Compensation Scheme) Order 2011;

'business' includes a trade or profession and includes any activity carried on by a body of persons (whether corporate or unincorporated);

'child' means a person under the age of eighteen;

'childbirth' means the birth of a living child or the birth of a child whether living or dead after 24 weeks of pregnancy;

'collective agreement' means a collective agreement within the meaning of section 178 of the Trade Union and Labour Relations (Consolidation) Act 1992, the trade union parties to which are independent trade unions within the meaning of section 5 of that Act;

'contract of employment' means a contract of service or apprenticeship, whether express or implied, and (if it is express) whether oral or in writing;

'disability living allowance' means the disability living allowance provided for in Part III of the Social Security Contributions and Benefits Act 1992;

'employee' means an individual who has entered into or works under (or, where the employment has ceased, worked under) a contract of employment;

'employer' means the person by whom an employee is (or, where the employment has ceased, was) employed;

'expected week of childbirth' means the week, beginning with midnight between Saturday and Sunday, in which it is expected that childbirth will occur, and 'week of childbirth' means the week, beginning with midnight between Saturday and Sunday, in which childbirth occurs;

'job', in relation to an employee returning after maternity leave or parental leave, means the nature of the work which she is employed to do in accordance with her contract and the capacity and place in which she is so employed;

'ordinary maternity leave' means leave under section 71 of the 1996 Act;

'parental leave' means leave under regulation 13(1);

'parental responsibility' has the meaning given by section 3 of the Children Act 1989, and 'parental responsibilities' has the meaning given by section 1(3) of the Children (Scotland) Act 1995;

'personal independence payment' means personal independence payment under Part 4 of the Welfare Reform Act 2012;

'statutory leave' means leave provided for in Part 8 of the 1996 Act;

'statutory maternity leave' means ordinary maternity leave and additional maternity leave;

'statutory maternity leave period' means the period during which the employee is on statutory maternity leave;

'workforce agreement' means an agreement between an employer and his employees or their representatives in respect of which the conditions set out in Schedule 1 to these Regulations are satisfied.

(2) A reference in any provision of these Regulations to a period of continuous employment is to a period computed in accordance with Chapter I of Part XIV of the 1996 Act, as if that provision were a provision of that Act.

(3) For the purposes of these Regulations any two employers shall be treated as associated if—

(a) one is a company of which the other (directly or indirectly) has control; or

(b) both are companies of which a third person (directly or indirectly) has control; and 'associated employer' shall be construed accordingly.

(4) [omitted]

3 [omitted]

PART II MATERNITY LEAVE

4 Entitlement to ordinary maternity leave and to additional maternity leave

(1) An employee is entitled to ordinary maternity leave and to additional maternity leave provided that she satisfies the following conditions—

(a) no later than the end of the fifteenth week before her expected week of childbirth, or, if that is not reasonably practicable, as soon as is reasonably practicable, she notifies her employer of—

(i) her pregnancy,

(ii) the expected week of childbirth, and

(iii) the date on which she intends her ordinary maternity leave period to start, and

(b) if requested to do so by her employer, she produces for his inspection a certificate from—

(i) a registered medical practitioner, or

(ii) a registered midwife, stating the expected week of childbirth.

(1A) An employee who has notified her employer under paragraph (1)(a)(iii) of the date on which she intends her ordinary maternity leave period to start may subsequently vary that date, provided that she notifies her employer of the variation at least—

(a) 28 days before the date varied, or

(b) 28 days before the new date,

whichever is the earlier, or, if that is not reasonably practicable, as soon as is reasonably practicable.

(2) Notification under paragraph (1)(a)(iii) or (1A)—

(a) shall be given in writing, if the employer so requests, and

(b) shall not specify a date earlier than the beginning of the eleventh week before the expected week of childbirth.

(3) Where, by virtue of regulation 6(1)(b), an employee's ordinary maternity leave period commences with the day which follows the day which follows the first day after the beginning of the fourth week before the expected week of childbirth on which she is absent from work wholly or partly because of pregnancy—

(a) paragraph (1) does not require her to notify her employer of the date specified in that paragraph, but

(b) (whether or not she has notified him of that date) she is not entitled to ordinary maternity leave or to additional maternity leave unless she notifies him as soon as is reasonably practicable that she is absent from work wholly or partly because of pregnancy and of the date on which the birth occurred and of the date on which her absence on that account began.

(4) Where, by virtue of regulation 6(2), an employee's ordinary maternity leave period commences on the day which follows the day on which childbirth occurs—

(a) paragraph (1) does not require her to notify her employer of the date specified in that paragraph, but

(b) (whether or not she has notified him of that date) she is not entitled to ordinary maternity leave or to additional maternity leave unless she notifies him as soon as is reasonably practicable after the birth that she has given birth and of the date on which the birth occurred.

(5) The notification provided for in paragraphs (3)(b) and (4)(b) shall be given in writing, if the employer so requests.

5 [revoked]

6 Commencement of maternity leave periods

(1) Subject to paragraph (2), an employee's ordinary maternity leave period commences with the earlier of—

(a) the date which she notifies to her employer in accordance with regulation 4, as the date on which she intends her ordinary maternity leave period to start or, if by virtue of the provision for variation in that regulation she has notified more than one such date, the last date she notifies, and

(b) the day which follows the first day after the beginning of the fourth week before the expected week of childbirth on which she is absent from work wholly or partly because of pregnancy.

(2) Where the employee's ordinary maternity leave period has not commenced by virtue of paragraph (1) when childbirth occurs, her ordinary maternity leave period commences on the day which follows the day on which childbirth occurs.

(3) An employee's additional maternity leave period commences on the day after the last day of her ordinary maternity leave period.

7 Duration of maternity leave periods

(1) Subject to paragraphs (2) and (5), an employee's ordinary maternity leave period continues for the period of 26 weeks from its commencement, or until the end of the compulsory maternity leave period provided for in regulation 8 if later.

(2) Subject to paragraph (5), where any requirement imposed by or under any relevant statutory provision prohibits the employee from working for any period after the end of the period determined under paragraph (1) by reason of her having recently given birth, her ordinary maternity leave period continues until the end of that later period.

(3) In paragraph (2), 'relevant statutory provision' means a provision of—

(a) an enactment, or

(b) an instrument under an enactment,

other than a provision for the time being specified in an order under section 66(2) of the 1996 Act.

(4) Subject to paragraph (5), where an employee is entitled to additional maternity leave her additional maternity leave period continues until the end of the period of 26 weeks from the day on which it commenced.

(5) Where the employee is dismissed after the commencement of an ordinary or additional maternity leave period but before the time when (apart from this paragraph) that period would end, the period ends at the time of the dismissal.

(6) An employer who is notified under any provision of regulation 4 of the date on which, by virtue of any provision of regulation 6, an employee's ordinary maternity leave period will commence or has commenced shall notify the employee of the date on which her additional maternity leave period shall end.

(7) The notification provided for in paragraph (6) shall be given to the employee—

(a) where the employer is notified under regulation 4(1)(a)(iii), (3)(b) or (4)(b), within 28 days of the date on which he received the notification;

(b) where the employer is notified under regulation 4(1A), within 28 days of the date on which the employee's ordinary maternity leave period commenced.

8 Compulsory maternity leave

The prohibition in section 72 of the 1996 Act, against permitting an employee who satisfies prescribed conditions to work during a particular period (referred to as a 'compulsory maternity leave period'), applies—

(a) in relation to an employee who is entitled to ordinary maternity leave, and

(b) in respect of the period of two weeks which commences with the day on which childbirth occurs.

9 Application of terms and conditions during ordinary maternity leave and additional maternity leave

(1) An employee who takes ordinary maternity leave or additional maternity leave—

(a) is entitled, during the period of leave, to the benefit of all of the terms and conditions of employment which would have applied if she had not been absent, and

(b) is bound, during that period, by any obligations arising under those terms and conditions, subject only to the exceptions in sections 71(4)(b) and 73(4)(b) of the 1996 Act.

(2) In paragraph (1)(a), 'terms and conditions' has the meaning given sections 71(5) and 73(5) by of the 1996 Act, and accordingly does not include terms and conditions about remuneration.

(3) For the purposes of sections 71 and 73 of the 1996 Act, only sums payable to an employee by way of wages or salary are to be treated as remuneration.

(4) In the case of accrual of rights under an employment-related benefit scheme within the meaning given by Schedule 5 to the Social Security Act 1989, nothing in paragraph (1)(a) concerning the treatment of additional maternity leave shall be taken to impose a requirement which exceeds the requirements of paragraph 5 of that Schedule.

10 Redundancy: pregnancy and maternity leave

(1) This regulation applies where it is not practicable by reason of redundancy for an employer to continue to employ an employee under her existing contract of employment during—

(a) the protected period of pregnancy;

(b) the statutory maternity leave period; or

(c) the additional protected period.

(1A) For the purposes of paragraph (1)(a) the protected period of pregnancy—

(a) begins, subject to paragraph (c), when the employer is informed of the pregnancy which may be after the end of the pregnancy,

(b) ends—

(i) if the employee has the right to statutory maternity leave, on the day on which the statutory maternity leave period commences, or

(ii) if the employee does not have the right to statutory maternity leave, at the end of the period of two weeks beginning with the end of the pregnancy, but,

(c) does not begin if the employer is informed of the pregnancy on or after the day on which, had the employer been informed of the pregnancy earlier, the protected period of pregnancy would have ended in accordance with either paragraph (b)(i) or (ii).

(1B) For the purposes of paragraph (1)(c) the additional protected period—

(a) begins with the day after the last day of the employee's statutory maternity leave period;

(b) continues during any period of continuous employment that includes the statutory maternity leave period referred to in sub-paragraph (a); and

(c) ends immediately before the relevant day.

(1C) For the purposes of paragraph (1B)(c) the relevant day—

(a) where paragraph (1D) does not apply, is the day after a period of 18 months beginning with the first day of the expected week of childbirth;

(b) where paragraph (1D) applies, is the day after a period of 18 months beginning with the day that childbirth occurred.

(1D) This paragraph applies where, before the end of the statutory maternity leave period or, if that is not reasonably practicable, as soon as is reasonably practicable thereafter, the employer has been notified by the employee of the day that childbirth occurred.

(1E) Notification under paragraph (1D) must be given in writing if the employer so requests.

(2) Where there is a suitable available vacancy, the employee is entitled to be offered (before the end of her employment under her existing contract) alternative employment with her employer or his successor, or an associated employer, under a new contract of employment which complies with paragraph (3) (and takes effect immediately on the ending of her employment under the previous contract).

(3) The new contract of employment must be such that—

(a) the work to be done under it is of a kind which is both suitable in relation to the employee and appropriate for her to do in the circumstances, and

(b) its provisions as to the capacity and place in which she is to be employed, and as to the other terms and conditions of her employment, are not substantially less favourable to her than if she had continued to be employed under the previous contract.

11 Requirement to notify intention to return during a maternity leave period

(1) An employee who intends to return to work earlier than the end of her additional maternity leave period, shall give to her employer not less than 8 weeks' notice of the date on which she intends to return.

(2) If an employee attempts to return to work earlier than the end of her additional maternity leave period without complying with paragraph (1), her employer is entitled to postpone her return to a date such as will secure, subject to paragraph (3), that he has 8 weeks' notice of her return.

(2A) An employee who complies with her obligations in paragraph (1) or whose employer has postponed her return in the circumstances described in paragraph (2), and who then decides to return to work—

(a) earlier than the original return date, must give her employer not less than 8 weeks' notice of the date on which she now intends to return;

(b) later than the original return date, must give her employer not less than 8 weeks' notice ending with the original return date.

(2B) In paragraph (2A) the 'original return date' means the date which the employee notified to her employer as the date of her return to work under paragraph (1), or the date to which her return was postponed by her employer under paragraph (2).

(3) An employer is not entitled under paragraph (2) to postpone an employee's return to work to a date after the end of the relevant maternity leave period.

(4) If an employee whose return to work has been postponed under paragraph (2) has been notified that she is not to return to work before the date to which her return was postponed, the employer is under no contractual obligation to pay her remuneration until the date to which her return was postponed if she returns to work before that date.

(5) This regulation does not apply in a case where the employer did not notify the employee in accordance with regulation 7(6) and (7) of the date on which her additional maternity leave period would end.

12 [revoked]

12A Work during maternity leave period

(1) Subject to paragraph (5), an employee may carry out up to 10 days' work for her employer during her statutory maternity leave period without bringing her maternity leave to an end.

(2) For the purposes of this regulation, any work carried out on any day shall constitute a day's work.

(3) Subject to paragraph (4), for the purposes of this regulation, work means any work done under the contract of employment and may include training or any activity undertaken for the purposes of keeping in touch with the workplace.

(4) Reasonable contact from time to time between an employee and her employer which either party is entitled to make during a maternity leave period (for example to discuss an employee's return to work) shall not bring that period to an end.

(5) Paragraph (1) shall not apply in relation to any work carried out by the employee at any time from childbirth to the end of the period of two weeks which commences with the day on which childbirth occurs.

(6) This regulation does not confer any right on an employer to require that any work be carried out during the statutory maternity leave period, nor any right on an employee to work during the statutory maternity leave period.

(7) Any days' work carried out under this regulation shall not have the effect of extending the total duration of the statutory maternity leave period.

PART III PARENTAL LEAVE

13 Entitlement to parental leave

(1) An employee who—

(a) [revoked]

(b) has, or expects to have, responsibility for a child,

is entitled, in accordance with these Regulations, to be absent from work on parental leave for the purpose of caring for that child.

(1A) [revoked]

(2) An employee has responsibility for a child, for the purposes of paragraph (1), if—

(a) he has parental responsibility or, in Scotland, parental responsibilities for the child; or

(b) he has been registered as the child's father under any provision of section 10(1) or 10A(1) of the Births and Deaths Registration Act 1953 or of section 18(1) or (2) of the Registration of Births, Deaths and Marriages (Scotland) Act 1965.

(3) [revoked]

14 Extent of entitlement

(1) An employee is entitled to eighteen weeks' leave in respect of any individual child.

(1A) [revoked]

(2) Where the period for which an employee is normally required, under his contract of employment, to work in the course of a week does not vary, a week's leave for the employee is a period of absence from work which is equal in duration to the period for which he is normally required to work.

(3) Where the period for which an employee is normally required, under his contract of employment, to work in the course of a week varies from week to week or over a longer period, or where he is normally required under his contract to work in some weeks but not in others a week's leave for the employee is a period of absence from work which is equal in duration to the period calculated by dividing the total of the periods for which he is normally required to work in a year by 52.

(4) Where an employee takes leave in periods shorter than the period which constitutes, for him, a week's leave under whichever of paragraphs (2) and (3) is applicable in his case, he completes a week's leave when the aggregate of the periods of leave he has taken equals the period constituting a week's leave for him under the applicable paragraph.

15 When parental leave may be taken

An employee may not exercise any entitlement to parental leave in respect of a child after the date of the child's 18th birthday.

16 Default provisions in respect of parental leave

The provisions set out in Schedule 2 apply in relation to parental leave in the case of an employee whose contract of employment does not include a provision which—

(a) confers an entitlement to absence from work for the purpose of caring for a child, and

(b) incorporates or operates by reference to all or part of a collective agreement or workforce agreement.

16A [omitted]

PART IV PROVISIONS APPLICABLE IN RELATION TO MORE THAN ONE KIND OF ABSENCE

17 Application of terms and conditions during periods of leave

An employee who takes parental leave—

(a) is entitled, during the period of leave, to the benefit of her employer's implied obligation to her of trust and confidence and any terms and conditions of her employment relating to—

(i) notice of the termination of the employment contract by her employer;

(ii) compensation in the event of redundancy, or

(iii) disciplinary or grievance procedures;

(b) is bound, during that period, by her implied obligation to her employer of good faith and any terms and conditions of her employment relating to—

(i) notice of the termination of the employment contract by her,

(ii) the disclosure of confidential information,

(iii) the acceptance of gifts or other benefits, or

(iv) the employee's participation in any other business.

18 Right to return after maternity or parental leave

(1) An employee who returns to work after a period of ordinary maternity leave, or a period of parental leave of four weeks or less, which was—

(a) an isolated period of leave, or

(b) the last of two or more consecutive periods of statutory leave which did not include—

(i) any period of parental leave of more than four weeks; or

(ii) any period of statutory leave which when added to any other period of statutory leave (excluding parental leave) taken in relation to the same child means that the total amount of statutory leave taken in relation to that child totals more than 26 weeks,

is entitled to return to the job in which she was employed before her absence.

(2) An employee who returns to work after—

(a) a period of additional maternity leave, or a period of parental leave of more than four weeks, whether or not preceded by another period of statutory leave, or

(b) a period of ordinary maternity leave, or a period of parental leave of four weeks or less, not falling within the description in paragraph (1)(a) or (b) above, is entitled to return from leave to the job in which she was employed before her absence or, if it is not reasonably practicable for the employer to permit her to return to that job, to another job which is both suitable for her and appropriate for her to do in the circumstances.

(3) The reference in paragraphs (1) and (2) to the job in which an employee was employed before her absence is a reference to the job in which she was employed—

(a) if her return is from an isolated period of statutory leave, immediately before that period began;

(b) if her return is from consecutive periods of statutory leave, immediately before the first such period.

(4) This regulation does not apply where regulation 10 applies.

18A Incidents of the right to return

(1) An employee's right to return under regulation 18(1) or (2) is a right to return—

(a) with her seniority, pension rights and similar rights as they would have been if she had not been absent, and

(b) on terms and conditions not less favourable than those which would have applied if she had not been absent.

(2) In the case of accrual of rights under an employment-related benefit scheme within the meaning given by Schedule 5 to the Social Security Act 1989, nothing in paragraph (1)(a) concerning the treatment of additional maternity leave shall be taken to impose a requirement which exceeds the requirements of paragraphs 5 and 6 of that Schedule.

(3) The provisions in paragraph (1) for an employee to be treated as if she had not been absent refer to her absence—

(a) if her return is from an isolated period of statutory leave, since the beginning of that period;

(b) if her return is from consecutive periods of statutory leave, since the beginning of the first such period.

19 Protection from detriment

(1) An employee is entitled under section 47C of the 1996 Act not to be subjected to any detriment by any act, or any deliberate failure to act, by her employer done for any of the reasons specified in paragraph (2).

(2) The reasons referred to in paragraph (1) are that the employee—

(a) is pregnant;

(b) has given birth to a child;

(c) is the subject of a relevant requirement, or a relevant recommendation, as defined by section 66(2) of the 1996 Act;

(d) took, sought to take or availed herself of the benefits of, ordinary maternity leave or additional maternity leave;

(e) took or sought to take—

(i) [revoked],

(ii) parental leave, or

(iii) time off under section 57A of the 1996 Act;

(ee) failed to return after a period of ordinary or additional maternity leave in a case where—

(i) the employer did not notify her, in accordance with regulation 7(6) and (7) or otherwise, of the date on which the period in question would end, and she reasonably believed that that period had not ended, or

(ii) the employer gave her less than 28 days' notice of the date on which the period in question would end, and it was not reasonably practicable for her to return on that date;

(eee) undertook, considered undertaking or refused to undertake work in accordance with regulation 12A;

(f) declined to sign a workforce agreement for the purpose of these Regulations, or
(g) being—
(i) a representative of members of the workforce for the purposes of Schedule 1, or
(ii) a candidate in an election in which any person elected will, on being elected, become such a representative;
performed (or proposed to perform) any functions or activities as such a representative or candidate.

(3) For the purposes of paragraph (2)(d), a woman avails herself of the benefits of ordinary maternity leave if, during her ordinary maternity leave period, she avails herself of the benefit of any of the terms and conditions of her employment preserved by section 71 of the 1996 Act and regulation 9 during that period.

(3A) For the purposes of paragraph (2)(d), a woman avails herself of the benefits of additional maternity leave if, during her additional maternity leave period, she avails herself of the benefit of any of the terms and conditions of her employment preserved by section 73 of the 1996 Act and regulation 9 during that period.

(4) Paragraph (1) does not apply in a case where the detriment in question amounts to dismissal within the meaning of Part X of the 1996 Act.

(5) Paragraph (2)(b) only applies where the act or failure to act takes place during the employee's ordinary or additional maternity leave period.

(6) For the purposes of paragraph (5)—
(a) where an act extends over a period, the reference to the date of the act is a reference to the last day of that period, and
(b) a failure to act is to be treated as done when it was decided on.

(7) For the purposes of paragraph (6), in the absence of evidence establishing the contrary an employer shall be taken to decide on a failure to act—
(a) when he does an act inconsistent with doing the failed act, or
(b) if he has done no such inconsistent act, when the period expires within which he might reasonably have been expected to do the failed act if it were to be done.

20 Unfair dismissal

(1) An employee who is dismissed is entitled under section 99 of the 1996 Act to be regarded for the purposes of Part X of that Act as unfairly dismissed if—
(a) the reason or principal reason for the dismissal is of a kind specified in paragraph (3), or
(b) the reason or principal reason for the dismissal is that the employee is redundant, and regulation 10 has not been complied with.

(2) An employee who is dismissed shall also be regarded for the purposes of Part X of the 1996 Act as unfairly dismissed if—
(a) the reason (or, if more than one, the principal reason) for the dismissal is that the employee was redundant;
(b) it is shown that the circumstances constituting the redundancy applied equally to one or more employees in the same undertaking who held positions similar to that held by the employee and who have not been dismissed by the employer, and
(c) it is shown that the reason (or, if more than one, the principal reason) for which the employee was selected for dismissal was a reason of a kind specified in paragraph (3).

(3) The kinds of reason referred to in paragraphs (1) and (2) are reasons connected with—
(a) the pregnancy of the employee;
(b) the fact that the employee has given birth to a child;
(c) the application of a relevant requirement, or a relevant recommendation, as defined by section 66(2) of the 1996 Act;
(d) the fact that she took, sought to take or availed herself of the benefits of, ordinary maternity leave or additional maternity leave;

(e) the fact that she took or sought to take—
  (i) [revoked]
  (ii) parental leave, or
  (iii) time off under section 57A of the 1996 Act;

(ee) the fact that she failed to return after a period of ordinary or additional maternity leave in a case where—
  (i) the employer did not notify her, in accordance with regulation 7(6) and (7) or otherwise, of the date on which the period in question would end, and she reasonably believed that that period had not ended, or
  (ii) the employer gave her less than 28 days' notice of the date on which the period in question would end, and it was not reasonably practicable for her to return on that date;

(eee) the fact that she undertook, considered undertaking or refused to undertake work in accordance with regulation 12A;

(f) the fact that she declined to sign a workforce agreement for the purposes of these Regulations, or

(g) the fact that the employee, being—
  (i) a representative of members of the workforce for the purposes of Schedule 1, or
  (ii) a candidate in an election in which any person elected will, on being elected, become such a representative,

performed (or proposed to perform) any functions or activities as such a representative or candidate.

(4) Paragraph (3)(b) only applies where the dismissal ends the employee's ordinary or additional maternity leave period.

(5) Paragraphs (3) and (3A) of regulation 19 apply for the purposes of paragraph (3)(d) as they apply for the purposes of paragraph (2)(d) of that regulation.

(6) [revoked]

(7) Paragraph (1) does not apply in relation to an employee if—

(a) it is not reasonably practicable for a reason other than redundancy for the employer (who may be the same employer or a successor of his) to permit her to return to a job which is both suitable for her and appropriate for her to do in the circumstances;

(b) an associated employer offers her a job of that kind, and

(c) she accepts or unreasonably refuses that offer.

(8) Where on a complaint of unfair dismissal any question arises as to whether the operation of paragraph (1) is excluded by the provisions of paragraph (7), it is for the employer to show that the provisions in question were satisfied in relation to the complainant.

21 Contractual rights to maternity or parental leave

(1) This regulation applies where an employee is entitled to—

(a) ordinary maternity leave,

(b) additional maternity leave, or

(c) parental leave,

(referred to in paragraph (2) as a 'statutory right') and also to a right which corresponds to that right and which arises under the employee's contract of employment or otherwise.

(2) In a case where this regulation applies—

(a) the employee may not exercise the statutory right and the corresponding right separately but may, in taking the leave for which the two rights provide, take advantage of whichever right is, in any particular respect, the more favourable, and

(b) the provisions of the 1996 Act and of these Regulations relating to the statutory right apply, subject to any modifications necessary to give effect to any more favourable contractual terms, to the exercise of the composite right described in sub-paragraph (a) as they apply to the exercise of the statutory right.

22 [omitted]

Regulation 2(1)

SCHEDULE 1

WORKFORCE AGREEMENTS

1. An agreement is a workforce agreement for the purposes of these Regulations if the following conditions are satisfied—

(a) the agreement is in writing;

(b) it has effect for a specified period not exceeding five years;

(c) it applies either—

(i) to all of the relevant members of the workforce, or

(ii) to all of the relevant members of the workforce who belong to a particular group;

(d) the agreement is signed—

(i) in the case of an agreement of the kind referred to in sub-paragraph (c)(i), by the representatives of the workforce, and in the case of an agreement of the kind referred to in sub-paragraph (c)(ii), by the representatives of the group to which the agreement applies (excluding, in either case, any representative not a relevant member of the workforce on the date on which the agreement was first made available for signature), or

(ii) if the employer employed 20 or fewer employees on the date referred to in sub-paragraph (d)(i), either by the appropriate representatives in accordance with that sub-paragraph or by the majority of the employees employed by him; and

(e) before the agreement was made available for signature, the employer provided all the employees to whom it was intended to apply on the date on which it came into effect with copies of the text of the agreement and such guidance as those employees might reasonably require in order to understand it in full.

2. For the purposes of this Schedule—

'a particular group' is a group of the relevant members of a workforce who undertake a particular function, work at a particular workplace or belong to a particular department or unit within their employer's business;

'relevant members of the workforce' are all of the employees employed by a particular employer, excluding any employee whose terms and conditions of employment are provided for, wholly or in part, in a collective agreement;

'representatives of the workforce' are employees duly elected to represent the relevant members of the workforce, 'representatives of the group' are employees duly elected to represent the members of a particular group, and representatives are 'duly elected' if the election at which they were elected satisfied the requirements of paragraph 3 of this Schedule.

3. The requirements concerning elections referred to in paragraph 2 are that—

(a) the number of representatives to be elected is determined by the employer;

(b) the candidates for election as representatives of the workforce are relevant members of the workforce, and the candidates for election as representatives of a group are members of the group;

(c) no employee who is eligible to be a candidate is unreasonably excluded from standing for election;

(d) all the relevant members of the workforce are entitled to vote for representatives of the workforce, and all the members of a particular group are entitled to vote for representatives of the group;

(e) the employees entitled to vote may vote for as many candidates as there are representatives to be elected; and

(f) the election is conducted so as to secure that—

(i) so far as is reasonably practicable, those voting do so in secret, and

(ii) the votes given at the election are fairly and accurately counted.

Regulation 16

SCHEDULE 2

DEFAULT PROVISIONS IN RESPECT OF PARENTAL LEAVE

Conditions of entitlement

1. An employee may not exercise any entitlement to parental leave unless—
   (a) he has complied with any request made by his employer to produce for the employer's inspection evidence of his entitlement, of the kind described in paragraph 2,
   (b) he has given his employer notice, in accordance with whichever of paragraphs 3 to 5 is applicable, of the period of leave he proposes to take, and
   (c) in a case where paragraph 6 applies, his employer has not postponed the period of leave in accordance with that paragraph.

2. The evidence to be produced for the purpose of paragraph 1(a) is such evidence as may reasonably be required of—
   (a) the employee's responsibility or expected responsibility for the child in respect of whom the employee proposes to take parental leave,
   (b) the child's date of birth or, in the case of a child who was placed with the employee for adoption, the date on which the placement began.
   (c) [revoked]

2A. Where regulation 13(1A) applies, and the employee's entitlement to parental leave arises out of a period of employment by a person other than the person who was his employer on 9th January 2002, the employee may not exercise the entitlement unless he has given his employer notice of that period of employment, and provided him with such evidence of it as the employer may reasonably require.

Notice to be given to employer

3. Except in a case where paragraph 4 or 5 applies, the notice required for the purpose of paragraph 1(b) is notice which—
   (a) specifies the dates on which the period of leave is to begin and end, and
   (b) is given to the employer at least 21 days before the date on which that period is to begin.

4. Where the employee is the father of the child in respect of whom the leave is to be taken, and the period of leave is to begin on the date on which the child is born, the notice required for the purpose of paragraph 1(b) is notice which—
   (a) specifies the expected week of childbirth and the duration of the period of leave, and
   (b) is given to the employer at least 21 days before the beginning of the expected week of childbirth.

5. Where the child in respect of whom the leave is to be taken is to be placed with the employee for adoption by him and the leave is to begin on the date of the placement, the notice required for the purpose of paragraph 1(b) is notice which—
   (a) specifies the week in which the placement is expected to occur and the duration of the period of leave, and
   (b) is given to the employer at least 21 days before the beginning of that week, or, if that is not reasonably practicable, as soon as is reasonably practicable.

Postponement of leave

6. An employer may postpone a period of parental leave where—
   (a) neither paragraph 4 nor paragraph 5 applies, and the employee has accordingly given the employer notice in accordance with paragraph 3;
   (b) the employer considers that the operation of his business would be unduly disrupted if the employee took leave during the period identified in his notice;

(c) the employer agrees to permit the employee to take a period of leave—
   (i) of the same duration as the period identified in the employee's notice,
   (ii) beginning on a date determined by the employer after consulting the employee, which is no later than six months after the commencement of that period, and
   (iii) ending before the date of the child's eighteenth birthday;

(d) the employer gives the employee notice in writing of the postponement which—
   (i) states the reason for it, and
   (ii) specifies the dates on which the period of leave the employer agrees to permit the employee to take will begin and end; and

(e) that notice is given to the employee not more than seven days after the employee's notice was given to the employer.

Minimum periods of leave

7. An employee may not take parental leave in a period other than the period which constitutes a week's leave for him under regulation 14 or a multiple of that period, except in a case where the child in respect of whom leave is taken is entitled to a disability living allowance, armed forces independence payment or personal independence payment.

Maximum annual leave allowance

8. An employee may not take more than four weeks' leave in respect of any individual child during a particular year.

9. For the purposes of paragraph 8, a year is the period of twelve months beginning—
   (a) on the date on which the employee first became entitled to take parental leave in respect of the child in question
   (b) [repealed]

and each successive period of twelve months beginning on the anniversary of that date.

The Part-Time Workers (Prevention of Less Favourable Treatment) Regulations 2000

(SI 2000 No. 1551)

PART I GENERAL AND INTERPRETATION

1 Citation, commencement and interpretation

(1) [omitted]

(2) In these Regulations—

'the 1996 Act' means the Employment Rights Act 1996;

'contract of employment' means a contract of service or of apprenticeship, whether express or implied, and (if it is express) whether oral or in writing;

'employee' means an individual who has entered into or works under or (except where a provision of these Regulations otherwise requires) where the employment has ceased, worked under a contract of employment;

'employer', in relation to any employee or worker, means the person by whom the employee or worker is or (except where a provision of these Regulations otherwise requires) where the employment has ceased, was employed;

'pro rata principle' means that where a comparable full-time worker receives or is entitled to receive pay or any other benefit, a part-time worker is to receive or be entitled to receive not less than the proportion of that pay or other benefit that the number of his weekly hours bears to the number of weekly hours of the comparable full-time worker;

'worker' means an individual who has entered into or works under or (except where a provision of these Regulations otherwise requires) where the employment has ceased, worked under—

(a) a contract of employment; or

(b) any other contract, whether express or implied and (if it is express) whether oral or in writing, whereby the individual undertakes to do or perform personally any work or services for another party to the contract whose status is not by virtue of the contract that of a client or customer of any profession or business undertaking carried on by the individual.

(3) In the definition of the pro rata principle and in regulations 3 and 4 'weekly hours' means the number of hours a worker is required to work under his contract of employment in a week in which he has no absences from work and does not work any overtime or, where the number of such hours varies according to a cycle, the average number of such hours.

2 Meaning of full-time worker, part-time worker and comparable full-time worker

(1) A worker is a full-time worker for the purpose of these Regulations if he is paid wholly or in part by reference to the time he works and, having regard to the custom and practice of the employer in relation to workers employed by the worker's employer under the same type of contract, is identifiable as a full-time worker.

(2) A worker is a part-time worker for the purpose of these Regulations if he is paid wholly or in part by reference to the time he works and, having regard to the custom and practice of the employer in relation to workers employed by the worker's employer under the same type of contract, is not identifiable as a full-time worker.

(3) For the purposes of paragraphs (1), (2) and (4), the following shall be regarded as being employed under different types of contract—

(a) employees employed under a contract that is not a contract of apprenticeship;

(b) employees employed under a contract of apprenticeship;

(c) workers who are not employees;

(d) any other description of worker that it is reasonable for the employer to treat differently from other workers on the ground that workers of that description have a different type of contract.

(4) A full-time worker is a comparable full-time worker in relation to a part-time worker if, at the time when the treatment that is alleged to be less favourable to the part-time worker takes place—

(a) both workers are—

(i) employed by the same employer under the same type of contract; and

(ii) engaged in the same or broadly similar work having regard, where relevant, to whether they have a similar level of qualification, skills and experience; and

(b) the full-time worker works or is based at the same establishment as the part-time worker or, where there is no full-time worker working or based at that establishment who satisfies the requirements of sub-paragraph (a), works or is based at a different establishment and satisfies those requirements.

3 Workers becoming part-time

(1) This regulation applies to a worker who—

(a) was identifiable as a full-time worker in accordance with regulation 2(1); and

(b) following a termination or variation of his contract, continues to work under a new or varied contract, whether of the same type or not, that requires him to work for a number of weekly hours that is lower than the number he was required to work immediately before the termination or variation.

(2) Notwithstanding regulation 2(4), regulation 5 shall apply to a worker to whom this regulation applies as if he were a part-time worker and as if there were a comparable full-time worker employed under the terms that applied to him immediately before the variation or termination.

(3) The fact that this regulation applies to a worker does not affect any right he may have under these Regulations by virtue of regulation 2(4).

4 Workers returning part-time after absence

(1) This regulation applies to a worker who—

(a) was identifiable as a full-time worker in accordance with regulation 2(1) immediately before a period of absence (whether the absence followed a termination of the worker's contract or not);

(b) returns to work for the same employer within a period of less than twelve months beginning with the day on which the period of absence started;

(c) returns to the same job or to a job at the same level under a contract, whether it is a different contract or a varied contract and regardless of whether it is of the same type, under which he is required to work for a number of weekly hours that is lower than the number he was required to work immediately before the period of absence.

(2) Notwithstanding regulation 2(4), regulation 5 shall apply to a worker to whom this regulation applies ('the returning worker') as if he were a part-time worker and as if there were a comparable full-time worker employed under—

(a) the contract under which the returning worker was employed immediately before the period of absence; or

(b) where it is shown that, had the returning worker continued to work under the contract mentioned in sub-paragraph (a) a variation would have been made to its term during the period of absence, the contract mentioned in that sub-paragraph including that variation.

(3) The fact that this regulation applies to a worker does not affect any right he may have under these Regulations by virtue of regulation 2(4).

PART II RIGHTS AND REMEDIES

5 Less favourable treatment of part-time workers

(1) A part-time worker has the right not to be treated by his employer less favourably than the employer treats a comparable full-time worker—

(a) as regards the terms of his contract; or

(b) by being subjected to any other detriment by any act, or deliberate failure to act, of his employer.

(2) The right conferred by paragraph (1) applies only if—

(a) the treatment is on the ground that the worker is a part-time worker, and

(b) the treatment is not justified on objective grounds.

(3) In determining whether a part-time worker has been treated less favourably than a comparable full-time worker the pro rata principle shall be applied unless it is inappropriate.

(4) A part-time worker paid at a lower rate for overtime worked by him in a period than a comparable full-time worker is or would be paid for overtime worked by him in the same period shall not, for that reason, be regarded as treated less favourably than the comparable full-time worker where, or to the extent that, the total number of hours worked by the part-time worker in the period, including overtime, does not exceed the number of hours the comparable full-time worker is required to work in the period, disregarding absences from work and overtime.

6 Right to receive a written statement of reasons for less favourable treatment

(1) If a worker who considers that his employer may have treated him in a manner which infringes a right conferred on him by regulation 5 requests in writing from his employer a written statement giving particulars of the reasons for the treatment, the worker is entitled to be provided with such a statement within twenty-one days of his request.

(2) A written statement under this regulation is admissible as evidence in any proceedings under these Regulations.

(3) If it appears to the tribunal in any proceedings under these Regulations—

(a) that the employer deliberately, and without reasonable excuse, omitted to provide a written statement, or

(b) that the written statement is evasive or equivocal,

it may draw any inference which it considers it just and equitable to draw, including an inference that the employer has infringed the right in question.

(4) This regulation does not apply where the treatment in question consists of the dismissal of an employee, and the employee is entitled to a written statement of reasons for his dismissal under section 92 of the 1996 Act.

7 Unfair dismissal and the right not to be subjected to detriment

(1) An employee who is dismissed shall be regarded as unfairly dismissed for the purposes of Part X of the 1996 Act if the reason (or, if more than one, the principal reason) for the dismissal is a reason specified in paragraph (3).

(2) A worker has the right not to be subjected to any detriment by any act, or any deliberate failure to act, by his employer done on a ground specified in paragraph (3).

(3) The reasons or, as the case may be, grounds are—

(a) that the worker has—

(i) brought proceedings against the employer under these Regulations;

(ii) requested from his employer a written statement of reasons under regulation 6;

(iii) given evidence or information in connection with such proceedings brought by any worker;

(iv) otherwise done anything under these Regulations in relation to the employer or any other person;

(v) alleged that the employer had infringed these Regulations;

(vi) refused (or proposed to refuse) to forgo a right conferred on him by these Regulations; or

(b) that the employer believes or suspects that the worker has done or intends to do any of the things mentioned in sub-paragraph (a).

(4) Where the reason or principal reason for dismissal or, as the case may be, ground for subjection to any act or deliberate failure to act, is that mentioned in paragraph (3)(a)(v), or (b) so far as it relates thereto, neither paragraph (1) nor paragraph (2) applies if the allegation made by the worker is false and not made in good faith.

(5) Paragraph (2) does not apply where the detriment in question amounts to the dismissal of an employee within the meaning of Part X of the 1996 Act.

8 Complaints to employment tribunals etc.

(1) Subject to regulation 7(5), a worker may present a complaint to an employment tribunal that his employer has infringed a right conferred on him by regulation 5 or 7(2).

(2) Subject to paragraph (3), an employment tribunal shall not consider a complaint under this regulation unless it is presented before the end of the period of three months (or, in a case to which regulation 13 applies, six months) beginning with the date of the less favourable treatment or detriment to which the complaint relates or, where an act or failure to act is part of a series of similar acts or failures comprising the less favourable treatment or detriment, the last of them.

(2A) [omitted]

(3) A tribunal may consider any such complaint which is out of time if, in all the circumstances of the case, it considers that it is just and equitable to do so.

(4) For the purposes of calculating the date of the less favourable treatment or detriment under paragraph (2)—

(a) where a term in a contract is less favourable, that treatment shall be treated, subject to paragraph (b), as taking place on each day of the period during which the term is less favourable;

(b) where an application relies on regulation 3 or 4 the less favourable treatment shall be treated as occurring on, and only on, in the case of regulation 3, the first day on which the applicant worked under the new or varied contract and, in the case of regulation 4, the day on which the applicant returned; and

(c) a deliberate failure to act contrary to regulation 5 or 7(2) shall be treated as done when it was decided on.

(5) In the absence of evidence establishing the contrary, a person shall be taken for the purposes of paragraph (4)(c) to decide not to act—

(a) when he does an act inconsistent with doing the failed act; or

(b) if he has done no such inconsistent act, when the period expires within which he might reasonably have been expected to have done the failed act if it was to be done.

(6) Where a worker presents a complaint under this regulation it is for the employer to identify the ground for the less favourable treatment or detriment.

(7) Where an employment tribunal finds that a complaint presented to it under this regulation is well founded, it shall take such of the following steps as it considers just and equitable—

(a) making a declaration as to the rights of the complainant and the employer in relation to the matters to which the complaint relates;

(b) ordering the employer to pay compensation to the complainant;

(c) recommending that the employer take, within a specified period, action appearing to the tribunal to be reasonable, in all the circumstances of the case, for the purpose of obviating or reducing the adverse effect on the complainant of any matter to which the complaint relates.

(8) [revoked]

(9) Where a tribunal orders compensation under paragraph (7)(b), the amount of the compensation awarded shall be such as the tribunal considers just and equitable in all the circumstances having regard to—

(a) the infringement to which the complaint relates; and

(b) any loss which is attributable to the infringement having regard, in the case of an infringement of the right conferred by regulation 5, to the pro rata principle except where it is inappropriate to do so.

(10) The loss shall be taken to include—

(a) any expenses reasonably incurred by the complainant in consequence of the infringement; and

(b) loss of any benefit which he might reasonably be expected to have had but for the infringement.

(11) Compensation in respect of treating a worker in a manner which infringes the right conferred on him by regulation 5 shall not include compensation for injury to feelings.

(12) In ascertaining the loss the tribunal shall apply the same rule concerning the duty of a person to mitigate his loss as applies to damages recoverable under the common law of England and Wales or (as the case may be) Scotland.

(13) Where the tribunal finds that the act, or failure to act, to which the complaint relates was to any extent caused or contributed to by action of the complainant, it shall reduce the amount of the compensation by such proportion as it considers just and equitable having regard to that finding.

(14) If the employer fails, without reasonable justification, to comply with a recommendation made by an employment tribunal under paragraph (7)(c) the tribunal may, if it thinks it just and equitable to do so—

(a) increase the amount of compensation required to be paid to the complainant in respect of the complaint, where an order was made under paragraph (7)(b); or

(b) make an order under paragraph (7)(b).

8A [omitted]

9 Restrictions on contracting out

Section 203 of the 1996 Act (restrictions on contracting out) shall apply in relation to these Regulations as if they were contained in that Act.

PART III MISCELLANEOUS

10 [omitted]

11 Liability of employers and principals

(1) Anything done by a person in the course of his employment shall be treated for the purposes of these Regulations as also done by his employer, whether or not it was done with the employer's knowledge or approval.

(2) Anything done by a person as agent for the employer with the authority of the employer shall be treated for the purposes of these Regulations as also done by the employer.

(3) In proceedings under these Regulations against any person in respect of an act alleged to have been done by a worker of his, it shall be a defence for that person to prove that he took such steps as were reasonably practicable to prevent the worker from—

(a) doing that act; or

(b) doing, in the course of his employment, acts of that description.

PART IV SPECIAL CLASSES OF PERSON

12 Crown employment

(1) Subject to regulation 13, these Regulations have effect in relation to Crown employment and persons in Crown employment as they have effect in relation to other employment and other employees and workers.

(2) In paragraph (1) 'Crown employment' means employment under or for the purposes of a government department or any officer or body exercising on behalf of the Crown functions conferred by a statutory provision.

(3) For the purposes of the application of the provisions of these Regulations in relation to Crown employment in accordance with paragraph (1)—

(a) references to an employee and references to a worker shall be construed as references to a person in Crown employment to whom the definition of employee or, as the case may be, worker is appropriate; and

(b) references to a contract in relation to an employee and references to a contract in relation to a worker shall be construed as references to the terms of employment of a person in Crown employment to whom the definition of employee or, as the case may be, worker is appropriate.

13–17 [omitted]

The Fixed-term Employees (Prevention of Less Favourable Treatment) Regulations 2002

(SI 2002 No. 2034)

PART 1 GENERAL AND INTERPRETATION

Citation, commencement and interpretation

1.—(1) [omitted]

(2) In these Regulations—

'the 1996 Act' means the Employment Rights Act 1996;

'collective agreement' means a collective agreement within the meaning of section 178 of the Trade Union and Labour Relations (Consolidation) Act 1992; the trade union parties to which are independent trade unions within the meaning of section 5 of that Act;

'employer', in relation to any employee, means the person by whom the employee is (or, where the employment has ceased, was) employed;

'fixed-term contract' means a contract of employment that, under its provisions determining how it will terminate in the normal course, will terminate—

- (a) on the expiry of a specific term,
- (b) on the completion of a particular task, or
- (c) on the occurrence or non-occurrence of any other specific event other than the attainment by the employee of any normal and bona fide retiring age in the establishment for an employee holding the position held by him,

and any reference to 'fixed-term' shall be construed accordingly;

'fixed-term employee' means an employee who is employed under a fixed-term contract;

'permanent employee' means an employee who is not employed under a fixed-term contract, and any reference to 'permanent employment' shall be construed accordingly;

'pro rata principle' means that where a comparable permanent employee receives or is entitled to pay or any other benefit, a fixed-term employee is to receive or be entitled to such proportion of that pay or other benefit as is reasonable in the circumstances having regard to the length of his contract of employment and to the terms on which the pay or other benefit is offered;

'renewal' includes extension and references to renewing a contract shall be construed accordingly;

'workforce agreement' means an agreement between an employer and his employees or their representatives in respect of which the conditions set out in Schedule 1 to these Regulations are satisfied.

Comparable employees

2.—(1) For the purposes of these Regulations, an employee is a comparable permanent employee in relation to a fixed-term employee if, at the time when the treatment that is alleged to be less favourable to the fixed-term employee takes place,

- (a) both employees are—
  - (i) employed by the same employer, and
  - (ii) engaged in the same or broadly similar work having regard, where relevant, to whether they have a similar level of qualification and skills; and
- (b) the permanent employee works or is based at the same establishment as the fixed-term employee or, where there is no comparable permanent employee working or based at that establishment who satisfies the requirements of sub-paragraph (a), works or is based at a different establishment and satisfies those requirements.

(2) For the purposes of paragraph (1), an employee is not a comparable permanent employee if his employment has ceased.

PART 2 RIGHTS AND REMEDIES

Less favourable treatment of fixed-term employees

3.—(1) A fixed-term employee has the right not to be treated by his employer less favourably than the employer treats a comparable permanent employee—

(a) as regards the terms of his contract; or

(b) by being subjected to any other detriment by any act, or deliberate failure to act, of his employer.

(2) Subject to paragraphs (3) and (4), the right conferred by paragraph (1) includes in particular the right of the fixed-term employee in question not to be treated less favourably than the employer treats a comparable permanent employee in relation to—

(a) any period of service qualification relating to any particular condition of service,

(b) the opportunity to receive training, or

(c) the opportunity to secure any permanent position in the establishment.

(3) The right conferred by paragraph (1) applies only if—

(a) the treatment is on the ground that the employee is a fixed-term employee, and

(b) the treatment is not justified on objective grounds.

(4) Paragraph (3)(b) is subject to regulation 4.

(5) In determining whether a fixed-term employee has been treated less favourably than a comparable permanent employee, the pro rata principle shall be applied unless it is inappropriate.

(6) In order to ensure that an employee is able to exercise the right conferred by paragraph (1) as described in paragraph (2)(c) the employee has the right to be informed by his employer of available vacancies in the establishment.

(7) For the purposes of paragraph (6) an employee is 'informed by his employer' only if the vacancy is contained in an advertisement which the employee has a reasonable opportunity of reading in the course of his employment or the employee is given reasonable notification of the vacancy in some other way.

Objective justification

4.—(1) Where a fixed-term employee is treated by his employer less favourably than the employer treats a comparable permanent employee as regards any term of his contract, the treatment in question shall be regarded for the purposes of regulation 3(3)(b) as justified on objective grounds if the terms of the fixed-term employee's contract of employment, taken as a whole, are at least as favourable as the terms of the comparable permanent employee's contract of employment.

(2) Paragraph (1) is without prejudice to the generality of regulation 3(3)(b).

Right to receive a written statement of reasons for less favourable treatment

5.—(1) If an employee who considers that his employer may have treated him in a manner which infringes a right conferred on him by regulation 3 requests in writing from his employer a written statement giving particulars of the reasons for the treatment, the employee is entitled to be provided with such a statement within twenty-one days of his request.

(2) A written statement under this regulation is admissible as evidence in any proceedings under these Regulations.

(3) If it appears to the tribunal in any proceedings under these Regulations—

(a) that the employer deliberately, and without reasonable excuse, omitted to provide a written statement, or

(b) that the written statement is evasive or equivocal,

it may draw any inference which it considers it just and equitable to draw, including an inference that the employer has infringed the right in question.

(4) This regulation does not apply where the treatment in question consists of the dismissal of an employee, and the employee is entitled to a written statement of reasons for his dismissal under section 92 of the 1996 Act.

Unfair dismissal and the right not to be subjected to detriment

6.—(1) An employee who is dismissed shall be regarded as unfairly dismissed for the purposes of Part 10 of the 1996 Act if the reason (or, if more than one, the principal reason) for the dismissal is a reason specified in paragraph (3).

(2) An employee has the right not to be subjected to any detriment by any act, or any deliberate failure to act, of his employer done on a ground specified in paragraph (3).

(3) The reasons or, as the case may be, grounds are—

(a) that the employee—

(i) brought proceedings against the employer under these Regulations;

(ii) requested from his employer a written statement under regulation 5 or regulation 9;

(iii) gave evidence or information in connection with such proceedings brought by any employee;

(iv) otherwise did anything under these Regulations in relation to the employer or any other person;

(v) alleged that the employer had infringed these Regulations;

(vi) refused (or proposed to refuse) to forgo a right conferred on him by these Regulations;

(vii) declined to sign a workforce agreement for the purposes of these Regulations; or

(viii) being—

(aa) a representative of members of the workforce for the purposes of Schedule 1, or

(bb) a candidate in an election in which any person elected will, on being elected, become such a representative,

performed (or proposed to perform) any functions or activities as such a representative or candidate, or

(b) that the employer believes or suspects that the employee has done or intends to do any of the things mentioned in sub-paragraph (a).

(4) Where the reason or principal reason for dismissal or, as the case may be, ground for subjection to any act or deliberate failure to act, is that mentioned in paragraph (3)(a)(v), or (b) so far as it relates thereto, neither paragraph (1) nor paragraph (2) applies if the allegation made by the employee is false and not made in good faith.

(5) Paragraph (2) does not apply where the detriment in question amounts to dismissal within the meaning of Part 10 of the 1996 Act.

Complaints to employment tribunals etc.

7.—(1) An employee may present a complaint to an employment tribunal that his employer has infringed a right conferred on him by regulation 3, or (subject to regulation 6(5)), regulation 6(2).

(2)–(5) [omitted]

(6) Where an employee presents a complaint under this regulation in relation to a right conferred on him by regulation 3 or 6(2) it is for the employer to identify the ground for the less favourable treatment or detriment.

(7) Where an employment tribunal finds that a complaint presented to it under this regulation is well founded, it shall take such of the following steps as it considers just and equitable—

(a) making a declaration as to the rights of the complaint and the employer in relation to the matters to which the complaint relates;

(b) ordering the employer to pay compensation to the complainant;
(c) recommending that the employer take, within a specified period, action appearing to the tribunal to be reasonable, in all the circumstances of the case, for the purpose of obviating or reducing the adverse effect on the complainant of any matter to which the complaint relates.

(8) Where a tribunal orders compensation under paragraph (7)(b), the amount of the compensation awarded shall be such as the tribunal considers just and equitable in all the circumstances having regard to—

(a) the infringement to which the complaint relates, and
(b) any loss which is attributable to the infringement.

(9) The loss shall be taken to include—

(a) any expenses reasonably incurred by the complainant in consequence of the infringement, and
(b) loss of any benefit which he might reasonably be expected to have had but for the infringement.

(10) Compensation in respect of treating an employee in a manner which infringes the right conferred on him by regulation 3 shall not include compensation for injury to feelings.

(11) In ascertaining the loss the tribunal shall apply the same rule concerning the duty of a person to mitigate his loss as applies to damages recoverable under the common law of England and Wales or (as the case may be) the law of Scotland.

(12) Where the tribunal finds that the act, or failure to act, to which the complaint relates was to any extent caused or contributed to by action of the complainant, it shall reduce the amount of the compensation by such proportion as it considers just and equitable having regard to that finding.

(13) If the employer fails, without reasonable justification, to comply with a recommendation made by an employment tribunal under paragraph (7)(c) the tribunal may, if it thinks it just and equitable to do so—

(a) increase the amount of compensation required to be paid to the complainant in respect of the complaint, where an order was made under paragraph (7)(b); or
(b) make an order under paragraph (7)(b).

7A. [omitted]

Successive fixed-term contracts

8.—(1) This regulation applies where—

(a) an employee is employed under a contract purporting to be a fixed-term contract, and
(b) the contract mentioned in sub-paragraph (a) has previously been renewed, or the employee has previously been employed on a fixed-term contract before the start of the contract mentioned in sub-paragraph (a).

(2) Where this regulation applies then, with effect from the date specified in paragraph (3), the provision of the contract mentioned in paragraph (1)(a) that restricts the duration of the contract shall be of no effect, and the employee shall be a permanent employee, if—

(a) the employee has been continuously employed under the contract mentioned in paragraph 1(a), or under that contract taken with a previous fixed-term contract, for a period of four years or more, and
(b) the employment of the employee under a fixed-term contract was not justified on objective grounds—
    (i) where the contract mentioned in paragraph (1)(a) has been renewed, at the time when it was last renewed;
    (ii) where that contract has not been renewed, at the time when it was entered into.

(3) The date referred to in paragraph (2) is whichever is the later of—

(a) the date on which the contract mentioned in paragraph (1)(a) was entered into or last renewed, and
(b) the date on which the employee acquired four years' continuous employment.

(4) For the purposes of this regulation Chapter 1 of Part 14 of the 1996 Act shall apply in determining whether an employee has been continuously employed, and any period of continuous employment falling before the 10th July 2002 shall be disregarded.

(5) A collective agreement or a workforce agreement may modify the application of paragraphs (1) to (3) of this regulation in relation to any employee or specified description of employees, by substituting for the provisions of paragraph (2) or paragraph (3), or for the provisions of both of those paragraphs, one or more different provisions which, in order to prevent abuse arising from the use of successive fixed-term contracts, specify one or more of the following—

- (a) the maximum total period for which the employee or employees of that description may be continuously employed on a fixed-term contract or on successive fixed-term contracts;
- (b) the maximum number of successive fixed-term contracts and renewals of such contracts under which the employee or employees of that description may be employed; or
- (c) objective grounds justifying the renewal of fixed-term contracts, or the engagement of the employee or employees of that description under successive fixed-term contracts,

and those provisions shall have effect in relation to that employee or an employee of that description as if they were contained in paragraphs (2) and (3).

Right to receive written statement of variation

9.—(1) If an employee who considers that, by virtue of regulation 8, he is a permanent employee requests in writing from his employer a written statement confirming that his contract is no longer fixed-term or that he is now a permanent employee, he is entitled to be provided, within twenty-one days of his request, with either—

- (a) such a statement, or
- (b) a statement giving reasons why his contract remains fixed-term.

(2) If the reasons stated under paragraph (1)(b) include an assertion that there were objective grounds for the engagement of the employee under a fixed-term contract, or the renewal of such a contract, the statement shall include a statement of those grounds.

(3) A written statement under this regulation is admissible as evidence in any proceedings before a court, an employment tribunal and the Commissioners of the Inland Revenue.

(4) If it appears to the court or tribunal in any proceedings—

- (a) that the employer deliberately, and without reasonable excuse, omitted to provide a written statement, or
- (b) that the written statement is evasive or equivocal,

it may draw any inference which it considers it just and equitable to draw.

(5) An employee who considers that, by virtue of regulation 8, he is a permanent employee may present an application to an employment tribunal for a declaration to that effect.

(6) No application may be made under paragraph (5) unless—

- (a) the employee in question has previously requested a statement under paragraph (1) and the employer has either failed to provide a statement or given a statement of reasons under paragraph (1)(b), and
- (b) the employee is at the time the application is made employed by the employer.

PART 3 MISCELLANEOUS

Restrictions on contracting out

10. Section 203 of the 1996 Act (restrictions on contracting out) shall apply in relation to these Regulations as if they were contained in that Act.

11. [omitted]

Liability of employers and principals

12.—(1) Anything done by a person in the course of his employment shall be treated for the purposes of these Regulations as also done by his employer, whether or not it was done with the employer's knowledge or approval.

(2) Anything done by a person as agent for the employer with the authority of the employer shall be treated for the purposes of these Regulations as also done by the employer.

(3) In proceedings under these Regulations against any person in respect of an act alleged to have been done by an employee of his, it shall be a defence for that person to prove that he took such steps as were reasonably practicable to prevent the employee from—

(a) doing that act, or

(b) doing, in the course of his employment, acts of that description.

13.–17. [omitted]

PART 5 EXCLUSIONS

18. [omitted]

Agency workers

19.—(1) Save in respect of paragraph 1 of Part 1 of Schedule 2, these Regulations shall not have effect in relation to employment under a fixed-term contract where the employee is an agency worker.

(2) In this regulation 'agency worker' means any person who is supplied by an employment business to do work for another person under a contract or other arrangements made between the employment business and the other person.

(3) In this regulation 'employment business' means the business (whether or not carried on with a view to profit and whether or not carried on in conjunction with any other business) of supplying persons in the employment of the person carrying on the business, to act for, and under the control of, other persons in any capacity.

20. [omitted]

SCHEDULE 1

WORKFORCE AGREEMENTS

1. An agreement is a workforce agreement for the purposes of these Regulations if the following conditions are satisfied—

(a) the agreement is in writing;

(b) it has effect for a specified period not exceeding five years;

(c) it applies either—

(i) to all of the relevant members of the workforce, or

(ii) to all of the relevant members of the workforce who belong to a particular group;

(d) the agreement is signed—

(i) in the case of an agreement of the kind referred to in sub-paragraph (c)(i), by the representatives of the workforce, and in the case of an agreement of the kind referred to in sub-paragraph (c)(ii) by the representatives of the group to which the agreement applies (excluding, in either case, any representative not a relevant member of the workforce on the date on which the agreement was first made available for signature), or

(ii) if the employer employed 20 or fewer employees on the date referred to in sub-paragraph (d)(i), either by the appropriate representatives in accordance with that sub-paragraph or by the majority of the employees employed by him;

(e) before the agreement was made available for signature, the employer provided all the employees to whom it was intended to apply on the date on which it came into effect with copies of the text of the agreement and such guidance as those employees might reasonably require in order to understand it fully.

2. For the purposes of this Schedule—

'a particular group' is a group of the relevant members of a workforce who undertake a particular function, work at a particular workplace or belong to a particular department or unit within their employer's business;

'relevant members of the workforce' are all of the employees employed by a particular employer, excluding any employee whose terms and conditions of employment are provided for, wholly or in part, in a collective agreement;

'representatives of the workforce' are employees duly elected to represent the relevant members of the workforce, 'representatives of the group' are employees duly elected to represent the members of a particular group, and representatives are 'duly elected' if the election at which they were elected satisfied the requirements of paragraph 3 of this Schedule.

3. The requirements concerning elections referred to in paragraph 2 are that—

(a) the number of representatives to be elected is determined by the employer;

(b) the candidates for election as representatives of the workforce are relevant members of the workforce, and the candidates for election as representatives of a group are members of that group;

(c) no employee who is eligible to be a candidate is unreasonably excluded from standing for election;

(d) all the relevant members of the workforce are entitled to vote for representatives of the workforce, and all the members of a particular group are entitled to vote for representatives of the group;

(e) the employees entitled to vote may vote for as many candidates as there are representatives to be elected;

(f) the election is conducted so as to secure that—

(i) so far as is reasonably practicable, those voting do so in secret, and

(ii) the votes given at the election are fairly and accurately counted.

The Paternity and Adoption Leave Regulations 2002

(SI 2002 No. 2788)

PART 1 GENERAL

1. [omitted]

Interpretation

2.—(1) In these Regulations—

'the 1996 Act' means the Employment Rights Act 1996;

'additional adoption leave' means leave under section 75B of the 1996 Act;

'additional maternity leave' means leave under section 73 of the 1996 Act;

'adopter', in relation to a child, means a person who has been matched with the child for adoption, or, in a case where two people have been matched jointly, whichever of them has elected to be the child's adopter for the purposes of these Regulations;

'adoption agency' has the meaning given, in relation to England and Wales, by section 2(1) of the Adoption and Children Act 2002 and, in relation to Scotland, by section 119(1) of the Adoption and Children (Scotland) Act 2007;

'adoption leave' means ordinary or additional adoption leave;

'child' means a person who is, or when placed with an adopter for adoption was, under the age of 18;

'contract of employment' means a contract of service or apprenticeship, whether express or implied, and (if it is express) whether oral or in writing;

'employee' means an individual who has entered into or works under (or, where the employment has ceased, worked under) a contract of employment;

'employer' means the person by whom an employee is (or, where the employment has ceased, was) employed;

'expected week', in relation to the birth of a child, means the week, beginning with midnight between Saturday and Sunday, in which it is expected that the child will be born;

'ordinary adoption leave' means leave under section 75A of the 1996 Act;

'parental leave' means leave under regulation 13(1) of the Maternity and Parental Leave etc. Regulations 1999;

'partner', in relation to a child's mother or adopter, means a person (whether of a different sex or the same sex) who lives with the mother or adopter and the child in an enduring family relationship but is not a relative of the mother or adopter of a kind specified in paragraph (2);

'paternity leave' means leave under regulation 4 or regulation 8 of these Regulations;

'placed for adoption' means—

(a) placed for adoption under the Adoption and Children Act 2002 or the Adoption and Children (Scotland) Act 2007; or

(b) placed in accordance with section 22C of the Children Act 1989 with a local authority foster parent who is also a prospective adopter;

'prospective adopter' means a person who has been approved as suitable to adopt a child and has been notified of that decision in accordance with regulation 30B(4) of the Adoption Agencies Regulations 2005;

. . .

'statutory adoption leave' means ordinary adoption leave and additional adoption leave;

'statutory adoption leave period' means the period during which the adopter is on statutory adoption leave;

'statutory leave' means leave provided for in Part 8 of the 1996 Act.

(2) The relatives of a child's mother or adopter referred to in the definition of 'partner' in paragraph (1) are the mother's or adopter's parent, grandparent, sister, brother, aunt or uncle.

(3) References to relationships in paragraph (2)—

(a) are to relationships of the full blood or half blood or, in the case of an adopted person, such of those relationships as would exist but for the adoption, and

(b) include the relationship of a child with his adoptive, or former adoptive, parents,

but do not include any other adoptive relationships.

(4)–(4A) [omitted]

(5) A reference in any provision of these Regulations to a period of continuous employment is to a period computed in accordance with Chapter 1 of Part 14 of the 1996 Act, as if that provision were a provision of that Act.

(6) For the purposes of these Regulations, any two employers shall be treated as associated if—

(a) one is a company of which the other (directly or indirectly) has control; or

(b) both are companies of which a third person (directly or indirectly) has control;

and 'associated employer' shall be construed accordingly.

3. [omitted]

PART 2 PATERNITY LEAVE

Entitlement to paternity leave: birth

4.—(1) An employee is entitled to be absent from work for the purpose of caring for a child or supporting the child's mother if he—

(a) satisfies the conditions specified in paragraph (2), and

(b) has complied with the notice requirements in regulation 6 and, where applicable, the evidential requirements in that regulation.

(1A) [repealed]

(2) The conditions referred to in paragraph (1) are that the employee—

(a) [repealed]

(b) is either—

(i) the father of the child; or

(ii) married to, the civil partner or the partner of the child's mother, but not the child's father;

(c) has, or expects to have—

(i) if he is the child's father, responsibility for the upbringing of the child;

(ii) if he is the mother's husband, the civil partner or partner but not the child's father, the main responsibility (apart from any responsibility of the mother) for the upbringing of the child.

(3) [repealed]

(4) An employee shall be treated as having satisfied the condition in paragraph (2)(b)(ii) if he would have satisfied it but for the fact that the child's mother has died.

(5) An employee shall be treated as having satisfied the condition in paragraph (2)(c) if he would have satisfied it but for the fact that the child was stillborn after 24 weeks of pregnancy or has died.

(6) An employee's entitlement to leave under this regulation shall not be affected by the birth, or expected birth, of more than one child as a result of the same pregnancy.

Options in respect of leave under regulation 4

5.—(1) An employee may choose to take either—

(a) a single period of leave of either one week or two weeks, or

(b) two non-consecutive periods of leave of a week each

in respect of a child under regulation 4.

(2) The leave may only be taken during the period which begins with the date on which the child is born and ends—

(a) except in the case referred to in sub-paragraph (b), 52 weeks after that date;

(b) in a case where the child is born before the first day of the expected week of its birth, 52 weeks after that day.

(3) Subject to paragraph (2) and, where applicable, paragraph (4), an employee may choose to begin his period of leave on—

(a) the date on which the child is born;

(b) the date falling such number of days after the date on which the child is born as the employee may specify in a notice under regulation 6, or

(c) a predetermined date, specified in a notice under that regulation, which is later than the first day of the expected week of the child's birth.

(4) [omitted]

6.—(1) An employee must give their employer—

(a) notice of their entitlement to take leave in respect of a child under regulation 4 which specifies the expected week of the child's birth, and

(b) a declaration in writing that the employee satisfies the conditions in regulation 4(2)(b) and (c).

(2) The employee must also give their employer, on each occasion that a period of leave is chosen in accordance with regulation 5—

(a) a notice that specifies the start day or date of the period of leave and its duration, and

(b) a declaration in writing that the purpose of that period of leave will be that specified in regulation 4(1).

(3) The notice and declaration in paragraph (1) must be given in or before the 15th week before the expected week of the child's birth or, if it is not reasonably practicable to do so, as soon as is reasonably practicable.

(4) The notice and declaration in paragraph (2) must be given at least 28 days before—

(a) the first day of the expected week of the child's birth, where the option in regulation 5(3)(a) is chosen;

(b) the date falling the specified number of days after the first day of the expected week of the child's birth, where the option in regulation 5(3)(b) is chosen;

(c) the predetermined date, where the option in regulation 5(3)(c) is chosen;

or, if it is not reasonably practicable to do so, as soon as is reasonably practicable.

(5) An employee who has previously given notice under paragraph (2)(a) or (8) or this paragraph may—

(a) vary the day or date chosen as the day or date on which a period of leave will begin or end, or

(b) cancel the period of leave chosen,

provided that notice of the variation or cancellation is given to the employer in accordance with paragraph (6).

(6) A notice under paragraph (5) must be given by whichever is the earlier of at least 28 days before—

(a) the original day or date referred to in paragraph (7)(a), or

(b) the new day or date referred to in paragraph (7)(b),

or, if it is not reasonably practicable to do so, as soon as is reasonably practicable.

(7) For the purposes of—

(a) paragraph (6)(a), where a notice has previously been given under paragraph (2)(a), (5) or (8), the original day or date is—

(i) the first day of the expected week of the child's birth, where the option in regulation 5(3)(a) was chosen in that notice;

(ii) the specified number of days after the first day of the expected week of the child's birth, where the option in regulation 5(3)(b) was chosen in that notice;

(iii) the predetermined date specified in that notice, where the option in regulation 5(3)(c) was chosen;

(b) paragraph (6)(b), the new day or date is—

(i) the first day of the expected week of the child's birth, where the option in regulation 5(3)(a) is chosen in the notice of variation;

(ii) the date falling the specified number of days after the first day of the expected week of the child's birth, where the option in regulation 5(3)(b) is chosen in the notice of variation;

(iii) the predetermined date specified in the notice of variation, where the option in regulation 5(3)(c) is chosen.

(8) In a case where—

(a) the employee has chosen to begin a period of leave on a particular predetermined date, and

(b) the child is not born on or before that date,

the employee must vary the choice of date by substituting a later predetermined date, or exercising an alternative option under regulation 5(3), and must give the employer notice of the variation as soon as is reasonably practicable.

(9) Where a notice is given under paragraph (5) or (8) which varies the days or dates of a period of leave, a declaration under paragraph (2)(b) in relation to that period must be given at the same time as that notice.

(10) An employee must give their employer a further notice, as soon as is reasonably practicable after the child's birth, of the date on which the child was born.

(11) Notice under paragraphs (1)(a), (2)(a), (5), (8) or (10) must be given in writing, if the employer so requests.

7. [omitted]

Entitlement to paternity leave: adoption

8.—(1) Subject to paragraph (1A), an employee is entitled to be absent from work for the purpose of caring for a child or supporting the child's adopter if he—

(a) satisfies the conditions specified in paragraph (2), and

(b) has complied with the notice requirements in regulation 10 and, where applicable, the evidential requirements in that regulation.

(1A) An employee is not entitled to be absent from work under paragraph (1) if the employee—

(a) has taken any shared parental leave in respect of the child;

(b) has exercised a right to take time off under section 57ZJ of the 1996 Act in respect of the child; or

(c) has already taken paternity leave in relation to the child as a result of the child being placed with a prospective adopter who is at the time of the placement the employee's spouse, civil partner or partner.

(2) The conditions referred to in paragraph (1) are that the employee—

(a) [repealed]

(b) is either married to, the civil partner or the partner of the child's adopter, and

(c) has, or expects to have, the main responsibility (apart from the responsibility of the adopter) for the upbringing of the child.

(3) [repealed]

(4) An employee shall be treated as having satisfied the condition in paragraph (2)(b) if he would have satisfied it but for the fact that the child's adopter died during the child's placement.

(5) An employee shall be treated as having satisfied the condition in paragraph (2)(c) if he would have satisfied it but for the fact that the child's placement with the adopter has ended.

(6) An employee's entitlement to leave under this regulation shall not be affected by the placement for adoption of more than one child as part of the same arrangement.

Options in respect of leave under regulation 8

9.—(1) An employee may choose to take either—

(a) a single period of leave of either one week or two weeks, or

(b) two non-consecutive periods of leave of a week each,

in respect of a child under regulation 8.

(2) The leave may only be taken during the period of 52 weeks beginning with the date on which the child is placed with the adopter.

(3) Subject to paragraph (2) and, where applicable, paragraph (4), an employee may choose to begin a period of leave under regulation 8 on—

(a) the date on which the child is placed with the adopter;

(b) the date falling such number of days after the date on which the child is placed with the adopter as the employee may specify in a notice under regulation 10, or

(c) a predetermined date, specified in a notice under that regulation, which is later than the date on which the child is expected to be placed with the adopter.

(4) [omitted]

Notice and evidential requirements for leave under regulation 8

10.—(1) An employee must give their employer—

(a) notice of their entitlement to take leave in respect of a child under regulation 8 which specifies—

(i) the date on which the adopter was notified of having been matched with the child, and

(ii) the date on which the child is expected to be placed with the adopter or, where the child has already been placed for adoption, the date of placement, and

(b) a declaration in writing that the employee satisfies the conditions in regulation 8(2)(b) and (c).

(2) The employee must also give their employer, on each occasion that a period of leave is chosen in accordance with regulation 9—

(a) a notice that specifies the start day or date of the period of leave and its duration, and

(b) a declaration in writing that the purpose of the period of leave will be that specified in regulation 8(1).

(3) The notices and declarations in paragraphs (1) and (2) must be given no more than seven days after the date on which the adopter is notified of having been matched with the child or, if it is not reasonably practicable to do so, as soon as is reasonably practicable.

(4) An employee who has previously given notice under paragraph (2)(a) or (7) or this paragraph may—

(a) vary the day or date chosen as the day or date on which a period of leave will begin or end, or

(b) cancel the period of leave chosen,

provided that notice of the variation or cancellation is given to the employer in accordance with paragraph (5).

(5) A notice under paragraph (4) must be given by whichever is the earlier of at least 28 days before—

(a) the original day or date referred to in paragraph (6)(a), or

(b) the new day or date referred to in paragraph (6)(b),

or, if it is not reasonably practicable to do so, as soon as is reasonably practicable.

(6) For the purposes of—

(a) paragraph (5)(a), where a notice has previously been given under paragraph (2)(a), (4) or (7), the original day or date is—

(i) the date provided under paragraph (1)(a)(ii) as the date on which the child is expected to be placed with the adopter, where the option in regulation 9(3)(a) was chosen in that notice;

(ii) the date falling the specified number of days after the date provided under paragraph (1)(a)(ii) as the date on which the child is expected to be placed with the adopter, where the option in regulation 9(3)(b) was chosen in that notice;

(iii) the predetermined date specified in that notice, where the option in regulation 9(3)(c) was chosen;

(b) paragraph (5)(b), the new day or date is—

(i) the date provided under paragraph (1)(a)(ii) as the date on which the child is expected to be placed with the adopter, where the option in regulation 9(3)(a) is chosen in the notice of variation;

(ii) the date falling the specified number of days after the date provided under paragraph (1)(a)(ii) as the date on which the child is expected to be placed with the adopter, where the option in regulation 9(3)(b) chosen in the notice of variation;

(iii) the predetermined date specified in the notice of variation, where the option in regulation 9(3)(c) is chosen.

(7) In a case where—

(a) the employee has chosen to begin a period of leave on a particular predetermined date, and

(b) the child is not placed with the adopter on or before that date,

the employee must vary the choice of date by substituting a later predetermined date or exercising an alternative option under regulation 9(3) and must give the employer notice of the variation as soon as is reasonably practicable.

(8) Where a notice is given under paragraph (4) or (7) which varies the days or dates of a period of leave, a declaration under paragraph (2)(b) in relation to that period must be given at the same time as that notice.

(9) An employee must give their employer a further notice, as soon as is reasonably practicable after the child's placement, of the date on which the child was placed, unless that information has already been provided under paragraph (1)(a)(ii).

(10) Notice under paragraphs (1)(a), (2)(a), (4), (7) or (9) must be given in writing, if the employer so requests.

11.–11A. [omitted]

Application of terms and conditions during paternity leave

12.—(1) An employee who takes paternity leave—

(a) is entitled, during the period of leave, to the benefit of all of the terms and conditions of employment which would have applied if he had not been absent, and

(b) is bound, during that period, by any obligations arising under those terms and conditions, subject only to the exception in section 80C(1)(b) of the 1996 Act.

(2) In paragraph (1)(a), 'terms and conditions of employment' has the meaning given by section 80C(5) of the 1996 Act, and accordingly does not include terms and conditions about remuneration.

(3) For the purposes of section 80C of the 1996 Act, only sums payable to an employee by way of wages or salary are to be treated as remuneration.

Right to return after paternity leave

13.—(1) An employee who returns to work after a period of paternity leave which was—

(a) an isolated period of leave, or

(b) the last of two or more consecutive periods of statutory leave which did not include any—

(i) period of parental leave of more than four weeks; or

(ii) period of statutory leave which when added to any other periods of statutory leave (excluding parental leave) taken in relation to the same child means that the total amount of statutory leave taken in relation to that child totals more than 26 weeks,

is entitled to return from leave to the job in which he was employed before his absence.

(2) An employee who returns to work after a period of paternity leave not falling within the description in paragraph (1)(a) or (b) above is entitled to return from leave to the job in which he was employed before his absence, or, if it is not reasonably practicable for the employer to permit him to return to that job, to another job which is both suitable for him and appropriate for him to do in the circumstances.

(3) The reference in paragraphs (1) and (2) to the job in which an employee was employed before his absence is a reference to the job in which he was employed—

(a) if his return is from an isolated period of paternity leave, immediately before that period began;

(b) if his return is from consecutive periods of statutory leave, immediately before the first such period.

Incidents of the right to return after paternity leave

14.—(1) An employee's right to return under regulation 13 is a right to return—

(a) with his seniority, pension rights and similar rights—

(i) in a case where the employee is returning from consecutive periods of statutory leave which included a period of additional adoption leave or additional maternity leave, as they would have been if the period or periods of his employment prior to the additional adoption leave or (as the case may be) additional maternity leave were continuous with the period of employment following it;

(ii) in any other case, as they would have been if he had not been absent, and

(b) on terms and conditions not less favourable than those which would have applied if he had not been absent.

(2) The provision in paragraph (1)(a)(i) concerning the treatment of periods of additional maternity leave or additional adoption leave is subject to the requirements of paragraphs 5, 5B and 6 of Schedule 5 to the Social Security Act 1989 (equal treatment under pension schemes: maternity absence and family leave).

(3) The provisions in paragraph (1)(a)(ii) and (b) for an employee to be treated as if he had not been absent refer to his absence—

(a) if his return is from an isolated period of paternity leave, since the beginning of that period;

(b) if his return is from consecutive periods of statutory leave, since the beginning of the first such period.

PART 3 ADOPTION LEAVE

Entitlement to ordinary adoption leave

15.—(1) Subject to paragraph (1A), an employee is entitled to ordinary adoption leave in respect of a child if he—

(a) satisfies the conditions specified in paragraph (2), and

(b) has complied with the notice requirements in regulation 17 and, where applicable, the evidential requirements in that regulation.

(1A) An employee is not entitled to be absent from work under paragraph (1) in relation to a child if the employee has already taken ordinary adoption leave as a result of that child being placed, or expected to be placed, with the employee under section 22C of the Children Act 1989.

(2) The conditions referred to in paragraph (1) are that the employee—

(a) is the child's adopter; and

(b) [revoked]

(c) has notified the agency that he agrees that the child should be placed with him and on the date of placement.

(3) [revoked]

(4) An employee's entitlement to leave under this regulation shall not be affected by the placement for adoption of more than one child as part of the same arrangement.

16.–17. [omitted]

Duration and commencement of ordinary adoption leave

18.—(1) Subject to regulations 22 and 24, an employee's ordinary adoption leave period is a period of 26 weeks.

(2) Except in the case referred to in paragraph (3), an employee's ordinary adoption leave period begins on the date specified in his notice under regulation 17(1), or, where he has varied his choice of date under regulation 17(4), on the date specified in his notice under that provision (or the last such date if he has varied his choice more than once).

(3) In a case where—

(a) the employee has chosen to begin his period of leave on the date on which the child is placed with him, and
(b) he is at work on that date,

the employee's period of leave begins on the day after that date.

Application of terms and conditions during ordinary adoption leave and additional adoption leave

19.—(1) An employee who takes ordinary adoption leave or additional adoption leave—
(a) is entitled, during the period of leave, to the benefit of all of the terms and conditions of employment which would have applied if he had not been absent, and
(b) is bound, during that period, by any obligations arising under those terms and conditions, subject only to the exceptions in sections 75A(3)(b) and 75B(4)(b) of the 1996 Act.

(2) In paragraph (1)(a), 'terms and conditions of employment' has the meaning given by sections 75A(4) and 75B(5) of the 1996 Act, and accordingly does not include terms and conditions about remuneration.

(3) For the purposes of sections 75A and 75B of the 1996 Act, only sums payable to an employee by way of wages or salary are to be treated as remuneration.

Additional adoption leave: entitlement, duration and commencement

20.—(1) An employee is entitled to additional adoption leave in respect of a child if—
(a) the child was placed with him for adoption,
(b) he took ordinary adoption leave in respect of the child, and
(c) his ordinary adoption leave period did not end prematurely under regulation 22(2)(a) or 24.

(2) Subject to regulations 22 and 24, an employee's additional adoption leave period is a period of 26 weeks beginning on the day after the last day of his ordinary adoption leave period.

21. [revoked]

Work during adoption leave period

21A.—(1) An employee may carry out up to 10 days' work for his employer during his statutory adoption leave period without bringing his statutory adoption leave to an end.

(2) For the purposes of this regulation, any work carried out on any day shall constitute a day's work.

(3) Subject to paragraph (4), for the purposes of this regulation, work means any work done under the contract of employment and may include training or any activity undertaken for the purposes of keeping in touch with the workplace.

(4) Reasonable contact from time to time between an employee and his employer which either party is entitled to make during an adoption leave period (for example to discuss an employee's return to work) shall not bring that period to an end.

(5) This regulation does not confer any right on an employer to require that any work be carried out during the statutory adoption leave period, nor any right on an employee to work during the statutory adoption leave period.

(6) Any days' work carried out under this regulation shall not have the effect of extending the total duration of the statutory adoption leave period.

22. [omitted]

Redundancy: adoption leave

23.—(1) This regulation applies where it is not practicable by reason of redundancy for an employer to continue to employ an employee under their existing contract of employment during—
(a) the statutory adoption leave period, or
(b) the additional protected period.

(1A) For the purposes of paragraph (1)(b) the additional protected period—

(a) begins with the day after the last day of the employee's statutory adoption leave period;
(b) continues during any period of continuous employment that includes the statutory adoption leave period referred to in sub-paragraph (a); and
(c) ends immediately before the relevant day.

(1B) For the purposes of paragraph (1A)(c) the relevant day is the day after a period of 18 months beginning with the day the child is placed with the employee for adoption.

(2) Where there is a suitable available vacancy, the employee is entitled to be offered (before the end of his employment under his existing contract) alternative employment with his employer or his employer's successor, or an associated employer, under a new contract of employment which complies with paragraph (3) and takes effect immediately on the ending of his employment under the previous contract.

(3) The new contract of employment must be such that—

(a) the work to be done under it is of a kind which is both suitable in relation to the employee and appropriate for him to do in the circumstances, and
(b) its provisions as to the capacity and place in which he is to be employed, and as to the other terms and conditions of his employment, are not substantially less favourable to him than if he had continued to be employed under the previous contract.

Dismissal during adoption leave

24.—(1) Where an employee is dismissed after an ordinary or additional adoption leave period has begun but before the time when (apart from this regulation) that period would end, the period ends at the time of the dismissal.

25. [omitted]

Right to return after adoption leave

26.—(1) An employee who returns to work after a period of ordinary adoption leave which was—

(a) an isolated period of leave, or
(b) the last of two or more consecutive periods of statutory leave which did not include any—
 (i) period of parental leave of more than four weeks; or
 (ii) period of statutory leave which when added to any other periods of statutory leave (excluding parental leave) taken in relation to the same child means that the total amount of statutory leave taken in relation to that child totals more than 26 weeks,

is entitled to return from leave to the job in which he was employed before his absence.

(2) An employee who returns to work after—

(a) a period of additional adoption leave, whether or not preceded by another period of statutory leave, or
(b) a period of ordinary adoption leave not falling within the description in paragraph (1)(a) or (b) above,

is entitled to return from leave to the job in which he was employed before his absence, or, if it is not reasonably practicable for the employer to permit him to return to that job, to another job which is both suitable for him and appropriate for him to do in the circumstances.

(3) The reference in paragraphs (1) and (2) to the job in which an employee was employed before his absence is a reference to the job in which he was employed—

(a) if his return is from an isolated period of adoption leave, immediately before that period began;
(b) if his return is from consecutive periods of statutory leave, immediately before the first such period.

(4) This regulation does not apply where regulation 23 applies.

Incidents of the right to return from adoption leave

27.—(1) An employee's right to return under regulation 26 is to return—

(a) with his seniority, pension rights and similar rights as they would have been if he had not been absent, and

(b) on terms and conditions not less favourable than those which would have been applied to him if he had not been absent.

(2) In the case of accrual of rights under an employment-related benefit scheme within the meaning given by Schedule 5 to the Social Security Act 1989, nothing in paragraph (1)(a) concerning the treatment of additional adoption leave shall be taken to impose a requirement which exceeds the requirements of paragraphs 5, 5B and 6 of that Schedule.

(3) The provisions in paragraph (1) for an employee to be treated as if he had not been absent refer to his absence—

(a) if his return is from an isolated period of ordinary adoption leave, since the beginning of that period;

(b) if his return is from consecutive periods of statutory leave, since the beginning of the first such period.

PART 4 PROVISIONS APPLICABLE IN RELATION TO BOTH PATERNITY AND ADOPTION LEAVE

Protection from detriment

28.—(1) An employee is entitled under section 47C of the 1996 Act not to be subjected to any detriment by any act, or any deliberate failure to act, by his employer because—

(za) the employee took or sought to take time off under section 57ZE of the 1996 Act;

(zb) the employer believed that the employee was likely to take time off under section 57ZE of the 1996 Act;

(zc) the employee took or sought to take time off under section 57ZJ or 57ZL of the 1996 Act;

(zd) the employer believed that the employee was likely to take time off under section 57ZJ or 57ZL of the 1996 Act;

(a) the employee took or sought to take paternity leave or ordinary or additional adoption leave;

(b) the employer believed that the employee was likely to take ordinary or additional adoption leave,

(bb) the employee undertook, considered undertaking or refused to undertake work in accordance with regulation 21A, or

(c) the employee failed to return after a period of additional adoption leave in a case where—

(i) the employer did not notify him, in accordance with regulation 17(7) and (8) or otherwise, of the date on which that period ended, and he reasonably believed that the period had not ended, or

(ii) the employer gave him less than 28 days' notice of the date on which the period would end, and it was not reasonably practicable for him to return on that date.

(2) Paragraph (1) does not apply where the detriment in question amounts to dismissal within the meaning of Part 10 of the 1996 Act.

Unfair dismissal

29.—(1) An employee who is dismissed is entitled under section 99 of the 1996 Act to be regarded for the purpose of Part 10 of that Act as unfairly dismissed if—

(a) the reason or principal reason for the dismissal is of a kind specified in paragraph (3), or
(b) the reason or principal reason for the dismissal is that the employee is redundant, and regulation 23 has not been complied with.

(2) An employee who is dismissed shall also be regarded for the purposes of Part 10 of the 1996 Act as unfairly dismissed if—

(a) the reason (or, if more than one, the principal reason) for the dismissal is that the employee was redundant;
(b) it is shown that the circumstances constituting the redundancy applied equally to one or more employees in the same undertaking who had positions similar to that held by the employee and who have not been dismissed by the employer, and
(c) it is shown that the reason (or, if more than one, the principal reason) for which the employee was selected for dismissal was a reason of a kind specified in paragraph (3).

(3) The kinds of reason referred to in paragraph (1) and (2) are reasons connected with the fact that—

(za) the employee took or sought to take time off under section 57ZE of the 1996 Act;
(zb) the employer believed that the employee was likely to take time off under section 57ZE of the 1996 Act;
(zc) the employee took or sought to take time off under section 57ZJ or 57ZL of the 1996 Act;
(zd) the employer believed that the employee was likely to take time off under section 57ZJ or 57ZL of the 1996 Act;
(a) the employee took, or sought to take, paternity or adoption leave;
(b) the employer believed that the employee was likely to take ordinary or additional adoption leave;
(bb) the employee undertook, considered undertaking or refused to undertake work in accordance with regulation 21A; or
(c) the employee failed to return after a period of additional adoption leave in a case where—
    (i) the employer did not notify him, in accordance with regulation 17(7) and (8) or otherwise, of the date on which that period would end, and he reasonably believed that the period had not ended, or
    (ii) the employer gave him less than 28 days' notice of the date on which the period would end, and it was not reasonably practicable for him to return on that date.

(4) [revoked]

(5) Paragraph (1) does not apply in relation to an employee if—

(a) it is not reasonably practicable for a reason other than redundancy for the employer (who maybe the same employer or a successor of his) to permit the employee to return to a job which is both suitable for the employee and appropriate for him to do in the circumstances;
(b) an associated employer offers the employee a job of that kind, and
(c) the employee accepts or unreasonably refuses that offer.

(6) Where, on a complaint of unfair dismissal, any question arises as to whether the operation of paragraph (1) is excluded by the provisions of paragraph (5), it is for the employer to show that the provisions in question were satisfied in relation to the complainant.

Contractual rights to paternity or adoption leave

30.—(1) This regulation applies where an employee is entitled to—

(a) paternity leave,
(b) ordinary adoption leave, or
(c) additional adoption leave,

(referred to in paragraph (2) as a 'statutory right') and also to a right which corresponds to that right and which arises under the employee's contract of employment or otherwise.

(2) In a case where this regulation applies—

(a) the employee may not exercise the statutory right and the corresponding right separately but may, in taking the leave for which the two rights provide, take advantage of whichever right is, in any particular respect, the more favourable, and

(b) the provisions of the 1996 Act and of these Regulations relating to the statutory right apply, subject to any modifications necessary to give effect to any more favourable contractual terms, to the exercise of the composite right described in sub-paragraph (a) as they apply to the exercise of the statutory right.

31. [omitted]

The Information and Consultation of Employees Regulations 2004

(SI 2004 No. 3426)

Arrangement of Regulations

PART I GENERAL

2 Interpretation
3 Application
3A Agency workers

PART III NEGOTIATED AGREEMENTS

7 Employee request to negotiate an agreement in respect of information and consultation
11 Employer notification of decision to initiate negotiations
12 Restrictions on employee request and employer notification
13 Dispute about employee request, employer notification or whether obligation in regulation 7(1) applies
14 Negotiations to reach an agreement
16 Negotiated agreements

PART IV STANDARD INFORMATION AND CONSULTATION PROVISIONS

18 Application of standard information and consultation provisions
20 Standard information and consultation provisions

PART V DUTY OF CO-OPERATION

21 Co-operation

PART VI COMPLIANCE AND ENFORCEMENT

22 Disputes about operation of a negotiated agreement or the standard information and consultation provisions
23 Penalties
24 Exclusivity of remedy

PART VII CONFIDENTIAL INFORMATION

25 Breach of statutory duty
26 Withholding of information by the employer

SCHEDULE 1 APPLICATION OF REGULATIONS

PART I GENERAL

1 [omitted]

2 Interpretation

In these Regulations—

'the 1996 Act' means the Employment Rights Act 1996;

'agency worker' has the same meaning as in regulation 3 of the Agency Workers Regulations 2010;

'Appeal Tribunal' means the Employment Appeal Tribunal;

'CAC' means the Central Arbitration Committee;

'consultation' means the exchange of views and establishment of a dialogue between—

(a) information and consultation representatives and the employer; or

(b) in the case of a negotiated agreement which provides as mentioned in regulation 16(1)(f)(ii), the employees and the employer;

'contract of employment' means a contract of service or apprenticeship, whether express or implied, and (if it is express) whether oral or in writing;

'date of the ballot' means the day or last day on which voting may take place and, where voting in different parts of the ballot is arranged to take place on different days or during periods ending on different days, the last of those days;

'employee' means an individual who has entered into or works under a contract of employment and in Part VIII and regulation 40 includes, where the employment has ceased, an individual who worked under a contract of employment;

'employee request' means a request by employees under regulation 7 for the employer to initiate negotiations to reach an agreement under these Regulations;

'employer notification' means a notification by an employer under regulation 11 that he wishes to initiate negotiations to reach an agreement under these Regulations;

'information' means data transmitted by the employer—

(a) to the information and consultation representatives; or

(b) in the case of a negotiated agreement which provides as mentioned in regulation 16(1)(f)(ii), directly to the employees,

in order to enable those representatives or those employees to examine and to acquaint themselves with the subject matter of the data;

'Information and Consultation Directive' means European Parliament and Council Directive 2002/14/EC of 11 March 2002 establishing a general framework for informing and consulting employees in the European Community;

'information and consultation representative' means—

(a) in the case of a negotiated agreement which provides as mentioned in regulation 16(1)(f)(i), a person appointed or elected in accordance with that agreement; or

(b) a person elected in accordance with regulation 19(1);

'negotiated agreement' means—

(a) an agreement between the employer and the negotiating representatives reached through negotiations as provided for in regulation 14 which satisfies the requirements of regulation 16(1); or

(b) an agreement between the employer and the information and consultation representatives referred to in regulation 18(2);

'negotiating representative' means a person elected or appointed pursuant to regulation 14(1)(a);

'parties' means the employer and the negotiating representatives or the information and consultation representatives, as the case may be;

'Pension Schemes Regulations' means the Occupational and Personal Pension Schemes (Consultation by Employers and Miscellaneous Amendment) Regulations 2006;

'pre-existing agreement' means an agreement between an employer and his employees or their representatives which—

(a) is made prior to the making of an employee request; and

(b) satisfies the conditions set out in regulation 8(1)(a) to (d),

but does not include an agreement concluded in accordance with regulations 17 or 42 to 45 of the Transnational Information and Consultation of Employees Regulations 1999 or a negotiated agreement;

'standard information and consultation provisions' means the provisions set out in regulation 20;

'suitable information relating to the use of agency workers' means information as to—

(a) the number of agency workers working temporarily for and under the supervision and direction of the employer,

(b) the parts of the employer's undertaking in which those agency workers are working, and

(c) the type of work those agency workers are carrying out.

'undertaking' means a public or private undertaking carrying out an economic activity, whether or not operating for gain;

'valid employee request' means an employee request made to their employer by the employees of an undertaking to which these Regulations apply (under regulation 3) that satisfies the requirements of regulation 7 and is not prevented from being valid by regulation 12.

3 Application

(1) These Regulations apply to undertakings—

(a) employing in the United Kingdom, in accordance with the calculation in regulation 4, at least the number of employees in column 1 of the table in Schedule 1 to these Regulations on or after the corresponding date in column 2 of that table; and

(b) subject to paragraph (2), whose registered office, head office or principal place of business is situated in Great Britain.

(2) Where the registered office is situated in Great Britain and the head office or principal place of business is situated in Northern Ireland or vice versa, these Regulations shall only apply where the majority of employees are employed to work in Great Britain.

(3) In these Regulations, an undertaking to which these Regulations apply is referred to, in relation to its employees, as 'the employer'.

3A Agency workers

(1) Paragraphs (2) and (3) apply to an agency worker whose contract within regulation 3(1)(b) of the Agency Workers Regulations 2010 (contract with the temporary work agency) is not a contract of employment.

(2) For the purposes of regulations 3, 4 and Schedule 1, any agency worker who has a contract with a temporary work agency shall be treated as being employed by that temporary work agency for the duration of that agency worker's assignment with the employer.

(3) In these Regulations 'assignment' has the same meaning as in regulation 2 and 'temporary work agency' has the same meaning as in regulation 4, of the Agency Workers Regulations 2010.

4–6 [omitted]

PART III NEGOTIATED AGREEMENTS

7 Employee request to negotiate an agreement in respect of information and consultation

(1) On receipt of a valid employee request, the employer shall, subject to paragraphs (8) and (9), initiate negotiations by taking the steps set out in regulation 14(1).

(2) Subject to paragraph (3), an employee request is not a valid employee request unless it consists of—

(a) a single request made by at least 2% of the employees in the undertaking; or

(b) a number of separate requests made on the same or different days by employees which when taken together mean that at least 2% of the employees in that undertaking have made requests, provided that the requests are made within a period of six months.

(3) Where the figure of 2% in paragraph (2) would result in less than 15 or more than 2,500 employees being required in order for a valid employee request to be made, that paragraph shall have effect as if, for the figure of 2%, there were substituted the figure of 15, or as the case may be, 2,500.

(4) An employee request is not a valid employee request unless the single request referred to in paragraph (2)(a) or each separate request referred to in paragraph (2)(b)—

(a) is in writing;

(b) is sent to—

(i) the registered office, head office or principal place of business of the employer; or

(ii) the CAC; and

(c) specifies the names of the employees making it and the date on which it is sent.

(5) Where a request is sent to the CAC under paragraph (4)(b)(ii), the CAC shall—

(a) notify the employer that the request has been made as soon as reasonably practicable;

(b) request from the employer such information as it needs to verify the number and names of the employees who have made the request; and

(c) inform the employer and the employees who have made the request how many employees have made the request on the basis of the information provided by the employees and the employer.

(6)–(8) [omitted]

(9) If an application is made to the CAC under regulation 13, the employer shall not be required to initiate negotiations unless and until if the CAC declares that there was a valid employee request or that the employer's notification was valid.

8–10 [omitted]

11 Employer notification of decision to initiate negotiations

(1) The employer may start the negotiation process set out in regulation 14(1) on his own initiative by issuing a written notification satisfying the requirements of paragraph (2), and where the employer issues such a notification regulations 14 to 17 shall apply.

(2) The notification referred to in paragraph (1) must—

(a) state that the employer intends to start the negotiating process and that the notification is given for the purpose of these Regulations;

(b) state the date on which it is issued; and

(c) be published in such a manner as to bring it to the attention of, so far as reasonably practicable, all the employees of the undertaking.

12 Restrictions on employee request and employer notification

(1) Subject to paragraph (2), no employee request or employer notification is valid if it is made or issued, as the case may be,—

(a) where a negotiated agreement applies, within a period of three years from the date of the agreement or, where the agreement is terminated within that period, before the date on which the termination takes effect;

(b) where the standard information and consultation provisions apply within a period of three years from the date on which they started to apply; and

(c) where the employer has held a ballot under regulation 8, or was one of the employers who held a ballot under regulation 9 and the result was that the employees did not endorse the valid employee request referred to in regulation 8(1), within a period of three years from the date of that request.

(2) Paragraph (1) does not apply where there are material changes in the undertaking during the applicable period having the result—

(a) where a ballot held under regulation 8 or 9 had the result that the employees did not endorse the valid employee request, that there is no longer a pre-existing agreement which satisfies paragraph (1)(b) and (c) of regulation 8 or in the case of a ballot held under regulation 9, that there is no longer an agreement satisfying paragraph (1)(b) of that regulation; or

(b) where a negotiated agreement exists, that the agreement no longer complies with the requirement in regulation 16(1) that it must cover all the employees of the undertaking.

13 Dispute about employee request, employer notification or whether obligation in regulation 7(1) applies

(1) If the employer considers that there was no valid employee request—

(a) because the employee request did not satisfy any requirement of regulation 7(2) to (4) or was prevented from being valid by regulation 12, or

(b) because the undertaking was not one to which these Regulations applied (under Regulation 3) on the date on which the employee request was made,

the employer may apply to the CAC for a declaration as to whether there was a valid employee request.

(2) If an employee or an employees' representative considers that an employer notification was not valid because it did not comply with one or more of the requirements in regulation 11(2) or was prevented from being valid by regulation 12, he may apply to the CAC for a declaration as to whether the notification was valid.

(3) The CAC shall only consider an application for a declaration made under paragraph (1) or (2) if the application is made within a one month period beginning on the date of the employee request or the date on which the employer notification is made.

14 Negotiations to reach an agreement

(1) In order to initiate negotiations to reach an agreement under these Regulations the employer must as soon as reasonably practicable—

(a) make arrangements, satisfying the requirements of paragraph (2), for the employees of the undertaking to elect or appoint negotiating representatives; and thereafter

(b) inform the employees in writing of the identity of the negotiating representatives; and

(c) invite the negotiating representatives to enter into negotiations to reach a negotiated agreement.

(2)–(7) [omitted]

15 [omitted]

16 Negotiated agreements

(1) A negotiated agreement must cover all employees of the undertaking and may consist either of a single agreement or of different parts (each being approved in accordance with paragraph (4)) which, taken together, cover all the employees of the undertaking. The single agreement or each part must—

(a) set out the circumstances in which the employer must inform and consult the employees to which it relates;

(b) be in writing;

(c) be dated;

(d) be approved in accordance with paragraphs (3) to (5);

(e) be signed by or on behalf of the employer;

(f) either—

(i) provide for the appointment or election of information and consultation representatives to whom the employer must provide the information and whom the employer must consult in the circumstances referred to in sub-paragraph (a);

(ii) or provide that the employer must provide information directly to the employees to which it relates and consult those employees directly in the circumstances referred to in sub-paragraph (a); and

(g) provide that where an employer is to provide information about the employment situation, under that agreement or under any part, such information shall include suitable information relating to the use of agency workers (if any) in that undertaking.

(2) Where a negotiated agreement consist of different parts they may provide differently in relation to the matters referred to in paragraph (1)(a) and (f).

(3) A negotiated agreement consisting of a single agreement shall be treated as being approved for the purpose of paragraph (1)(d) if—

(a) it has been signed by all the negotiating representatives; or

(b) it has been signed by a majority of negotiating representatives and either—

(i) approved in writing by at least 50% of employees employed in the undertaking, or

(ii) approved by a ballot of those employees, the arrangements for which satisfied the requirements set out in paragraph (5), in which at least 50% of the employees voting, voted in favour of approval.

(4) A part shall be treated as being approved for the purpose of paragraph (1)(d) if the part—

(a) has been signed by all the negotiating representatives involved in negotiating the part; or

(b) has been signed by a majority of those negotiating representatives and either—

(i) approved in writing by at least 50% of employees (employed in the undertaking) to which the part relates, or

(ii) approved by a ballot of those employees, the arrangements for which satisfied the requirements set out in paragraph (5), in which at least 50% of the employees voting, voted in favour of approving the part.

(5)–(6) [omitted]

17–17A [omitted]

PART IV STANDARD INFORMATION AND CONSULTATION PROVISIONS

18 Application of standard information and consultation provisions

(1) Subject to paragraph (2)—

(a) where the employer is under a duty, following the making of a valid employee request or issue of a valid employer notification, to initiate negotiations in accordance with regulation 14 but does not do so, the standard information and consultation provisions shall apply from the date—

(i) which is six months from the date on which the valid employee request was made or the valid employer notification was issued, or

(ii) information and consultation representatives are elected under regulation 19, whichever is the sooner; and

(b) if the parties do not reach a negotiated agreement within the time limit referred to in regulation 14(3) (or that period as extended by agreement under paragraph (5) of that regulation) the standard information and consultation provisions shall apply from the date—

(i) which is six months from the date on which that time limit expires; or

(ii) information and consultation representatives are elected under regulation 19, whichever is the sooner.

(2) Where the standard information and consultation provisions apply, the employer and the information and consultation representatives elected pursuant to regulation 19 may, at any time, reach an agreement that provisions other than the standard information and consultation provisions shall apply.

(3) An agreement referred to in paragraph (2) shall only have effect if it covers all the employees of the undertaking, complies with the requirements listed in regulation 16(1)(a) to (c), (e) and (f), and is signed by a majority of the information and consultation representatives.

19 [omitted]

20 Standard information and consultation provisions

(1) Where the standard information and consultation provisions apply pursuant to regulation 18, the employer must provide the information and consultation representatives with information on—

(a) the recent and probable development of the undertaking's activities and economic situation;

(b) the situation, structure and probable development of employment within the undertaking (and such information must include suitable information relating to the use of agency workers (if any) in that undertaking) and on any anticipatory measures envisaged, in particular, where there is a threat to employment within the undertaking; and

(c) subject to paragraph (5), decisions likely to lead to substantial changes in work organisation or in contractual relations, including those referred to in—

(i) sections 188 to 192 of the Trade Union and Labour Relations (Consolidation) Act 1992; and

(ii) regulations 13 to 16 of the Transfer of Undertakings (Protection of Employment) Regulations 2006.

(2) The information referred to in paragraph (1) must be given at such time, in such fashion and with such content as are appropriate to enable, in particular, the information and consultation representatives to conduct an adequate study and, where necessary, to prepare for consultation.

(3) The employer must consult the information and consultation representatives on the matters referred to in paragraph (1)(b) and (c).

(4) [omitted]

(5) The duties in this regulation to inform and consult the information and consultation representatives on decisions falling within paragraph (1)(c) cease to apply once the employer is under a duty under—

(a) section 188 of the Act referred to in paragraph (1)(c)(i) (duty of employer to consult representatives);

(b) regulation 13 of the Regulations referred to in paragraph (1)(c)(ii) (duty to inform and consult representatives), or

(c) any of regulations 11 to 13 of the Pension Schemes Regulations,

and he has notified the information and consultation representatives in writing that he will be complying with his duty under the legislation referred to in sub-paragraph (a) or (b), or (c) as the case may be, instead of under these Regulations, provided that the notification is given on each occasion on which the employer has become or is about to become subject to the duty.

(6) Where there is an obligation in these Regulations on the employer to inform and consult his employees, a failure on the part of a person who controls the employer (either directly or indirectly) to provide information to the employer shall not constitute a valid reason for the employer failing to inform and consult.

PART V DUTY OF CO-OPERATION

21 Co-operation

The parties are under a duty, when negotiating or implementing a negotiated agreement or when implementing the standard information and consultation provisions, to work in a spirit of co-operation and with due regard for their reciprocal rights and obligations, taking into account the interests of both the undertaking and the employees.

PART VI COMPLIANCE AND ENFORCEMENT

22 Disputes about operation of a negotiated agreement or the standard information and consultation provisions

(1) Where—

(a) a negotiated agreement has been agreed; or

(b) the standard information and consultation provisions apply,

a complaint may be presented to the CAC by a relevant applicant who considers that the employer has failed to comply with the terms of the negotiated agreement or, as the case may be, one or more of the standard information and consultation provisions.

(2) A complaint brought under paragraph (1) must be brought within a period of three months commencing with the date of the alleged failure.

(3) In this regulation—

'failure' means an act or omission; and

'relevant applicant' means—

(a) in a case where information and consultation representatives have been elected or appointed, an information and consultation representative, or

(b) in a case where no information and consultation representatives have been elected or appointed, an employee or an employees' representative.

(4) Where the CAC finds the complaint well-founded it shall make a declaration to that effect and may make an order requiring the employer to take such steps as are necessary to comply with the terms of the negotiated agreement or, as the case may be, the standard information and consultation provisions.

(5) An order made under paragraph (4) shall specify—

(a) the steps which the employer is required to take; and

(b) the period within which the order must be complied with.

(6) If the CAC makes a declaration under paragraph (4) the relevant applicant may, within the period of three months beginning with the date on which the declaration is made, make an application to the Appeal Tribunal for a penalty notice to be issued.

(7) Where such an application is made, the Appeal Tribunal shall issue a written penalty notice to the employer requiring him to pay a penalty to the Secretary of State in respect of the failure unless satisfied, on hearing representations from the employer, that the failure resulted from a reason beyond the employer's control or that he has some other reasonable excuse for his failure.

(8) Regulation 23 shall apply in respect of a penalty notice issued under this regulation.

(9) No order of the CAC under this regulation shall have the effect of suspending or altering the effect of any act done or of any agreement made by the employer or of preventing or delaying any act or agreement which the employer proposes to do or to make.

23 Penalties

(1) A penalty notice issued under regulation 22 shall specify—

(a) the amount of the penalty which is payable;

(b) the date before which the penalty must be paid; and

(c) the failure and period to which the penalty relates.

(2) No penalty set by the Appeal Tribunal under this regulation may exceed £75,000.

(3) Matters to be taken into account by the Appeal Tribunal when setting the amount of the penalty shall include—

(a) the gravity of the failure;

(b) the period of time over which the failure occurred;

(c) the reason for the failure;

(d) the number of employees affected by the failure; and

(e) the number of employees employed by the undertaking or, where a negotiated agreement covers employees in more than one undertaking, the number of employees employed by both or all of the undertakings.

(4) The date specified under paragraph (1)(b) must not be earlier than the end of the period within which an appeal against a declaration or order made by the CAC under regulation 22 may be made.

(5) If the specified date in a penalty notice has passed and—

(a) the period during which an appeal may be made has expired without an appeal having been made; or

(b) such an appeal has been made and determined,

the Secretary of State may recover from the employer, as a civil debt due to him, any amount payable under the penalty notice which remains outstanding.

(6) The making of an appeal suspends the effect of a penalty notice.

(7) [omitted]

24 Exclusivity of remedy

The remedy for infringement of the rights conferred by Parts I to VI of these Regulations is by way of complaint to the CAC, and not otherwise.

PART VII CONFIDENTIAL INFORMATION

25 Breach of statutory duty

(1) A person to whom the employer, pursuant to his obligations under these Regulations, entrusts any information or document on terms requiring it to be held in confidence shall not disclose that information or document except, where the terms permit him to do so, in accordance with those terms.

(2) In this regulation a person referred to in paragraph (1) to whom information or a document is entrusted is referred to as a 'recipient'.

(3) The obligation to comply with paragraph (1) is a duty owed to the employer, and a breach of the duty is actionable accordingly (subject to the defences and other incidents applying to actions for breaches of statutory duty).

(4) Paragraph (3) shall not affect any legal liability which any person may incur by disclosing the information or document, or any right which any person may have in relation to such disclosure otherwise than under this regulation.

(5) No action shall lie under paragraph (3) where the recipient reasonably believed the disclosure to be a 'protected disclosure' within the meaning given to that expression by section 43A of the 1996 Act.

(6) A recipient to whom the employer has entrusted any information or document on terms requiring it to be held in confidence may apply to the CAC for a declaration as to whether it was reasonable for the employer to require the recipient to hold the information or document in confidence.

(7) If the CAC considers, on an application under paragraph (6), that the disclosure of the information or document by the recipient would not, or would not be likely to, harm the legitimate interests of the undertaking, it shall make a declaration that it was not reasonable for the employer to require the recipient to hold the information or document in confidence.

(8) If a declaration is made under paragraph (7), the information or document shall not at any time thereafter be regarded as having been entrusted to the recipient who made the application under paragraph (6), or to any other recipient, on terms requiring it to be held in confidence.

26 Withholding of information by the employer

(1) The employer is not required to disclose any information or document to a person for the purposes of these Regulations where the nature of the information or document is such that,

according to objective criteria, the disclosure of the information or document would seriously harm the functioning of, or would be prejudicial to, the undertaking.

(2) If there is a dispute between the employer and—

(a) where information and consultation representatives have been elected or appointed, such a representative; or

(b) where no information and consultation representatives have been elected or appointed, an employee or an employees' representative,

as to whether the nature of the information or document which the employer has failed to provide is such as is described in paragraph (1), the employer or a person referred to in sub-paragraph (a) or (b) may apply to the CAC for a declaration as to whether the information or document is of such a nature.

(3) If the CAC makes a declaration that the disclosure of the information or document in question would not, according to objective criteria, be seriously harmful or prejudicial as mentioned in paragraph (1), the CAC shall order the employer to disclose the information or document.

(4) An order under paragraph (3) shall specify—

(a) the information or document to be disclosed;

(b) the person or persons to whom the information or document is to be disclosed;

(c) any terms on which the information or document is to be disclosed; and

(d) the date before which the information or document is to be disclosed.

27–43 [omitted]

SCHEDULE 1

APPLICATION OF REGULATIONS

Number of employees	Date Regulations apply
At least 150	6 April 2005
At least 100	6 April 2007
At least 50	6 April 2008

The Transfer of Undertakings (Protection of Employment) Regulations 2006

(SI 2006 No. 246)

1. [omitted]

Interpretation

2.—(1) In these Regulations—

'assigned' means assigned other than on a temporary basis;

'collective agreement', 'collective bargaining' and 'trade union' have the same meanings respectively as in the 1992 Act;

'contract of employment' means any agreement between an employee and his employer determining the terms and conditions of his employment;

references to 'contractor' in regulation 3 shall include a sub-contractor;

'employee' means any individual who works for another person whether under a contract of service or apprenticeship or otherwise but does not include anyone who provides services under a contract for services and references to a person's employer shall be construed accordingly;

'insolvency practitioner' has the meaning given to the expression by Part XIII of the Insolvency Act 1986;

references to 'organised grouping of employees' shall include a single employee;

'recognised' has the meaning given to the expression by section 178(3) of the 1992 Act;

'relevant transfer' means a transfer or a service provision change to which these Regulations apply in accordance with regulation 3 and 'transferor' and 'transferee' shall be construed accordingly and in the case of a service provision change falling within regulation 3(1)(b), 'the transferor' means the person who carried out the activities prior to the service provision change and 'the transferee' means the person who carries out the activities as a result of the service provision change;

'the 1992 Act' means the Trade Union and Labour Relations (Consolidation) Act 1992;

'the 1996 Act' means the Employment Rights Act 1996;

'the 1996 Tribunals Act' means the Employment Tribunals Act 1996;

'the 1981 Regulations' means the Transfer of Undertakings (Protection of Employment) Regulations 1981.

(2) For the purposes of these Regulations the representative of a trade union recognised by an employer is an official or other person authorised to carry on collective bargaining with that employer by that trade union.

(3) [omitted]

A relevant transfer

3.—(1) These Regulations apply to—

(a) a transfer of an undertaking, business or part of an undertaking or business situated immediately before the transfer in the United Kingdom to another person where there is a transfer of an economic entity which retains its identity;

(b) a service provision change, that is a situation in which—

(i) activities cease to be carried out by a person ('a client') on his own behalf and are carried out instead by another person on the client's behalf ('a contractor');

(ii) activities cease to be carried out by a contractor on a client's behalf (whether or not those activities had previously been carried out by the client on his own behalf) and are carried out instead by another person ('a subsequent contractor') on the client's behalf; or

(iii) activities cease to be carried out by a contractor or a subsequent contractor on a client's behalf (whether or not those activities had previously been carried out by the client on his own behalf) and are carried out instead by the client on his own behalf,

and in which the conditions set out in paragraph (3) are satisfied.

(2) In this regulation 'economic entity' means an organised grouping of resources which has the objective of pursuing an economic activity, whether or not that activity is central or ancillary.

(2A) References in paragraph (1)(b) to activities being carried out instead by another person (including the client) are to activities which are fundamentally the same as the activities carried out by the person who has ceased to carry them out.

(3) The conditions referred to in paragraph (1)(b) are that—

(a) immediately before the service provision change—

(i) there is an organised grouping of employees situated in Great Britain which has as its principal purpose the carrying out of the activities concerned on behalf of the client;

(ii) the client intends that the activities will, following the service provision change, be carried out by the transferee other than in connection with a single specific event or task of short-term duration; and

(b) the activities concerned do not consist wholly or mainly of the supply of goods for the client's use.

(4) Subject to paragraph (1), these Regulations apply to—

(a) public and private undertakings engaged in economic activities whether or not they are operating for gain;

(b) a transfer or service provision change howsoever effected notwithstanding—

(i) that the transfer of an undertaking, business or part of an undertaking or business is governed or effected by the law of a country or territory outside the United Kingdom or that the service provision change is governed or effected by the law of a country or territory outside Great Britain;

(ii) that the employment of persons employed in the undertaking, business or part transferred or, in the case of a service provision change, persons employed in the organised grouping of employees, is governed by any such law;

(c) a transfer of an undertaking, business or part of an undertaking or business (which may also be a service provision change) where persons employed in the undertaking, business or part transferred ordinarily work outside the United Kingdom.

(5) An administrative reorganisation of public administrative authorities or the transfer of administrative functions between public administrative authorities is not a relevant transfer.

(6) A relevant transfer—

(a) may be effected by a series of two or more transactions; and

(b) may take place whether or not any property is transferred to the transferee by the transferor.

(7) [omitted]

Effect of relevant transfer on contracts of employment

4.—(1) Except where objection is made under paragraph (7), a relevant transfer shall not operate so as to terminate the contract of employment of any person employed by the transferor and assigned to the organised grouping of resources or employees that is subject to the relevant transfer, which would otherwise be terminated by the transfer, but any such contract shall have effect after the transfer as if originally made between the person so employed and the transferee.

(2) Without prejudice to paragraph (1), but subject to paragraph (6), and regulations 8 and 15(9), on the completion of a relevant transfer—

(a) all the transferor's rights, powers, duties and liabilities under or in connection with any such contract shall be transferred by virtue of this regulation to the transferee; and

(b) any act or omission before the transfer is completed, of or in relation to the transferor in respect of that contract or a person assigned to that organised grouping of resources or employees, shall be deemed to have been an act or omission of or in relation to the transferee.

(3) Any reference in paragraph (1) to a person employed by the transferor and assigned to the organised grouping of resources or employees that is subject to a relevant transfer, is a reference to a person so employed immediately before the transfer, or who would have been so employed if he had not been dismissed in the circumstances described in regulation 7(1), including, where the transfer is effected by a series of two or more transactions, a person so employed and assigned or who would have been so employed and assigned immediately before any of those transactions.

(4) Subject to regulation 9, any purported variation of a contract of employment that is, or will be, transferred by paragraph (1), is void if the sole or principal reason for the variation is the transfer.

(5) Paragraph (4) does not prevent a variation of the contract of employment if—

(a) the sole or principal reason for the variation is an economic, technical, or organisational reason entailing changes in the workforce, provided that the employer and employee agree that variation; or

(b) the terms of that contract permit the employer to make such a variation.

(5A) In paragraph (5), the expression 'changes in the workforce' includes a change to the place where employees are employed by the employer to carry on the business of the employer or to carry out work of a particular kind for the employer (and the reference to such a place has the same meaning as in section 139 of the 1996 Act).

(5B) Paragraph (4) does not apply in respect of a variation of the contract of employment in so far as it varies a term or condition incorporated from a collective agreement, provided that—

(a) the variation of the contract takes effect on a date more than one year after the date of the transfer; and

(b) following that variation, the rights and obligations in the employee's contract, when considered together, are no less favourable to the employee than those which applied immediately before the variation.

(5C) Paragraphs (5) and (5B) do not affect any rule of law as to whether a contract of employment is effectively varied.

(6) Paragraph (2) shall not transfer or otherwise affect the liability of any person to be prosecuted for, convicted of and sentenced for any offence.

(7) Paragraphs (1) and (2) shall not operate to transfer the contract of employment and the rights, powers, duties and liabilities under or in connection with it of an employee who informs the transferor or the transferee that he objects to becoming employed by the transferee.

(8) Subject to paragraphs (9) and (11), where an employee so objects, the relevant transfer shall operate so as to terminate his contract of employment with the transferor but he shall not be treated, for any purpose, as having been dismissed by the transferor.

(9) Subject to regulation 9, where a relevant transfer involves or would involve a substantial change in working conditions to the material detriment of a person whose contract of employment is or would be transferred under paragraph (1), such an employee may treat the contract of employment as having been terminated, and the employee shall be treated for any purpose as having been dismissed by the employer.

(10) No damages shall be payable by an employer as a result of a dismissal falling within paragraph (9) in respect of any failure by the employer to pay wages to an employee in respect of a notice period which the employee has failed to work.

(11) Paragraphs (1), (7), (8) and (9) are without prejudice to any right of an employee arising apart from these Regulations to terminate his contract of employment without notice in acceptance of a repudiatory breach of contract by his employer.

Effect of relevant transfer on contracts of employment which incorporate provisions of collective agreements

4A.—(1) Where a contract of employment, which is transferred by regulation 4(1), incorporates provisions of collective agreements as may be agreed from time to time, regulation 4(2) does not transfer any rights, powers, duties and liabilities in relation to any provision of a collective agreement if the following conditions are met—

(a) the provision of the collective agreement is agreed after the date of the transfer; and

(b) the transferee is not a participant in the collective bargaining for that provision.

(2) For the purposes of regulation 4(1), the contract of employment has effect after the transfer as if it does not incorporate provisions of a collective agreement which meet the conditions in paragraph (1).

Effect of relevant transfer on collective agreements

5. Where at the time of a relevant transfer there exists a collective agreement made by or on behalf of the transferor with a trade union recognised by the transferor in respect of any employee whose contract of employment is preserved by regulation 4(1) above, then—

(a) without prejudice to sections 179 and 180 of the 1992 Act (collective agreements presumed to be unenforceable in specified circumstances) that agreement, in its application in relation to the employee, shall, after the transfer, have effect as if made by or on behalf of the transferee with that trade union, and accordingly anything done under or in connection with it, in its application in relation to the employee, by or in relation to the transferor before the transfer, shall, after the transfer, be deemed to have been done by or in relation to the transferee; and

(b) any order made in respect of that agreement, in its application in relation to the employee, shall, after the transfer, have effect as if the transferee were a party to the agreement.

Effect of relevant transfer on trade union recognition

6.—(1) This regulation applies where after a relevant transfer the transferred organised grouping of resources or employees maintains an identity distinct from the remainder of the transferee's undertaking.

(2) Where before such a transfer an independent trade union is recognised to any extent by the transferor in respect of employees of any description who in consequence of the transfer become employees of the transferee, then, after the transfer—

(a) the trade union shall be deemed to have been recognised by the transferee to the same extent in respect of employees of that description so employed; and

(b) any agreement for recognition may be varied or rescinded accordingly.

Dismissal of employee because of relevant transfer

7.—(1) Where before or after a relevant transfer, any employee of the transferor or transferee is dismissed, that employee is to be treated for the purposes of Part 10 of the 1996 Act (unfair dismissal) as unfairly dismissed if the sole or principal reason for the dismissal is—

(a) the transfer itself; or

(b) a reason connected with the transfer that is not an economic, technical or organisational reason entailing changes in the workforce.

(2) This paragraph applies where the sole or principal reason for the dismissal is an economic, technical or organisational reason entailing changes in the workforce of either the transferor or the transferee before or after a relevant transfer.

(3) Where paragraph (2) applies—

(a) paragraph (1) does not apply;

(b) without prejudice to the application of section 98(4) of the 1996 Act (test of fair dismissal), for the purposes of sections 98(1) and 135 of that Act (reason for dismissal)—

(i) the dismissal is regarded as having been for redundancy where section 98(2)(c) of that Act applies; or

(ii) in any other case, the dismissal is regarded as having been for a substantial reason of a kind such as to justify the dismissal of an employee holding the position which that employee held.

(3A) In paragraph (2), the expression 'changes in the workforce' includes a change to the place where employees are employed by the employer to carry on the business of the employer or to carry out work of a particular kind for the employer (and the reference to such a place has the same meaning as in section 139 of the 1996 Act).

(4) The provisions of this regulation apply irrespective of whether the employee in question is assigned to the organised grouping of resources or employees that is, or will be, transferred.

(5) Paragraph (1) shall not apply in relation to the dismissal of any employee which was required by reason of the application of section 5 of the Aliens Restriction (Amendment) Act 1919 to his employment.

(6) Paragraph (1) shall not apply in relation to a dismissal of an employee if the application of section 94 of the 1996 Act to the dismissal of the employee is excluded by or under any provision of the 1996 Act, the 1996 Tribunals Act or the 1992 Act.

Insolvency

8.—(1) If at the time of a relevant transfer the transferor is subject to relevant insolvency proceedings paragraphs (2) to (6) apply.

(2) In this regulation 'relevant employee' means an employee of the transferor—

(a) whose contract of employment transfers to the transferee by virtue of the operation of these Regulations; or

(b) whose employment with the transferor is terminated before the time of the relevant transfer in the circumstances described in regulation 7(1).

(3) The relevant statutory scheme specified in paragraph (4)(b) (including that sub-paragraph as applied by paragraph 5 of Schedule 1) shall apply in the case of a relevant employee irrespective of the fact that the qualifying requirement that the employee's employment has been terminated is not met and for those purposes the date of the transfer shall be treated as the date of the termination and the transferor shall be treated as the employer.

(4) In this regulation the 'relevant statutory schemes' are—

(a) Chapter VI of Part XI of the 1996 Act;

(b) Part XII of the 1996 Act.

(5) Regulation 4 shall not operate to transfer liability for the sums payable to the relevant employee under the relevant statutory schemes.

(6) In this regulation 'relevant insolvency proceedings' means insolvency proceedings which have been opened in relation to the transferor not with a view to the liquidation of the assets of the transferor and which are under the supervision of an insolvency practitioner.

(7) Regulations 4 and 7 do not apply to any relevant transfer where the transferor is the subject of bankruptcy proceedings or any analogous insolvency proceedings which have been instituted with a view to the liquidation of the assets of the transferor and are under the supervision of an insolvency practitioner.

Variations of contract where transferors are subject to relevant insolvency proceedings

9.—(1) If at the time of a relevant transfer the transferor is subject to relevant insolvency proceedings these Regulations shall not prevent the transferor or transferee (or an insolvency practitioner) and appropriate representatives of assigned employees agreeing to permitted variations.

(2) For the purposes of this regulation 'appropriate representatives' are—

(a) if the employees are of a description in respect of which an independent trade union is recognised by their employer, representatives of the trade union; or

(b) in any other case, whichever of the following employee representatives the employer chooses—

(i) employee representatives appointed or elected by the assigned employees (whether they make the appointment or election alone or with others) otherwise than for the purposes of this regulation, who (having regard to the purposes for, and the method by which they were appointed or elected) have authority from those employees to agree permitted variations to contracts of employment on their behalf;

(ii) employee representatives elected by assigned employees (whether they make the appointment or election alone or with others) for these particular purposes, in an election satisfying requirements identical to those contained in regulation 14 except those in regulation 14(1)(d).

(3) An individual may be an appropriate representative for the purposes of both this regulation and regulation 13 provided that where the representative is not a trade union representative he is either elected by or has authority from assigned employees (within the meaning of this regulation) and affected employees (as described in regulation 13(1)).

(4) [omitted]

(5) Where assigned employees are represented by non-trade union representatives—

(a) the agreement recording a permitted variation must be in writing and signed by each of the representatives who have made it or, where that is not reasonably practicable, by a duly authorised agent of that representative; and

(b) the employer must, before the agreement is made available for signature, provide all employees to whom it is intended to apply on the date on which it is to come into effect with copies of the text of the agreement and such guidance as those employees might reasonably require in order to understand it fully.

(6) A permitted variation shall take effect as a term or condition of the assigned employee's contract of employment in place, where relevant, of any term or condition which it varies.

(7) In this regulation—

'assigned employees' means those employees assigned to the organised grouping of resources or employees that is the subject of a relevant transfer;

'permitted variation' is a variation to the contract of employment of an assigned employee where—

(a) the sole or principal reason for it is the transfer itself or a reason connected with the transfer that is not an economic, technical or organisational reason entailing changes in the workforce; and
the sole or principal reason for the variation is the transfer and not a reason referred to in regulation 4(5)(a); and

(b) it is designed to safeguard employment opportunities by ensuring the survival of the undertaking, business or part of the undertaking or business that is the subject of the relevant transfer;

'relevant insolvency proceedings' has the meaning given to the expression by regulation 8 (6).

Pensions

10.—(1) Regulations 4 and 5 shall not apply—

(a) to so much of a contract of employment or collective agreement as relates to an occupational pension scheme within the meaning of the Pension Schemes Act 1993; or

(b) to any rights, powers, duties or liabilities under or in connection with any such contract or subsisting by virtue of any such agreement and relating to such a scheme or otherwise arising in connection with that person's employment and relating to such a scheme.

(2) For the purposes of paragraphs (1) and (3), any provisions of an occupational pension scheme which do not relate to benefits for old age, invalidity or survivors shall not be treated as being part of the scheme.

(3) An employee whose contract of employment is transferred in the circumstances described in regulation 4(1) shall not be entitled to bring a claim against the transferor for—

(a) breach of contract; or

(b) constructive unfair dismissal under section 95(1)(c) of the 1996 Act,

arising out of a loss or reduction in his rights under an occupational pension scheme in consequence of the transfer, save insofar as the alleged breach of contract or dismissal (as the case may be) occurred prior to the date on which these Regulations took effect.

Notification of employee liability information

11.—(1) The transferor shall notify to the transferee the employee liability information of any person employed by him who is assigned to the organised grouping of resources or employees that is the subject of a relevant transfer—

(a) in writing; or

(b) by making it available to him in a readily accessible form.

(2) In this regulation and in regulation 12 'employee liability information' means—

(a) the identity and age of the employee;

(b) those particulars of employment that an employer is obliged to give to an employee pursuant to section 1 of the 1996 Act;

(c) information of any—

(i) disciplinary procedure taken against an employee;

(ii) grievance procedure taken by an employee,

within the previous two years, in circumstances where a Code of Practice issued under Part IV of the Trade Union and Labour Relations (Consolidation) Act 1992 which relates exclusively or primarily to the resolution of disputes applies;

(d) information of any court or tribunal case, claim or action—
    (i) brought by an employee against the transferor, within the previous two years;
    (ii) that the transferor has reasonable grounds to believe that an employee may bring against the transferee, arising out of the employee's employment with the transferor; and

(e) information of any collective agreement which will have effect after the transfer, in its application in relation to the employee, pursuant to regulation 5(a).

(3) Employee liability information shall contain information as at a specified date not more than fourteen days before the date on which the information is notified to the transferee.

(4) The duty to provide employee liability information in paragraph (1) shall include a duty to provide employee liability information of any person who would have been employed by the transferor and assigned to the organised grouping of resources or employees that is the subject of a relevant transfer immediately before the transfer if he had not been dismissed in the circumstances described in regulation 7(1), including, where the transfer is effected by a series of two or more transactions, a person so employed and assigned or who would have been so employed and assigned immediately before any of those transactions.

(5) Following notification of the employee liability information in accordance with this regulation, the transferor shall notify the transferee in writing of any change in the employee liability information.

(6) A notification under this regulation shall be given not less than 28 days before the relevant transfer or, if special circumstances make this not reasonably practicable, as soon as reasonably practicable thereafter.

(7) A notification under this regulation may be given—

(a) in more than one instalment;

(b) indirectly, through a third party.

Remedy for failure to notify employee liability information

12.—(1) On or after a relevant transfer, the transferee may present a complaint to an employment tribunal that the transferor has failed to comply with any provision of regulation 11.

(2) An employment tribunal shall not consider a complaint under this regulation unless it is presented—

(a) before the end of the period of three months beginning with the date of the relevant transfer;

(b) within such further period as the tribunal considers reasonable in a case where it is satisfied that it was not reasonably practicable for the complaint to be presented before the end of that period of three months.

(2A) [omitted]

(3) Where an employment tribunal finds a complaint under paragraph (1) well-founded, the tribunal—

(a) shall make a declaration to that effect; and

(b) may make an award of compensation to be paid by the transferor to the transferee.

(4) The amount of the compensation shall be such as the tribunal considers just and equitable in all the circumstances, subject to paragraph (5), having particular regard to—

(a) any loss sustained by the transferee which is attributable to the matters complained of; and

(b) the terms of any contract between the transferor and the transferee relating to the transfer under which the transferor may be liable to pay any sum to the transferee in respect of a failure to notify the transferee of employee liability information.

(5) Subject to paragraph (6), the amount of compensation awarded under paragraph (3) shall be not less than £500 per employee in respect of whom the transferor has failed to comply with a provision of regulation 11, unless the tribunal considers it just and equitable, in all the circumstances, to award a lesser sum.

(6) In ascertaining the loss referred to in paragraph (4)(a) the tribunal shall apply the same rule concerning the duty of a person to mitigate his loss as applies to any damages recoverable under the common law of England and Wales, Northern Ireland or Scotland, as applicable.

(7) Sections 18A to 18C of the 1996 Tribunals Act (conciliation) shall apply to the right conferred by this regulation and to proceedings under this regulation as it applies to the rights conferred by that Act and the employment tribunal proceedings mentioned in that Act.

Duty to inform and consult representatives

13.—(1) In this regulation and regulations 13A, 14 and 15 references to affected employees, in relation to a relevant transfer, are to any employees of the transferor or the transferee (whether or not assigned to the organised grouping of resources or employees that is the subject of a relevant transfer) who may be affected by the transfer or may be affected by measures taken in connection with it; and references to the employer shall be construed accordingly.

(2) Long enough before a relevant transfer to enable the employer of any affected employees to consult the appropriate representatives of any affected employees, the employer shall inform those representatives of—

- (a) the fact that the transfer is to take place, the date or proposed date of the transfer and the reasons for it;
- (b) the legal, economic and social implications of the transfer for any affected employees;
- (c) the measures which he envisages he will, in connection with the transfer, take in relation to any affected employees or, if he envisages that no measures will be so taken, that fact; and
- (d) if the employer is the transferor, the measures, in connection with the transfer, which he envisages the transferee will take in relation to any affected employees who will become employees of the transferee after the transfer by virtue of regulation 4 or, if he envisages that no measures will be so taken, that fact.

(2A) Where information is to be supplied under paragraph (2) by an employer—

- (a) this must include suitable information relating to the use of agency workers (if any) by that employer; and
- (b) 'suitable information relating to the use of agency workers' means—
  - (i) the number of agency workers working temporarily for and under the supervision and direction of the employer;
  - (ii) the parts of the employer's undertaking in which those agency workers are working; and
  - (iii) the type of work those agency workers are carrying out.

(3) For the purposes of this regulation the appropriate representatives of any affected employees are—

- (a) if the employees are of a description in respect of which an independent trade union is recognised by their employer, representatives of the trade union; or
- (b) in any other case, whichever of the following employee representatives the employer chooses—
  - (i) employee representatives appointed or elected by the affected employees otherwise than for the purposes of this regulation, who (having regard to the purposes for, and the method by which they were appointed or elected) have authority from those employees to receive information and to be consulted about the transfer on their behalf;
  - (ii) employee representatives elected by any affected employees, for the purposes of this regulation, in an election satisfying the requirements of regulation 14(1).

(4) The transferee shall give the transferor such information at such a time as will enable the transferor to perform the duty imposed on him by virtue of paragraph (2)(d).

(5) The information which is to be given to the appropriate representatives shall be given to each of them by being delivered to them, or sent by post to an address notified by them to the employer, or (in the case of representatives of a trade union) sent by post to the trade union at the address of its head or main office.

(6) An employer of an affected employee who envisages that he will take measures in relation to an affected employee, in connection with the relevant transfer, shall consult the appropriate representatives of that employee with a view to seeking their agreement to the intended measures.

(7) In the course of those consultations the employer shall—

(a) consider any representations made by the appropriate representatives; and

(b) reply to those representations and, if he rejects any of those representations, state his reasons.

(8) The employer shall allow the appropriate representatives access to any affected employees and shall afford to those representatives such accommodation and other facilities as may be appropriate.

(9) If in any case there are special circumstances which render it not reasonably practicable for an employer to perform a duty imposed on him by any of paragraphs (2) to (7), he shall take all such steps towards performing that duty as are reasonably practicable in the circumstances.

(10) Where—

(a) the employer has invited any of the affected employees to elect employee representatives; and

(b) the invitation was issued long enough before the time when the employer is required to give information under paragraph (2) to allow them to elect representatives by that time,

the employer shall be treated as complying with the requirements of this regulation in relation to those employees if he complies with those requirements as soon as is reasonably practicable after the election of the representatives.

(11) If, after the employer has invited any affected employees to elect representatives, they fail to do so within a reasonable time, he shall give to any affected employees the information set out in paragraph (2).

(12) The duties imposed on an employer by this regulation shall apply irrespective of whether the decision resulting in the relevant transfer is taken by the employer or a person controlling the employer.

Variation to the duty to inform and consult where no appropriate representatives

13A.—(1) This regulation applies if, at the time when the employer is required to give information under regulation 13(2)—

(a) at least one of the following conditions is satisfied—

(i) the employer employs fewer than 50 employees;

(ii) there are fewer than 10 transferring employees.

(b) there are no appropriate representatives within the meaning of regulation 13(3); and

(c) the employer has not invited any of the affected employees to elect employee representatives.

(1A) For the purposes of paragraph (1)(a)(ii), 'transferring employees' means the employees who work for the transferor and who are to be (or are likely to be) transferred to the transferee's employment under a relevant transfer.

(2) The employer may comply with regulation 13 by performing any duty which relates to appropriate representatives as if each of the affected employees were an appropriate representative.

Election of employee representatives

14.—(1) The requirements for the election of employee representatives under regulation 13(3) are that—

(a) the employer shall make such arrangements as are reasonably practicable to ensure that the election is fair;

(b) the employer shall determine the number of representatives to be elected so that there are sufficient representatives to represent the interests of all affected employees having regard to the number and classes of those employees;

(c) the employer shall determine whether the affected employees should be represented either by representatives of all the affected employees or by representatives of particular classes of those employees;

(d) before the election the employer shall determine the term of office as employee representatives so that it is of sufficient length to enable information to be given and consultations under regulation 13 to be completed;

(e) the candidates for election as employee representatives are affected employees on the date of the election;

(f) no affected employee is unreasonably excluded from standing for election;

(g) all affected employees on the date of the election are entitled to vote for employee representatives;

(h) the employees entitled to vote may vote for as many candidates as there are representatives to be elected to represent them or, if there are to be representatives for particular classes of employees, may vote for as many candidates as there are representatives to be elected to represent their particular class of employee;

(i) the election is conducted so as to secure that—

  (i) so far as is reasonably practicable, those voting do so in secret; and

  (ii) the votes given at the election are accurately counted.

(2) Where, after an election of employee representatives satisfying the requirements of paragraph (1) has been held, one of those elected ceases to act as an employee representative and as a result any affected employees are no longer represented, those employees shall elect another representative by an election satisfying the requirements of paragraph (1)(a), (e), (f) and (i).

Failure to inform or consult

15.—(1) Where an employer has failed to comply with a requirement of regulation 13 or regulation 14, a complaint may be presented to an employment tribunal on that ground—

(a) in the case of a failure relating to the election of employee representatives, by any of his employees who are affected employees;

(b) in the case of any other failure relating to employee representatives, by any of the employee representatives to whom the failure related;

(c) in the case of failure relating to representatives of a trade union, by the trade union; and

(d) in any other case, by any of his employees who are affected employees.

(2) If on a complaint under paragraph (1) a question arises whether or not it was reasonably practicable for an employer to perform a particular duty or as to what steps he took towards performing it, it shall be for him to show—

(a) that there were special circumstances which rendered it not reasonably practicable for him to perform the duty; and

(b) that he took all such steps towards its performance as were reasonably practicable in those circumstances.

(3) If on a complaint under paragraph (1) a question arises as to whether or not an employee representative was an appropriate representative for the purposes of regulation 13, it shall be for the employer to show that the employee representative had the necessary authority

to represent the affected employees except where the question is whether or not regulation 13A applied.

(3A) If on a complaint under paragraph (1), a question arises as to whether or not regulation 13A applied, it is for the employer to show that the conditions in sub-paragraphs (a) and (b) of regulation 13A(1) applied at the time referred to in regulation 13A(1).

(4) On a complaint under paragraph (1)(a) it shall be for the employer to show that the requirements in regulation 14 have been satisfied.

(5) On a complaint against a transferor that he had failed to perform the duty imposed upon him by virtue of regulation 13(2)(d) or, so far as relating thereto, regulation 13(9), he may not show that it was not reasonably practicable for him to perform the duty in question for the reason that the transferee had failed to give him the requisite information at the requisite time in accordance with regulation 13 (4) unless he gives the transferee notice of his intention to show that fact; and the giving of the notice shall make the transferee a party to the proceedings.

(6) In relation to any complaint under paragraph (1), a failure on the part of a person controlling (directly or indirectly) the employer to provide information to the employer shall not constitute special circumstances rendering it not reasonably practicable for the employer to comply with such a requirement.

(7) Where the tribunal finds a complaint against a transferee under paragraph (1) well-founded it shall make a declaration to that effect and may order the transferee to pay appropriate compensation to such descriptions of affected employees as may be specified in the award.

(8) Where the tribunal finds a complaint against a transferor under paragraph (1) well-founded it shall make a declaration to that effect and may—

- (a) order the transferor, subject to paragraph (9), to pay appropriate compensation to such descriptions of affected employees as may be specified in the award; or
- (b) if the complaint is that the transferor did not perform the duty mentioned in paragraph (5) and the transferor (after giving due notice) shows the facts so mentioned, order the transferee to pay appropriate compensation to such descriptions of affected employees as may be specified in the award.

(9) The transferee shall be jointly and severally liable with the transferor in respect of compensation payable under sub-paragraph (8)(a) or paragraph (11).

(10) An employee may present a complaint to an employment tribunal on the ground that he is an employee of a description to which an order under paragraph (7) or (8) relates and that—

- (a) in respect of an order under paragraph (7), the transferee has failed, wholly or in part, to pay him compensation in pursuance of the order;
- (b) in respect of an order under paragraph (8), the transferor or transferee, as applicable, has failed, wholly or in part, to pay him compensation in pursuance of the order.

(11) Where the tribunal finds a complaint under paragraph (10) well-founded it shall order the transferor or transferee as applicable to pay the complainant the amount of compensation which it finds is due to him.

(12) An employment tribunal shall not consider a complaint under paragraph (1) or (10) unless it is presented to the tribunal before the end of the period of three months beginning with—

- (a) in respect of a complaint under paragraph (1), the date on which the relevant transfer is completed; or
- (b) in respect of a complaint under paragraph (10), the date of the tribunal's order under paragraph (7) or (8),

or within such further period as the tribunal considers reasonable in a case where it is satisfied that it was not reasonably practicable for the complaint to be presented before the end of the period of three months.

(13) [omitted]

Failure to inform or consult: supplemental

16.—(1) Section 205(1) of the 1996 Act (complaint to be sole remedy for breach of relevant rights) and sections 18A to 18C of the 1996 Tribunals Act (conciliation) shall apply to the rights conferred by regulation 15 and to proceedings under this regulation as they apply to the rights conferred by those Acts and the employment tribunal proceedings mentioned in those Acts.

(2) An appeal shall lie and shall lie only to the Employment Appeal Tribunal on a question of law arising from any decision of, or arising in any proceedings before, an employment tribunal under or by virtue of these Regulations; and section 11(1) of the Tribunals and Inquiries Act 1992 (appeals from certain tribunals to the High Court) shall not apply in relation to any such proceedings.

(3) 'Appropriate compensation' in regulation 15 means such sum not exceeding thirteen weeks' pay for the employee in question as the tribunal considers just and equitable having regard to the seriousness of the failure of the employer to comply with his duty.

(4) Sections 220 to 228 of the 1996 Act shall apply for calculating the amount of a week's pay for any employee for the purposes of paragraph (3) and, for the purposes of that calculation, the calculation date shall be—

(a) in the case of an employee who is dismissed by reason of redundancy (within the meaning of sections 139 and 155 of the 1996 Act) the date which is the calculation date for the purposes of any entitlement of his to a redundancy payment (within the meaning of those sections) or which would be that calculation date if he were so entitled;

(b) in the case of an employee who is dismissed for any other reason, the effective date of termination (within the meaning of sections 95 (1) and (2) and 97 of the 1996 Act) of his contract of employment;

(c) in any other case, the date of the relevant transfer.

16A.–17. [omitted]

Restriction on contracting out

18. Section 203 of the 1996 Act (restrictions on contracting out) shall apply in relation to these Regulations as if they were contained in that Act, save for that section shall not apply in so far as these Regulations provide for an agreement (whether a contract of employment or not) to exclude or limit the operation of these Regulations.

19.–21. [omitted]

The Agency Workers Regulations 2010

(SI 2010 No. 93)

PART 1 GENERAL AND INTERPRETATION

2 Interpretation
3 The meaning of agency worker
4 The meaning of temporary work agency

PART 2 RIGHTS

5 Rights of agency workers in relation to the basic working and employment conditions
6 Relevant terms and conditions
7 Qualifying period
8 Completion of the qualifying period and continuation of the regulation 5 rights
9 Structure of assignments
12 Rights of agency workers in relation to access to collective facilities and amenities
13 Rights of agency workers in relation to access to employment

PART 3 LIABILITY, PROTECTIONS AND REMEDIES

14 Liability of temporary work agency and hirer
15 Restrictions on contracting out
17 Unfair dismissal and the right not to be subjected to detriment
18 Complaints to employment tribunals etc.
19 Calculating a week's pay
20 Liability of employers and principals

PART 1 GENERAL AND INTERPRETATION

2 Interpretation

In these Regulations—

'the 1996 Act' means the Employment Rights Act 1996);

'assignment' means a period of time during which an agency worker is supplied by one or more temporary work agencies to a hirer to work temporarily for and under the supervision and direction of the hirer;

'contract of employment' means a contract of service or of apprenticeship, whether express or implied, and (if it is express) whether oral or in writing;

'employee' means an individual who has entered into or works under or, where the employment has ceased, worked under a contract of employment;

'employer', in relation to an employee or worker, means the person by whom the employee or worker is (or where the employment has ceased, was) employed;

'employment'—

(a) in relation to an employee, means employment under a contract of employment, and

(b) in relation to a worker, means employment under that worker's contract,

and 'employed' shall be construed accordingly;

'hirer' means a person engaged in economic activity, public or private, whether or not operating for profit, to whom individuals are supplied, to work temporarily for and under the supervision and direction of that person; and

'worker' means an individual who is not an agency worker but who has entered into or works under (or where the employment has ceased, worked under)—

(a) a contract of employment, or

(b) any other contract, whether express or implied and (if it is express) whether oral or in writing, whereby the individual undertakes to do or perform personally any work or services for another party to the contract whose status is not by virtue of the contract that of a client or customer of any profession or business undertaking carried on by the individual,

and any reference to a worker's contract shall be construed accordingly.

3 The meaning of agency worker

(1) In these Regulations 'agency worker' means an individual who—

(a) is supplied by a temporary work agency to work temporarily for and under the supervision and direction of a hirer; and

(b) has a contract with the temporary work agency which is—

(i) a contract of employment with the agency, or

(ii) any other contract with the agency to perform work or services personally.

(2) But an individual is not an agency worker if—

(a) the contract the individual has with the temporary work agency has the effect that the status of the agency is that of a client or customer of a profession or business undertaking carried on by the individual; or

(b) there is a contract, by virtue of which the individual is available to work for the hirer, having the effect that the status of the hirer is that of a client or customer of a profession or business undertaking carried on by the individual.

(3) For the purposes of paragraph (1)(a) an individual shall be treated as having been supplied by a temporary work agency to work temporarily for and under the supervision and direction of a hirer if—

(a) the temporary work agency initiates or is involved as an intermediary in the making of the arrangements that lead to the individual being supplied to work temporarily for and under the supervision and direction of the hirer, and

(b) the individual is supplied by an intermediary, or one of a number of intermediaries, to work temporarily for and under the supervision and direction of the hirer.

(4) An individual treated by virtue of paragraph (3) as having been supplied by a temporary work agency, shall be treated, for the purposes of paragraph (1)(b), as having a contract with the temporary work agency.

(5) An individual is not prevented from being an agency worker—

(a) because the temporary work agency supplies the individual through one or more intermediaries;

(b) because one or more intermediaries supply that individual;

(c) because the individual is supplied pursuant to any contract or other arrangement between the temporary work agency, one or more intermediaries and the hirer;

(d) because the temporary work agency pays for the services of the individual through one or more intermediaries; or

(e) because the individual is employed by or otherwise has a contract with one or more intermediaries.

(6) Paragraph (5) does not prejudice the generality of paragraphs (1) to (4).

4 The meaning of temporary work agency

(1) In these Regulations 'temporary work agency' means a person engaged in the economic activity, public or private, whether or not operating for profit, and whether or not carrying on such activity in conjunction with others, of—

(a) supplying individuals to work temporarily for and under the supervision and direction of hirers; or

(b) paying for, or receiving or forwarding payment for, the services of individuals who are supplied to work temporarily for and under the supervision and direction of hirers.

(2) Notwithstanding paragraph (1)(b) a person is not a temporary work agency if the person is engaged in the economic activity of paying for, or receiving or forwarding payments for, the services of individuals regardless of whether the individuals are supplied to work for hirers.

PART 2 RIGHTS

5 Rights of agency workers in relation to the basic working and employment conditions

(1) Subject to regulation 7, an agency worker (A) shall be entitled to the same basic working and employment conditions as A would be entitled to for doing the same job had A been recruited by the hirer—

(a) other than by using the services of a temporary work agency; and

(b) at the time the qualifying period commenced.

(2) For the purposes of paragraph (1), the basic working and employment conditions are—

(a) where A would have been recruited as an employee, the relevant terms and conditions that are ordinarily included in the contracts of employees of the hirer;

(b) where A would have been recruited as a worker, the relevant terms and conditions that are ordinarily included in the contracts of workers of the hirer,

whether by collective agreement or otherwise, including any variations in those relevant terms and conditions made at any time after the qualifying period commenced.

(3) Paragraph (1) shall be deemed to have been complied with where—

(a) an agency worker is working under the same relevant terms and conditions as an employee who is a comparable employee, and

(b) the relevant terms and conditions of that comparable employee are terms and conditions ordinarily included in the contracts of employees, who are comparable employees of the hirer, whether by collective agreement or otherwise.

(4) For the purposes of paragraph (3) an employee is a comparable employee in relation to an agency worker if at the time when the breach of paragraph (1) is alleged to take place—

(a) both that employee and the agency worker are—

(i) working for and under the supervision and direction of the hirer, and

(ii) engaged in the same or broadly similar work having regard, where relevant, to whether they have a similar level of qualification and skills; and

(b) the employee works or is based at the same establishment as the agency worker or, where there is no comparable employee working or based at that establishment who satisfies the requirements of sub-paragraph (a), works or is based at a different establishment and satisfies those requirements.

(5) An employee is not a comparable employee if that employee's employment has ceased.

(6) [revoked]

6 Relevant terms and conditions

(1) In regulation 5(2) and (3) 'relevant terms and conditions' means terms and conditions relating to—

(a) pay;

(b) the duration of working time;

(c) night work;

(d) rest periods;

(e) rest breaks; and

(f) annual leave.

(2) For the purposes of paragraph (1)(a), 'pay' means any sums payable to a worker of the hirer in connection with the worker's employment, including any fee, bonus, commission, holiday pay or other emolument referable to the employment, whether payable under contract or otherwise, but excluding any payments or rewards within paragraph (3).

(3) Those payments or rewards are—

(a) any payment by way of occupational sick pay;

(b) any payment by way of a pension, allowance or gratuity in connection with the worker's retirement or as compensation for loss of office;

(c) any payment in respect of maternity, paternity, parental bereavement or adoption leave;

(d) any payment referable to the worker's redundancy;

(e) any payment or reward made pursuant to a financial participation scheme;

(f) any bonus, incentive payment or reward which is not directly attributable to the amount or quality of the work done by a worker, and which is given to a worker for a reason other than the amount or quality of work done such as to encourage the worker's loyalty or to reward the worker's long-term service;

(g) any payment for time off under Part 6 of the 1996 Act or section 169 of the Trade Union and Labour Relations (Consolidation) Act 1992 (payment for time off for carrying out trade union duties etc.);

(h) a guarantee payment under section 28 of the 1996 Act;

(i) any payment by way of an advance under an agreement for a loan or by way of an advance of pay (but without prejudice to the application of section 13 of the 1996 Act to any deduction made from the worker's wages in respect of any such advance);

(j) any payment in respect of expenses incurred by the worker in carrying out the employment; and

(k) any payment to the worker otherwise than in that person's capacity as a worker.

(4) For the purposes of paragraphs (2) and (3) any monetary value attaching to any payment or benefit in kind furnished to a worker by the hirer shall not be treated as pay of the worker except any voucher or stamp which is—

(a) of fixed value expressed in monetary terms, and
(b) capable of being exchanged (whether on its own or together with other vouchers, stamps or documents, and whether immediately or only after a time) for money, goods or services (or for any combination of two or more of those things).

(5) In this regulation—

'financial participation scheme' means any scheme that offers workers of the hirer—
(a) a distribution of shares or options, or
(b) a share of profits in cash or in shares;

'night time' in relation to an individual, means—
(a) a period—
(i) the duration of which is not less than seven hours, and
(ii) which includes the period between midnight and 5 a.m.,
which is determined for the purposes of these Regulations by a working time agreement, or
(b) in default of such a determination, the period between 11 p.m. and 6 a.m.;

'night work' means work during night time;

'relevant training' means work experience provided pursuant to a training course or programme, training for employment, or both, other than work experience or training—
(a) the immediate provider of which is an educational institution or a person whose main business is the provision of training, and
(b) which is provided on a course run by that institution or person;

'rest period', in relation to an individual, means a period which is not working time, other than a rest break or leave to which that individual is entitled either under the Working Time Regulations 1998 or under the contract between that individual and the employer of that individual;

'working time', in relation to an individual means—
(a) any period during which that individual is working, at the disposal of the employer of that individual and carrying out the activity or duties of that individual,
(b) any period during which that individual is receiving relevant training, and
(c) any additional period which is to be treated as working time for the purposes of the Working Time Regulations 1998 under a working time agreement; and

'working time agreement', in relation to an individual, means a workforce agreement within the meaning of regulation 2(1) of the Working Time Regulations 1998, which applies to the individual any provision of—
(a) a collective agreement which forms part of a contract between that individual and the employer of that individual, or
(b) any other agreement in writing which is legally enforceable as between the individual and the employer of that individual.

7 Qualifying period

(1) Regulation 5 does not apply unless an agency worker has completed the qualifying period.

(2) To complete the qualifying period the agency worker must work in the same role with the same hirer for 12 continuous calendar weeks, during one or more assignments.

(3) For the purposes of this regulation and regulations 8 and 9, the agency worker works in 'the same role' unless—
(a) the agency worker has started a new role with the same hirer, whether supplied by the same or by a different temporary work agency;
(b) the work or duties that make up the whole or the main part of that new role are substantively different from the work or duties that made up the whole or the main part of the previous role; and
(c) the temporary work agency has informed the agency worker in writing of the type of work the agency worker will be required to do in the new role.

(4) For the purposes of this regulation, any week during the whole or part of which an agency worker works during an assignment is counted as a calendar week.

(5) For the purposes of this regulation and regulations 8 and 9, when calculating whether any weeks completed with a particular hirer are continuous, where—

(a) the agency worker has started working during an assignment, and there is a break, either between assignments or during an assignment, when the agency worker is not working,

(b) paragraph (8) applies to that break, and

(c) the agency worker returns to work in the same role with the same hirer,

any continuous weeks during which the agency worker worked for that hirer before the break shall be carried forward and treated as continuous with any weeks during which the agency worker works for that hirer after the break.

(6) For the purposes of this regulation and regulation 8, when calculating the number of weeks during which the agency worker has worked, where the agency worker has—

(a) started working in a role during an assignment, and

(b) is unable to continue working for a reason described in paragraph (8)(c) or (8)(d)(i), (ii) or (iii),

for the period that is covered by one or more such reasons, that agency worker shall be deemed to be working in that role with the hirer, for the original intended duration, or likely duration of the assignment, whichever is the longer.

(7) Where—

(a) an assignment ends on grounds which are maternity grounds within the meaning of section 68A of the 1996 Act, and

(b) the agency worker is deemed to be working in that role in accordance with paragraph (6),

the fact that an agency worker is actually working in another role, whether for the same or a different hirer during the period mentioned in paragraph (6) or any part of that period, does not affect the operation of that paragraph.

(8) This paragraph applies where there is a break between assignments, or during an assignment, when the agency worker is not working, and the break is—

(a) for any reason and the break is not more than six calendar weeks;

(b) wholly due to the fact that the agency worker is incapable of working in consequence of sickness or injury, and the requirements of paragraph (9) are satisfied;

(c) related to pregnancy, childbirth or maternity and is at a time in a protected period;

(d) wholly for the purpose of taking time off or leave, whether statutory or contractual, to which the agency worker is otherwise entitled which is—

(i) ordinary, compulsory or additional maternity leave;

(ii) ordinary or additional adoption leave;

(iii) paternity leave;

(iv) time off or other leave not listed in sub-paragraph (d)(i), (ii) or (iii); or

(v) for more than one of the reasons listed in sub-paragraph (d)(i) to (iv);

(e) wholly due to the fact that the agency worker is required to attend at any place in pursuance of being summoned for service as a juror under the Juries Act 1974, the Coroners Act 1988, the Court of Session Act 1988 or the Criminal Procedure (Scotland) Act 1995, and the break is 28 calendar weeks or less;

(f) wholly due to a temporary cessation in the hirer's requirement for any worker to be present at the establishment and work in a particular role, for a pre-determined period of time according to the established custom and practices of the hirer; or

(g) wholly due to a strike, lock-out or other industrial action at the hirer's establishment; or

(h) wholly due to more than one of the reasons listed in sub-paragraphs (b), (c), (d), (e), (f) or (g).

(9) Paragraph (8)(b) only applies where—

(a) the break is 28 calendar weeks or less;

(b) paragraph (8)(c) does not apply; and

(c) if required to do so by the temporary work agency, the agency worker has provided such written medical evidence as may reasonably be required.

(10) For the purposes of paragraph (8)(c), a protected period begins at the start of the pregnancy, and the protected period associated with any particular pregnancy ends at the end of the 26 weeks beginning with childbirth or, if earlier, when the agency worker returns to work.

(11) For the purposes of paragraph (10) 'childbirth' means the birth of a living child or the birth of a child whether living or dead after 24 weeks of pregnancy.

(12) [omitted]

8 Completion of the qualifying period and continuation of the regulation 5 rights

Where an agency worker has completed the qualifying period with a particular hirer, the rights conferred by regulation 5 shall apply and shall continue to apply to that agency worker in relation to that particular hirer unless—

(a) that agency worker is no longer working in the same role, within the meaning of regulation 7(3), with that hirer; or

(b) there is a break between assignments, or during an assignment, when the agency worker is not working, to which regulation 7(8) does not apply.

9 Structure of assignments

(1) Notwithstanding paragraphs (1) and (2) of regulation 7, and regulation 8, if paragraphs (3) and (4) apply an agency worker shall be treated as having completed the qualifying period from the time at which the agency worker would have completed the qualifying period but for the structure of the assignment or assignments mentioned in paragraph (3).

(2) Notwithstanding paragraphs (1) and (2) of regulation 7, and regulation 8, if paragraphs (3) and (4) apply an agency worker who has completed the qualifying period and—

(a) is no longer entitled to the rights conferred by regulation 5, but

(b) would be so entitled but for the structure of the assignment or assignments mentioned in paragraph (3),

shall be treated as continuing to be entitled to those rights from the time at which the agency worker completed that period.

(3) This paragraph applies when an agency worker has—

(a) completed two or more assignments with a hirer (H),

(b) completed at least one assignment with H and one or more earlier assignments with hirers connected to H, or

(c) worked in more than two roles during an assignment with H, and on at least two occasions has worked in a role that was not the 'same role' as the previous role within the meaning of regulation 7(3).

(4) This paragraph applies where—

(a) the most likely explanation for the structure of the assignment, or assignments, mentioned in paragraph (3) is that H, or the temporary work agency supplying the agency worker to H, or, where applicable, H and one or more hirers connected to H, intended to prevent the agency worker from being entitled to, or from continuing to be entitled to, the rights conferred by regulation 5; and

(b) the agency worker would be entitled to, or would continue to be entitled to, the rights conferred by regulation 5 in relation to H, but for that structure.

(5) The following matters in particular shall be taken into account in determining whether the structure of the assignment or assignments mentioned in paragraph (3) shows that the most likely explanation for it is that mentioned in paragraph (4)(a)—

(a) the length of the assignments;
(b) the number of assignments with H and, where applicable, hirers connected to H;
(c) the number of times the agency worker has worked in a new role with H and, where applicable, hirers connected to H, and that new role is not the 'same role' within the meaning of regulation 7(3);
(d) the number of times the agency worker has returned to work in the same role within the meaning of regulation 7(3) with H and, where applicable, hirers connected to H;
(e) the period of any break between assignments with H and, where applicable, hirers connected to H.

(6) For the purposes of this regulation hirers are connected to a hirer if one hirer (directly or indirectly) has control of the other hirer or a third person (directly or indirectly) has control of both hirers.

10–11 [revoked]

12 Rights of agency workers in relation to access to collective facilities and amenities

(1) An agency worker has during an assignment the right to be treated no less favourably than a comparable worker in relation to the collective facilities and amenities provided by the hirer.

(2) The rights conferred by paragraph (1) apply only if the less favourable treatment is not justified on objective grounds.

(3) 'Collective facilities and amenities' includes, in particular—

(a) canteen or other similar facilities;
(b) child care facilities; and
(c) transport services.

(4) For the purposes of paragraph (1) an individual is a comparable worker in relation to an agency worker if at the time when the breach of paragraph (1) is alleged to take place—

(a) both that individual and the agency worker are—
    (i) working for and under the supervision and direction of the hirer, and
    (ii) engaged in the same or broadly similar work having regard, where relevant, to whether they have a similar level of qualification and skills;
(b) that individual works or is based at the same establishment as the agency worker or, where there is no comparable worker working or based at that establishment who satisfies the requirements of sub-paragraph (a), works or is based at a different establishment and satisfies those requirements; and
(c) that individual is an employee of the hirer or, where there is no employee satisfying the requirements of sub-paragraphs (a) and (b), is a worker of the hirer and satisfies those requirements.

13 Rights of agency workers in relation to access to employment

(1) An agency worker has during an assignment the right to be informed by the hirer of any relevant vacant posts with the hirer, to give that agency worker the same opportunity as a comparable worker to find permanent employment with the hirer.

(2) For the purposes of paragraph (1) an individual is a comparable worker in relation to an agency worker if at the time when the breach of paragraph (1) is alleged to take place—

(a) both that individual and the agency worker are—
    (i) working for and under the supervision and direction of the hirer, and
    (ii) engaged in the same or broadly similar work having regard, where relevant, to whether they have a similar level of qualification and skills;

(b) that individual works or is based at the same establishment as the agency worker; and
(c) that individual is an employee of the hirer or, where there is no employee satisfying the requirements of sub-paragraphs (a) and (b), is a worker of the hirer and satisfies those requirements.

(3) For the purposes of paragraph (1), an individual is not a comparable worker if that individual's employment with the hirer has ceased.

(4) For the purposes of paragraph (1) the hirer may inform the agency worker by a general announcement in a suitable place in the hirer's establishment.

PART 3 LIABILITY, PROTECTIONS AND REMEDIES

14 Liability of temporary work agency and hirer

(1) Subject to paragraph (3), a temporary work agency shall be liable for any breach of regulation 5, to the extent that it is responsible for that breach.

(2) The hirer shall be liable for any breach of regulation 5, to the extent that it is responsible for that breach.

(3) A temporary work agency shall not be liable for a breach of regulation 5 where it is established that the temporary work agency—

(a) obtained, or has taken reasonable steps to obtain, relevant information from the hirer—
  (i) about the basic working and employment conditions in force in the hirer;
  (ii) if needed to assess compliance with regulation 5, about the relevant terms and conditions under which an employee of the hirer is working where—
    (aa) that employee is considered to be a comparable employee in relation to that agency worker for the purposes of regulation 5(4), and
    (bb) those terms and conditions are ordinarily included in the contract of such a comparable employee; and
  (iii) which explains the basis on which it is considered that the employee referred to in sub-paragraph (ii)(aa) is a comparable employee;
(b) where it has received such information, has acted reasonably in determining what the agency worker's basic working and employment conditions should be at the end of the qualifying period and during the period after that until, in accordance with regulation 8, the agency worker ceases to be entitled to the rights conferred by regulation 5; and
(c) ensured that where it has responsibility for applying those basic working and employment conditions to the agency worker, that agency worker has been treated in accordance with the determination described in sub-paragraph (b),

and to the extent that the temporary work agency is not liable under this provision, the hirer shall be liable.

(4) [revoked]

(5) Where more than one temporary work agency is a party to the proceedings, when deciding whether or not each temporary work agency is responsible in full or in part, the employment tribunal shall have regard to the extent to which each agency was responsible for the determination, or application, of any of the agency worker's basic working and employment conditions.

(6) The hirer shall be liable for any breach of regulation 12 or 13.

(7) In relation to the rights conferred by regulation 17—

(a) a temporary work agency shall be liable for any act, or any deliberate failure to act, of that temporary work agency; and
(b) the hirer shall be liable for any act, or any deliberate failure to act, of the hirer.

15 Restrictions on contracting out

Section 203 of the 1996 Act (restrictions on contracting out) shall apply in relation to these Regulations as if they were contained in that Act.

16 [omitted]

17 Unfair dismissal and the right not to be subjected to detriment

(1) An agency worker who is an employee and is dismissed shall be regarded as unfairly dismissed for the purposes of Part 10 of the 1996 Act if the reason (or, if more than one, the principal reason) for the dismissal is a reason specified in paragraph (3).

(2) An agency worker has the right not to be subjected to any detriment by, or as a result of, any act, or any deliberate failure to act, of a temporary work agency or the hirer, done on a ground specified in paragraph (3).

(3) The reasons or, as the case may be, grounds are—

(a) that the agency worker—

(i) brought proceedings under these Regulations;

(ii) gave evidence or information in connection with such proceedings brought by any agency worker;

(iii) made a request under regulation 16 for a written statement;

(iv) otherwise did anything under these Regulations in relation to a temporary work agency, hirer, or any other person;

(v) alleged that a temporary work agency or hirer has breached these Regulations;

(vi) refused (or proposed to refuse) to forgo a right conferred by these Regulations; or

(b) that the hirer or a temporary work agency believes or suspects that the agency worker has done or intends to do any of the things mentioned in sub-paragraph (a).

(4) Where the reason or principal reason for subjection to any act or deliberate failure to act is that mentioned in paragraph (3)(a)(v), or paragraph 3(b) so far as it relates to paragraph (3)(a)(v), neither paragraph (1) nor paragraph (2) applies if the allegation made by the agency worker is false and not made in good faith.

(5) Paragraph (2) does not apply where the detriment in question amounts to a dismissal of an employee within the meaning of Part 10 of the 1996 Act.

18 Complaints to employment tribunals etc.

(1) In this regulation 'respondent' includes the hirer and any temporary work agency.

(2) Subject to regulation 17(5), an agency worker may present a complaint to an employment tribunal that a temporary work agency or the hirer has infringed a right conferred on the agency worker by regulation 5, 12, 13 or 17(2).

(3) [revoked]

(4) Subject to paragraph (5), an employment tribunal shall not consider a complaint under this regulation unless it is presented before the end of the period of three months beginning—

(a) in the case of an alleged infringement of a right conferred by regulation 5, 12 or 17(2), with the date of the infringement, detriment or breach to which the complaint relates or, where an act or failure to act is part of a series of similar acts or failures comprising the infringement, detriment or breach, the last of them;

(b) in the case of an alleged infringement of the right conferred by regulation 13, with the date, or if more than one the last date, on which other individuals, whether or not employed by the hirer, were informed of the vacancy.

(4A) [omitted]

(5) A tribunal may consider any such complaint which is out of time if, in all the circumstances of the case, it considers that it is just and equitable to do so.

(6) For the purposes of calculating the date of the infringement, detriment or breach, under paragraph (4)(a)—

(a) where a term in a contract infringes a right conferred by regulation 5, 12 or 17(2), that infringement or breach shall be treated, subject to sub-paragraph (b), as taking place on each day of the period during which the term infringes that right or breaches that duty;
(b) a deliberate failure to act that is contrary to regulation 5, 12 or 17(2) shall be treated as done when it was decided on.

(7) In the absence of evidence establishing the contrary, a person (P) shall be taken for the purposes of paragraph (6)(b) to decide not to act—
(a) when P does an act inconsistent with doing the failed act; or
(b) if P has done no such inconsistent act, when the period expires within which P might reasonably have been expected to have done the failed act if it was to be done.

(8) Where an employment tribunal finds that a complaint presented to it under this regulation is well founded, it shall take such of the following steps as it considers just and equitable—
(a) making a declaration as to the rights of the complainant in relation to the matters to which the complaint relates;
(b) ordering the respondent to pay compensation to the complainant;
(c) recommending that the respondent take, within a specified period, action appearing to the tribunal to be reasonable, in all the circumstances of the case, for the purpose of obviating or reducing the adverse effect on the complainant of any matter to which the complaint relates.

(9) Where a tribunal orders compensation under paragraph (8)(b), and there is more than one respondent, the amount of compensation payable by each or any respondent shall be such as may be found by the tribunal to be just and equitable having regard to the extent of each respondent's responsibility for the infringement to which the complaint relates.

(10) Subject to paragraphs (12) and (13), where a tribunal orders compensation under paragraph (8)(b), the amount of the compensation awarded shall be such as the tribunal considers just and equitable in all the circumstances having regard to—
(a) the infringement or breach to which the complaint relates; and
(b) any loss which is attributable to the infringement.

(11) The loss shall be taken to include—
(a) any expenses reasonably incurred by the complainant in consequence of the infringement or breach; and
(b) loss of any benefit which the complainant might reasonably be expected to have had but for the infringement or breach.

(12) Subject to paragraph (13), where a tribunal orders compensation under paragraph (8)(b), any compensation which relates to an infringement or breach of the rights—
(a) conferred by regulation 5; or
(b) conferred by regulation 17(2) to the extent that the infringement or breach relates to regulation 5,

shall not be less than two weeks' pay, calculated in accordance with regulation 19.

(13) Paragraph (12) does not apply where the tribunal considers that in all the circumstances of the case, taking into account the conduct of the claimant and respondent, two weeks' pay is not a just and equitable amount of compensation, and the amount shall be reduced as the tribunal consider appropriate.

(14) Where a tribunal finds that regulation 9(4) applies and orders compensation under paragraph (8)(b), the tribunal may make an additional award of compensation under paragraph 8(b), which shall not be more than £5,000, and where there is more than one respondent the proportion of any additional compensation awarded that is payable by each of them shall be such as the tribunal considers just and equitable having regard to the extent to which it considers each to have been responsible for the fact that regulation 9(4)(a) applies.

(14A) In relation to an infringement or breach for which a tribunal orders a respondent to pay compensation under paragraph (8)(b), the tribunal may order the respondent also to pay a penalty under section 12A of the Employment Tribunals Act 1996 only if the tribunal decides not to exercise the power under paragraph (14) to make an additional award of compensation against the respondent.

(15) Compensation in respect of treating an agency worker in a manner which infringes the right conferred by regulation 5, 12 or 13, shall not include compensation for injury to feelings.

(16) In ascertaining the loss the tribunal shall apply the same rule concerning the duty of a person to mitigate loss as applies to damages recoverable under the common law of England and Wales or (as the case may be) the law of Scotland.

(17) Where the tribunal finds that the act, or failure to act, to which the complaint relates was to any extent caused or contributed to by action of the complainant, it shall reduce the amount of the compensation by such proportion as it considers just and equitable having regard to that finding.

(18) If a temporary work agency or the hirer fails, without reasonable justification, to comply with a recommendation made by an employment tribunal under paragraph (8)(c) the tribunal may, if it thinks it just and equitable to do so—

- (a) increase the amount of compensation required to be paid to the complainant in respect of the complaint, where an order was made under paragraph (8)(b); or
- (b) make an order under paragraph (8)(b).

18A [omitted]

19 Calculating a week's pay

(1) For the purposes of regulation 18(12)—

- (a) a week's pay shall be the higher of—
  - (i) the average weekly pay received by the agency worker, in relation to the assignment to which the claim relates, in the relevant period; and
  - (ii) the average weekly pay the agency worker should have been receiving by virtue of regulation 5, in relation to the assignment to which the claim relates, in the relevant period; and
- (b) for the purposes of this paragraph, only payments in respect of basic pay whether by way of annual salary, payments for actual time worked or by reference to output or otherwise shall be taken into account.

(2) The relevant period is—

- (a) where the assignment has ended on or before the date the complaint was presented to the tribunal under regulation 18(2), the four week period (or in a case where the assignment was shorter than four weeks, that period) ending with the last day of the assignment to which the claim relates; or
- (b) where the assignment has not so ended the four week period (or in the case where that assignment was shorter than four weeks, that period) ending with the date of the complaint.

20 Liability of employers and principals

(1) Anything done by a person in the course of employment shall be treated for the purposes of these Regulations as also done by their employer, whether or not it was done with that employer's knowledge or approval.

(2) Anything done by a person as agent for the employer with the authority of the employer shall be treated for the purposes of these Regulations as also done by the employer.

(3) In proceedings under these Regulations against any person in respect of an act alleged to have been done by an employee of that person, it shall be a defence for that person to prove that he or she took such steps as were reasonably practicable to prevent the employee from—

- (a) doing that act; or
- (b) doing, in the course of his or her employment, acts of that description.

21–25 [omitted]

The Employment Relations Act 1999 (Blacklists) Regulations 2010

(SI 2010 No. 493)

1 [omitted]

2 Interpretation

(1) In these Regulations—

'employment agency' means a person who, for profit or not, provides services for the purposes of finding employment for workers or supplying employers with workers, and does not include a trade union by reason only of the services a trade union provides only for and in relation to its members;

'office', in relation to a trade union, means any position—

(a) by virtue of which the holder is an official of the trade union, or

(b) to which Chapter 4 of Part 1 of the Trade Union and Labour Relations (Consolidation) Act 1992 (duty to hold elections) applies,

and 'official' has the meaning given by section 119 of that Act;

'prohibited list' has the meaning given by regulation 3(2);

'services', in relation to an employment agency, means services for the purposes of finding employment for workers or supplying employers with workers;

'use', in relation to a prohibited list, includes use of information contained in the list.

(2) References in these regulations to information supplied by a person who contravenes regulation 3 include information supplied by a person who would contravene that regulation if that person's actions took place in Great Britain.

General prohibition

3 General prohibition

(1) Subject to regulation 4, no person shall compile, use, sell or supply a prohibited list.

(2) A 'prohibited list' is a list which—

(a) contains details of persons who are or have been members of trade unions or persons who are taking part or have taken part in the activities of trade unions, and

(b) is compiled with a view to being used by employers or employment agencies for the purposes of discrimination in relation to recruitment or in relation to the treatment of workers.

(3) 'Discrimination' means treating a person less favourably than another on grounds of trade union membership or trade union activities.

(4) In these Regulations references to membership of a trade union include references to—

(a) membership of a particular branch or section of a trade union, and

(b) membership of one of a number of particular branches or sections of a trade union;

and references to taking part in the activities of a trade union have a corresponding meaning.

4 Exceptions to general prohibition

(1) A person does not contravene regulation 3 in the following cases.

(2) The first case is where a person supplies a prohibited list, but—

(a) does not know they are supplying a prohibited list, and

(b) could not reasonably be expected to know they are supplying a prohibited list.

(3) The second case is where a person compiles, uses or supplies a prohibited list, but—

(a) in doing so, that person's sole or principal purpose is to make known a contravention of regulation 3 or the possibility of such a contravention,

(b) no information in relation to a person whose details are included in the prohibited list is published without the consent of that person, and

(c) in all the circumstances compiling, using or supplying the prohibited list is justified in the public interest.

(4) The third case is where a person compiles, uses, sells or supplies a prohibited list, but in doing so that person's sole or principal purpose is to apply a requirement either—

(a) that a person may not be considered for appointment to an office or for employment unless that person has experience or knowledge of trade union matters, and in all the circumstances it is reasonable to apply such a requirement, or

(b) that a person may not be considered for appointment or election to an office in a trade union unless he is a member of the union.

(5) The fourth case is where a person compiles, uses, sells or supplies a prohibited list, but the compilation, use, sale or supply of the prohibited list is required or authorised—

(a) under an enactment,

(b) by any rule of law, or

(c) by an order of the court.

(6) The fifth case is where a person uses or supplies a prohibited list—

(a) for the purpose of, or in connection with, legal proceedings (including prospective legal proceedings), or

(b) for the purpose of giving or obtaining legal advice,

where the use or supply is necessary in order to determine whether these regulations have been, are being or will be complied with.

Refusal of employment or employment agency services

5 Refusal of employment

(1) A person (P) has a right of complaint to an employment tribunal against another (R) if R refuses to employ P for a reason which relates to a prohibited list, and either—

(a) R contravenes regulation 3 in relation to that list, or

(b) R—

(i) relies on information supplied by a person who contravenes that regulation in relation to that list, and

(ii) knows or ought reasonably to know that the information relied on is supplied in contravention of that regulation.

(2) R shall be taken to refuse to employ P if P seeks employment of any description with R and R—

(a) refuses or deliberately omits to entertain and process P's application or enquiry;

(b) causes P to withdraw or cease to pursue P's application or enquiry;

(c) refuses or deliberately omits to offer P employment of that description;

(d) makes P an offer of such employment the terms of which are such as no reasonable employer who wished to fill the post would offer and which is not accepted; or

(e) makes P an offer of such employment but withdraws it or causes P not to accept it.

(3) If there are facts from which the tribunal could conclude, in the absence of any other explanation, that R contravened regulation 3 or relied on information supplied in contravention of that regulation, the tribunal must find that such a contravention or reliance on information occurred unless R shows that it did not.

6 Refusal of employment agency services

(1) A person (P) has a right of complaint to an employment tribunal against an employment agency (E) if E refuses P any of its services for a reason which relates to a prohibited list, and either—

(a) E contravenes regulation 3 in relation to that list, or

(b) E—

(i) relies on information supplied by a person who contravenes that regulation in relation to that list, and

(ii) knows or ought reasonably to know that information relied on is supplied in contravention of that regulation.

(2) E shall be taken to refuse P a service if P seeks to make use of the service and E—

(a) refuses or deliberately omits to make the service available to P;

(b) causes P not to make use of the service or to cease to make use of it; or

(c) does not provide P the same service, on the same terms, as is provided to others.

(3) If there are facts from which the tribunal could conclude, in the absence of any other explanation, that E contravened regulation 3 or relied on information supplied in contravention of that regulation, the tribunal must find that such a contravention or reliance on information occurred unless E shows that it did not.

7 Time limit for proceedings under regulation 5 or 6

(1) Subject to paragraph (2), an employment tribunal shall not consider a complaint under regulation 5 or 6 unless it is presented to the tribunal before the end of the period of three months beginning with the date of the conduct to which the complaint relates.

(1A) [omitted]

(2) An employment tribunal may consider a complaint under regulation 5 or 6 that is otherwise out of time if, in all the circumstances of the case, it considers that it is just and equitable to do so.

(3) The date of the conduct to which a complaint under regulation 5 relates shall be taken to be—

(a) in the case of an actual refusal, the date of the refusal;

(b) in the case of a deliberate omission—

(i) to entertain and process P's application or enquiry, or

(ii) to offer employment,

the end of the period within which it was reasonable to expect R to act;

(c) in the case of conduct causing P to withdraw or cease to pursue P's application or enquiry, the date of that conduct;

(d) in a case where R made but withdrew an offer, the date R withdrew the offer;

(e) in any other case where R made an offer which was not accepted, the date on which R made the offer.

(4) The date of the conduct to which a complaint under regulation 6 relates shall be taken to be—

(a) in the case of an actual refusal, the date of the refusal;

(b) in the case of a deliberate omission to make a service available, the end of the period within which it was reasonable to expect E to act;

(c) in the case of conduct causing P not make use of a service or to cease to make use of it, the date of that conduct;

(d) in the case of failure to provide the same service, on the same terms, as is provided to others, the date or last date on which the service in fact was provided.

8 Remedies in proceedings under regulation 5 or 6

(1) Where an employment tribunal finds that a complaint under regulation 5 or 6 is well-founded, it shall make a declaration to that effect and may make such of the following as it considers just and equitable—

(a) an order requiring the respondent to pay compensation;

(b) a recommendation that the respondent take within a specified period action appearing to the tribunal to be practicable for the purpose of obviating or reducing the adverse effect on the complainant of any conduct to which the complaint relates.

(2) Compensation shall be assessed on the same basis as damages for breach of statutory duty and may include compensation for injury to feelings.

(3) Where an award of compensation is made, the amount of compensation before any increase or reduction is made under paragraph (4), (5) or (6) shall not be less than £5,000.

(4) If the respondent fails without reasonable justification to comply with a recommendation under paragraph (1)(b), the tribunal may increase its award of compensation or, if it has not made such an award, make one.

(5) Where the tribunal considers that any conduct of the complainant before the refusal to which the complaint under regulation 5 or 6 relates was such that it would be just and equitable to reduce the award of compensation, the tribunal shall reduce that amount accordingly.

(6) The amount of compensation shall be reduced or further reduced by the amount of any compensation awarded by the tribunal under section 140 of the Trade Union and Labour Relations (Consolidation) Act 1992 in respect of the same refusal.

(7) The total amount of compensation shall not exceed £65,300.

Detriment

9 Detriment

(1) A person (P) has a right of complaint to an employment tribunal against P's employer (D) if D, by any act or any deliberate failure to act, subjects P to a detriment for a reason which relates to a prohibited list, and either—

- (a) D contravenes regulation 3 in relation to that list, or
- (b) D—
  - (i) relies on information supplied by a person who contravenes that regulation in relation to that list, and
  - (ii) knows or ought reasonably to know that information relied on is supplied in contravention of that regulation.

(2) If there are facts from which the tribunal could conclude, in the absence of any other explanation, that D contravened regulation 3 or relied on information supplied in contravention of that regulation, the tribunal must find that such a contravention or reliance on information occurred unless D shows that it did not.

(3) This regulation does not apply where the detriment in question amounts to the dismissal of an employee within the meaning in Part 10 of the Employment Rights Act 1996.

10 Time limit for proceedings under regulation 9

(1) Subject to paragraph (2), an employment tribunal shall not consider a complaint under regulation 9 unless it is presented before the end of the period of three months beginning with the date of the act or failure to which the complaint relates or, where that act or failure is part of a series of similar acts or failures (or both) the last of them.

(1A) [omitted]

(2) An employment tribunal may consider a complaint under regulation 9 that is otherwise out of time if, in all the circumstances of the case, it considers that it is just and equitable to do so.

(3) For the purposes of paragraph (1)—

- (a) where an act extends over a period, the reference to the date of the act is a reference to the last day of the period;
- (b) a failure to act shall be treated as done when it was decided on.

(4) For the purposes of paragraph (3), in the absence of evidence establishing the contrary D shall be taken to decide on a failure to act—

- (a) when D does an act which is inconsistent with doing the failed act, or
- (b) if D has done no such inconsistent act, when the period expires within which D might reasonably have been expected to do the failed act if it was done.

11 Remedies in proceedings under regulation 9

(1) Where the employment tribunal finds that a complaint under regulation 9 is well-founded, it shall make a declaration to that effect and may make an award of compensation to be paid by D to P in respect of the act or failure complained of.

(2) Subject to the following paragraphs, the amount of the compensation awarded shall be such as the tribunal considers just and equitable in all the circumstances having regard to the act or failure complained of and to any loss sustained by P which is attributable to D's act or failure.

(3) The loss shall be taken to include—

(a) any expenses P reasonably incurred in consequence of the act or failure complained of; and

(b) loss of any benefit which P might reasonably be expected to have had but for that act or failure.

(4) In ascertaining the loss, the tribunal shall apply the same rule concerning the duty of a person to mitigate his loss as applies to damages recoverable under the common law of England and Wales or Scotland.

(5) Where an award of compensation is made, the amount of compensation before any increase or reduction is made under paragraphs (6), (7) and (8) of this regulation and section 207A of the Trade Union and Labour Relations (Consolidation) Act 1992 shall not be less than £5,000.

(6) Where the conduct of P before the act or failure complained of was such that it would be just and equitable to reduce the amount of compensation, the tribunal shall reduce that amount accordingly.

(7) Where the tribunal finds that the act or failure complained of was to any extent caused or contributed to by action of P, it shall reduce or further reduce the amount of the compensation by such proportion as it considers just and equitable having regard to that finding.

(8) The amount of compensation shall be reduced or further reduced by the amount of any compensation awarded by the tribunal under section 149 of the Trade Union and Labour Relations (Consolidation) Act 1992 in respect of the same act or failure.

(9) In determining the amount of compensation to be awarded no account shall be taken of any pressure exercised on D by calling, organising, procuring or financing a strike or other industrial action, or by threatening to do so; and that question shall be determined as if no such pressure had been exercised.

(10) Where P is a worker and the detriment to which P is subjected is the termination of P's contract, and that contract is not a contract of employment, the compensation awarded to P under this regulation shall not exceed £65,300.

12 [omitted]

Action for breach of statutory duty

13 Action for breach of statutory duty

(1) A contravention of regulation 3 is actionable as a breach of statutory duty.

(2) If there are facts from which the court could conclude, in the absence of any other explanation, that the defendant has contravened, or is likely to contravene, regulation 3, the court must find that such a contravention occurred, or is likely to occur, unless the defendant shows that it did not, or is not likely to, occur.

(3) In proceedings brought by virtue of this regulation, the court may (without prejudice to any of its other powers)—

(a) make such order as it considers appropriate for the purpose of restraining or preventing the defendant from contravening regulation 3; and

(b) award damages, which may include compensation for injured feelings.

(4) A person may complain to an employment tribunal under regulation 5, 6 or 9, or under Part 10 of the Employment Rights Act 1996 (unfair dismissal) as it applies by virtue of these Regulations and bring an action for breach of statutory duty in respect of the same conduct for the purpose of restraining or preventing the defendant from contravening regulation 3.

(5) Except as mentioned in paragraph (4), a person may not bring an action for breach of statutory duty and complain to an employment tribunal under regulation 5, 6 or 9, or under Part 10 of

the Employment Rights Act 1996 (unfair dismissal) as it applies by virtue of these Regulations, in respect of the same conduct.

14–18 [omitted]

The Equality Act 2010 (Disability) Regulations 2010

(SI 2010 No. 2128)

1–2 [omitted]

3 Addictions

(1) Subject to paragraph (2) below, addiction to alcohol, nicotine or any other substance is to be treated as not amounting to an impairment for the purposes of the Act.

(2) Paragraph (1) above does not apply to addiction which was originally the result of administration of medically prescribed drugs or other medical treatment.

4 Other conditions not to be treated as impairments

(1) For the purposes of the Act the following conditions are to be treated as not amounting to impairments:—

(a) a tendency to set fires,
(b) a tendency to steal,
(c) a tendency to physical or sexual abuse of other persons,
(d) exhibitionism, and
(e) voyeurism.

(2) Subject to paragraph (3) below, for the purposes of the Act the condition known as seasonal allergic rhinitis shall be treated as not amounting to an impairment.

(3) Paragraph (2) above shall not prevent that condition from being taken into account for the purposes of the Act where it aggravates the effect of any other condition.

5 Tattoos and piercings

For the purposes of paragraph 3 of Schedule 1 to the Act, a severe disfigurement is not to be treated as having a substantial adverse effect on the ability of the person concerned to carry out normal day-to-day activities if it consists of—

(a) a tattoo (which has not been removed), or
(b) a piercing of the body for decorative or other non-medical purposes, including any object attached through the piercing for such purposes.

6 Babies and young children

For the purposes of the Act, where a child under six years of age has an impairment which does not have a substantial and long-term adverse effect on the ability of that child to carry out normal day-to-day activities, the impairment is to be taken to have a substantial and long-term adverse effect on the ability of that child to carry out normal day-to-day activities where it would normally have that effect on the ability of a person aged 6 years or over to carry out normal day-to-day activities.

7 Persons deemed to have a disability

A person is deemed to have a disability, and hence to be a disabled person, for the purposes of the Act where that person is certified as blind, severely sight impaired, sight impaired or partially sighted by a consultant ophthalmologist.

8–15 [omitted]

Shared Parental Leave Regulations 2014

(SI 2014 No. 3050)

PART 2

Chapter 1

4 Mother's entitlement to shared parental leave
5 Father's or partner's entitlement to shared parental leave
6 Calculation of total amount of shared parental leave available (birth)
7 Periods when shared parental leave may be taken
8 Mother's notice of entitlement and intention to take shared parental leave
9 Father's or partner's notice of entitlement and intention to take shared parental leave

PART 4

35 Continuity of employment test
36 Employment and earnings test

1–3 [omitted]

PART 2 ENTITLEMENT TO SHARED PARENTAL LEAVE (BIRTH)

Chapter 1

Entitlement to leave—general

4 Mother's entitlement to shared parental leave

(1) M is entitled to be absent from work to take shared parental leave in accordance with Chapter 2 to care for C if she satisfies the conditions specified in paragraph (2) and P satisfies the conditions specified in paragraph (3).

(2) The conditions are that—

(a) M satisfies the continuity of employment test (see regulation 35);

(b) M has, at the date of C's birth, the main responsibility for the care of C (apart from the responsibility of P);

(c) M is entitled to statutory maternity leave in respect of C;

(d) M has ended any entitlement to statutory maternity leave by curtailing that leave under section 71(3)(ba) or 73(3)(a) of the 1996 Act (and that leave remains curtailed) or, where M has not curtailed in that way, M has returned to work before the end of her statutory maternity leave;

(e) M has complied with regulation 8 (notice to employer of entitlement to shared parental leave);

(f) M has complied with regulation 10(3) to (5) (evidence for employer); and

(g) M has given a period of leave notice in accordance with regulation 12.

(3) The conditions are that—

(a) P satisfies the employment and earnings test (see regulation 36); and

(b) P has, at the date of C's birth, the main responsibility for the care of C (apart from the responsibility of M).

(4) Entitlement under paragraph (1) is not affected by the number of children born or expected as a result of the same pregnancy.

5 Father's or partner's entitlement to shared parental leave

(1) P is entitled to be absent from work to take shared parental leave in accordance with Chapter 2 to care for C if P satisfies the conditions specified in paragraph (2) and M satisfies the conditions specified in paragraph (3).

(2) The conditions are that—

(a) P satisfies the continuity of employment test (see regulation 35);

(b) P has, at the date of C's birth, the main responsibility for the care of C (apart from the responsibility of M);

(c) P has complied with regulation 9 (notice to employer of entitlement to shared parental leave);

(d) P has complied with regulation 10(3) to (5) (evidence for employer); and

(e) P has given a period of leave notice in accordance with regulation 12.

(3) The conditions are that—

(a) M satisfies the employment and earnings test (see regulation 36);

(b) M has, at the date of C's birth, the main responsibility for the care of C (apart from the responsibility of P);

(c) M is entitled to statutory maternity leave, statutory maternity pay, or maternity allowance in respect of C; and

(d) where—

(i) M is entitled to statutory maternity leave, she has ended any entitlement to statutory maternity leave by curtailing that leave under section 71(3)(ba) or section 73(3)(a) of the 1996 Act (and that leave remains curtailed) or, where M has not curtailed in that way, M has returned to work before the end of her statutory maternity leave,

(ii) M is not entitled to statutory maternity leave but is entitled to statutory maternity pay, she has curtailed the maternity pay period under section 165(3A) of the 1992 Act (and that period remains curtailed), or

(iii) M is not entitled to statutory maternity leave but is entitled to maternity allowance, she has curtailed the maternity allowance period under section 35(3A) of that Act (and that period remains curtailed).

(4) Entitlement under paragraph (1) is not affected by the number of children born or expected as a result of the same pregnancy.

6 Calculation of total amount of shared parental leave available (birth)

(1) Where M is entitled to statutory maternity leave, subject to paragraph (10), the total amount of shared parental leave available to M and P in relation to C is 52 weeks less—

(a) where there is a leave curtailment date, the number of weeks of statutory maternity leave beginning with the first day of statutory maternity leave taken by M and ending with the leave curtailment date (irrespective of whether or not M returns to work before that date), or

(b) where M's statutory maternity leave ends without her curtailing that leave under section 71(3) or section 73(3) of the 1996 Act, the number of weeks of statutory maternity leave taken.

(2) Where M is not entitled to statutory maternity leave, but is entitled to statutory maternity pay, subject to paragraph (11), the total amount of shared parental leave available to P in relation to C is 52 weeks less—

(a) where M returns to work without reducing her statutory maternity pay period under section 165(3A) of the 1992 Act, the number of weeks of statutory maternity pay payable to M in respect of C before M returns to work, or

(b) in any other case, the number of weeks of statutory maternity pay payable to M in respect of C up to the pay curtailment date.

(3) Where M is not entitled to statutory maternity leave, but is entitled to maternity allowance, the total amount of shared parental leave available to P in relation to C is 52 weeks less—

(a) where M returns to work without reducing her maternity allowance period under section 35(3A) of the 1992 Act, the number of weeks of maternity allowance payable to M in respect of C before M returns to work, or

(b) in any other case, the number of weeks of maternity allowance payable to M in respect of C up to the allowance curtailment date.

(4) The total amount of shared parental leave which M is entitled to take in relation to C is the product of the calculation in paragraph (1) less—

(a) any shared parental leave which P has notified under regulation 12 (as varied by any notice under regulation 15),

(b) any period of leave which is required to be taken in accordance with paragraph (2) of regulation 18, and

(c) any weeks of statutory shared parental pay to which P is entitled and during which P is not absent on shared parental leave.

(5) The total amount of shared parental leave which P is entitled to take in relation to C is the product of the calculation in paragraph (1), (2) or (3), as the case may be, less—

(a) any shared parental leave which M has notified under regulation 12 (as varied by any notice under regulation 15),

(b) any period of leave which is required to be taken in accordance with paragraph (1) of regulation 18, and

(c) any weeks of statutory shared parental pay to which M is entitled and during which M is not absent on shared parental leave.

(6) For the purposes of paragraphs (4)(a) and (5)(a), any leave notified but, as a result of M giving a revocation notice, not taken must be disregarded.

(7) For the purposes of paragraph (1), a part of a week in which maternity leave is taken is to be treated as a whole week.

(8) For the purposes of paragraph (2) and (3)—

(a) a part of a week in respect of which statutory maternity pay or maternity allowance is payable is to be treated as a whole week, and

(b) 'week' has the meaning given by section 165(8) of the 1992 Act, in relation to statutory maternity pay, and the meaning given by section 122(1) of that Act, in relation to maternity allowance.

(9) For the purposes of paragraphs (4) and (5), any week of leave or pay notified by M or P, as the case may be, to be taken concurrently from more than one employer is to be treated as one week.

(10) Where M is entitled to take statutory maternity leave from more than one employment, any calculation under paragraph (1) of the total amount of shared parental leave available must be calculated using—

(a) the first day of statutory maternity leave taken by M in relation to C from any employment; and

(b) the later of—

(i) the leave curtailment date, or

(ii) the last day of statutory maternity leave taken by M from any employment in relation to C where that leave ends without her curtailing it under section 71(3) or section 73(3) of the 1996 Act.

(11) Where M is not entitled to statutory maternity leave, but has more than one entitlement to statutory maternity pay—

(a) paragraph (2)(a) is to apply as though it read—

'(a) where M returns to work for all of her employers without reducing her statutory maternity pay periods under section 165(3A) of the 1992 Act, the number of weeks of statutory maternity pay payable to M in respect of C before the last date on which M returns to work, or', and

(b) paragraph (2)(b) is to apply as though it read—

'(b) in any other case, the number of weeks of statutory maternity pay payable to M in respect of C up to the latest pay curtailment date.'.

7 Periods when shared parental leave may be taken

(1) Shared parental leave may be taken at any time within the period which begins on the date C is born (or, where more than one child is born as the result of the same pregnancy, the date on which the first child is born) and ends the day before C's first birthday.

(2) Shared parental leave must be taken in complete weeks.

(3) Shared parental leave may be taken as one continuous period or in discontinuous periods.

(4) The minimum period of shared parental leave which may be taken is one week.

(5) An employee may be absent on shared parental leave in relation to C at the same time that another employee is—

(a) absent on leave provided for in Part 8 of the 1996 Act in relation to C;

(b) in receipt of pay under section 35 or Part 12, 12ZA, or 12ZC of the 1992 Act in relation to C.

8 Mother's notice of entitlement and intention to take shared parental leave

(1) M must, not less than eight weeks before the start date of the first period of shared parental leave to be taken by M, give her employer a written notice which contains the information specified in paragraph (2) and is accompanied by the declarations specified in paragraph (3).

(2) The specified information is—

(a) M's name;

(b) P's name;

(c) the start and end dates of any period of statutory maternity leave taken or to be taken by M;

(d) the total amount of shared parental leave available (in accordance with regulation 6(1));

(e) C's expected week of birth and C's date of birth (except as provided for in paragraph (5));

(f) how much shared parental leave M and P each intend to take;

(g) an indication as to when M intends to take shared parental leave (including the start and end dates for each period of leave).

(3) The specified declarations are—

(a) a declaration signed by M that—

(i) M satisfies, or will satisfy, the conditions in regulation 4(2);

(ii) the information given by M in the notice is accurate;

(iii) M will immediately inform her employer if she ceases to care for C;

(b) a declaration signed by P—

(i) specifying P's name, address, and national insurance number (or a declaration that P does not have a national insurance number);

(ii) that P satisfies, or will satisfy, the conditions in regulation 4(3);

(iii) that P is the father of C, or the person who is married to, or the civil partner or the partner of, M;

(iv) that P consents to the amount of leave which M intends to take (as set out in the notice for the purposes of paragraph (2)(f));

(v) that P consents to M's employer processing the information in P's declaration.

(4) The references to P in paragraphs (2) and (3) are references to the individual who satisfies paragraph (3) of regulation 4.

(5) Where a notice is given under paragraph (1) before C is born, M must give C's date of birth to her employer as soon as reasonably practicable after the birth of C and, in any event, before the first period of shared parental leave to be taken by M.

(6) The indication provided in accordance with paragraph (2)(g) is non-binding and must not be treated as a period of leave notice unless otherwise indicated in the notice.

9 Father's or partner's notice of entitlement and intention to take shared parental leave

(1) P must, not less than eight weeks before the start date of the first period of shared parental leave to be taken by P, give P's employer a written notice which contains the information specified in paragraph (2) and is accompanied by the declarations specified in paragraph (3).

(2) The specified information is—

(a) P's name;

(b) M's name;

(c) the start and end dates of any—

(i) period of statutory maternity leave taken or to be taken by M;

(ii) period in respect of which statutory maternity pay received or to be received by M (where statutory maternity leave was not taken or is not be taken in relation to that period) is payable; or

(iii) period in respect of which maternity allowance received or to be received by M (where statutory maternity leave was not taken or is not be taken in relation to that period) is payable;

(d) the total amount of shared parental leave available (in accordance with regulation 6(1), (2) or (3));

(e) C's expected week of birth and C's date of birth (except as provided for in paragraph (4));

(f) how much shared parental leave P and M each intend to take;

(g) an indication as to when P intends to take shared parental leave (including the start and end dates for each period of leave).

(3) The specified declarations are—

(a) a declaration signed by P that—

(i) P satisfies, or will satisfy, the conditions in regulation 5(2);

(ii) the information given by P in the notice is accurate;

(iii) that P is the father of C, or the person who is married to, or the civil partner or the partner of, M;

(iv) P will immediately inform P's employer if P ceases to care for C or if M informs P that she has ceased to satisfy the condition in regulation 5(3)(d);

(b) a declaration signed by M—

(i) specifying M's name, address, and national insurance number (or a declaration that M does not have a national insurance number);

(ii) that M satisfies, or will satisfy, the conditions in regulation 5(3);

(iii) that M consents to the amount of leave which P intends to take (as set out in the notice for the purposes of paragraph (2)(f));

(iv) that M will immediately inform P if she ceases to satisfy the conditions in regulation 5(3)(d);

(v) that M consents to P's employer processing the information in M's declaration.

(4) Where a notice is given under paragraph (1) before C is born, P must give C's date of birth to P's employer as soon as reasonably practicable after the birth of C and, in any event, before the first period of shared parental leave to be taken by P.

(5) The indication provided in accordance with paragraph (2)(g) is non-binding and must not be treated as a period of leave notice unless otherwise indicated in the notice.

PART 4 CONDITIONS OF ENTITLEMENT RELATING TO EMPLOYMENT AND EARNINGS

35 Continuity of employment test

(1) For the purposes of entitlement to shared parental leave (see regulations 4, 5, 20 and 21), an employee satisfies the continuity of employment test if the employee—

(a) has been continuously employed with an employer for a period of not less than 26 weeks ending with the relevant week (see paragraph (3)); and

(b) remains in continuous employment with that employer until the week before any period of shared parental leave taken by the employee.

(2) Where Part 2 applies and C is born earlier than the relevant week and an employee would have satisfied the condition in sub-paragraph (a) of paragraph (1) if the employee's employment had continued until the end of the week immediately preceding that week, the employee must be treated as having satisfied that condition.

(3) In this regulation—

'relevant week' means—

(a) where Part 2 applies, the week immediately preceding the 14th week before the expected week of birth;

(b) where Part 3 applies, the week in which A was notified of having been matched for adoption with C.

36 Employment and earnings test

(1) An individual satisfies the employment and earnings test if that individual—

(a) has been engaged in employment as an employed or self-employed earner for any part of the week in the case of at least 26 of the 66 weeks immediately preceding the calculation week; and

(b) has average weekly earnings (determined in accordance with paragraph (2)) of not less than the amount set out in section 35(6A) of the 1992 Act in relation to the tax year preceding the tax year containing the calculation week.

(2) An individual's average weekly earnings are determined by dividing by 13 the specified payments made, or treated as being made, to or for the benefit of that individual, in the 13 weeks (whether or not consecutive) in the period of 66 weeks immediately preceding the calculation week in which the payments are greatest.

(3) Where an individual receives any pay after the end of the period in paragraph (2) in respect of any week falling within that period, the average weekly amount is to be determined as if such sum had been paid in that period.

(4) Where an individual is not paid weekly, the payments made, or treated as made, to or for the benefit of that individual or for that individual's benefit for the purposes of paragraph (2), must be determined by dividing the total sum paid to that individual by the nearest whole number of weeks in respect of which that sum is paid.

(5) In this regulation—

'calculation week' means—

(a) where Part 2 applies, the expected week of birth;

(b) where Part 3 applies, the week in which A was notified of having been matched for adoption with C.

'employed earner' has the meaning given by section 2 of the 1992 Act, subject for these purposes to the effect of regulations made under section 2(2)(b) of that Act;

'self-employed earner' has the meaning given by section 2 of the 1992 Act, subject for these purposes to the effect of regulations made under section 2(2)(b) of that Act;

'specified payments'—

(a) in relation to a self-employed earner who satisfies the conditions in paragraph (6), are to be treated as made to the self-employed earner at an amount per week equal to the amount set out in section 35(6A) of the 1992 Act that is in force at the end of the week;

(b) in relation to an employed earner, are all payments made to the employed earner or for the employed earner's benefit as an employed earner specified in regulation 2 (specified payments for employed earners) of the Social Security (Maternity Allowance) (Earnings) Regulations 2000; and

'tax year' means the 12 months beginning with the 6th April in any year.

(6) The conditions referred to in paragraph (a) of the definition of 'specified payments' are that, in respect of any week, the self-employed earner—

(a) does not hold a certificate of exception issued pursuant to regulation 44(1) of the Social Security (Contributions) Regulations 2001 and has paid a Class 2 contribution (within the meaning of section 1 of the 1992 Act), or

(b) holds such a certificate of exception.

37–46 [omitted]

The Exclusivity Terms in Zero Hours Contracts (Redress) Regulations 2015

(SI 2015 No. 2021)

1 [omitted]

2 Unfair dismissal and the right not to be subjected to detriment

(1) An employee who works under a zero hours contract is to be regarded for the purposes of Part 10 of the 1996 Act as unfairly dismissed if the reason (or, if more than one, the principal reason) for the dismissal is the reason specified in paragraph (3).

(2) A worker who works under a zero hours contract has the right not to be subjected to any detriment by, or as a result of, any act, or any deliberate failure to act, of an employer done for the reason specified in paragraph (3).

(3) The reason is that the worker breached a provision or purported provision of the zero hours contract to which section 27A(3) of the 1996 Act applies.

(4) Paragraph (2) does not apply where the detriment in question amounts to a dismissal of an employee within the meaning of Part 10 of the 1996 Act.

(5) Section 108 of the 1996 Act (qualifying period of employment) does not apply in relation to a dismissal to which paragraph (1) applies.

3 Complaints to employment tribunals

(1) Subject to regulation 2(4), a worker may present a complaint to an employment tribunal that an employer has infringed the right conferred on the worker by regulation 2(2).

(2) Subject to paragraph (3), an employment tribunal must not consider a complaint under this regulation unless it is presented before the end of the period of three months beginning with the date of the act or failure to act to which the complaint relates or, where that act or failure is part of a series of similar acts or failures, the last of them.

(2A) [omitted]

(3) A tribunal may consider any such complaint which is out of time if, in all the circumstances of the case, it considers that it is just and equitable to do so.

(4) For the purposes of paragraph (2)—

(a) where an act extends over a period, the 'date of the act' means the last day of that period; and

(b) failure to do something is to be treated as occurring when the person in question decided on it.

(5) In the absence of evidence to the contrary, a person (P) is to be taken to decide on failure to do something—

(a) when P does an act inconsistent with doing it, or

(b) if P does no inconsistent act, on the expiry of the period in which P might reasonably have been expected to do it.

(6) Where a worker presents a complaint under this regulation it is for the employer to identify the ground on which any act, or deliberate failure to act, was done.

3A [omitted]

4 Remedies

(1) Where an employment tribunal finds that a complaint presented to it under regulation 3 is well founded, it must take such of the following steps as it considers just and equitable—

(a) making a declaration as to the rights of the complainant and the employer in relation to the matters to which the complaint relates; and

(b) ordering the employer to pay compensation to the complainant.

(2) Subject to paragraphs (5) and (6), where a tribunal orders compensation under paragraph (1)(b), the amount of the compensation awarded must be such as the tribunal considers just and equitable in all the circumstances having regard to—

(a) the infringement to which the complaint relates; and

(b) any loss which is attributable to the act, or failure to act, which infringed the complainant's right.

(3) The loss must be taken to include—

(a) any expenses reasonably incurred by the complainant in consequence of the act, or failure to act, to which the complaint relates; and

(b) loss of any benefit which the complainant might reasonably be expected to have had but for that act or failure to act.

(4) In ascertaining the loss the tribunal must apply the same rule concerning the duty of a person to mitigate loss as applies to damages recoverable under the common law of England and Wales or (as the case may be) the law of Scotland.

(5) Where—

(a) the detriment to which the worker is subjected is the termination of the worker's contract, but

(b) that contract is not a contract of employment,

any compensation awarded under paragraph (1)(b) must not exceed the limit specified in paragraph (6).

(6) The limit is the total of—

(a) the sum which would be the basic award for unfair dismissal, calculated in accordance with section 119 of the 1996 Act, if the worker had been an employee and the contract terminated had been a contract of employment; and

(b) the sum for the time being specified in section 124(1ZA) of the 1996 Act which is the limit for a compensatory award to a person calculated in accordance with section 123 of the 1996 Act.

(7) Where the tribunal finds that the act, or failure to act, to which the complaint relates was to any extent caused or contributed to by action of the complainant, it must reduce the amount of the compensation by such proportion as it considers just and equitable having regard to that finding.

5 [omitted]

The Exclusivity Terms for Zero Hours Workers (Unenforceability and Redress) Regulations 2022

(SI 2022 No. 1145)

2 Interpretation

In these Regulations—

'the 1996 Act' means the Employment Rights Act 1996;

'exclusivity term' means any provision or purported provision of a contract which—

(a) prohibits the worker from doing work or performing services under another contract or under any other arrangement; or

(b) prohibits the worker from doing so without the employer's consent;

'the lower earnings limit' is the amount specified for the purpose of section 5(1)(a) of the Social Security Contributions and Benefits Act 1992;

'specified contract' has the meaning given in regulation 3(2);

'wages' has the same meaning as in section 27 of the 1996 Act;

'zero hours contract' has the same meaning as in section 27A of the 1996 Act.

PART 2 UNENFORCEABILITY

3 Unenforceability

(1) Any provision of a specified contract which contains an exclusivity term is unenforceable against a worker.

(2) In these Regulations, a 'specified contract' is a contract of employment or other worker's contract which is not a zero hours contract and entitles a worker to be paid under that contract, net average weekly wages that do not exceed the lower earnings limit.

(3) A specified contract is specified for the purpose of section 27B(2)(c) of the 1996 Act.

PART 3 CALCULATION OF NET AVERAGE WEELY WAGES

4 Permanent contracts of employment or other worker's contracts

Where the contract of employment or other worker's contract is permanent, the average weekly wages are calculated by dividing by 52 the total remuneration to which the worker is entitled under that contract in respect of a period of 52 weeks.

5 All other contracts of employment or other worker's contracts

Where regulation 4 does not apply, the average weekly wages are calculated by dividing the total remuneration to which the worker is entitled under their contract by the number of weeks during which their contract is expected to continue.

6 Net average weekly wages

The net average weekly wages are calculated by subtracting all deductions of whatever nature from the average weekly wages.

PART 4 REDRESS AND REMEDIES

7 Unfair dismissal and the right not to be subjected to a detriment

(1) An employee who works under a specified contract is to be regarded for the purpose of Part 10 of the 1996 Act as unfairly dismissed if the reason (or, if more than one, the principal reason) for the dismissal is the reason specified in paragraph (3).

(2) A worker who works under a specified contract has the right not to be subjected to any detriment by, or as a result of, any act, or any deliberate failure to act, of an employer done for the reason specified in paragraph (3).

(3) The reason is that the worker breached an exclusivity term of their specified contract.

(4) Paragraph (2) does not apply where the detriment in question amounts to a dismissal of an employee within the meaning of Part 10 of the 1996 Act.

(5) Section 108 of the 1996 Act (qualifying period of employment) does not apply in relation to a dismissal to which paragraph (1) applies.

8 Complaints to employment tribunals

(1) Subject to regulation 7(4), a worker may present a complaint to an employment tribunal that an employer has infringed the right conferred on the worker by regulation 7(2).

(2) Subject to paragraph (3), an employment tribunal must not consider a complaint under this regulation unless it is presented before the end of the period of three months beginning with the date of the act or failure to act to which the complaint relates, or where that act or failure is part of a series of similar acts or failures, the last of them.

(2A) [omitted]

(3) A tribunal may consider any such complaint which is out of time if, in all the circumstances of the case, it considers that it is just and equitable to do so.

(4) For the purposes of paragraph (2)—

- (a) where an act extends over a period, the 'date of the act' means the last day of that period; and
- (b) failure to do something is to be treated as occurring when the person in question decided on it.

(5) In the absence of evidence to the contrary, a person (P) is to be taken to decide on failure to do something—

- (a) when P does an act inconsistent with doing it, or
- (b) if P does no inconsistent act, on the expiry of the period in which P might reasonably have been expected to do it.

(6) Where a worker presents a complaint under this regulation it is for the employer to identify the ground on which any act, or deliberate failure to act, was done.

8A [omitted]

9 Remedies

(1) Where an employment tribunal finds that a complaint presented to it under regulation 8 is well founded, it must take such of the following steps as it considers just and equitable—

- (a) making a declaration as to the rights of the complainant and the employer in relation to the matters to which the complaint relates; and
- (b) ordering the employer to pay compensation to the complainant.

(2) Subject to paragraphs (5) and (6), where a tribunal orders compensation under paragraph (1)(b), the amount of compensation awarded must be such as the tribunal considers just and equitable in all the circumstances having regard to—

- (a) the infringement to which the complaint relates; and
- (b) any loss which is attributable to the act, or failure to act, which infringed the complainant's right.

(3) The loss must be taken to include—

- (a) any expenses reasonably incurred by the complainant in consequence of the act, or failure to act, to which the complaint relates; and
- (b) loss of any benefit which the complainant might reasonably be expected to have had but for that act or failure to act.

(4) In ascertaining the loss the tribunal must apply the same rule concerning the duty of a person to mitigate loss as applies to damages recoverable under the common law of England and Wales or (as the case may be) the law of Scotland.

(5) Where—

- (a) the detriment to which the worker is subjected is the termination of their specified contract, but
- (b) that contract is not a contract of employment,

any compensation awarded under paragraph (1)(b) must not exceed the limit specified in paragraph (6).

(6) The limit is the total of—

(a) the sum which would be the basic award for unfair dismissal, calculated in accordance with section 119 of the 1996 Act, if the zero hours worker had been an employee and the specified contract terminated had been a contract of employment; and

(b) the sum for the time being specified in section 124(1ZA) of the 1996 Act which is the limit for a compensatory award to a person calculated in accordance with section 123 of the 1996 Act.

(7) Where the tribunal finds that the act, or failure to act, to which the complaint relates was to any extent caused or contributed to by action of the complainant, it must reduce the amount of the compensation by such proportion as it considers just and equitable having regard to that finding.

10 [omitted]

The Carer's Leave Regulations 2024

(SI 2024 No. 251)

PART 1 GENERAL

Application

2.—(1) Subject to paragraphs (2) to (5), these Regulations apply in relation to employees who give notice of an intention to take carer's leave on or after 6th April 2024.

(2) Regulation 11 (protection from detriment) has effect only in relation to an act or failure to act which takes place on or after 6th April 2024.

(3) For the purposes of paragraph (2)—

(a) where an act extends over a period, the reference to the date of the act is a reference to the last day of that period, and

(b) a failure to act is to be treated as done when it was decided on.

(4) For the purposes of paragraph (3)(b), in the absence of evidence establishing the contrary an employer shall be taken to decide on a failure to act—

(a) when they do an act inconsistent with doing the failed act, or

(b) if they have done no such inconsistent act when the period expires within which they might reasonably have been expected to do the failed act if it was to be done.

(5) Regulation 12 (unfair dismissal) has effect only in relation to dismissals where the effective date of termination (within the meaning of section 97 of the 1996 Act) falls on or after 6th April 2024.

Interpretation

3. In these Regulations—

'the 1996 Act' means the Employment Rights Act 1996;

'carer's leave' means leave under section 80J of the 1996 Act;

'day' means a period of 24 hours beginning at midnight, for the purposes of this regulation and regulations 7 and 8;

'relevant period' means a period of 12 months which ends on the last day of the carer's leave the employee has requested;

'statutory leave' means leave provided for in Part 8 of the 1996 Act;

'week' means a seven day period starting at midnight between Sunday and Monday.

PART 2 CARER'S LEAVE

Entitlement to carer's leave

4.—(1) An employee is entitled to be absent from work to take carer's leave where they—

(a) satisfy the conditions in paragraph (2), and

(b) comply with the notice requirements in regulation 7.

(2) The conditions referred to in paragraph (1)(a) are that the employee—

(a) has a dependant with a long-term care need(3),

(b) wants to be absent from work to provide or arrange care for that dependant, and

(c) has not exceeded their entitlement under regulation 5(1).

Extent of entitlement

5.—(1) An employee who satisfies the conditions in regulation 4 is entitled one week of carer's leave during the relevant period.

(2) The minimum period of carer's leave an employee may take is half a working day.

(3) The maximum period of carer's leave an employee may take is one continuous week.

(4) Where an employee chooses to take carer's leave it need not be taken on consecutive days.

(5) In this regulation 'working day' means the period in which an employee is normally expected or required to work on the day the leave is to be taken.

Calculation of a weeks leave

6.—(1) In respect of regulation 5 a week of carer's leave is a period of absence from work equal in duration to the period the employee is normally expected or required to work in a week at the time of making the request, calculated in accordance with paragraphs (2) to (5).

(2) Where the period for which an employee is normally expected or required, under their contract of employment, to work in the course of a week does not vary, a week's leave for the employee is a period of absence from work which is equal in duration to the period for which the employee is normally required to work during the course of a week in the relevant period.

(3) Where the period for which an employee is normally required, under their contract of employment, to work in the course of a week varies from week to week or over a longer period, or where they are normally required under their contract to work in some weeks but not in others, a week's leave for the employee is a period of absence from work which is equal in duration to the period calculated by dividing the total of the periods for which the employee is normally required to work during the course of a week in the relevant period by 52.

(4) In the case of an employee who has worked for their employer for at least one week but less than 52 weeks during the relevant period, a week's leave is a period of absence from work which is equal in duration to the period calculated by dividing the total of the periods for which the employee is normally required to work during the course of a week by the number of weeks the employee has been employed.

(5) In the case of an employee who has worked for their employer for less than a week, a week's leave is a period of absence from work which is equal in duration to the period for which the employee is expected to work in that week.

7.–14. [omitted]

The Employment Rights (Increase of Limits) Order 2026

(SI 2026 No. 310)

SCHEDULE*

Relevant statutory provision		Subject of provision	Old limit	New limit
1	Section 145E(3) of the 1992 Act	Amount of award for unlawful inducement relating to trade union membership or activities, or for unlawful inducement relating to collective bargaining.	£5,735	£5,993
2	Section 156(1) of the 1992 Act	Minimum amount of basic award of compensation where dismissal is unfair by virtue of sections 152(1) or 153 of the 1992 Act.	£8,763	£9,157
3	Section 176(6A) of the 1992 Act	Minimum amount of compensation where individual excluded or expelled from union in contravention of section 174 of the 1992 Act and not admitted or re-admitted by date of tribunal application.	£13,384	£13,986
4	Section 27M(1) of the 1996 Act	Limit on amount of compensatory award for failure to allocate and pay tips fairly.	£5,135	£5,366
5	Section 27O(2) of the 1996 Act	Limit on amount of compensatory award for failure to have a written policy on dealing with qualifying tips, gratuities and service charges, or failure to create a record of how they have been dealt with.	£5,135	£5,366
6	Section 31(1) of the 1996 Act	Limit on amount of guarantee payment payable to an employee in respect of any day.	£39	£41
7	Section 120(1) of the 1996 Act	Minimum amount of basic award of compensation where dismissal is unfair by virtue of sections 100(1)(a) and (b), 101A(d), 102(1) or 103 of the 1996 Act.	£8,763	£9,157
8	Section 124(1ZA)(a) of the 1996 Act	Limit on amount of compensatory award for unfair dismissal.	£118,223	£123,543**
9	Section 186(1)(a) and (b) of the 1996 Act	Limit on weekly amount payable to an employee, pro-rated where referable to a shorter period, in respect of a debt to which Part 12 of the 1996 Act applies and which is referable to a period of time.	£719	£751
10	Section 227(1) of the 1996 Act	Maximum amount of 'a week's pay' for the purpose of calculating a redundancy payment or for various awards including the basic or additional award of compensation for unfair dismissal.	£719	£751

* **Editor's Note:** the new limits came into effect on 6 April 2026.

** **Editor's Note:** the limit for compensatory award is expected to be removed in 2027.

The National Minimum Wage (Amendment) Regulations 2026*

(SI 2026 No. 357)

1. [omitted]

Amendments to the National Minimum Wage Regulations 2015

2.—(1) The National Minimum Wage Regulations 2015 are amended as follows.

(2) In regulation 4 (the national living wage) for '£12.21' substitute '£12.71'.

(3) In regulation 4A(1) (workers who qualify for the national minimum wage at a different rate)—

(a) in sub-paragraph (b) for '£10.00' substitute '£10.85';

(b) in sub-paragraph (c) for '£7.55' substitute '£8.00';

(c) in sub-paragraph (d) for '£7.55' substitute '£8.00'.

(4) In regulation 16(1) (amount for provision of living accommodation) for '£10.66' substitute '£11.10'.

* **Editor's Note:** these figures are updated annually.

Part III

Non-Statutory Materials

ACAS Code of Practice 1 Disciplinary and Grievance Procedures*

(Revised 2015)

Introduction

1. This Code is designed to help employers, employees and their representatives deal with disciplinary and grievance situations in the workplace.

- Disciplinary situations include misconduct and/or poor performance. If employers have a separate capability procedure they may prefer to address performance issues under this procedure. If so, however, the basic principles of fairness set out in this Code should still be followed, albeit that they may need to be adapted.
- Grievances are concerns, problems or complaints that employees raise with their employers.

The Code does not apply to redundancy dismissals or the non-renewal of fixed term contracts on their expiry.

2. Fairness and transparency are promoted by developing and using rules and procedures for handling disciplinary and grievance situations. These should be set down in writing, be specific and clear. Employees and, where appropriate, their representatives should be involved in the development of rules and procedures. It is also important to help employees and managers understand what the rules and procedures are, where they can be found and how they are to be used.

3. Where some form of formal action is needed, what action is reasonable or justified will depend on all the circumstances of the particular case. Employment tribunals will take the size and resources of an employer into account when deciding on relevant cases and it may sometimes not be practicable for all employers to take all of the steps set out in this Code.

4. That said, whenever a disciplinary or grievance process is being followed it is important to deal with issues fairly. There are a number of elements to this:

- Employers and employees should raise and deal with issues **promptly** and should not unreasonably delay meetings, decisions or confirmation of those decisions.
- Employers and employees should act consistently.
- Employers should carry out any necessary **investigations**, to establish the facts of the case.
- Employers should **inform** employees of the basis of the problem and give them an opportunity to **put their case** in response before any decisions are made.

- Employers should allow employees to be **accompanied** at any formal disciplinary or grievance meeting.
- Employers should allow an employee to **appeal** against any formal decision made.

Discipline

Keys to handling disciplinary issues in the workplace

Establish the facts of each case

5. It is important to carry out necessary investigations of potential disciplinary matters without unreasonable delay to establish the facts of the case. In some cases this will require the holding of an investigatory meeting with the employee before proceeding to any disciplinary hearing. In others, the investigatory stage will be the collation of evidence by the employer for use at any disciplinary hearing.

6. In misconduct cases, where practicable, different people should carry out the investigation and disciplinary hearing.

7. If there is an investigatory meeting this should not by itself result in any disciplinary action. Although there is no statutory right for an employee to be accompanied at a formal investigatory meeting, such a right may be allowed under an employer's own procedure.

8. In cases where a period of suspension with pay is considered necessary, this period should be as brief as possible, should be kept under review and it should be made clear that this suspension is not considered a disciplinary action.

Inform the employee of the problem

9. If it is decided that there is a disciplinary case to answer, the employee should be notified of this in writing. This notification should contain sufficient information about the alleged misconduct or poor performance and its possible consequences to enable the employee to prepare to answer the case at a disciplinary meeting. It would normally be appropriate to provide copies of any written evidence, which may include any witness statements, with the notification.

10. The notification should also give details of the time and venue for the disciplinary meeting and advise the employee of their right to be accompanied at the meeting.

Hold a meeting with the employee to discuss the problem

11. The meeting should be held without unreasonable delay whilst allowing the employee reasonable time to prepare their case.

12. Employers and employees (and their companions) should make every effort to attend the meeting. At the meeting the employer should explain the complaint against the employee and go through the evidence that has been gathered. The employee should be allowed to set out their case and answer any allegations that have been made. The employee should also be given a reasonable opportunity to ask questions, present evidence and call relevant witnesses. They should also be given an opportunity to raise points about any information provided by witnesses. Where an employer or employee intends to call relevant witnesses they should give advance notice that they intend to do this.

Allow the employee to be accompanied at the meeting

13. Workers have a statutory right to be accompanied by a companion where the disciplinary meeting could result in

- a formal warning being issued;
- the taking of some other disciplinary action; or
- the confirmation of a warning or some other disciplinary action (appeal hearings).

14. The statutory right is to be accompanied by a fellow worker, a trade union representative, or an official employed by a trade union. A trade union representative who is not an employed official

must have been certified by their union as being competent to accompany a worker. Employers must agree to a worker's request to be accompanied by any companion from one of these categories. Workers may also alter their choice of companion if they wish. As a matter of good practice, in making their choice workers should bear in mind the practicalities of the arrangements. For instance, a worker may choose to be accompanied by a companion who is suitable, willing and available on site rather than someone from a geographically remote location.

15. To exercise the statutory right to be accompanied workers must make a reasonable request. What is reasonable will depend on the circumstances of each individual case. A request to be accompanied does not have to be in writing or within a certain time frame. However, a worker should provide enough time for the employer to deal with the companion's attendance at the meeting. Workers should also consider how they make their request so that it is clearly understood, for instance by letting the employer know in advance the name of the companion where possible and whether they are a fellow worker or trade union official or representative.

16. If a worker's chosen companion will not be available at the time proposed for the hearing by the employer, the employer must postpone the hearing to a time proposed by the worker provided that the alternative time is both reasonable and not more than five working days after the date originally proposed.

17. The companion should be allowed to address the hearing to put and sum up the worker's case, respond on behalf of the worker to any views expressed at the meeting and confer with the worker during the hearing. The companion does not, however, have the right to answer questions on the worker's behalf, address the hearing if the worker does not wish it or prevent the employer from explaining their case.

Decide on appropriate action

18. After the meeting, decide whether or not disciplinary or any other action is justified and inform the employee accordingly in writing.

19. Where misconduct is confirmed or the employee is found to be performing unsatisfactorily it is usual to give the employee a written warning. A further act of misconduct or failure to improve performance within a set period would normally result in a final written warning.

20. If an employee's first misconduct or unsatisfactory performance is sufficiently serious, it may be appropriate to move directly to a final written warning. This might occur where the employee's actions have had, or are liable to have, a serious or harmful impact on the organisation.

21. A first or final written warning should set out the nature of the misconduct or poor performance and the change in behaviour or improvement in performance required (with timescale). The employee should be told how long the warning will remain current. The employee should be informed of the consequences of further misconduct, or failure to improve performance, within the set period following a final warning. For instance that it may result in dismissal or some other contractual penalty such as demotion or loss of seniority.

22. A decision to dismiss should only be taken by a manager who has the authority to do so. The employee should be informed as soon as possible of the reasons for the dismissal, the date on which the employment contract will end, the appropriate period of notice and their right of appeal.

23. Some acts, termed gross misconduct, are so serious in themselves or have such serious consequences that they may call for dismissal without notice for a first offence. But a fair disciplinary process should always be followed, before dismissing for gross misconduct.

24. Disciplinary rules should give examples of acts which the employer regards as acts of gross misconduct. These may vary according to the nature of the organisation and what it does, but might include things such as theft or fraud, physical violence, gross negligence or serious insubordination.

25. Where an employee is persistently unable or unwilling to attend a disciplinary meeting without good cause the employer should make a decision on the evidence available.

Provide employees with an opportunity to appeal

26. Where an employee feels that disciplinary action taken against them is wrong or unjust they should appeal against the decision. Appeals should be heard without unreasonable delay and

ideally at an agreed time and place. Employees should let employers know the grounds for their appeal in writing.

27. The appeal should be dealt with impartially and wherever possible, by a manager who has not previously been involved in the case.

28. Workers have a statutory right to be accompanied at appeal hearings.

29. Employees should be informed in writing of the results of the appeal hearing as soon as possible.

Special cases

30. Where disciplinary action is being considered against an employee who is a trade union representative the normal disciplinary procedure should be followed. Depending on the circumstances, however, it is advisable to discuss the matter at an early stage with an official employed by the union, after obtaining the employee's agreement.

31. If an employee is charged with, or convicted of a criminal offence this is not normally in itself reason for disciplinary action. Consideration needs to be given to what effect the charge or conviction has on the employee's suitability to do the job and their relationship with their employer, work colleagues and customers.

Grievance

Keys to handling grievances in the workplace

Let the employer know the nature of the grievance

32. If it is not possible to resolve a grievance informally employees should raise the matter formally and without unreasonable delay with a manager who is not the subject of the grievance. This should be done in writing and should set out the nature of the grievance.

Hold a meeting with the employee to discuss the grievance

33. Employers should arrange for a formal meeting to be held without unreasonable delay after a grievance is received.

34. Employers, employees and their companions should make every effort to attend the meeting. Employees should be allowed to explain their grievance and how they think it should be resolved. Consideration should be given to adjourning the meeting for any investigation that may be necessary.

Allow the employee to be accompanied at the meeting

35. Workers have a statutory right to be accompanied by a companion at a grievance meeting which deals with a complaint about a duty owed by the employer to the worker. So this would apply where the complaint is, for example, that the employer is not honouring the worker's contract, or is in breach of legislation.

36. The statutory right is to be accompanied by a fellow worker, a trade union representative, or an official employed by a trade union. A trade union representative who is not an employed official must have been certified by their union as being competent to accompany a worker. Employers must agree to a worker's request to be accompanied by any companion from one of these categories. Workers may also alter their choice of companion if they wish. As a matter of good practice, in making their choice workers should bear in mind the practicalities of the arrangements. For instance, a worker may choose to be accompanied by a companion who is suitable, willing and available on site rather than someone from a geographically remote location.

37. To exercise the statutory right to be accompanied workers must make a reasonable request. What is reasonable will depend on the circumstances of each individual case. A request to be accompanied does not have to be in writing or within a certain time frame. However, a worker should provide enough time for the employer to deal with the companion's attendance at the meeting. Workers should also consider how they make their request so that it is clearly understood, for instance by letting the employer know in advance the name of the companion where possible and whether they are a fellow worker or trade union official or representative.

38. If a worker's chosen companion will not be available at the time proposed for the hearing by the employer, the employer must postpone the hearing to a time proposed by the worker provided that the alternative time is both reasonable and not more than five working days after the date originally proposed.

39. The companion should be allowed to address the hearing to put and sum up the worker's case, respond on behalf of the worker to any views expressed at the meeting and confer with the worker during the hearing. The companion does not however, have the right to answer questions on the worker's behalf, address the hearing if the worker does not wish it or prevent the employer from explaining their case.

Decide on appropriate action

40. Following the meeting decide on what action, if any, to take. Decisions should be communicated to the employee, in writing, without unreasonable delay and, where appropriate, should set out what action the employer intends to take to resolve the grievance. The employee should be informed that they can appeal if they are not content with the action taken.

Allow the employee to take the grievance further if not resolved

41. Where an employee feels that their grievance has not been satisfactorily resolved they should appeal. They should let their employer know the grounds for their appeal without unreasonable delay and in writing.

42. Appeals should be heard without unreasonable delay and at a time and place which should be notified to the employee in advance.

43. The appeal should be dealt with impartially and wherever possible by a manager who has not previously been involved in the case.

44. Workers have a statutory right to be accompanied at any such appeal hearing.

45. The outcome of the appeal should be communicated to the employee in writing without unreasonable delay.

Overlapping grievance and disciplinary cases

46. Where an employee raises a grievance during a disciplinary process the disciplinary process may be temporarily suspended in order to deal with the grievance. Where the grievance and disciplinary cases are related it may be appropriate to deal with both issues concurrently.

Collective grievances

47. The provisions of this code do not apply to grievances raised on behalf of two or more employees by a representative of a recognised trade union or other appropriate workplace representative. These grievances should be handled in accordance with the organisation's collective grievance process.

Equality Act 2010 Statutory Code of Practice on Equal Pay*

(Issued 2011)

2 GOOD EQUAL PAY PRACTICE

Introduction

158. Despite the implementation of equal pay and sex discrimination legislation in the 1970s, there is still a significant gender pay gap. It could take an estimated 20 years to close the gap without further corrective action. This section of the code of practice therefore provides information and

* **Editor's Note:** the copyright in the document in this publication has been adapted from and all other intellectual property rights in that material are owned by, or licensed to, the Equality and Human Rights Commission (EHRC). The full document can be found at https://www.equalityhumanrights.com/sites/default/files/equalpaycode.pdf (accessed 15 April 2026).

guidance on steps that employers can take which go beyond compliance with legal requirements. These steps, taken in consultation with the workforce and trade union or other employee representatives, should help accelerate the achievement of substantive gender equality at work.

159. The financial loss to women arising out of unequal pay is well documented, but organisations also lose out by failing to properly value and reward the range of skills and experience that women bring to the workforce.

The most commonly recognised risk of failing to ensure that pay is determined without sex discrimination is the risk of time-consuming and costly equal pay litigation. The direct costs to an organisation of a claim can include not only any eventual equal pay award to the woman or women bringing the claim but also the costs of time spent responding to the claim, and the costs of legal representation.

The indirect costs are harder to quantify, but could include lower productivity on the part of those employees who consider that they are not getting equal pay and on the part of managers whose time is taken up in dealing with staff dissatisfaction and other repercussions.

160. Tackling unequal pay can also increase efficiency and productivity by attracting the best employees, reducing staff turnover, increasing commitment, and reducing absenteeism. Pay is one of the key factors affecting motivation and relationships at work. It is therefore important to develop pay arrangements that are right for the organisation and that reward employees fairly. Providing equal pay for equal work is central to the concept of rewarding people fairly for what they do.

161. Employers should not discriminate on any protected ground in their pay arrangements. The information on good practice set out here focuses on eliminating gender pay inequalities, which are the subject of this code of practice. However, the methods used to identify and remedy unlawful gender pay discrimination can also be used to remedy unlawful pay discrimination on other grounds.

Reviewing or auditing pay

162. Employers are responsible for providing equal pay for equal work and for ensuring that pay systems are transparent. Where a pay system lacks transparency the employer must be able to prove there is no sex discrimination behind a pay differential.

Pay arrangements are often complicated and the features that can give rise to discrimination in pay are not always obvious. A structured pay system, based on sound, bias-free job evaluation, is more transparent and more likely to provide equal pay than a system that relies primarily on managerial discretion.

ACAS can advise on how to structure a pay system

163. Most employers believe that they provide equal pay for equal work, irrespective of the sex of the job holders or whether they work full or part time. An equal pay audit is the most effective way of establishing whether an organisation is in fact providing equal pay.

Organisations subject to the gender equality duty must pay due regard to the need to eliminate sex discrimination in pay. Although conducting an equal pay audit is not mandatory, it demonstrates appropriate action to identify and eliminate gender pay discrimination. It provides a risk assessment tool for pay structures.

The Commission recommends all employers carry out regular equal pay audits. A model for carrying out an equal pay audit is described below.

164. A number of common pay practices, listed below, pose risks in terms of potential non-compliance with an employer's legal obligations:

- lack of transparency and unnecessary secrecy over grading and pay
- discretionary pay systems (for example, merit pay and performance-related pay) unless they are clearly structured and based on objective criteria
- different non-basic pay, terms and conditions for different groups of employees (for example, attendance allowances, overtime or unsocial hours payments)

- more than one grading and pay system within the organisation
- long pay scales or ranges
- overlapping pay scales or ranges, where the maximum of the lower pay scale is higher than the minimum of the next higher scale, including 'broad-banded' structures where there are significant overlaps
- managerial discretion over starting salaries
- market-based pay systems or supplements not underpinned by job evaluation
- job evaluation systems which have been incorrectly implemented or not kept up to date
- pay protection policies.

There is detailed guidance on the Commission's website about the law and risk management in relation to these issues. In many cases, this will involve carrying out a few straightforward checks or reviewing a relevant policy.

165. Risks of equal pay challenges generally arise not out of any intention to discriminate, but through pay systems not being kept under review and up to date. ACAS provides basic advice on the various different types of pay systems and on job evaluation.

The benefits of conducting an equal pay audit

166. The benefits to an organisation of carrying out an equal pay audit include:

- identifying, explaining and, where unjustifiable, eliminating pay inequalities
- having rational, fair and transparent pay arrangements
- demonstrating to employees and to potential employees a commitment to equality, and
- demonstrating the organisation's values to those it does business with.

167. An equal pay audit may be the most effective method of ensuring that a pay system is free from unlawful bias. An audit should include:

- comparing the pay of men and women doing equal work—ensuring that this considers work that is the same or broadly similar (like work), work rated as equivalent and work that can be shown to be of equal value or worth
- identifying and explaining any pay differences, and
- eliminating those pay inequalities that cannot be explained on non-discriminatory grounds.

168. A process that does not include these features cannot claim to be an equal pay audit. The Commission's extensive guidance for employers on conducting equal pay audits is available on its website.

169. An equal pay audit is not simply a data collection exercise. It entails a commitment to put right any unjustified pay inequalities. This means that the audit must have the involvement and support of managers who have the authority to deliver the necessary changes.

170. The validity of the audit and the success of subsequent action taken will be enhanced if the pay system is understood and accepted by the managers who operate the system, by the employees and by their unions. Employers should therefore aim to secure the involvement of employees and, where possible, trade union and other employee representatives, when carrying out an equal pay audit.

A model for carrying out an equal pay audit

171. The Commission recommends a five-step equal pay audit model.

Step 1: Decide the scope of the audit and identify the information required.

Step 2: Determine where men and women are doing equal work.

Step 3: Collect and compare pay data to identify any significant pay inequalities between roles of equal value.

Step 4: Establish the causes of any significant pay inequalities and assess the reasons for them.

Step 5: Develop an equal pay action plan to remedy any direct or indirect pay discrimination.

The Commission's Equal Pay Resources and Audit Toolkit provides detailed guidance on how to conduct an audit.

Equality Act 2010 Statutory Code of Practice on Employment*

(Issued 2011)

PART 2

Chapter 16 Avoiding discrimination in recruitment

Introduction

16.1 Ensuring fair recruitment processes can help employers avoid discrimination. While nothing in the Act prevents an employer from hiring the best person for the job, it is unlawful for an employer to discriminate in any of the arrangements made to fill a vacancy, in the terms of employment that are offered or in any decision to refuse someone a job (see Chapter 10). With certain limited exceptions, employers must not make recruitment decisions that are directly or indirectly discriminatory. As with other stages of employment, employers must also make reasonable adjustments for disabled candidates, where appropriate.

16.2 It is recognised that employers will have different recruitment processes in place depending on their size, resources, and the sector in which they operate. Whichever processes are used, applicants must be treated fairly and in accordance with the Act. This chapter examines the main issues arising in the recruitment of both external and internal applicants and explains the steps that should be taken to avoid unlawful conduct within each of the recruitment stages that are commonly used. It also makes some recommendations for good practice.

Defining the job

General principles

16.4 The inclusion of requirements in a job description or person specification which are unnecessary or seldom used is likely to lead to indirect discrimination. Employers who use job descriptions and person specifications should therefore review them each time they decide to fill a post. Reliance on an existing person specification or job description, may lead to discrimination if they contain discriminatory criteria.

Example: An employer uses a person specification for an accountant's post that states 'employees must be confident in dealing with external clients' when in fact the job in question does not involve liaising directly with external clients. This requirement is unnecessary and could lead to discrimination against disabled people who have difficulty interacting with others, such as some people with autism.

Job Descriptions

16.5 Job descriptions should accurately describe the job in question. Inclusion of tasks or duties that workers will not, in practice, need to perform has two pitfalls. It may discourage appropriately qualified people from applying because they cannot perform the particular task or fulfil the

* **Editor's Note:** the copyright in the document in this publication has been adapted from and all other intellectual property rights in that material are owned by, or licensed to, the Equality and Human Rights Commission (EHRC). The full document can be found at https://www.equalityhumanrights.com/sites/default/files/employercode.pdf (accessed 15 April 2026).

particular duty specified. It may also lead to discrimination claims if such people believe they have been unfairly denied an opportunity of applying.

16.6 Job titles should not show a predetermined bias for the recruitment of those with a particular characteristic. For example, 'shop girl' suggests a bias towards recruiting a younger woman, and 'office boy' suggests a bias towards recruiting a younger man.

16.7 Tasks and duties set out in the job description should be objectively justifiable as being necessary to that post. This is especially important for tasks and duties which some people may not be able to fulfil, or would be less likely to be able to fulfil, because of a protected characteristic. Similarly, the job description should not overstate a duty which is only an occasional or marginal one.

Example: A job description includes the duty: 'regular Sunday working'. In reality, there is only an occasional need to work on a Sunday. This overstated duty written into the job description puts off Christians who do not wish to work on a Sunday, and so could amount to indirect discrimination unless the requirement can be objectively justified.

16.8 Where there are different ways of performing a task, job descriptions should not specify how the task should be done. Instead, the job description should state what outcome needs to be achieved.

Example: A job description includes the task: 'Using MagicReport software to produce reports about customer complaints'. This particular software is not accessible to some disabled people who use voice-activated software. Discrimination could be avoided by describing the task as 'Producing reports about customer complaints'.

16.9 Job descriptions should not specify working hours or working patterns that are not necessary to the job in question. If a job could be done either part-time, full-time, or through job share arrangements, this should be stated in the job description. As well as avoiding discrimination, this approach can also widen the group of people who may choose to make an application.

Example: A job description for a manager states that the job is full-time. The employer has stated this because all managers are currently full-time and he has not considered whether this is an actual requirement for the role. The requirement to work full-time could put women at a disadvantage compared with men because more women than men work part-time or job share in order to accommodate childcare responsibilities. This requirement could amount to indirect discrimination unless it can be objectively justified.

Person specifications

16.10 Person specifications describe various criteria—including skills, knowledge, abilities, qualifications, experience and qualities—that are considered necessary or desirable for someone fulfilling the role set out in the job description. These criteria must not be discriminatory. Discrimination can be avoided by ensuring that any necessary or desirable criteria can be justified for that particular job.

16.11 Criteria that exclude people because of a protected characteristic may be directly discriminatory unless they are related to occupational requirements.

Example: Stating in a job description for a secretary that the person must be under 40 would amount to direct age discrimination against people over 40. In some circumstances, age criteria can be objectively justified, but in this case it is very unlikely.

16.12 Criteria that are less likely to be met by people with certain protected characteristics may amount to indirect discrimination if these criteria cannot be objectively justified.

Example: Asking for 'so many years' experience could amount to indirect discrimination because of age unless this provision can be objectively justified.

Example: A requirement for continuous experience could indirectly discriminate against women who have taken time out from work for reasons relating to maternity or childcare, unless the requirement can be objectively justified.

16.13 The person specification should not include criteria that are wholly irrelevant.

Example: A requirement that the applicant must be 'active and energetic' when the job is a sedentary one is an irrelevant criterion. This requirement could be discriminatory against some disabled people who may be less mobile.

16.14 Employers should ensure that criteria relating to skills or knowledge are not unnecessarily restrictive in specifying particular qualifications that are necessary or desirable. It is advisable to make reference to 'equivalent qualifications' or to 'equivalent levels of skill or knowledge' in order to avoid indirect discrimination against applicants sharing a particular protected characteristic if this group is less likely to have obtained the qualification. The level of qualification needed should not be overstated. Employers should avoid specifying qualifications that were not available a generation ago, such as GCSEs, without stating that equivalent qualifications are also acceptable.

Example: Requiring a UK-based qualification, when equivalent qualifications obtained abroad would also meet the requirement for that particular level of knowledge or skill, may lead to indirect discrimination because of race, if the requirement cannot be objectively justified.

16.15 As far as possible, all the criteria should be capable of being tested objectively. For example, attributes such as 'leadership' should be defined in terms of measurable skills or experience.

Health requirements in person specifications

16.16 The inclusion of health requirements can amount to direct discrimination against disabled people, where such requirements lead to a blanket exclusion of people with particular impairments and do not allow individual circumstances to be considered. Employers should also be aware that, except in specified circumstances, it is unlawful to ask questions about health or disability before the offer of a job is made or a person is placed in a pool of people to be offered a job (see paragraphs 10.25 to 10.43).

Example: A person specification states that applicants must have 'good health'. This criterion is too broad to relate to any specific requirement of the job and is therefore likely to amount to direct discrimination because of disability.

16.17 The inclusion of criteria that relate to health, physical fitness or disability, such as asking applicants to demonstrate a good sickness record, may amount to indirect discrimination against disabled people in particular, unless these criteria can be objectively justified by the requirements of the actual job in question.

16.18 Person specifications that include requirements relating to health, fitness or other physical attributes may discriminate not only against some disabled applicants, but also against applicants with other protected characteristics—unless the requirements can be objectively justified.

Example: A person specification includes a height requirement. This may indirectly discriminate as it would put at a disadvantage women, some disabled people, and people from certain racial groups if it cannot be objectively justified for the job in question.

Advertising a job

16.19 An employer must not discriminate in its arrangements for advertising jobs or by not advertising a job. Neither should they discriminate through the actual content of the job advertisement (see paragraphs 3.32 and 10.6).

Content of job advertisements

16.23 Job advertisements should accurately reflect the requirements of the job, including the job description and person specification if the employer uses these. This will ensure that nobody will be unnecessarily deterred from applying or making an unsuccessful application even though they could in fact do the job.

16.24 Advertisements must not include any wording that suggests the employer may directly discriminate by asking for people with a certain protected characteristic, for example by advertising for a 'salesman' or a 'waitress' or saying that the applicant must be 'youthful'.

Example: An employer advertises for a 'waitress'. This suggests that the employer is discriminating against men. By using a gender neutral term such as 'waiting staff' or by using the term 'waiter or waitress', the employer could avoid a claim of discrimination based on this advert.

16.25 Advertisements must not include any wording that suggests the employer might indirectly discriminate. Wording should not, for example, suggest criteria that would disadvantage people of a particular sex, age, or any other protected characteristic unless the requirement can be objectively justified or an exception under the Act applies.

16.26 A job advertisement should not include wording that suggests that reasonable adjustments will not be made for disabled people, or that disabled people will be discriminated against, or that they should not bother to apply.

Example: An employer advertises for an office worker, stating, 'This job is not suitable for wheelchair users because the office is on the first floor'. The employer should state instead, 'Although our offices are on the first floor, we welcome applications from disabled people and are willing to make reasonable adjustments'.

When is it lawful to advertise for someone with a particular protected characteristic?

16.27 Where there is an occupational requirement for a person with a particular protected characteristic that meets the legal test under the Act, then it would be lawful to advertise for such a person; for example, if there is an occupational requirement for a woman (see paragraphs 13.2 to 13.15). Where the job has an occupational requirement, the advertisement should state this so that it is clear that there is no unlawful discrimination.

Example: An employer advertises for a female care worker. It is an occupational requirement for the worker to be female, because the job involves intimate care tasks, such as bathing and toileting women. The advert states: 'Permitted under Schedule 9, part 1 of the Equality Act 2010'.

16.28 An employer can lawfully advertise a job as only open to disabled applicants because of the asymmetrical nature of disability discrimination (see paragraph 3.35).

Example: A private nursery advertises for a disabled childcare assistant. This is lawful under the Act.

16.29 An employer may include statements in a job advertisement encouraging applications from under-represented groups, as a voluntary 'positive action' measure (see Chapter 12). An employer may also include statements about their equality policy or statements that all applications will be considered solely on merit.

Example: The vast majority of workers employed by a national retailer are under the age of 40. Consequently, people over the age of 40 are under-represented in the organisation. The retailer is looking to open new stores and needs to recruit more staff. It would be lawful under the Act for that retailer to place a job advert encouraging applications from all groups, especially applicants over the age of 40.

Application process

General principles

16.32 An employer must not discriminate through the application process. A standardised process, whether this is through an application form or using CVs, will enable an employer to make an objective assessment of an applicant's ability to do the job and will assist an employer in demonstrating that they have has assessed applicants objectively. It will also enable applicants to compete on equal terms with each other. A standardised application process does not preclude reasonable adjustments for disabled people (see below).

Example: An application form asks applicants to provide 400 words stating how they meet the job description and person specification. Applicants are marked for each criterion they satisfy and short-listed on the basis of their marks. This is a standardised application process that enables the employer to show that they have assessed all applicants without discriminating.

Chapter 17 Avoiding discrimination during employment

Flexible working

17.8 There are statutory rules which give employees with caring responsibilities for children or specified adults the right to have a request for flexible working considered. The right is designed to give employees the opportunity to adopt working arrangements that help them to balance their commitments at work with their need to care for a child or an adult.

17.11 It is also important to bear in mind that rigid working patterns may result in indirect discrimination unless they can be objectively justified. Although a flexible working request may legitimately be refused under the statutory rules, such a refusal may still be indirectly discriminatory if the employer is unable to show that the requirement to work certain hours is justified as a proportionate means of achieving a legitimate aim. For example:

- A requirement to work full-time hours may indirectly discriminate against women because they are more likely to have childcare responsibilities.
- A requirement to work full-time hours could indirectly discriminate against disabled people with certain conditions (such as ME). It could also amount to a failure to make reasonable adjustments.
- A requirement to work on certain days may indirectly discriminate against those with particular religious beliefs.

Example: An employee's contractual hours are 9am–3pm. Under the flexible working procedures, she has formally requested to work from 10am–4pm because of childcare needs. Her employer refuses, saying that to provide staff cover in the mornings would involve extra costs. This refusal would be compatible with the flexible working procedures, which do not require a refusal to be objectively justified. However, in some circumstances, this could amount to indirect sex discrimination. Where a refusal to permit certain working patterns would detrimentally affect a larger proportion of women than men, the employer must show that it is based on a legitimate aim, such as providing sufficient staff cover before 10am, and that refusing the request is a proportionate means of achieving that aim.

17.12 Employers should also be particularly mindful of their duty to make reasonable adjustments to working hours for disabled workers.

Example: A worker with a learning disability has a contract to work normal office hours (9am to 5.30pm in this particular office). He wishes to change these hours because the friend whom he needs to accompany him to work is no longer available before 9am. Allowing him to start later is likely to be a reasonable adjustment for that employer to make.

Sickness and absence from work

17.16 Sickness and absence from work may be governed by contractual terms and conditions and/or may be the subject of non-contractual practices and procedures. Regardless of the nature of these policies, it is important to ensure that they are non-discriminatory in design, and applied to workers who are sick or absent for whatever reason without discrimination of any kind. This is particularly important when a policy has discretionary elements such as decisions about stopping sick pay or commencing attendance management procedures.

17.17 To avoid discrimination, sickness and absence procedures should include clear requirements about informing the employer of sickness and providing medical certificates. They should also specify the rate and the maximum period of payment for sick pay.

Disability-related absences

17.20 Employers are not automatically obliged to disregard all disability-related sickness absences, but they must disregard some or all of the absences by way of an adjustment if this is reasonable. If an employer takes action against a disabled worker for disability-related sickness absence, this may amount to discrimination arising from disability.

Example: During a six-month period, a man who has recently developed a long-term health condition has a number of short periods of absence from work as he learns to manage this condition. Ignoring these periods of disability-related absence is likely to be a reasonable adjustment for the employer to make. Disciplining this man because of these periods of absence will amount to discrimination arising from disability, if the employer cannot show that this is objectively justified.

Pregnancy-related absences

17.25 All pregnancy-related absences must be disregarded for the purposes of attendance management action. Workers who are absent for a pregnancy-related reason have no automatic right to full pay but should receive no less than the contractual sick pay that might be due for the period in question. However, employers have no obligation to extend contractual sick pay beyond what would usually be payable. Sickness absence associated with a miscarriage should be treated as pregnancy-related sickness. Pregnancy-related absence is covered in more detail in Chapter 8.

Example: A worker has been off work because of pregnancy complications since early in her pregnancy. Her employer has now dismissed her in accordance with the sickness policy which allows no more than 20 weeks' continuous absence. This policy is applied regardless of sex. The dismissal is unfavourable treatment because of her pregnancy and would be unlawful even if a man would be dismissed for a similar period of sickness absence, because the employer took into account the worker's pregnancy-related sickness absence in deciding to dismiss.

Emergency leave

17.32 Employees have a statutory right to take reasonable unpaid time off which is necessary to deal with immediate emergencies concerning dependants. Dependants include a spouse or civil partner or partner, a child or a parent, or a person living in the employee's household. In dealing with cases where emergency leave is required, employers should ensure that they do not discriminate.

Example: A worker receives a telephone call informing him that his civil partner has been involved in an accident. The worker has been recorded as next of kin on his civil partner's medical notes and is required at the hospital. The employer has a policy that only allows emergency leave to be taken where a spouse, child or parent is affected and refuses the worker's request for leave. This would amount to discrimination because of sexual orientation. It would also be a breach of the worker's statutory rights.

Annual leave

17.33 Annual leave policies and procedures must be applied without discrimination of any kind. It is particularly important for employers to avoid discrimination when dealing with competing requests for annual leave, or requests that relate to a worker's protected characteristic such as religion or belief.

17.34 The Working Time Regulations 1998 provide a minimum annual holiday entitlement of 5.6 weeks, which can include public and bank holidays; however, employers may offer workers more holiday than their minimum legal entitlement. The procedure in the Regulations for requesting annual leave and dealing with such requests may be replaced by agreement between the employer and worker. All policies and procedures for handling annual leave requests should be non-discriminatory in design and the employer must not refuse a request for annual leave because of a protected characteristic.

17.35 A policy leading to a refusal is also an application of a provision, criterion or practice. The policy could be indirectly discriminatory if it places the worker and people sharing the worker's characteristic at a particular disadvantage, unless the provision, criterion or practice is a proportionate means of achieving a legitimate aim.

17.36 A worker may request annual leave for a religious occasion or to visit family overseas. To avoid discrimination, employers should seek to accommodate the request—provided the worker has sufficient holiday due to them and it is reasonable for them to be absent from work during the period requested.

Example: An Australian worker requests three weeks' leave to visit his family in Australia. He works for a large employer, whose annual leave policy normally limits periods of annual leave to a maximum of two weeks at any one time. The two-week limit could be indirectly discriminatory because of nationality, unless it can be objectively justified. In this case, the employer has sufficient staff to cover the additional week's leave. They operate the annual leave policy flexibly, and agree to allow the worker to take three weeks' leave to visit his family.

17.37 Many religions or beliefs have special periods of religious observance, festivals or holidays. Employers should be aware that some of these occasions are aligned with lunar phases. As a result, dates can change from year to year and may not become clear until quite close to the actual day.

> **Example:** Last year, a Sikh worker took annual leave on 1 and 2 March to celebrate Hola Mohalla. This year, he requests annual leave on 6th and 7th March to celebrate the same holiday. No other staff members in his department have requested leave on these dates. The employer refuses the request but says that the worker can take off the same days as he did last year. Festivals in Sikhism are based on the lunar calendar, so the dates on which they fall differ every year. It could be indirect discrimination for the employer to expect the worker to take annual leave on the same days every year, unless this can be objectively justified.

17.38 Employers who require everyone to take leave during an annual closedown should consider whether this creates a particular disadvantage for workers sharing a protected characteristic who need annual leave at other times, for example, during specific school holidays or religious festivals. This practice could amount to indirect discrimination, unless it can be objectively justified. Although the operational needs of the business may be a legitimate aim, employers must consider the needs of workers in assessing whether the closure is a proportionate means of achieving the aim (see paragraphs 4.25 to 4.32).

Avoiding discrimination—accommodating workers' needs

Dress and business attire

17.39 Many employers enforce a dress code or uniform with the aim of ensuring that workers dress in a manner that is appropriate to the business or workplace or to meet health and safety requirements. However, dress codes—including rules about jewellery—may indirectly discriminate against workers sharing a protected characteristic. To avoid indirect discrimination, employers should make sure that any dress rules can be justified as a proportionate means of achieving a legitimate aim such as health and safety considerations.

17.40 It is good practice for employers to consult with workers as to how a dress code may impact on different religious or belief groups, and whether any exceptions should be allowed—for example, for religious jewellery.

> **Example:** An employer introduces a 'no jewellery' policy in the workplace. This is not for health and safety reasons but because the employer does not like body piercings. A Sikh worker who wears a Kara bracelet as an integral part of her religion has complained about the rule. To avoid a claim of indirect discrimination, the employer should consider allowing an exception to this rule. A blanket ban on jewellery would probably not be considered a proportionate means of achieving a legitimate aim in these circumstances.

Language in the workplace

17.44 A language requirement for a job may be indirectly discriminatory unless it is necessary for the satisfactory performance of the job. For example, a requirement that a worker have excellent English skills may be indirectly discriminatory because of race; if a worker really only needs a good grasp of English, the requirement for excellent English may not be objectively justified. A requirement for good spoken English may be indirectly discriminatory against certain disabled people, for example, deaf people whose first language is British Sign Language. (See Chapter 4 for more information on indirect discrimination.)

Example: A superstore insists that all its workers have excellent spoken English. This might be a justifiable requirement for those in customer-facing roles. However, for workers based in the stock room, the requirement could be indirectly discriminatory in relation to race or disability as it is less likely to be objectively justified.

17.47 An employer might also wish to impose a requirement on workers to communicate in a common language—generally English. There is a clear business interest in having a common language in the workplace, to avoid misunderstandings, whether legal, financial or in relation to health and safety. It is also conducive to good working relations to avoid excluding workers from conversations that might concern them.

17.51 Inappropriate or derogatory language in the workplace could amount to harassment if it is related to a protected characteristic and is sufficiently serious. Workplace policies—if the employer has these in place—should emphasise that workers should not make inappropriate comments, jokes or use derogatory terms related to a protected characteristic (see Chapter 7 on harassment).

Example: A male worker has made a number of offensive remarks about a worker who is pregnant, such as 'women are only good for making babies'. The employer's equality policy makes it clear that inappropriate and offensive language, comments and jokes related to a protected characteristic can amount to harassment and may be treated as a disciplinary offence. The employer may bring disciplinary proceedings against the male worker for making offensive comments that relate to the pregnant worker's sex.

Chapter 19 Termination of employment

Introduction

Terminating employment

19.3 Those responsible for deciding whether or not a worker should be dismissed should understand their legal obligations under the Act. They should also be made aware of how the Act might apply to situations where dismissal is a possibility. Employers can help avoid discrimination if they have procedures in place for dealing with dismissals and apply these procedures consistently and fairly. In particular, employers should take steps to ensure the criteria they use for dismissal—especially in a redundancy situation—are not indirectly discriminatory (see paragraph 19.11 below).

19.4 It is also important that employers ensure they do not dismiss a worker with a protected characteristic for performance or behaviour which would be overlooked or condoned in others who do not share the characteristic.

Example: A Sikh worker is dismissed for failing to meet her set objectives, which form a part of her annual performance appraisal, in two consecutive years. However, no action is taken against a worker of the Baha'i faith, who has also failed to meet her objectives over the same period of time. This difference in treatment could amount to direct discrimination because of religion or belief.

19.5 Where an employer is considering dismissing a worker who is disabled, they should consider what reasonable adjustments need to be made to the dismissal process (see Chapter 6). In addition, the employer should consider whether the reason for dismissal is connected to or in consequence of the worker's disability. If it is, dismissing the worker will amount to discrimination arising from disability unless it can be objectively justified. In these circumstances, an employer should consider whether dismissal is an appropriate sanction to impose.

Example: A disabled worker periodically requires a limited amount of time off work to attend medical appointments related to the disability. The employer has an attendance management policy which results in potential warnings and ultimately dismissal if the worker's absence exceeds 20 days in any 12-month period. A combination of the worker's time off for disability-related medical appointments and general time off for sickness results in the worker consistently exceeding the 20 day limit by a few days. The worker receives a series of warnings and is eventually dismissed. This is likely to amount to disability discrimination.

19.6 Based on the facts in the example above, it is very likely to have been a reasonable adjustment for the employer to ignore the absences arising out of the worker's disability or increase the trigger points that would invoke the attendance policy. By making one or both of these adjustments, the employer could have avoided the possibility of claims for both a failure to make adjustments and discrimination arising from disability.

19.7 Employers must not discriminate against a transsexual worker when considering whether to dismiss the worker for absences or other conduct because of gender reassignment (see paragraphs 9.31 to 9.33). To avoid discrimination because of gender reassignment when considering the dismissal of a transsexual worker, employers should make provision within their disciplinary policy for dealing with such dismissals.

Example: A transsexual worker who experiences gender dysphoria and is considering gender reassignment takes time off from work because of his condition. The employer's attendance management policy provides that absence exceeding eight days or more in a 12-month rolling period will trigger the capability procedure. As the worker has had over eight days off, the employer invokes the procedure and consequently decides to dismiss him. However, over a previous 12-month rolling period, the worker was absent from work for more than eight days with various minor illnesses. The employer took no action against the worker because they viewed these absences as genuine. The dismissal could amount to an unlawful dismissal because of gender reassignment.

Dismissal for reasons of capability and conduct

19.8 As noted in Chapter 17, employers must not discriminate against or victimise their workers in how they manage capability or conduct issues. To avoid discrimination in any disciplinary decision that leads to a dismissal (or could lead to a dismissal after a subsequent disciplinary matter), employers should have procedures in place for managing capability and conduct issues. They should apply these procedures fairly and in a non-discriminatory way.

Example: A white worker and a black worker are subjected to disciplinary action for fighting. The fight occurred because the black worker had made derogatory remarks about the white worker. The employer has no disciplinary policy and consequently does not investigate the matter. Instead, the employer decides to dismiss the white worker without notice and give the black worker a final written warning. This could amount to a discriminatory dismissal because of race. Had the employer had a disciplinary procedure in place and applied it fairly, they could have avoided a discriminatory outcome.

19.9 Where an employer is considering the dismissal of a disabled worker for a reason relating to that worker's capability or their conduct, they must consider whether any reasonable adjustments need to be made to the performance management or dismissal process which would help improve the performance of the worker or whether they could transfer the worker to a suitable alternative role.

How can discrimination be avoided in capability and conduct dismissals?

19.10 To avoid discrimination when terminating employment, an employer should, in particular:

- apply their procedures for managing capability or conduct fairly and consistently (or use Acas's Guide on Disciplinary and Grievance at Work, if the employer does not have their own procedure);
- ensure that any decision to dismiss is made by more than one individual, and on the advice of the human resources department (if the employer has one);
- keep written records of decisions and reasons to dismiss;
- monitor all dismissals by reference to protected characteristic;
- encourage leavers to give feedback about their employment; this information could contribute to the monitoring process.

Please see the prelims for the following tables of contents:

Alphabetical *v*
Chronological *viii*